Acclaim for Susan Hertog's

Anne Morrow Lindbergh

"A delight to read. . . . Lindbergh's life, set against the backdrop of the early twentieth century, is an engrossing one."
—*San Antonio Express-News*

"Whether soaring into the sky or deep in mourning, Anne Morrow Lindbergh comes vividly to life in this poignant, haunting and lyrical work."
—Ron Chernow

"A charming book. . . . Without trying to force Lindbergh into a mold, [Hertog] portrays her as an early example of the modern feminist dilemma, a woman so completely identified as her husband's wife, yet who fought successfully to define her own soul."
—*St. Petersburg Times*

"A wonderful biography, truly worthy of its subject; Anne Morrow Lindbergh's was one of the extraordinary lives of the century, shaped by all its forces from politics and fame, from violent crime to feminism. And she emerges in the end as a woman of great faith and conviction. Susan Hertog has captured this groundbreaking life with depth, breadth and feeling."
—Peggy Noonan

"A full and interesting portrait of one of the twentieth century's notable women."
—*The Indianapolis Star*

"Susan Hertog's *Anne Morrow Lindbergh* restores this important poet to her rightful place in the pantheon of twentieth century writers, one of the spirits by which this century knew itself and named itself. . . . It should bring Anne Morrow Lindbergh to a new generation of readers."
—Erica Jong

"Intriguing. . . . Susan Hertog's biography explores the thoughts of a woman who reflects upon the conflicts of women of her generation."
—*Pittsburgh Post-Gazette*

Susan Hertog

Anne Morrow Lindbergh

Susan Hertog was born in New York City, and graduated from Hunter College. After earning her M.F.A. from Columbia University, she became a freelance journalist and photographer while raising her three children. She lives in Manhattan with her family.

Ms. Peggy J. Weyhrich
PO Box 234
Randolph, NE 68771

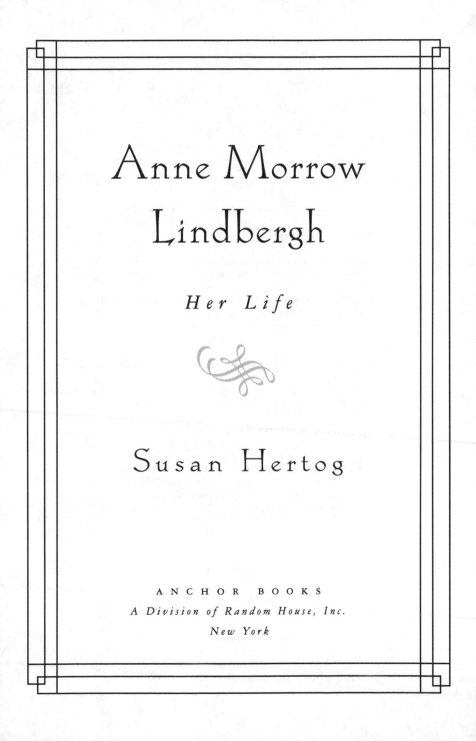

Anne Morrow Lindbergh

Her Life

Susan Hertog

ANCHOR BOOKS
A Division of Random House, Inc.
New York

FIRST ANCHOR BOOKS EDITION, NOVEMBER 2000

Copyright © 1999 by Susan Hertog

The Library of Congress has cataloged the Nan A. Talese / Doubleday edition as follows:
Anne Morrow Lindbergh: her life / Susan Hertog. — 1st ed.
in the United States of America.
p.   cm.
Includes bibliographical references.
ISBN 0-385-46973-X
1. Lindbergh, Anne Morrow, 1906–   . 2. Women authors,
American—20th Century Biography.   3. Women air pilots—United
States—Biography.   4. Air pilots' spouses—United States—Biography.
5. Lindbergh, Charles A. (Charles Augustus), 1902–1974—Marriage.   I. Title.
PS3523.I516Z69   1999
818'.5209—dc21
[B]   99–28759   CIP

Anchor ISBN: 0-385-72007-6

Book design by Deborah Kerner
Author photograph © Nancy Crampton

www.anchorbooks.com

Printed in the United States of America
10   9   8   7   6   5   4   3   2   1

THIS BOOK
IS DEDICATED
WITH LOVE
TO MY MOTHER,
MARILYN REINFELD GORELL

Acknowledgments

One of the great joys of finishing a book ten years in the making is the opportunity to thank the many people who helped me along the way. Writing a book, no matter how many hours one spends alone, is a collaborative effort—from the encouragement of friends, to the skill and perseverance of archivists and librarians, to editors and copy editors and research assistants, to the scholars whose erudition has cleared the path, to smiling strangers who nod and pass. All efforts rise and converge to produce some shadow of truth, some flash of perception, that might never have been.

I am profoundly grateful to Anne Lindbergh for permitting me the privilege to share and record her thoughts and memories during our many conversations between 1985 and 1989.

So many people at so many institutions helped to facilitate my research that I could not possibly thank them all. Professionals and volunteers from small elementary schools to large universities, from private museums and libraries to city, state, and federal archives, from remote island historical societies to special collections in large urban centers went beyond necessity to make certain I could find the information and photographs I needed. Standing tall among them were Mark Falzini, archivist at the New Jersey State Police Archives, Charlene Roice and her staff at Hess-Roice Research Consultants, Minneapolis, Minnesota, Ruth Brine at Time/Life. Among the Lindbergh scholars, the late Alden Whitman, journalist and gentleman, understood the Lindberghs in all their complexity and graciously shared his experience and insights with me.

I especially want to thank my research assistant, Julie Bertles Greicius, whose passion for Anne and her work matched my own. Her tireless efforts, unflagging enthusiasm, and insatiable curiosity contributed immeasurably to the substance and spirit of the book.

My gratitude, as well, to Stephen Koch, teacher and friend, whose encouragement led me to my editor, Nan Talese at Doubleday. Through these long years she taught me the difference between a good idea and a good book. She, along with my agent, Georges Borchardt, gave me an opportunity to write a biography few novice writers are privileged to have. Their patience and support through my many drafts enabled my project to come to fruition. Thank you, as well, to Alicia Brooks, assistant editor at Nan A. Talese/Doubleday, who spent many long hours playing midwife to its publication, easing and expediting its safe passage, and to Sandee Yuen, Publicity Director, whose abundant expertise moved my private journey into the public eye. My gratitude, as well, to my photo-editors, Alexandra Truitt and Jerry Marshall, to Midge Decter, and to the many people who read and critiqued the manuscript.

If one can thank a friend for her character and constancy, for her love of me and her love of life, Wendy Donn Podos deserves much praise. And if one can thank a mentor for her faith and courage, Lila Kalinich has earned my deepest gratitude. These ten years she has walked beside me, teaching me to trust the process and to see "the mountains in the darkest gorge."

My children Allison, Justin, and David deserve a medal for their forbearance—finally, their mother's obsession has come to an end. It was my love for my daughter Allison, my first child, that brought me to Anne Lindbergh and I hope my work serves her well. As a young wife and a lawyer, she strives to become the "modern woman" whom Anne imagined in *Gift from the Sea.*

But there are certain "mysteries," as Anne would say, that no one can measure or articulate. Those I reserve for my husband, Roger, who was enough of a hero to teach me about Charles and enough of a teacher to make me feel like a hero.

SUSAN HERTOG
SUNDAY, APRIL 4, 1999

Table of Contents

And there is a Catskill eagle in some souls that can alike dive down into the blackest gorges, and soar out of them again and become invisible in the sunny spaces. And even if she forever flies within that gorge, that gorge is in the mountains; so that even in her lowest swoop the mountain eagle is still higher than the other birds upon the plain, even though they soar.

HERMAN MELVILLE,
Moby-Dick

Anne Morrow Lindbergh

HER LIFE

Prelude

*A*nne Morrow Lindbergh *on the balcony of her chalet*
in Vevey, Switzerland, August 1988. (*Photographed by the author*)

The first time I saw Anne Lindbergh was in Minnesota, in 1985, at an annual meeting of the Lindbergh Fund, the environmental organization established in honor of her late husband, Charles. In spite of the urgings of family and friends, Mrs. Lindbergh refused to meet me. For four days, I watched from afar as she bristled at the obsequity of admirers, as she exploded with warmth among friends, as she accepted awards and gave them graciously; I wished I could meet her face to face, if only for a moment.

But a tight circle of friends protected her with a fervor attendant on a holy shrine. Her presence lingered like incense behind closed doors. If, by chance, one approached the "forbidden," angry voices rose in protest, forming a protective circle around her. Some who shielded her seemed proud to be part of this inner circle. Others appeared angered, even imprisoned by it. All seemed creatures of habit rather than of conviction, trapped in a script rehearsed for half a century.

They protected her, they said, because she was "weak"; weak with the scars of age and tragedy. And yet there was a paradox that begged to be understood. Those who treated her as though she were weak knew she was strong.

"Strong as steel," they whispered to me in corners of the room while they tended their priestess as if she were a lost lonely child.

Fascinated by her mask, and by the intricate mythology she had created in its service, I wondered why this disciplined writer, this pioneering aviator, this fervent conservationist, this mother of five, and the wife of the indomitable Charles Lindbergh chose to appear weak? What was she concealing behind this elaborate charade?

With a notebook full of observations and a bitterness common among those who pursue the Lindberghs, I sat at the departure gate, waiting for the plane home to New York, when Mrs. Lindbergh, quite by chance, sat down beside me. Not believing the good fortune the gods had granted me, I reveled at being, for the first time, in the physical presence of a subject I had been studying for twenty years.

I sat very still, taking note of her deeply lined cheek, her angular profile, and her frail curved body, as she sat, Sphinx-like, in thought. How small and insignificant she seemed, sitting in that blue vinyl chair, her head turned away from the bustling traffic of people, toward the glass-walled balcony overlooking the airfield. She sat cross-legged, drawing energy inward, not so much a presence as a receptacle for the sights and sounds that are the kaleidoscope of airport life. More striking than her posture or her stature was the fact that she was alone. No one recognized or followed her. No imposing husband sat beside her. None of her five children was there to disturb her thoughts or to demand her attention. She was a gentle sylph of a woman, girlish even in her old age, slightly bent and dressed in blue, watching the comings and goings of airport life behind dark, passably fashionable glasses. At any moment, I expected her to turn and greet me. I, after all, knew her well.

At the age of twenty-one, I had given birth to my daughter. We spent the summer at an island beach, and I read Anne Lindbergh's book *Gift from the Sea*. It spread clear across my life like a finely focused lens. It was the mid-sixties, in the heat of an escalating war, when presidents and statesmen, visionaries and children were beaten and killed in the fevered anarchy of the streets. To those raised in the quiescence of the fifties, the line between law and lawlessness was nothing more than a matter of opinion.

Looking at history through our newspapers, we ordinary house-wives, neither soldiers nor protesters, had no voice and had no answers. We had only questions—gnawing questions that consumed our neatly fashioned lives, turning every certainty into a battleground of ideas. My friends and I, finely dressed young matrons behind our proper English prams, walked our babies along city streets, stalking ideas as if we were jungle cats. What did it mean to be a woman? How did one live out one's needs without violating oneself or those one loved? How could a woman be free and independent, yet part of a constellation of social expectations and relationships that threatened to eclipse her?

In little more than a hundred pages, in language so simple and lyrical that it was more poetry than prose, Anne Morrow Lindbergh set forth the answers in *Gift from the Sea*. Look inside yourself, she said. Strip life of its conventions; reach down to the essentials. Find the core of your being. Make it an *oasis* for yourself and others. Take strength from it and create a space, sacred and inviolable, in which to become and express yourself. Do it gently, do it gracefully, without anger or destruction. Do it because the quality of your life—in fact, the quality of Western civilization!—depends on your authenticity.

I had read her book without knowledge of her past, her husband, or her fame. And yet understanding the genesis of her philosophy became an increasing obsession. How and where did she find these answers? How dare she answer with certainty the questions that threatened the fabric of our lives? I unearthed her books in libraries and bookstands. I read her diaries and letters as they appeared off the press.

Through her writing, Anne Lindbergh became my mentor and my friend. I walked alongside her, like some metaphysical voyeur, dusting myself off when she fell and applauding myself for her every victory. Her thoughts and her anguish became a laboratory for me to study my role as wife and mother, as well as to cultivate my literary ambition. I came to believe that if I were to understand Anne Lindbergh and the choices she had made, I could chart the process of female creativity, finding feminine consciousness in crises, heightened by the anguish and isolation of fame. I would know not only myself, but something more: the anatomy of a woman who had chosen to become a writer.

Now, after twenty years, and merely by chance, Anne Morrow Lindbergh, total stranger and intimate friend, was sitting beside me. I introduced myself and reached for her hand. Her touch was like a fluttering bird; energy and movement without flesh or place. She raised her eyebrow like a camera clicking its shutter. My image recorded, she withdrew. Out of indifference, she turned away.

Fueled by that chance meeting in 1985, I pursued her, making circles of words and relationships around her, forcing her to acknowledge my intent to write her story. Slowly, I pierced the inner circle.

Two years later, out of weariness as much as curiosity, Anne Morrow Lindbergh invited me to her mountain chalet in a small town east of Geneva, Switzerland.

The invitation held the fire of Old Testament sin. It was an act of intimidation hidden between the folds of social grace and literary allusion.

"I feel an aversion to having my LIFE written," she wrote. "The aversion has to do with the appalling amount of publicity we have already had and my intense desire to escape from it . . . The aversion is not to you but to publicity, public scrutiny and the falsity of public images. In fact, *all* images. A man called Stiller once wrote about images in a novel. One of the characters says to another 'You have made me an image . . . Every image is a "sin." ' "

In this country steeped in Calvinism, the language of the Ten Commandments had a forbidding ring: "You shall not make for yourself a graven image . . . for I the Lord am a jealous God."

My mind both rejected and obeyed her warning. I too had Old Testament beginnings. Eastern European Orthodox Jews observed the ancient prescript, much like the Midwestern or New England fundamentalists. I too had ancestors whose lives had been spent in prayer and public service. Their voices "murmured in my blood" like rain-filled streams, ready to overflow. They told me that Life, not Art, was the true sphere of man. And woman? A woman who makes "images"? My grandmother would have mocked me with laughter, then narrowed her eyes in anger. What was I doing in this strange and Gentile city without my husband and my children? Why wasn't I content to live God's will? What was I trying to prove?

I was not trying to prove anything, I thought; I was trying to understand. I wanted to find a pattern—a way of living that would permit me to balance love and work without the scars of sacrifice. It was a personal journey, perhaps a selfish one, but if I could bring order to one woman's life, wouldn't my words and images serve others?

Anne Lindbergh was tired, she would later say, of "sugary images" that made her appear "sweet and kind." She was "a rebel," she said with pride and anger. I began to realize that my task was to find the rebel beneath the saint, the steel beneath the porcelain—the psychological reality that obscured the myth.

My problems, however, would prove to be less esoteric. I had written no books, and I was not a historian. I was a housewife and a mother of three, with a fascination for Anne Lindbergh and a desire to write. Paradoxically, my lack of public reputation persuaded Mrs. Lindbergh to take me at my word. I had no past and I made no promise except my commitment to honest scholarship. In a period of two years, I cultivated relations with members of the family. It was clear that I had no political or ideological motives, and, for the moment at least, was welcomed as a friend. But as I met with Anne Lindbergh again and again, ten times in all, her advisers grew suspicious. Who was this "housewife" Susan Hertog? And what did she really want? Was she as earnest as she appeared to be, or was she part of a news media conspiracy? By the time Anne had her stroke, in 1991, many established writers were banging on her door, and, in the end, I was not given access to her unpublished papers. Nonetheless, I persevered.

The story, I realized, was mine for the taking, and it was more grand than any I might have imagined. To my advantage, Anne and Charles were writers. They wrote about everything to everybody. They had published diaries, articles, and books—travelogues, novels, memoirs, and poetry. I visited private and public archives and traveled throughout the United States and Europe to visit friends and relatives of the Morrow and Lindbergh families. But my most precious and telling moments were those spent with Anne.

Our first meeting in Vevey, Switzerland, on a warm August afternoon still holds the thrill of reunion with a friend I knew so little and yet so well. As I emerged from the tunnel of the train station, I waved to Anne excitedly, but of course she did not recognize me. We entered a small gray car, and Anne drove. I was surprised by her confidence at the wheel. How difficult to see this frail woman in a white cotton sweater as the girl who had blazed uncharted routes to places where no

woman had ever been. In my mind, I stripped the veneer of her aged
skin to seek, once again, the smooth-faced girl.

The road narrowed into a driveway, and we chugged slowly up an
incline. To an American unschooled in the nuances of Swiss architecture, the chalet looked like a cottage, like so many found in the woods
of rural New York. It was a modest A-frame, deep reddish-brown, and
unadorned, except for a few flower pots that hung from the balcony like
beads on a summer necklace.

We walked up the narrow stone steps to the main room, which was
both kitchen and living space, opening on a balcony overlooking the
mountains. She was proud of this house. Charles had called it Anne's
Chalet.

Anne served a generous lunch: meat, cheese, dark bread with raw
mountain butter, and salad. As we passed the salad and the bread, the
conversation turned personal, with Anne skillfully orchestrating it. Yet
beneath the placid surface of Anne's talk was a relentless and piercing
scrutiny. I had been warned of her intensity, of her finely tuned antennae hidden beneath her gentility and reserve. She scanned my face and
hands, examined my jewelry and my clothes for traces of falsity and indiscretion. She probed my eyes to seek my intent.

"I learned a lot about you," she said as we sat after lunch on the balcony.

I did not question her. I had passed a test.

As she spoke, she removed her dark glasses and I saw for the first time
her violet, almond-shaped eyes. She leaned back into the worn,
plastic-flowered chaise, looking up, unfocused, at the sky, as though
seeking divine acknowledgment. She gazed at the hillside and the mountains, commenting on the birds as they fed at her window, enthralled by
their beauty and by the intricacies of their play. They connected her, she
said, to the "great forces of nature"; they renewed her energy and re-
asserted the creative essence of the universe. In this setting, amid the un-
shorn trees, the cowbells, and the mountains, she seemed strong and
lucid, confident and proud of her ability to think and to remember.

Because she knew few strangers, she spoke to me as a friend, relieved, even grateful to unburden her thoughts. In spite of her reticence, she loved to talk. Slowly, our conversation began to take shape.

I spoke of her books; Anne spoke of Charles.

I spoke of her poetry; Anne spoke of Charles.

I spoke of her father; Anne spoke of Charles.

"I want to set the record straight," she finally said. "That's all I have
left of him."

Her monologue seemed to hang in space—bold and unadorned. It
was as though she were renouncing something old and dear; as though
she knew it was time to confront the inevitable. Her face grew soft as
her words changed fragments of memory into a story.

"My life began when I met Charles Lindbergh."

1

A New Beginning

*Charles Lindbergh on the steps of the American
Embassy in Mexico City, December 1927.*

(Amherst College Archives)

I have no life but this,
To lead it here;
Nor any death, but lest
Dispelled from here;
Nor tie to earths to come,
Nor action new,
Except through this extent,
The realm of you.

— EMILY DICKINSON

DECEMBER 14, 1927, VALBUENA FIELD, MEXICO CITY

It was nearly noon, and Colonel Lindbergh was late. Thousands of people lined the broad airfield, flooding the valley between the snow-covered mountains with a frenzied rush of sound and color. It was as if all of Mexico had gathered for the spectacle: men in overalls, their serapes pulled tight against the chill morning air, women in brightly colored shawls, and children kicking gaily in the dust. They had trudged the roads before dawn, only to wait for hours in the midday sun. Worn by heat and delay, the crowd loosened and fragmented. Once stiff with expectation, the people settled into a carnival mood, making the soldiers who paced the lines twitch with uncertainty. Anything could happen with a crowd this size; its energy unleashed could easily turn destructive. When Lindbergh had arrived in Paris after his transatlantic flight only seven months earlier, the crowd had surged toward him, mauling his plane in a wild stampede.[1]

United States Ambassador Dwight Morrow waited impatiently. A lot was riding on Lindbergh's safe arrival, and Morrow was not one to take disappointment lightly. At fifty-four, he was an accomplished lawyer and a Wall Street millionaire, but he was new to Mexico, this "cemetery" of political reputations, and he had much to prove.

Standing five feet four inches tall, Dwight Morrow was less than imposing. Dressed like a banker in a three-piece pinstripe suit, in spite of the heat, he posed for the cameras, fumbled with his glasses and smiled nervously at the press. His clothes, as usual, fit poorly; this time they seemed to swallow him whole. His large head, topped by a blue fedora, rested on the edge of a thickly starched collar, and his trousers bagged shapelessly over his shoes. He was a Chaplinesque figure, a parody of a gentleman, like a poor man dressed in a rich man's clothes. His body looked like an uninvited guest, self-indulgently diverting the issues at hand.[2]

The issues at hand were heavy indeed. Mexico and the United States were on the brink of war. The Mexican government, wracked with internecine struggle and hopelessly in debt, had threatened to nationalize American oil companies. The business community was up in arms, and diplomatic relations were at their ebb. President Calvin Coolidge had concluded it meant sending in Morrow or the U.S. Marines.[3]

While Coolidge worried that Morrow's connection to J. P. Morgan would link him to American business interests, he banked on his pristine style and reputation. Morrow could outreason and outquote any lawyer around. He could preach the Bible and bore his listeners with Thucydides, but his true gift lay in the realm of compromise. Resisting the taint of marketplace pragmatism, Morrow decided that his mission was to compose differences, as a conductor might orchestrate a melody or a tune. The plain truth was that he was a master of deals.

Rigorously trained in mathematics by his father, Dwight believed in the morality of logic. James Elmore Morrow, a fundamentalist Presbyterian of Scottish-Irish descent, had taught his precocious second-born son the art and method of systematic thought. Relentlessly, as though it were the very stuff of salvation, he had drilled his boy in mathematics and syllogism, along with the hundred and seven questions of the Presbyterian catechism. Logic, James believed, was intrinsic to ethics—the outward manifestation of God's ordinance, no less binding than prayer and church. It made one deal with realities rather than appearances and put the burden of proof on the inquirer. Dwight dealt with issues, not with men. He could make wrathful negotiators talk as if they were comrades, yet have each side think it was outwitting the other. It was a gift that his partners at J. P. Morgan and Company had deemed priceless.

And this priceless gift had earned him a fortune. When he left Morgan, only two months earlier, after fourteen years as its chief counsel, he was a full partner, earning more than a million dollars a year. Now, his money permitted him the luxury of public service—his dream since he had been a law clerk at the age of twenty-two. Money, he believed, turned dreamers into men of action, allowing them to participate in history. It wasn't that he wanted to be rich; he just didn't want to be poor. His father's inability to earn a good salary was underlined by his mother's obvious disappointment. Although Clara Morrow, a Campbellite fundamentalist Presbyterian,[4] considered it natural to submit to her husband, she made plain that she preferred "bonnets" to books. Wishing to please his mother, Dwight imagined himself a "dragon-slayer," bringing home the spoils of his conquest. It was a fantasy he would often need to replay.[5]

While some saw him as a man of ruthless ambition, each career move, in fact, caused him anguish. He saw himself as a statesman—a philosopher king—removed from the rabble of the political arena. He served God by serving the community, certain that his good works would place him among the elect.[6] Yet he felt guilty about his money, as if he were a renegade academic seduced by the pleasures of commerce and status. He was a reluctant Horatio Alger hero who would have rather been an Abraham Lincoln.

Perched high on the flag-draped grandstand above the field, scanning the horizon for Lindbergh's plane, Morrow's tiny figure beside the robust presence of Mexican President Plutarco Calles was a reminder of the chasm between the two men. The twelfth president in the seventeen years since the revolution, Calles was a clever politician, a Machiavellian leader cloaking his aims in the rhetoric of nationalism and peace. His enemies called him an "iron man," no less a despot than the man he had ousted. But in these weeks preceding the election, he had gone too far, murdering his competitors and their supporters to clear the way for his nationalist party. For all his bravado, revolution seemed imminent; he could no longer rely on the loyalty of the army.

Dark-eyed and grim behind his close-cropped mustache, President Calles looked nervously at his watch. He had been up all night, calling his staff for news of Lindbergh's flight. The bloody events of the last few weeks had imbued everything, even this midweek master stroke of public relations, with bitter irony. Charles Lindbergh's arrival would be a humbling reminder of Calles's dependence on American money. If he were to survive, he would need the good will of the American government and some old-fashioned Yankee theater.

Suddenly, the sky roared. Five escort planes, zooming in formation, dazzled the crowd like a jolt of electricity. People jumped to their feet, pointing and shouting at the approaching aircraft.

Morrow was relieved. The flight, after all, had been his idea. With no air routes or radios to guide a pilot, even the best could go down. There were fears that Lindbergh had cracked up; that his motor had failed him in one of the rocky districts where no plane could land safely. Morrow had tried to dissuade Lindbergh from making a nonstop flight from Washington, but Lindbergh had been adamant. If his flight connected the nations' capitals, it would have greater political significance, Lindbergh said, especially by drawing the attention of Congress.[7]

Morrow, who had met Lindbergh at the White House a few months earlier, quickly learned that he was no backwoods farm boy.[8] Born to a line of skillful politicians, Lindbergh understood Washington, understood Congress, and understood the power and whim of public opinion. His paternal grandfather, Ola Månsson, had been one of the few landholding peasants in Sweden to serve in the Riksdag. Although his was a voice of social reform, Månsson blatantly abused his position. As an officer of a Malmö bank with connections to government officials, he was accused of bribery and embezzlement. In 1859, to escape imprisonment, Månsson changed his name to August Lindbergh,[9] left his wife and seven children, and fled to America with his nineteen-year-old mistress, Louisa Carline, and their illegitimate son, Charles, to begin a new life in central Minnesota.[10]

Bypassing the fertile prairies of the Swedish colonies, the Lindberghs bought a hundred and sixty acres of woodlands and pasture in Melrose, Minnesota, a new community of German immigrants. While August tilled the land to grow oats and wheat, and set up a blacksmith shop a mile outside town, his peasant-girl wife tended her baby and worked in the fields. Lonely and despairing of their future, Louisa, in her rosebud bonnets, milked the cows and pined for home, family, and Sweden.[11] With time, the farm prospered, and their handwrought sod hut was transformed into the biggest frame house in the county. Still an outspoken agent of reform, Lindbergh was appointed postmaster and village secretary and, later, clerk of school districts and justice of the peace. When the four children born to him and Louisa were grown, he married her secretly in the town church and put the scandals of Sweden behind him. But, as if in mourning for something forever lost, Louisa wore a black dress beneath her kitchen apron all her life.

August, however, had few regrets. Unlike the unforgiving God of James Morrow, August Lindbergh's God demanded no penance.[12] According to Lindbergh's Lutheran-based theology, sin was inherent in the human condition, and faith in Christ justified salvation. The individual served God through the institutions of the community, but divine will superseded its structures and its laws. Some men were called upon to wear the "mask of God"; sometimes this meant breaking the rules.

Independence and self-reliance were August Lindbergh's defining principles, and he handed them down as gospel to his son, Charles August. When C.A. was six years old, Lindbergh gave him a gun, permitting him the run of the surrounding woods to shoot game and duck for the family table. But if C.A. learned to love the freedom of the wilderness and the open sky, he also witnessed the vicissitudes of farming. Crop failures, falling prices, and the unregulated growth of railroads nearly disenfranchised the small Midwest farmer. In 1883, determined not to bend to an elitist government controlled by the "Eastern money," C. A. Lindbergh enrolled in the law school of the University of Michigan.

By the turn of the century, he emerged a gentleman, much as his father had been forty years earlier. Five feet eleven inches tall, he wore elegant three-piece suits, a gold pocket watch, and a hat worn stylishly askew. In the lumber town of Little Falls, Minnesota, northeast of Melrose, he became a commercial and residential landholder and a shareholder in several banks, accruing assets of nearly a quarter of a million dollars. In 1887, he married Mary, the sweet-faced daughter of his landlord, Moses La Fond, a French-Canadian settler who had carved a niche for himself in the state legislature. Pious, unschooled, and dedicated, Mary nonetheless had ambitions of her own. After finishing her domestic chores, she devoted her time to painting and sewing, and won prizes for her needlework. Determined also to learn the art of photography, she took pictures of her three children and developed the film in a laboratory she devised in the hollow behind the front hall staircase.

Soon, Mary and Charles moved to a large brick house close to town and raised their daughters in the Congregational church, straddling the mores of the backwoods settlers and the new and affluent middle class. When Mary died in 1898, during surgery for the removal of a tumor that turned out to be a fetus, C.A. was bereft, yet her death brought the possibility of transforming his life. Still an ambitious young man of forty, he stood at the edge of a booming community that held the promise of wealth and political power. In 1900 he sent his daughters to boarding school and moved to a large hotel in the center of town.

There he met Evangeline Lodge Land, a high school chemistry teacher newly arrived from Detroit, and was immediately taken with her beauty and youth, her rippling Irish laugh, her regal capes and long lacy dresses. His first marriage had the air of an arranged convenience, but his courtship of Evangeline was steeped in romance. It was clear that he had met his match in this fiery, ambitious woman of twenty-four who was determined not to settle for a backwoods life. And it was clear to Evangeline that the handsome widower with the razor wit and the pocketful of cash offered her more than a career in teaching.

Within nine months they were married, and the following year, on February 4, 1902, Charles Augustus, was born. C.A. had purchased a

hundred and twenty acres, two and a half miles southwest of Little
Falls, bordered by the Mississippi River and bisected by Pike Creek.
Although the Lindberghs called it "the farm," it was not a farm at all;
it was mostly wild land with huge white pines, oaks, lindens, elms, and
poplars. The three-story house, with its sweeping porches and oak-paneled walls, towered on a bluff above the trees and the plum orchard in
the valley along the river.[13] It was equipped with bathrooms, hot-water
radiators, and water pumped by gas from a well, and it held four second-floor bedrooms and a third floor with servants' quarters and a bil-
liard room. It had cost so much, by Little Falls standards—$8000—that
C.A. was ashamed to let anyone know. He and his wife gave lavish parties for the Little Falls elite, serving delicacies brought in from Chicago
and Minneapolis on imported china and crystal. C.A. hired men to
work the farm and the stables, and Evangeline hired a maid, a cook, and
a nurse to help care for C.A.'s daughters and the infant son. Now the
country squire's wife, Evangeline wanted to spend her leisure painting
flowers on glass and practicing her scales on the piano.

But there was a dark side to this romantic idyll. Shortly after
Charles was born, Evangeline grew bitter, angry, sometimes violent,
making a mockery of the family's status and their home, shaming C.A.
in front of family and friends. His daughters thought she was "crazy"
and accused her of child abuse; others construed her behavior as "schizophrenia," a turn-of-the-century label for any inexplicable female dis-
turbance. But there was a psychological reality that went unnoticed by
those too willing to cast her as a gold-digger and madwoman.[14]
Evangeline's postpartum mood swings may well have been extreme, reflecting a family tendency toward mania and depression, but she was
also reacting to relations and circumstances.

More educated, sophisticated, and ambitious than the small-town
wives of the moneyed men whom she befriended for C.A.'s benefit,
Evangeline was alienated in a town worlds apart from everyone and
everything she had ever known. Furthermore, C.A. had taken a mistress, and Evangeline was left alone in the big pine house with their
small son and C.A.'s teenage daughters. Feeling abandoned and be-

trayed, she became the prisoner of a man who would neither love her nor let her go. Employment was not suitable for a woman of her class, and divorce would have meant public shame and the end of C.A.'s political aspirations. While Evangeline's behavior may have seemed inexplicable, the asylums were full of women who could not escape the restrictions of marriage or motherhood through employment or divorce. It was in the context of her marriage to a sadistic man and the loneliness of the circumstances she had unwittingly chosen that Evangeline rebelled.[15]

On August 6, 1905, the charade came to an end. A fire that began on the third floor, in a closet frequented by the maid, burned the house to its foundation. Within twenty minutes, everything Charles had known was consumed in flames. Three-year-old Charles peeked out from behind the backyard barn at the black cloud of smoke funneling through the roof of his home. The next morning, the ashes still smoldering beneath the roof beams, Evangeline plodded through the wreckage to find her pearl-and-diamond engagement ring.[16] Afterward, she always saw the fire as a symbol of the rage festering beneath the surface of her marriage; young Charles came to see it as the end of an illusion.

With the destruction of the house, the Lindberghs' tenuous marriage lost its hold. Evangeline took Charles back to Detroit, and C.A. moved to an apartment in Minneapolis. Maintaining the semblance of family life, Evangeline and her son returned to Little Falls each summer and stayed in a cottage C.A. had built on the wild bluff above the river. It stood on the leveled remains of the old mansion, and they called it their "camp." But they never really went "home" again.

Although Charles would savor the memories of long summer days, swimming with his friends in a nearby creek and navigating logs down the Mississippi River, in truth, after the age of three, he lived a solitary and fragmented life. Shuttled between his grandparents' home in Detroit, "camp" in Little Falls, and his father's apartment in Minneapolis, he attended eleven primary schools, never completing a full year of study.[17] Left to fend for themselves, with little money, Charles and his mother lived like pariahs at the edge of a society that had no place for single mothers and little tolerance for separation or divorce.[18] While C.A. controlled the purse strings from afar, Evangeline held her only child close. Demanding his companionship and needing his competence, she came to expect more than her son could give, and he, in turn, acted bigger than he was, trying to fill the emptiness of his mother's life with a heightened sense of his power and achievements.

C.A.'s politics, meanwhile, were becoming radical. When his real estate and credit operations failed in 1905, he turned against the capitalist system and was elected to Congress in 1906 as a champion of farmers' rights. Representing the Sixth District of Minnesota, he moved to Washington, D.C., with his secretary, reputed to be his long-time mistress. But his Populist fervor quickly turned paranoid, and he labeled Catholics and capitalists the political forces bent on destroying the farmers of America. C.A.'s friends called him a martyr and a saint, his constituents, however, thought him a xenophobe and a Bolshevik. He called for a more direct democracy to reward all the "energies of labor," and he condemned the unfair distribution of wealth and the commercial and industrial "evil" of the cities. In 1916, when he ran for governor, he was endorsed by the Non-Partisan League, but was plagued by verbal threats and physical abuse, and his campaign ended in defeat. No longer in Congress, C.A. hustled real estate in Florida but barely managed to survive one day at a time. In 1924, he died of a brain tumor in Little Falls, homeless, penniless, broken, and alone.

By way of compensation, Charles was to crave a life of success measured according to objective standards. Disgusted by what he called the "spineless subjectivity" evident in most people's lives, the young Lindbergh learned to value the clear-cut language of science and the precise methodology of his physician grandfather, Charles H. Land,[19] whose laboratory in Detroit provided him a refuge from relations and controversies he could neither control nor understand. He came to believe that "science held the key to the mystery of Life; Science was truth; Science was power."[20] With this key, he would later write that man "could taste the wine of the gods, of which they would know nothing." Yet, he wondered if flying was too "godlike" and arrogant.

He wanted to be a physician, but fearing he was too "stupid" to complete the necessary course work, Lindbergh enrolled at the University of Wisconsin, aiming for an engineering degree.[21] Unprepared for the rigors of college life, and intolerant of authority, he dropped out after his first year, before he was thrown out. In 1922, at the age of twenty, Lindbergh left Madison, Wisconsin, on his motorcycle with nothing more than a vague notion that he wanted to fly.

Quite simply, he wanted "a new life," one that would rise above the "dusty moss of danger." Later, he wrote that flying encompassed all he loved: "the air, the sky, the lure of adventure, the appreciation of beauty."[22] It lay beyond the descriptive words of men—where life meets death on an equal plane; where man is more than man, and existence both supreme and valueless at the same instant.

After rumbling southwest to Nebraska, he became an apprentice pilot, hiring himself out as a stuntman and barnstormer with a "flying circus" in exchange for flying lessons. He walked on the wings of primitive one-engine planes, earning the nickname "Daredevil Lindbergh." A year later, in 1923, without the skill or license of a solo pilot, Lindbergh bought himself a monoplane, a salvaged World War I Curtiss "Jenny." As an apprentice at the Nebraska Standard Aircraft Corporation, he earned both his license and his freedom, and by the summer was on his own, barnstorming through Alabama and Mississippi, offering rides for cash along the way.

By the turn of the year, Lindbergh was committed to a career as a professional pilot. He joined the Army Flight School in San Antonio, Texas, and graduated first in his class. Within a few months, at the age of twenty-three, he became chief pilot for the Robinson Aircraft Corporation in St. Louis, laying out routes for the U.S. mail. It was on one of those long-distance night flights that he suddenly thought of competing for the prize offered by Raymond Orteig to a pilot for a nonstop transatlantic flight. His mind held only one question: "Why not?"[23]

Charles would later call it "a vision born of night, altitude, and moonlight"; now he was quick to convert the desire into an efficient

plan. In a sharp reversal of his father's ideology, Lindbergh courted industrial capitalists, hoping to raise money for the experimental flight.
He felt "uncomfortable" on the "posh" upholstery of bank offices, he
later wrote, but he clearly understood the influence of "a felt hat and a
silk scarf" and the power of well-conceived "propaganda." Confident of
his commitment and skill, he accelerated the course of his operation,
and within weeks had backers, a plane, and a public following.[24]

Other flyers from England, France, and Italy—famous, experienced,
and with unlimited funds—had been thwarted by accident, poor judgment, and craft design. But Lindbergh conceived of a single-man, single-engine plane, built to his specifications by the Ryan Company, with
220 horsepower and a flying range of 4000 miles. On May 21, 1927,
he took off from Roosevelt Field in Long Island, New York, and, at the
speed of a hundred and seven miles per hour, arrived in Paris 33½ hours
later, to the cheers of a hundred and fifty thousand Frenchmen. Charles
was stunned by the magnitude of his welcome; the government of
France treated him like a monarch. He was paraded through the streets
of Paris, asked to address the French assembly, and awarded the Cross
of the Legion of Honor.

A week later, Charles went to London, where the crowds once again
were nearly out of control. He had hoped to fly around the world, stopping to see his grandfather's native Sweden, but President Coolidge
called him home to be honored by the American people. Ground had
been gained; much had been conquered. His flight symbolized the hope
of the future, but it also captured a nostalgia for the past. His spartan
simplicity mirrored an aspect of the collective psyche that Americans
feared they were losing. The sandy-haired boy with the modest grin and
borrowed suits too tight in the chest confirmed some notion of heart-
land integrity. Lindbergh was both firm and implacable, humble and
shy, and when he spoke, he used the language of the farm laborer and
the workingman—direct, concise, and down-home practical. The technology that had grown out of the exigencies of World War I had extended the perimeters of ordinary consumers with the crank of a motor
and the turn of a dial. The prism of radio and the motion picture screen

had brought them the power to see themselves and to measure their lives according to new standards of wealth, beauty, and glamour. These standards were the very stuff of Hollywood fantasy, creating, in turn, new expectations. Americans knew what they had gained even as they feared the price they were paying. Lindbergh told them that nothing had been lost. They could keep all the freedom that technology promised without selling their lusty souls to the devil.

Within the first week after his flight, Lindbergh had received $5 million of commercial offers—books, records, cosmetics, clothing, cigarettes, furniture, movies. Scores of popular songs and hundreds of poems had been written about his flight. And while Lindbergh would soon grow tired of the sound and touch of the crowd, it was clear that, in spite of his sincere humility, he enjoyed the public adulation.

Dwight Morrow had met Lindbergh by chance on the day of his arrival home from England. When Lindbergh's ship, the *Memphis,* sailed into port in Virginia, Morrow, head of the newly formed Aircraft Board, was having lunch with President Coolidge.[25] Lindbergh arrived at the presidential mansion, and the magnetism between the two men was immediate. Standing six feet two inches tall, the lean, beautiful flyer was everything Morrow had wanted to be—the dragon-slaying man of action, courage, and moral rectitude. The small, Bible-quoting philosopher with his pants too long would see Lindbergh as a conquering prince whose confidence came from a place so deep that it seemed to redefine the meaning of virtue.

Seeing, as well, the naïveté of his own youth in this ambitious young man, Morrow had a paternal desire to embrace him. He recruited twenty-two of his J. P. Morgan associates to raise $10,500 to pay Lindbergh's St. Louis debts, and offered his services as financial adviser to invest the young man's rapidly accumulating wealth. For all Lindbergh's courage and extraordinary competence, he struck Morrow as a bit of a waif. He was certain that Lindbergh, despite his well-honed political instincts, did not have the street knowledge to match his new fast-paced, media-hounded life.

Lindbergh was grateful. Unlike the other men who were riding his coattails, Morrow was warm, genuine, and protective. As self-appointed liaison between Charles and the financial community, Morrow shielded him from the strain of public demand. When Morrow was appointed ambassador to Mexico, Lindbergh asked him if he could be of help. Morrow quickly replied, "A little flying in Latin-America . . . would be a fine adventure."[26]

Once again, Morrow's political instincts were sharp; Lindbergh's flight was exactly what he needed to assuage American dissension with the Calles regime. It was the perfect confluence of three men and their causes, wrapped and sealed in one glorious metaphor. For President Calles, Lindbergh's flight was a seductive distraction, a grand illusion of peace and reconciliation. For Morrow, Lindbergh's presence offered credibility and clout. For Lindbergh, it was a chance to fly, long and fast, for the second time, and to prove the viability of commercial air-flight.

The escort planes disappeared over the mountains, and a dead silence enveloped the crowd. Suddenly, a soldier pushed through the lines and ran to the grandstand. President Calles listened to him, then rose to the microphone. The sighting had been false, he said. What had passed was an oil plane. There was no sign of the *Spirit of St. Louis.* He begged their patience.

Dwight's wife, Elizabeth Morrow, felt she had been patient long enough.[27] She was hot, hungry, and tired of exchanging pleasantries with the president. Small and birdlike, Betty, as she was called, had a delicacy that belied the force of her will. Prim and voguish in her cloche hat and caped navy dress, she appeared more like a clubwoman awaiting her butler than a dignitary about to meet an aviator-hero in the godforsaken dustbowl of a tropical airfield. With perfect composure, she chatted with Mrs. Weddell, wife of the British foreign minister, who served her a proper English lunch of sandwiches and lemonade from her hand-woven, neatly packed picnic basket.

If Betty shared her husband's impatience, she did not share his distress. For her, Lindbergh's flight was theater at its best. She loved embassy life—the costume and the ritual, the deference and the decorum. Except for the heat, she might have relished the drama of Lindbergh's late entrance, which made the prospect of meeting him that much sweeter.

All the years of struggle and waiting for the right post for Dwight had finally come to fruition. Like Dwight, she had a thirst for status and wealth which rose from fundamentalist roots. Wealth was the crown of a virtuous life, and she too had known the sting of poverty. As the eldest daughter of a ne'er-do-well lawyer, she had fought like a general in an all-out war to leave Cleveland, Ohio, and her mother's domestic "slavery." She had primed herself for upper-crust society, earning a degree at Smith College, wanting not only prestigious credentials, but the chance for financial independence. Marriage to a schoolmaster's unpolished son may have been a capitulation, but her failure at a literary career and the eight years served as the functional head of her downtrodden family had brought her to the brink of desperation. The family's dependence on her good-natured competence had become a burden and a social liability. It was now clear that Dwight Morrow was going places, and that her own ambition would amount to nothing. Morrow's determination and his desire to please her was a reasonable bargain for a woman of nearly thirty who was feeling the smart of spinsterhood. And the brash Mr. Morrow had not let her down. By the time she turned forty, she was living the comfortable and well-connected life of a suburban New Jersey matron. With maids to tend her house and nannies for her children, she filled her days with the "municipal housekeeping" of a female philanthropist.

At first she had objected to Dwight's Mexican assignment, calling it a "penny whistle" post, a trinket tossed to a whining child. She had hoped for Britain or, at the very least, France. But the Mexican people had taken her by surprise. She hadn't been prepared for the opulence and the grandeur of the American Embassy or for the generosity and reverence of the people who served them. She wrote to her daughter Anne at Smith College that she had fourteen servants who didn't permit her "to lift a pin." It was a long way from Cleveland and her mother's middle-class, threadbare drudgery.

But the sweet excitement of embassy life had its price. While their youngest child, Constance, sturdy and confident, traveled with them, Betty worried about her three older children. Elisabeth, the eldest, had recently graduated from Smith and was teaching at a Montessori school at home in Englewood, New Jersey. Anne was a senior at Smith; Dwight Jr. was a freshman at Groton.

Betty had been apart from her children before, but never for so long and never with so much uncertainty. Anne had written her not to worry about her children, that her responsibility to her father in Mexico was paramount. But Betty sensed that old patterns were breaking. In spite of the fact that Betty and Dwight had been moving toward this moment for twenty-five years, Dwight's appointment to Mexico somehow took them by surprise. Betty feared that they were losing touch with ordinary life, that they were paying a price for their status and pleasure.

Lindbergh's impending arrival made her eldest daughter's absence particularly painful. Elisabeth would have been a comfort to Betty. So easy with people, so poised and confident, Elisabeth was nothing like Betty at that age and everything she had wanted to be.[28] She was a bit of a miracle, after all the self-doubt Betty had known. Blond, long-legged, filled with vitality in spite of a weak heart, Elisabeth was self-possessed and in control. She would make a perfect match for "the beautiful young Colonel," and Betty was pleased that Lindbergh's arrival coincided with Elisabeth's impending visit for the Christmas holiday.

Anne, the Morrows' "second daughter," was to accompany Elisabeth. She, however, was cause for worry. More like a Morrow—small, brainy, brown-haired—Anne seemed vulnerable, like a bird you could frighten away by a wrong move or the slant of an eye. She was pretty enough, lithe and graceful, with violet-blue eyes, soft wavy hair, and, when she wasn't trying to hide it, a full lovely figure. But she was slow and tentative, almost apologetic for her presence.[29] She played the role of invisible observer, skirting a room with downcast eyes, sheathing herself in her own flesh. At times she cultivated her shyness, using it to keep others at a distance. Her acute sensitivity and solitary bent were far different from Betty's gregarious nature. Betty and Elisabeth were usually in harmony, but Betty and Anne seemed at odds. Even as a child, Anne had played at the edge, posturing conformity while flouting her mother's rules. When Anne made it clear that she wanted to go to Vassar instead of Smith, Betty felt her foundations shaking. Anne had capitulated like a good little girl, but the tension between them remained.

Dwight Jr., however, was the most fragile of all. Born on the eve of Morrow's entry into international finance, he was the only son and the heir apparent to Morrow's ambition, but he had been sickly from the start. As an infant he had suffered from a digestive disorder that left him malnourished and frail, and in spite of his strong intelligence, his natural athletic gifts, and handsome, chiseled face, he had been plagued by physical and mental illness.[30]

Betty made excuses. He was a genius like his father and his grandfather before him. That explained his weak nerves and delicate constitution; of course he broke down now and then. How could a genius survive in this imperfect world?[31] If he could only relax and take things as they came. Betty was relieved that he wasn't in Mexico now. The long trip and the attendant publicity would have been a terrible strain on his nerves. By the time he and the girls came for the Christmas holiday the following week, the tumult would be over. Until then, she and precocious "little Con" would entertain the famous young Colonel.

Lindbergh was two hours late, and there was still no sign. All of Mexico, said one observer, was holding its breath.

America's Viking of the Air had taken off at Bolling Field, in Washington, D.C., under the cover of low-hanging clouds that promised to follow him straight to Mexico. As he had prepared the *Spirit of St. Louis* for the second time to cross thousands of miles of uncharted territory, there had been no crowds, none of the drama of the transatlantic flight. Those who observed his businesslike attention to the last details of preparation felt that his intense efficiency had robbed them of the thrill of his impending departure. He was slow and meticulous, but as the weather began to clear, he had quickened his pace. When he emerged from the hangar, he was seen to have changed from his business attire into the brown leather jumpsuit that had become his uniform. The earflaps of his aviator's hood dangled at his chin, and a pair of goggles was pushed back from his forehead.

He moved toward the plane, and the cameramen crept closer and closer, encircling him like small black spiders with their tripods and hoods. Afraid that he might injure them as he taxied the plane to the runway, he yelled to them to move away. "If you play ball with me, I'll treat you fair. If you don't, I'll turn the other way."

The cameramen moved back, and Lindbergh, carrying three meat sandwiches and two quarts of water meant to last him over twenty-one hundred miles, prepared to climb into the plane.

"Wave to us!" the photographers shouted. Lindbergh, his face calm and serious, posed obligingly as he stepped into the "big machine."

The long flight to Mexico City was a welcome relief after months of pit stops across the states, preaching airplane safety to skeptical crowds. He had visited eighty-two cities and flown twenty-two thousand miles, making speeches, attending dinners, and marching in parades. Now, the tropical air would rest and stretch his mind, bringing him into a sensual contact with the terrain below. For a few hours there would be no hounding by the press nor demands of petty social necessities that had beleaguered him in the preceding months.[32]

He believed that flying posed little danger to one who was prepared. Even if there was danger, the nearness of death excited him—focusing, even purifying, his every thought and action—so that it was like living at the crux of life and death. The beauty and freedom of flight were worth more than anything he had known on the ground below. He would rather be killed in a crash than live the "antlike days" of a frightened spectator.[33]

The crowds no longer bothered him as much. Nothing could be as bad as it had been in London and Paris. Most amusing were the women—so fawning and silly, always trying to impress him. He, who had found women to be a problem all his life, was now the most coveted man in the world. He received hundreds of letters from female admirers, declaring their love and proposing marriage to the Prince of the

Air. Girls were everywhere, and for the first time he knew he could have his pick. Lindbergh had never liked to date; he hated the small talk and the pretense. His childhood had taught him that intimacy meant pain. Abandonment and suffocation—the two ends of the emotional spectrum—were integral to his notions of love and marriage. He felt in control only when he was alone. Yet in recent months he had begun observing young women more carefully. His public acclaim seemed to heighten his loneliness. A wife would be someone to fly with—a friend, "a crew."[34] Every time he shook hands with a girl, the press promptly had him "engaged." A movie company had offered him a flat million dollars for close-ups of his face during a marriage ceremony. Who the bride was didn't matter.

This was his second record-breaking flight, and he felt confident. The flight to Mexico City was fifteen hundred miles shorter than the distance from New York to Paris. The engine would not be overloaded, and the strength of his wings would not be tested by the calm tropical weather, yet the flight proved to be more difficult than he had expected. Unlike the northeast route to Paris, he flew southwest into the night. Fog and rain-streaked darkness followed him through Houston, Texas, and for six hundred and fifty miles he flew blind, forced to gauge his route by instruments. When he reached Tampico, on the gulf coast of Mexico, he expected to fly straight to Mexico City, two hundred and fifty miles away, but, engulfed by fog and without a plotted course, he drifted three hundred miles west to the state of Guadalajara, deep into the mountains of the Sierra Madre. Twenty-five hours into the flight he was lost, meandering over nameless territory, unmarked by rivers, railroads, and towns.[35]

At precisely sixteen minutes before three, Lindbergh's silver-winged plane dropped into view. It had taken him twenty-seven hours and fifteen minutes, only six hours under his meticulously planned flight to Paris. Still, it was nothing short of a miracle, compared with the Morrows' torturous week-long journey in a railroad car.

Saluting the hundred and fifty thousand people who now waited in the hot sun, Lindbergh flew his plane until "it seemed to hang in the air" and then descended in a long sweeping curve over the presidential box. Dwight Morrow, it was said, was the most pleased man in Mexico.

As if in gratitude, those on the field shouted bravos and hurled their broad-brimmed hats into the air. Unlike the Parisians, who had gouged his plane for souvenirs, these admirers took him up on their shoulders and carried him to the hangar. Instead of the ticker tape thrown by New Yorkers, the Mexicans deluged him with bouquets of flowers.

Morrow, driving with Captain Winslow, first secretary of the embassy, in his open car to greet Lindbergh, certainly did not expect an apology. As far as he and the thousands of impassioned spectators were concerned, the flight had been perfect. Lindbergh, however, was embarrassed at being two hours late. His railroad map had failed him, and his ignorance of Spanish kept him circling the towns, mistaking bathroom signs for station stops, challenging every ounce of his piloting sense, in spite of the clearing weather and the broad daylight. It had been, he felt, a poor showing for a friend.

The crowd, unconcerned with nuance, jumped the fences and swarmed the field, shouting "Viva Lindbergh," and "Bravo, Lindy." Lindbergh sat high on the rear fender of the car, just to make sure that everyone could see him. The throng on the field shouted with joy and stampeded toward the ambassador's car, clinging to its doors and blocking its way back to the grandstand. Trapped by the crowds, Betty was terrified; people grabbed at her clothes, nearly tearing them off.[36]

To Constance Morrow, the fourteen-year-old-daughter of Ambassador and Mrs. Morrow waiting at the stand, it seemed forever before the car returned. When it approached, she was nearly jammed through the railings by the photographers who rushed to see Lindbergh. While President Calles made a short speech and the mayor of Mexico City presented him with the keys, Constance kept her eyes glued on Lindbergh. Taken with the tall, sandy-haired flyer, she sent her impressions in a letter to Anne, still at Smith, preparing to leave for

Mexico.[37] To Anne's amusement, Constance had enclosed a hand-drawn portrait.

Sitting in her room at school, Anne felt no excitement at the thought of meeting Lindbergh. Elisabeth, she was certain, would thoroughly captivate him, as she did all the other boys they knew, while Anne would sit awkwardly, feeling like a fool. As usual, she would find herself alone in her room, ashamed and inadequate, eloquently rehashing the conversation before the mirror. Men brought out the best in Elisabeth but made Anne feel stupid and worthless.[38]

Her only consolation was the thought of seeing her mother and father. Returning to Smith without Elisabeth for her junior and senior years, and saying good-bye to her parents when they left for Mexico, had given Anne a taste of loneliness she had never known. And yet there was a feeling of separateness and strength she had never before permitted herself. No longer bound by her mother's circle of vigilance, Anne relaxed and stretched beyond the edge.

She had always resented her mother's double standard. Betty Morrow took the liberty of having her way. She went where and when she wanted, leaving the children at home with the nanny. Anne and Elisabeth, Dwight Jr., and Con spent many lonely nights in the nursery while their mother traveled through Europe, dining and entertaining, shopping for clothes, furniture, and art. It was for Morgan and Company, her mother would say, and later, during the war, for the Military Board. But her mother needn't have gone with her father, and she needn't have stayed so long. Betty Morrow was the perfect executive, Anne thought; she organized her children's lives and left.

The truth was that Anne really didn't know her father or her mother. They "never really talked to her," she later said. They were constantly moving, never touching ground.

But Christmas at home had always been different. Time stopped, and the world was reordered. Life itself seemed reconfirmed. The whole family assembled under one roof, and nothing was more important than home and one another. In October, Anne had written to her mother that

Christmas away from the social mania of New York held the promise of a quiet family holiday.[39]

But by December, she was beginning to wonder whether Mexico would be more of the same: dinners, parties, public events. More than ever, she would have to share her parents with others, to forgo the short moments of intimacy she treasured. Lindbergh's arrival in Mexico the week before sounded more like the "French Revolution" than a diplomatic reception. She could not imagine her place in this brash timpani of personalities and diplomatic decorum.

A week on the sleeper train was enough to extinguish any glimmer of excitement. Never in her twenty-two years had she been more bored or more cold. It was a bit like "dying," she wrote in her diary.[40] After boarding in New York, where she met Elisabeth and Dwight Jr., Anne had traveled to Chicago and then through St. Louis toward Laredo. The desolation and poverty of the small Texas towns seen through the window of her velvet-seated private car filled her with sadness. She was repelled by her parents' affluence, by the "waste" and "artificialities" of their indulgent "walled garden" life, and yet she was comforted, even grateful for its insulation. How terrible to be left behind in this "savage" land of mud-built houses, she mused.[41]

Elisabeth's unaccustomed presence by her side rekindled her jealousy. Her sister's delicately sculpted face, as smooth and translucent as fine alabaster, shone with new confidence. In the two years since graduating from Smith, Elisabeth had earned the respect of her parents. To their pleasure, she had become what they prized most: a teacher. The Morrows came from a long line of teachers, and nothing was more satisfying than passing on the tradition to their daughters. A teacher was a spiritual leader, her father had written, the finest goal of an educated woman.[42]

Elisabeth pleased them so easily, just by being herself; Anne always seemed to fall short. The only thing she could do was write. But writing had always been for her more a necessity than a skill, a way of understanding people and sorting out her feelings and thoughts. She could say things on paper that she could never say to someone's face. At

Smith she had learned to value her writing as a craft. She was praised for her insight and her scholarship and was encouraged by friends and teachers to publish. She thought about becoming a writer but feared that she lacked the tenacity to carry it through. She often wondered whether she really was talented. She had a boyfriend, known as P, a friend of the family, but he was painfully conventional and predictable. She was certain he saw her only in stereotype; he didn't seem to know who she was at all. Perhaps, like her mother, she would give up a career for the "humdrum divinity" of married life. Marriage loomed like a grave inevitability—something large and yet too small to capture the "fire" she felt inside. She who "loved Scarlet" wore "a gown of black," she wrote in a poem.[43]

Suddenly the train arrived in Mexico City. They saw bright lights and small close streets as it slid into the railway station. Finding themselves on the back platform, they watched Con leap over the tracks from behind a car. Then they fell into one another's arms.[44]

There was so much to talk about that they could barely sort it out. Everyone talked so fast, asking questions and hardly waiting for answers. Were they all right? Were they safe and well? Where was the embassy? Could they meet Colonel Lindbergh?

If they hurried, their parents told them, they could meet him now. While their father jumped into another car, racing to see Lindbergh at the embassy, the children and their mother followed behind, hoping to catch Lindbergh before he left the reception.

Instinctively, Anne withdrew. Something had changed. This wasn't like home at all. Things were different, faster, out of control. The way people looked at her, the way her mother spoke—the cars, the drivers, the clothes her mother wore. Lindbergh was breaking into their family party with all his "public hero stuff," and she didn't like it.[45]

They sped, car behind car, through the brightly lit streets of the old city, and stopped before a huge eagle-crested iron gate. Once they honked loudly, the gate opened and they approached the embassy. Anne could see a massive door and, in the distance, a stone staircase. The steps were covered with red velvet, like a carpet laid out for a royal wedding.

Of course, Anne thought, Lindbergh would be "nice," a "regular news-paper hero, the baseball-player type," but he was certainly no one who would interest her—not of her world, not at all an intellectual.[46] Besides, she disliked good-looking men—"lady-killers," self-absorbed and inaccessible.[47] Should she, she wondered, "worship Lindbergh like everyone else?"[48] They tumbled out of the car, dazed and shaken, as uni-formed officers stood at attention on the steps. Climbing the plush stairway between the line of soldiers, Anne whispered to Elisabeth, "How ridiculous!"[49] Exhausted, at last they reached the top.

Then Anne saw a "tall slim boy in evening dress" standing against a "great stone pillar." He was "so much slimmer, so much taller, so much more poised than I had expected. Not at all like the grinning 'Lindy' pictures."[50]

Betty hurried the introductions, breathlessly pushing Elisabeth for-ward. "Colonel Lindbergh, this is my oldest daughter, Elisabeth."

From behind, Anne observed his fine-bone face and clear blue eyes. "And this is Anne," her mother said.

Lindbergh didn't smile. He took her hand and bowed.

The attributes of True Womanhood, by which a woman judged herself and was judged by her husband, her neighbors, and society, could be divided into four cardinal virtues—piety, purity, submissiveness and domesticity. Put them all together and they spelled mother, daughter, sister, wife-woman. Without them no matter whether there was fame, achievement or wealth, all was ashes. With them she was promised happiness and power.

— BARBARA WELTER,
The Cult of True Womanhood

CHRISTMAS 1927, MEXICO CITY

Anne scampered through the halls of the embassy buildings like a girl on a school holiday. She peeked in and out of the stone-walled rooms, draped with curtains and crimson tapestries. The smell of tuberoses wafted through the windows, and the cavernous fireplaces were laden with lilies. Growing tired of the darkened rooms lit only by the sun through slatted shades, Anne climbed to the roof of the embassy residence to peer over the garden wall. She felt the searing heat rise from the streets and heard the marketplace cries of the young native boys, herding their turkeys like flocks of sheep. She imagined herself a medieval princess in a royal tower, cloistered from the tumbledown squalor of the shanties below.[1]

There were those back home who heartily agreed that the new American Embassy was a "decadent" extravagance. Several members of Congress were outraged by the appropriation of $150,000 for the neoclassic European "palace," with its iron gate and white pillared façade. It was to them a piece of "pernicious political architecture," a symbol of monarchy and corruption rather than of democratic equality. Nonetheless, the State Department deemed it a necessity to preserve the "dignity" of the American ambassador. America, after all, had won

2

Coming Home

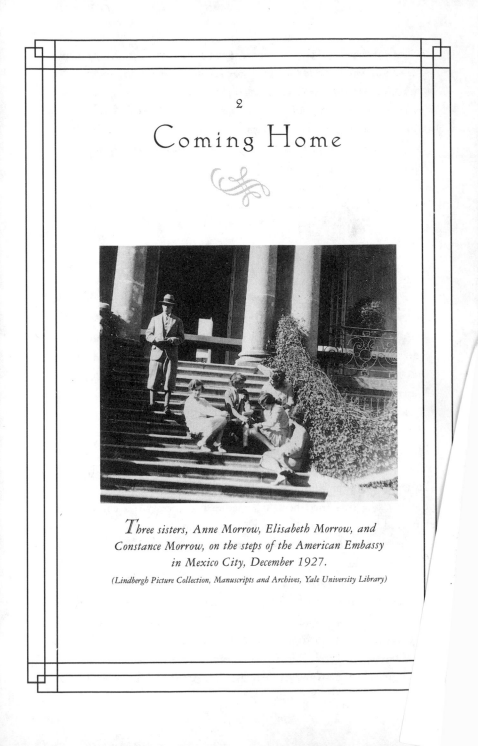

Three sisters, Anne Morrow, Elisabeth Morrow, and Constance Morrow, on the steps of the American Embassy in Mexico City, December 1927.
(Lindbergh Picture Collection, Manuscripts and Archives, Yale University Library)

the Great War, and Mexico was merely the "backyard" of Texas.[2] Lindbergh's presence justified their vision.

By the time Anne arrived, Lindbergh had been in Mexico City nearly a week. The Mexicans had kept their promise to receive him with a grandeur rivaling that of the capitals of Europe. It was Paris and London all over again. Calling him the "unaccredited Ambassador of the Air," the parliament summoned him to address a special session. "Humanity," said one deputy, "has taken wings." Their countries would move together toward a common destiny, aware that war would be as destructive to the victor as to the vanquished. We are, said the minister, brothers who must rise above petty concerns, "triumphantly traveling toward the sun."[3]

They paraded Lindbergh through their streets and along the waterways, showering him with flowers and serenading him with music. Lindbergh's straight-laced, laconic style made him all the more regal and elegant. In the seven months since his transatlantic flight, he had cultivated a public persona. Instinctively, he understood the power of his fame and leaped at the chance to mold the public's view of aviation. He spoke with a steady, determined intensity, as though the future of flight had become his personal cause. His manner had lost some of its baby-faced naïveté; his jaw and cheekbones were angular and lean. And when he walked, he sometimes strutted, hands in pockets, leaning easily into his stride. No longer content to be led like a puppy, he walked in front of the official entourage, savvy in the ways of government ceremony and facile in his handling of the crowds.[4]

On the night of Anne's arrival, Morrow was entertaining Lindbergh alone in the public rooms of the embassy. Great fires burned in the stone fireplaces as waistcoated manservants attended to their every need. After dinner, Morrow and Lindbergh returned to the family residence, stopping to chat in Morrow's study. Betty, preoccupied with her children in the second-storey rooms, was surprised to hear voices in the study below.

"Anyone there?" she called from the top of the stairs.

"Oh, no," said Morrow, restraining his pride. "Only Colonel Lindbergh."

Collecting her daughters, Betty marshaled them into the study to greet him. While Morrow welcomed the presence of his family, the entrance of the women seemed to faze Lindbergh. He stood by the desk, shifting from foot to foot, as Morrow relinquished the floor to the women.

Betty and Anne sat silently on the sofa while Elisabeth gently took control. Skillfully, she directed the course of conversation, juggling small talk with the "marvelous executiveness" of a "Lady of the White House."[5]

Betty had warned her daughters to stick to the subject of aviation. Lindbergh, she told them, was uncomfortable with talk of other topics. But Elisabeth brazenly tested the borders.[6] "How did you like the bull-fight?" she asked, knowing full well that Lindbergh had caused a stir with his attendance.

Shifting nervously, Lindbergh replied that it wasn't exactly his idea of a good time.

In fact, Lindbergh had thumbed his nose at the American groups intent on protecting animal rights. The Mexicans, he said, had the right to choose their national sport. He would not insult his hosts in the name of righteousness.

Convinced, now, of her mother's wisdom, Elisabeth retreated behind small talk.

Would he show them the sombrero he had received as a gift? she asked.

Relieved, Lindbergh left the room to retrieve the hat and then, steadied by the prop, passed it around like a laboratory specimen, articulating in detail its distinctive features.

To Anne, his cool, impersonal performance was nothing short of "breathtaking." So restrained and direct, he seemed as classic as the pillared room in which he stood. To Anne, he was "the most beautiful, most stupendous achievement of our age," a medieval "cathedral," standing in testimony to all that was virtuous and good.[7]

When Morrow authoritatively brought the evening to a close, Anne was grateful and thoroughly exhausted. Once she returned to her room, she felt out of control. "I cannot express this delicate thing . . . all I can feel is: my instruments are too small, too inadequate . . ."[8] All she had was the strength of her will to keep her from falling apart until she could make sense of her feelings and hear a signal from the gods.

The next day, while Elisabeth toyed with Lindbergh as if he were a younger brother, playing on his self-consciousness with the clever banter of a sophisticated elder, Anne grew silent and withdrawn. Wide-eyed and frozen, she found it almost impossible to talk. She stuttered and mumbled when he asked her questions, finally admitting it was her habit to "listen."[9] And yet they were drawn like magnets, observing each other across the vastness of rooms, colliding in the courtyard when they least expected to, playing visual games of hide and seek. But for all their flirting, Anne could not permit her eyes to meet his. So bright, so blue, she couldn't bear their intensity.[10]

That night at dinner in the residence, Elisabeth and the Colonel argued fiercely about the relative merits of Western and Chinese civilization and philosophy, as Anne watched quietly, analyzing the dynamics of their exchanges.

Charles was measured and controlled, setting forth his arguments with focused confidence. Elisabeth, Anne noted, argued well, but she was no match for his disciplined intelligence.

Fencing with his saber-sharp mind, Elisabeth was intimidated by his logical precision. It was obvious, even to her, that she had lost the game.[11]

Unaware of her sister's feelings of inadequacy, Anne envied her courage. Elisabeth's bold manner, however, was not the stuff of fortitude; it was the simple fact of romantic indifference. Elisabeth had set her sights not on marriage, but on friendship and career. Her polished and cerebral attitude belied her sensuous and romantic nature. While she obliged her parents with the behavior of ideal femininity, in truth she had little interest in men. She found them arrogant and dull, not half as interesting as Connie Chilton, whom she had met at Smith. Tall and husky, with a commanding presence, Connie showered Elisabeth with love and attention.

In the two years since Elisabeth left Smith, her love for Connie had become consuming, eclipsing her interest in those around her. In fact, Lindbergh's presence heightened her certainty. The face Lindbergh saw across the table was the cover of a confused and fragile young woman who feared her instincts and prayed for her salvation.[12]

As the dinner progressed, there were shouts outside the walls of the residence, as though a great crowd were assembling. To Anne the sound was terrifying; it was like the crowds who had battered the palace walls during the French Revolution. Feeling somewhat like Marie Antoinette as she clinked her crystal goblet and ate from her china plate, Anne was frightened by Lindbergh's equanimity. While she shivered to the sounds of the chanting crowd, Lindbergh, she noted, "went on unconsciously eating."[13]

After dinner, a delegation of students called on Lindbergh, addressing him in childlike, flowery English. Lindbergh listened carefully, leaning forward in his seat, lending them his dignity as they spoke. In gratitude, he merely shook their hands, accepting their praise with silent restraint. And then he walked to the balcony window, the Morrow family following, and waved to the pushing, jostling crowd.

"Viva Lindbergh," the mob roared, as boys scaled the walls to touch his hands. Lindbergh hailed the crowd from the balcony while Anne watched from behind. The faces seemed strange, the sounds and songs were primitive. Anne wondered what would happen if the people's energy turned bad, if the fervor of their admiration became anger. She wondered how Lindbergh interpreted his "mad popularity," but he seemed not to think about it at all.[14]

Lindbergh let the warmth of the household embrace him and reveled in the easy reciprocity of the Morrow family. There was something familiar, intuitively akin; they all knew exactly what he wanted and accepted him according to his own rules. In fact, Anne and Elisabeth were working hard behind the scenes to make it appear that way.

He was so fragile, such a boy. They tried to be lighthearted and nonchalant in his presence,[15] as one would try to win the trust of a child.

With Christmas approaching, the Morrows encouraged Lindbergh to extend his stay. At their urging, he telephoned his mother, Evangeline, and invited her to join him at the embassy and then arranged for a Ford trimotor plane to carry her the twenty-two hundred miles from Detroit to Mexico City.

On the periphery of her son's life since he left five years earlier, Evangeline Lindbergh had expected to spend the holidays alone. She was more than pleased to accept the invitation. After four days of flying over the United States, stopping each night in a different town, Evangeline landed in Mexico City on December 21. Thousands of people gathered to greet her; the public reception rivaled her son's. She was, after all, a piece of Lindbergh, and the press insisted on making her a hero. Without her intent, Evangeline had achieved a long-distance record for passenger flight; no woman had ever flown so long or so far. When her plane touched down, the crowd charged, and Evangeline, frightened, opened her cabin window, trying to shoo the people away from the deadly force of the propellers.

At fifty-five, Charles's mother had lost the elegance of her youth. Once beautiful and slim, she had grown thick and fleshy. Now that Charles was gone and her husband and her parents were dead, she lived in Detroit with her brother, teaching chemistry at a local high school. Stylish enough in her broad-brimmed hat and flowered silk dress, Evangeline had an air of forced gentility, as though she had to marshall all her strength to keep herself under control. With great effort, she had channeled her sweeping moods and compulsive habits into neat compartments; the volatility of her youth seemed to have been mere eccentricity. But Evangeline had never wanted to fit into a mold; the public life of her husband had held no appeal to her. Now, suddenly, as Charles Lindbergh's mother, she felt a part of "the real thing." The invitation to spend Christmas with the Morrows at the American Embassy filled her with hope and gratitude.[16]

Elated by her adventure and the cheering of the crowd, Evangeline amused the press with stories of her travels. The airplane, she announced with certainty, was a mode of travel here to stay, and Mexico was more beautiful than she had ever imagined. No, she hadn't brought her son a Christmas present; his only interest was in machines. She apologized for the inadequacy of her words. She was saturated with feelings, but none she wished to share with the public. One should never "air one's emotions," she asserted firmly, to the disappointment of the hungry press.

Flattered and photographed, Evangeline sipped her tea in the embassy reception hall, waiting anxiously for Charles to arrive. Fresh and eager from a stunt performance, he moved swiftly through the doors to greet her. She rose in response and they smiled warmly, clasping each other's hands in greeting. He ushered her toward the Morrows and their entourage of American officials, and then into the quiet of a private room, beyond the glare of lights and reporters.

While Elisabeth saw only Evangeline's strength, Anne saw straight through to her sadness. Mrs. Lindbergh, used to small-town politics, was like an actress suddenly thrust onto the stage. She did, however, rise to the occasion, immediately sensing what was required and readily aware of its implications for her son. There was perfect harmony between mother and son, Anne noted in her diary.[17]

The consonance of mother and son was testimony to their common past—the past they had lived together for twenty years on the periphery of a society that had denied their legitimacy. They had learned to accept, even to savor, their isolation, making it the outward sign of their superiority. And yet the full, rich Morrow household evoked their sense of loss. For the first time, Evangeline understood what might have been had she stayed married and played by the rules. The Morrows were the family she and Charles had never had.

Evangeline's arrival in a trimotor plane, large enough to accommodate many people, opened the possibility that the Morrows could go on a flying excursion with Charles. When Lindbergh insisted on taking the Morrow children for a ride, they were politely demure but secretly "thrilled." Anne quietly prayed for "consciousness," not her ordinary half-asleep daze. She wanted to truly experience flying; she wanted to remain aware.

A crowd gathered around the hangar, and the silver plane glimmered in the morning sun. When Anne, Elisabeth, and Con boarded the plane, it felt as if they were in one of Ford's cars, but instead of the straight velvet seats, the chairs were wicker and tipped at an angle by the nose of the plane. Excited yet afraid, she looked out at the photographers and the press, feeling the separateness that came with celebrity. Lindbergh, smiling, sauntered across the field in a business suit and gray felt hat. He stepped inside, greeted the girls, and, bowing to protect his head, took his place at the controls.

As the engine raced, Anne shivered with excitement. The plane rolled faster and faster, and she heard the wind "hiss" through the window. She saw the trees and hangars whirl by; she hardly noticed the plane ascending. Thrilled to be together and flying with Lindbergh, the three young women moved forward to the cockpit to watch him. He sat quietly at ease, one hand on the wheel, looking relaxed and perfectly in control. Anne noted his "tremendous hands," with their strong grasp, and his harmonious movements. Once she had summoned the courage to look out the window, she savored every small sensation, trying to keep a semblance of composure as her body pulsed to each gentle lift of the ascent.

Their shadow seemed like a "great bird"[18] soaring above the lakes and meadows. Suddenly, Anne understood: she was inside the bird and part of its shadow. The city below looked like a child's toy; everything her parents knew as grand and imposing now seemed small and insignificant. Only the mountains retained their majesty, and even they seemed to bow in awe.

Flying with Lindbergh as he cut through the sky, Anne understood why he feared nothing. She felt as if, like him, "life had found her—and death, too."[19]

Later that night, she wrote in her diary: "The idea of this clear, direct, straight boy—how it has swept out of sight all other men I have ever known . . . my little embroidery beribboned world is smashed."[20]

3

The Early Years

Dwight and Elizabeth Morrow, home from their honeymoon. Englewood, New Jersey, 1903.

(Amherst College Archives)

FAMILY ALBUM[1]

My parents, my children:
Who are you, standing there
In an old photograph—young married pair
I never saw before, yet see again?
You pose somewhat sedately side by side,
In your small yard off the suburban road.
He stretches a little in young manhood's pride
Broadening his shoulders for the longed-for load,
The wife that he has won, a home his own;
His growing powers hidden as spring, unknown,
But surging in him toward their certain birth,
Explosive as dandelions in the earth.

She leans upon his arm, as if to hide
A strength perhaps too forward for a bride,
Feminine in her bustle and long skirt;
She looks demure, with just a touch of flirt
In archly tilted head and squinting smile
At the photographer, she watches while
Pretending to be girl, although so strong,
Playing the role of wife ("Here I belong!"),
Anticipating mother, with man for child,
Amused at all her roles, unreconciled.

And I who gaze at you and recognize
The budding gestures that were soon to be
My cradle and my home, my trees, my skies . . .

—ANNE MORROW LINDBERGH

SPRING 1893, NORTHAMPTON, MASSACHUSETTS

Betty Cutter was in an awful temper the day she met Dwight Morrow at a school dance. Local dances had a clandestine air, and Betty liked to play by the rules. Her friends who waited at the Northampton station for the boys from Amherst to arrive were a bit too eager for Betty's taste, risking their Smith College "dignity" in a frivolous breach of self-restraint. Smith parties, held inside the college gates, perfectly suited Betty's sensibilities. Church-like socials, more like conversations set to music, they were tightly monitored by faculty chaperones, and Betty could be back in her room by ten. But this was an informal dance, held at the local girls' school and although it was slated for midmorning, it had live music, "round" dancing, and lax rules. Ungoverned by the rituals of dance cards and numbers, the girls enjoyed the chaos in the gym as, nearly tripping on their long dresses, they raced to find partners for the first dance. The beautiful girls got their pick; the others trailed, fearing they would be left behind. Betty, plain-faced and delicate, with a pug nose and a slight build, lingered at the edge of the dance floor in a defiant pose. But Dwight, eager for the challenge, was thoroughly "beguiled." To Betty's surprise, they danced all day.[2]

Nearly twenty years old, and well into her sophomore year, Betty had to face reality. Graduation was only two years away, and she dreaded the thought of going home. Home meant submitting to the tight restrictions of her parents and carrying out part-time care of her younger sisters, one of whom was severely retarded.[3] Marriage, against Betty's deepest instincts for independence and a literary career, was a distasteful yet sensible alternative. And the determined Mr. Morrow, as tenacious and as ambitious as she, was, for the moment, a pleasant companion.

As they waltzed around the school gym that spring morning of 1893 at their first meeting, Betty could only have felt the harmony of their views. Like the Morrows, the Cutters were educated and pious, affected by the same turn-of-the-century mix of Puritan energy and the drive for upward mobility. The Morrow ancestors had been farmers in the highlands of Ireland, immigrating to America in the early 1700s; the Cutters had arrived nearly a century before from the mining towns of northeastern England, where they earned their living as glaziers, shoemakers, millers, blacksmiths, and coopers. In America they stayed one step behind the frontier settlers, who required their services to sustain their communities. Urban dwellers, the Cutters settled first in Boston and then moved to New Hampshire, Vermont, Pennsylvania, and Ohio. There they became teachers, doctors, lawyers, and merchants, rising quickly through the social strata.[4]

The Cutter scion to whom Betty and her twin sister, Mary, were born on May 29, 1873, had deserted the farmlands of Vermont to follow the inland seaways and lakes to the port town of Cleveland, Ohio. While her grandfather had been an uneducated farmer who made his money in the marketplace, her step-grandfather was a blue-blooded Yankee, educated at Yale and ambitious for his stepsons. Her father, Charles, temperamentally unsuited to his legal profession or any other formal vocation, was a sensitive and gentle man who loved his books, his garden, and the comforts of home. Frustrated by his inability to earn a living, he soon grew tired, weak, and depressed, and sought refuge with his wife and four daughters in his parents' sprawling three-generation home.

Like Dwight's mother, Clara, Betty's mother, Annie Spencer, would always feel that her husband had failed her. And like Dwight, Betty believed herself responsible for her mother's domestic burdens and economic disappointments. Nonetheless, the Cutters, like the Morrows, drew strength from their religion. Annie Cutter, a descendent of a "long line of roaring fundamentalist Congregationalist preachers," made the Bible, with its parables and its ethics, the fulcrum of her children's daily lives. And Betty, using the Hebrew Bible and the New Testament as her primers, cultivated a love of stories and poetry.

At the age of ten, after a long bout of tuberculosis, Betty's twin sister died. The family eulogized Mary as God's "little angel," and Betty, uncertain of the purity of her own soul, struggled to find her place alone.[5] Hiding beneath the front hall stairs from her grandparents, her parents, and her sisters, Betty read books and wrote in her diary. While visits to her wealthy cousins, the Dillinghams, would teach Betty the privileges and pleasures of the rich, she also saw the emotional poverty of women whose pleasure in life was defined by their husbands' wealth and status. Books, she believed, would be her "ticket out." Independence required a college education.

After persuading her parents to let her attend a girls' preparatory school, Betty got "the wish of her life." In the fall of 1892, she boarded the train to Northampton, Massachusetts, en route to Smith College, with two new dresses, made by her mother, a desk donated by her Uncle Arthur, and a painting by her Aunt Mary intended to lend "homeliness" to her college room. The 108 students in Betty's freshman class were among the 2.8 percent of women who went to college in the 1890s.[6] Even those who could afford the "Eastern elites" often tutored their daughters at home. While the parents of most college women had incomes twice as high as the national average, the Cutters felt the financial burden. If it hadn't been for Uncle Arthur, who had nurtured her after her twin's death and who understood her need for autonomy, Betty would have remained at home.

But back in Cleveland after graduation, in the summer of 1896, Betty realized that her "ticket out" had been nothing more than a round-trip ticket home. Caught, once again, in the quagmire of her family's needs, Betty understood, perhaps for the first time, the depth of her mother's sadness. Annie Cutter was exhausted and depressed, as much from the effort of hiding the family's poverty beneath genteel postures as she was from the poverty itself. Her unhappiness elicited Betty's sympathy, along with her guilt. It was an old guilt, perhaps, based on Betty's desire to fill the emotional vacuum made by her twin's death.

Betty wrote in her diary, "My blessed mother, she shall have happiness from now on if I can give it to her." Betty wanted to make her mother happy by staying at home and helping her to care for the children, but her own ambition—her desire to write—constantly cracked through to the surface. "I must accomplish something, I must do something, I must be something." By September, only three months out of college, Betty understood that autonomy would require money. "Oh if only I were a boy," she wrote in her diary, "how gladly would I go to work."[7]

Although her success at Smith had convinced her that she could find a career in writing, within a year after graduation Betty's hopes were dashed, so in the fall of 1896, she devised a new plan for making money. If she could not publish fiction, she would teach it. Betty secured the elegant front room in the house of a well-off cousin and tried her hand at "parlor-teaching." Although in one semester she earned the astonishing sum of $574, she came to "despise" the work. She doubted both the quality of her skills and the worth of her students. In a sense, she had become a caricature of herself, preaching the insights of Ibsen's *Doll's House* to a group of middle-aged "ladies" from town.

Betty was frustrated that she had achieved nothing, while Dwight was "marching straight ahead with no worries." She was beginning to believe that her task was impossible: to be "historical and social and domestic all at once." Although her confinement at home made her "mean and little and tired of spirit," she had not lost her love of parties and travel.[8] By the spring of 1897 she was through with parlor talks, and the possibility of marrying Dwight Morrow resurfaced with new meaning. Yet moving away from home seemed out of the question; how could she leave her mother behind? "My dear mother, how can I ever go away?"

Dwight, who had entered Amherst College on academic probation, had graduated in 1895 as class orator, had been elected to Phi Beta Kappa, and was noted as one of those most likely to succeed. Then, after a year back home in Pittsburgh, working as an office boy for his cousin Richard Scandrett, he went to New York and enrolled in Columbia University's School of Law, where his tuition was covered by his father and a part-time job. At Columbia he met the sons of lawyers and businessmen, who introduced him to the life of the New York rich, with their townhouses and Long Island estates. Dwight may have been ashamed of his shabby clothes and unpolished manner, but he won his new friends' admiration with his mind and his morals. He did protest that his "rich" friends heightened the value of his "poor friends," but he was hungrier and more ambitious than ever before. And Betty Cutter, with her aspirations for a "Madison Avenue" life, seemed within Dwight's reach.[9]

Hoping to impress her with his "grand move," he wrote to Betty in Cleveland to tell her the news. She clearly admired his courage and his success; still, one can sense her painful recognition that her own career as a writer was doomed.

> *Your life now is about as different as possible from mine. But I call yours more satisfactory, just because you can say along with St. Paul and all other grand people, "this is the one thing I do," whereas I have to say, "these sixteen things I do and none of 'em amount to a row of pins."*[10]

Two years later, in 1899, Betty's father lost his job at the Ohio and Pennsylvania Coal Company and had little promise of further employment. Camouflaging their financial problems, the Cutters went abroad, where living was cheaper and Papa would have a chance to regain his strength and perspective. Betty used her language skills and her practicality to settle the family into a comfortable routine, but she was lonely, much as she had been as a child. Surrounded by relatives, she communicated with none. Now, however, she had the solace of a responsive mind. Through the steady flow of letters to and from Dwight, Betty found a means of self-scrutiny. Expressing her disappointments and her hopes, she tested her ideas against the touchstone of Dwight's growing confidence.

Excited by the prospect of seeing Dwight, Betty returned home in May 1901, only to find herself incapable of responding to the demands of the relationship. Dwight's need for emotional and sexual intimacy frightened her, summoning up memories of her mother's consuming needs after the death of her sister Mary and the pain of her father's constant failures. An explosive confrontation left Betty and Dwight exhausted and bereaved. What might have been a passionate reunion turned into a metaphysical dissection of the nature of love.[11]

But Dwight, "a fatalist," continued to pursue her. When they found themselves invited to the same Massachusetts resort the following summer, Dwight was the first to recognize the irony of their chance reunion. He wrote, "I'm coming, unless you object . . . If our little flower isn't entirely dead." Claiming it would do their "flower" good, Betty agreed. With "internal nervous prostration," she met Dwight in her most becoming blue Swiss cotton dress. Whether it was the breeze from the bay, the beauty of the sun on the Ipswich pastures, or the sheer exhaustion from seven years of fighting the inevitable, Miss Cutter and Mr. Morrow ended their day in "perfect understanding."[12]

On June 16, 1903, Betty and Dwight were married at the Cutter home in Cleveland, surrounded by their parents, their sisters, and their college friends. As soon as they returned from their honeymoon in the hills of Vermont and the Connecticut Valley they had come to love, they quickly defined their aspirations. Nothing, said Dwight's friends, was good enough for him and his young bride, and yet no place good enough was also affordable. It would either be east of Fifth Avenue or not at all, Dwight declared. As a compromise to "not at all," the Morrows chose Englewood, New Jersey, a mere ten miles across the Hudson River from Times Square.

Even as they sat in their Cottage Lane house on the other side of Englewood's tracks, they knew hard work would carry them up the rolling terraces of the Palisades and into the fine stone houses occupied by the young Olympians of government and Wall Street. Men like Thomas A. Lamont and Henry P. Davison of J. P. Morgan and Company, Seward Prosser of Banker's Trust, and Cornelius Bliss, former Secretary of the Interior, dominated the political and social circles of this northern New Jersey enclave, still untouched by bridge or highway. Once rolling farmland, occupied by the Calvinist Dutch and the Presbyterian British, Englewood, at the turn of the century, had been molded by the rich into huge manicured estates with stables and greenhouses, proper English gardens, and well-placed decorative trees. The large lawns sloped gently and unmarked into one another's back doors, and the owners' lives inter-twined like partners in an intricate minuet, nonetheless passionate for their stately elegance. The men traveled to and from Wall Street on a yacht docked in Englewood. Breakfast was served outbound and cocktails inbound. Of course, one could always take the train to Jersey City and cross by ferry, but the sacrifice of rising early to catch the seven o'clock boat was a small price to pay for hobnobbing with the town's elite.

After the Morrows arrived in July of 1903, Dwight took the train and the Hudson ferry. While they were still on the outer rim of the town's social circle, Betty and Dwight felt much at home in this civic-minded, staunchly Presbyterian, five-mile-square oasis of woodlands and meadows, fine private schools and prestigious clubs.[13]

By the time their first child, Elisabeth, was born in March 1904, Dwight's diligence had begun to pay off. Within three years, he had doubled his salary and advanced from junior clerk to partner in the law firm of Reed, Simpson, Thacher and Barnum. Now, with a salary of nearly $4000, the Morrows moved across the tracks to Spring Lane, a small street in the foothills of town, and dubbed their Victorian house "Number 1." "The house is fine, fine," Dwight wrote to his college friend, Charles Burnett. It had a parlor, a library, a dining room, and a kitchen on the first floor, four bedrooms on the second floor, a cellar with a laundry, and even a porch. "In the morning," he wrote, "we take our chops and eggs off doilies . . . Elizabeth has been fortunate in get-ting a good girl from Richmond, Virginia—a colored girl who makes fine rolls and good buckwheat cakes . . . I feel like a grownup."[14]

Betty, too, had everything she wanted—a husband, a home, a maid, and now a child. Shortly after Elisabeth's birth, Betty celebrated their good fortune in her diary. She and Dwight were as happy as two people could be. His name went on the office letterhead, and life seemed nearly "perfect."

The birth of Anne Spencer Morrow, on June 22, 1906, seemed in-cidental; a pause in the movement of a well-oiled machine. Well into her thirties, Betty no longer ached to become a writer, just as Dwight no longer flirted with academia. Their childhood aspirations had become avocations, placed aside by convention and responsibility. They knew what they wanted from each other and from life: winters in Englewood, summers on Long Island, and the social prestige and opportunity for public service that accompanied the affluence earned by hard work.

The birth of another daughter was not greeted with enthusiasm. Cutter women seemed to produce girls, and Betty may have worried that, like her mother, she would never have a son. Anne's arrival had confirmed that fear. Their first daughter, Elisabeth Reeve, was frail, irritable, and difficult to control. But if Elisabeth was willful beyond reason, she was also beautiful beyond words. "Perfection" was the word Betty used to define her finely cut features and porcelain skin, framed by golden ringlets. She had an aura of delicate feminine beauty that assuaged Betty's fears of her own inadequacies.

Anne, neither the male child they desired nor a female beauty to rival Elisabeth, sensed from the beginning her tenuous place in the family circle. The best she could do was "fit in." And fitting in meant nothing short of the strict self-discipline and good deeds that had brought the Morrows so far so fast. Not fitting in would not be tolerated, as though the wildest of weeds could become a rose, simply by an act of will.

But Anne required little prodding to conform to Morrow standards. Compared with her sister, she was obedient and angelic—pure gold. But her docile nature worked against her; she was promptly rewarded by being ignored.

At two years old, her mother found her curious and attentive, constantly talking and pointing at objects, hungry to know the names of things. But often, Anne was serious and withdrawn, refusing to participate or even to smile.[15]

If the dear little girl was aware that she was good, she may also have been aware that she would never be good enough. Sickly Elisabeth grew more beautiful, witty, and clever each year, casting a shadow over Anne. While Elisabeth received constant praise from her parents and her peers, Anne received perfunctory tolerance.

"Nobody," Anne would later say, "said I was good at anything." Her grandmother Clara Morrow would repeat, over and over, "Praise to the face is open disgrace."

But as Anne grew, her shroud became her mantle. In bed at night, separated from her sister by a screen with blue roses, Anne would invent stories, a fantasy world of royalty and adventure, in which she was always beautiful and over which she always reigned. She imagined herself as Queen Bessie, like her mother, endowed with magical powers to change the course of the Morrow household with no more than the turn of a phrase.[16]

But the real Queen Bessie was feeling less than regal. With the birth of a second child, and not quite as much wealth as she had hoped for, she began to see her life as resembling her mother's. The confinement to home and nursery, without the domestic help she wanted, made her bored and restless. But, like her mother, Betty knew how to "stage" her life, to give the impression of ease and wealth while waiting for her husband to make them realities. Being in the right place at the proper season was an important aspect of the show, and summers in Englewood would not suffice. Beginning in 1907, the summer after Anne was born, Betty took her two daughters to Quogue, a small town seventy-five miles east of New York on the southern shore of Long Island.[17]

Once a desertlike stretch of sand and pastures in a cove between two bays, Quogue had become a fashionable summer resort. By the time the Morrows made their trek east from Brooklyn through the town of Riverhead and on to Quogue, the stagecoach had given way to the railroad, and the God-fearing hamlet of farmers and fishermen was lined with carriages and boardinghouses. And though the hotels lacked the status of the private clubs and cottages that dotted the sandy lanes down to the beach, they offered a genteel life with public bathhouses set on the broad white dunes of the newly established public beach. Considered socially, even morally inferior, the boarders were barred from the clubhouse golf courses, the afternoon teas, and the evening dances, but they cultivated an elegance of their own, with horse-drawn surreys to the beach, parties and teas, bike rides through pastures, and boat rides in the bay.

With its cool winds and its high style, Quogue was the place to be and to be seen. And Betty, always a stickler for propriety, sought legitimacy among her peers.

But many nights, Betty cried herself to sleep, embarrassed by her naughty and willful daughter, Elisabeth.[18] Meanwhile, Anne sat quietly by, watching the waves shatter and crash, race and pound against the sand. This was her first glimpse of the blue Atlantic, a "boundless" stretch "beyond the edge."[19] From now on, when she climbed the hills of Englewood up to the tops of the Palisades, Anne would know where the boats on the Hudson went, as they made their way south to the open sea.

On New Year's Day of 1910, Betty declared that their struggle was over. They finally had the money to live as they wished. Two years before, in November of 1908, she had given birth to a son, Dwight Jr. Now, with three children and Dwight's yearly income at $25,000, they sold their Spring Lane house for $27,000 and moved up to Palisades Avenue into a larger but still modest home at the edge of Englewood's finest estates.[20] Elisabeth described it as "a mild example of late gingerbread architecture with fancy trimming around the windows and a little tower over the front door."[21]

The house stood on an acre of land planted with shapely old trees and a lush garden. Anne and her brother and sister played under the sweet gum trees, listening to the trains hooting in the valley below. From their bedroom window, Betty and Dwight could look west over their neighbors' sweeping lawns to the curving Hackensack River and the skyline above the hills of Paterson. The couple, feeling they had reached the pinnacle of their aspirations, vowed that, barring "ill fortune," this would be their lifelong home.

But even as they relished their contentment, Dwight planned his entry into the heady world of Englewood politics, a town that proved to be the right place for someone with "lofty views" and the instinct to make the most of political opportunities. Dwight's instincts, to his surprise, were flawless.

In 1912, he ran for mayor and lost, but won 90 percent of the

Republican vote and, perhaps more important, the attention of a J. P. Morgan partner, Thomas Lamont. From that time on it was "what to do" with this diminutive, ubiquitous upstart of an unconnected lawyer with no family standing and no banking credentials, but an engaging personality and unquestioned integrity. After weighing the possible effects of Morrow's physical stature and shoddy appearance—not up to the standards of the fashionable and athletic Morgan men—Tom Lamont, in December 1913, offered Dwight a job as an "understudy," with the prospect of becoming a partner.

The Calvinist ethic of his father had made Dwight fear the temptation of money. He saw himself, after all, as a waylaid academic, conceding to the marketplace for "higher" ends. His father had never earned more than $1800 a year; Dwight now had assets over $100,000, surely a sum sufficient for his needs. But his work at Simpson and Thacher had become a tiresome set of routines, and his career stretched before him like a "desert" of familiar challengers.

He understood the power of Morgan. The Wall Street panic of 1907 had made it a one-man federal reserve, raising millions in minutes to save faltering banks and New York City's payroll. The nineteenth-century consolidators of the nation's rail network, the Morgan partners were now the country's most powerful trust builders in farming, shipping, and steel. They underwrote foreign government bonds and helped to finance Britain's war in South Africa. In December 1913, the company was about to become the official wartime purchasing agent for Great Britain in the United States.[22]

More than the partners' power, Dwight valued their honesty and good character. The fine reputation of Morgan and Company was as important as its influence. The firm had achieved a rare coalescence—high-minded conscience with international power. Even Teddy Roosevelt, a conservationist who had cringed at the way Morgan bartered railroads for Alaska's land resources, believed in the integrity of the Morgan partners. There were others, of course, who disagreed; one was the congressional representative from the Sixth District of Minnesota, Charles A. Lindbergh. The year before, Lindbergh had spearheaded the Pujo Commission to investigate the Eastern "money trusts," a code term, it was said, for J. P. Morgan and Company.

Morrow assured his friends and family that the work at Morgan was important enough to justify its responsibilities. But faith, not logic, ultimately governed his choice. Faith, he wrote to a friend, was the only valid premise of "big decisions."[23] He was determined to use his position at Morgan to earn the money and the reputation that would permit him the opportunity for public service. With access to a network of four banks in three countries, the law clerk who had dreamed of being a Supreme Court justice might, indeed, make it to the top.

Betty too was climbing higher. Once she entered the Morgan circle, her life assumed a new pace and rhythm. Although she was now the mother of four children—Elisabeth, ten; Anne, eight; Dwight, five; and Constance, six months—Betty was hardly ever home. Taking her cues from Flo Lamont, the grande dame of Morgan, Betty spent her evenings at dinner with the partners or in New York City entertaining dignitaries. In Englewood, her days merged one into the other at endless meetings of clubs and organizations. Like many of her educated contemporaries, Betty wanted more than the promise of suffrage. She valued the community of other women and a chance to engage in public service. Just as the women's colleges had offered its students escape from their parents' homes, the clubs provided young mothers with a door out of the nursery. Viewing themselves as a sisterhood of social and cultural custodians, these women built hierarchies of power that reflected but did not overshadow the male structures.[24]

Fortunately for Betty, Englewood was fertile ground for women with time and money to spare. While the men were in New York, running their law offices and investment banks, the women wielded influence in the hospitals, churches, and clubs. The Community Chest, the Red Cross, the Children's Aid Society, the Missionary Society, the Presbyterian Church, the Shakespeare Literary Club, and, of course, the Smith College Club were among the organizations Betty served.

Her daily life became little more than a sequence of club meetings and dates with friends, punctuated with the mild regret of one who sensed she was paying a price for an ambition she did not understand. Rarely did she visit the children at school, and more and more she traveled with Dwight, leaving them at home with the nurse. She wondered why Anne sobbed and clung to her when she returned from an extended shopping tour in Europe; she regretted leaving Anne when the girl had the flu, but tending the nursery was more than she could bear.[25] Unable to acknowledge or clarify her motives, even to herself, Betty played her domestic and social roles one against the other. Without a model for quantifying her needs, among the first generation of women with both education and leisure, she could not define her role as a mother. She simply had no time for her children.

The children were tended by a German nanny, who ran their lives with an iron hand.[26] She demanded restraint and complete obedience, and the children, in trepidation, complied. The upstairs nursery was a world apart, a place to rehearse social poses and manners and to earn the right to join the grown-ups downstairs. Elisabeth, Anne, and Dwight ate their meals at a small white table that doubled as a playhouse on rainy days. Acting out their fantasies in dramatic games, they staged imaginary rebellions. Donned in their parents' coats and hats, they would play librarian, detective, and nurse. Elisabeth was usually the librarian, Dwight loved the cops-and-robbers chase, and Anne was always the nurse or nanny. Her job was both to emulate and to taunt their guardian, who watched their movements from the upstairs hall. Leaving the nursery, having assumed a haughty, nanny-like demeanor, Anne would suddenly return to surprise the children. The goal of the game was for the players to learn the art of perfect silence at the snap of a verbal command. Anne may have feared her nanny's wrath, but she loved the excitement of the role. If only for a moment, she was the judge and executor, wielding power over her siblings.

As though Betty understood the price of a "proper life," she required each of her children to keep a diary, which she presented as a tool for a disciplined life. Betty's requirement, in fact, was a gift, inspired perhaps by her own rebellion, which had found its voice in the privacy of her diaries. For Anne, it was both a release and a comfort; a mirror to her fears and a means of self-mastery. Instead of ordering her life, it permitted her to live between the rules, to free the force of her imagination. Protected from the censure of her nurse and her mother, Anne lost herself in thoughts and feelings, confessing all that inhibited her in daily life.

Like her mother, Anne with her diary at her side lived the double life of an obedient child and a probing observer. Yet her confessions filled her with guilt. Afraid that she had transgressed divine law, fearing the wrath of a vengeful God, Anne paced the garden of her Palisades Avenue home, counting her sins and praying for mercy.[27] The diary, in turn, nourished her confidence to share her stories with other children. Her parents, following the suit of the Morgan partners, took their yearly midwinter vacation in Nassau, the capital of the Bahamas. The heart of a cotton-smuggling operation during the Civil War, Nassau was now an international banking center and a winter resort for the American and British business elite.[28] In the backyard of a rented cottage on the bay, down a private lane that may once have been forbidding, Anne wrote, directed, and produced plays for the children of her parents' friends. Never again, Anne later said, would she have the same belief in the power of her words.[29]

Anne's memories of Nassau, recorded in sensual imagery, became the core of the spiritual "gifts" that Anne believed came from the sea. Impressionistic vignettes, awash in sunlight and steeped in native culture, they defined the perimeters of subjective time. Swept into contemplative reverie, Anne wrote the detailed descriptions of flower, sun, sky, and sea that presaged her later writings.[30]

In 1919, once again following the path of the Morgan partners, the Morrows purchased an apartment in New York City, relegating their Englewood home to a weekend retreat. While their "seven-thousand-square-foot home in the sky"[31] at Four East Sixty-Sixth Street did not rival the Lamonts' custom-built townhouse, its high ceilings and huge rooms became the perfect stage for their social lives. For Anne, the move was an opportunity. Elisabeth had chosen to leave the public schools in Englewood and board at Milton Academy in Massachusetts;

Anne preferred to stay in New York with her parents and attend Miss Chapin's School for Girls.

With Elisabeth away, Anne basked in her mother's attention. Perhaps for the first time since Anne was a child, Betty recognized the acuity and sensitivity that lay behind Anne's timid exterior. On Anne's fourteenth birthday, on the eve of her entry into Chapin, Betty gave her oil paints, brushes, and a portfolio, in the hope that her little artist would sketch and paint during the long summer days ahead.[32]

Out of Englewood and in the mainstream of city life, Anne saw her world begin to expand. Like Elisabeth, she had attended the Dwight School in Englewood, and, though it was a fine academy, dedicated to the individual needs of girls, it was a conservative school in a suburban enclave. Miss Chapin's School, located in two brownstones on East Fifty-seventh Street in Manhattan, was a window into the larger world of politics and suffragism, personal rights and public responsibilities. The intention of Miss Chapin, who founded the school in 1901, was to make it a paradigm for women's education. Here, girls were deemed capable of academic as well as athletic and civic excellence. Bible study and prayers were integral to the daily program, but the focus was on individual accomplishment. With an enrollment of only seventy-five girls, the small classes were able to focus on each student's needs. The school's innovative club system comprised extracurricular classes that encouraged the members' artistic expression.

At Chapin, Anne found a way to transform the "secret life" of her diary into literature, honing her thoughts and fantasies into poetry, stories, and essays. With the encouragement of a teacher, Anne submitted her work to *The Wheel,* Chapin's new literary magazine. Her writing had the naughtiness of a child who had found the hole in a hermetic system. At home and in class, she concentrated on being "good"; on paper, she was playful and devilish. In the stories she wrote as a first-year student, she blithely set the "fairy tale" tradition on its head by having the dragon eat the beautiful but vacuous princess and the brave but insipid prince. Gaining confidence as she went on, she turned her formal poetic quatrains into mischievous displays of rebellion. She flaunted her sins—pride, sloth, jealousy, disobedience, anger—knowing they were safe behind the curtain of her page. In her sophomore year, in an essay on ambition, Anne declared that she would be "a singer or a dancer or an artist." And although she might need a magic potion for the task, she was resolved to be "very tall and beautiful!"[33] In recognition of her achievements, Anne was named Head of the School, "a position," one of her friends later said, "that wasn't one a dreamer got elected to."[34]

Before her senior year Anne had composed an essay called "Disillusions of Childhood." Grown-ups, she wrote, feel pain. There are no fairies. Clouds are not solid. Balloons always break. And while she wanted to marry someone named "Rosebride . . . one can't choose one's husband for his name." Somehow, Anne protested, it didn't seem "right."

But there were compensations for Anne's growing awareness: the possibility of adventure and travel, even if only in her imagination. In an essay on "the enchantment of distance," Anne acknowledged the beauty and mystery of far-off places, and the magnitude of the seas that separated her from them. She was "lured" by travel and by the sea, she wrote, but not yet old enough to follow her whim. With memorabilia, articles, and photographs that she spread across the table in her bedroom, she played like a child with seashells at the beach, savoring little rituals and conjuring up daydreams. Her images of places and people, flowers and gardens and the horizon of the sea, became anodynes to dull routine. Perhaps, she concluded, imaginary voyages were truly the best. She could go anywhere she wanted at any time, on the impulse of a moment and the sail of a wish.[35]

As her senior year approached, Anne wondered how to measure her success and worried that she would not be able to achieve it alone. On the night before graduation, in June 1924, the seniors were asked by the Chapin headmistress to record their hopes for the future. Anne wrote unabashedly, "I want to marry a hero."[36]

With college only a few months away, Anne's fears of being over-shadowed by her sister and her mother acquired a keen immediacy. She did not want to follow them by going to Smith. She wanted to join some of her Chapin friends who were going to Vassar, where life seemed free and avant-garde. But Betty was determined that all her daughters would go to Smith, no matter how much they protested.[37]

Anne's rebellion was far from ordinary. Her desire for autonomy was not only a breach of the family ethic, but a rare display of personal defiance. While women made up nearly half the college student pop-ulation, only 7.6 percent of the women at the age of eighteen had the opportunity to go to college. At a time when most Americans, male or female, did not receive a high school diploma, the upper-middle-class parents who encouraged a daughter to go to school demanded, in return, proper obedience. Along with their checks for $800 for room, board, and tuition came the prerogative of choosing the child's school.[38]

In a letter to Elisabeth, Anne begged her to plead her cause. She didn't see why she had to follow her mother's wishes. Wasn't Elisabeth's compliance enough? She admitted she was weak and lacked the nerve to sever the ties which bound her to family tradition, but she couldn't hold back her anger. She wanted to strike out on her own—to assert her independence and her strength.[39] With all her power, she resisted her mother, but, forced once again to acquiesce, she donned the mask of obedience.

When Anne entered Smith in the fall of 1924, along with 528 other young women,[40] she would have been pleased to know that from its inception, in 1871, the college was dedicated to fostering female au-tonomy. Clearly an institution run by men and predicated on Victorian notions of femininity, it was nevertheless a groundbreaking experiment in social theory and female education. The Congregationalist clergymen and Amherst scholars who had founded the school broke ranks with prevalent social dogma, which perceived the female brain as being in-herently inferior to the male's. Determined to bring women into the prevailing activities of academic and social life, to dispel the cloister-like ambiance of earlier women's schools, they developed the "cottage system," which called for multiple structures situated on a central street. The trustees refused to build a college library or chapel, thereby inducing the students to use the town facilities. And they insisted that there be nothing in the curriculum or in the academic buildings that would denote the gender of the student body.[41]

While she was not quite ready to define her womanhood, Anne found Smith a serious place. Within a few months, the confidence and playfulness she had displayed in her high school years were gone. Although she felt hampered by her mother's reputation as a Smith alumna and her sister's academic accomplishments, Anne tried to play down her feelings of discontent. She wrote to her father that she had found her place at Smith; she only wished she could keep her perspective.[42] She worried, however, about her grades, and apologized to her mother for not meeting the high academic standards of the Morrow family.[43]

Anne's one sweet victory lay in her ability to write, but she was certain her mother wouldn't approve. Her letters begged her mother for acceptance, urging her to remember her own youthful ambitions to be a writer. She buried her anger beneath "Mother Darling" and gratitude, as if her words might exorcise her mother's contempt. Eager for praise, but afraid that her mother would not approve of her free-form style, so different from her own classical quatrains, Anne did not send her poems or stories home.[44] Her hunger for the approval of an older woman, however, was satisfied by the admiration of her writing teacher, Mina Kirstein.

Tall, dark, and elegant, Mina Kirstein was a charismatic teacher with high expectations and a generous disposition. If she believed a student was both talented and "serious," there was "nothing she wouldn't do to encourage her."[45] The brilliant and ambitious daughter of wealthy German Jews, also a graduate of Smith, she overflowed with ideas and energy. She could dominate a classroom like "a ship at full sail." Unfortunately, she also dominated her students' lives. Anne, uncertain of her own worth, was drawn to Mina's nurturing will. In 1924, when she enrolled in Miss Kirstein's creative writing course, she was unaware of the teacher's life of promiscuous sex and social-climbing adultery, and was delighted by the encouragement to submit her works for publication in *The Smith College Monthly,* the literary magazine. Anne wrote to her mother that the praise was "heart-warming." Perhaps it wasn't true and it wouldn't last, but nonetheless it was satisfying.

But try as she might to rekindle the spontaneity of her high school writing, she was overwhelmed by self-doubt. She wrote in her diary, "There is a kind of wall made of paper and the pen and the scratchy noise of the two; a wall between my thoughts and wishes and their expression."

In her junior year, happily, the wall itself became her inspiration. If she couldn't penetrate it, she could wish it away. In her poem "Caprice,"[46] written for the magazine, she tried to persuade an Angel to make her into a scarlet Spanish dancer:

> *I should like to be a dancer,*
> *A slim persuasive dancer,*
> *A scarlet Spanish dancer,*
> *If you please! . . .*

But, says the Angel, there is only room for brown-haired Quaker Maidens.

> *So I play the role of Quaker*
> *And I do not blame my maker*
> *For I think I wear the Quaker*
> *With a grace!*
> *But when a tune is tilting,*
> *Like a scarlet skirt is lilting,*
> *That my rebel heart is lilting*
> *No one sees . . .*

By the time Anne arrived in Mexico for the Christmas holiday during her senior year, her independence had begun to crystallize. Long disenchanted with her parents' restraint and pretensions, hungry for something substantial and real, Anne had already left her "beribboned" childhood behind. Charles Lindbergh was the mirror of her ambitions, someone capable of making his own rules. From the moment her eyes locked into his, even before she flew in his plane, she heard the melody of her "scarlet" dance.

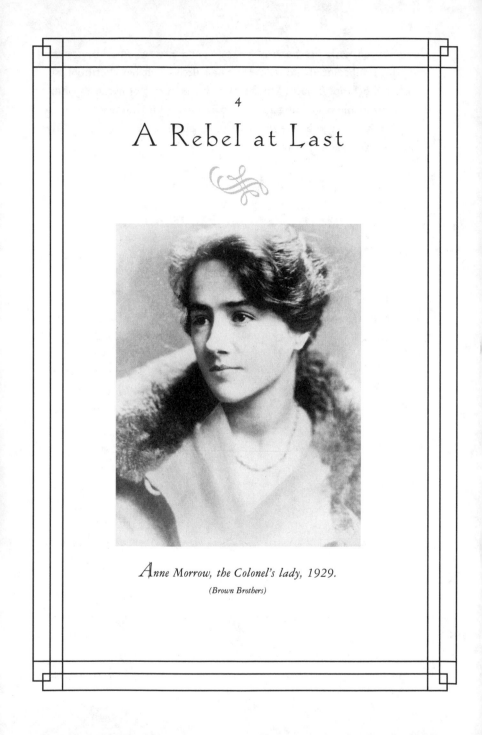

4

A Rebel at Last

Anne Morrow, the Colonel's lady, 1929.

(Brown Brothers)

Lovers and madmen have such seething brains,
Such shaping fantasies that apprehend
More than cool reason comprehends.

—WILLIAM SHAKESPEARE,

A Midsummer Night's Dream,

ACT V, SCENE I

JANUARY 1928, NORTHAMPTON, MASSACHUSETTS

After the sunlit gardens of Mexico, Anne found Northampton bleak and oppressive. The winter light cast ashen shadows, covering the campus in a heavy pall. But inside the walls, the air was conflagatory. Anne learned that a freshman, Frances Smith, had disappeared, and rumors of her suicide swept through its halls.[1]

The "horror," Anne wrote, was beyond words or imagining. The questions—the relentless interrogations by police and reporters shrouded an enveloping cloud that changed the face of everything. Most terrible was the realization that her friend had died and that she had done nothing to stop it.

Before the Christmas holiday, Anne had been asked to give Frances counsel. But Frances's fears were much like her own. Feelings of inadequacy, along with a vivid imagination, had made her shy, lonely, and withdrawn. Even as a child, Anne learned, Frances had fallen into trance-like states, in which she isolated herself from family and friends; this time, however, she had no hope of return. Feeling "weightless," as though she could "fly," she had thrown herself into the Connecticut River.[2] Several months later, the police found her body bloated and misshapen, but not decomposed, in an orange dress and a red coat.

Anne, preoccupied by Lindbergh, feared she might meet a similar end. She, too, had flying fantasies and wondered whether she was going mad. Frances's mother insisted that Anne could have helped her daughter; that Anne was the only friend Frances loved. Sleepless with guilt

and anxiety, wondering what she should have done, Anne waited for each dawn by counting the hours. Every morning at exactly four-thirty, she would rehearse her memories of Lindbergh's take-off from Mexico.[3] She recalled their breakfast by the embassy fireplace, their drive through the deserted streets to the airport, the excitement of watching his silver plane rise defiantly over the earth, catching the first glow of morning.[4]

While Anne cloaked herself in darkness, she wrote in her diary, Lindbergh transformed life with his "burning intensity."[5] The American public agreed.

Lindbergh, counted among the miracles of the New Year, was hailed by American clergy as the quintessence of Christian virtue.[6] Leaving Mexico City on December 28, 1927, he flew 9,060 miles, circling the coast of Central and South America, through the islands of the Caribbean, and back along the gulf coast of Florida through Georgia and Texas to St. Louis, Missouri. Hailed as a divine emissary of peace and good will,[7] he received a hero's welcome in every capital. Once again, thousands of people stormed his plane, surging toward him with frightening force and lifting him high above them.[8] Parades were staged; holidays declared.[9] Stamps were issued, and streets were named in his honor.

The *New York Times* quoted the chairman of the Senate Library Committee as saying:

> *Lindbergh achieved what no person, living or dead, had ever accomplished . . . {He} had occupied the first page on every cosmopolitan newspaper in Europe and America . . . he has made himself the hero of every son, the sweetheart of every daughter.*[10]

Little did the press know that the daughter of Dwight and Betty Morrow was already sweet on Lindbergh. But just as Anne's spirits rose with his memory, she was "terrified" by a call from Elisabeth. Their brother, Dwight Jr., was "very ill."[11] In fact, Dwight had had a nervous breakdown when he returned to Groton after the Christmas holiday.

The father had tried to rally young Dwight by writing him letters like those of a football coach, hoping to inspire moral rectitude. But nothing Morrow said or wrote was able to penetrate Dwight's fear and self-doubt.[12]

Two thousand miles away in Mexico, Betty and Dwight tried to deny the severity of Dwight's illness, insisting to each other that his breakdown would be swift and passing. On Valentine's Day, 1928, drowning in a deluge of diplomatic celebrations, Dwight Sr. wrote a letter of gratitude to Elisabeth, who had taken a leave of absence from her teaching post at school in Englewood to help care for her brother. He reassured her that Dwight would recover as soon as he was able to get some rest.[13] But the breakdown was more serious than the Morrows were willing to admit. Their son was hallucinatory and delirious.

Anne had a special feeling for Dwight. In spite of his intelligence and driving ambition, he was as sensitive and vulnerable as she. Dwight always seemed a piece of herself, and now his illness made her question her sanity. Exploring madness in her diary, Anne projected herself into the mind of Frances, alienated, alone, and the object of ridicule.[14] Trying to understand Dwight's breakdown, trying to grasp his pain, she imagined her death. "Useless" and good for nothing, she would gladly have exchanged her life for his.

The thoughts of madness turned back to Lindbergh and love, however, when her old boyfriend P announced his engagement. She hadn't wanted to marry him; she just didn't like being left behind. Resolutely, Anne denounced romantic love, affirming only the love for her family.[15] Yet her parents were far away, and their house in Englewood was no longer a refuge. She returned to school from a weekend visit feeling "poked . . . pulled . . . hurried."[16] Lonely and confused, Anne at times felt small and worthless; at others, strong and in control. Consolation and perspective came only through writing and observations of nature.

"I must say over and over to myself, Make your world count."[17] She wanted to live an honest and purposeful life. Perhaps she would teach or find the courage to write. She would immerse herself in the things she loved—literature, art, music, and nature—but, like her mother and father, she would dedicate herself to others, finding happiness as a wife and a mother.

By March, spring held the promise of reconciliation. For the first time since Anne's return from Mexico, she had faith in the rhythm and goodness of life.[18] She wondered if it was selfish to want happiness and love when the mere turning of the seasons offered so many "miracles."[19]

The real miracle she wanted was Charles Lindbergh, and try as Anne did to hide her feelings from family and friends, Elisabeth had caught on. Anne's need to idolize others, noted Elisabeth, was an old pattern. With Lindbergh, it had reached a new dimension.[20] The only way to dispel her anguish, Anne decided, was to erase Lindbergh from her thoughts. She turned to books, gardening, and food in an attempt to regain her composure.

But Lindbergh felt out of control, too. By the time he returned from his Latin American tour, in mid-February 1928, he had had enough of the limelight. Mauled by overzealous fans, exhausted from giving speeches and signing autographs, he was weary of good-will flights. At a luncheon given by the Guggenheim Fund, he announced that it would be his last official function. It was time for him to "retire to a private life."[21]

Lindbergh's desire for privacy ignited a debate about his rights and responsibilities as a public figure. While the media justified their intrusion by declaring Lindbergh's life a matter of "public record," private citizens urged compassion for the "boy-hero" whom "Fame" had taken in her hand.[22]

Nonetheless, the *New York Times* pursued him. Interpreting Lindbergh's desire for a "private" life as a wish to marry, the newspaper launched a drive to snag him a wife. Like a matchmaker, the newspaper reported him in "perfect health" (although a little thin for his six-feet-two-inches),[23] and blessed with a small fortune (estimated between $400,000 and $1 million).[24] If any woman was seen within Lindbergh's proximity, he was, reportedly, "engaged." And Lindbergh was constantly swarmed by suitors—from the daughters of wealthy businessmen and high public officials to street walkers and starlets who demanded his attention. The protection of friends worked against him. Guarded in the grand salons and country estates of the rich and powerful, safe from the intrusive press, he had little time alone with women. Charles was now twenty-six years old, and he had never had a date.

Before the flight he wasn't interested in girls; after the flight he was suspect and cold.[25] A wunderkind in an adult society of aviators, statesmen, and politicians, Charles had a social life that was frozen in time. When he left his friends and his mother in Wisconsin five years earlier, he had left his boyhood behind. And all that he had ever known of intimacy was his father's abandonment and his mother's suffocation. Everything in between—easy conversation, dating, and sexuality—was nothing more than a pleasant abstraction.

Nonetheless, the rumors were right: Lindbergh was ready to take a wife. Embarking on a "girl-meeting project," much as he charted a map for a flight, he reviewed in his mind the possibilities. Thoughts of Anne Morrow never surfaced. She had seemed so young, shy, and naïve, more like a schoolgirl than a prospective mate.[26]

Insulated at Smith from news of Lindbergh's travels and the public debate, Anne wondered why he was so silent. Hadn't he promised to teach her and Elisabeth to fly? Nearly three months without a call from him, and Anne was feeling rejected. It never crossed her mind that Lindbergh had met hundreds of young women and had invited many to fly in his plane; she chose to protect herself from disappointment. Extolling the virtues of Platonic love, she asked her diary whether it was possible to love someone "objectively"—to view Lindbergh as an "oracle" rather than as a "carnal" presence. It was the perfect solution. The "divinity" of the relationship would be preserved, as though the absence of one's beloved was merely a "condensed presence."[27] But she considered her envy of Elisabeth's happiness with Constance to be selfish and sinful. It would be better to find solace in nature, she concluded.[28]

Dwight Jr.'s illness brought the Morrow family together, but it sent a chill through their long-awaited Easter holiday. Elisabeth, at the request of her brother, accompanied him to Southern Pines, a rest home in

North Carolina, where they were met by their maternal grandmother, Annie Cutter. It seemed all too appropriate that Betty had called her mother for help. Betty saw her son as she had seen her father—a sensitive, high-strung "genius" unable to "cope" with the pressures of conventional masculine life. Although the medical jargon had changed in the thirty years since Betty's father was labeled neurasthenic, Dwight Jr. was considered "of nervous temperament." Who better than her mother, a nursemaid to her husband all his life, to help raise the spirits of a boy who felt inadequate to the demands of manhood?[29]

Strangely, Dwight Jr. drew strength from his madness. Perhaps for the first time, in the aftermath of his breakdown, he was aware that he was different from his father. While his father could easily harness his intellect, Dwight fractured in the process, succumbing to paroxysms of fear and self-doubt. Sheltered in the rest home, he sought to prove himself worthy to his family by challenging his father's standards. The father was certain that ancient and European literature and history were the core of Western civilization; Dwight Jr. studied the "mysteries" of Native American culture. The father played a mediocre game of golf; the son sought mastery. On the golf course at Southern Pines, he practiced the game with a passion. When he finally hit a hole in one, he cabled his father: "CURED."[30] Dwight Jr.'s words shouted through the wires; finally he too was a winner.

Since Elisabeth was occupied with helping Dwight Jr., Anne went to Mexico on holiday alone. Certain that her stay would be cast in "shadows" without the "sunlight" of her sister's presence,[31] she nonetheless threw herself into the beauty of the Mexican landscape. Her diary assumed a new dimension, building on the multisensory style of her adolescent essays. She absorbed the line, color, and sound of the landscape—the montage of sun and shade, fire and ice—splashing it onto her pages as though she were composing an expressionist painting.[32]

To Anne's surprise, she did not miss Elisabeth. She found the solitude both naughty and exhilarating. On Easter Sunday, April 8, two

days after Dwight's cable to his father, Anne echoed her brother's call
for self-confirmation. She would no longer be weak and self-apologetic,
pining away for recognition from Charles. "Colonel. L." was not to be
her standard; he would have to rise to her measure.[33]

Elisabeth, too, had found release. Alone in Englewood, out of sight
of her mother, she reveled in her autonomy. Playing responsibility
against desire, she used her devotion to Dwight Jr. to garner time alone
with Connie. Connie's presence was an anodyne; with Connie, Elisabeth
didn't feel sick. Plagued with poor health since a bout with pneumonia
during her freshman year at Smith, Elisabeth was short of breath and
easily fatigued. Her mother, perhaps thinking of the death of Mary, her
twin, had spun webs of restrictions around Elisabeth until the daughter screamed in suffocation. But only Connie seemed to hear.

Elisabeth had met Constance in a philosophy class in 1924, during
her junior year at Smith. There was an immediate bond between them,
strengthened by their belief in God and prayer. Connie, the daughter
of a wealthy leather merchant, was worldly, assertive, and practical,
with searing blue eyes, curly blond hair, and a tall husky frame that
radiated confidence. She alone seemed capable of piercing Elisabeth's
persona, exposing her fearful and fragile personality. With Connie,
Elisabeth could talk about everything—personal relationships, literature, and philosophy. As Charles did to Anne, Connie appeared to
Elisabeth as a member of superior breed, capable of raising her to a
higher moral realm. Elisabeth made a pact with Connie not to love
anyone else, least of all a man. They believed that sexuality tainted
love, debasing and diminishing the spiritual bond. Whether Elisabeth
was frightened of sexual intimacy, was in need of Connie's maternal
warmth, or was homosexual is not clear. Their love, rooted in
Presbyterian piety and Victorian virtue, was strangely naïve.
Frightened of their feelings for each other, they implored God to give
them wisdom and guidance.[34]

To Dwight and Betty Morrow, the fundamentalist teachings of the
Hebrew Bible condemned love between women as alien and abhorrent;

it was even more distressful to them because their family was in the public eye. It is difficult to separate their desire to protect Elisabeth's health from their need to keep her apart from Connie, and it is difficult to discount the psychosomatic aspects of Elisabeth's illness—the digestive problems, the nervousness, and the fatigue—from the guilt she may have felt in loving another woman.

Yet Betty had had "crushes" on women at Smith, and her own adjustment to heterosexuality had been both slow and difficult.[35] Had mother and daughter shared these feelings, they might have alleviated the tension, but there is no evidence of such conversations. As it was, Elisabeth staged an underground war.

While Anne saw Elisabeth as gracefully confident, she was, in fact, nervous and sad. Anne sensed Elisabeth's pulling away but could not understand the reason. Elisabeth's preoccupation with Connie angered Anne. A friend of Connie's later said, "Anne would always feel that it was Connie Chilton who stole her sister."[36]

By necessity, Anne moved closer to her younger sister, Con. Just as ready to adore her as she had worshiped Elisabeth, Con was to Anne the ideal woman, a height to which she could only aspire. When Con joined her in Mexico, they had a "perfect" time. They shared the warmth and beauty of the landscape and established a rhythm and a reciprocity that would later serve as Anne's paradigm for the perfect heterosexual relationship.[37] It was like being in love, she wrote.[38]

Anne had found victory in her trip to Mexico. Feeling productive and back in control, she was eager to return to school. But no sooner had she boarded the train for Northampton than her obsession with Charles Lindbergh returned. This time, she rejoiced in his superiority. She knew she would never be a great aviator; she took solace in her admiration for him. After all, she wrote, if she were more like him, she would never have recognized his greatness.[39]

Back at Smith life resumed its nightmarish quality. Anne felt confused and irrational, as though her center would not hold.[40]

Determined to fly again, with or without Lindbergh, Anne hired an instructor at an airfield near Northampton. Flying opened to her a "fifth dimension"—a state of higher consciousness—but she condemned her efforts as "trivial" and "hysterical."[41] She felt like a child back in the nursery, pretending to be grown-up in her mother's clothes.

While Anne watched Charles Lindbergh, Lindbergh, no doubt, watched Dwight Morrow. In fact, most of America was watching. Morrow had attracted the support of a powerful journalist, Walter Lippmann, the editor of *World Magazine.* Because he had an audience of more than ten million Americans, he was courted and feared by officials and politicians. His soft line on Latin American debt and his noninterventionist stance were construed by his critics as Bolshevik and un-American. But, like Morrow, Lippmann saw himself as a philosopher and a historian, a would-be academic coerced into the political arena by the force of his moral conscience.

When the Mexican government threatened to nationalize the oil industry, Lippmann and Morrow worked to protect American property rights. They negotiated a deal with the Mexican government that granted ownership to American oil companies and also tightened the restrictions on salable land.[42] Emboldened by their success, they sought to resolve the church-government controversy that had split the country into warring factions. Establishing the key issue as the registration of priests, Morrow and Lippmann struck a deal whereby the church could keep its land if it permitted the government to regulate the clergy. The agreement was sealed, and the churches reopened. The hallmark of the achievement, Morrow wrote to his son, was that neither side could claim a victory.[43]

While time would reveal that Morrow's negotiations had achieved nothing of enduring consequence, his diplomatic style gave the illusion that United States–Mexican rapprochement was possible. He was hailed as victorious on both sides of the table.[44]

By the end of March 1928, five months into Morrow's service, his name was mentioned in Washington as the next Republican candidate for president. Will Rogers wrote:

> *Being President is child's play compared to pacifying Mexico . . . He is the biggest ad Wall Street ever sent out. He almost makes 'em look respectable.*[45]

Insulated from politics and unaware of her brother's and sister's rebellions, Anne began to enjoy her freedom. By May 1928, on her graduation from Smith, Anne felt more creative and more in tune with her body than ever before. She began to see herself apart from her mother and her sisters and beyond the "towering shadow" of Lindbergh.[46]

A career in writing seemed a possibility. That spring, she had won two prestigious academic prizes: the Elizabeth Montagu Prize for her essay on women of the eighteenth century and Madame d'Houdetot, and the Mary Augusta Jordan Literary Prize for her work of fiction called "Lida Was Beautiful." The Comtesse d'Houdetot was a French aristocrat who defied her parents and the conventions of marriage by keeping a lover who held a key to her private garden. Intent on deceiving no one, she chose to live authentically, viewing life as would an innocent child.[47] Implicit was Anne's wish to judge life according to her own standards.

"Lida Was Beautiful" is a wicked little piece about a young woman's misfortune of having a beautiful cousin. Poetic and carefully executed, it was a thinly veiled account of Anne's envy of Elisabeth. But it ends on a note of self-appreciation. Like Anne, the protagonist, a plain Jane, was young, slim, and worthy of admiration.[48]

Anne was proud of her prizes and enjoyed the attention they elicited from her family. Still, the notion of her "smallness"—her insignificance—whispered through the bravada.[49]

Anne returned home in the summer of 1928, as her mother had done thirty-two years earlier. Even though she did not carry her mother's economic and family burdens, she felt stripped of purpose. With only the hope of a literary career and vague notions of teaching and marriage, Anne had nothing to do and no plans for the future. Alone in Englewood, thousands of miles away from her parents, Anne wrote incessantly in her diary, pushing her observations toward form and cohesion. The diary became a laboratory in which to examine art and love. They were, she wrote, rooted in the same source—the need to infuse ordinary life with the unifying "magic" of perfection. But metaphysics often gave way to fantasy. Anne created a pantheistic world moved by mysteries she could not explain. Thrilled yet frightened by the power of her vision, sensing that she was on the verge of self-discovery, she longed for "fusion" with someone or something larger than herself.

Avidly, Anne followed Lindbergh's movements in the news. While Lindbergh protested that he wanted to retire, he kept going, much as before. Each day the newspapers reported his flights and the accolades he received, from leaders who deemed him another Abraham Lincoln to showgirls who insisted he was their lover. Called everything from a "tool of American imperialism" to "Jesus Christ at the gates of Jerusalem,"[50] Lindbergh accepted foreign and domestic awards, gave radio and written addresses, and flew survey flights for the airline TAT. It was rumored that he planned a trip around the world and a Pacific flight northwest to the Orient.

In the six months since Anne met Lindbergh, she had made him into the "newspaper hero" she claimed to detest. She imagined him above human pain, seeing him as both the artist and the art, the idol and the ideal. He spanned all chasms and merged all distinctions. He was life itself—free and unadorned, yet superbly civilized.

But she had no hope of marrying him herself. The marriage of Charles and Elisabeth was "inevitable."[51] *Life* magazine would probably print a special issue. The fact that they had neither dated nor spent time alone with each other seemed irrelevant. How could he resist Elisabeth's "perfection"?

Lindbergh, though, had no interest in Elisabeth. In spite of her beauty and her "sparkling vivacity," Lindbergh was thinking of the ambassador's "second daughter." He reminded himself that she was "extremely pretty," dark-haired and blue-eyed, graceful and sensitive. His wife-seeking "project" was not going well; he had not met one woman he wanted to date.

On a trip to New York in the fall of 1928, he learned that Anne was living alone at the Morrows' Palisades Avenue home in Englewood. Carefully, he began "laying [his] plans."[52]

When the phone rang, on the warm morning of an ordinary day in the middle of October, it nearly paralyzed Anne with fear. Her mother's secretary, Jo Greame, told her that Lindbergh had telephoned the day before and said he would ring her again in the morning.[53] Though she had imagined this moment for nearly ten months, Anne was hardly able to maintain her composure.

She stared at the telephone as though it were a bottle of "castor oil," certain it would churn her system.[54] Then, in a barely audible voice, she said, "Hello-o."

Lindbergh declared his presence in his brusque manner: "Hello, this is . . . Lindbergh himself."

"H-how do you do," replied Anne softly.

Lindbergh boldly stated his intent. "When I was south last winter, I promised to take you up sometime here in the East. I called up to tell you I'd be very glad to arrange a flight—if you'd care to go?"

Dazed, Anne paused and then replied, "I—I'd love to."

But as if conspiring in her own rejection, she told him she couldn't see him for a week. She was going to the hospital for a minor operation. That, she implied, changed everything. To her surprise, Lindbergh held firm. "No," he said, he had plenty of time. He was determined, even eager, to teach her to fly.

Anne prepared for the trip, still certain that she was a substitute for Elisabeth. When he telephoned a week later to ask whether he might visit her in Englewood to discuss plans for their flight, Anne, once again, was dumbstruck with fear.

Feeling cornered by his persistence and precision, Anne agreed to meet him at four o'clock the following afternoon.[55]

"Sick with excitement,"[56] Anne waited in the fading October garden for Lindbergh's chauffeured car to arrive. By 3:45, nearly "hysterical" with fear, she paced the courtyard. Just as she had given up hope, the maid called to her from the upstairs window. Lindbergh just phoned to say he had been delayed.[57]

When he arrived, it was nearly dusk. They stood in the courtyard, silhouetted against the open door, suddenly stunned by each other's presence. Lindbergh apologized for being late; Anne nodded in polite forgiveness. Relieved and smiling, they entered the house, moving through the center hall into the living room. Charles strolled about confidently, hand in pocket, and Anne rang for the maid to bring them tea. They sat face to face by the fireside, discussing the flight and their strategy for avoiding the press.[58]

Anne had forgotten how tall he was, how thin and fair and "sunny." She loved the ruddy cast of his skin and his easy, wide grin. Even his hair seemed to "laugh."[59]

His manner, on the contrary, was businesslike, even cold.[60] Anne felt like an octopus, tentacles spread, ready to ensnare him,[61] but he conducted the meeting as though he were "a small boy" on a fishing trip who would come and go as he pleased.[62] She blamed his awkwardness on her frailty, as though it were her presence that brought out the worst in him. She didn't deserve his kindness.

And yet Charles seemed familiar, like someone she had known in a dream.[63] In the garden the next morning, contemplating the trees, Anne defined the dynamics of marriage. He, Charles Lindbergh, was like the big oak tree; cock-combed in red. She was small and frail, with a lacy crown. They would stand together, protecting each other.[64]

Three days later, wary of meeting at an airfield lest they be labeled "engaged" by the press, Anne and Charles met at the New York apartment of Cornelius Bliss, a friend of the Morrows. Anne remarked that she felt "like a deer, hunted by smiling, smirking, sure-of-themselves, relentless hunters."[65]

Determined to survive the flight by adopting the persona of a sophisticated woman, she arrived in her gray riding trousers and an old leather coat, apologetic and certain that she looked ridiculous.[66] Lindbergh at once set her at ease. She looked fine, he said, and he was certain she would learn how to fly.

Once in the air, Anne relaxed. In a de Havilland Moth—the open plane having been Anne's suggestion—they circled the New York and

New Jersey coastline. Lindbergh, anticipating the noise of wind and engine, had devised a sign language; by tapping his helmet, he could let her know they should shift the controls from one to the other. Anne at first was "terrified" when he waved his hands to signal her turn. The plane was as stubborn as an elephant, and she pleaded silently with the rudders to obey her. Soon, losing her fear in a fit of laughter, she managed to bumble through the interlude, with Lindbergh controlling the rudder and stick with his feet and knees. Graciously, he turned and smiled as he resumed control with a light tap of his helmet.[67]

Their secret adventure bound them, strong and fast. But word had leaked to the press. Three days later, their second meeting was short and hurried. Stalked by reporters, they flew from Teterboro in New Jersey across the Hudson and the East River to Long Island City and back again. Mammoth clouds, gray and rolling, hollowed a tunnel for their plane. And, like a "commanding hawk," at 160 miles an hour, they flew down the coast back to Teterboro, skimming the tops of trees. Again Anne took control of the plane, this time rising above self-doubt. Flying now felt easy and natural, and she delighted in the beauty of the sky and the earth. It was not only an escape from books and introspection but a chance to transcend the boundaries of imagination.[68]

Anne wrote to Con that she always thought she had seen the limits of the world. But now, "at one breath-taking instant, I saw *beyond!*"[69]

That evening Lindbergh returned to the Morrow home and asked to take Anne for a ride in his car. For hours they rambled through the back country roads around Englewood in Lindbergh's new black Franklin sedan. Charles wore a fedora, brim turned jauntily down on his forehead, and a bright blue tie that matched his eyes. Anne was surprised at how easily they slipped into a rhythm, discarding preconception for the give-and-take of honest conversation. Charles seemed eager to lift his mask of perfection, and Anne was grateful that the hero image was gone. She enjoyed his playful nonchalance, his dry humor, and the subtlety of his wit. For all his coolness and reserve, Charles was gentle and seductive. He treated her tenderly, buoying her confidence and assuaging her fears.

Of course she had the courage to fly, he said; of course she could learn to master a plane. He told her she shouldn't act like a schoolgirl. Rules, he said, were meant to be broken, and much of academic learning was "useless."[70] But in spite of the certainty of his demeanor, Charles Lindbergh was learning, too. He learned that beneath Anne's façade of timidity was wanderlust, curiosity, and warmth. She offered him love without the suffocation that had attended his mother's. At the end of the evening, Charles asked Anne to marry him.

"You must be kidding!" Anne blurted in astonishment. "You don't know me."[71]

"Oh, I do know you," he replied.

And one can only take him at his word. In the short weeks since their first date, Anne had shown him her competence and her character. After just one lesson, she had flown Lindbergh's plane with ease and grace. She had proven herself capable of his peripatetic life and had instinctively protected him from the press. Her sense of adventure, her childlike curiosity, her sheer delight in the beauty of nature were evident wherever they went, whenever they flew. Finally he had found someone who understood him, someone he could teach and mold. Her quick mind and agile body would make her an efficient and able "crew"—willing to follow, willing to comply, and willing to let him do as he pleased.

Stunned and flattered, Anne agreed. His proposal seemed impulsive and absurd—almost laughable—yet Anne knew she was to take it seriously. How could she dare to say no to Charles Lindbergh, coveted by millions of women? Wasn't his love what she had always wanted?

There remained, however, a "hideous chasm" between them, Anne wrote to Con.[72] Charles, it seemed, never opened a book. She wondered whether they could bridge such a gap. How could anyone so different be so wonderful?[73]

Anne was "completely turned upside down," overflowing with feelings she couldn't understand or control.[74] With Charles, she had crossed into another sphere, she noted, like the boy who had flown too close to the sun.[75] Charles's presence was almost like a sleeping potion. She couldn't write. She couldn't read. Nothing interested her. He seemed to call up every ounce of her energy, and when he left, he took everything with him, leaving nothing of himself behind.

Betrothed in secrecy, they waited for the right moment to tell the Morrows. While Anne remained in Englewood, wondering when they would make their announcement, Charles disappeared. On October 29, he left for a hunting trip in northern Mexico with an American friend. Within three hours of their first expedition, the press reported that he had bagged a deer. Something else was in the air, and the reporters sensed that the trip to Mexico was more than a holiday. While Charles parried with the reporters' questions, changing his story each time they spoke to him, he quietly made plans to meet Anne in Mexico.

The Morrows, now privy to the secret, joined in the evasion of the press. Dwight arranged an official invitation by Secretary of War Alex McNab, and Charles arrived at Valbuena Field on the evening of November 9. Two hundred people greeted him at the airport; Ambassador Morrow was nowhere to be seen. Carefully, Charles was "whisked" to the embassy and on the next day was driven to the Morrows' Cuernavaca retreat. Although the Mexican newspapers reported the couple engaged, the embassy continued to disclaim any romance between Anne and Charles. Lindbergh, hounded by reporters, stayed with the Morrows for two weeks. The couple was sighted in Lindbergh's rented Curtiss Falcon and Dwight Morrow's official embassy car, and the Mexican people, fed by the press, relished the rumors that Lindbergh had married the ambassador's daughter.

5

Presentiment

*A*nne Morrow and her mother,
Elizabeth Cutter Morrow, 1929.

(Lindbergh Picture Collection,

Manuscripts and Archives,

Yale University Library)

PRESENTIMENT

I am still as an Autumn tree
In which there is no wind
No breath of movement
Yet, there on a top branch
For no cause I can see
A single leaf oscillates
Violently
To what thin melody does it dance?
What lost note vibrates in me?
From the past or the future?
Memory or presentiment?

—ANNE MORROW LINDBERGH[1]

DECEMBER 31, 1928, ENGLEWOOD, NEW JERSEY

On New Year's Eve, 960 people gathered at the Morrows' new Englewood home.[2] This was Betty's house, the one that would erase the poverty of her childhood. Modeled on the Smith president's house in Northampton, it had been designed by Delano and Aldrich, architects to the Rockefellers, the Lamonts, and the United States Government. It had been constructed by fine European craftsmen, who laid its brick, paneled its walls, secured its antique marble mantels, and set its sprawling stone floors and verandahs. After two years of construction, at a cost of $400,000, it was completed in the fall of 1928.[3]

Betty, the poor girl from Cleveland who had hated the drudgery of housework, was now the mistress of twenty-four servants, who swept her paths, cultivated her gardens, cleaned her floors, her crystal, and her silver, and drove her in her shiny black limousines. The schoolmaster's son from the back streets of Pittsburgh had built her a home worthy of her bargain. Betty had made the anglophilic life of the wealthy intelligentsia her own and had climbed Palisades Avenue into the hills.

This was a house fit for an ambassador's wife, and this was a party beyond "her wildest hopes." By seven-thirty "everybody" from Englewood and "crowds" from New York streamed down Lydecker Avenue toward the Morrow home. Twenty policemen steered the traffic while the guests walked through the iron gates and up the winding drive toward the crest of the eastern hill. Evening had fallen warm and dry, and the towering oaks, leafless against the winter sky, framed the fifty-two acres of woodlands and meadows around them. Rounding the curve, the guests walked down the slope into a courtyard sheltered by shrubs and gardens.[4] The house, dubbed Next Day Hill,[5] was a symmetrical red brick Georgian Colonial flanked by northern and southern wings, two stories high, with arched bay windows and a door on a huge stone pediment.

The guests entered the wood-paneled foyer and crossed its terracotta floor, through the French doors, and on to a brick-walled verandah. Hemlock wreaths, poinsettias, and Christmas trees lined its length, and a Mexican band played in the glass-enclosed piazza on its southern end. Flowers gushed from crystal vases which stood on mirrored mahogany stands, while accordions, guitars, and trumpets played, and white-gloved waiters passed ruby red sangria.

The crowd was as various as the professional and social circles of the Morrows' twenty-five years of marriage. Pittsburgh and Cleveland mingled with Mexico and Wall Street, hometown teachers and lawyers brushed against New York money and diplomats. Betty's sister Annie, Dwight's sister Agnes, and his Amherst friend Charles Burnett chatted and laughed with Morgan partner Thomas Lamont, Great Britain's Ambassador to Mexico, Esmond Ovey, and the wife of the late Woodrow Wilson.[6]

When the reception was over, sixty-nine people sat down to dinner at two tables, one hosted by Dwight and Betty, the other by Elisabeth and Anne. At the end of the meal, Betty spoke about her long-held dream to build the house, which germinated while she was still a student at Smith. Dwight, shining with pride, rose to toast his wife, praising the life and home she had made. His only regret, he said to his family and friends, was that he had not obeyed Betty and built the house ten years earlier.[7]

As if inspired by her parents' happiness, Anne danced the *jarabe* in the ballroom after dinner.[8] To the sound of trumpets and the beat of maracas, her heels clicked and her red skirt twirled and her black, braided wig flew out behind her. At the end, Anne thrust her hat on the floor and danced triumphantly on its brim. The crowd broke into the Mexican anthem and a lively chorus of "The Star-Spangled Banner."

The timing of Anne's dance seemed less than accidental. Charles Lindbergh was scheduled to arrive after dinner. The opulence and the joy of the celebration moved him. The wine, the food, the mahogany, and the silver again evoked memories of his childhood on the Mississippi and the life he and his parents had wanted and lost. This was the Morrow family at its best, choreographed with precision by Betty. During her year at the embassy, Betty had cultivated a style of her own—proper and sophisticated, interlaced with strands of Latin custom and culture. The soft sounds of a New England Christmas meshed with the brash cheer of a Mexican band.

Still flushed by her scarlet dance, Anne was ushered by Charles into an empty room. There, amid the faint sounds of Mexico, Charles asked for reassurance that she would marry him. Although they had told Anne's parents of their betrothal, they did not yet want a public announcement. But because it was two months since their decision, Charles feared that Anne had doubts.

He was right. Despite Anne's initial consent, she was unconvinced that either one of them was ready to marry. She had resigned herself to a conventional life; she wanted to write and she wanted to marry, but she wanted a husband who shared her interests, a man so close to her in "mind, spirit, and understanding," he would feel like "home."[9] For the first time, she had met a man who understood her, and it was frightening. Charles saw the rebel heart inside the timid girl, and his piercing eye both pleased and threatened her. She knew that, with Charles, her ambitions could run free and her deepest instincts would be valued. But she also knew that marriage to the "hero" would change her life forever, and there would be no turning back.

But why, she wondered, had her parents accepted her betrothal to Lindbergh when her own wishes had counted for nothing? Why as his appendage was she suddenly whole? Her doubts grew as much from fear as from confusion and the feeling that she simply had no choice.[10]

How could Anne refuse to marry Charles Lindbergh? Could she tell her parents that he didn't read enough books? Could she justify a career in writing or teaching instead of being Lindbergh's wife and co-pilot? And then there was his physical beauty, the beauty she could not stop thinking or writing about—his tall, muscular body, his sandy hair, which seemed to "laugh," his hands and wrists, which burst with vitality. Most of all, it was the intensity of his eyes; they did not "seem his nor any man's but as though many bright skies and clear horizons were behind them."[11]

The Morrows had not been surprised by Lindbergh's proposal. It was Anne's indecision that bewildered them. They took their usual January vacation in Nassau and, on its white beaches, had weighed the prospect of Anne's marriage to Charles. Anne and Elisabeth sat in the sun, eating tomato sandwiches dripping with mayonnaise, and talking incessantly of love and heroes. Elisabeth took a maternal view of Anne's soul-baring honesty, feeling at once the intensity of her confusion and wondering when she would have the courage to make up her mind.[12] It may have puzzled Anne that Elisabeth wasn't jealous. Perhaps, for the first time, Elisabeth confided the depth of her feelings for Connie, and Anne understood Elisabeth's need to pull away.

While Anne wallowed in indecision, Lindbergh held to a clever strategy. He kept his silence and did not call or write, leaving Anne to deal alone with her uncertainty. As a result, she missed him twice as much.[13]

In January 1929 the Morrow family had other concerns. Dwight

Morrow's political ambitions were thwarted by President Herbert Hoover's unwillingness to appoint him secretary of state. Hoover feared that if Mellon were secretary of the treasury and Morrow secretary of state, his administration would be viewed as "big business government." The matter was explained in the press as Mexico's continuing need for Morrow in a time of crisis, but the truth behind his failure to obtain the appointment slowly surfaced.[14]

Suddenly, in the midst of the publicity, the Morrows received a call from the headmaster of Groton. Dwight Jr. had had another breakdown.[15] Immediately, Betty and Dwight took the train to New York and set off in their private car for Pittsfield, Massachusetts. On January 30 they rode twelve miles in subzero weather to Stockbridge, where Dwight had been taken to a rest home.[16]

Once again, Dwight Jr.'s illness held Betty and Dwight hostage. They lived as though the events of their lives were disconnected from the mental torture of their son. Yet the emotional instability of Dwight Jr. served as a barometer to the pressures in their lives. Anne's betrothal to Charles Lindbergh and Morrow's ascendance in the political arena exacerbated Dwight Jr.'s conflicts. Behind the scenes, he played ragtime to their melody, forcing his parents to appraise their vulnerability—to reflect on both their standards and their ambition. Morrow's letters to his son during the following months alternated between endearing words of encouragement and grim lectures on moral conduct, obviating the possibility of true emotional exchange. To Morrow, virtue and sanity were the same—a moral debt owed to ourselves, our friends, the community, and God. Like a preacher shaking his finger at his wayward flock, he listed the hallmarks of a virtuous life: self-restraint, knowledge, integrity, courage, and excellence within the limits of one's ability.[17]

Anne too had a debt to pay. She had kept Lindbergh waiting another month. As if her decision were nothing less than a gift, on February 3, one day before Lindbergh's twenty-seventh birthday, Anne gave her consent. In the end, logic and reason meant nothing; preconception and fear slipped away. All that remained was her love for Charles. Never had she met anyone "so fine, so clear, so utterly good, so real."[18] Their marriage was a matter of fate.

Anne had wanted a quiet intellectual life, unlike her parents' fast-moving pace. But now she was doomed to follow Lindbergh across the continents of time and space. She wrote to her friend Corliss Lamont: "Don't wish me happiness . . . Wish me courage and strength and a sense of humor—I will need them all."[19]

Released from the grip of indecision, Anne was suddenly eager to give the "news to the world." Nine days later, Dwight Morrow announced from his private office at the embassy in Mexico the engagement of Anne Spencer Morrow to Charles Augustus Lindbergh.[20] The notice was handed to foreign correspondents and disseminated to newspapers throughout the world.

In the left-hand column of the first page of the *New York Times,* upstaging the 280,000 people who had congregated in St. Peter's Square to pay homage to the Pope, the headline read: COLONEL LINDBERGH BE-TROTHED TO MISS ANNE S. MORROW.[21]

The announcement of the engagement surprised some, inspired others, and elicited global expressions of congratulations. Lindbergh's friends in St. Louis were stunned. "Girls," they said, "had never interested 'Slim.' "[22]

But if his social reluctance seemed odd to his colleagues, it was the stuff of royalty to the foreign eye. The United States minister to Canada, William Phillips, saw Lindbergh's social restraint as a princely virtue: "Colonel Lindbergh occupies a perfectly unique position in our country, very much like the Prince of Wales in Great Britain and Canada, because he represents to us, as does the Prince of Wales to you, all that is finest in man."[23]

The public response to Lindbergh's choice as bride was uniform and unequivocal. Anne Morrow was portrayed as the perfect mate for the perfect hero. She was "proper" in demeanor, newspapers wrote, "moderate" in taste and inclination, "beautiful," and "demure."

The *New York Times* reported that Anne was the Morrows' "second daughter," that she was Presbyterian, "like her father and her family," and that she had a commitment to both academic study and domesticity.[24] It added that she was a good student without being "a grind"[25] and, though she was not athletic, she conformed to notions of "prudent" activity.

This "sweet, quiet, and attractive girl," it stated, was slender; her luxuriant brown hair framed "very large and pansy-colored" eyes. Furthermore, she was a brilliant, prize-winning authoress.[26]

Restrained yet ambitious, intelligent yet beautiful, Anne was the epitome of Victorian womanhood, the consummate bride for the consummate man. For the moment, in the midst of public acclaim, Anne was transformed. To her family, Anne looked more radiant and beautiful than ever.[27] But she was already paying a price for her decision to marry the boy-hero who conducted his life like a fishing trip. For ten days, she sat alone in the embassy without so much as a word from Charles. Daily, the servants brought her the newspapers that reported his itinerary, his whereabouts, and his safety.[28] Anne's fears had come to pass. She had lost control of her life. Betrothed to the Prince, she had become his handmaiden, obediently awaiting his return.

6

The Mermaid's Bargain

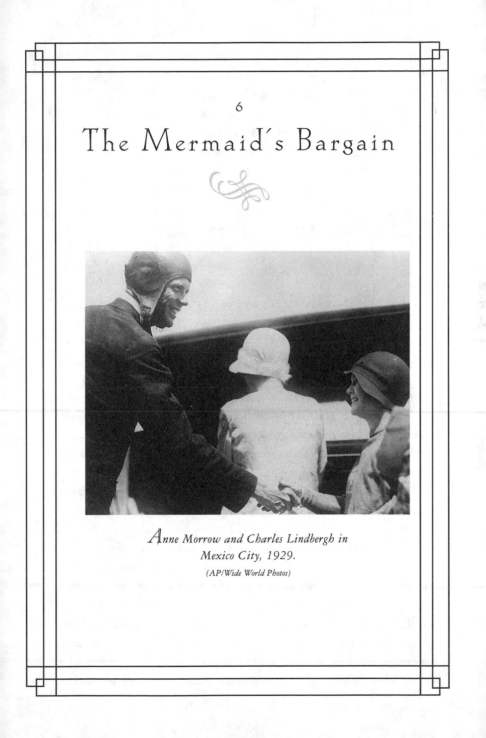

*Anne Morrow and Charles Lindbergh in
Mexico City, 1929.*
(AP/Wide World Photos)

THE LITTLE MERMAID

Only the little mermaid knows the price
One pays for mortal love, what sacrifice . . .
The magic sweetness of a mermaid's song,
She must abandon, if she would belong
To mortal world, the gift—of fatal choice—
That would have won the Prince, her golden voice.

— ANNE MORROW LINDBERGH[1]

FEBRUARY 1929, MEXICO CITY

Reporters surrounded the American Embassy, swooping like vultures in search of prey, hoping to catch the perfect vignette, the symbolic gesture, the definitive glance. The Morrows had thought they understood fame, but the adulation of the Mexican people, consumed by political chaos, bore no resemblance to the idolatry that now began to envelop them. The public wanted to possess Lindbergh—even at the expense of Lindbergh himself. And the Morrows were part of the spoils.

Hundreds of letters and telegrams made their way to the embassy, congratulating Betty and Dwight on their daughter's engagement. When Charles returned to the United States for "a maiden voyage" of the new Latin America mail routes of Pan Am Airways, Anne stayed in Mexico with her parents. Day after day, she sat at her desk, responding to those with familiar names, hiding her frustration beneath the jargon of etiquette and social amenity. More than anything, she wanted to be worthy of her parents' legacy and live up to the standards set by Charles Lindbergh. But there was a piece of Anne that wondered whether Lindbergh could measure up to her. The initial relief that came with her decision had quickly faded again into doubt. She whose life was defined by contemplation and study, she who thrived on sharing her thoughts with her sisters and analyzing her experiences in her diary, was suddenly unable to write or to move freely. Still, she tried to put on a strong face for Charles.

On Valentine's Day, 1929, she wrote him a letter hoping to put his mind at ease, but her anger seeped through to its surface. His absence had put an unfair burden on her, and she confided her fears and her loneliness. Everything, she wrote, seemed "horribly unreal" and her doubts seemed ridiculous when everyone was telling her how lucky she was.[2] But more than anything, she resented Charles's warning not to write letters.[3] It was as if he had sucked the life out of her—writing was her only way of keeping perspective. Now her words, if leaked to the press, could be used against them.

Yet Anne had a gnawing fear that even if she were to write, Charles would not hear her. She feared that their differences—their needs and ways of loving—would have no common ground.[4]

Yet whenever she remembered his eyes, their beauty and intensity left her without a choice.[5] But where were they? Lindbergh came and went at will. Except from newspaper reports, Anne had no idea where he was. Her finest instincts suddenly seemed wrong or dangerous. Moments of solitude, once filled with "dark creativity," did not bring her solace. Nothing had any substance. She was an image, a plaything of the press, and even those close to her found it difficult to be sympathetic. She had, after all, won the prize.[6]

After two weeks, which seemed to Anne like years, Charles sent notice of his arrival. Hoping to outrun the press, the Morrow family packed their bags to meet Charles at their mountain retreat in Cuernavaca.

After eleven hours in the air from El Paso to Mexico City, Charles motored by car from the embassy, arriving at the Morrow home at nine that evening. Looking delightfully ruffled and carefree, he seemed eager to be alone with Anne. They climbed up to the *mirador* and talked in the moonlight, happy just to be together again.[7] The whole family reveled in Charles's presence as they watched the couple sit together, heads bent close, nodding intently, just like lovers about to be married.[8]

After two days of dealing with family and reporters, Anne and Charles were eager for time alone. Secretly, they planned a day of flying into the mountains and the valleys beyond. On February 27, Charles rose early to speak with correspondents. Observers noted that he was more reticent and evasive than usual. Later that morning, Anne and Charles took an embassy car to Valbuena airport and flew off, unannounced, in a borrowed Travelair cabin monoplane.

Once in flight, they set their course for the desolate prairieland beyond the city, where they could picnic alone. On the way home, Anne took the controls while Charles surveyed the land below. He noticed that a wheel had fallen off the plane, and feared that the axle would catch the ground and capsize the plane when they tried to land. Anticipating the danger of explosion on impact, he reduced the gasoline on board by flying around for several hours. Aware that he and Anne would be tossed around the cabin, Charles put Anne in the back seat, padded her with a big flying suit and cushion, and told her to open the windows and hold on to the seat bottom. He planned to fly the controls with one hand and grip the fuselage with the other. An attempt to land on one wheel did not work; as he had anticipated, the plane caught the ground and accelerated forty miles an hour through the thin mountain air.[9]

Anne was certain this was a test she had to pass, and she was certain, if she failed, he would think her a coward.[10] But the test came and went without her notice. Anne emerged from the aircraft frightened but unscathed; Charles, unshaken, had dislocated his shoulder. Who and what had been tested was a matter of opinion. For Anne, it was a test of her trust in Charles. For Betty Morrow, it was a test of how well Charles could protect her daughter. But for Charles, it was a test of the future of aviation. From the moment he left the plane, he was careful to assuage the fears of the anxious public. As rescuers helped him out of the cockpit, he grinned and clutched his injured right shoulder. Pale beneath his deep Mexican tan, aware that his words would echo around the world, he called the crash a minor "mishap" that might have happened to anyone.[11] "Mishap." It was a new word for Anne, and a new way of talking about her experience. She too would have to choose her words.

Anne smiled tentatively as Charles answered the reporters' questions. Taking her by the arm, Charles led her toward the hangar, several hundred yards away, but as they went to their car, the reporters turned to Anne.

"How do you feel?" they asked.

"Augustus will speak for me,"[12] Anne answered, shielding herself behind Charles. In one nearly invisible moment, by using Lindbergh's royal middle name,[13] Anne had defined her public stance. Her own words would not suffice. From now on Charles would be her voice. It was one more price she paid for her Prince.

As the public response began to reach a crescendo, Charles knew he had to act quickly. That night, with his shoulder and arm bandaged, he and Anne returned to the site of the crash. Three days later, they went flying again.[14]

The public was enthusiastic. "Lindy" was praised for his social commitment and Anne and her parents for their indomitable courage. Will Rogers summed it up:

> So bravo, Lindy: You are bigger tonight than you ever was before, and that's saying a lot. And bravo, little Miss Anne, you have helped aviation more today than you will ever know. And Mr. and Mrs. Morrow, bless your hearts for your splendid help. That's why you gave your daughter to him, because you knew he could take care of her.[15]

While "Little Miss Anne" was at a loss for words, Betty Morrow was suddenly prolific. In the days following Anne and Charles's engagement, Betty's entries in her stark, shopping-list diary became self-conscious literary essays, alive with detail and local color. The regime of President Calles had been threatened by revolt, and with uncharacteristic interest, Betty probed its meaning as if she had taken her place in

history. She accused Calles of starting a revolution and conducting himself like a dictator. Betty felt like a prisoner of Mexico—none of them
could leave the country now.[16]

In the national election of 1928, Calles was precluded from succeeding himself as president, according to the 1917 constitution. He
had stepped aside for Alvaro Obregón, a radical reformer and political
ally who, as president from 1920 to 1924, had carried the country
through the bloodiest years of the civil war to prosperity. When
Obregón was assassinated by a religious fanatic who resented his anti-
clerical views, Calles formed the National Revolutionary Party and appointed himself its leader.

But the revolution had an unintended consequence. It distracted the
press from Anne and Charles and had the salutary effect of locking
Charles into the Morrows' country retreat for nearly three weeks. Anne
and Charles spent more time together during those weeks than in the
fifteen months since they had met. Lindbergh's presence, however, set
the household on edge. Constrained inside the country villa, Charles
seemed to explode with energy, tearing through the rooms like a run-
away train.[17]

Elisabeth's loneliness became more intense with Lindbergh's presence, and she poured it out in letters to Connie. She too was a target of
publicity and a never-ending slave to embassy propriety. Most of all, she
was crazy with boredom. Tired of parties and the social scene, Elisabeth
wanted to teach in the nearby Catholic orphanage. She complained of
intestinal grippe and low spirits; only Connie assuaged her loneliness.
Unlike Anne, who doubted that Charles was listening, Elisabeth knew
that she was being heard.

As the revolution raged outside the walls, there was a minor insurrection within. With hours alone and time to pass, Charles, Anne,
Betty, and Dwight discussed wedding plans. Betty wanted a traditional
Presbyterian ceremony and a properly decorous affair; Anne and Charles
had in mind something simpler. While Betty made her plans with
great excitement, devising a list of essential guests,[18] Anne wondered
why she even had to wear a wedding dress. Anne wanted her own kind

of wedding, one not bound by her parents' rules. Using Charles as her buffer, she challenged her parents' wishes. With Charles now speaking for both of them, Betty and Dwight had to listen. By the time Charles left, on March 14, Anne's happiness was evident. She announced she was certain that Charles was the "right" person. She told her family she was "sure *sure sure.*"[19]

But within twenty-four hours of Charles's leaving, Anne's fears returned. She began to see both sides of the ledger; Charles's voice was obliterating her own. Handling her parents and the press were practical necessities, but she would not trade marriage for her love of literature and philosophy or the possibility of becoming a writer. She had to be sure that Charles would respect her differences and her needs.

On March 15, Anne began a long letter to Charles, and continued it over the course of several days.[20] It was a kaleidoscopic representation of her thoughts, sometimes philosophical, sometimes reflective, sometimes wistful and poetic. She quoted from Shakespeare and Wordsworth, seeking, she wrote, "recollection in tranquillity;" she described "sunlight through a jar of marmalade" and told him of her mysterious longing for the sea. But somewhere in the middle she lost her nerve. Desperately seeking the words with which to gain Charles's notice and approval, Anne realized she was talking to herself, perhaps risking more than she knew. By the end of the letter, she apologized profusely, begging Charles to forgive her foolish thoughts.

But everything without Charles seemed absurd. Since the announcement of the engagement a month earlier, the embassy staff, along with her family, were still trying to regain their balance. On March 16, 1929, the night before Elisabeth's twenty-fifth birthday, the staff officials threw Elisabeth a party. With the obvious cooperation of her parents, the men dressed up like St. Patrick's Day kittens, with large green bow ties and black tuxedoes. Knowing Elisabeth's love of rabbits, with whose skittish whimsy she felt akin, her mother's secretary presented her with a live rabbit on a bed of greens. Elisabeth was at once the centerpiece of the celebration and fair game for everyone's ridicule.

Then there were gifts that sent the party guests into fits of laughter and Elisabeth into fits of shame. Allen, one of Elisabeth's friends, gave her a Victrola record addressed to "Miss Clay Pigeon" and signed "Augustus." The song was "Consolation," from an Otto Harbach and Oscar Hammerstein show.[21] Its refrain was supposed to be a comment on Elisabeth's feelings at being rejected by Charles Lindbergh:

> *I'll tell you what I need, I need your consolation*
> *Just a touch of tender demonstration*
> *I need a little more than friendly conversation*
> *What I need I cannot get by phone*
> *I need to feel that pressure upon my lips*
> *   as they caress your own.*
> *I'll tell you what I'll do to show appreciation,*
> *I'll let no one console me but you alone!*

Another friend, Fred, composed a huge collage—framed in glass and ready to hang—of more than fifty newspaper clippings that parodied Elisabeth's alleged rejection by Charles. To ensure her immediate recognition, he placed a photograph of Elisabeth in the middle of the tabloid pieces, bearing headlines that ridiculed her appearance and her personal habits and predicted a tragic life as a spinster without Lindbergh.[22]

While Elisabeth seemed to take it all in fun, for the first time she was seeing herself as the public saw her—passed over, rejected, and without a future. She fantasized about running away with Connie but knew they couldn't run far. For, alas, she was the ambassador's daughter and had to be careful to do the right thing.

Throughout the month of March, Anne continued to write letters to Charles, acting out roles like a bit performer, hoping to hear at least a little applause. How could she define herself to Charles? Was she a literary connoisseur? A schoolmarm? A preacher? Or a giggling, foolish child? Again, her frustration became self-contempt. She just wanted to know that she had pleased him. Her cloistered life at the embassy had given her too much time to think about trivial things. Nothing she did

seemed important or purposeful. She begged his forgiveness, hoping her pettiness was not tiresome.[23]

In truth, it was Anne who was bored—bored and angry. The unending fabrications of the press had become unbearable. They goaded her with fantastic rumors, hoping to incite her to speak. The whole world, apparently, wanted to know where and when she would marry Charles Lindbergh.[24] Defiantly, Anne refused to see the reporters. While rumors proliferated that she would marry Charles in Englewood, she considered playing the press the fool by marrying Charles right there at the embassy in Mexico.[25]

Three days later, without notice, Charles arrived. Anne was so happy to see him that his mere presence assuaged her fears. Immediately, she announced to her parents that she was very much in love and wished to be married as soon as possible. In swift response, the Morrows planned to leave for Englewood on April 28, setting the date for the wedding at the end of May.

Elisabeth was more than pleased. She intended to head straight for Boston. For the first time, Elisabeth contemplated the possibility of her own marriage. Lonely, and confused about her feelings for Connie, Elisabeth wondered whether there was a man capable of awaking her love. Perhaps he had died in the Great War, she wondered, unknown and buried in France. Within a week after Charles's arrival, Elisabeth took to her bed with crying spasms.[26] She was caught in a web of expectations contrary to her deepest instincts.

When Charles left, Anne became depressed and listless. The thought of another month without him was so difficult that for ten days she could not even write to him. She felt selfish, apathetic, and unresponsive—a burden to everyone around her.[27] " 'Oh god!' " she finally wrote to him, quoting *Hamlet,* " 'I could be bounded in a nutshell, and count myself a king of infinite space, were it not that I have bad dreams.'"[28] Consoling herself that his return to Mexico would quell her fears, nonetheless, she dreaded standing up to the press alone.

The Morrows left Mexico City, as planned, on Sunday, April 28. On

May 2, after three days with Grandma Cutter in Cleveland, they arrived in New York. Their arrival, however, had been leaked to the press, and they were greeted in Englewood by a hungry mob of reporters and thrill-seekers. Ringed by Secret Service men, Anne, Betty, and Elisabeth fought their way through the crowd into the house, only to find threats against their lives in the mail.[29] Anne's bad dreams had been prescient. The Morrows were subjected to a barrage of public adulation and newspaper publicity.

Nonetheless, for Elisabeth the moment was filled with possibility. Her parents, preoccupied with the logistics of the wedding, would loosen their grip on her. Anticipating her trip to Boston, Elisabeth wrote to Connie that she would love her so deeply and so well that she would never look or feel the same way again.[30]

Betty and Dwight, meanwhile, were fighting an all-out battle with a foe so fierce, they could not anticipate its moves. Anne and Charles had formed a powerful alliance, the goal of which, short of blatant impropriety, was to break free from the traditions and restraints of the Morrow family. The wedding plans had become a contest of wills.

To Betty, Anne seemed cold and detached, as if she had shifted her allegiance to Charles. Betty was disappointed that neither of them wanted to be married by a minister in a church. They found the idea hypocritical, since neither one had the habit of attending church. Saddened by their flouting of ritual and tradition, Betty worried that her relationship with Anne would never be the same.[31]

Four days later, Betty had a productive talk with Charles. His distrust of organized religion and the ministry was rooted in memories of his father's small-town politics, when churchgoing had been a part of the public show. He would agree to marriage by a minister, he finally told Betty, but would not tolerate the presence of politicians.[32]

Elisabeth's weekend in Boston with Connie made her even more certain of their love. Theirs was a simple communion, and Elisabeth offered her eternal affection. Thrilled by the beauty of their physical and spiritual intimacy, Elisabeth declared that being with Connie was all she lived for. They shared so much joy, in so many ways; she was con-

vinced that their complete and perfect understanding would keep them lovers forever.[33]

While Elisabeth was buoyed by thoughts of spending a long quiet summer alone with Connie, Anne was exhausted by her wedding plans. On Anne's behalf, Elisabeth called Mr. Russell Leffingwell, a former partner of their father's at J. P. Morgan and Company, to request the use of his home in Oyster Bay before they took their scheduled trip to Maine. Mr. Leffingwell consented, and the very next day Anne and Elisabeth were off.

But the beauty and peacefulness of Oyster Bay were fleeting. Betty Morrow wrote that Con, now boarding at Milton Academy, near Boston, was receiving life-threatening phone calls. Furious at the relentless press, they wondered if they should take Con out of school.

On May 18, the Morrows left for their home in North Haven, Maine, in Lindbergh's plane. Betty was delighted that the trip took only four hours, although for most of the ride, her air sickness prevented her from looking down. Nonetheless, she remarked with pride that Anne had flown the plane during part of the trip. Grateful when the flight was over, Betty was glad to see her beautiful island and the lavender hills which swept the horizon beyond Deacon's Point.

When Charles landed the plane in the meadow, it looked like a woolly monster, an oversized yellow and black hippopotamus quietly taking its evening meal in the fertile pastures behind their house. They arrived, of course, to a band of reporters—thirteen, to be precise—from the *Portland Telegram,* who stalked them all the way from the plane to their house. Three Secret Service men had to patrol the estate; one of them slept in the house.[34]

Charles rejected Betty's offer of a formal introduction to a select group of friends and relatives; he hoped to keep the visit as private as possible. On May 20, the Morrows quietly celebrated the anniversary of Charles's transcontinental flight. Again locked in the house, this time because of bad weather, Charles and the Morrows spent much time alone—talking, reading, playing jacks, and bantering. For the moment, there was a truce. Charles told stories about his flight and filled the long hours by the fire with memories of where he had been and what he'd been doing exactly two years earlier.

On May 23, with less than a week until the wedding, the Morrows began their journey to Englewood. Returning home was filled with the bittersweet memories of a family in transition. It was sweet with presents and letters from friends, bitter with anticipated emptiness. With Anne about to be married, the family's time together would never be the same. The present already belonged to the past, and every gesture became an artifact. In a sense, the rite of passage had already taken place, but they were about to make it sacred, and, for the Morrows, that made all the difference.

Anne sat by silently while Betty and Charles conducted final negotiations. They examined each paragraph of the traditional Presbyterian wedding service, line by line. Betty feared liturgical violation; Charles feared violating his integrity. At last, Betty was relieved to find that the essential rituals would be performed—the Lord's Prayer and the Benediction. And Charles was satisfied that his integrity would be preserved. He shyly practiced his wedding vows, but only when he was alone with Anne.[35]

Straddling both sides, fearful of offending either, Anne said nothing. It was clear that Charles and her mother were fighting for control. Her mother, who still wanted to lay down the rules, would not easily renounce her power. To Betty, Anne was her little girl, grown more precious since her betrothal to Charles. Four days before the wedding, as if wanting to freeze Anne's childhood in time, Betty knocked on Anne's bedroom door. As they sat next to one another on Anne's bed, Betty shared her deep sorrow. Hugging one another tightly, they moved toward the little white chair that used to be in Anne's nursery room. There they sat together, Anne snuggled close in her mother's arms. As if rocking against the strains of an old melody, Betty comforted both of them.

For Anne, the days before the wedding bore a sense of loss. Most of all, she would miss her sisters. In bedroom by bedroom, Anne said good-bye.

"She came out of Con's room, crying, 'I love them both!' " wrote Betty. Betty consoled her. "She held me close—so close!"[36]

As the wedding grew near, Dwight Jr.'s distance from the family became poignantly clear. Yet in her diary, Betty, strangely, treated his absence with nonchalance. Her formal list of wedding guests did not include him. Later, she would explain to friends that his physician, Dr. Riggs, had cautioned the family not to press him to attend; being there might cause a setback of weeks or months. Betty noted that Dwight dreamed of coming to the wedding but feared a breakdown.

Betty carefully numbered her wedding guests. She and Dwight Sr., Elisabeth and Con—four. Mrs. Lindbergh—one. Her mother and sisters, Annie and Edith, and Edith's husband, Shelton Yates—four more. Dwight's sisters, Alice Morrow and Agnes Scandrett, both of whom lived in Englewood, and Agnes's son, Richard—three. Dwight's brother Jay and his wife, Hattie—two more. And their neighbors—the Vernon Munroes, the C. W. Hulsts (Aunt Maud and Uncle Dutch), Betty's college friend Amey Aldrich, and the Presbyterian minister, Dr. William Allen Brown. Altogether, twenty.

On Sunday, May 26, the day before the wedding, the Morrows laid out a grand charade. The house brimmed with spring flowers cut from their gardens as the staff worked overtime to prepare the food for a coterie of friends and family who would attend Betty's fifty-fourth birthday party. The guests paraded up the winding tree-lined drive, past reporters and police, in cars and by foot, in their summer finery. The women wore peach, yellow, and ivory chiffon dresses and matching straw hats. The men wore light blue and gray suits with Panama hats. Betty and Dwight greeted their guests at the front door and ushered them through the foyer, also thick with flowers, and out on to the stone verandah. In full view of the reporters, watching the grounds from the driveway below, the servants passed the tea and served the punch to the light-hearted group celebrating Betty's birthday.

Meantime, the Morrows had the wedding cake smuggled into the house. A reporter noted that one of the guests who attended the reception carried "a huge box." A neighbor, perhaps Vernon Munroe, had been appointed by the Morrows to select the cake and arrange to have the initials L and M interwoven on top of the rosebud frosting. Amid the flowers and teacups, they devised plans and codes and set times and procedures for the following day. Knowing that reporters would record each detail of her wardrobe, Anne made certain that she was noticed in her new "French ensemble" of cross-bar printed blue-and-white crêpe.

A warm haze blanketed the northeast on the morning of May 27. Camouflaging their anxiety beneath a flurry of activity, Anne, Con, and Elisabeth walked through the "old" courtyard garden to pick forget-me-nots for Anne's bouquet. While Elisabeth arranged the larkspur and columbine, Con and Anne walked together through the gardens on the hills above the house. Sworn to secrecy, the servants diligently attended to their chores, ensuring that the routine would remain unbroken.

Later that morning, in a gambit to distract the press, Anne and Charles went driving in Charles's car, wearing the clothes they had worn the day before at Betty's birthday reception. They visited the home of friends, Dr. and Mrs. H. G. Ward, where formal photographs of the bride and groom were taken.

Shortly after noon, twelve of the guests assembled for lunch in the grand dining hall: the Morrows, Evangeline Lindbergh, Betty's mother and sisters, Vernon Munroe, Aunt Maud, Uncle "Dutch," and Betty's friend Amey Aldrich. Anne loved the warmth of her family and friends and was too nervous, she later wrote, to eat her favorite asparagus dish.

After lunch, as if to taunt the press one more time, Anne and Charles took a ride about town. Dressed in the same clothes they had worn that morning, they nodded to the reporters as they whisked by.

At three-fifteen, according to an arranged telephone code, the wedding guests, also in the clothes they had worn the preceding day, walked casually up the winding drive and into the sunken courtyard. Greeted, this time, by Betty alone, they went through the main foyer, now shaded, and into the large drawing room. With the shades closed to the afternoon sun, the room with its elaborately carved oak walls and fifteen-foot ceilings was like a church.

Anne, meanwhile, prepared herself in the downstairs ladies' dressing room, adjusting her full floating gown and lacing the larkspur and columbine her sisters had gathered into her handmade Brussels cap.[37] At a signal from her maid, Charles came into the room, wanting again to reassure her. He was followed by Betty, Elisabeth, and Con, who kissed her before leaving her with their father. Gently, he offered his arm, and they walked through the hall and down the three stone steps, pausing at the double doors of the drawing room.

On cue from Betty, Minister William Allen Brown, tall and stately, rose to his feet. Everyone, in hushed excitement, turned to see the bride.

Betty sighed with joy at her daughter's loveliness as she walked toward Charles. She seemed like a vision in her crème white chiffon dress, worn with the silver French veil she and Elisabeth had chosen. The veil, set in her soft wavy hair, fell to her shoulders, resting like a cloud in the folds of her dress.

Smiling proudly, Dwight escorted Anne through the arc of family and friends toward the fireplace to meet Charles.

The service, Betty noted, was spare but elegant, and no one seemed to notice Charles's required changes in the ceremony. The ring was passed in a circle of blessings, from Charles to Betty, then to Minister Brown, and finally back to Charles. Charles, in a plain blue suit, placed it on Anne's finger. No one, to the public's chagrin, dared to describe the wedding kiss.

Nonetheless, the proclamation of marriage was met with a flood of emotion from family and friends, who embraced them with good wishes, hugs, and kisses. Afterward, Anne and Charles cut the cake, and everyone lingered to eat and talk.

The frosting, wrote Betty, was as hard as cement, and the punch was perfectly awful. Anne, however, noticed little more than the circle of love in her family. To her delight, Charles felt the same.[38] To Anne, it was as if his approval confirmed their worth.

After the reception, Anne returned to her bedroom with her sisters and Betty to change her clothes for the wedding trip. She wore a dark blue traveling dress and a blue hat of felt and straw. Rushing out the door, Anne turned to wave goodbye, stopping one last time to relish the moment. Raising her arms in sad farewell, she steadied herself against the rising summer wind.[39]

In a note written to her mother on the day of her wedding, Anne described her feelings upon leaving: "I have a permanent happy solid feeling of holding hands with both you and Charles."[40]

7

Honeymoon Politics

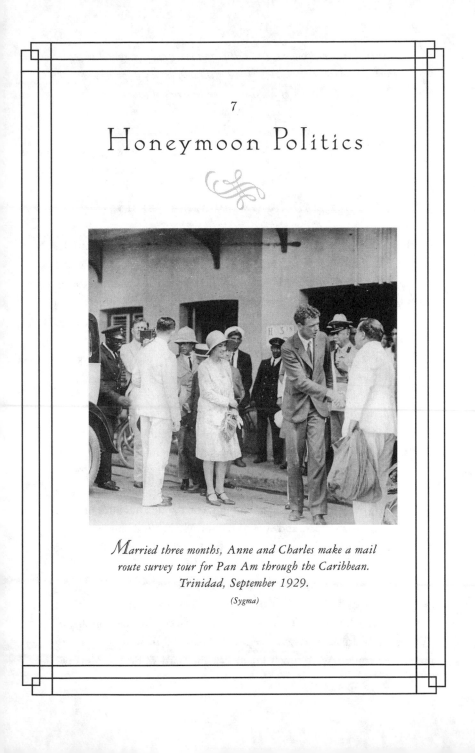

Married three months, Anne and Charles make a mail route survey tour for Pan Am through the Caribbean. Trinidad, September 1929.

(Sygma)

Within marriage, power is the ability to impose one's imaginative
vision and make it prevail . . . Love is the momentary or prolonged
refusal to think of another person in terms of power.

—PHYLLIS ROSE, *Parallel Lives*

MAY 1929, ENGLEWOOD, NEW JERSEY

At six-fifteen in the evening, two hours after Anne and Charles had slipped through the cordon of police and reporters with a casual nod, Morrow's friend Dutch Hulst came motoring down the driveway. He stopped at the gate and said to Fitzpatrick, a young policeman, "Tell the boys that Colonel Lindbergh and Miss Morrow were married by Dr. Brown."[1]

Within the hour, and with an unmistakable air of victory, Dwight Morrow drove down the hill, accompanied by his secretary, A. H. Springer. The car came to a stop and the reporters crowded around to congratulate him and to ask for details of the wedding. Always the gentleman, Morrow apologized for their trouble but refused to discuss particulars. Nodding politely toward his secretary, he informed them that Mr. Springer would explain "everything you want to know."[2]

On Morrow's departure, Springer pulled from his pocket a stack of duplicate, typewritten slips of paper, which he handed out after reading aloud the message: "Mr. and Mrs. Dwight W. Morrow announce the marriage of their daughter Anne to Charles A. Lindbergh at Englewood, New Jersey, May 27, 1929.[3]

"That is all," he said firmly, and turned back up the hill.

The reporters scrambled for their cars, and everyone inside the house was jubilant. Elisabeth, Con, and Connie stood in the middle of Elisabeth's bedroom and screamed at the top of their lungs, just to prove they could.[4] With much ingenuity and hard work, the Morrows had beaten the press at its own game and had savored the sweetness of a family wedding beyond the glare of camera lights and gawking mobs.

If the price of their hoax was to be public derision, the Morrows were more than glad to pay it. The press treated them like thieves who had robbed it of a story, but their friends applauded their cleverness and courage. Hundreds of telegrams arrived at the Morrow estate, singing their praises and wishing the bride and groom a safe journey.

A tirade of criticism broke out in the newspapers, igniting a national debate about who owned Lindbergh. The issue was a matter of property rights: what constituted public domain? Did Lindbergh, "a Grade A public figure,"[5] have the right to remove himself from the adoring American public?

"We made him," the reporters railed. "Why won't he play ball with us?" They admitted that they hadn't flown his plane across the ocean, but, they reasoned, had it not been for their publicity, Lindbergh would not have become a hero. Furthermore, without the press he would not have met Anne Morrow or started "on the road to riches."

The problem, of course, was the element of truth, but it was tantamount to saying that astrologists owned the moon. For the first time, the press had the technology to create a global commodity distinct from the person it represented. The question was not who owned Lindbergh; it was who owned Lindbergh's public persona. And the answer was becoming eminently clear. The press would tell Lindbergh's story at its discretion, with or without his knowledge or consent. The Lindberghs, after all, were the best show in town.

The editors of *The New Republic* wrote, "Lindy and Anne were a motion picture come true. They convinced every idealistic person that there was some justice in the world, after all."[6] But the line between fantasy and reality had blurred, wrote the editors. The public demanded to be entertained like "a vaudeville audience on a hot summer afternoon." Its inability to empathize with the "beleaguered" pair would stir up this kind of rebellion, but it was exactly the family's secrecy, warned the editors, that would excite their predators.

Alone on their honeymoon yacht, Anne and Charles had little knowledge of the public commotion they had caused. They sailed up Long Island Sound and up the waters of the New England coast on a thirty-eight-foot motorboat, the *Mouette,* French for "seagull," borrowed from their friend Harold Bixby, one of the backers of Charles's transatlantic flight. Working in the hull of the boat in the heat of midday, Anne was not thinking about their public image. She was trying to make sense of Charles's notions of marine "housekeeping." She spent most of her time arranging cans and boxes of food in the ship's pantry. She could understand neither the purpose of her task nor the absurd amounts of gourmet food—shrimp, pâté de foie gras, even plum pudding.[7] Either Charles expected an impending disaster or a formal dinner party for twelve—in any case, she was certain they would never run out of food.

Intent upon laying down his rules from the beginning, Charles Lindbergh played his honeymoon like an upscale version of an army boot camp. The press may have cast him in the role of romantic lover, but Charles drew on the only example of intimacy he had ever known— father and son on a camping trip in the woods. And while Anne had a visceral sense that something was wrong, as usual she blamed herself. She wondered why she was dissatisfied at spending the whole day cleaning the boat. The completion of her daily tasks did give her a feeling of self-sufficiency, she wrote home; the problem was that the chores were never-ending. Charles navigated the boat while Anne played the docile housewife, cooking meals and washing dishes, mopping the floors and the decks, making the bed and cleaning the bathroom, only to begin again the next morning. Charles's demands were strange, and yet, at the same time, "natural." Nonetheless, she didn't feel like a bride. In fact, she didn't feel female at all. She felt more like Charles's "little boy."[8]

Even as Charles was training Anne as a petty officer, Anne was brewing a mutinous plan. Before she left, she had packed a book of poetry, a collection of ditties and pleasant poems; something unintimidating that she thought would capture Charles's attention. On a quiet morning, with the yacht at anchor, Anne seated Charles on a deck chair in the sun and read to him. "He was bored to tears," Anne later said. She was about to give up when he grabbed the book and leafed through it. To Anne's surprise and pleasure, he chose a romantic poem by a A. E. Housman and read it aloud. "Never underestimate the basic instincts of a fine mind," she later told a friend. "Even if it is uneducated."[9]

Back in Englewood, Betty settled into her rigorous social routine, and Elisabeth welcomed the solitude of the empty house. Sitting on the floor of her room, in the shadow of her four-poster bed, she wrote to Connie, apologizing for her dreadful behavior during the days before the wedding, and reminding Connie that life was good even in the face of adversity. Life could play tricks that were cruel, not funny. The only satisfaction for the soul, she concluded, was to search for truth and beauty.[10]

The cruel joke, of course, was that Elisabeth was alone. In spite of her acknowledged beauty and cultivated mind, the "golden girl" of the Morrow family was facing the prospect of spinsterhood. Elisabeth knew she was different from Anne. She felt different, in fact, from most women—less desirous of men, more fragile, more lonely, and certainly more ambitious. She would not settle for an ordinary marriage, like so many of her friends and millions of women. For the first time, as if exchanging one dream for another, she articulated the idea of establishing a school.[11]

At the age of twenty-five, Elisabeth saw a school as a surrogate family. Her only escape from her parents' gilded cage was to play the system against itself, converting her wealth and social standing into tools of influence and revolt. And in 1929, establishing a nursery school for the rich was an act of rebellion. Such schools may have been considered suitable for the poor and orphaned, but "progressive" upper-class nursery schools were seen as radical institutions. They took children away from their mothers and homes, challenging the families' mores and structure. Steeped in John Dewey's belief in developing the individual child, progressive schools wrested power from the parents and handed it to professional educators, who had redefined their roles. No longer taskmasters whipping the wayward, teachers were the "guides" and "co-workers" of the child. For Elisabeth, this was a petticoat insurrection clothed in the patrician culture of her parents. It was an attempt to give children the voice and autonomy that neither she nor her siblings had had.[12]

The same ordinary people who chilled Elisabeth with their meaningless lives now heatedly awaited news of her sister. For more than a week, the press cruised the coast by air and boat from the Long Island Sound to the coast of Maine, searching for the celebrated newlyweds.

On June 4, the Lindberghs' honeymoon came to a swift end when a big yellow flying boat swooped down past their yacht as it nosed into the harbor at Wood's Hole, Massachusetts. Anne disappeared into the cabin, and Charles, sun-tanned and relaxed in his white duck trousers and open shirt, remained at the wheel. As he approached the wharf, a reporter and a cameraman cornered him. For a week, Anne and Charles had lived like "nobodies," moving and drifting as they pleased, but now the hunt that had started at Englewood was resumed with a vengeance. Hundreds of planes and boats surged up the New England coast to find them. For three or four days, they raced their pursuers out into the open sea, daring to anchor only at night along the fishing banks. To make matters worse, the weather had turned stormy, and the waves crashing around their yacht threw them out of their bunk at night. Anne confessed that it wasn't terribly comfortable, but she did not succumb to seasickness.[13]

After several days, Charles managed to outrun the press. Free again to move at leisure, they meandered through the small islands off the coast of Maine and then set out for home. Retracing their path down the New England coast, they arrived in New York—tanned, rested, and resigned to the demands of their adoring public.

After checking into the Berkshire Hotel on June 18, Anne wrote to her mother that they would awaken early the next day for their first public appearance together at a Long Island aviation show. She dreaded the ceremony and the mobs and the constant stalking of photographers and reporters. Nonetheless, she was content to do it for Charles.[14]

A week later, having completed business in New York and paid a short visit to Englewood, Anne and Charles set out to inspect and inaugurate the new transcontinental air and rail route for TAT airlines, for which Charles was a technical adviser. In an open Curtis-Falcon biplane, they flew across four states in three days—New Jersey, Pennsylvania, Ohio, and Indiana—through rain and a thick fog that brought "cold terror" to Anne. When they stopped to inspect the transfer station at Columbus, Ohio, Anne was struck by the homage paid to Charles. Always an observer, but never so close, she had not understood that Charles was treated like a king. Teasingly referring to him as Charlemagne, she wrote to her mother that no one could bend too deep or fawn too much in his presence.

When they were alone, however, the thrill of flying was unimaginable. The beauty of flying two thousand feet above the hills of Pennsylvania and the lush farmlands of Ohio catapulted her into a wonderland, where nothing made sense and everything was possible.

As she slipped into the rhythm of flight, her eyes became a lens through which, perhaps for the first time, the metaphysics of flight were defined by a woman. Anne wrote narratives in her head, later putting them on paper in her letters home. She compared the swirl of clouds and the prisms of light to religious visions, and described the configurations of sea and land with the breathless excitement of a child. Her lack of scientific knowledge and her aesthetic perception infused her experience with poignancy and innocence, transforming description into poetry. Anne recorded her vision, from eight thousand feet, of their arrival in St. Louis. In the half-light of a darkened night, she watched the Missouri and Mississippi converge. The two great rivers "joined, broad, peaceful and gleaming, between the dark shores."[15]

The press followed their voyage closely, referring to Anne alternately as "bride" and "passenger." She, in fact, was beginning to feel like a partner to Charles—unequal, certainly, but nonetheless a protégée, capable of learning anything he could teach. Merely being with him made her confident; when he was behind her, she stood straight and tall. Alone for hours on long-distance flights, they passed notes to each other, playing like schoolchildren on summer holiday.

From St. Louis they flew west to Kansas City on July 1, to Wichita two days later, and then on to Albuquerque and Winslow in New Mexico.

"It was an education in America," Anne later said. She had read Willa Cather and books about the plains, but there was an excitement about seeing the West firsthand that was beyond her expectation. The rich, fertile farmland sprawled beneath her, and she marveled at the tiny houses clustered beside the winding lattice of railroad tracks and at the rivers that cut like silver streaks through the prairies and farmlands. Charles loved the expanse of space; Anne was just as interested in the people. The crowds that greeted them each night when they landed were "funny" and strange, like none she had ever known.[16]

For the first time, Anne could see herself in a broad social context. Her education and upbringing had made her different from the women she met in the small towns—aware, curious, intellectual, and ambitious. She had little patience for uneducated women, she wrote home.[17] Furthermore, she noted with a touch of self-consciousness, the average man, educated or not, was more interesting than any woman.

But there was a type of woman who earned her complete admiration, embodied for the moment in Mrs. Bixby, the wife of the St. Louis banker who had backed Charles's flight. Mrs. Bixby was educated, well-groomed, sensitive, and interesting. Whole and self-contained, she was still dedicated to home and family, content in her self-created world. She treated herself with grace and generosity—with the kind of energy one usually reserved for others. Anne was certain this was the key to happiness.[18]

On July 6, the Lindberghs completed their flight, making a "perfect landing" at the Glendale Airfield outside Los Angeles. They were cheered by thousands and greeted by aviation and public officials; then they posed for photographers and motion picture cameras. Escorted to the TAT terminal, Lindbergh pressed a button that signaled sixteen passengers in New York's Pennsylvania Station to board a train on the first leg of their westward journey. They were to disembark at

Columbus, Ohio, where they would transfer to a plane for the flight over the Mississippi Valley to Waynoka, Oklahoma. At Waynoka they would board a Santa Fe coach for an overnight trip to Clovis, New Mexico. From there, at a pace thought miraculous, they would fly to Los Angeles the next day, arriving within forty-eight hours of their departure. For the inaugural flight, Charles would pilot an eastbound flight to Waynoka, where he would turn around and pilot the westward flight back to Los Angeles. On the flight west, Amelia Earhart and Will Rogers were to be among his passengers.

Anne was amazed at the luxuries of the commuter TAT flight. Unlike Charles's plane, the fuselage was decorated like a Pullman car, with lush leather seats, window curtains, and lamps.[19] The passengers were even served a mid-morning snack, and in addition to lunch, a proper tea. They were shuttled from plane to train by specially designed automobiles, and were given rest rooms to wash and change.[20]

Anne, feeling self-conscious among the movie stars and celebrities who gathered for the inaugural, watched as Mary Pickford cracked a bottle of champagne over the nose of the plane. Anne was given an enormous bunch of yellow roses, but when the photographers were about to snap the picture, Miss Pickford took the roses, and Anne assumed the role of dutiful observer.

The pressure of public life was beginning to take its toll. The strain of avoiding questions, quickly and politely, was like "fencing," she wrote home. Although Charles managed quite easily, Anne became mired in the social amenities of the exchange. In desperation, she confided to her sister Con, she would foil them all by adopting a "Bright-Insane Smile."[21]

Even with the game mastered and the job done, Anne was lonely. Locked out of the airline meetings that Charles attended day and night, she felt useless and disconnected. This was Charles's life, not hers; home and family were more substantive and real, even at a distance. Anne wondered whether the price she was paying for her marriage was too high. She was frightened by the realization of her dependency on Charles, his needs, and his unpredictable schedule. The letters from her family were like a protective shield she carried with her as she moved from place to place and meeting to meeting.

But away from the formalities of public life, driving alone through the pastures and farmlands of the California countryside, they were enveloped in their own private world. There was a "golden bloom" over everything. "Maybe it's just the way we feel, C. and I, when we get off together, alone—all gold"[22]

They flew over places never before seen from the air, inaccessible to archaeologists without months of travel on horseback or by foot. Their jaunt across the Yucatán peninsula more than a year earlier had earned them a high reputation as aerial photographers. Now, on their flight back from the West Coast, Anne and Charles photographed Native American ruins that predated Coronado in the painted deserts of New Mexico.

For Anne, the highlight of the return trip was their stopovers in Cleveland and in Detroit to see their families. The visit to Grandma Cutter in Cleveland was like returning home, and the one in Detroit permitted her to see a new aspect of Charles. He was playful and spoiled among his family, and she joined in the game, treating him like a pampered child. The contrast made her own childhood seem long ago, stolen prematurely and without warning.

During a detour to Englewood, Anne confronted the razing of the house on Palisade Avenue, the home in which she had spent her childhood. The emptiness was terrifying, as though someone close to her had died. Her childhood, so rich with feelings and memories, had simply "vanished."[23]

The shock of that loss Anne carried with her, even as she and Charles headed south to Washington, D.C., and to President Hoover's mountain retreat in Virginia. Amid the ceremonial necessities of a visit with the president, Anne saw only the poignancy of ordinary life. Reality, she wrote home, belonged not to the president or to celebrated fliers, but to the illiterate, impoverished, Bible-loving mountaineers, in tune with one another and with the beauty of the land. Their knowledge was clear, deep, and ineffable, untainted by pretense or convention.[24]

To Betty, Anne exuded a new confidence—bright, lovely and radiant.[25] Flying, it seemed, suited her well. She had already passed her physical exam, and was preparing for her student pilot's license.

In fact, Charles was tutoring Anne daily at the Aviation Club on Long Island. Each morning they made the long trek from Englewood to Hicksville, where they arrived at eight-thirty to make practice runs. In a dual control plane, with Charles behind her, Anne would take off, circle several hundred feet above the field, and land. After each landing, with Anne still at the controls, Charles would discuss her flight. At times Anne's lessons were cut short because reporters in planes flew dangerously close, hanging out the windows to take her photograph.[26]

On August 24, having given her nine hours of instruction, Charles judged Anne ready for a solo flight. After several runs and a few words of caution, he sent her off alone. Anne climbed into the cockpit and took off across the field, gaining speed rapidly. As the plane rose, she pulled back the throttle, circling until she gained an altitude of five hundred feet, and then landed. She tried this again; on the third round, she stayed aloft longer, circling several minutes above the field. Obviously pleased, Charles sat on the porch of the clubhouse and read the newspaper, glancing, every few seconds, at the sky.[27] When they arrived in Englewood, Charles was flushed with pride for Anne.[28]

Charles was pleased. Anne was coming along well, in spite of her fears and fits of homesickness. And she was as quick and as sharp as he had hoped. Eager to please him and to earn his approval, she was a sturdy and disciplined crewman. But she touched him in ways he hadn't anticipated. Charles had been lonelier than he knew.[29] Now, Anne's presence in the back cockpit, within the touch of his hand and the call of his voice, filled the long, empty hours of flying. With training and experience, Anne would be able to co-pilot Charles's plane, and he was becoming more ambitious. He planned to extend his mail route and survey tours, and to make the long-delayed flight to Asia.

For the moment, Charles was content to remain on Long Island. Even though the Morrow family had gone to their end-of-summer retreat in Maine, Charles stayed an extra week to watch the air races in

Westhampton.[30] Relaxed and satisfied, Charles made a sudden truce with reporters, permitting them to take photographs and conduct interviews. Anne, meanwhile, was bursting with impatience to see her family. She missed her parents and her sisters. "I dream of North Haven every night," Anne wrote to her mother.[31]

8

The Odyssey

Anne and Charles, Chaco Canyon, New Mexico, 1929.
(Lindbergh Picture Collection, Manuscripts and Archives,
Yale University Library)

And this should give you pause my son; don't stay too long away
from home, leaving your treasures there and brazen suitors near.
They'll squander all you have and take it from you, and then how
will your journey serve?

—HOMER, *The Odyssey*

SEPTEMBER 11, 1929, NORTH HAVEN, MAINE

A t last, Anne and Charles arrived!
Elisabeth shouted wildly to her mother as she watched their red sports plane[1] swoop down at sunset onto the meadow behind the house. Thrilled to see Anne safe on the ground, Betty rushed out the back door waving her arms in circles of joy.

Having been called on a search mission for a TAT airliner lost in the mesas of Arizona and New Mexico, they had arrived three weeks later than expected. It was not surprising, considering their eagerness to return home, that the Lindberghs set a new speed record on their flight from St. Louis: 905 miles in five hours and twenty-one minutes. Elisabeth remarked that Anne looked very tired, as though the trip had frayed her nerves.

But Anne was pleased to be "home" again. Even this remote eighty-four-acre estate on the northwest coast of a tiny island in Penobscot Bay was warm and inviting after four months of nomadic life. Set on a windswept point, surrounded by meadows and lawns, the house was a rambling New England farmstead with a touch of Colonial style. While it lacked the majesty of the Lamonts' Sky Farm, it rivaled the neighboring summer estates inhabited since the turn of the century by Boston bankers and Wall Street financiers. Betty had commissioned Delano and Aldrich to build the house in 1928, at the same time she had authorized Next Day Hill, and she designed a separate cottage for her children, hoping to give them privacy and space.[2]

Now, after many weeks of waiting, Anne and Charles were finally there.

They had missed the social highpoint of the summer: the Pulpit Harbor sailboat race, capped by a party on the Lamonts' back lawn. And there was already a chill in the evening air and a tinge of crimson on the ridge of maples. But the days were still warm enough to sail and picnic, and to walk along the cliffs and wildflower meadows of the outlying islands. The next day Betty packed lunch, and they sailed southwest through the jagged maze of inlets and harbors to the White Islands. As Charles, Betty, and Dwight lingered behind, Anne and Con, in blue jeans and red scarves, leaped across the rocks with childlike abandon.[3]

Three months apart had been painful to all of them; they were so pleased to be together again. But Dwight had serious matters on his mind. Since Anne's marriage to Charles and the constant risk she took in flying, Dwight feared her premature death. He wanted to bequeath Anne some money, but he worried that it would pass out of the Morrow family if Anne and Charles were to die at the same time. Dwight talked to Anne and Charles about his making such a will, but Dwight and Charles disagreed about the terms. Finally, however, Dwight decided to leave $1 million in trust to Anne, money that would revert to the Morrow family on her death.[4]

Because of the thick fog blanketing North Haven, Betty, Dwight, Anne, and Charles delayed their flight to Englewood. Elisabeth, however, left by boat for Boston. She wrote to Connie that a strange happiness had enveloped her those last few days. She felt certain she would never get married and vowed to find happiness by establishing her school.[5]

She then set about surveying the grammar schools of Massachusetts, sending a running narrative to Connie as she did so. Anne and Charles, back in Englewood, prepared for a three-week air mail and survey tour. It was to be a 7000-mile flight, the longest since Charles's 1928 goodwill tour. Meticulously planned, minute by minute, the flight would circle the Caribbean through the islands to the northern coast of South

America and back through Central America to Cuba and Florida. The goal was to survey existing Pan Am routes from Miami to Paramaribo, Dutch Guyana, and to study the possibility of passenger travel across the Canal Zone.[6] Flying in a German-owned, state-of-the-art, Sikorsky twin-engine amphibian plane, the Lindberghs were to be accompanied by Juan Trippe, the president of Pan American Airlines, and his wife, Betty.[7]

At dawn on September 18, Anne and Charles set off from Roosevelt Field on Long Island, accompanied by a co-pilot and a radio operator, to meet the Trippes in Washington.[8] Unlike their previous survey flights alone in their private monoplane, this was a public relations event designed to convince sixteen governments, along with the American people, of the viability of commercial flight. An arduous, back-breaking tour, it was brilliantly staged by Trippe to have the look and feel of an upper-class excursion—socialites embarking on a leisurely cruise. Charles wore a gray business suit, his helmet discreetly held in his hand, and Anne wore a pastel chiffon dress and a brimmed straw hat. Trippe, who didn't particularly like to fly, followed Lindbergh like his "shadow" in a white Panama suit and brown-and-white saddle shoes. Only his wife exuded ease, joking with reporters and charming the officials.[9]

They rose each morning at four and were in the air by seven. When they stopped every few hours to refuel and to deliver and pick up mail, they were met by cheering, flag-waving crowds. And when they weren't at receptions, dinners, or parties, Anne sat on the plane in a comfortable lounge chair, writing in her diary and reading books.[10] She may have appeared absurd to those around her, like a misplaced matron on her suburban front porch; in fact, she was examining the metaphysics of spatial and human relationships during flight. She concluded that distance was mental, not physical. The sound and touch of people back home were as vital as the quality of one's imagination.[11]

They toured the Caribbean islands, stopping in Cuba, Haiti, Puerto Rico, and Trinidad. In lyrical images, Anne describes the magnificent beauty of the land and sea, never before viewed from the sky—the "rich green" land, the "iridescent" seas,[12] and the majestic cliffs "plunging" into "turquoise" waters.[13]

But as they flew across the constellation of islands, Anne worried that she and Charles were the harbingers of change that might destroy both the culture and the land. Progress, Anne realized, could be an illusion. She deplored the arrogance that led to the exploitation of people and land.[14] She marveled at Charles's prediction that the islands would be only a day's journey from the U.S. coastline, and wondered whether this access would breed the commercialism she had seen in Nassau.

As news of their flights rippled through the foreign press, the size of the crowds swelled to thousands. Symbols of "progress," they were embraced—sometimes too heartily. When they arrived at the final mail-route stop in Paramaribo on September 23, government officials were determined to parade them through the streets, like icons of American technology, in a car hung with red, white, and blue lanterns. Charles declined, but was compelled by sheer courtesy to ride behind the official limousine in an unmarked car. The torches were lit, the band played "Lucky Lindy," and people ran and shouted alongside their car. "Charles," wrote Anne, "gritted his teeth and didn't look to left or right—that look of contained bitterness . . . a wild mad dream."[15]

On October 10, on the way back to Florida through Central America, they made an unannounced detour from Belize across unexplored territory between Yucatán and the British Honduras. Unlike their jaunt the year before, this time they were accompanied by the Carnegie Institute archaeologist Alfred V. Kidder and by a coterie of reporters more interested in the drama inside the plane than in the Mayan ruins they had come to document. They reported that, even at ten thousand feet, Anne was the ideal hostess, serving a two-course meal during the flight, tidying up the cabin after the men, and intermittently acting as Charles's navigator and photographer. The reporters were awed as much by her precision as by her grace.[16]

While Anne and Charles were living like vagabond performers in a circus, the Morrows were trapped by illness and circumstance. Dwight

Jr. had been sent home from Amherst College, depressed, confused, and on the edge of a breakdown. Once again, Betty and Dwight struggled with their feelings as they prepared to send him to a sanitarium, this time in Stockbridge, Massachusetts. His physician, Dr. Austen Riggs,[17] said he was much improved; he could not, however, assure them that their son's sweeping moods of depression and elation would not return.

As usual, Dwight tried to convince his son that health was an act of will. For the first time Betty wondered whether her son was overwhelmed by his father's expectations, but her Puritan ethic prevailed. She decided he needed to stand straight and tall, meeting the challenge on its own terms. Only then could his ambitions be fulfilled. Resolved to help him, Betty hired a professional tutor.[18]

Once Dwight Jr. was settled in Stockbridge, the Morrows prepared to return to Mexico. Anne and Charles were flying at record speed up the coast and around the gulf at the same time that the Morrows lumbered by Pullman train through the Midwest on their week-long journey south. They were welcomed in Mexico City by huge crowds, but nothing was quite the same. Mexico was no longer at the center of their lives. Betty missed Englewood and Anne, Dwight had his mind on New Jersey politics, and Elisabeth, now living in Mexico and ill with heart disease, was homesick even in the presence of her parents.[19]

Anne, too, was lonely, and missing home, which had now assumed a new definition. It was not a place so much as an ideal, clothed in family relationships. When the Morrows were together, they were "home." Formerly, they had moved as if in concentric circles, but Anne was about to find a new orbit on the outer rim. After nearly a week in Englewood Anne wrote to her mother in Mexico that she was expecting a baby. The news sent Betty Morrow into fits of anxiety.

Betty was consumed with thoughts of Anne, no matter where she went or what she did. Even a game of golf with Elisabeth couldn't distract her. It was as if she could hear Anne's loneliness through her words, and Betty longed to hold and comfort her as she had done in the days before her wedding.[20]

When Anne and Charles had arrived in Englewood during the last week of October, the house was empty. Anne reveled in the comfort and familiarity; she rearranged the furniture in her room and rummaged through the closets and attics to find objects from her childhood. The thought of a baby of her own stirred the wish to hold on to the past, even though she couldn't remember having been happier than in the present. Released for the moment from Charles's schedule, for the first time since her marriage, Anne had time for herself. When Charles went off to Panama on business for Pan Am, Anne wrote sonnets,[21] read Chekhov and Tolstoy, and visited childhood friends.

The press had no inkling of Anne's pregnancy. Experienced in the art of survival, the Morrows had learned to keep their secrets. There was, though, one secret they could not keep—Dwight Morrow's political career had taken a new turn. Anne's marriage to Charles made Dwight the perfect candidate for just about everything. He was appointed to a five-power conference on naval limitation in London at the same time as he was offered the New Jersey Republican Senate seat occupied by Walter E. Edge, who had just been appointed Ambassador to France.[22] While it was clear to Morrow he was playing in the big leagues, it was also clear that he had to follow the rules.

Morrow was recognized as a shrewd negotiator and gifted diplomat; now his image was enhanced by the Lindbergh name. The mere sound of it was like an elixir to an electorate still mourning the loss of thousands of men in the war fought little more than a decade earlier. With his son-in-law at his side, Morrow could woo voters from a platform beyond party affiliation: "Peace through progress."

Although Dwight was flattered, he had a measure of contempt for political machinations, and Betty noted that he felt "forced" and "tricked" at having to make a fast decision at a long distance. He did not know that his friend Joseph Frelinghuysen was also a candidate for Ambassador Edge's seat.[23] Betty, aware of her husband's indecision, recruited her friends George Rublee and Reuben Clark, at the embassy, to encourage Dwight to accept the Senate post. And when he did, she was overjoyed. This was the life she had hoped for. The appointment was surely just the beginning; there were already rumbles of a presidential draft for 1936.[24]

As Betty packed their bags to leave Cuernavaca, she was suddenly overwhelmed by Mexico's beauty—its white mountains against an azure sky, the pristine water, the sun-soaked countryside. Nothing, though, could compare with the thought of being home in Englewood with Anne.[25]

But to Betty's disappointment, Anne did not plan to stay. Pregnant or not, she was expected to fly. Charles had commitments he wanted to keep and still harbored hopes of an Asian flight. Anne, on the other hand, wanted to find a home, a farmhouse in Connecticut or on Long Island. She would live anywhere, she wrote to her mother, just to feel self-sufficient.[26]

Once again, Christmas overtook the Morrows. The decoration of the tree, the poinsettias in the halls, the fires burning from room to room, embraced them in a familiar island of consolation. For the Morrows, Christmas held the promise of salvation, illuminating and sanctifying their daily lives. But Christmas at home was a luxury that Anne did not dare to savor. Nauseated in her early pregnancy, Anne reluctantly planned her flights with Charles. They would bring in the New Year with an inspection tour of the TAT lines, and, after flying to Columbus and Indianapolis, would arrive in St. Louis on New Year's Eve.

Determined not to let go of home, Anne tried to bring it with her. She memorized poetry at night so that she could amuse herself during the long hours of flying. She categorized the poems according to the emotions they evoked, regretting that few permitted her either joy or sorrow. To her, most of them were either pleasant or melancholy. Only Dante Gabriel Rossetti, Beaumont, and Shakespeare could bring the pure distilled sounds that satisfied her. She consoled herself and her mother with letters, but they rippled with a sense of loss. Anne did take pleasure in seeing Charles happy, yet she felt uprooted, caught in a way of life that was not her own.

She wrote to her sister Con on January 14, from Los Angeles, that the

California rain was cold and penetrating, all the more painful because it was unexpected. Snuggled between a desk and a radiator, she wrote an ode to a New England spring, exploding with color, energy, and light. Imagining the beauty of Next Day Hill with its red fires burning and its gushing white blooms, Anne washed away the gray winter sky. The room itself became her garden, radiant with flowers everywhere.[27]

While flying brought mastery to the level of art, Anne still let her fears overtake her. Unable to share them with Charles or with her family, Anne found a willing listener in Charles's mother. When two TAT passenger planes crashed, killing everyone aboard, Anne, now in her third month of pregnancy, railed against the senseless loss of life. There had been no defects in the plane, and the weather report had been clear and favorable, yet sixteen lives had hung on the judgment of a single pilot. Would Charles be up to the task, she wondered in her letters to Evangeline? Would Charles know when to turn back? Perhaps they were deluding themselves; they might be the next to go down.

She apologized to Evangeline for her frailty. Like Charles, she equated strength with reason, having learned her parents' lessons well. Feelings sapped courage and resolve. Reason was at the crux of duty and virtue; everything else was self-indulgence. Determined not to succumb to her fears, Anne cultivated the manner of confidence, challenging herself to fly.

By the end of January, with relentless coaching from Charles, Anne had mastered the Lockheed biplane and anxiously awaited the delivery of Charles's new low-winged Speedster. Her real triumph was yet to come.

Convinced that motorless flight—fast, cheap, and accessible— would be a spark for popular interest, Charles learned how to glide. With the help of Hawley Bowlus, a record-breaking pilot, Charles taught Anne, who delighted in the ease with which she learned and in the grace and beauty of the glider as it sailed. She wrote to her family that the plane was first towed across a field by a car; then, as the car went faster, it pulled the glider up into the air. When the rope was cut, the plane, like a kite, rode the air currents.

After several practice runs, Charles encouraged Anne to take the glider pilot's test. The day before her flight, he chose the ideal place—the Soledad Mountains, the highest peaks in San Diego. No one had ever sailed from them before, but Charles was convinced that the thermal lifts would raise Anne's plane to a steady soar.

Anne, less certain, climbed reluctantly to the peak of the mountain. But once she saw the glider "perched" at the edge of the cliff, Anne felt comfortable and confident. As the cameramen poised and the coach yelled commands, Anne was shot like an arrow off a bow, cutting the air and catching the wind.

It was instinct that carried Anne off the cliff—instinct and Charles's belief that she could do it. Wondering if she was about to be sacrificed to one of Charles's grand ideals, Anne pretended it was a dream. But when she heard the keel scrape off the side of the mountain, her fears melted into serenity, and she felt in control. Gliding smoothly through the currents, she angled down the mountainside. Then she stopped with barely a warning "like a sled" into crusted snow.[28]

It was only later, through the eyes of observers, that Anne understood what she had done. As she sailed down into the meadow beside the highway, cars stopped dead in their tracks; people rushed out to see what had fallen from the sky. "She's all right!" yelled one woman. "This little girl fell all the way down the mountain, and she's all right."

Dressed in white duck trousers, a sylph of a woman despite her pregnancy, Anne surmised that she must have looked positively insane.

"But how will you get back up?" the woman asked, scaling the mountain with her eyes.

"Oh, I'm not going up again," Anne said. "This is where I meant to come."[29]

In fact, Anne had maneuvered her ship more than well. She had stayed aloft the required six minutes for a first-class license and became the first woman to qualify as a glider pilot. Her mother was in a frenzy, chastising her daredevil daughter for her dangerous acts. Young women across the country, though, responded by forming girls' glider clubs, with Anne Lindbergh as a charter member.

The success of her flight dissipated Anne's ambivalence, and she began earnestly to study the mechanics of flight. The luxury of their new Falcon monoplane, with its isinglass windows and roomy cockpit, made her feel safe and comfortable. Charles had installed a generator to keep them warm, and they brought plenty of food and lined the cockpits with pillows and coats to prevent drafts. Best of all, the isinglass cover did not separate her from Charles. She shouted and poked at him playfully as they flew.

To their adoring public, Anne and Charles were achieving a marital harmony in the air that few achieved in the comfort of home. The press, however, gave little credit to Anne for their success.

The Literary Digest noted:

> *When one recalls how few women are able to learn such a simple thing as driving an automobile from their husbands, with whom they are in other matters (with the possible exception of bridge) able to get along perfectly, one begins to suspect that as a teacher Lindbergh must have an unusual tact and patience.*[30]

In truth, Anne was a willing and able student who needed little more than Charles's confidence to motivate and sustain her. In preparation for high-altitude flying, she was required to learn sextant navigation. Now the laws of physics that had eluded her as a student at Smith suddenly became crucial to her work as a navigator. With Charles's help, Anne mastered the theory and mechanics of celestial navigation. Using a sextant to calculate the position of the sun, moon or stars, Anne triangulated their precise position.[31]

She had forgotten the pleasure of focusing on one task and the joy of working with someone toward a common goal. Six months pregnant, she wrote to her mother that the difficult parts were the extremes of weather, boarding the plane, and climbing back out. But worst of all were her stiff limbs and body aches from sitting too long in a small seat.[32]

Although she wished for nothing but home, Anne loved the wild beauty of California, with its cliffs plunging into the sea, and its rocky coast dotted with sandy white beaches.[33]

Finally, on April 21, after a journey of four months, Anne and Charles set their course for home. Dressed, this time, in their electrically warmed flying suits and fur-lined jumpers and helmets, they flew their custom Lockheed Sirius high-altitude monoplane at 20,000 feet at a speed of 190 miles per hour. Choosing to break the time record rather than to fly low and slowly to conserve fuel, they stopped for gas in Wichita, Kansas. They made the trip from Glendale, California, to Roosevelt Field on Long Island in 14 hours, 45 minutes, and 32 seconds, nearly three hours under the record set the previous June. While Charles played down the value of their flight, the five thousand people who had waited all day and night at the airfield saw the Lindberghs as homecoming heroes.[34]

When the plane came to a full stop, it was surrounded by the reporters and cameramen, as well as the scores of pilots, who had spent the night in the light-drenched field. Exhausted and nauseated, Anne was embarrassed to step out of the cockpit into the camera lights. But with genuine admiration, the photographers encircling her broke into applause.

One year and thirty thousand miles later, the girl for whom flying had been "cold terror" was greeted by an adoring public and the approbation of her peers. Anne was an equal among aviators and a pioneer of commercial flight. She smiled and waved at the cheering crowd.

She was finally home.

THE LITTLE MERMAID[1]

Into the smoky cauldron she must throw
A mermaid's kingdom, gleaming far below
The restless waves and filtered light that falls
Through dim pellucid depths on palace walls.

All childhood haunts must go, all memories;
Her swaying garden of anemones
Circled by conch-shells, where the sea-fans dance
To unheard music bending in a trance.

—ANNE MORROW LINDBERGH

MAY 1930, NEWARK, NEW JERSEY

On Memorial Day 1930, Charles Lindbergh set a new record. He flew the 110 miles from Atlantic City to Newark in forty-five minutes.[2] A mere puddle jump in the annals of aviation history, it was nonetheless noted nationwide. Sitting behind him in the cockpit was Dwight Morrow, suddenly the most interesting political figure in the country. Six months after his temporary appointment, Morrow was running in the primary race to retain his Senate seat. In less than an hour, without a word of testimony or endorsement, Lindbergh, his pilot-chauffeur, had clothed Morrow in his aura, teaching him the subtleties of media manipulation.

As he swept down into Newark Metropolitan airport in the same Lockheed Sirius monoplane he and Anne had used on their record-breaking transcontinental flight a month earlier, Lindbergh sheathes Morrow, a symbol of old-fashioned values, in his silver flying machine. He gave Morrow the essence of his popularity—moral stability in a

9

Into the Cauldron

*Charles and Anne, Dwight and Elizabeth Morrow
in North Haven, Maine, en route to Asia, July 1931.*

(UPI/Corbis-Bettmann)

technological age. It was a generous gift to his ambitious father-in-law, one he might have given his own father had he lived to witness Lindbergh's fame.

They arrived to the din of fire engines, brass bands, and a huge cheering holiday crowd. As officials greeted them and reporters closed in, Lindbergh made certain he was in full view of the cameras, with Morrow by his side. Morrow, his usual disheveled self, was whisked into a waiting limousine and escorted by police on motorcycles to Krueger Hall, in downtown Newark. There, his head barely rising above the lectern, Morrow delivered an elegant speech on the pivotal issue of the campaign: Prohibition. Stunning his opponents and pleasing the Republican Party, Morrow made a persuasive argument for its repeal, stripping the law of its moral weight and presenting it as an unenforceable rule. He advocated the passage of the Volstead Act, which would grant each state the right to determine its policy toward the traffic of liquor. His challengers, two "dries," Joseph F. Frelinghuysen, a former senator, and Representative Frank Fort, faded into the background as Morrow staged his "battle of words."

His opponents called him as idealistic but weak, out of touch with the electorate. The writer Edmund Wilson dubbed him a mechanical, unimpressive little man who promoted old-time religion—faith, confidence, and moral fiber—as an anodyne for complex social and economic problems. He was a puppet, Wilson said, "the gigantic ventriloquial voice . . . of American capitalism."[3] Apparently the electorate disagreed. Two weeks later, on June 17, Morrow made a landslide, winning the primary by three hundred thousand votes over his opponent, Representative Fort. An anonymous critic summed it up this way: "You might beat Morrow, but you could not beat Morrow and Will Rogers and Anne and Lindy combined."

Her father's campaign made Anne nervous. Her pregnancy was constantly in the news. Not only was her husband thrown into the political turmoil; her unborn baby was, as well. Reporters stalked the gates outside Next Day Hill, querying the Lindberghs and Morrows as they passed and trying to bribe the servants for news. Anne was angry at the press. While she understood her responsibility as a public figure, she and Charles held firm to their decision to give out no information.[4]

Heightening the tension was a mild heart attack suffered by Elisabeth. Later, it was revealed that she was dangerously ill; the Morrows had been informed by physicians that lesions were forming on the heart muscle and there was nothing they could do.[5] Confined to bed, Elisabeth felt helpless, cheated of time and possibility. Nevertheless, she expected to open her Montessori school, as planned, in the first week of October. She and Connie had rented a small Victorian house in Englewood with a white fence around it, a big garden behind with apple trees, horse chestnuts, a mulberry tree, and a pig farm. She named it the Little School because the children were young. Her big dream, however, was coming true: they had enrolled forty children under the age of six.[6]

With the Morrow and the Lindbergh families under one roof in Englewood, the days passed in a series of personal dramas and crises. Even though she was on "rest-cure," Elisabeth invited her teaching staff to the house to swim, play tennis, and plan for the fall. Morrow continued at his mad pace, like a man running out of time. Charles, more or less grounded until the baby arrived, made himself busy with household chores, and Anne luxuriated in the simple pleasures of sleep, food, and long walks with their terrier. Now in her ninth month, she succumbed to a state of hazy consciousness, and longed for the slender, vital body she once had had, a body that yielded to her wishes. But as usual, nature was her consolation, reflecting and molding the contours of her mind, giving her faith in the cycle of the seasons. As she walked in the woods surrounding the Morrow home, she savored the sights and sounds of spring, stopping to admire the pure white dogwood. Later, in her poems reminiscent of Rilke, "No Angels" and "Dogwood," the dogwood tree became a symbol of hope and new life.

But new life, Anne sensed, had a hierarchy of its own, and some forms were more welcome than others. As she entered the last two weeks of pregnancy, she worried that the child might not be a boy, and confessed her fear in a letter to her mother-in-law. She arranged a code to elude the press. For a girl, the telegram would be "advising accepting terms of contract." For a boy, it would be "advising purchasing property." "Advise" and "accepting" each had an A, Anne explained to Evangeline, and the baby would be named Anne. There would be no question of a boy's name—Charles. Besides the obvious alliteration, one can ponder her allusion to female acceptance and male control, to the ancient laws of kinship and property rights. But beyond the names was the fear itself, the inadequacy symbolized by not producing a male child.

She wondered if Evangeline, for whom a male child had been salvation, would be disappointed and apologized in advance for falling short of expectation. Charles, she noted, seemed blasé about the baby's sex, but Anne knew a boy would please him.[7]

When Anne went into labor on Saturday, June 21, the Morrow estate became a fortress. Dr. Everett M. Hawks, associated with the Fifth Avenue Hospital in New York City, pushed his way through the crowds of reporters who stood at the Morrows' gate. With him were four specialists and a nurse, Marie Cummings, who had resigned her position as head nurse of the Knickerbocker Hospital for the privilege of assisting at the Lindbergh birth. Present, as well, in addition to the immediate family, was Brigadier General J. J. Morrow, Dwight's older brother. While the wires buzzed and reporters poised, the Morrow home grew still. Without real information, the reporters fabricated fanciful portraits of the expectant father nervously pacing the rooms of the mansion, seeking little company and comfort from others. It was probably not far from the truth. One imagines Charles solitary and withdrawn as he waited for news of the birth of his child.

At 1:10 P.M. on Sunday, June 22, Anne gave birth to a baby boy, 7 pounds and 12.8 ounces. It was reported that Lindbergh ate his Sunday dinner and took a dive into the Morrows' pool. The *Daily News* noted that it "seemed almost an omen, in view of the horoscope predicting the Eaglet will be a waterman rather than an airman."[8]

The euphoria, the unqualified joy of the moment, dissipated Anne's antipathy toward the press. Reversing her pledge of silence, she sent a message to the reporters outside the gates, informing them that it was a double birthday celebration—the day of her son's birth was on her twenty-fourth birthday.

As greetings from friends came pouring in, a steady stream of outsiders tried to gain admission to the Morrow home but were turned away by private guards. Within hours, the baby's birth was front-page news across the nation and the world. The announcement of the Lindbergh birth in the *New York Times* elbowed aside Admiral Byrd's return from Antarctica, even as he was taking time from his celebration schedule to congratulate Colonel Lindbergh in person. In France, the Lindbergh baby was honored as one of "our own,"[9] and four thousand miles away, in Kenosha, Wisconsin, "the infant son" was honored by the Kenosha Junior Optimist Club as a member in the highest standing.[10]

Anne felt "gloriously happy" since her boy had been born. At first she had worried it would look like her, with brown hair and a big nose, but then she noticed that he had Charles's mouth and chin. Relieved, she felt certain she had satisfied everyone.[11]

Several days later, the *Times* reported that Anne had filed a birth certificate at the Englewood Department of Health without registering the baby's name. As if the baby's birth had eclipsed her own and obliterated her connection with her past, Anne gave her occupation as "flyer" and her city of permanent residence as St. Louis, Missouri.[12]

In the wake of Morrow's victory and the baby's birth, the Lindberghs began to withdraw from the press. Anne and Charles appeared and disappeared at will, and the press soon felt manipulated. Under the guise of public interest, they wanted the news. It wasn't Lindbergh's flaws that irked them; it was his persona of perfection. In an article entitled "What's Wrong with Lindbergh?" John S. Gregory of *Outlook* magazine warned that if Lindbergh persisted in being perfect and "Godlike," the press, out of sheer boredom, would be forced to fabricate his baser qualities.[13]

Ironically, the press did not understand the power of its fabrications. The media image of Lindbergh was molding the family's psychological reality. The Lindberghs and Morrows began to see one another as idealized personalities; Anne, who sensed the distortion, believed it beyond her control. Dwight Jr. felt the curse of his "presidential" father and his "godlike" brother-in-law, and Elisabeth also struggled with Anne's portrait of perfection. Since Anne's marriage and the birth of the baby, the tables had turned. In Elisabeth's eyes, Anne was the one who had everything. It was her own life that seemed uncertain.

In the days succeeding the birth of Charles Jr., Elisabeth, recuperating in Maine, wrote a letter begging Anne for her understanding and sympathy. Anne was ruffled by her sister's jealousy; her self-doubt evoked Anne's guilt. Nonetheless, Anne responded elegantly, portraying the birth of her son as just another milestone Elisabeth could easily match.[14]

Deferring to Elisabeth as an authority on childrearing, Anne sought her advice in the care of her son. She thought the Montessori method "enlightening" and played with the idea of Watsonian motherhood. John B. Watson, an American psychologist, preached a detached and scientific stance, encouraging mothers to be physically and emotionally removed, scientific and objective, without selfish or neurotic motives.[15] Anne joked that she easily fit the ideal. She had no desire to cuddle her baby.[16]

Throughout the fall, Charles became increasingly restless. He wanted to return to his flying schedule, and he wanted Anne to fly with him. Her rebounding health signaled to him that she was ready. Reluctantly, Anne agreed to hire a nurse to care for the baby while she and Charles traveled. But Marie Cummings, the nurse who had attended the baby's birth and had promised to stay, now gave word of her wish to leave. She was a hospital nurse used to big-city tumult, and was tired of the crowded house, small-town life, and unpredictable schedule. Elisabeth's personal maid, Mary Beatties, told a friend, Betty Gow, of an opening on the Lindbergh-Morrow staff and suggested that she ask for an interview.

Betty Gow, dark-eyed and graceful, with a delicate beauty much like Anne's, was a salesgirl who had quit school at the age of fourteen. She had come from Glasgow, Scotland, in May 1929 to earn her living as a domestic servant. Since her arrival, she had held five jobs, three of them in Detroit, where she had visited her boyfriend in the hope that he would marry her. When the relationship ended in a quarrel in September 1930, Betty returned to New Jersey as a nursemaid for a local family. On February 23, 1931, Betty Gow was interviewed by Betty Morrow's secretary, Kathleen Sullivan, and sent up the hill to the Morrow estate. Banks, the butler, who also served as Dwight Morrow's valet, met her at the door and ushered her upstairs to Anne and Charles, who greeted her on the second-floor landing. The interview, a half-hour in length, was conducted as they stood in the hallway.

To Betty Gow, Charles seemed "nobody special"—not at all like the image drawn by the press. She was struck by his lack of sophistication when he complimented Betty on her English and then, realizing it was her native tongue, turned red with embarrassment. But Betty liked Anne right away.[17] Unpretentious, without makeup and fancy clothes, Anne seemed accessible, familiar, and as naïve as Betty herself.

Betty saw herself as a novice servant, untutored in the ways of the educated and rich. In spite of her short stints as nursemaid, she had little knowledge of child care and was, in fact, surprised that the Lindberghs trusted her. When they called the very next morning to engage her services, she was thrilled. Later, Betty came to believe that her naïveté had been her biggest asset. She was gentle and earnest and willing to learn, and the Lindberghs must have sensed that they could train her to fill their idiosyncratic needs. In many ways, it was a perfect match. Not knowing what to expect, Betty expected nothing, and not knowing what to give, the Lindberghs gave nothing. With little time off on a daily or even weekly basis, Betty simply made do, freeing the Lindberghs to follow their peripatetic schedule.

For one week, Marie Cummings tutored Betty in Watsonian precepts. The baby's schedule, unlike his parents', was regular and strict. He ate at the same hours every day, and to prevent him from waking at night, he was roused at ten P.M., had his "nappy" changed, and was put on the toilet. He was so annoyed by this that he went back to sleep and did not wake up until morning. Betty Gow and the baby, nicknamed Charlie, moved to the third floor and into Dwight Jr.'s childhood quarters. Now that they were parents, Anne and Charles were more uncomfortable than ever with the crowded house and their dependence on the Morrows. If they disagreed on how much time Anne should spend with their child, they passionately agreed on the need to find a home of their own.

During his flying tours over Long Island, Connecticut, and New Jersey, Charles surveyed tracts of land. He had found a parcel of 382 acres near Princeton, in the town of Hopewell,[18] and returned with Anne by car so that she could see it. Only an hour and five minutes by train from New York, with its sprawling university, its small English Tudor village, and its lush farmland, Princeton seemed to marry the East and Midwest, and wrap up all the best in storybook fashion with a New England white picket fence. The land, nineteen minutes from Princeton, had a brook and fields and woodlands filled with beautiful oaks. Until they could build a house, they would live in a rented cottage near town, with a field sufficient for a landing strip.[19]

Their rented farmhouse, along with the promise of a home of their own, assuaged Anne's fears of leaving the baby. The Colonial farmhouse had two stories, two bedrooms, and servants' quarters, and was on a quiet back road surrounded by big trees. Anne hired a newly arrived English couple, the Whateleys, to run the house and garden, and within a month she prepared Betty Gow and the baby to make the move. Enthralled with the newness of it all, Anne relished setting up the house, buying sheets and towels, kitchenware, and inexpensive furniture.

The early months in Princeton were a happy time for Anne. She adored the baby and missed him terribly when she had to leave with Charles. If she was not home by his bedtime, she consoled herself with visions of his scrunched-up, squinty smile. On the days she was home, she played with the baby, cranking up the gramophone and singing and dancing to the music throughout the day.

Hoping to pass some of her joy to her mother, Anne wrote long letters to her. She lived only two hours from Englewood, but the letters were Anne's way of capturing the beauty and texture of her motherhood. It was a gift her mother deserved. The letters had a new quality—mellow, peaceful, and observant—as though she had earned her legitimate place. Free of self-justification, they were alive with images of small-town life—football games, gardens, and hands smelling of leaves, her pleasure in reading Katherine Mansfield by the fire, and her hours of contemplative solitude. Most of all, she wrote of her "lamb," sleeping in the barn, shielded by windowed doors that flooded it with light and kept out the wind. He had become so responsive to her and Charles, longing for their hugs and delighting in their games. Most of all, he loved when Charles swung him through the air, as if he were flying in his father's plane.[20]

Charles, too, was thriving, supervising the building of their new house and chopping down trees for firewood, as he had done with his father on the banks of the Mississippi. The foundation of the house, reported to be sixty by forty feet, was nearing completion, and the long road to the highway was finally done. When Charles wasn't at home, he was at work at the Rockefeller Institute with Alexis Carrel, a Nobel Prize–winning surgeon and biologist. Elisabeth's health was deteriorating, and Charles, encouraged by Anne, hoped he could apply his mechanical skills to designing laboratory apparatus that would help Carrel repair damaged heart valves.

She sensed that her precious time at home was running out. For the moment, Charles was content with his work, but she knew she could not remain home for long. Charles expected her, at the very least, to attend public receptions and ceremonies. She wrote to Evangeline that it was as if she "jumped from bed into a plane"; the double life of wife and mother was a tightrope of loyalties and responsibilities.[21] Already sensing future conflicts between her and Charles, Anne tried to rally her family behind her. But Elisabeth was ill and preoccupied with her school; their mother, now the grand dame of New Jersey, was more consumed by public events than before; and Con was still a schoolgirl at Milton Academy. Anne's best hope for friendship lay with Evangeline, whom she tried to lure into her fold. It was as if she were making a deal: in exchange for her friendship and support, she would give Evangeline a backstage view of her son's life. Instinctively, Anne played on Evangeline's sympathy, pulling her close with news of the baby and connecting the baby to Charles in every way.

But her efforts ran like water through a sieve. Evangeline would come to visit, but she did not stay; she seemed incapable of the intimacy Anne required. Charles, too, had an ambivalent streak, which Anne and Betty Gow found strange and troubling; he sometimes pushed the baby away. Anne wrote to Evangeline that Charles held his hands out "for your lamb" and then squeezed him around the neck. Betty noticed that, under the guise of promoting independence, Charles locked the baby out of the house without any toys and forbade others to answer his cries. She also thought it cruel of Charles to shave Skean, the Scottish terrier, a periodic procedure that made the dog antisocial and skittish. The dog had taken to hiding under chairs when people were around.

But if these strange occurrences were unsettling, they paled beneath the real threat. The baby was the object of so much public interest that Anne's anxiety about his safety was becoming ever more intense. News of their land purchase had leaked to the press. The exact location, the amount of acreage, along with the dimensions of the house, were printed in newspapers around the country. Reporters had even tracked them to their rented farmhouse. And the more the public learned, the more insatiable it grew. Strangers would call them at home in Princeton and demand to see the baby. One woman said "she *must* see that baby—life or death."[22] In Little Falls, Minnesota, Charles's hometown, souvenir collectors had ransacked his childhood house, leaving little standing other than its shell.[23]

Worst of all, sightseers had broken through the guarded gates in Englewood and had killed Elisabeth's dog, Daffin, with their car. They left the dog howling without even bothering to stop.[24]

By the beginning of April 1931, Anne's domestic routine was all but forgotten. Charles was planning a trip to California and was talking about a long summer flight to the Orient. Without her family to take care of the baby in Princeton, Anne asked Whateley to bring

Charlie to Englewood. At least Aunt Annie, her mother's sister, would come to see him, she wrote to her mother. She and Charles would stay for Easter and leave the following week.

But Charles must have sensed Anne's anxiety, for he canceled the trip. Anne was so relieved, she could do nothing but rave about the baby—his curly golden hair, his beautiful smile, his tanned face, which flushed with excitement in the warmth of the spring sunshine, and his growing discernment of people. He was beginning to be afraid of strangers, and kept a steady grip on Anne or Betty Gow.[25]

Meanwhile, Elisabeth made an astonishing announcement. She would marry in June—June 6, to be exact. She had met a man, she revealed, on the beach in Nassau that May while her parents were in Europe and Con, Dwight Jr., and Connie had left for home. She was sitting alone when he introduced himself, and they had spent that day and many days afterward strolling along the beach and talking. At week's end, Elisabeth was certain—they were both certain—that each had found the person divinely ordained as spouses.[26]

His name was Clyde Roddy; he was a thirty-three-year-old Presbyterian minister from Arlington, New Jersey, recently widowed. Attractive, athletic, smart, and well-educated, Roddy was a graduate of Yale, the Union Theological Seminary, and Southern Methodist University.[27] To Anne, he seemed a little too ardent in his attentions to Elisabeth and premature in his expectations of marriage. With help from Con, Anne tried to dissuade Elisabeth, but Elisabeth refused to listen. Ecstatic at the possibility of marriage, she was not ashamed by the clandestine manner and brevity of her romance.

Two weeks later, on May 6, Dwight and Betty Morrow returned from Europe. Shocked at Elisabeth's news, they were convinced that no man of honor would have acted with such impropriety, proposing to a woman in her parents' absence and not asking them for her hand in marriage. They implored Elisabeth to reconsider, but their daughter was adamant. The power of Clyde's love filled her with a divine radiance, the light of God. She knew her mother had expected her to marry a different kind of man,[28] someone like a J. P. Morgan partner or a diplomat. But she could not see a life of pouring tea for dignitaries in the stuffy salons of Europe. No—Clyde was neither brilliant nor rich, but the money he had he spent on the laborers in his parish who needed help.[29]

Elisabeth's engagement was a brash rebellion against everything for which her parents stood. Yet once again it was clothed in high nobility—church, God, service to man. Finally she was free of her parents' upper-class pretensions, their moneyed life style and social demands. And finally she was free of her love for Connie and Connie's desire to possess her. Marriage to a minister would resolve the problem of her sexuality. It was physical love, perfunctory and procreative, without the weight of carnal sin. Marriage to Clyde, in effect, offered her autonomy in the midst of constraint. But Elisabeth's plan for subterfuge failed. Betty and Dwight forbade her to marry a bridegroom who acted too eager for a minister of God. Elisabeth reluctantly bowed to her parents' wishes, breaking her engagement to Clyde.

While Elisabeth had been determined to please no one, Anne dedicated herself to Charles. As Anne had feared the short holiday trip Charles planned had mushroomed into a three-month jaunt across Canada, northwest to Alaska, Japan, China, and the Soviet Union. In preparation, Charles was starting her on a rough training course at the Aviation Country Club on Long Island. By mid-May, she was spending so many hours flying that she had little time to be with her baby. Charles was a taskmaster with a critical streak, always expecting Anne to do her best. He worked her daily, into the night, and when she was not up to standard, he treated her like a wayward child. Nonetheless, she was moving along; soon she would have ten hours of solo flight and she could apply for her pilot's license.[30]

Without intent, Anne had capitulated to Charles. She renounced her desire to stay at home and committed herself to preparing for the flight. On May 30, as Charles beamed with approval, Anne made four landings, spiraled from an elevation of two thousand feet, executed figure-eights, and performed all the requirements for becoming licensed.[31]

But for Anne, the victory was bittersweet. Now that she was a pilot,

Charles planned to equip their monoplane with dual controls so that she could relieve him on long flights. Charles's ambition seemed to have no geographical or cultural bounds; he planned a trip of mythological proportions. They would fly seventy-one hundred miles through what the newspapers were to call "the wildest and least inhabited portions of the globe," attempting to carve an aerial passage northwest to the Orient. It was a feat that had taken explorers four centuries to achieve by boat.[32]

Their monoplane, the Sirius, equipped with its 600–horsepower Cyclone engine and new pontoons, would have gasoline tanks capable of holding enough fuel for two thousand miles, thus giving them the potential to navigate the inland rivers and lakes of North America and the Bering Sea.[33] Charles's goal was simple, Anne later wrote: to link the continents by air and to find the shortest surface route from New York to Tokyo, pointing a straight line through Canada along the coast of the Arctic Ocean to Asia. While the strategic and commercial value of such an air route was indisputable, Anne later noted that their motives were entwined with the "glamour and magic" of the Orient and the realization that they would see inaccessible, unexplored territory.[34]

Reflecting the adulation of the American press, the Japanese expressed their pleasure at the prospect of welcoming the Lindberghs. Captain Kodama, chief of the technical section of the Japanese Air Bureau, said, "Japan will be delighted to welcome Colonel and Mrs. Lindbergh, whose names, features, and exploits are as familiar here as in the United States . . . The visit to the Far East by air of the first American to conquer the Atlantic is a matter of great interest to us all."

The Soviet Union, the Philippines, and Denmark followed suit, granting the Lindberghs the right to land and to refuel.

During the month of June, Anne practiced Morse code on a buzzer in the comfort of her bedroom in Princeton. As an aid, she identified the foreign sounds and symbols with familiar images from myths and fairy tales, and she passed her third-class radio operator's test along with Charles—though with a lower grade. By month's end, she and Charles had increased their speed to seventeen words a minute. They planned to have two radio sets on the plane, one of them the conventional type and the other an emergency device.[35]

On June 22, 1931, Anne and Charlie held a quiet birthday party for Charlie. The immediate family and the servants gathered in the front courtyard of the house in Englewood and, in loving unison, sang "Happy Birthday." Anne lit one candle in the cake on a small wooden table; Charles took photographs. The curly-haired baby had grown chubby, with a large head and short torso. While Anne could see him only as a reflection of Charles, others saw a resemblance to her father.[36] Neither the press nor the staff was reminded that it was Anne's birthday too, but in the evening, the Morrows and the Lindberghs celebrated in town.

As preparations for the trip expanded, so did Anne's fears. Her mother, sensing Anne's sadness, offered to keep the baby with her at their home in North Haven. Anne was grateful that the baby would be with her mother. It quelled her anxiety about leaving home. She knew he would be protected and loved.[37]

Twelve days later, the Lindberghs began their arduous trip with a ceremonial stop in Washington, D.C. It was a gracious nod to the State Department and to the press. Two hundred people lined the banks of the Potomac to witness their take-off, and scores of cars came to a halt on the highways. On the same day, the baby and Betty Gow took the train to Bar Harbor. Anne's parting instructions to Betty were that she keep a diary and photograph him once a month. She asked Betty to refrain from kissing and hugging him, fearing that he might become spoiled.[38] Hoping they would not be followed by the press, Anne prayed for their safe arrival. But unknown to Anne, reporters had spotted Betty and Charlie at the train station. Within days, the nation knew that the Lindbergh baby and his nurse were in North Haven.

The first official stop was to be Ottawa in Canada, but Anne and Charles detoured to Maine to say good-bye. All the Morrows were gathered for the occasion—Aunt Agnes, Aunt Alice, Aunt Hilda, Aunt Hattie, and Uncles Edwin and Jay. Their friends and neighbors throughout North Haven thronged to the pier to watch them land.

While the Morrows motored in their yacht to greet Anne and Charles, numerous motorboats, rowboats, and sailboats angled around the bay to embrace them.

After a quiet family evening at the Morrow home, riddled with anxiety as well as good spirits, Anne and Charles lifted off early the next morning. Their black-bodied ship with its scarlet wings and silver pontoons rose above the blue bay in a spray of foam. As their plane rose, higher, Anne and Charles shot their hands out of the cockpit to wave at the shrieking crowd. In a gesture of humility, almost a curtsey, Charles circled the harbor, dipped his wings, and disappeared into the sky above the Camden Hills.[39]

For Anne, this was a breathtaking moment, uniting the past and the future, stopping time, and holding life in a perfect family tableau.

10

Black October

Dwight Morrow in Lindbergh's plane, waving to the crowd on his senatorial campaign tour, May 1930.

(Amherst College)

*Nothing in human affairs deserves anxiety, and grief stands in the way
to hinder the self-succour that our duty immediately requires of us.*

—PLATO, *The Republic*

AUTUMN 1931, ENGLEWOOD, NEW JERSEY

S hortly before midnight on Sunday, October 4, 1931, Dwight
Morrow leaned on the arm of his waiting valet and walked
slowly up the stairs of his darkened house. Morrow usually
wasn't one to lean, but he had never felt so tired. He and Banks
climbed up the winding, lantern-lit stairway to the second floor and
turned toward the double wooden doors of the master suite. As
Morrow wished Banks a "good night," Banks noted that Morrow
looked uncommonly pale.[1]

Since his return from Maine at summer's end, Morrow's campaign
for the senatorial seat had quickened its pace. With the election now
only weeks away, even his weekends were consumed by political events.
On the previous afternoon, Dwight and Betty had been hosts to six
thousand Bergen County Republicans at their home, in honor of
Dwight's colleague, Senator Baird, who was seeking reelection.[2]
Morrow's hands were pained and blistered from greeting his guests.
Earlier that Sunday evening, he had addressed several hundred people
at a black-tie dinner of the Federation of Jewish Philanthropies at the
Waldorf-Astoria in New York. Praising the work of an entire generation of Jews who organized and sustained ninety-one charities with the
"blood and sacrifice" it required for their "dream," he admonished them
that they "dare not fail," not only for their own sake but for the thousands of philanthropic societies of all faiths throughout America who
were seeking inspiration from their deeds. It is "tragic," he said, when
a new generation, falling on hard times, renounces the dreams and accomplishments of their fathers.[3] Again, he had courted the crowd until

Dwight and Elizabeth Morrow, married twelve years and well ensconced in the New York and Englewood financial and social communities, posing with their children on the back lawn of their Palisades Avenue home, 1915. (Amherst College Archives and Special Collections, Amherst College Library)

Anne, unsmiling, dressed in ribbons and bows, possibly on her first birthday, with her grandmother, circa 1907. (Lindbergh Picture Collection, Manuscripts and Archives, Yale University Library)

Charles Lindbergh with his father, Charles A. Lindbergh, Sr., a real estate lawyer elected as a Congressman to the 6th District of Minnesota in 1906, serving for ten years, circa 1912. (Photo by David B. Edmonston, Minnesota Historical Society)

A lighthearted Anne, age ten, smiles jauntily at the camera in a rare show of her mischievous side, Englewood, New Jersey, circa 1916. (Lindbergh Picture Collection, Manuscripts and Archives, Yale University Library)

Anne as a teenager, serious and contemplative, too old to be carefree, too young to be adventurous. Recognized as a poet and an essayist at the Chapin School in New York City, Anne has a nuanced and penetrating eye, circa 1920. (Lindbergh Picture Collection, Manuscripts and Archives, Yale University Library)

Anne spends a quiet summer afternoon reading on the back porch swing of the Morrows' Palisades Avenue home in Englewood, circa 1916. (Lindbergh Picture Collection, Manuscripts and Archives, Yale University Library)

The Morrow children – Elisabeth, Anne, Dwight Jr., and Constance – perfectly composed and lined in a row, circa 1920. (Corbis/Underwood & Underwood)

Elizabeth Morrow escorting her daughter Elisabeth to England on a passenger ship, circa 1926. Elisabeth has a flair for fashion and charade, easily hiding the painful effects of her heart disease from her family and friends. (UPI/Corbis-Bettmann)

Anne Morrow, fall 1927, clowns with her friends in the first row as they pose for a class picture, soon to graduate from Smith College. (Lindbergh Picture Collection, Manuscripts and Archives, Yale University Library)

Charles Lindbergh with his mother, Evangeline Lodge Land Lindbergh, posing for the press before takeoff for his transatlantic flight, May 1927. (Rinhart; George/Corbis-Bettmann)

Charles Lindbergh, after completing his second record-breaking flight, 2200 miles from Washington, D.C., strikes a sophisticated pose for the Morrow sisters, Elisabeth and Anne, on the grounds of the U.S. Embassy in Mexico City, December 1927. (Lindbergh Picture Collection, Manuscripts and Archives, Yale University Library)

*T*he house and gardens of the Morrow estate, called Next Day Hill (to-Morrow), Englewood, New Jersey, circa 1929. Today it houses the Elisabeth Morrow School. (UPI/Corbis-Bettmann)

*E*lizabeth and Dwight Morrow stand at the front door of their sprawling new home in Englewood, set into the hills of the Palisades, custom built by European craftsmen on fifty-two acres of meadows and woodlands, circa 1929. (Amherst College Archives and Special Collections, Amherst College Library)

*A*nne and Charles with Gloria Swanson at an official reception during their 1929 flight to California for TAT, introducing coast-to-coast service in forty-eight hours by train and plane. Anne, tired of the public ceremony, wants to go home to her sisters and her parents. (Culver Pictures)

In July of 1930, Anne nurses her newborn son, Charles A. Lindbergh, Jr., in the garden of her parents' Englewood estate. Frustrated without a home of their own, the Lindberghs nonetheless choose to remain in the comfort and security of Next Day Hill. (New York Times Co./Archive Photo)

After a three-month tour west to California, Anne and Charles pose in front of their Lockheed Sirius at the Los Angeles airport before their record-breaking transcontinental flight home to New York, March 21, 1930. Anne, the first woman to receive a glider pilot's license, is now seven months pregnant. (AP/Wide World Photos)

*C*harles A. Lindbergh, Jr., surrounded by his great-grandmother Annie Cutter, his grandmother Elizabeth Morrow, and his mother, Anne, January 1931. *(UPI/Corbis-Bettmann)*

*A*nne Morrow and Charles Lindbergh at Mitchell Field, Long Island, on their honeymoon, July 1929. *(Lindbergh Picture Collection, Manuscripts and Archives, Yale University Library)*

*T*he road leading up to the Morrow estate on Deacon's Point on North Haven, an island off the coast of Maine. The house was built at the same time as Next Day Hill, while Dwight Morrow was Ambassador to Mexico, circa 1929-1930. *(Lindbergh Picture Collection, Manuscripts and Archives, Yale University Library)*

On a survey tour north to Asia, Anne and Charles arrive in Ottawa, Canada, August 1931, before crossing the icy tundra toward Alaska. (Roger-Viollet/Liaison Agency)

Anne posing with Eskimos in Point Barrow, Alaska, August 1931. (Underwood & Underwood/Corbis-Bettmann)

Anne and Charles land in Aklavik, Alaska, en route to Japan and China, August 1931. (AP/Wide World Photos)

his blisters oozed, but a friend noted that he didn't look tired at all; he had spoken with the "force and fire" of a young man.

The tiredness had come on gradually during the long limousine ride home through the deserted city streets, across the Hudson by ferry, and down the hills of the Palisades. By the time he met Banks waiting at the door, the fatigue had overtaken him.

In his dressing room, he carefully placed his tuxedo, shoes, and shirt in appropriate parts of the wooden niches designed by his wife to curb his untamed sense of order; then he slipped into bed beside her. As usual, he had told Betty not to wait up. An early riser, she was planning a morning round of golf before the official luncheon they were to host the next afternoon. Dwight must have fallen swiftly to sleep, for Betty was not disturbed by his movement.

The next morning Betty rose quietly, dressed quickly, and walked softly down the stairs to have breakfast with Elisabeth. Around eleven, Morrow's secretary, Arthur Springer, began to worry. He had planned to meet Morrow before the official business of the day, and it was unlike Morrow to be late. He spoke to Banks, who remembered the look of fatigue on his employer's face the night before, and together they hurried up the stairs and knocked at his door. On receiving no answer, they opened the door and found Morrow unconscious on his bed, his chest heaving as he gasped for air. Banks called an ambulance and paged Betty at the club. Two and a half hours later, Dwight Morrow died at Englewood Hospital without having regained consciousness. Betty, still in her golf shoes and trousers, was dry-eyed and silent. She summoned the chauffeur to take her home, in the company of Elisabeth, Dwight's sister Agnes Scandrett, and Agnes's daughter, Lucien Greathouse.

In spite of her grief, Betty was in control, and her first priority was to tell the other children. She cabled Anne and Charles aboard the British aircraft carrier *Hermes,* en route to Shanghai. They had made their way through the tundra of northern Canada, through the endless nights of the Arctic Ocean, down through the Bering Strait and the enveloping fog of the Japanese islands, to Tokyo and Osaka. But on landing in Nanking, China, they learned that millions of people were homeless and starving because of the Grand Canal and Yangtze River flood. Only their state-of-the-art amphibian plane had the range and equipment to do the survey essential to making decisions on flood relief. Anne and Charles flew rescue missions to stranded villagers in need of medicine and supplies. Then, just as they prepared to leave Hangkow for one last rescue flight, their plane capsized, and they were forced to travel by boat to Shanghai to await its repair.[4]

Betty telegraphed Con, on her way to visit Charlie in Maine, and she telephoned Dwight Jr., now back at Amherst. Most Americans learned of Morrow's death against the loud cheering of baseball spectators. The third game of the World Series was being played at Shibe Park in Philadelphia when the news was sent from the offices of NBC to the announcers at the field. As the fans roared, radio listeners heard the news: Dwight Morrow, distinguished lawyer, financier, and statesman, was dead at fifty-eight.[5]

For twenty-four hours, his body lay in a simple coffin in the library of his home, beside his favorite chair, among the books he loved. Only his intimate friends and family members were admitted to the house. On October 7, at two o'clock, the coffin was draped in a blanket of lilies that had been sent by President Hoover, who could not attend, and was carried into the hearse waiting in the courtyard. Neighbors and friends lined the three-mile stretch between the Morrow home and the church, where four thousand people waited outside. The service started promptly at three—the thousand seats of the church were filled with family and friends as well as delegations from the House and the Senate, cabinet officials, Vice President Curtis, and former President Coolidge. The Reverend Carl Hopkins Elmore, minister of the Presbyterian Church and a long-time friend of the Morrow family, officiated. Dressed in black, Elisabeth, Dwight, and Con escorted Betty to her pew. Reporters noted that Charles Lindbergh, Jr., had not been brought back from Maine for his grandfather's funeral.[6]

That afternoon, Morrow was buried with a private graveside ceremony, almost within sight of the Morrow estate. In an odd departure from the usual Presbyterian service, a prayer of Socrates that Plato had written in *The Phaedrus* was read. It was one Morrow had quoted often:

> *Give me beauty in the inward soul, and may the outward and inward man be at one. May I reckon the wise to be wealthy, and may I have such a quantity of gold as a temperate man and he only can bear and carry.*[7]

It was this struggle—to reconcile the irreconcilable—that had undermined Morrow's health during his last years. Even as he rose to unanticipated heights of accomplishment, wealth, and public office, he had longed for the life he had known as a child in Pittsburgh. Scholar turned politician, humanist turned partisan, pauper turned millionaire, he could never match his simple tastes to the money and esteem he garnered. The statesman's life was more than he had bargained for; at times he wondered whether it had been worth the price. After only three months of his Senate term, Morrow had become thoroughly demoralized. Forced to make decisions without time to study the issues, he found the work difficult and puzzling.[8] The hurry and chaos of Senate procedure violated his intellectual integrity. Morrow saw himself as a man of ideas, as a Philosopher King who had left academia to serve the public. Somewhere, he had made a turn that weakened his control. Perhaps Betty understood and found it more than she could bear. As the coffin was lowered into the grave, she picked up a handful of earth and let it slide through her fingers onto the lily-covered coffin. Her grief found no words.

Words of sympathy and praise, in the hundreds of letters from friends, colleagues, and associates, poured into the Morrow household.[9] Now that he was dead, there was no praise sufficient for the senator from New Jersey. Republicans and Democrats, dries and wets alike, lauded his skill as a negotiator founded on his erudition and honesty. The editors of *Outlook* stated it well: "It was his habit to stand aside and study a question and then, entering the discussion himself, make it seem as if it had never been discussed before." Through the prism of Morrow's mind the problem took on a new shape.

But Morrow's strength was also his frailty. The logic that cut to the heart of an issue sapped him of vigor. By denying anything that smacked of the irrational, he locked up his feelings until he burst with pain. He treated his body as if it were a disposable machine, an instrument designed solely for performance. Still under his father's influence, he deified "reason" until it overshadowed his spirit. This, too, was Morrow's legacy—the mask of reason and virtue which destroyed him.

For months after his death, Anne could not reconcile the loss of her father. She could not imagine life without his playful smile, his fierce idealism, and his agile mind. She wondered how her mother could bear the pain. He had been the center of her life.

If Betty felt that her "center" had dropped, Anne felt her own center had been restored. The truth was, her father's death was bringing her home—home to the baby and a life of her own. Her grief couldn't quell her feelings of joy, which brought on moments of guilt and despair. On October 8, she and Charles had left their plane in Shanghai for repairs, and crossed the Japanese islands by rail. After sailing to Seattle, they borrowed a plane and they arrived home in Englewood on the nineteenth.

Anne kept her father's death at a distance, wishing like a child that he could be there to comfort her. But even as she felt robbed of his strength, her spirits were buoyed by the vitality of her son. Finally, she was home with her baby, and what a beautiful boy he was.

In her letters to Evangeline, she began to refer to Charlie as "the boy," much as Charles's father had referred to him. To Anne, it confirmed his proper place. He was categorically male—confident, bold, and independent.

The praise for Charlie's strength belonged to Betty Gow. She had been alone with him for more than two months. Betty Morrow, busy with her husband's campaign, rarely came to North Haven. She relied on news of the baby's health and progress from the diaries Betty Gow sent to her in Englewood. The only other servant in the house, Emily, the cook, apparently ignored the baby. The days passed slowly, and the nights were long, and much as she enjoyed the beauty of the house and the island, Betty felt abandoned by the Lindberghs and the Morrows.[10]

She began to spend her evenings with Henrik Finn (Red) Johnson, who had been introduced to her at a dance by Alfred Burke, the Morrows' chauffeur. Johnson was a seaman with restless energy and little ambition who had "jumped ship" in March 1927, when he was twenty-two. He flitted from job to job, using his paychecks to fund vacations and living off his brother and the kindness of relatives. A year before he met Betty, in April 1930, he had secured a job on Thomas Lamont's yacht in Brooklyn Harbor and was aboard when Lamont sailed the following August to North Haven. He and Betty went to several village dances and, in the company of other Morrow and Lamont servants, to night parties at the local beaches. Soon, Red was visiting Betty alone in the evenings at the Morrow estate. She was taken with his fun-loving manner, his dimpled cheeks, and his shock of red hair. Well built and dapper, he had an easy and mischievous smile that spread through the corners of his eyes. While he wasn't the marrying kind, Betty was pleased with the attention he paid her. They talked about the baby and the "little different things he did," and Red quickly became her confidant and friend.

Red stayed in North Haven until the second week of September, when he sailed back to New Jersey with the Lamonts. After the boat was docked in Brooklyn at the beginning of October, Red was once again out of a job. Hoping to maintain their friendship, Red and Betty corresponded while she remained in North Haven with Charlie. When she returned with the baby to Englewood shortly after Morrow's death, Red took a room in town in order to be "near to her" again.

Anne, arriving on October 19, found the baby healthy, sturdy, and strong. Betty had seen to it that Charlie looked his best. Since he had outgrown his nightclothes and his shoes, she spent part of her wages to buy him new clothes. The family had not given her money for expenses, but she feared that she would look neglectful if Charlie was not well dressed.

Anne was grateful to Betty for her care of the baby; Charlie had the warmth of a child who had been loved and protected. Although he did not recognize his parents on their return, neither was he afraid of them. Best of all, Charles adored "the boy." To her surprise, he spoiled him with treats.[11]

Anne hoped to move into their new house in Hopewell, New Jersey, shortly before Thanksgiving and was determined to be Charlie's full-time mother. For the moment, Charles consented. She allowed Betty Gow to take a three-month holiday, and, for the first time since their marriage, Charles traveled alone. Anne relished the time in her mother's company, falling into a domestic routine, bound to the rhythms of her child and the slow-moving pace beyond the boom and rush of the city.[12]

Her quiet life prompted rumors in the press that she was pregnant again. When she did not accompany Charles on the survey routes, Walter Winchell blasted the news over the radio, as if challenging Anne to respond. She and Charles denied the report—but it was true; they were expecting their second child.

Terribly nauseated again, Anne welcomed the help of the Morrow servants, as well as Elisabeth's invitation to have Charlie attend her school. In mid-November, at the age of seventeen months, Charlie, nearly half a year younger than any of the other children, started at the Little School. On his first day, all the children gathered around him and made a fuss, but the boy previously the youngest became jealous and punched Charlie in the back.[13]

"Charlie sat down and cried." No one had intentionally hurt him before. With the objectivity of a Watsonian mother, Anne stood by as the other boy hit him five times for five different reasons before anyone intervened. The faculty, she wrote, tongue-in-cheek, called a conference with the psychologist. He suggested that Charlie play alone for a while to become "accustomed to his environment" before he tried to "make social adjustments."

There were adjustments in the Morrow home, too. Now the sole man of the house, Charles played a familiar role. Morrow was dead, and Charles felt both the responsibility and the license to fill the void. For the first time, he gave public voice to his political views; they echoed the Populist philosophy of his father and struck a consonant chord with the public, which, in 1931, was devastated by poverty and unemployment.

By the end of the year, banks in more than thirty states had closed, and millions of people, homeless and out of work, roamed the land. State and city governments were swamped with welfare cases, and families wandered from place to place in search of hospitable communities. The vagrants were largely agricultural workers and young men who had finished school only to find there were no jobs. The following summer they congregated in Washington, surrounded the White House, and made their squalor a form of protest. President Hoover, unmoved, locked himself in his quarters.[14]

Just one month after Morrow died, Lindbergh was urging a "readjustment" of the nation's industrial structure.

> *We must strike a balance where the abundance of labor and material which now exists can be properly distributed. When this is accomplished, we will be in an even better position than during the past period of prosperity. Until it is done the system we have established is under test. Whether we progress to new standards or fall back to the old depends upon our individual ability to assist and cooperate in the emergency we now face.*[15]

The notion of redistribution, which would have been abhorrent to Morrow, appealed to Charles and many of his contemporaries in America and in Europe; it was an answer to what they perceived as the failure of capitalism.

Anne, meanwhile, noticed little beyond her white picket fence. She had planned to settle in Hopewell by the holidays, but the house still needed painting inside, and she was reluctant to stay there alone with the baby. They were not planning much for Christmas, just enough to entertain Charlie. Her father's death had dampened everyone's spirits.[16]

By January, however, Anne was back to her writing and had finished the first chapter of what promised to be a book, an account of their trip to Asia, beginning with the stopover at North Haven. She was satisfied with her writing because she had been wholly conscious of the joy she felt at that gathering of the family. It was the last time she saw her father, and "like a bee tasting a whole summer in one honey-suckle,"[17] his memory now gave her strength and faith.

She was beginning to see her trip as a journey beyond the bounds of ordinary narrative. Like Edward Hopper, she tried to paint the bare sides of barns, hoping that the canvas would reflect her emotions.

While Anne nestled into a quiet life, Charles accelerated his work as technical consultant to Pan Am and TAT, charting passenger routes from North to South America, and inspecting transcontinental routes between New York and Los Angeles. On February 4, he celebrated his thirtieth birthday to more public acclaim, and with more public influence and faith in the future of commercial aviation, than he could have imagined during his transatlantic flight five years earlier. Hailed as the American Prince of Wales, he was urged by foreign leaders to continue his tours. Aviation, Lindbergh advised the United States military, should be added to the curriculum at West Point.[18]

By mid-February, Anne and Charles were living part time in Englewood, spending their weekends in Hopewell. Anne was finally in her own home with her baby, and everything else seemed a diversion, even her writing. Charles, perhaps thinking of his mother's entrapment, saw Anne's domesticity as self-indulgence. He urged her to continue writing her book. Hoping to coax her out of the house, he asked her to help his public drive for flood relief in China and to join him on a short trip to the air races in Los Angeles. Reluctantly, Anne agreed.

On February 7, with Charlie playing at her feet, Anne wrote a letter to Evangeline, describing the child's every word and move. Charmed by her baby's determination and sense of humor, and eager to share her joy in his games and laughter, she rambled on for pages, until Charles demanded that the letter stop. He wondered, he teased, whether she was writing another book.[19]

On February 22, leaving Betty to care for the baby, Anne kept her promise to Charles. Wooden and doll-like, Anne spoke on behalf of the Federal Council of Churches before the microphones of the Columbia and National Broadcasting Systems and addressed the public on the state of the flooded regions of China.

The *New York Times* reported:

> *It was her first appearance before the microphone, but listeners detected no trace of nervousness, and her words, spoken in a pleasing voice and perfectly enunciated, came clearly over the air.*[20]

Charles sat by her side, nodding and smiling as she spoke, chatting in whispers with studio executives. Once more, Anne had earned his approval.

11

Within the Wave

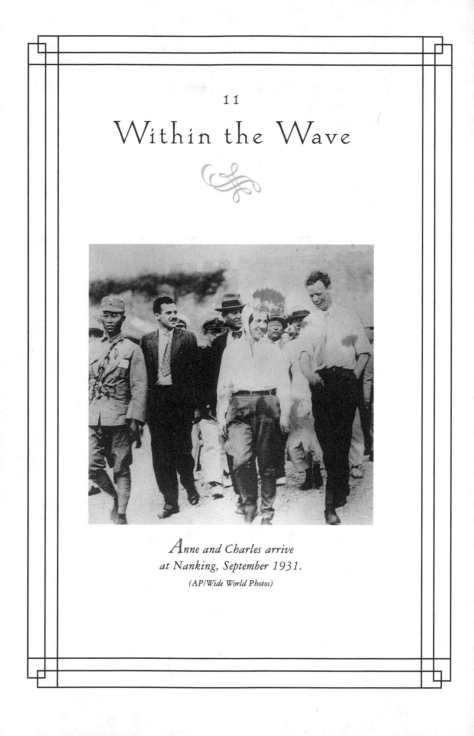

*Anne and Charles arrive
at Nanking, September 1931.*

(AP/Wide World Photos)

WITHIN THE WAVE[1]

Within the hollow wave there lies a world,
Gleaming glass-perfect, rising to be hurled
Into a thousand fragments on the sand,
Driven by tide's inexorable hand . . .
Smooth mirror of the present, poised between
The crest's "becoming" and the foam's "has been"—
How luminous the landscape seen across
The crystal lens of an impending loss!

—ANNE MORROW LINDBERGH

TUESDAY, MARCH 1, 1932, HOPEWELL, NEW JERSEY

A continent away, the floods of the Yangtze raged, but two days after Anne's radio plea for help, she and Charles had left the center stage of New York to spend a quiet weekend in Hopewell. Their four hundred acres of farmland and forest had proven a perfect retreat, far from the highway, along rambling country roads, unpaved and little traveled.[2] With a mile of driveway between them and the nearest road, Anne and Charles were comfortable in their privacy; they rarely drew their shutters closed, and had fired the guard who had stood at their gate warding off souvenir hunters during construction.

The stone manor, stark and angular against the fields, played counterpoint to the dense woodlands beyond. Its white fieldstone walls formed a U-shaped structure, which at once embraced those who entered and held the relentless wind at bay. It had rained for nearly forty-eight hours, and the March wind whipped about the house, hissing through the windows and doors. Inside, the fires were lit, and Elsie Whateley, a handsome English woman of forty-seven who served as housekeeper and cook, prepared a late dinner in the west wing. Charles had left the previous morning for business in New York, and Anne sat in the living room, awaiting his return. She glanced constantly at her watch, listening for the familiar sounds of Charles's approach, eager to see him after his two days away.[3]

It was rare for Anne to be in Hopewell on a Tuesday. She and Charles usually rose early on Monday morning and returned to Englewood with the baby by midday. But the baby, now twenty months old, had a cold, and Anne, three months pregnant, was fighting the fatigue of the long days and interrupted nights of caring for him. While Anne prized her weekends without the nurse, the baby's schedule was strict and demanding, even more so now with the onset of his cold. It called for breakfast at six-thirty, lunch at noon, a nap at two-thirty, dinner at six, and bedtime at eight. Anne had been giving Charlie her constant attention, oiling his chest, putting drops in his nose, keeping him warm and dry, and getting up several times at night to check his breathing.[4]

On Monday morning, Anne had awakened to a blustery rain and the noise of Charlie's congested breathing. Charles urged Anne to stay home, and took off as usual for business in New York. Anne telephoned Betty Gow at Next Day Hill, informing her of Charlie's cold and her intention to remain in Hopewell for another day. But on Tuesday morning, exhausted by another sleepless night, Anne told Elsie Whateley's husband, Oliver, serving as butler, to call the station for a schedule and to summon Betty Gow to come from Englewood by train.[5]

It was nearly ten-thirty when Whateley rang the Morrow residence. Violet Sharpe answered the phone. A vivacious English country girl with rosy cheeks and big hips, Violet had a weakness for men, loose talk, and illicit beer.[6] Popular among the Morrows' twenty-nine servants, she was admired most by Septimus Banks, the butler and head of the domestic staff. Violet had thoughts of marrying Banks, hoping he would rescue her from spinsterhood and domestic service. But it turned out that he was a drunkard, and there were rumors that Violet had decided to abort their baby. Betty Morrow had come close to dismissing Banks several times for drunkenness on duty, but had chosen to retain him. His aristocratic speech and manner, cultivated in the homes of the Carnegies and Vanderbilts, suited Betty's notions of propriety and breeding.[7] Banks knew he was there to stay; Violet, however, was becoming restless. Now twenty-eight years old, she sought the company of other men and earned a reputation as an easy mark at the bars she frequented on her nights off.[8] Within the Morrow home, however, Violet was the model of the proper downstairs maid. She helped the other servants in the kitchen, cleaned the public quarters of the house, and answered the phone when Banks was busy or away.[9]

When Violet summoned Betty Gow to the phone, Whateley informed her of Anne's request. Anne, too, spoke to Betty, giving her details of the baby's cold. Betty didn't relish the idea of traveling to Hopewell by train in the storm, and, with the permission of Mrs. Morrow, she asked the Morrow chauffeur, Henry Ellerson, to drive her in one of the family cars.[10]

Ellerson was also flirting with dismissal. A drunk and a gambler, a truck driver turned chauffeur, he had been destitute until he was hired by the Morrows as a gateman. Doubling as the family's second-string driver, he had taken Charlie to Elisabeth's school every day and knew the Lindbergh's habits well. Although he was married and had two children, he rarely lived at home, frequenting the speakeasies around Englewood and dating a local woman. For a time, he had lived in a rooming house with Betty's boyfriend Red and other Morrow servants.[11]

Before leaving Englewood, Betty telephoned Red at his rooming house. While they had seen each other for dinner with several Morrow and Lamont servants[12] on Sunday and Monday, they had planned a date for Tuesday evening with a German couple named Marguerite and Johannes Junge.[13] Marguerite, an American of German descent born to a wealthy Hamburg family that had lost its money after the war, had been a dressmaker and seamstress on the Morrow staff for nearly a year. Although the Morrows had known her as a spinster named Jantzen, recommended by a German friend of theirs, she had been married for nine years to Johannes, a street-smart and articulate marine surveyor and export agent, newly arrived and unemployed.[14] Marguerite and Red

Johnson had become "intimate friends," living in the same boarding house along with Ellerson. In the three months since Johannes's arrival, he, Marguerite, Betty, and Red had become a foursome.

This would be Betty's fourth visit to the Hopewell house, but only her second visit when the Lindberghs were there. She had visited twice before with Red; once at the end of November and again, only two weeks earlier, on St. Valentine's Day. Oliver and Elsie Whateley, lonely in Hopewell, were grateful for the company of their two young friends. New to domestic service, Elsie had been a clerk and an aspiring singer in England and Oliver had been a jeweler by trade. Bald and stocky, Oliver had neither the stature nor the instincts of a seasoned butler. To pass the long days while the Lindberghs were away, Oliver gave unauthorized tours of the house and grounds to curious visitors and passersby.[15] Betty's friend Red, easygoing and friendly, was a welcome companion for an afternoon. They walked the rooms, the halls, and the stairwells, and paced the hard frozen fields. Stretching the bounds of a casual tour, Oliver took Red into the surrounding woods, following the underground electrical lines until they surfaced into the trees.[16]

Unable to reach Red at his rooming house, Betty left a message with his landlady and asked Marguerite to let him know about her sudden trip to Hopewell. Betty and Henry Ellerson left the Morrow home at approximately 11:45, making one stop in town to buy candy at a drugstore. Ellerson would later note that Betty had the "blues" and was uneasy at the thought of "being confined" in Hopewell.[17] They arrived at the estate around two, and after a quick lunch with Ellerson and the Whateleys in the kitchen, Betty joined the baby at two-thirty in the nursery.[18]

In the gray light of the winter afternoon, Charlie, a round-faced child with golden curls, his mother's violet eyes and father's dimpled chin, played on the bare tiled floor with his blocks and trucks. As he played, he engaged Betty in his familiar babble, pointing to the objects on the walls and floor, and wandering around the small, gaily decorated room in sudden moments of purposeful activity. While the room echoed Anne's childhood nursery, a miniature world of toys and furniture, it seemed the center of this house, far different from the nanny-governed island Anne had known.

Betty Gow's arrival and a break in the weather permitted Anne to walk down the driveway and to wander in the mud-soaked clearing that surrounded the house. At about three-thirty, she stopped below the nursery to throw pebbles at the southeast window in the hope of attracting Charlie's attention. The flutter aroused Betty, who lifted Charlie up to the window to smile and wave to his mother.[19] Satisfied with her walk, Anne returned to the house to have her tea and requested that the baby join her in the living room. At five o'clock, Charlie came to play. He stayed for a while, and then wandered into the servants' sitting room to visit with Betty and Elsie. Rambunctious and playful, Charlie ran twice around the kitchen table before surrendering to Betty's arms. She carried him upstairs to the nursery, while Elsie prepared the Lindberghs' dinner.[20] At five-thirty, Whateley received a call from Charles advising him that he would arrive home later than expected.[21]

At six o'clock, Anne visited the nursery to find Charlie finishing his cereal at his small maple table in the center of the room. She stayed to help Betty feed him and prepare him for bed. As Betty was dressing Charlie for the night, he spit up his medicine on his nightsuit. In the course of changing his clothes, Betty worried that he would soil another new suit with his chest oil. An experienced seamstress, Betty offered to make a nightshirt with an extra high neck and sleeves to go under his usual sleeveless shirt. Pleased with her suggestion, Anne offered to go down to Elsie for scissors and thread. On Anne's return, Betty cut a pattern from her old flannel petticoat and sewed the shirt while Charlie and Anne played.[22]

It was late, nearly thirty minutes past Charlie's bedtime, when he was ready for bed. Betty rubbed his chest once again with oil and dressed him in three layers: first, her handmade flannel shirt, then his store-bought sleeveless nighty, then his new gray Dr. Denton's suit. As usual, Betty covered his thumbs with metal guards to prevent his thumb-sucking and fastened the strings around his wrists. She lowered the crib's rail and placed him in it, face down. Anne and Betty closed the windows and tried to bolt closed the warped southeast shutter. In order to do so, they leaned over the large black suitcase set on a long, low cedar chest, being careful not to topple Charlie's Tinkertoy car, perched on its wheels on the windowsill.[23] But even with the force of their combined strength, the shutters refused to catch.[24]

It was seven-thirty when Anne left the room, turning off the nursery lights behind her. She told Betty she usually opened the French window halfway, depending on the direction of the wind. Betty washed the baby's dishes and clothes in the bathroom adjoining the nursery. It was nearly eight o'clock when she was through; satisfied that Charlie was asleep, she pinned his blanket to the mattress cover, opened a window, and closed both doors. Before retiring to the kitchen to have her dinner, Betty stopped in the living room to assure Anne that the baby was comfortable and fast asleep.[25]

At about ten minutes after eight, Anne thought she heard Charles's tires on the gravel driveway. She crooked her head toward the front door, and then, uncertain, turned back to her writing. It was 8:25 when Anne finally heard Charles honk his horn and pull his sedan into the garage.[26] It was a late return home, but it should have been later. Charles was scheduled to speak at an alumni dinner at New York University, but he had confused the dates and had driven home to Hopewell to see Anne and the baby, as he had promised the morning before.[27] He had spent two full days at the offices of TAT and at the Rockefeller Institute, working with Alexis Carrel. Tired from the two-hour commute, he walked through the garage into the kitchen, where Betty and Elsie were having dinner. He inquired about the baby's health, went to the pantry to greet Oliver Whateley, and then walked through the dining room to the living room, where Anne sat writing at her desk. They went upstairs to the bathroom that adjoined the nursery on the other side, and she talked with him while he washed for dinner. It was 8:35 when Anne and Charles went down to the dining room, where they were served by Whateley, and nine when they returned to the living room, after telling the servants they did not wish to be disturbed.[28]

Their afterdinner talks had become something of a ritual. It was time alone, valued more than ever because they spent their days apart. In Englewood, Anne had her mother and Elisabeth to keep her company. Here, in Hopewell, she had no one but the servants. The pregnancy made her feel foggy and old—too tired for productive work; it was difficult to write anything but letters. She missed the agility of her mind and body. Her only compensation was the sheer beauty of Charlie and the chance to be with him and watch him grow. After all the loneliness she had known as a child, Anne refused to have barriers of servants between her and her little boy.

For the moment, however, Anne basked in the richness of her husband's mind, flushed with the stimulation of city and laboratory, and capable, she believed, of mastering anything. His mental agility and range of interests surpassed Anne's expectations; what appeared to be mechanical prowess had shown the depths of creativity. Proof was the eagerness with which Dr. Carrel had enlisted Charles in his laboratory projects. Disciplined, persistent, and confident in his judgment, Charles solved problems with scientific rigor. Even without professional training, he could think beyond some of Carrel's illustrious colleagues.

Anne was engrossed in their conversation when Charles jumped up, startled by a noise.

"What's that?" he asked. Anne listened but heard nothing.

Later, Charles would remember a strange cracking noise, but it was a "kitchen" sound, he would say, like the breaking of the slats of a wooden crate.[29] Assuming that Whateley had things under control, Charles took no further notice. Tired and not feeling well, Anne cut their talk short. Sometime between 9:10 and 9:15, they retired to the second floor, where Charles bathed and changed his clothes. Anne bathed and read while Charles went to his study, just below the nursery, to work.[30]

Earlier, at 8:35, while Charles and Anne were dining, Betty had been summoned to the kitchen telephone by Whateley to talk to her boyfriend, Red Johnson. They spoke for a few minutes about her trip to Hopewell and the baby's health, and then, with sadness, said their good-byes. Red was leaving early the next morning for his brother's home in West Hartford, Connecticut. He asked Betty whether he should await her return, but Betty encouraged him to go as planned. Then Betty chatted with Oliver and Elsie while they cleaned up the kitchen and, after that, accompanied Elsie to the Whateleys' apartment over the garage while Oliver remained in the sitting room to read.[31]

At ten o'clock, as usual, Betty went up the west-wing stairs and crossed the landing to check on the baby before she went to sleep. With only the light from the hall to guide her, she walked into the baby's bathroom and opened the door to the nursery. The air seemed uncommonly cold. She closed the window, stopping for a moment to turn on the electric heater, and then made her way in the half-light of the bathroom toward the baby's crib. As she approached, the silence alarmed her. She could not hear the baby breathing. Nervously, she ran her hands over the bed linens and then rushed to Anne, who was coming out of the bathroom.[32]

"Do you have the baby, Mrs. Lindbergh?" asked Betty.

"No," said Anne. "Maybe the Colonel has him."

Disturbed by Anne's answer, Betty hurried down to Charles.

"Do you have the baby, Colonel?" she asked. "Don't fool me."[33] Charles was a practical joker and had occasionally hidden the baby to tease Betty. But this was beyond laughter. Frightening Betty with his leap, Charles catapulted up the stairs to the nursery. Finding the crib empty and the sheets in disarray, as though his child had been yanked up by his head, he crossed through the bathroom to the bedroom to find Anne. Pale and dazed, Anne asked, "Do you have the baby, Charles?" Then he turned away. The silence confirmed Anne's worst fears.[34] In the twenty months since the baby's birth, Anne believed they had been fighting a "war," against their enemy, the public.[35]

While Anne searched the baby's room, Charles took his rifle from the bedroom closet and instructed Whateley to inform the local police. On hearing the news, Elsie ran up the west stairway to comfort Anne, who was leaning out the window, wildly scanning the field for Charlie. Anne thought she heard a baby cry, but before she could speak, Elsie told her it was the shrill of a cat. Later, Anne was certain it was the howl of the wind.[36]

Elsie helped Anne dress, and the three women scoured each closet and drawer, looking everywhere the baby might be hiding. Charles and Whateley searched the grounds. After finding nothing, Charles called his lawyer, Henry Breckinridge, in New York, and the New Jersey State Police. By 10:40 state troopers joined the local police on the scene, and by 10:46 the news had been teletyped on the open wires: Charles A. Lindbergh, Jr., had been abducted from his crib in the Lindbergh home between 7:30 and 10:00 P.M.[37]

Soon, the world was shocked by an event nearly as traumatic as a presidential assassination or an outbreak of war. But for the moment it was the Lindberghs' private nightmare, a terrifying betrayal by the American public who adored them. Anne had sometimes wondered what their arrogance had wrought as they flew the skies into unseen lands, disturbing the flow of native life with their big silver flying machine. Was this the punishment for their "intruding gaze," mirrored back through the half-closed shutters of a darkened nursery? Was this the fire of an angry sun that had scorched the wings of Icarus? Forever, Anne would ask herself those questions.

12

The War

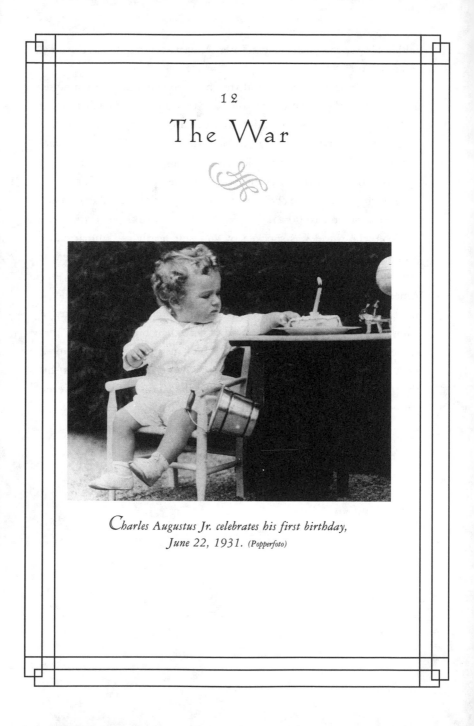

*Charles Augustus Jr. celebrates his first birthday,
June 22, 1931. (Popperfoto)*

. . . Listen, my heart as only
saints have listened . . .
Listen to the voice of the wind
And the ceaseless message that forms itself out of silence.
It is murmuring toward you now
From those who died young.

—RAINER MARIA RILKE,
  The First Elegy,
  TRANSLATED BY STEPHEN MITCHELL

MARCH 1, HOPEWELL, NEW JERSEY

Swaddled in warmth and darkness only an hour before, the Lindbergh home was now ablaze with light. When the Hopewell police arrived, Charles stood, gun in hand, waiting for them at the door. He led the officers up to the nursery and then outside, to the grounds beneath the southeast window, to search for signs of the intruders. They found two deep impressions in the mud and two sets of footprints,[1] one of which led southeast to a ladder. Assuming it had been used by the kidnappers to climb up to the window, they left it untouched, and returned to the house to wait for the state troopers.

In his initial search of the child's room, Charles had found a small white envelope on the windowsill beneath the warped shutters. Assuming it contained a note from the kidnappers, he had left it unopened. Now, Corporal Frank Kelly, an expert in fingerprints and crime-scene photography, dusted the envelope for prints. Finding only a single smudge, he handed the envelope to Major Schoeffel, the state official in charge, who, in turn, gave it to Lindbergh. Inside, Charles found a note written in a large scrawling hand in blue ink.

Dear Sir!

Have 50,000$ redy 25000$ in 20$ bills 15000$ in 10$ bills
and 10000$ in 5$ bills. After 2–4 days we will inform you were to
deliver the Mony. We warn you for making anyding public or for the
Polise. the child is in gut care. Indication for all letters are signature
and 3 holds. [2]

The signature was a symbol on the bottom right-hand corner of the
note: two blue interlocking circles joined by a solid red mark pierced
by three square holes.

Fifty thousand dollars. It wasn't a huge sum. Small, in fact, for a
"professional gang," but to anyone else, it must have seemed a fortune.
Nineteen thirty-two was the darkest year of the Depression. The stock-
market crash of 1929 had initiated a steady and broad decline in the
country's economy. With the failure of banks worldwide and a quagmire of unpaid war debts, the American economy was shrinking fast.
During the three years following the crash, the GNP shrank by nearly
a half, and unemployment tripled. In New York City alone, a million
people were unemployed. [3]

Violence had become a tool for economic survival. Organized gangs
multiplied to protect bootleggers, and a new professional class of criminals emerged. Gunmen and racketeers, hired to ward off competing
gangs, made the easy slide into gambling, extortion, and kidnapping.
In 1931 there were 279 kidnapping cases in the United States, and it
was estimated that six hundred cases had gone unreported. Kidnapping
had become a highly organized business, requiring a division of labor
among as many as twenty people. They preyed upon the powerful and
the well-to-do, choosing and studying their targets with mathematical
precision. [4] The Lindberghs' wealth, publicly estimated at half a million
dollars, made them prime targets for those harboring greed or dissatisfaction. [5] While millions walked the land homeless and hungry, the
Lindberghs, silent and seemingly immune, shuttled from the Morrows'
lavish Englewood estate to their $50,000 mountain retreat in the com-
fort of chauffeur-driven limousines.

By eleven o'clock on the night of March 1, only twenty minutes after Lindbergh called the police but two hours after he had heard the inexplicable "crack," every major bridge, tunnel, ferry, and highway leading to New York was blocked, and every incoming vehicle and its driver was searched and recorded. In New Jersey, roads were barricaded and hospitals were alerted. Within hours, criminals and suspects across the state were summoned for investigation.[6] The crime had turned the mirror back on the public. This time the public was being hunted, and Charles Lindbergh was at the head of the pack.

By midnight, Colonel H. Norman Schwarzkopf,[7] superintendent of the New Jersey State Police, was on the scene. He was an experienced military man and administrator, but he was not a criminal investigator. He had served on the front in France during World War I, and his command of the German language and his administrative skills had made him a prime choice as a law official in the occupation force in Germany after the war. In 1921, back in the States, and having resigned from the military, he was appointed superintendent of the newly formed state police. During the force's fledgling years, he found it difficult to maintain discipline. Harmless incidents of neglect and poor judgment had mushroomed into a public issue in 1926, when fourteen troopers were found guilty of various offenses, including murder, while serving a warrant to a family suspected of abusing its cattle. Thereafter, Schwarzkopf tightened his control, modeling the organization on the army's structure of command and discipline. Although some resented his style of leadership, Schwarzkopf, an imposing figure at six feet, had the respect of his troopers and officers. He was a friendly and gregarious man, as congenial as he was authoritative and demanding; a man bound by friendship as much as by duty.[8]

Schwarzkopf admired Lindbergh for his pioneering flights, and from the moment he walked onto the crime scene he was bent on cultivating Lindbergh's friendship. To prove his sincerity and his admiration, Schwarzkopf gave Lindbergh free run within the bounds of his command.

Henry C. Breckinridge, a tall and dashing Wall Street attorney, arrived in Hopewell soon after Lindbergh's call. A former assistant secretary of war, he had been Lindbergh's adviser after his transatlantic flight, earning his complete trust and confidence. But he, too, was intimidated by Lindbergh and was willing enough to let him rule. While both men made it clear to Lindbergh that he was in charge, the truth was Lindbergh didn't know what to do. A meticulous strategist who left nothing to chance, he prided himself on his logic and methodology, but his reason was fading with his mounting desperation. Lindbergh wanted his baby back, and he made it clear to Schwarzkopf and Breckinridge that he would do anything to ensure his safety.

At one A.M., while the experts combed the house and grounds for clues, Lindbergh and several state officers formed an old-fashioned posse. For three and a half hours they penetrated the darkness of the roads and nearby homes with their flashlights, questioning all who walked, drove, and lived in the area.

Although Schwarzkopf and his troopers attempted to protect the southeast corner of the residence, by morning the crime scene was out of control. Once Wednesday dawned, no one could keep the swarms of reporters, photographers, and sightseers from overrunning the grounds and stamping out clues. No one knew how much evidence was lost.[9] A fruitless night had left Lindbergh, Breckinridge, and Schwarzkopf exhausted and depressed, sitting in the living room, attempting to formulate a plan.

Charles was ubiquitous, but Anne seemed to disappear. Since the evening before, she felt that nothing and no one was real. Sequestered with her mother and Elisabeth in the upstairs bedroom, Anne knew that to maintain hope, she had to stay in control—and hope was the essence of survival. Betty Morrow, as usual, was disciplined and stoic, trying to nourish Anne with courage and optimism, but her efforts could only buffer the chaos.[10]

Local, state, and federal police moved in and out of the house at will. The public rooms became dormitories and, even in her bedroom, Anne lost her privacy. The garage was converted into a command station; the west wing became a meetinghouse. Policemen lounged in the kitchen along its walls and stairways, talking to one another, reading newspapers, and making telephone calls, and Whateley served them coffee as if they were houseguests.[11]

In the town of Hopewell, the local telephone exchange was forced to expand to three times its normal size, which required huge quantities of equipment and help. Temporary telephones were installed in private homes, where reporters vied for accommodations. The hotel lobby was a mass of reporters and curiosity seekers twenty-four hours a day.

Anne remained in her room, supported by her mother and sister. By the afternoon of March 2, she was tired from not sleeping but was sufficiently in control to compose a letter—straight, factual, and full of optimism—swearing her mother-in-law to secrecy. After relating the details of the crime as she knew them, Anne relayed the information that had not been released.[12] The intruder knew their schedule in Englewood and Hopewell and was familiar with the baby's room. But the search had yielded no fingerprints, because everything was handled with gloves. Meticulously done and precisely planned, it seemed like the work of a professional. "I was afraid of a lunatic," Anne wrote.[13]

And so was Schwarzkopf. While Anne relayed small bits about the investigation, Schwarzkopf and his dogged investigator, Arthur T. Keaton, thought the unthinkable. They believed the baby was dead. The appearance of the crib suggested that he had been yanked from the bed sheets by his head, and the ransom note, uncharacteristically, contained no threats against the baby's life.[14] While they tried to assuage Anne's fears, they believed that what had taken place was a cold-blooded killing—desperate and mercenary, but not the work of professionals. Nonetheless, they encouraged Anne's guarded optimism and begged her patience and understanding. They hoped the nationwide dragnet of police along with the outpouring of media coverage and public interest would coerce the kidnappers to return the child.

In fact, the sympathy and the publicity were working against them. While the world chattered, the kidnappers kept silent. Broadcasters and reporters clogged the radio and telegraph wires with sentimental talk devoid of substance, and the newspapers, seeking to feed the public interest, cranked out thousands of stories more imagined than real. Newspapers worldwide had made the kidnapping front-page copy. From Pittsburgh to Paris, news about the Lindbergh baby superseded issues of domestic and foreign concern. On March 2, millions of Chinese peasants were still being battered by floods as thousands of their soldiers were killed by the Japanese invaders.[15] Nonetheless, all eyes were on Hopewell, New Jersey.

The rivalry grew intense among city, state, and national agencies, which vied for power and jurisdiction. Each wanted to be "the charging knight on horseback, slaying the dragon for public acclaim."[16] Since there was no federal kidnapping law permitting the police to apprehend criminals across state lines, and the crime had occurred outside the city in a rural town, the New Jersey State Police held their ground. Bent on proving that he and his troopers were worthy of their task, Schwarzkopf eschewed the help of the New York City police and the FBI. He would not share his information, and J. Edgar Hoover, head of the FBI, was riddled with jealousy.[17] He wanted the spotlight and the center stage, and was put out by his inferior status. Still, it was estimated that 100,000 policemen, including the 35,000 local officers, were searching for Charlie, as well as thousands of ordinary citizens.[18] Calling the Lindberghs a testimony to American youth and decency, *Commonweal* magazine wrote, "It is hardly an exaggeration to say . . . these two young people . . . are under the whole world's protection."[19]

But Lindbergh didn't want protection. He feared that the authorities would scare the kidnappers away and thwart his efforts at communication. To make matters worse, Governor Harry A. Moore of New Jersey had publicly announced that he would seek to make kidnapping a capital crime, and he offered a $25,000 reward to anyone who could guarantee the baby's safe return. Deeply concerned that public sentiment would alienate the kidnappers, Charles persuaded the governor to rescind the offer.[20] Charles continued to remind the police that the safety of his child, not justice, was his prime concern. Schwarzkopf, whose moves were complicated by his friendship with Lindbergh, tried to play the middle ground. Outwardly, he complied with Lindbergh's rules; covertly, he authorized Keaton to circumvent them.

Thirty-five policemen representing the state as well as adjacent cities and counties patrolled the Lindbergh estate, screening all visitors who entered on foot or by car. Despite an illusion of progress, by the end of the second day the police had come up with nothing. False leads abounded, yet the police could hardly ignore anyone with a reasonable story. Well-intentioned housewives, thrill-seeking teenagers, good-hearted neighbors, and observant and earnest citizens had produced nothing but false leads and further intrusion.[21]

Anne was the primary object of curiosity. Everyone wanted a glimpse of the bereaved mother. The press observed her every move, following her even on her daily walk. One man, suited like a "gentleman," convinced the police as well as Charles that he had made contact with the kidnapper. He demanded to speak with Anne immediately, but once in her private quarters, he began to rant and rave, in Shakespearean cadences, about the "slings and arrows" of human fortune. He had to be tackled and dragged out the door.[22]

The Lindberghs received thousands of letters, requiring the efforts of two policemen eight hours a day to sort and peruse. Beginning the day after the kidnapping, the mail—about seven hundred letters a day—was dumped, pound by pound, into barrels.[23] The dreams, tears, and idiocies of the public clamored for the Lindberghs' attention, even in their grief.

Nonetheless, Anne, knowing her mother-in-law's keen sense of order and public decorum, wrote to her on March 2 that everything was under control. Charles was remaining cool and lucid in the face of so much confusion.

In fact, nothing was under control, and nothing was happening. Frustrated by the lack of progress, Keaton quietly interrogated the servants, against Charles's instructions. From the beginning, Charles had made it clear that the Lindbergh and Morrow servants were above suspicion. The equation was simple. To suspect them was to implicate himself—to expose his flawed judgment. Not only was his reputation at stake; his psychological integrity was, too. If the servants had duped him, then no one was in control. That burden was more than Charles could bear, and he instinctively protected himself and Anne.

Keaton, however, pursued his theory that it was an "inside job."[24] Although it was clear that someone could have gleaned sufficient information from newspapers and newsreels and from careful observation of the patterns of the household, it was possible that some of the thirty-odd servants inside the Lindbergh and Morrow homes had worked in concert to inform the abductors or to protect their movements.[25] Any one of the servants might have had reason enough; several of them could have created a phalange of lies. While coincidence is always the enemy of the truth, the servants' relations with one another and with the Lindberghs raised questions that begged to be asked.

Except for a factor of incredible luck, it was nearly impossible to time the crime with precision. The servants had reported that no one but the baby was on the second floor between 8:35 and 9:10, and the Lindberghs' dog, Wahgoosh,[26] had not barked. Had he heard strangers, Wahgoosh, a fox terrier with acute hearing, would have made their presence known. But he had not been on guard as usual outside the baby's room on the second-floor landing.[27]

Anne was haunted by the dog's silence, but was too frightened to ask the obvious. Instead of confronting the servants, questioning why the dog had been removed, she tried to think of reasons for his not barking. The extreme force of the wind, she reasoned, had drowned the sounds of the intruders' movements. Furthermore, Charles had designed the house with eighteen-inch-thick stone walls and reinforced concrete floors and ceilings to prevent a fire from destroying it, as had happened to his childhood home in Minnesota. Ironically, the fortress Charles built against his fears muffled the sounds that might have permitted him to save his child.

Anne continued to believe that all was well. Aside from her unanswered queries about the dog, Anne renounced any role in the investigation. Like those around her, she gave Charles complete control.

On March 3, two days after the kidnapping, Charles shocked Schwarzkopf by permitting his emissary, Colonel Breckinridge, to make contact with the underworld. Charles was ready to pay the $50,000 ransom, but he had no clue as to whom or where to bring it. The kidnappers had failed to respond to the plea he had broadcast over the open wire,[28] so he resolved to find them on his own, to meet them on their terms, outside the law and beyond the auspices of the authorities. It was a desperate effort to sustain his hope. He knew that the kidnappings in 1931 were linked to an estimated two thousand criminals with ties to the mob.[29] And they had never bartered for the body of a dead person.

In spite of the pleas from Schwarzkopf and his lieutenants, Charles and Breckinridge commissioned a local racketeer, Morris (Mickey) Rosner, to act on Lindbergh's behalf. Rosner, a petty criminal with a smooth tongue and big ideas, had been recently indicted for a stock scam that cheated his "investor" of nearly $2 million. Nevertheless, Charles and Breckinridge were impressed by him. They invited him to Hopewell, made him privy to unpublicized details of the crime, and gave him $2500 dollars in cash to cover his expenses.[30] In effect, Rosner became Charles's private secretary,[31] answering his calls, lounging on his sofa, and fraternizing with the family and police.

Charles's approach to the underworld stirred a fierce national debate. It was difficult to fault Lindbergh for playing the game according to prevailing rules. Corruption in politics and business was rampant. The media rang with diatribes against capitalism and individualism gone haywire and a government too weak to control the criminal elements that threatened the bulwarks of society. The Lindbergh baby was a symbol of all that was good and innocent in America, and now he had been cruelly stolen. It was a personal crime against the body politic, one that somehow justified Lindbergh's decision. It seemed to everyone an all-out war.[32]

Playing on the confused state kidnapping laws, which were based on outmoded perceptions of transportation, gangs took victims across states lines in cars, trains, and planes in order to move beyond the state's jurisdiction. Two decades earlier, an attempt to pass legislation making the crime a federal offense, punishable by death, had failed. As recently as one week before Charlie was abducted, there had been a new congressional effort to put kidnapping under the aegis of interstate commerce, subject to imprisonment or death. But as of March 1932, the laws were outdated and uneven. In New Jersey, the crime was punishable by thirty years in prison. In New York, it was a minor felony, punishable by only five to fifteen years. The mob played on these discrepancies, manipulating the public and the police.[33]

Anne supported Charles's decision. She was convinced that the baby would be released unharmed.

While an air of optimism prevailed inside the walls of the estate, the press felt abandoned. Used only as vehicles for disseminating selected information, the newspapers jockeyed for power by creating poignant portraits of a mother in grief. Kept off the grounds of the Lindbergh estate, the reporters and photographers gathered at a closed train station in Hopewell, where they were unable to spy on the estate. They could barely discern what Anne wore on her daily stroll, let alone her thoughts and feelings, but that did not deter them from creating an image of a Madonna-like heroine, above the smut of crime and police investigation though a prime force in the recovery of her child. On March 3, the *New York Times* wrote:

> *Thousands of eyes have been trained on her. Thousands of telegraph wires, of typewriters tapped out the infinite detail of her private and her public life. She has always remained calm, gracious. Now she is not calm, except for the outer shell of her. For all the combined drama of her young life is as a leaf on a willful breeze in comparison with the tragedy that has come in it at the open window of her home on the mountain top. She keeps a hold on her taut nerves. She keeps her brain clear for whatever direction she may be called to give in the greatest manhunt in history. She keeps her body poised for action. She has been unable to eat or to sleep. All the first day of her baby's absence she wore a plain navy*

blue sports frock with a white collar, and she has kept a blue plaid scarf
tied about her dark hair so that she will be ready to go—to the end of
the world, if need be.[34]

In fact, except for the first night, Anne had been eating and sleeping normally. Optimistic because of the efforts of those around her, and
cushioned by the company of her mother and sister, Anne was determined not to jeopardize her pregnancy. She felt no need to go anywhere;
Charles had become her mind and body. It was he who would go to the
"end of the world" to bring the baby home.

Anne did not want to be a heroine, but playing the role of Madonna
served her notions of feminine virtue well. She could rail against the
immorality while exonerating herself from responsibility. In her grief,
Anne took the Morrows' Victorian pose—seeing herself as a woman,
pure and submissive, without independent social or moral agency. If, as
she assumed, Charlie was alive, her purpose was to teach the kidnappers
how to keep him healthy. Concerned that they would not feed him according to his needs or his schedule, Anne published his diet in the
Times on March 3:

1 quart of milk during the day
3 tbsp of cooked cereal morning and night
2 tbsp of cooked vegetables once a day
1 yolk of egg daily
1 baked potato or rice once a day
2 tbsp of stewed fruit daily
$^{1}/_{2}$ cup of orange juice on waking
$^{1}/_{2}$ cup of prune juice after the afternoon nap
14 drops of medicine called Viosterola during the day[35]

While Anne concentrated on the health of her "lamb," Schwarzkopf
reached into the lion's den. Still convinced it may have been an inside
job, he suggested to Charles that he be allowed to polygraph the servants, thereby providing conclusive evidence of their complicity or in-

nocence. Charles refused.[36] Unable to carry out the polygraphs, he and his lieutenants pursued the servants, one by one, in direct defiance of Charles's instructions.

Betty Gow was first. The last person to see the baby alive and the servant most intimately involved in the private lives of the Lindberghs, she was in an excellent position to act as informant. The questions centered on the movements of her boyfriend, Red Johnson.[37] Betty echoed the story Red had told the police the day after the kidnapping: he had spent the night of March 1 with the Junges, taking them for a ride in his automobile to an ice cream parlor north of Englewood, and had arrived home at approximately eleven and gone to bed.

Schwarzkopf had traced him to his brother's house in West Hartford, and had asked the local police to bring him in. Unruffled by the accusations against him, in spite of the relentless grilling of the police, he had refused to change his story or confess to the crime. "How can I confess to a crime I did not do?" he said.[38] There was no hard evidence to implicate Red, but at the time of his arrest, the police had found his car, a green coupe that a Lindbergh neighbor thought he had spotted on the night of the crime, with an empty bottle of milk in the back seat. They also found a postcard, at the West Hartford post office, that resembled in handwriting and content a card sent to the Lindberghs from Newark the day after the kidnapping. The West Hartford postcard was addressed to Charles A. Lindbergh in Princeton, New Jersey. Echoing the card sent several days before, it read: "Baby still safe. Get things quiet." Though he could not trace the cards to Red, Schwarzkopf still considered him as a prime suspect.

Red had known about the baby's illness since the evening before, and about Betty's need to be in Hopewell since four o'clock that afternoon, when he had called the Morrows' house and had spoken to Marguerite Junge. It was the Junges, in fact, who gave Red an alibi— an alibi they would later reverse.[39] Strangely, the Junges' story, placing Red in Englewood with them between the hours of eight and eleven, meshed with Violet Sharpe's story of a date with a stranger, and the police wondered whether their two stories were one. Johannes Junge told police of seeing Violet in a car with a man just as he was driving his wife to the estate. Later, he would say the man was Red Johnson.[40]

The servants, once a tight circle of friends, now began to turn on one another. Marguerite denied her involvement, including her year-long friendship with Red. Her husband, Johannes, acted like a cornered animal, spewing forth statement after statement, oral and written, to the police, hoping to dissociate himself from Red. While he tried to protect Violet from suspicion, he portrayed Ellerson as a shady figure capable of succumbing to temptation. And Red, too, turned on his friends. When he was questioned two weeks after the crime by the Newark police, he told them it was "an inside job." Quickly, however, he exonerated all the servants and refused to give the police any details.[41] Without further evidence, the police could not detain Johnson. And without Charles's permission, they could not further investigate the servants. When Schwarzkopf discovered, though, that Johnson was an illegal alien, he used the information as both a hook and a threat. Unless Johnson cooperated, Schwarzkopf made clear, he would be deported.[42]

Charles, meanwhile, continued to take the matter into his own hands. On March 4, three days after the kidnapping, he wrote the kidnappers a message, published in the *Times,* pledging his trust and confidence and assuring them that he and his wife would accept their rules and accommodate any people they appointed for the safe return of their child.[43]

New Jersey Attorney General Will A. Stevens was appalled. He, too, issued a statement to the press. The Lindberghs, he said, had no power to offer criminals immunity. The State of New Jersey would exercise the full power of the law to make sure that justice was served.[44] To Charles, that declaration was further confirmation that his own needs were not being met by the demands of the law.

Three days had gone by, with no word from the kidnappers. The *New York Times* wrote, "The world waits hopefully." Never had the fate of a child evoked such worldwide concern. There were "no boundaries" to the grief, wrote the *Times.*[45]

Anne waited. She had come down with a severe cold and was finding it difficult to sleep. Her mother began to worry that the stress would jeopardize her pregnancy. Anne worried, too. Waiting without the power to help was more painful than she had imagined.

But at the end of the day, the Lindberghs had received another letter, bearing the same signature and insignia as the ransom note. Schwarzkopf and Charles considered the scrawling, handwritten message legitimate. It read:

> *Dear Sir: We have warned you note to make anything public also notify the police now ou have to take consequences—means we wil have to hold the baby until everything is quite. We can note make any appointment just now. We know very well what it means to us. It is realy necessary to make a world affair out of this, or to get your baby back as soon as possible to settle those affair in a quick way will be better for both—don't by afraid about the baby—keeping care of us day and night. We also will feed him according to the diet.*

The kidnappers were angry. The public and the police had intervened, and Lindbergh would have to take the consequences. Get the world out of the way, they were saying and we may comply. Later, a psychiatrist hired to study the case would interpret the allusion to "a world affair" as a kind of victory for the kidnappers.[46] In a perverse way, they were now as famous as the Lindberghs, sharing their celebrity. But to Charles, there was only one message: cut the publicity and restrain police activity.

Anne was pleased; the baby was well. While she didn't want to build false hope, she wrote to her mother-in-law on March 5 that she had received "word that the baby is safe."[47] But chaos continued to rule their home. The police and the publicity had become intolerable.

Meanwhile, Lindbergh's man Mickey Rosner continued to work the underworld. He charged two men, Salvy Spitale and Irving Blitz, to act as intermediaries with the mob, and Charles and Anne were pleased.[48]

Spitale and Blitz were powerful men in the Mafia; their influence among the gangs was renowned. Everyone believed they were on the right track, and everyone was convinced the baby was safe. To her surprise, the criminal kingpins seemed more sympathetic and sincere than many of the politicians who had come to call. Charles, she wrote, was more hopeful than ever.

It seemed the whole underworld was coming clean to help the Lindberghs. Offering his sympathy, Al Capone volunteered his services from his cell in federal prison. If the government would let him out of jail, he told the press, he was certain he could find the kidnappers. In a generous display of good will, he told the authorities they could keep his brother, Mitzi, as hostage.[49] But Elmer Irey, the IRS officer who had convicted Capone, came to Hopewell to persuade Lindbergh not to comply. Irey said that Capone had already tried to pin the crime on a member of his own gang. In truth, Capone had no idea who the kidnapper was, and he was using the Lindberghs to leave jail and flee the country. Irey also believed Spitale and Blitz were nothing more than bootleggers—petty thieves preying on Lindbergh's naïveté. Irey's condemnation of Capone and the underworld connection stiffened Lindbergh's view.[50]

Breckinridge, though, was convinced of the mob's foul play, and persuaded Charles to make contact with Frank Costello, head of the Luciano family in New York. Costello was blunt. The baby was dead, he said. Tell Lindbergh not to pay the ransom. His words fell on deaf ears.[51]

With all the resources of the American justice system ready to serve him, Lindbergh chose to walk the path alone. The same determination that had propelled him across the Atlantic strengthened his resolve to remain, at all costs, in control. Charles wanted to get in touch with the kidnappers, and he would defy anyone for that end. There was a strange twist to his notions of social justice; there was a hierarchy of criminals and a hierarchy of crimes. Rules and laws were meant to be broken by violators capable of justifying their cause. Like his Lutheran grandfather and his father, Charles saw the law as an artifact of man, not as the will of God. But to those around him, Charles's defiance was hubris, obstructive and eventually destructive. Even so, the magnetism of his confidence drew many to his side, among them Dr. John F. Condon.

Dr. Condon was a seventy-two-year-old retired schoolteacher with a walrus-sized mustache as flamboyant as his personality. Proud of his superlative moral standing, he considered himself a Renaissance man, athletic and strong yet contemplative and philosophical. He contributed poems and essays to his local newspaper, the *Bronx Home News,* and he had a reputation among his neighbors as an egotist and a grandstanding patriot. He believed that Charles A. Lindbergh represented the best of American values and youth, and that the kidnapping was a national disgrace. It was his duty, he believed, to redress the desecration and to sanctify the status of his hero.[52]

Against the wishes of his family, Condon wrote a letter to the *Bronx Home News* on March 7, six days after the kidnapping, offering his services as an intermediary between the Lindberghs and the kidnappers, as well as a thousand dollars of his own money to supplement the ransom. Although his children balked and his neighbors laughed, friends applauded his splendid show of patriotism. The *News* may have been unknown outside the Bronx, but an estimated hundred thousand people read it every day. Condon was certain that someone would take notice. The very next day, he was proven right.

It was the kidnappers who responded. Within hours, Condon was in Hopewell, basking in his idol's attention. Moved by the authenticity of the kidnapper's logo on the bottom of the letter Condon had received, Lindbergh agreed to designate him an intermediary. Schwarzkopf had once again lost control. Lindbergh was wholly in charge, accepting the word of a complete stranger. Astounding the authorities, Lindbergh also gave Condon instructions for the exchange of the ransom with a note verifying his position. That night, Condon slept on the floor of the nursery and prayed to God for help in finding the baby's abductors. When Charles came in to see him the next morning, Condon was searching through the baby's toys for an object the baby would immediately recognize. He took three carved wooden animals—a lion, a camel, and an elephant—and asked whether he might take the safety pins that had secured the blanket as verification of his identity to the kidnappers.[53]

As stipulated by the kidnappers in the note to Condon, Colonel Breckinridge placed an ad in the *New York American,* indicating that the ransom money was ready, and signed it with an acronym of Condon's initials—Jafsie.

More firmly than before, the press was barred from the Lindbergh estate, now blazing with light and expectancy. The reporters and national broadcasters, however, continued to grind out their bulletins, repeating to their ravenous readers and listeners the latest statements of those on the periphery of the investigation. Whatever legitimate news there was could have been printed in three-quarters of a column, but day after day thousands of words appeared on the front page of every newspaper in the country. The Associated Press, acting with restraint, sent out ten thousand words a day; the Hearst organization managed to churn out three times as many. After all, Charles Lindbergh, Jr., heralded only twenty months earlier with the fanfare of a royal prince, was "the best known baby in the world."[54]

The lack of official information tempted the tabloids to fabricate. Often, the stories they printed were flagrant lies intended to incite public frenzy. Anne was comforted, however, by the sympathy and the indignation of hundreds of people all over the country, all hoping for the return of her baby. The collective good will of the country, Anne wrote, was heartening. In Madison Square Garden, she noted, the referees had stopped a boxing match so that all could stand and pray for the baby.

As Charles and Breckinridge were working to transfer the money to Condon, another man came forward as an intermediary with the kidnappers. John Hughes Curtis, head of a large ship-building company in Virginia, told his story to the rector of the Christ Episcopal Church in Norfolk, the Reverend Dobson-Peacock, who had served in Mexico when Dwight Morrow was the ambassador. One of his workers, he said, claiming to be an emissary of the mob, had told him that the New York–New Jersey contingent was on "the take," trying to swindle Lindbergh. His worker, named Sam, told him that his people wanted to deal directly with Lindbergh. Out of a strong sense of duty, Curtis told his rector, he felt compelled to help Lindbergh.[55]

Dobson-Peacock was impressed with Curtis's credentials. He was a successful entrepreneur, the president of the local country club, and the commodore of the Norfolk Yacht Club. There was no reason to doubt his story. Dobson-Peacock volunteered to help him get through to Lindbergh, and as coincidence would have it, when he called the Lindbergh house, Mickey Rosner answered the phone.

After Rosner identified himself as Lindbergh's personal secretary, the rector put John Curtis on the line. Not knowing that Rosner was a rival to Sam's gang, Curtis relayed the story of mob corruption in the north. Rosner barely responded, leaving Dobson-Peacock and Curtis confused and angry.[56]

While Lindbergh and Breckinridge were engrossed in their plans for Condon's meeting with the kidnappers, the state police, still in defiance of Lindberghs' wishes, continued to interview the Lindbergh and Morrow servants.

Violet Sharpe, above all, was causing problems. She was arrogant, uncooperative, and, worst of all, evasive, creating the very doubt she wished to erase. From the beginning, she could not remember the name of the man she saw on the evening of March 1, nor the names of the man and woman who had accompanied them. Furthermore, her account of the evening was riddled with contradictions. At first she said that they had all gone to see a movie but later admitted that they had been at a speakeasy, the Peanut Grille, in East Orange, New Jersey. There were enough inconsistencies in Violet's story to make the police suspicious, and the more they pressed her, the more she resisted. Angry at their intruding into her personal life, Violet refused to speak to them any further. They dismissed her but made a note to question her again.[57]

Anne continued to believe there was progress. By March 10, Spitale, Mickey Rosner's underworld emissary, had become convinced it was not a gangland "snatch." Interviewed by a reporter who trailed him and Blitz during their underworld search, Spitale said, "If it was someone I knew, I'll be god-damned if I wouldn't name him. I been in touch all around, and I come to the conclusion that this one was pulled by an in-dependent."[58]

In fact, the experts who had been engaged to study the crime were beginning to believe that the gang theory was wrong. If Lindbergh's status was what had provoked the crime, wrote the forensic psychiatrist Dudley Schoenfeld, the man himself was not someone the gangs would "hit." He was too ethical and upright, and too much in the public eye, unlike the corrupt and wealthy targets of the mob who were easy marks for extortion. Schoenfeld believed that it was the work of one man, a megalomaniac who wanted more than money. He wanted to bring Lindbergh down, and there could be no attack on Lindbergh's manhood more fierce than snatching his male child.[59]

Even as Lindbergh turned a deaf ear to those who tried to dash his hopes, he welcomed the news from Condon that the kidnappers were about to give further instructions. He decided as well not to dismiss Curtis and his story.

The kidnappers made contact with Condon on March 11, leaving word with his wife that he was to expect instructions. But in Norfolk, Virginia, Curtis had come up with a new strategy for getting Lindbergh's attention. He convinced Admiral Burrage, commander of the *Memphis,* the ship that had brought Charles back to America after his flight to Paris, to speak on his behalf. In view of Condon's apparent success, Charles was not convinced of Curtis's story but he was unwilling to shut the door on a possible lead. Reluctantly, he consented to further communication, but his hopes remained with Condon, who was preparing to meet the alleged kidnappers.[60]

On that day, Schwarzkopf worked behind the scenes, following his theory that it was the work of an amateur. He himself questioned Red Johnson, hoping to talk him into a confession, but Johnson, as usual, was steady, controlled, and consistent. He apparently was exactly as he appeared: a Norwegian sailor with a penchant for milk and Scottish women. Disappointed that the investigation of the servants had not turned up useful information, Schwarzkopf appealed once again to the press and the public. But word had leaked about the Lindberghs' making new contacts with the mob. Angered by what it considered Schwarzkopf's dissembling, the press branded him a failure.[61]

Meanwhile, Condon was secretly preparing for his first meeting with the kidnappers. Again using a courier, they wrote, "We trust you." They told Condon to go to the last subway stop on Jerome Avenue in the Bronx, where he would find further instructions. Bring the money, they wrote. In fact, Lindbergh had not raised the money. When Condon decided to go anyway, Schwarzkopf pleaded with Lindbergh to let his men accompany him, but Lindbergh refused.

The note containing further instructions was under the porch of a deserted frankfurter stand. It directed Condon to cross the street to the Woodlawn Cemetery. Fifteen minutes passed before a man signaled him into the cemetery with a white handkerchief, with which he muffled his mouth when speaking to Condon. It did not hide the same heavy German accent and contorted English of the man who had spoken to Condon on the phone. The man, whom Condon estimates at about five foot ten, about thirty-five years old, asked for the money. Condon replied to Cemetery John, as he later called him, that there would be no money unless he could see the baby. He then played on the young man's guilt and tried to persuade him to defect from the gang. Though his strategy failed, he kept the man in conversation for an hour and fifteen minutes, during which he gleaned important information. The man told him that the baby was alive and well, that he was on a boat, being cared for by two women, and that the head of the gang had raised the ransom to $70,000. Cemetery John promised to send Condon the baby's sleeping suit as proof of the gang's possession of the child, and the two arranged to communicate again through the *Bronx Home News* when the ransom money was ready. As Condon watched the man disappear into the woods, he was satisfied,[62] but Schwarzkopf later was furious. Charles had refused to let his men follow Condon, and now the kidnapper had got away.

After learning from Condon the gist of the exchange at the cemetery, Lindbergh requested the U.S. Treasury Department to help him assemble the ransom money. Three days later, with the notes tied in a bundle, Lindbergh was ready to make the transfer. On the morning of Sunday, March 13, twelve days after the kidnapping, the ad appeared in the *Bronx Home News*. Later that afternoon, Cemetery John called to say there would be a delay in sending the sleeping suit.[63]

Anne, demoralized, found refuge in a back bedroom, trying to keep her feelings under control by writing a letter to Elisabeth. Everything was disjointed and absurd, as though logic and reason and trust had no meaning. The ordinary expectations of daily life had turned into a nightmare. She wrote in her diary:

> *Time has not continued since that Tuesday night. It is as if we just stepped off into one long night, or day. And I have a sustained feeling— like one high note on an organ that has got stuck—inside me.*[64]

All lines of communication to the press were pulled short, but the more information Schwarzkopf withheld, the more perverse and intrusive were the press's efforts. Daily the tabloids fabricated stories, stoking the interest of the public. On Friday, March 18, a new form of public espionage emerged. Spurred by the warm spring weather, a company operating from an emergency airfield three miles from Hopewell offered sightseers aerial tours of the Lindbergh estate for $2.50 a ticket.[65] While Schwarzkopf's men and local authorities worked on the ground to direct traffic away from the house, the sightseeing planes zoomed overhead.

On Tuesday, Condon received a brown paper bundle in the mail. Within an hour, Breckinridge was at his side, and together they examined the gray sleeping suit and the one-page note attached to it. The suit, without doubt, had been taken from the baby and laundered and neatly folded. It was either a sign of cooperation or a twist of ruthless cruelty designed to manipulate Lindbergh. The kidnappers were now demanding their ransom without further delay. No more meetings or exchanges, they wrote. They wanted their $70,000, and they wanted confirmation that Lindbergh was ready to do business.

Charles was more than ready. Responding to a call at midnight, he arrived at Condon's house at one-thirty A.M. Wearing a hunting cap and glasses so that he could pass unnoticed, Charles examined the baby's gray suit, and, satisfied that it was his son's, pushed for an immediate exchange. Condon wanted to see the baby first, but Charles insisted that they play according to the kidnapper's rules. He urged Condon to place the ad exactly as the kidnappers had requested.[66]

He got home just before dawn. Before leaving, he had told Anne about the package sent to Condon. All night Anne had listened in bed for Charles's car. When Charles unwrapped the bundle, she too was sure it was Charlie's suit. For the parents, the suit was proof that the kidnappers had the baby. Now they had to keep their side of the bargain.

But Lindbergh was having trouble raising the money. Selling his TAT stock had not raised enough; he would have to draw on other sources. He could have asked for help from Betty Morrow or his wealthy friends, but he was determined to do this on his own. Furthermore, he believed time was running out. The "Jafsie" advertisements were attracting attention. The press, figuring that the kidnappers had responded to Condon's advertisements, camped out in Condon's front yard, forcing him to leave and enter his home in disguise. And it was clear that the kidnappers were getting nervous, their communications were slower and their words were harsher. Curiously, they never threatened to hurt the baby. They were ready to wait until they could get what they wanted. And though waiting would cost Lindbergh money—another $20,000—they seemed to have nothing but time. Condon continued to push to see the baby, but Charles insisted on compliance with the kidnappers' stipulations. Condon also urged Breckinridge to make a list of the serial numbers on the ransom bills, but this, too, Charles rejected. On March 17, both the *Home News* and the *New York American* carried Condon's message: "I accept. Money is ready. John, your package is delivered and is OK. Direct me. Jafsie."

Two days passed without a response. Condon ran a new ad in the *Bronx Home News*. Still no response. He was worried that the kidnappers had missed his ads. He was not sure what the silence meant, but something was changing. He and Lindbergh needed to act fast. He ran still another ad, with the consent of Breckinridge, in which he proposed the immediate return of the child for cash.

Meanwhile, John Hughes Curtis said the kidnappers were getting nervous. The baby was all right, but they wanted proof that Lindbergh would come through with the money. He was to deposit $25,000 in a Norfolk bank, but he refused to make the payment unless there was proper identification. Furthermore, Lindbergh told Curtis he thought his story was a sham. Curtis and his group, feeling spurned and disillusioned, left Hopewell. Rumors that began to proliferate in the Norfolk press became headlines in New York. Lindbergh was furious. If Cemetery John read the newspapers, he would certainly feel double-crossed.

Anne, however, was more optimistic than ever. She trusted Condon, she trusted Charles, and she was gaining faith in the process. Waiting, she wrote to her mother-in-law, was difficult, but she could bear it as long as there was hope. Her letters assumed a familiar quality. She permitted herself to get lost in the commonplace. Her life had assumed a pattern again. Even spring was beginning to feel warm.

Anne's poignant awareness of joy and sorrow, reflected in nature and integral to the fabric of ordinary life, would later be expressed in her poem "Security."[67] The poem implies that women sit at the edge of life, gleaning strength from ordinary tasks and the majesty of nature. Unlike men, who turn the working wheels of the world, women live in the great abyss between the earth and sky: "There is refuge in a sea-shell—/Or a star;/But in between,/Nowhere."

Meanwhile, the ugly business of negotiation moved forward. As if in revenge for being dismissed by Lindbergh, Curtis and his men loosed rumors to the press that Lindbergh had given them authority to negotiate. Again Condon tried to reassure John that they were following his rules. He put another ad in the paper, but Cemetery John was silent. Finally, on Tuesday, March 28, Condon received word. The kidnappers were upset. They couldn't understand why Lindbergh was negotiating with others, and if he didn't hurry, they would raise their price.

Charles resolved there would be no more delays. Condon must tell the kidnappers that he would accept their terms. On Thursday, March 31, Condon ran his fifth ad. The next day, Cemetery John replied by messenger. The money should be ready by Saturday. If there was no trap, the baby would be returned after eight hours.

Schwarzkopf wanted to keep Condon under surveillance. Once the baby was safe, he reasoned, they could arrest John. But again Lindbergh insisted that the police stay out. While Schwarzkopf believed he had no choice but to do as Lindbergh requested, there were others who thought he was wrong to comply. Elmer Irey stated that Lindbergh was obstructing justice. The baby, he suspected, was dead.[68] The negotiations were for nothing, and the kidnappers would escape. When he insisted that Lindbergh include gold notes and record the serial numbers that were on the ransom bills, Lindbergh backed down and consented. But he forbade police intervention, and Schwarzkopf, as usual, acceded to his demand.

Under Irey, the IRS reassembled the ransom money according to the new specifications, and tied it into two bundles. The first contained $50,000, all but $14,000 in gold notes. The second contained $20,000, divided according to John's requirements, all in gold notes. Condon stuffed the $50,000 into a box built according to John's instructions, but the bundle containing the $20,000 would not fit and had to be packaged separately.

On Friday, April 1, the same morning the money was tied and bound, Betty Gow and Elsie Whateley strolled the grounds of the Lindbergh estate, returning along the gravel driveway, a path they had walked many times before. On this day they spotted something gleaming among the stone pebbles half a mile from the entrance to the estate. Leaning down, Betty recognized it as one of the baby's thumb guards and ran back to the house to show Anne.[69] To Anne, it was an omen of hope. To the investigators, it was a strange coincidence.

John Curtis continued to demand Lindbergh's attention. The closer Lindbergh drew to negotiation with the kidnappers, the more desperate Curtis became. The kidnappers, he said, had reduced the ransom by half. Once again, Lindbergh brushed Curtis away and prepared to drive to the Bronx with Breckinridge.

On Saturday evening, the day the ad appeared in the *Bronx Home News,* Lindbergh, Breckinridge, and Condon waited in Condon's living room. Afraid that things might get out of hand once the exchange had taken place, Lindbergh carried a small revolver. Condon noticed and grew concerned. There was no way he could anticipate Lindbergh's reactions once he came face to face with his son's abductors, so he had to keep Lindbergh under control. When Lindbergh offered to go alone, Condon insisted on carrying things through. Lindbergh deferred to Condon, and they agreed to drive a car belonging to Condon's friend to the drop-off point.

At 7:45, a messenger wearing a taxi driver's cap rang the doorbell and left an envelope. Condon tore it open and read aloud the note, signed with the familiar scrawl and insignia, that directed Condon to take the money by car to a designated site in the northeast Bronx within the hour. It was the Bergen Greenhouse at 3225 Tremont Avenue. There, on a table outside the door, he would receive further instructions. On the reverse side of the note were the usual admonitions: no police; bring the money.

Lindbergh drove the small Ford sedan two and a half miles east to the nursery. There, under a rock on a table outside its door, was a note instructing Condon to walk alone across Tremont Avenue to St. Raymond's Cemetery and then follow an adjacent road south. Lindbergh wanted to go with him, but Condon, eager to keep Lindbergh away from the exchange, reminded him that the kidnappers demanded he come alone. Condon walked off without the money and disappeared down the unlit cemetery road. Standing among the tombstones and statues, Condon surveyed the cemetery and saw no one. Just as he started back to the car, a voice cried out, "Hello, Doctor!" Condon recognized the voice as Cemetery John's. For the first time, Lindbergh heard it too.

Condon walked back to the cemetery and saw a man crouched behind a bush. When Condon told him to stand up, he recognized the man as John. Making no attempt to hide his face this time, John asked for the money, which Condon told him was in the car with Lindbergh. John told Condon he could not get the baby for six or eight hours and made Condon promise not to pursue him so that the kidnappers would have time to escape. When pressed further, he told Condon the baby was with his "Father."[70] Condon demanded directions to the place where he could find the baby; then he would release the money. John retreated, saying he would return in ten minutes, and told Condon to get the money.

Hoping to save Lindbergh the extra $20,000 in the second bundle, he told John that Lindbergh had not been able to raise more than $50,000. John agreed to that amount, and Condon went back to the car, where Lindbergh gave him the money.

When Condon returned to the cemetery for the exchange, he once again begged John to let him see the child before he handed over the money. He warned John not to commit a double-cross. "The baby is all right," said John, so Condon shook his hand and returned to Lindbergh.

Lindbergh, feeling successful, was jubilant. The note in his hand would take him to his baby. They discussed Condon's promise to John not to open the note for six hours, and Lindbergh considered himself bound by Condon's promise. Amazed at Lindbergh's decision, especially in light of his consistent defiance of others, Condon worked hard to persuade him to read the note. Lindbergh agreed to open the note but was determined not to break Condon's promise to John. The baby, said the note, was on a twenty-eight-foot boat called *Nelly,* cruising the waters between Martha's Vineyard and Elizabeth Island.

Congratulating each other like old war buddies, Lindbergh and Condon drove to Manhattan to meet Breckinridge and Irey for a debriefing at the Morrow apartment on East Sixty-sixth Street. Irey was less than pleased. If Condon had been surprised by Lindbergh's conscience, Irey was taken aback by Condon's lack of judgment. He claimed that Condon had made a crucial error in withholding the second bundle. That was the bundle that contained the gold notes, and when the country went off the gold standard in the following year, all gold coins and gold certificates would be recalled. The serial numbers on those gold notes might have accelerated the apprehension of the kidnappers. Since Irey thought the baby was dead, he regarded the ransom payment as a gambit in a game of chess. And they seemed to be losing the game.

Condon was crestfallen at the possibility that he had unwittingly obstructed justice. Irey retracted his accusation and blamed Schwarzkopf for relinquishing his authority.

Lindbergh waited the requisite six hours, putting the time to good use. Enlisting the help of President Hoover, Lindbergh requested that navy planes assist in his surveillance, and he arranged to have a Sikorsky amphibious aircraft waiting at the airport on the outskirts of Bridgeport, Connecticut. At two A.M., Lindbergh, Breckinridge, and Condon drove there and at dawn they flew east to the Connecticut shore, and then northeast up Long Island Sound toward Martha's Vineyard. The three men were in high spirits and had high expectations as they flew up the coast. Later Breckinridge said that Condon had acted strangely, spouting Shakespeare and the Bible above the din of the airplane engine. But for the moment they were comrades on a grand mission.

Lindbergh wove between the islands, flying so low that they could scan the boats beneath them. None, however, matched the description of the *Nelly*. As the morning wore on, the excitement waned and Lindbergh's desperation grew. How could he have trusted the kidnappers? Why would they risk exposure; why would they remain with the baby on the boat? He flew randomly, inspecting everything that sailed. By noon, he was exhausted. When they stopped for lunch, Lindbergh refused to eat. All day they continued to search the waters off southern Massachusetts. By nightfall, there was nothing to do but go home.

Lindbergh landed at Teterboro airport at six-thirty. Carrying a small suitcase and the baby's favorite blanket, which he had taken with him, Lindbergh got into his car and drove to Hopewell. It was dark when he pulled into the driveway, but the house was blazing with light. Anne ran downstairs to greet him. His face said everything.

"I'm sorry," he said, as they embraced. And then it was Anne's turn to comfort Charles.[71] Perhaps it was only a delay. Perhaps the navy planes had scared them off. But Anne knew it was time to prepare herself for the worst. Hope was becoming a delusion.

A month had passed since the baby's abduction, and the press was at a loss. The Curtis rumors dominated the newspapers. Schwarzkopf denied everything, including speculations about Charles's mysterious excursions. But the next day, the story broke. After scanning the waters of the Atlantic coastline from Massachusetts to Virginia without success, Charles was ready to talk. The press blasted the story over the open wire: Lindbergh had paid the ransom and had been double-crossed.[72] Within two days, the U.S. Treasury Department authorized the distribution of a 57–page pamphlet listing the serial numbers of the 4750 bills that had been given to Cemetery John.

Condon later said that he had been shocked by Charles's naïveté; he himself thought from the beginning that the kidnappers could not be trusted. How could Charles believe that the people who had kidnapped his baby would keep their word about returning the child?[73]

Yet Charles continued to hope. Perhaps Curtis's story was true. Maybe the gang wanted a double payoff. It was not unusual for kidnappers to demand more than one ransom. Charles resolved to become his own investigator, ignoring, even defying, the advice of the police. Buoyed, once again, by Charles's determination, Anne maintained the semblance of optimism. She had permitted Charles to construct their reality, and she could not bear to let it crumble—if only for his sake.

John Curtis was finally in the spotlight, and for the first time everyone listened to him. There was, he told the press, no doubt about it. "I made contact with the person I went to see regarding the kidnapped son of Colonel Lindbergh and was informed that the child is well."[74]

The let-down after the week of high tension gave Charles a chance to rest. Anne closeted herself in her room with her mother; Charles did target practice with the state troopers in his woods. Even the public was beginning to calm down. Letters fell off to about a hundred a day, and fewer people called. The demands for money, however, were constant. Anne was astonished how many people promised the safe return of the child for payment without assurance or credentials of any kind.[75]

Anne blamed the press. She wrote to her mother-in-law on April 10 that the baby would be back if it had not been for the incessant publicity. The tabloids, she noted, were unconscionable. But the tone of her letters was changing. For the first time, she raised the possibility that the baby was dead. Although the police still offered her consolation, and Charles continued to encourage her, she was beginning to lose hope.[76]

While the newspapers rode the wave of the latest gossip, the magazines sought distance and meaning. Most blamed the kidnapping and the double-cross on a laissez-faire government that did not rein in American "individualism." It was the dark side of the courageous individualism that had made Lindbergh a hero: too much power, too little government. Mirroring public sentiment, the press could not accept that all hope was lost. The *Boston Herald* saw the double-cross as a reason for optimism: "If contact has been established with the kidnapper, it should not be impossible to re-establish it."[77]

Condon agreed. He would do his best to set things right. He put another ad in the *Bronx Home News*: "Please, better direction." As usual, Breckinridge arrived every evening between six and ten o'clock, hoping for a phone call or a message. Meanwhile, the banks were given the serial numbers of the bills.

Schwarzkopf tried to press the newspapers into silence, but they would not be governed. Condon was prime material; he was the closest reporters could get to the Lindbergh case, and they would not let him go. Condon, caught in the Lindbergh glitter, was treated with much the same mixture of deference and abuse. He was praised for his courage and accused of complicity. Most of all, he was hounded, day and night, by the public and the press.

Condon's standing with the police also changed. Now, even he was a suspect, no different from the servants who worked at the Lindbergh home. Schwarzkopf realized that he could not alienate Condon, the only one who had seen Cemetery John. So he treated him gently, even as he began a slow, steady, and thorough interrogation. Condon was cooperative but subtly antagonistic, ashamed, and even angry that he who had jeopardized his life was being treated like a criminal.[78]

Schwarzkopf believed there was more to be learned from the servants as well. The questions he had asked the very first day were still not fully answered. Violet Sharpe had lost her virtue and her reputation; she had nearly given up thoughts of marrying Banks. But was she desperate enough to barter the spoils of Charlie's abduction for the penniless future of a domestic servant? Had Betty Gow, in her loneliness and desire to marry, been duped by an ingratiating thug? And why had she made the baby a new shirt? Did she know he was going to be exposed to the cold night air? Had Henry Ellerson, a nomad with a thirst for booze, finally succumbed to his wild streak? Had Banks, demoralized by poverty and liquor, sold his honor for a "gentleman's cut?" And why was Marguerite Jantzen Junge, the American with a taste for money, trusted as a friend of the Morrows? Was she the docile woman she appeared to be? A calculating conspirator with Red Johnson? The scheming wife of a penniless German refugee? The liaison between the two worlds, the servants and the hitmen?

Why, on an ordinary Tuesday night, in the wake of a rainstorm, did the servants exchange a flurry of phone calls to confirm their scheduled meetings and dates? Was Red Johnson in Englewood when he called Betty? Did he go for a ride with the Junges as they had planned? Violet, too, had a date on Tuesday night—who was she with and where did they go? Had the Whateleys conspired with Ellerson, Red, Violet, and the Junges, providing a cover for their tracks?

Now that Lindbergh's attempts had failed, Schwarzkopf finally took control. Violet Sharpe was first on his list. On April 13, he sent Inspector Harry Walsh, a colleague and friend, to interview her at the Morrows' home. Violet's responses, unclear and contradictory, raised more questions than they answered.

The investigation, Anne was certain, had come to a halt. Every clue seemed to lead them nowhere.[79]

But on April 12, nine days after the ransom was paid, the first bill surfaced. In a bakery in Greenwich, Connecticut, "a smartly-dressed middle-aged woman" used it to pay for her purchases. When she saw that the shopkeeper recognized the bill, she snatched it back and walked out to her green chauffeur-driven sedan.[80] No one thought to record the license number.

By now, Condon's name was all over the newspapers. Reporters rang his doorbell, tapped on his window, and trampled over his frontyard. Condon studiously tried to finesse the truth, hoping not to alienate the kidnappers, to protect himself, and to stay in the game. Speaking from his front porch, he said:

> *I had contacts with the kidnappers and have direct contacts with them still. I have never identified them nor said a word against them. I value my life as they value theirs, and I know my life would not be worth anything if I said anything against them. I would be the happiest man in the world if I could place the baby's arms around his mother's neck.*[81]

The press continued to hound him, camping at his door and badgering him for more information. Lindbergh was worried, communication was impossible. Blaming the kidnappers' silence on the press, Anne and Charles issued a statement on April 15:

> *It is still of the utmost importance for us and our representatives to move about without being questioned and followed, and we are again requesting the complete cooperation of the press to that end.*[82]

Then another bill surfaced. In New York, David Isaacs, a retired clothing merchant, found that a twenty-dollar bill given to him was marked, and he turned it over to a Secret Service agent. He received it on April 6 from the East River Saving Bank, not long after the ransom was paid. Apparently the kidnappers had tried to dispose of some of the money before the banks were alerted.[83] And soon a pattern began to emerge: the notes were passing north and south along the East Side.

In a letter to Evangeline on April 18, Anne expressed her anger at the many rumors and unsubstantiated claims.[84] As if in response, Schwarzkopf issued an explanatory statement, and then shut down communication with the press. But, public interest gained new momentum. A constant stream of cars, thousands of them, passed along the road leading to the Lindbergh estate.[85] The only good news, Anne wrote, was her doctor's assurance that her pregnancy was going well.

When Elisabeth came to Hopewell the following weekend, Anne managed to maintain an air of quiet stoicism. But, in truth, she was exhausted and didn't know how much longer she could keep up her spirits.[86] Yet Elisabeth wrote to Connie Chilton, on April 22, that they had spent a lovely day exploring the woods, which were beginning to burst with bloom. Anne was magnificent, she wrote, praising her strength and fortitude. Never once did she appear to break down. And yet, Elisabeth observed that Anne had withdrawn from the horror of the event, blocking out the chaos around her. The newspapers, the reporters, and the police meant nothing to Anne. What did they have to do with Charlie?[87]

Betty Morrow, however, was terrified. She seemed to have absorbed all the tension and fear. She wondered how much Anne could endure before endangering herself or her pregnancy. Like Betty's saintlike mother, who had tended her twin sister, she spent all her time making sure that Anne was sleeping and eating well.

Life at Hopewell adopted a predictable pattern. Police activity, which was distant from the Lindberghs' living quarters, grew less as expectations diminished. Even Condon was beginning to doubt that the baby would be found alive.

On April 23, fifty-two days after the kidnapping and three weeks after the payment of the ransom, Condon stopped running his ad in the *Bronx Home News.* The press concluded that the Lindbergh baby hunt was "futile;" Charles thought otherwise. Unknown to the press, Charles had agreed to accompany John Curtis on a search along the Virginia coast for a ship called the *Mary B. Moss,* now said to be the one housing his baby.

With a detailed description of the kidnappers as well as an explanation for their motives and movement, Curtis had finally convinced Lindbergh that his story was true. Schwarzkopf, who thought Curtis's story to be a hoax, acknowledged that he had produced nothing, so once again he permitted Charles to have his way. But after a week at sea in stormy waters off the Virginia coast, Lindbergh and Curtis had had no sight of the *Mary B. Moss.* Lindbergh, exhausted, irritable, and furious at the press, somehow continued to believe that Curtis held out the only hope. By the first week in May, the press, having got word of Lindbergh's whereabouts, plastered the coastline with ships. Curtis said it was time to move to a sturdier boat. The gang was probably moving to rougher waters up north for the rendezvous. Lindbergh was elated. This was surely the last stop. The baby, Curtis told him, was in the waters near Cape May, off the coast of New Jersey.

After weeks of waiting for Charles to return, Anne was now convinced that Curtis was a liar. No one believed his story—no one but Charles.[88] Anne and the police tried to dissuade him, but Charles insisted on sailing Curtis's yacht, the *Cachelot.*

He set sail for Cape May on May 9. For three days he and Curtis sailed aimlessly in search of the *Mary B.* while Curtis spun stories of gang dissension and fragmentation. Though Lindbergh continued to take Curtis's word, Anne had had enough. Tired of the talk and deception, she turned inward, trying to find consolation in her own thoughts and memories. After three months of silence, Anne began to write in her diary. On May 11, 1932, she wrote that the kidnapping had an "eternal quality." She was condemned to see her boy "lifted out of his crib forever and ever, like Dante's hell."[89]

Anne didn't want to possess the baby; she wanted only to see him, to comfort him, to touch his beauty. She didn't want what she couldn't have; she wanted only that life would make sense.

Schwarzkopf tried to encourage her, and Anne was grateful, but she knew that he could not sway Charles. Commander, interrogator, and now family friend, Schwarzkopf was as frustrated as she. He had tried to keep in touch with Lindbergh on the yacht, but the storms at sea had prevented communication. On May 12, however, there was a message that demanded Lindbergh's immediate attention.

Once again defeated by storms, Curtis and Lindbergh had dropped anchor along the New Jersey coast. Curtis went ashore, telling Lindbergh he needed to talk to the kidnappers through his gang contacts. Lindbergh, helpless, did some menial chores on the ship to keep himself busy. On reaching shore, Curtis received the coded message from Schwarzkopf and, unable to decipher its meaning, called police headquarters in New York. Immediately, two detectives set out for Cape May.

While the news was hitting the wires and the evening papers, Schwarzkopf drove to the Lindbergh estate, where he spoke briefly with Mrs. Morrow. Together they walked up the center stairs to Anne, sitting in her bedroom and reading in the light of a dreary afternoon. Schwarzkopf told her that the baby's decomposed body had been found an hour earlier, buried beneath dirt and leaves in the woodlands of Melrose, no more than five miles southeast of the Lindbergh home.

Rocking her daughter in her arms, Betty said the words as gently as she could: "Anne, the baby is with Daddy."[90]

13

Ascent

*Anne and Charles, after the kidnapping,
fall 1932. (Sygma)*

Plunge deep
Into the sky
O wing
Of the Soul.

Reach
Past the last pinnacle
of speech
Into the vast
Inarticulate face
of Silence.

— ANNE MORROW LINDBERGH[1]

MAY 12, 1932, HOPEWELL, NEW JERSEY

Standing on the deck of Curtis's *Cachelot* as it sailed north toward Cape May, defying all that seemed logical, Charles had never been more certain he would bring the baby home to Anne. Each day he had cabled her from the ship, buoying her hope, raising her expectations. And Anne had so much wanted to believe that this time Curtis's story would be true. Even when she could no longer bear it, even when Curtis seemed to her just another melting "face," she took hope because Charles believed him. Now that she knew the baby was dead, she had to summon enough strength for both of them. She had to think clearly and stay in control.

Within half an hour of learning of her baby's death, Anne wrote once again to her mother-in-law. Her cool words and measured phrases turned the death of her blue-eyed lamb with the golden curls she loved to touch into an event she had to process and document. He was no longer "Charlie," but merely a body identified by its teeth and hair, dressed in a nightsuit and killed in an instant[2] by a savage stranger indifferent to her pain.

Anne blamed the baby's death on the press, as if it had conspired with the kidnappers. But on the discovery of the baby's body, the reporters turned their rancor, only days before directed toward the Lindberghs, toward the perpetrators of the crime. The media saw the kidnapping as a desecration of America, a crime against the hero and his state. The editors of the *New York Times* wrote that those who committed this "most merciless, perfidious, and despicable of deeds" against "the 'Little Friend of all the World' " were less than human, not even welcomed "by fallen angels in hell." Their crime, wrote the *Times,* was more hideous than Pharaoh's, more fiendish than Herod's, because, while theirs were intended to defend of the state, the killing of the Lindbergh baby was a gratuitous act.[3]

As if in agreement, Schwarzkopf pulled out all the stops. Furnished with descriptions from Curtis, he authorized a land, sea, and air search from the New Jersey shore to Cape Cod. Not to be outdone by Curtis, Condon declared he knew exactly to whom he paid the ransom and could pick the man "out of a thousand."

Anne, frankly, didn't care. On May 16, she wrote in her diary, "Justice does not need my emotions."[4]

The next day, however, Anne's emotions took over. And once her tears started, they would not stop. It was the physical loss that overwhelmed her—the knowledge that she would never see or touch her child again. Memories flooded back, and moment by moment she had to barter for self-control. Anne's tears permitted her to feel the cruelty of her baby's death.[5] And yet her thoughts echoed the official police report: "death due to external violence to the head." "External violence"—someone, something so depraved and hideous, it could not be human.

Anne walked the Hopewell estate, now in the full bloom of spring, with her mother and Elisabeth. When she saw the graceful blossoms of dogwood "like white stars cascading . . . upturned to the sun," she couldn't bear the pain.[6]

Later, her feelings were captured in a poem, "Dogwood." Expressing
the recognition of nature's indifference to human death was to become
the purpose, the justification of her art, moving from her diaries and
letters to her poems, essays, and books. Like Rilke, Anne began to hear
"demon voices" condemning her blindness and neglect. She had failed
to protect Charlie, to hear the ordinary sounds and signs that might
have warned her of his death. Now everything around her was seared,
and she was determined to transmit the sting of her senses. In her poem
"No Angels," she asks, as Rilke did in *Duino Elegies,* a faceless but intimate listener why she had not heard the message:

> *You think there are no angels any more—*
> *No angels come to tell us in the night*
> *Of joy or sorrow, love or death . . .*
> *Oh, do you not recall*
> *It was a tree,*
> *Springing from earth so passionately straight*
> *and tall,*
> *That made you see, at last, what giant force*
> *Lay pushing in your heart?*
> *And was it not that spray*
> *Of dogwood blossoms, white across your road*
> *That all at once made grief too great a load to bear?*[7]

While Anne turned the searchlight inward, the police hunted for
the gang, four men and one woman, who may have acted as nurse. They
reasoned that the baby was stolen for money and killed in panic.[8] As
pressure mounted for them to find the "vermin," a danger to the "freedom and security of every little child among us,"[9] Condon was getting
nervous; he went to Charles for help. Now that hell had broken loose
and everything was up for grabs, he was afraid that he would be pegged
as the murderer. On May 15, three days after the baby's body was found,
Lindbergh wrote Condon a letter, a copy of which he released to the
press:

My dear Mr. Condon:

> *Mrs. Lindbergh and I want to thank you for the great assistance you have been to us . . . Our sincere appreciation for your courage and cooperation.*[10]

But, in truth, the Lindberghs no longer knew whom to trust. They woke up several times each night, in need of sharing their thoughts and feelings. Security, they had come to believe, was a delusion—a matter of self-deception, something only fools would trust. The "god of chance," Anne wrote, reigned upon the earth.[11] She would look for Charlie forever, in the face of every child she met.[12]

The police were living a different nightmare: they could not find the face of the kidnapper anywhere. They wore Condon out, moving him from one police station to another to look at photographs that might be Cemetery John. Fantastic rumors filtered through the press. Like novelists in search of the perfect crime, reporters fabricated elaborate theories, accusing Condon of being the killer and Betty Gow his accomplice.[13]

Anne, disgusted by the publicity, turned to her diary; it became both her laboratory and her primer, a place to learn how to mourn and to find a new purpose in life. Here she could re-create Charlie, watch him play and walk and smile, touch his face and curls, hold him in her arms and carry him up to bed.[14]

For so long, Anne wrote, the terror had been outside her. Even before they took their trip, she had feared that they would be punished for their happiness. She had desperately wanted her mother-in-law to stay with Charlie in Maine while she and Charles were away. It was as though she had had a premonition; no one else saw the possible effects of the relentless publicity on the baby's safety. If only she had had the courage to voice her fears. Now, she vowed to confront the terror and find the courage to let Charlie go. He was whole and real, and yet untainted by the outside world.[15] But thoughts of the new baby brought her comfort; when he was born, she could begin again.[16]

She would sort out the infant clothes and perhaps make some, she said, but she could not write her book, the account of their trip to Asia. It would force her to face her sorrow and her fear. She would fly with Charles and she would play the piano—nursery songs, like those she might have played for Charlie. But something else had died with her son. "I'll never believe in anything again . . . faith and goodness and security in life."[17]

Even words lost their meaning. Language, the articulation of civilized life, held no power. There was nothing to say, no place to hide, nowhere to rest. They were still fighting the "war," said Charles.[18] And John Hughes Curtis was intent on proving him right.

Schwarzkopf, who now had Curtis in custody, was afraid that Lindbergh would use his clout to set him free. Even after the baby's body was found, Lindbergh had welcomed Curtis at Hopewell. When Schwarzkopf finally made it clear to Lindbergh that Curtis was a suspect, Lindbergh reluctantly agreed not to interfere with the investigation. In the end, it was Lieutenant Walsh who made Curtis crack. Broken and ashamed, Curtis released an official statement. He had been driven insane by financial worry, he said. The "gang" had never existed; it comprised merely "creatures of a distorted mind."[19]

The finding of the body brought the police and press back to Hopewell and back into the Lindbergh's living room. Anne again locked herself in her bedroom while Charles immersed himself in the details of the investigation. On May 18, Charles called a meeting of the chief investigators to stage a re-enactment of the crime. Schwarzkopf, playing the kidnapper, climbed up to the nursery window on a ladder and began to climb down with a burlap bag containing a thirty-pound weight, simulating the baby. Amazingly, the ladder split at the sixteenth rung as he was on the way down—the exact spot at which the original ladder had split. The burlap bag dropped on to the concrete foundation just below Charles's study, leading Schwarzkopf immediately to suggest that the baby had died from the fall on his head.[20]

Anne was appalled. "I will never climb out of this hell that way," she wrote.[21]

Charles's grief was expressed far differently. He sought justice; Anne sought to redeem her faith. While he pursued the criminals with fanatical passion, Anne longed to recapture her innocence, her belief that life was good and safe and that Hopewell could once again be her home. The investigation, though, was essential for Charles to diffuse his helplessness and rage.

But where was Anne's rage? Was heightened awareness enough? Where was her anger at Charles for demanding her constant presence on his flights, for taking her away from Charlie and home, leaving him vulnerable to harm? Where was her rage against the press, which had exposed every detail of their private lives, whetting the appetite of malcontents and madmen? Where was her anger at her mother for not keeping her promise to care for Charlie in Maine? He had been alone with the servants long enough for an outsider to penetrate their tight circle, to learn everything about Charlie and the family. And what about the servants? Why did she not want to question their loyalty?

For Anne, rage was not a possibility; it was not part of her lexicon. It was too extreme. And, like Charles, she felt that she somehow had been complicit. Anne's God was the Calvinist God of her parents. Justice was not ethically bound to man. Good deeds did not necessarily bestow happiness; evil did not always lead to suffering. She could blame herself, but even that was self-indulgent. Either you were "saved" or you weren't; "grace" was a state you could not earn. Had her father been alive, he would have counseled forbearance; nothing could change the finality of Charlie's death. Duty remained.

The police continued to produce nothing. Everyone was frustrated and blaming someone else. The FBI blamed the Internal Revenue Service. The IRS blamed Schwarzkopf. Schwarzkopf was beginning to turn on Condon, and Condon blamed Curtis for getting in the way of Cemetery John and his gang. The press hurled accusations at Schwarzkopf for missing the obvious—five miles outside the Lindberghs' front door. Criminal experts all over the world aligned themselves for or against Schwarzkopf. Everyone was eager to find the real killer, and the obvious fact was that Schwarzkopf had produced nothing. Governor Harry Moore endorsed Schwarzkopf's efforts, but his statement summed up the situation: "The cop who arrests the murderer of the Lindbergh child is made for life."[22] While the whole world was intent on re-creating the crime, Anne sat in the quiet of her room, trying to confront its reality.

On the 25 of May, two weeks after the body was found, Anne walked through the nursery door to find "her boy." Like an explorer braving the jungle, Anne opened his closet. Expecting fear, she was instead flooded with warmth. The description of her feelings as she discovers his clothes explodes with Charlie's vitality. When she found his shoes, coat, and mittens, she felt as though she has touched his skin. Through her tears she had found the joy she wanted.[23]

Despite her grief, Anne took pleasure in the victory of Amelia Earhart.[24] In a plane twice as fast and as powerful as Lindbergh's, Earhart had sought to commemorate his flight of five years earlier with a transatlantic flight of her own.[25] While the international press heralded their new heroine, the reporters at Hopewell yawned with boredom.[26] But in the "lull" between suspects, another blow hit the Morrow family. A report from Rockefeller Medical Center revealed that the damage to Elisabeth's heart valve had become severe. She would be increasingly susceptible to infectious disease, and there was little chance she would survive beyond five years.[27] Once again, Anne felt helpless in the face of death.[28]

Determined to put the past behind him, Charles went back to work. He resumed his research at the Rockefeller Institute and his duties at TAT. In Anne's little Cessna, he flew to Mitchell Field on Long Island for his annual transport license exam. While their lives assumed the semblance of normality, Anne had lost her will to fight. She was tired of excitement. Tired of talk. Tired of putting up a front. Elisabeth buoyed up her own spirits by parading in a polka-dot chiffon dress, Con came home from college bursting with possibility, but Anne stood on the periphery of life at Next Day Hill, lonely and heartbroken.[29] Once again the uninvolved observer, she let life wash over her. She sat in the sun as the colors, sounds, and stirrings of nature filled her mind and smoothed the wrinkles of memory.[30] Frozen in time, unable to write, Anne "plunged deep into the face of silence."

Elisabeth, as usual, was the mistress of charade. The more her health faded, the more she exhibited style and flourish. With her hat atilt and her furs on her arm, she set off to visit family friends in England.[31] Anne remained in Englewood, a prisoner of her own solitude, condemned to live.

The police, meanwhile, stalked Violet Sharpe. After a bout of tonsillitis, Violet was physically enervated. But something had happened to her mind as well. Along with her vitality, her spirit had dwindled. Her doctor warned Schwarzkopf's officers against further questioning.

Defying the doctor, the irrepressible Inspector Walsh arranged an interview with Violet at the Morrow home. On May 23, in the presence of Schwarzkopf, Keaton, and Lindbergh, Walsh again put Violet's memory to the test. Under the gaze of the august tribunal, Violet not only changed her story, but dismissed her lies as unimportant. She had originally told the police that she went to a movie with a stranger on the night of the kidnapping. Now the movie became a roadhouse, and the stranger a man named Ernie. When pressed, Violet alluded to her relationship with the butler, Banks. She admitted that Banks had a drinking problem, but she refused to reveal details of their relationship. The police, however, had already uncovered at least five sexual liaisons between Violet and men she had met at local bars, one a reporter for the *Daily News,* who had tried to bribe her for photographs and news of the Lindbergh baby. The situation, Violet said, made her sad.[32]

When the interview was over, Lindbergh still refused to consider Violet a suspect. But Inspector Walsh, intent on hooking Violet, called on her again on June 9. Although it was only seventeen days since he had seen her, Walsh was shocked at Violet's appearance. Since March, she had lost forty pounds.[33] The vivacious young woman now looked haggard and old. In the company of one of the Morrows' secretaries, Laura Hughes, Walsh showed Violet photographs of a man named Ernest Brinkert, a taxi dispatcher from White Plains, New York, whose business cards had turned up during an early search of Violet's room. With a strange nonchalance, Violet confirmed that Brinkert was the man she had been with on the night of the kidnapping. And now her manner turned bizarre. She trembled and cried when speaking, she screamed her answers when pressed. Frightened when Violet's tears turned to uncontrollable sobs, the secretary defied Walsh and called Violet's doctor. He arrived ten minutes later to find Violet collapsed in the secretary's arms. Casting Walsh an accusing look, the doctor examined Violet and then stated that she could be questioned no further. She was, he said, on the edge of "hysteria." Walsh dropped the questioning but told the doctor he would be back the next day.[34] As Violet rose to walk out of the room, she flashed a sly smile at Laura Hughes and gave her a wink.[35] That wink would forever haunt those who knew Violet. The next day, she committed suicide.[36]

The police interpreted Violet's suicide as a sign of her possible complicity in the kidnapping, but her friends blamed it on Banks.[37] Nearly thirty years old, without the promise of marriage or employment, with word of her possible link to the kidnapping and of her sexual liaisons about to be sent out on news wires around the world, Violet was desperate. In England, it was discovered that she had been married to George Payne, a butler in a house where she had served. He would deny the legality of their union, and the stain of adultery would deepen her shame. What was she to do? Her only choice would have been to return to her parents' crowded cottage in Brookshire, England. When she had heard that Walsh was coming to see her again, she was terrified and went to Banks for consolation. He had turned away. Violet took a measuring cup from the pantry shelf and walked up the back stairs to her room. She dissolved in water in her bathroom cup a measured amount of the cyanide crystals she had brought from England to clean silver. Then she drank the mixture, staggered down the stairs, and collapsed in the pantry. Moments later she died at her lover's feet.[38]

Some blamed Walsh, and others blamed Banks. Anne saw Violet as another figure in a surreal world of dissolving images.[39] So many stories, so many blind alleys, so many reasons to doubt and distrust; Anne tried to wash Violet from her mind.[40] The posthumous investigation by Inspector Walsh yielded no evidence to link Violet to Charlie's death, and within days, she was cleared of any connection. But her tarnished honor was a different story.

Violet's fear of disgrace came to pass; her parents refused to accept her body. On June 15, Violet was buried at the Brookside Cemetery, not far from the grave of Dwight Morrow. The Sharpe family asked that a wreath of roses be placed on her grave.[41]

Once again they were front page news. Anne feared that Charlie would be lost forever in the torrent of tragedy that followed his death.[42]

The next day, Anne and Charles drove to Sands Point, Long Island, to Falaise, the home of Harry and Carol Guggenheim. Harry Guggenheim[43] had taken a paternal interest in Charles ever since they met in 1927. After Lindbergh's transatlantic flight, Guggenheim worked with Dwight Morrow to protect him from the press and the demands of the public. Lindbergh's marriage to Anne deepened their friendship, and the Guggenheims opened their home as a haven to the young couple during the early years of their marriage. Anne liked Guggenheim's wife, Carol Morton, who struck her as someone not seduced by social expectations. Like the woman Anne wanted to become, Carol was creative and steeped in traditional values, uncompromised by convention or prevailing opinion. But more than that, Anne was envious of her faith. She comforted herself with Emily Dickinson's words: 'The loss of faith surpasses the loss of an estate.'[44]

Now, Anne walked in the cool darkness along the shore that bordered the ninety-acre estate on a cliff above the Sound. The peace and beauty of the enclave quieted her mind and fed her courage. It was as though she were "back from the war," she wrote. She wanted to start over, even though the future was laden with uncertainty.

Harry Guggenheim gave Anne and Charles advice about dealing with publicity:

As long as you do anything constructive all your life, you will have to meet it, you can't get away from it. Conquer it inside of you so you don't mind . . . You've got to stop fighting it, stop trying to get away from it.[45]

While Anne agreed with Guggenheim in principle, "we quiver when we're touched," she wrote.[46]

Under a barrage of letters and phone calls threatening their unborn baby's life, Anne and Charles had to acknowledge that they could not live in Hopewell without armed guards. They had already begun, reluctantly, to return to Englewood instead of Hopewell after their weekends away. Next Day Hill was not immune to danger, but there was a security system in place. The grounds were patrolled around the clock by state troopers and three private guards. Not that this stopped reporters from camping outside the gates, however, or sightseers by the hundreds trying to catch a glimpse of the Lindberghs.

Caught again in the web of her mother's life, Anne felt like an adolescent struggling to define her values. As though her Calvinist grandfather were thundering at her, she attempted to justify the blasphemy of a writer's life. Writing implied a narcissistic life with no concern for public service. Was her parents' ethic of charitable works the only criterion for a virtuous life? Was giving public service the only gift worth making? Paralyzed by guilt, Anne was still unable to write the narrative of the Asian trip. It was as though her writing and their flight had been acts of hubris that called down on them the death of Charlie. Though she believed her inability to write was a lack of connection between the book and her life, it is possible, as some professionals say, that the obstacle was her unexplored rage. It was the nexus between her feelings and her work that crippled the writing process. She would sit for hours on end, unable to find words that expressed her thoughts.[47]

With a generosity and sensitivity for which Anne would always be grateful, Charles understood that writing was Anne's lifeline. Aided by his encouragement, she tried to form her notes and letters into a narrative, but her letters and diaries, written in snippets in hotel rooms and the back cockpit of the plane, were of little help. They were devoid of emotion; they were the empty notations of a dutiful observer who wanted only to return home to Charlie.

As she moved toward her twenty-sixth birthday, she reassessed her life.[48] She resolved to capture eternal moments before they were stolen. Her diary flowered with detailed descriptions of everyday life. Every movement of Charles, every gathering of family and friends, resonated with meaning.

She found a kindred soul in the British novelist Charles L. Morgan.[49] Her sense of the eternal was heightened when she read his novel *The Fountain*. "This is it," she wrote in her diary. "This is what I want—*here*. This man knows!"[50]

"Death is the answer," Morgan had written: "When someone takes death inside himself, he relinquishes feelings of relative importance to others . . . He is suffused with humility and born again. He is the true saint and philosopher."[51] Man, is a creature divided against himself. "His desires cry in his silences." The solution is to withdraw within the circles of consciousness toward the center of one's being. Only at the core can one find the union of imagination and immortality.

Finding in Morgan's book a metaphor that would permeate her writing, she copied the lines into her diary: "[One must seek] the stilling of the soul within the activities of the mind and body so that it might be still as the axis of a revolving wheel is still."[52] The axis of the wheel "moves forward but it never revolves. It is the core of sanity in the heart of madness."[53]

Unaware that the process had begun, and terrified by the possibility, Anne gradually began to move apart from those around her. She knew that her awareness made her different from those immersed in the world of action. She knew she had to find another way of life, a means by which she could redefine her values and stand alone. But self-confirmation implied a separation from Charles and her mother, a loneliness she could not bear. Abandoned by her Presbyterian notions of God, she reached through Charles Morgan beyond Christianity toward a theology that challenged the duality of good and evil and the boundaries between life and death.

On June 22, 1933, Anne celebrated her birthday with thoughts of Charlie. He would have been two years old. Family and friends gathered in the garden of the Morrow estate for supper. As she watched Aunt Alice's home movies of Charlie, Anne realized that he could live only in her mind. But more and more, her dreams were filled with visions of the new baby. Strange—it always looked like Charlie.[54]

While Anne was contemplating the birth of her new child, Congress was preparing the law that would transfer the crime of kidnapping from state to federal jurisdiction. The act, known as the Lindbergh Law, stipulated that unless the victim was returned within a week, it would be presumed that he or she had been carried across state lines. The maximum penalty was life imprisonment. (A year later, the law was amended to make kidnapping an offense punishable by death.) Before the enactment of the law, kidnapping had been a misdemeanor punishable by a sentence of five years to life.[55]

Once Charlie's birthday passed, a cloud seemed to lift, and Anne's quest for strength and answers became more determined. She took daily pleasure in the plans for the new wing they would add to the Morrow home for her and Charles and the baby. She felt as if it were a new beginning. But just as she was releasing herself into the present, she and Charles were summoned to Hopewell for the trial of John Hughes Curtis.

Anne dreaded the trip, but when they got there, they saw the house, white and gleaming, cool and peaceful—with little trace of the crime. A picture of the baby, a burn mark from the fingerprinting on the stairway, but, on the whole, welcoming and peaceful. Anne went to the nursery and opened wide the big French window, sinking into the security of her life before the kidnapping. When she walked out of the room, she left the door open behind her.[56]

Buoyed by the prospect of the birth of her child, Anne began again to write her book. The process exorcised whatever demons remained. She wanted to concentrate her thoughts on a central theme, but was capable only of straight narratives. The themes, the focal point, she wrote, had not emerged.[57]

She tried to infuse Hopewell with new life, banishing memories of

Charlie's kidnapping. But just as she began to master her fears, more threatening letters arrived. Now she and Charles decided to hire a guard and buy a police dog, trained to attack intruders, so that they could live in their own home, not in Englewood. The dog trainer explained that it would take two weeks to establish a relationship, but, he assured them, the dog, a trained German shepherd, would be completely loyal and obedient. With the fearlessness of "a liontamer," Charles got inside the dog's cage. Within hours, Charles had mastered the dog and taken him out for a stroll on a leash.[58]

Anne delighted in the absurdity of having a canine bodyguard. He made her feel very important as he followed her up and down the stairs. It was like having a lovesick boyfriend.[59]

Back at Next Day Hill to spend the remaining weeks of her pregnancy in the comfort of her parents' home, Anne cherished and enjoyed the baby growing within her. While Charles studied bacteriology at the Rockefeller Institute, Anne sat in the sun and swam in the pool, feeling young and slim in the weightlessness of the water.[60]

Sadly, she noted she was letting go of Charlie. The "numbness," she theorized, was a kind of physical protection from the finality of death. She quoted Emily Dickinson in her diary:

This is the hour of lead
Remembered if outlived
As freezing persons recollect
The snow—
First chill, then stupor, then
The letting go.

Thoughts of death enveloped Anne; it was as though she owed a cosmic debt. There were times when she could not bear the guilt of her survival or the joy of giving birth to another child. Her guilt and rage, still unexpressed, made her fear that she would lose control.

At midnight on August 16, Anne's birth pangs began. By dawn, she was at her parents' apartment on East Sixty-sixth Street in New York.

As with Charlie's birth, she was attended by Marie Cummings, the nurse, Dr. E. M. Hawks, the obstetrician, and Dr. P. J. Flagg, the anesthetist. The gas was administered, and Anne descended into unconsciousness.

While Charlie's birth had felt like a hazy banishment from youth, this time it was like a fall into an abyss.[61] As if her self-contempt were pursuing her, she heard a voice, like the Grand Inquisitor, taunting her with questions.

Sometimes the voice told her the answer: Life was a "cheap trick," vacant of meaning. She screamed out in rebellion against the lie.

Moving in and out of consciousness, feeling contempt for the petty concerns of those around her, and for men, who could not possibly understand a woman's experience, she wondered whether the heightened awareness of birth was analogous to the experience of death.[62]

While Anne struggled for consciousness and release, the doctors worried about the effect her long labor might have on the baby. After several hours, they delivered the baby by cesarean section.[63]

Finally, Anne became conscious, feeling sore but weightless, and alert to the unmistakable bleat of her baby. Her mother's voice, quiet, dear, and full of humor, told her, "A little boy, Anne." That night, Anne wrote in her diary, "Out of the teeth of sorrow—a miracle. My faith had been reborn."[64]

14

Death Is the Answer

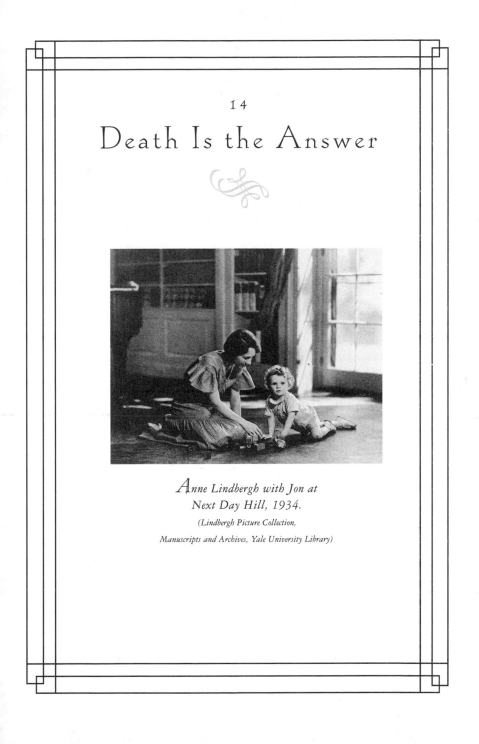

*Anne Lindbergh with Jon at
Next Day Hill, 1934.*
(Lindbergh Picture Collection,
Manuscripts and Archives, Yale University Library)

And so you died like women long ago,
died in the old warm house, old-fashionedly,
the death of those in child-bed, who are trying to close
themselves again, but cannot do it, because that darkness
which they also bore returns and grows importunate, and enters.

—RAINER MARIA RILKE,

Requiem, For A Friend,[1]

TRANSLATED BY J. B. LEISHMAN

AUGUST 1932, ENGLEWOOD, NEW JERSEY

Anne was so pleased to have a child—strong and male, a Lindbergh. But his birth was not the miracle she had expected. Anne found death everywhere—even in the breath of her newborn son. Conjuring up images of the night of the kidnapping, she wrote, "Nearer at night than morning, nearer in winter than in summer, nearer when the wind is howling or when I hear a child breathing peacefully asleep."[2]

"Death [is] the answer," Anne reminded herself, quoting again the words of Charles Morgan. Death was part of a natural cycle; the pinnacle of a life in service to a larger ideal. It was no different from the fulfillment of love or work; it was a consummation with immortality.[3]

On August 30, after two weeks of rest at the Morrows' apartment in New York, Anne and the baby returned to Englewood. Charles carried Anne out to the lawn, where she sat beneath a tree and watched her baby take his morning bottle from the nurse. The dogs, excited to see her after so many weeks away, leaped wildly up to greet her, and licked the toes of the baby in the nurse's arms.

Home from England, Elisabeth sat in the shade beside Anne. In her new chic hair wave, her black dress, and her black-and-white Paris hat,

Elisabeth related the simple joys of life in the English countryside, so different from the frenzied pace of New York.[4]

As they passed the last days of summer at Next Day Hill, Elisabeth dared to talk about a man she had come to know in England. Anne sensed that Elisabeth was in love again.[5]

Elisabeth had first met Aubrey Morgan in London in the winter of 1930, at a party given by a family friend. While Anne and Charles were flying on their inspection tour for TAT, Elisabeth had sailed to England with her parents for the Disarmament Conference. Aubrey pursued Elisabeth with letters and later "came courting" to the Morrows' apartment in New York. Aubrey, so unlike the reclusive minister Clyde, was a big man, "a real presence," not so much handsome as good-natured and jovial.[6] He was a practical man of commerce, descended from a family of wealthy merchants from Cardiff, Wales, and he had the breeding of a gentleman. Restrained, proper, and cultivated, he was exactly the husband Betty Morrow might have chosen to care for her sick, precious girl. Marriage, she may have reminded Elisabeth, was the "crown" of a selfless female life. Elisabeth understood that her time was short and that she had no future with Connie. Afraid of being sick and alone, Elisabeth saw marriage as a ticket out of her parents' house and a statement of her social legitimacy. With Aubrey, Elisabeth said, she felt sturdy and confident, as though "anything seem[ed] possible."[7] To an observer, it may have been another charade: the pretense of health and new beginnings just as her illness was about to tighten its hold. And sex was no longer an issue. The severity of the damage to Elisabeth's heart valve precluded frequent sexual intercourse; Aubrey would have to get her doctor's permission each time they wanted to make love.[8]

Even as Anne rejoiced in Elisabeth's happiness, she was beginning to understand that most of her life was beyond her control. Two weeks later, Elisabeth's announcement of her engagement to Aubrey was another sign that Anne's childhood was far behind. Elisabeth, too, was slipping away. Her mother was still at the center of their lives, but she and her sisters and brother looked outward toward the world, building new loyalties and establishing new patterns of living.[9]

The presence of her new baby softened everything. She would catch herself thinking of him as Charlie. She had to remind herself over and over that this baby was separate and different from him.[10] He was quick, lean, and muscular—not her "fat little lamb." They named him Jon, a name they had found in a Scandinavian history book. Jon, she implied, would be his own person—nobody's brother and nobody's junior.[11] Once again, Anne measured the beauty of her son by his resemblance to Charles.[12]

As the leaves began to fall from the tulip trees, Anne wrestled with the idea of "time." Time was not linear, she concluded; it was determined by associations, moods, and sensations.[13] As usual, she searched for literary paradigms with which to clarify and crystallize her thoughts. She attributed her understanding to her reading of Proust, but she had also discovered Freud's notion of memory—a web of memories encircling a core. One wrong thought, one dark feeling, and she was caught in the net of the kidnapping. Unfortunately, Anne's fears were continually confirmed.

A week after she arrived at her mother's with Jon, a deranged man broke through the guarded gate and called to Betty Gow at night through the window. Anne and Charles decided immediately to have someone with Jon at all times. Perhaps she was right; the kidnapping was "eternal." Perhaps they would always live in its shadow.[14] But at least the press had slackened its pace. Charles had made a public plea that reporters leave their new son alone. Publicity, he said, may have brought about the death of their first child. Their children had the right to grow up like "normal Americans."[15]

Anne still felt hunted. When she left the confines of the estate, even for an afternoon in the city, she felt out of place and in danger. One day, as she shopped in Macy's, someone recognized her, and a crowd of thrill-seekers began to pursue her. It was a "madhouse," she wrote. Catching herself in the store mirror, Anne was shocked by what she saw. She looked pale, worried, and out of shape. Barely twenty-six, she felt haggard and old. She rushed back to Englewood where she belonged—to her family and the fortress of her mother's home.[16]

Safety, however, exacted its price. Anne was rarely alone with Charles. Even though Jon was only a month old, on September 13 she left him in the care of Betty Gow at Next Day Hill and flew to North Haven in the same rented biplane Charles had used when teaching her to fly. When they reached Portland, Anne took the controls. As always, flying gave her balance and perspective.[17]

During these early days of September in North Haven, tinged with the red-leafed promise of fall, Anne sharpened her skills of observation. Everything was vulnerable, so she tried to preserve each moment in images—of Elisabeth and her mother walking the dogs, golf among the shimmering birch trees, tennis on the lawn, the fiery northern lights of a summer night, an afternoon picnic with Charles on the White Islands. Her diary had almost a pointillistic pattern, bathed in the refractions of soft island light. They were literary portraits, family tableaux, hung in sequence as if in a museum, preserved in the art of her words.

Anne was happy again, but even in North Haven, the wind and darkness brought their terror. She still could not accept the death of Charlie.[18]

Sadly, Anne was alone in her grief. Except for the investigation, Charles had put the kidnapping behind him. It was only seven months since the baby was taken, yet Charles could not tolerate Anne's sorrow or tears. She was beginning to see that their emotional needs were pushing them apart. Charles' persona of "strength" lay in his denial of the very emotions which might have healed her. Depriving herself of the right to mourn, Anne prayed for the courage to survive.

When she returned to Englewood on September 27, after two weeks away, Anne saw Jon with fresh eyes; he was big, round, pink, and long. She was thrilled to tend to him again—and his nose even looked smaller.[19]

But the vulnerability of their fame was made evident. In November, Charles L. Jodney, an unemployed carpenter and father of nine children, was jailed for threatening Betty Morrow.[20] Destitute and unemployed, Jodney had sent Betty two letters, pleading for money. When Betty wrote back that he must ask his community for help, he threatened her and her family with bodily harm. It was the first case in New England under the new federal extortion statute, enacted after the kidnapping.

Afraid for Jon's safety, Anne and Charles decided not to return to Hopewell. It was Charles who made the final decision; they would give the home and the land to the state to be used as a sanctuary for children.[21] It made Anne feel she was giving something back—restoring the life that Charlie had lost. Helping children would "make good out of evil."[22]

Charles, Anne wrote, was working hard and seemed happier and more productive than he had in a long time. He continued his research at the Rockefeller Institute, under the direction of Alexis Carrel. By the fall of 1932, the Nobel Laureate, impressed by Charles's intelligence and skill, had invited him to join the technical staff.[23] At sixty, Carrel was old enough to be Charles's father, and while there was a mentor-student quality to their relationship, he treated Charles as a peer.[24] Charles and Carrel were refining the perfusion pump, which perfused animal organs in such a way as to mimic certain aspects of the body's biochemistry. They hoped to devise a method for repairing human organs outside the body. When Carrel was chided in the press for his flamboyance—his strange habit of wearing a black robe and cap in the operating room—Charles publicly applauded him for his innovative methods and his generosity of spirit. Anne would later say that Carrel gave Charles the chance to fulfill the dream he had had as a child, working with his grandfather in his laboratory in Detroit.[25]

Fall moved swiftly into winter, but Christmas didn't bring its usual consolation. It was eclipsed by preparations for Elisabeth's wedding, which took place on December 28 at the Morrows' home in Englewood. On the day of the wedding, preoccupied with memories of her marriage to Charles when her father was alive, three years earlier, Anne quietly set out the glasses and the wine, recorded presents, mingled with the guests. Relieved not to be the center of attention, Anne was pleased to play a secondary role; it was her true nature. Consonant with her father's notions of "composing differences," Anne tried to harmonize the varied strains of the guests, to orchestrate the voices and memories. She greeted every guest with a smile and introduced each to the other. Balancing the numbers on each side of the room, she made certain that everyone felt important and comfortable. In her parents' home, among her family and friends, she had the luxury of just being "Anne."

Suddenly the music began and everyone found a place to view the procession. Aubrey and Uncle Jay, her father's brother, strode down the aisle. Uncle Jay tried not to cry.[26] And then came the wedding march: Con, a bridesmaid, enveloped in blue velvet and pink orchids, looked serious and demure. Even as Elisabeth came into view, Anne's eyes could not leave her little sister.

Dwight Jr. escorted Elisabeth down the aisle, reminding Anne of her father. A flood of emotion overtook her as she focused her eyes on Elisabeth. But it wasn't only Elisabeth she saw. In her sister's clear and penetrating beauty, Anne saw the essence of Elisabeth, the prototype of femininity. As so many times before, Anne was content to be in her sister's shadow. Yet even at this joyous occasion, one of rebirth and communion, Charlie's death haunted her. As she watched the wedding procession, she chastised herself for her baby's death. Over and over, she repeated to herself that "it could not have happened. It could have been another way."[27]

For now, Anne tried to run from her feelings, busying herself with activities she usually shunned. She went shopping, often, "like a man to drink."[28] She visited sick friends in the hospital and dined in New York with Charles's colleagues and visiting dignitaries.

As she rode the subway in Manhattan, she bitterly scanned the crowd. "Which one of you killed my boy?" she thought to herself, trying not to cry. These people—these horrible street people who read the tabloids; they were already dead, she wrote.[29]

By the turn of the year, Anne knew she could no longer hide. She had to permit herself to feel and to think. She had to write.

Conceived in December 1931 and completed in January 1934, *North to the Orient*[30] is the account of Anne's 1931 flight with Charles through Canada, Alaska, Russia, Japan, and China. But it is also an allegorical prose poem filled with the clarity and spirituality that grew out of her sorrow. It is an act of faith inextricably linked to the birth of Jon. While the kidnapping of Charlie stole the meaning of words, the birth of a new son resurrected Anne's faith in the creative process. It is not a book Anne could have written before the death of her father or the kidnapping of her infant son. It is too free-ranging in its speculation, too assertive, too metaphysical to be other than the product of profound suffering. It is, in fact, the very act of suffering that imbues the Lindberghs' flight with meaning and converts Anne's simple diary notes and letters into moral allegory. It is Anne's rage diffused and codified to achieve reconciliation and universality. It is an odyssey, written by one with an almost "animal desire" to find her way "home."

But at the time of her writing, Anne had no home. North Haven and Next Day Hill no longer existed as Anne remembered them; she would not return to Hopewell. The "home" she left in the summer of 1931 was the scene of her childhood, full of a loving and enveloping family, which could never be the same. Her father was dead and her son had been murdered. Nonetheless, Anne knew that she must find her way back to the "knot," which fastened her faith to life before they died, if she were to make sense of her experience and go forward with hope. She had to return to the innocence that belied her vulnerability in order to unravel its "mysteries."

Implicit in Anne's narrative is the myth of Theseus and the Minotaur. Anne is Ariadne, the king's daughter, who waits at the entrance of the Labyrinth for her hero to return, guided by the ball of thread she has given him. But Anne's Ariadne is a technological heroine in a technological age, with the skill and freedom to ride alongside her prince, capable of as much conquest as he. Anne is at once the lovesick maiden and the agent of their safe return. She, like Ariadne, devises

the plan that brings them home. This is Anne's moment of triumph—
the story that renews her faith and hope.

The Lindberghs' seven-thousand mile flight, which soared above
geographic and cultural boundaries, is the perfect metaphor for her psychological journey. Isolated in her sorrow, Anne uses the narrative to
rail against a universe indifferent to human suffering. Through the art
of narrative, she grieves and searches for reconciliation. It is a "day-
dream" in the Freudian sense, a creative vision in which the author
splinters her psyche into literary representations whose conflict and resolution will make her whole.

Anne is both the protagonist and the narrator, the observer and the
heroine. The people she meets on her flight are pilgrims; each a different person to test her virtue and teach her lessons.

At their first stop, Baker Lake, an isolated trading post on the flatlands of the Northwest Territory, Anne is the first white female the
Eskimos have ever seen and the first woman to visit the European fur
traders at their camp. As if reinventing herself through their eyes, Anne
examines the Victorian notions of the feminine ideal, the symbol of delicate beauty, moral purity, and "home." Laughing at the discrepancy between herself and the symbol, Anne probes the universal need for
intimacy and security. Like the animals they trap, the traders at Baker
Lake burrow beneath the ice, hiding from their feelings in order to survive the loneliness. Anne becomes the object of their projected fantasies; they treat her as warmly as if she were sister, mother, or wife. A
feminine ideal, Anne cracks their icy surface with the magical power of
her words. Language, she concludes, can crystallize memories raised
from the dark seas of the unconscious.

They fly deeper through the white summer nights of the Northwest
Territory to the Mackenzie delta, on its northern shore. There, in the
bleak and frozen land, Anne feels like an exile in time and space. They
stop at Aklavic, a sophisticated settlement of twenty-eight houses and
two churches in frequent contact with the "outside world." Unlike the
people of Baker Lake, the Eskimos and settlers here have radio appara-

tus and are visited yearly by a boat that brings letters and packages, food and dry goods from the mainland. To Anne, the arrival of the boat seems to symbolize the longing of men, women, and children for the comfort and possessions of "home."

As they span the Arctic Sea to the northernmost part of the Alaskan peninsula, Port Barrow, they are enveloped by fog. In the gray half-light of the Arctic sun, as they move farther into an abyss, Anne loses hope of arrival or retreat. Aided by the good will and competence of the stationmaster at Point Barrow, they blindly climb the walls of white fog. Once again, in exile in a barren and icy land, Anne explores the power of the spoken word. Their host, a doctor, is also a preacher who translates portions of the New Testament into the language of the Eskimos. Through the doctor's renditions of biblical stories and hymns, Anne confirms her need for a connection to a spiritual force, one that transcends the particularity of culture and language. Words, while they are limited instruments of human experience, connect not only man with man but man with God.

Their next stop is Nome, an old mining village on the south coast of the Seward Peninsula on the Bering Sea. There in the busy harbor, among the tarnished remnants of a gold rush town, Anne sees examples of the folly of human narcissism. By observing the chief of an ancient Eskimo tribe who is forced to sell trinkets to tourists in order to survive, Anne studies the social mythology of demigods, pathetic symbols of power in a universe beyond human control. The chief is taller and stronger than any of his tribesmen—he belongs to the "born rulers of the earth." And yet, Anne says, he is nothing more than a clown who ceases to be the king when he does not perform. He is worshipped as an image of royal invincibility. But he is, in fact, the court jester. Narcissistic, arrogant, and domineering, he mistakes his image for reality. Like Charles, Anne implies, he is the plaything of Nature, a "flying fool" deified by man.

Once again, they fly across the Bering Sea to its northeast peninsula and the Sea of Okhotsk. On the tiny Russian island of Karaginskiy, the secular concerns of a scientific and industrial society have obscured the spiritual aspects of life. This, Anne writes, is another barren land, no less sterile for its civilized modernity. Nonetheless, Anne finds a common bond with these women, whose culture and language are alien to her own. Spreading her photographs of Charlie on the table, Anne becomes connected to them and to "the boy" she left at home. While the Communist Party has replaced the priesthood, the human spirit cannot be crushed. Feelings and relations are the basis of what it means to be human.

Leaving Russia, they follow the chain of islands linking the Kamchatka Peninsula to Japan. The small island of Ketoi, with its little harbor cupped inside green volcanic peaks draped in fog, looks like the idyllic scene in a Japanese print—timelessly tranquil.

Like the skilled writer of a mystery tale, Anne slowly builds toward an overwhelming realization. Both writer and protagonist, ubiquitous surveyor and helpless victim, Anne spins a tale of pursuit by a monstrous Giant—the menacing fog. Her intent is to depict a battle of wills, confrontation between Man and Nature. Slowly the "shimmering unreal world," too beautiful to be threatening, succumbs to the enveloping fog. As fear creeps over her, Anne tries to keep it away with cold analysis, only to find herself imprisoned within it.

The Japanese stationmaster advises them to turn back, but his power, demonstrated only in words, is impotent against the force of Nature. Charles, her husband, is the true hero, the one who can conquer the Giant. He is the perfect shape of manhood—or is he? Until now, Charles has been the absent, invisible pilot-operator. Suddenly, he moves to center stage. He is the hero, tested to the very edge of the warrior's courage. Yet, writes Anne, Charles looks like a skeleton, flattened against the wind, a man "gritting his teeth in his lost fight." His is the very face of death. He, the jester who once made the princes laugh, is silenced by the power of death.

The flight slips further into allegory as Anne confirms her insights among the kind-hearted and provincial inhabitants of the remote islands of Japan. But all symbolic references cohere in her description of the Japanese tea ceremony, an event that does not have a geographic center. Even the reader though understands that it takes place on the outskirts of a city on one of the larger Japanese islands. Anne leaves the ritual remote from time and space, disconnected from the social realities of life in Japan. The tea garden is an oasis, an aesthetic setting apart from the turmoil of daily routine. If language has expressed the magic, silence is now the harmonizing melody. Words breed meaning, and yet they cannot touch the essential core.

All the people Anne meets on her pilgrimage "home" share one need: to be participants in a human and spiritual community. Anne asks, "What is essential to human life?" and carefully strips humanity of its social and cultural artifacts: language, convention, and technology. "Home" is no longer a physical refuge; it is the stillness at the center of one's mind, giving rise to self-knowledge and reconciliation. Silence is the alchemy that changes the artifacts of language and culture into the "gold" of beauty and art. Words and symbols, though no more than representations of human experience, are the only means for deriving understanding from the past.

Contrary to Hebrew scripture, Anne does not decry the graven image, the semblance of life through art. It does not presume power; it imbues life with meaning.

Death is the finality that cannot be challenged. But, Anne writes, it does not mean oblivion. Those we love must die, yet aesthetic symbols can re-create our memories and sustain our love. The bridge of words is like a beautifully woven "band of cloth" spanning the space between lovers. And, by implication, so is her book.

Anne cannot return to the home of her childhood. North Haven is forever changed; she cannot know again the joy of seeing her father and the baby wave good-bye. But life, stripped of certainty and magic, still holds room for affirmation. The scars of loss have been healed by art, the "beautiful abyss" between earth and sky. Anne has defied the God of her ancestors and justified the blasphemy of the written word. She has unthroned Charles, crowned Nature and Chance, and has begun to find her long way "home."

15

Purgatory

*A*nne prepares for the Hauptmann trial,
Englewood, 1935. (Lindbergh Picture Collection,
Manuscripts and Archives, Yale University Library)

*With rage or despair, cries as of troubled sleep or of a tortured shrill-
ness—they rose in a coil of tumult, along with noises like a slap of beat-
ing hands, all fused in a ceaseless flail that churns and frenzies that
dark and timeless air like sand through a whirlwind.*

—DANTE,

The Inferno,

FOREHELL, CANTO 3

JANUARY 1933, ENGLEWOOD, NEW JERSEY

The New Year resounded with life. The baby was growing fat and
strong, and more and more Anne released herself into the moment, feeling "younger and gayer" than she had in the long dark
months before. Thoughts of Charlie's death intruded, but Jon's presence
soothed everything.

While New York sank deeper into the Depression, and the restaurants and hotels were somber and half-empty, Anne and Charles moved
in the rarefied circles of the wealthy and the famous, insulated from a
country in turmoil. Foreign governments vied to honor them; the giants of industry and commerce pulled them to their side. Face to face
with the beautiful, coiffed, and velvet-gloved women of New York society, Anne set aside her "mask." Her own feelings, so close to the surface, made her self-conscious and vulnerable.[1]

They went to Amelia Earhart Putnam's house for dinner. But it was
to be a "prickly" evening. Earhart seemed to look right through her,
disdaining Anne's conventional femininity. Extending her long and
gracious hand, Earhart asked coolly, "Have you read *A Room of One's
Own?*"[2]

It was as if Earhart knew how difficult it was for Anne to break free
of Charles. Among female pilots, Anne never earned a reputation as a

true flyer. To this small coterie of women, Anne, who didn't fly solo, was viewed as an appendage to Charles. Earhart's question was almost rhetorical.

During the first week in January, Harold Nicolson and Vita Sackville-West arrived in town for their "American tour." Nicolson, a British foreign officer, a novelist, and a biographer who had recently abandoned his diplomatic career, was feeling middle-aged and depressed. His new career as a journalist and a radio broadcaster was unsatisfying. His wife, Vita, however, a bisexual with enough energy and optimism for both of them, had earned herself a reputation as a novelist. Both had become popular among the British avant-garde as social commentators and literary critics. Their public speeches and radio broadcasts supplemented Nicolson's uncertain income and Vita Sackville-West's shrinking family funds.[3]

On their first night in America, the Nicolsons dined with the Lindberghs at a private dinner at the Waldorf-Astoria. Nicolson was "shy to meet them," he wrote in his diary, after all they had been through. Charles was more complex than he had imagined. Nicolson was struck by Charles's physical beauty, as well as his "intellectual forehead, shy engaging manner, and his thin, nervous, capable fingers." His wife, wrote Nicolson, not referring to Anne by name, was "shy and retreating rather interested in books, with a tragedy at the corner of her mouth." Anne felt an immediate kinship with Harold. Vita appeared "veiled," but Anne found him open and warm, interested in her and in literature. Their conversation, which moved quickly from author to author, finally centered on Virginia Woolf. They talked about her books, sharing one another's impressions. Nicolson was admiring of Woolf's work, though critical.[4] Anne was puzzled by his comments on Woolf's books. She did not then know that Woolf was one of his wife's lovers.

As March 1, the anniversary of Charlie's death, grew near, Anne could not stop the flood of memory. Try as she did to dam it up, it swept over what she most wanted. And every night Anne recounted to herself the events in the last moments of her boy's life.[5]

But the reddening maples and the crack of the tulips through the frozen soil relieved her pain. She walked through the woods and sat on a log in the sun. In lyrical cadence, she wrote an ode to the eternal flow of life.[6]

Writing and flying were her only consolations. Flying, like art, Anne would later write, cut her free from the "strings" of memory and her daily routine.

Cut her free. This was the puzzle, one she had not yet solved. How to be grounded in daily life, yet be alive and creative, open to the beauty and adventure of flying and art? Her instincts pushed her into solitude, and her desire to fly took her away from Jon. While her writing had brought her self-reflection, she had not applied her insight to life. She knew she had to separate Charles's needs from her own, but for the moment, her ambivalence was paralyzing. She could neither commit herself fully to the care of Jon, nor could she ignore Charles's demands that she fly.

On April 16, she did consent to accompany Charles on an inspection tour for Transcontinental and Western Air. In October of 1930, Transcontinental Air Transport and Western Air Express had merged, establishing America's first all-air coast-to-coast passenger service.[7] Charles continued to work for the new conglomerate, purchasing planes and mechanical parts. On this trip, Charles was to inspect a new super-speed transport that would carry passengers between New York and Los Angeles in eighteen hours. Anne dreaded the publicity and the long hours in the back cockpit, but soon the sheer beauty of the countryside won her over. Distracting herself by reciting poetry, and delighted by the good weather and their safe landings, Anne relaxed. Once again, as she had during her early flights west with Charles, she felt that "the world was made for us."[8]

Baltimore, Washington, Pittsburgh, Columbus, St. Louis, Kansas City, Kingman—thousands of people came out to greet them each time they landed. As if to help them leave their tragedy behind, the public cheered their heroes on. After twelve days, Anne and Charles arrived in Los Angeles, the Promised Land—and she found that the broad green valleys, neat orchards, and big highways reminded her of Charlie. She had been pregnant with him on their flight to Los Angeles in 1930, and Charlie was still more real than Jon, even though Jon waited at home. Feeling like Alice in Wonderland, growing big and small, Anne tried to get back to "the right size" by amusing herself on the beaches of Los Angeles Bay. While Charles met with technicians and officials, Anne walked the shoreline, absorbed by the "unfold and slide" of the waves. Disguised in beach pajamas and smoked glasses, she roller-skated on the big concrete walk above the Palisades.[9]

But quickly her mood turned grim when, three weeks later, they were caught in a fog while flying back east. They were playing hide and seek with death and she closed her eyes and cried in terror that Death would "flow" right through her.[10] She chastised herself for not having faith in Charles; she believed her terror grew from her lack of faith.

In mid-May, a month after they had left, Anne and Charles returned to Englewood and Anne was happy to be home again with Jon. Charles, encouraged by the success of their California trip, began to plan another long-range survey. This time, he decided, they would fly across the Atlantic, first to Greenland and Iceland, and then to the continent. From France, they would fly south through Africa and circle home by way of South America. Charles estimated that the trip would take five months and planned to leave in early July. Jon would be eighteen months old when they returned, and their flights would have taken them from him for a third of his life. Yet Anne agreed. Perhaps her acquiescence was not merely to please Charles. Those around her believed she was afraid of getting too close to Jon.

They painted the Lockheed Sirius they had flown to Asia red and black and equipped it with a 710–horsepower Wright Cyclone engine and pontoons for landing on water. Their goal was to "link the continents by water routes," the last remaining barrier to commercial flight. They would test new equipment and gather slides of airborne microbes at high altitudes. Charles designed the plane for "total independence,"[11] with sophisticated radios and large fuel reserves, ensuring their safety in the icy north and along the sweltering Equator.

By June, Anne was back to practicing her Morse code. But all her preparations for the flight were infused with memories of Charlie; she worried about the safety of Jon in their absence. This time, her mother-in-law agreed to keep watch in Maine, along with Betty Gow, Elsie Whateley, and hired guards. Evangeline's presence, along with the promise of an escort ship and a radio base in Greenland, eased her fears.[12]

By month's end, however, death was again on her trail. Elisabeth had suffered another heart attack at her home in Wales. This time, Anne resolved not to be afraid. She had rehearsed everyone's death, even her own. Determined to leave a written legacy should she die in flight, Anne wrote a statement on July 8 and tucked it into her diary; it outlined her philosophy of mothering and her hopes for Jon. She wanted him to be sensitive and self-sufficient, but she feared he would be overprotected and lose the strength to stand alone. She hoped he would "meet [life] with optimism and courage and zest like his father and his grandfather."[13]

Anne and Charles left on July 9 from North Beach, New Jersey, stopping in North Haven to say good-bye to the Morrows, just as they had done two years earlier. Once more the townspeople crowded the harbor in their boats to greet them. Anne was struck by the frailty of her family alongside the permanent beauty of the islands. And yet she knew they would always protect her, and she could always come home.[14]

Anne would write home often, she promised her mother; her letters would give a purpose to her trip.[15]

As they flew east through Greenland and Iceland, though, Anne's letters glazed with distance. She sent home detailed descriptions of the mountains and the sky, the buildings and the houses, the lush gardens and the colorful dress of the Eskimos, but there was little expression of her emotions. While it was Anne's duty to keep a record of her impressions, she had left at home all that was real. Only when she watched the Eskimos dance did she begin to feel alive again. Expressing a theme which permeates her writing, she compares the perfect pattern of their music to the rhythms of the cycles of life.[16]

As they flew through the Shetland Islands toward the Continent, Anne's fears did become manifest; they were like an animal "hunger." Now deep into the trip, nearly six weeks, Anne realized it would be months before she could return home. All at once, her rage at Charles surfaced. He was asking her to live a life that was not her own. She had wanted to "stand alone" and survive in Charles's world, she wrote, but she knew she would always, in other people's eyes, be an extension of him, an appendage.[17] And her love for Charles was not the same, she concluded in her diary. It was no longer the "young-girl love" built on a dream and an ideal.[18] "Damn, damn, damn! I am sick of being this 'handmaid to the Lord.' "[19]

She wanted the "world of her own" she had tasted with Charlie during their first summer in Princeton—a world of creativity, home, and children. She wanted to "live simply, and have a garden and sun and work and a little girl—to play with Jon."[20] But as they carved their circle from the Shetland Islands across Denmark, Norway, Russia, and back to England, Anne had little hope that this world would ever be. She knew Charles would not accept her need to stay home.

Arriving in Cardiff on October 5, Anne and Charles visited Elisabeth and Aubrey. The weather was damp and dreary, but Elisabeth's rented house was "ablaze" with flowers. Beyond the white gate and fence, the drive was lined with fiery dahlias, and the old stone-wall house was covered with webs of tangled ivy. Elisabeth, at the door, looked as long and thin as a painted "portrait."[21] All her vitality flowed from her eyes—her eyes and her flaming red shoes, which clicked along the stone path as she ran to greet them.

She was at once strange and familiar, like an actress playing a role in someone else's dream of the way life ought to be. Elisabeth conducted her life with the skill of "one of Chaucer's model housewives," Anne wrote. And there was a new sobriety in Elisabeth's words. She was beginning to accept the facts of her illness, she told Anne, and was trying to come to terms with her constant chest pain.[22] After two days of polite talk and playful banter, Elisabeth said good-bye to Anne and Charles at the door. To Anne, she still looked like a portrait—life arrested in the glaze of art. Once again, her life had become a sequence of rituals dictated by social propriety. It was as if Elisabeth had traded her parents' "golden cage" for Aubrey's country squire landscape. Anne thought the prospect of death had made reality more inaccessible. She did not burden Elisabeth with her doubts about Charles.

They flew east to Southampton, then north to Scotland and Ireland, and circled down the coast of France to Paris. Paris was "one hectic rush," Anne wrote, full of ceremony and an intrusive press.[23] The French still regarded Charles as the Fairy Prince, and she and he had to fight crowds wherever they went. But it was not the crowds who were their enemy. Fog stalked them on their way to Amsterdam, and memories of the "white walls" of Japan gripped Anne with terror. She tried to keep her faith in Charles, but suddenly she lost control. "Wildly" she thought of going home, of taking the train back to Paris, of leaving Charles and never flying again. But imagining the headlines was enough to rivet her in place.[24]

"Are you getting a divorce, Mrs. Lindbergh?" the reporters would ask.

"Damn the newspapers," concluded Anne.

Filled with physical terror, Anne resolved never to live this way again. When she returned home, she would find her place. Now, however, it was her duty to go on with the trip, to go "the whole way" with her husband, as she wrote to her mother.[25]

Impatient to get home, counting the days as Thanksgiving and Christmas approached, Anne forced herself to restrain her emotions. But her letters assumed a haunting quality during the flight through Spain and Portugal toward the islands off the coast of Africa. Anne listened to the wind as it whirled and howled, reminding her of the night of the kidnapping, making them its plaything, determining the course and pace of their flight. Without the wind, they could not fly; once in its grip, they lost control. It became for her a defining metaphor, and Anne hunted for its meaning. The more they were tossed by the whim of the wind, the more frenetically Anne wrote in her diary.

The Cape Verde Islands were parched and brown. The once bustling

French seaport of Praia reeked with disease and death. Now a nearly abandoned port-of-call, to Anne it was a remnant of a dying empire. They were forced to stay overnight in the stationmaster's house, which Anne feared was contaminated by yellow fever. She felt lost in the land of "the Damned." Again they were playthings of the wind as they waited impatiently for it to rise. The next day, November 27, it blew cold and hard, and three days later, Thanksgiving Day, Anne held her breath as they took flight, first bouncing and stalling on the choppy sea and then suddenly aloft and free, she wrote, bound for the English colony of Bathurst on the western coast of Gambia.[26]

Despite the veneer of English gentility and the careful impression of propriety and order, Bathurst was another vacuous land. Even amid the lavish government houses, plentiful food, elegant dress and manners of their hosts, Anne felt no less a prisoner of the wind. And Charles felt his ship had failed him. He tried to lighten the plane by siphoning off fuel and unloading equipment, but the only reasonable course was to wait for the deadening calm of the air to change. The nights at Bathurst once again echoed the night of the kidnapping, when life was snuffed out by the howl of the wind.

"Listen!" Anne wrote in her diary, quoting Humbert Wolf's poem entitled "Autumn: Resignation": "The wind is rising, and the air is wild with leaves."[27] But if the wind was the instrument of death, it was also Anne's only hope for Christmas at home with Jon. Two days later, their plane was up and rising. The engine sounded like "a person breathing, easily, freely, almost like someone singing, ecstatically climbing."[28]

Even as Anne counted the days and wished for home, Charles, unhindered by anyone's schedule, conducted himself like a boy on a fishing trip. After flying southwest to Natal, Brazil, he decided to take a thousand-mile side trip up the Amazon to Manaus, Port-of-Spain, and Puerto Rico, delaying their return home by three weeks. Anne, crestfallen, refrained from complaining and chose once more to obey.[29] When they landed in Miami on December 16, the city seemed to explode with life—signs and shops and billboards and people. So close to home, Anne was thrilled to receive a wire from her mother in New York: the baby was fine and waiting for them in Englewood.[30]

But three days later, hours from home, flying from Charleston up the coast to New York, Anne was overtaken by fear. The abstract notion of "home," which had propelled her forward day by day, buttressing her strength and galvanizing her will, seemed another ring of Hell. Already, she felt torn by pressures and obligations: the press, the ceremonious fawning of officials, caring for the baby, finding a place to live, writing a new book, making Charles happy. The flight, in retrospect, seemed easy. She had had one task to do, and Charles was her master. Now, she had to please the world. She must, she wrote in her diary,[31] have the courage to say "no."

After a chase by cameramen in planes dangerously close to theirs, Anne and Charles landed at College Point, Long Island. Once on the ground, they slipped by reporters into the Edo Aircraft factory and out the front door. To the press, the Lindberghs were heroes returning from a grand adventure. They raised the world above the squalor and hopelessness of the Depression. Home safe after thirty thousand miles of flight, tanned, vibrant, and smiling, they seemed nothing less than a miracle. The *New York Tribune* pictured the hand of God, cupped over white-capped waves, cradling a silver biplane. Although the plane was misrepresented—the *Tingmissartoq*[32] was a low-winged monoplane—the message was clear: the Lindberghs' mission had been worthy of God's protection. The irony, of course, was that news about the Lindberghs sold newspapers, and while God might protect them, the press would not.

Back in the routine of Next Day Hill, Anne found life on the ground chaotic. Jon was "spoiled," and everyone seemed to know how to handle him better than she did.[33] She took him out to Falaise to visit the Guggenheims for three days, hoping to establish again their old rapport. But a return to Next Day Hill to face Christmas at home without her mother, Con, and Dwight Jr. was more than Anne could handle. They had gone to spend the holidays with Elisabeth and Aubrey, who had moved to Pasadena.

Disheartened by her prognosis but still optimistic, Elisabeth was wheeled around her garden in a custom-made bed, certain that she was shocking the neighbors with her unconventional vehicle for sunbathing. Again like an actress on the stage, she told everyone that it was actually fun to stay in bed, and that she felt certain—down to the very marrow of her bones—that she was healing. In truth she felt like a kept woman, an invalid who had to paint her face to please her master.[34] She missed her family in Englewood and she missed her school. When she married Aubrey the year before, Elisabeth had delegated the school's directorship to her mother and its daily operations to Connie Chilton. Although Elisabeth believed that her vision was being honored, she missed the sense of fulfillment she had gained with it.

Elisabeth had a gift for pretense; Anne had none. In the weeks after Christmas she was miserable in Englewood, and everyone knew it. After being alone with Charles for five months, Anne was restrained by the surveillance of her mother. There were too many opinions, she wrote, too many servants, and no privacy. Concerned about the safety of Jon, now sixteen months old, Anne and Charles decided to rent an apartment in the city rather than a house in the country. She had found a "rather small place," she wrote to her mother-in-law, a penthouse with two terraces, a sunny one for Jon and the other with beautiful views of the skyline for her and Charles. Jon would sleep in the adjoining room, and they would keep the dogs with them for protection. And she would begin to write the narrative of their transatlantic trip.[35]

While Anne wrestled with her discontent, her public image shone brighter than ever. The only female flyer who had crossed the Atlantic or the Pacific to Japan, Anne was awarded the Hubbard Gold Medal by the National Geographic Society. Her skill on the wireless radio, the society declared, ranked her as a world expert. The course of her flights, wrote the *New York Times,* "should be marked on every map in every school room. The boys already have their circumnavigator. The girls now have theirs."[36]

The Lindberghs' popularity was at an all-time high. *Newsweek* reported that Charles Lindbergh's signature was worth more than that of any celebrity alive—at least fifty dollars. Organizations, schools, and the media used the Lindbergh name to bring honor and profit to themselves. The Veteran Wireless Operators Association gave Anne a gold medal, Smith College honored her sister Constance, and even Charles Lindbergh, Sr., was resurrected as a prophet. The publishers Dorrance and Company reprinted his 1918 book, *Your Country at War,* claiming that his writings had foreshadowed the National Recovery Act and Roosevelt's New Deal legislation.[37] They hoped that his son would be pleased by their actions. Charles was pleased, probably more than he let on. He was learning to use his popularity as a political tool.

On February 9, 1934, citing collusion, President Roosevelt ordered the cancellation of all commercial airmail contracts. Although it appeared to be an act of belligerence against the airline industry, it was the culmination of a long series of investigations. Ever since the Kelly Act of 1925, when the airplane was recognized as a viable adjunct to the postal service, the postmaster general had had the authority to award airline contracts at his discretion. But it wasn't until the McNary-Watres Act of 1930, which gave him the power to transmit airmail payments to commercial carriers, that his authority began to have real implications for the airline industry.

In May and June of 1930, Postmaster General Walter F. Brown hosted what became known as the "Spoils Conferences." The purpose of the meetings was to divide the airmail contracts among invited representatives of all the major airlines. Uninvited smaller operators were not welcome. These secret meetings led to wild stock promotions and tens of millions of dollars to airline promoters, who invested little or no cash. The larger companies gobbled up the smaller ones, creating huge conglomerates and millions of dollars for entrepreneurs and stock owners, who in large part happened to be Republicans. In the summer of 1931, a small airline spurned by Brown leaked the news to the press. The result was a congressional investigation that exposed the machinations of Brown and the airlines.[38]

Lindbergh was linked to the scandal when it became known that he had received twenty-five thousand shares of TAT stock, valued at $250,000, as well as the option for twenty-five thousand shares at a preferential price when he became a technical adviser in 1928. When the Democrats and Roosevelt came to power in March 1933, the pressure was high to redress the injustice.

Lindbergh, who had begun his career as an airmail pilot, and who worried that his name would be smeared, along with that of his employer, TAT, now TWA, sent a telegram to Roosevelt the very next day, leaking it simultaneously to the press. He wrote that the entire industry was being condemned without a trial, which transgressed the right of all citizens, especially those who had worked so hard to ensure its success. Roosevelt was appalled by Lindbergh's action. It was unethical, he believed, in view of Lindbergh's popular acclaim, to register his protest publicly without giving him the opportunity to respond in private. But Lindbergh was implacable. He feared not only for the safety of all the inexperienced army personnel who had taken over the airmail routes, but for the future of commercial aviation. On February 15, he received a "polite telegram" from the postmaster general, chastising him for his unjust accusations made without knowledge of the facts. It was sent to the Morrow estate, where, the next day, Lindbergh received it on his return from New York.

Immediately, he duplicated the telegram and sent it to the newspapers, using it to further condemn the Roosevelt administration. Pitting his power to manipulate public opinion against the authority of the government, Lindbergh deepened the wound. Roosevelt had tried to squelch Lindbergh's protestations by offering him a place on a new committee formed to study the army operation of airmail, but Lindbergh, growing more bold, threw the offer back in his face and used it to deride Roosevelt.

Unfortunately, Lindbergh's prediction of disaster came true. By the end of the first week of army operations, five pilots were dead, six were injured, and eight planes were wrecked. By May, twelve pilots were dead, and the cost to the government was almost four million dollars.

In June the Air Mail Act of 1934 was passed, giving the air routes back to the airlines and placing them under the jurisdiction of the Interstate Commerce Commission.

The incident, however, had made clear to Lindbergh the breadth of his influence on the press and public opinion. He was beginning to believe that he had a moral imperative to take a stand on public issues.

As the airline scandal thrust Lindbergh's name back into the public arena, it had the unintended consequence of making Betty Morrow's poetry famous. A window into the Morrow and Lindbergh lives, her poetry was the coveted treasure of *The Atlantic Monthly*. With the death of her husband, the murder of her grandson, and the impending death of her daughter Elisabeth, Betty began to break with conventional rhyme and form, creating a dialogue between language and emotion. In April 1934, three of her poems were published by *The Atlantic Monthly*: "Saint of the Lost," "Asphodel," and "Hostage." "Saint of the Lost" is the least personal of the trio, an ode to Saint Anthony, watchman of the fallen, the hurt, and the lost. "Asphodel" is a retreat into myth, riddled with the sadness of her husband's death and the presentiment of her oldest daughter's passing. But "The Hostage," written in the masculine third person, is a clear expression of her anguish in the wake of Charlie's kidnapping. She speaks of violent murder and its forms—strangling, stabbing, shooting, throwing, starving, drowning—and the vicarious death of those who wait for the "hostage" to return, exploring the evil that is human and the emotions it evokes. The poem reflects the family's rage and marks a turning point in Betty's work.

Through this time of grief and foreboding, Anne and her mother gave each other courage and consolation. But in spite of the similarities in their writings, Anne never shared the intimacy enjoyed by her mother and Elisabeth. Especially in the face of Elisabeth's illness, reminiscent of the slow and painful death of Betty's twin, Mary, Anne felt inadequate and pushed aside. Like Betty, Anne sensed she could never fill her sister's loss in her mother's life, and both of them knew that Elisabeth was dying.

Within three months, Elisabeth had gained seventeen pounds. Hoping her plumpness would project an image of health to her friends, she protested that she really looked wonderful. In truth, she was growing weaker by the day. In a letter written to her mother about the future of her school, Elisabeth began to come to terms with the closeness of her death. The letter carried the solemnity of one who wanted to make her wishes known. Wrapped in salutations of love for her mother, it was a statement of Elisabeth's educational philosophy.

Her school meshed progressive and traditional values. She wanted to keep "the best of the old and the best of the new." She would find a way of educating children that would free them from the constraints of mindless conformity. While she would draw upon the ancient principles of Plato, there would be those who would call her a rebel. Nonetheless, she believed that the quality of life depended on self-knowledge and relationships. It was her goal to help children confront "the truth."[39]

Reflecting her parents' commitment to the community, yet unaccepting of their Calvinist predilections, Elisabeth's plan to foster individual needs was a desire for her own legitimacy and, with it, a kind of self-absolution.

While Elisabeth approached reconciliation, Anne was at odds with her life in New York. She and Charles hated the tumult of the city and thought about moving to California. Anne wrote to Elisabeth that she and Charles had bought a new single-engine, high-wing monoplane, built by the Monocoupe Corporation of St. Louis. It would be ready at the end of July, and they planned to visit her and Aubrey in California.

In early July, Anne luxuriated in the peace and beauty of the Morrow home in North Haven. The lull between trips let her slip into a midsummer torpor. She reveled in the island sun and soaked herself in long days with Jon, living a child's life again.[40]

For the first time, Anne was beginning to appreciate the past without dredging up the darkness of the kidnapping. Jon was just Jon—not a baby like Charlie, not Charlie's brother, but her child—unique, sufficient. And yet, she did distance herself from him; practicing a survival mechanism to protect herself from loss. Anne resolved to see the "essentials of life," the essence of childhood, not Jon alone.

She left North Haven feeling healthy and strong, she wrote, at one with her family and with nature. Charles, too, was well. Tanned and rested, on August 2 he flew a 3000-horsepower Sikorsky seaplane, under the auspices of Pan Am, and topped all records for a seaplane flight.[41] The craft, it was anticipated, would cut two days off the run from Miami to Buenos Aires, putting South America only five and a half days from New York. With planes like these, the 710-horsepower *Tingmissartoq* was quickly becoming a relic. Anne and Charles had arranged to have it displayed at New York's Museum of Natural History.[42]

By early fall, Anne and Charles had given up their apartment in the city and moved back to Englewood. Living in an apartment doesn't work, wrote Anne, but she didn't want to spend another winter in her mother's home. Nonetheless, something had lifted. Anne felt "young and gay," capable of ordinary conversation, dancing, and the companionship of friends. Even the press recognized it in her work. They called her first travel article for *The National Geographic* "a fast and friendly narrative," written in a "gay humor."[43] While the article was of great interest to the public, the narrative was uninspired. The language was terse, and the descriptions threadbare, except for the rare moments when Anne's poetic rhythms took hold. It was written too close in time to the experience, and its meaning was buried beneath fact and convention. But for Anne it was a tour de force, detailed and comprehensive, a rich source material for her new writings.

Finally, after two months, their new monocoupe was ready, and on September 12 they flew to St. Louis to pick it up. The craft, however, proved defective. They were grounded twice for minor repairs, once in Wichita, when a wheel support broke on landing, and again in Woodward, Oklahoma, for motor trouble. In Oklahoma, they were forced to land on a farm owned by Homer Atkins. Although Mr. Atkins didn't recognize the Lindberghs when he invited them home for supper, his wife knew immediately who they were. Thrilled to have them in their hometown, hundreds of ranchers and their families came to meet them. With an air of generosity, Anne and Charles sat on the front porch of the Atkins' ranch and discussed the problems of Depression farming—crops, drought, and federal subsidy. It was a moment of closeness with the public who adored them; a successful attempt at empathy and understanding. Charles felt at home with the farmers, immediately picking up the rhythm of ranch life. He accompanied his host on his morning chores and milked the cows in a neighbor's barn. Anne talked to the children, smiling and laughing at their stories, and spent time in the kitchen with Mrs. Atkins.[44]

After three days of delay, Anne and Charles arrived in Los Angeles, on September 17. Will Rogers, a friend of the Morrows, had offered his Santa Monica ranch to accommodate both the Lindberghs and Elisabeth and Aubrey Morgan. "Elisabeth looks marvelous," Anne wrote to her mother; she seemed healthy and indomitable. As usual, Elisabeth bowled Anne over with her energy, her perspective, and her sense of accomplishment.[45]

But one day later, as Anne and Charles basked in the California sunshine, they received a call from Colonel Schwarzkopf. On September 20, after a chance remark to a gas station attendant to whom he had passed a $20 gold ransom note, Bruno Richard Hauptmann, characterized by the press as a "blond-haired, tight-lipped carpenter" and former German Army machine-gunner, was arrested at his home in the Bronx as a suspect in the kidnapping.[46] As the Lindberghs flew toward Englewood, they were sucked back into the belly of darkness. "Flailing their arms like sand through a whirlwind," they arrived at the Morrow estate.

16

The Arrest

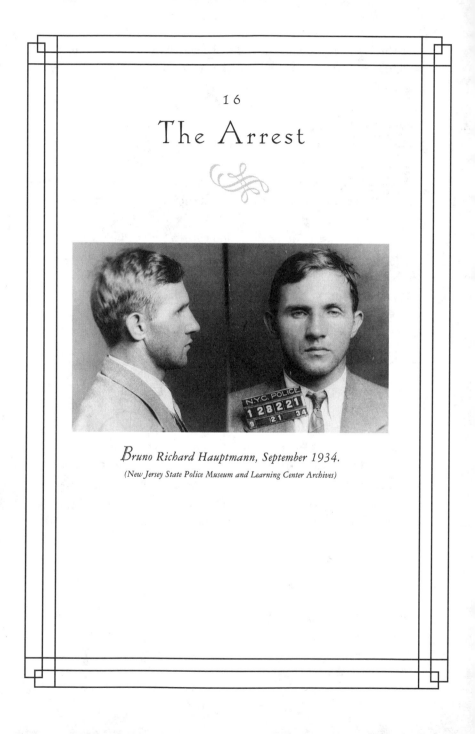

Bruno Richard Hauptmann, September 1934.
(New Jersey State Police Museum and Learning Center Archives)

God's purpose is justice. I am a friend of Nature since I was a child.
I see God growing up in the grass, and I hear the winds.

— BRUNO RICHARD HAUPTMANN,

OCTOBER 3, 1934[1]

TUESDAY, SEPTEMBER 18, 1934, THE BRONX, NEW YORK

Anna Schoeffler Hauptmann stood among the goldenrod and the mountain daisies on the terraced lawn beside her family's home. Her robust eighteen-month-old son, Manfred, named for the German air ace Manfred von Richthofen, romped in the warm autumn air as Anna watched, in her flowered robe and slippers, in the shade of the fading oaks. From the street, she noticed a man watching her. He approached and showed her his badge.[2] "I would like to see you, upstairs," he said.

Anna carried Manfred into the house, gave him to the care of her downstairs neighbor, Louisa Schuessler, and followed the man up the wooden stairs and into her apartment. Moments before, the rooms had been neat and spotless. Now, they were swarming with policemen, shoving aside furniture, rummaging through drawers, and emptying the contents of closets onto the floor. She found her husband, Richard, stooped next to their bed, handcuffed to a policeman and surrounded by agents, battering him with questions.

"What is this?" she yelled.

Richard didn't answer.

Putting her arms around him, she asked in German, "Did you do anything wrong?"

"No, Anna," Richard replied in German.

She yelled louder, this time breaking down in tears, "Tell me! Tell me if you did anything wrong! What are they doing here?"

"They're here over a gambling problem I had the other night," Richard replied.

Satisfied, Anna backed down. As she was led outside, she noticed the police had stripped the bedclothes off Manfred's new ivory-colored crib.

Two hours earlier, three black police cars had lain in wait as Richard pulled his dark blue Dodge out of the garage.

At thirty-five, Bruno Richard Hauptmann had an air of tutored breeding. He knew how to dress and how to flash his money with the nonchalance of a man-about-town. His face had a boyish quality, but his deep-set eyes spoke of cool determination. He was pleasing rather than handsome, and his delicate features contrasted with his athletic frame. His brawny arms and large powerful hands, strengthened by years at a carpenter's lathe, hung gracelessly beside his muscular legs. He looked like a laborer in rich man's clothing, surly and arrogant yet strangely serene.

His laconic mien and self-conscious speech belied a fun-loving, impulsive personality. He liked to hunt deer and rabbits, to gamble on the stock market, and to drink and play the mandolin with friends. While he had a taste for women other than his wife, he considered himself a dedicated father and a family man. He believed in God, was loyal to his friends, loved children, and delighted in the beauties of nature.[3] By all appearances, Bruno Richard Hauptmann was a gentle man with good Christian values—a self-made success with an eye on the American Dream.

In September 1934, while many of his friends and family were out of work and out of luck, Richard Hauptmann was building his fortune. He had suffered a loss in the early winter of 1932, but he seemed to have an instinct for picking stocks. He bragged to friends that he could make $2000 in one day, as much as $50,000 with any luck.[4] When he met Isidor Fisch, a skinny, short, big-eared German Jew, in the summer of 1932,[5] they became friends and business partners. Hauptmann continued to invest in the market, and Fisch traded in pelts and furs.

Each morning at about nine, Hauptmann would leave his five-room apartment in the tree-lined suburban section of the northeast Bronx, and drive his sedan down to his stockbroker's office. No one knew exactly how much money Hauptmann had made, but it was enough to buy him expensive suits, walnut furniture, a new radio and phonograph, vacation trips, and fashionable dresses for his wife. Meanwhile, those around him were scavenging for jobs and learning the art of self-denial.[6]

Hauptmann had emigrated from Germany eleven years earlier, but not through the usual channels. Born in 1899, the son of a stone mason in a small town in Saxony, Bruno Richard was the youngest of the five children of Paulina and Herman Hauptmann. When he quit school, at the age of fourteen, he went to trade school to study carpentry, drawing, and architecture. In 1917, he was conscripted into the army and served on the German front with a regiment in Königsburg. Six weeks before the end of the war he was hit on his right temple with shrapnel. He lay unconscious for hours and was left for dead, but he crawled back to his post on his hands and knees. Though dizzy and disoriented, unable to fit his helmet back on his swollen head, he resumed his duties.[7]

When he returned to his small native town of Kamenz in 1919, life was different. He was dizzy and forgetful most of the time. His father had died, and his two brothers had been killed in the war. He lived alone with his mother, working as a mechanic during the day and helping her at home at night. Frustrated by his work and his poverty, Hauptmann committed a series of assaults and robberies, for which he was convicted and jailed.[8] One of the crimes consisted of robbing two women as they wheeled their baby carriages along a deserted street; another, of climbing a ladder into the mayor's window in search of jewelry and cash. Later, Hauptmann said that the war had taught him that nothing was sacred.

After his third arrest, Hauptmann escaped from jail. Considered a hardened and dangerous criminal by the authorities, he was quick to realize there was no place to hide. In the fall of 1923, Hauptmann left Germany as a stowaway on a passenger ship bound for the States. After another abortive attempt on a German ship, he successfully evaded discovery on an American cruiser, the *George Washington,* bound for New Jersey. On November 26, 1923, his twenty-fourth birthday, Hauptmann walked down the gangplank on the pier at Hoboken, a free man. He had no passport and only two cents in his pocket. His intent was to save five hundred dollars and to move to California to be with his sister.

By memorizing English phrases, Hauptmann secured a job as a dishwasher and then as a mechanic. Through the kindness of friends, he met Anna Schoeffler in the spring of 1924, and by summer they decided to marry. Anna, sturdy, red-haired, and blue-eyed, was a twenty-six-year-old factory-worker and maid, who had legally emigrated from her hometown in Germany. She was attractive to Richard for her wholesome good looks, her good Christian character, and her $2500 savings account in a bank. She reminded him, he later said, of his saintly mother. Richard secured a steady job as a carpenter, and they married in the fall of the following year. During the next four years, the Hauptmanns prospered. They moved from a furnished room to an apartment of their own, and then north to Needham Avenue in the Bronx, where they rented the upstairs floor of a two-story home owned by Mr. and Mrs. Rauch, German Jews.

For two and a half years, the New Jersey State Police, along with the New York City cops and the FBI, had searched for the kidnapper. Clues had shifted the focus of the investigation across the river to New York City. The head of the investigation was James Finn, a doggedly ambitious city cop who had been on the New York City force for twenty-seven years. He had been assigned to protect Lindbergh during his return to New York after his flight in 1927, and Harry Bruno, Lindbergh's public relations man, had never forgotten him. After the New Jersey investigation floundered, Bruno requested that Finn be assigned to the job. In January 1933, Finn was put on full-time investigation of the crime, and was promoted to lieutenant. Frustrated by Schwarzkopf's unwillingness to share information, he had taken it on himself to chart the track of the gold ransom notes as they had surfaced.

By the fall of 1933, he could see a pattern.[9] At first, the bills seemed to have been deliberately scattered throughout the city, but after a year and a half, the bills started to surface in two specific areas—along Lexington and Third Avenues in Upper Manhattan, and in the German-speaking area of Yorkville. As a rule, they were folded in signature fashion, in eight parts, by a man who had the habit of throwing them on the counter for retrieval by the clerk. When those who had received the bills were questioned, they consistently remembered a man identical with Condon's description of Cemetery John: about forty, of middle height and weight, with small features and a triangular face, and wearing a soft felt hat. The chance comment to a gas station attendant in upper Manhattan, who had written Hauptmann's license number on the bill, brought the police to his blue Dodge and his Needham Avenue home.[10]

Once the New York police identified Hauptmann as the suspect, they informed Schwarzkopf and Hoover. Immediately, city, state, and federal agents streamed into the Needham Avenue vicinity to watch the area and the house. Still fighting for jurisdiction, like children grabbing for the prize, each demanded the right to have an equal number of agents present on the scene. The men caused a ruckus in the streets, blaming one another for creating suspicion that might tip off the suspect. They were warned by neighbors, bitten by a dog, and admonished by the local police. After several days of negotiations, they developed a plan, agreeable to all agencies, for arresting Hauptmann with the least resistance.[11]

Cautioned by the forensic psychiatrist Dudley Schoenfeld, the officers agreed that it would be better not to take him from his home. By studying the ransom notes and the kidnapper's bargaining behavior, Schoenfeld had deduced that he was a schizophrenic who viewed himself at once as helpless and powerful. Schoenfeld believed that he would have homosexual tendencies and would be quiet and restrained. Furthermore, he predicted that the man would carry a ransom note with him at all times as an emblem of his victory.[12]

As Hauptmann drove at a fast clip down White Plains Avenue toward Manhattan, the black police sedans followed, but with enough space to avoid detection. Hauptmann nonetheless saw them through his rearview mirror and sped through the streets at forty miles per hour. When traffic was blocked by a city sprinkler truck a half-block north of East Tremont Avenue, the lead police car pushed Hauptmann's Dodge to the side of the road and brought it to a stop. One detective rushed into the passenger seat beside the driver; the other police stopped behind and scrambled toward him. At gunpoint, they pulled Hauptmann out of the car, frisked him, and handcuffed him.

In deference to Schwarzkopf and the New Jersey State Police, Arthur (Buster) Keaton had been called to the scene to make the arrest. He pulled Hauptmann's wallet out of his pocket, and had what must have been the inestimable pleasure of removing from it a $20 gold ransom note.

To Anne and Charles, visiting with Elisabeth and Aubrey at Will Rogers's ranch in Santa Monica, Schwarzkopf's call came with little warning.[13] While the hunt for the kidnapper had been unrelenting, so too had been their efforts to put Charlie's murder behind them. Now they were forced to confront it again. Anne and Charles flew east, retracing the route they had flown at leisure just a few weeks earlier, and Jon was rushed by train from North Haven back to Englewood.[14] There, the family gathered once more to decide what to do.

Things were happening fast, and evidence was quickly mounting.[15] In spite of Hauptmann's cool denial of complicity in the crime, within hours of his arrest the police found two stashes of Lindbergh gold notes, totaling $14,600, hidden between the joists of his garage. Along with the notes, they found fieldglasses, several maps of New Jersey, drawings of a homemade ladder and two windows, lumber and nails that matched those used to build the ladder, a small, empty green bottle marked "ether,"[16] a loaded pistol, paper that matched that of the ransom notes, and Condon's phone number scribbled on his closet wall.[17] The next morning, the FBI called Schwarzkopf to congratulate him. Hauptmann's handwriting samples, spelling, and grammar matched those of the ransom notes.[18] Within a week, on the same day that Anne wrote to Evangeline, Charles, disguised in a hat and horn-rimmed glasses, had come face to face with Hauptmann in a line-up. Unknown to Hauptmann, Lindbergh had unequivocally identified his voice as that of Cemetery John.[19] Another half-century of archival investigation would turn scholars into detectives and facts into allegations, but within a week of his arrest, a worldwide network of police, reporters, and criminologists were convinced that Hauptmann was the kidnapper of the Lindbergh baby. MYSTERY SOLVED, declared the *New York Times*.[20]

While Schwarzkopf commandeered Hauptmann's extradition to New Jersey, Hauptmann's lawyers gathered evidence to support a plea of insanity. State examiners, however, deemed Hauptmann sane and morally cognizant.[21] He exuded not "evil" but humanity insensate; intelligence unmediated by common emotion. He spoke in a low, barely audible voice and displayed no excitement, perspective, or imagination, consonant with a man of above normal intelligence. Born with a speech defect and a form of disgraphia, which caused him to affix an *e* to the ends of words, he suffered spells of imbalance and dizziness resulting from his wartime head injury.[22]

Day after day, Hauptmann sat in a wooden chair answering the questions of police and psychiatrists. He spoke matter-of-factly in his high-pitched voice, showing no signs of doubt or fear. With his physical endurance and his steadfast denial of guilt, he wore out everyone; he never asked for his wife or his lawyer. Yet he could not account for his actions on the day of the crime and had no alibi.[23] He had sought employment at the Majestic Apartments in Manhattan on the morning of March 1, but he had been turned away, had driven home, put his car in the garage, and, as far as anyone knew, had disappeared. Lacking proof "beyond a reasonable doubt" that Hauptmann was not in New Jersey on the day of the kidnapping, the New York City police had no choice but to release him to the custody of Colonel Schwarzkopf.[24] His trial was set for January 2 at the State Courthouse in Flemington, New Jersey.

17

Testament

Anne testifying in the trial of
Bruno Richard Hauptmann, January 3, 1935.
(AP/Wide World Photos)

TESTAMENT

But how can I live without you?—*she cried.*

I left all the world to you when I died:
Beauty of earth and air and sea;
Leap of a swallow or a tree;
Kiss of rain and wind's embrace;
Passion of storm and winter's face;
Touch of feather, flower, and stone;
Chiseled line of branch or bone;
Flight of stars, night's caravan;
Song of crickets—and of man—
All these I put in my testament,
All these I bequeathed you when I went.

But how can I see them without your eyes
Or touch them without your hand?
How can I hear them without your ear,
Without your heart, understand?

These too, these too
I leave to you!

—ANNE MORROW LINDBERGH[1]

CHRISTMAS 1934, ENGLEWOOD, NEW JERSEY

It was the week before Christmas 1934, but no one in the Morrow home felt like celebrating. To the friends who had gathered for Sunday dinner, Next Day Hill reeked of death.[2] The silver was laid, the china was set, the Christmas holly was about to be hung, but the stately blue dining room, once bustling with warmth and vitality, seemed cold and bare.

Elisabeth had died three weeks earlier of pneumonia in the wake of abdominal surgery. The doctors had believed her appendix was diseased, but surgery revealed a thick adhesion that had strangled her bowel.[3] Three days later, Elisabeth contracted pneumonia and, within a week, was dead.

When Anne received the phone call from her mother in the early morning hours of December 3, she instinctively knew it signaled "the end." For Anne, Elisabeth had died too soon—they had so much left to see and share with each other. There were roads without ends, sentences half-finished, and sketches of the future only half-drawn, and now there would be no completion. Life had a "pasteboard" reality—ephemeral, illusory, suspended in time.

Again, birth and death commingled, turning Anne's thoughts to Charlie, imbuing her daily life with sorrow. As she paced the gravel paths in the Morrow estate, the trees and sky were disconnected from her "former life." Her desire to preserve the memory of Elisabeth was reflected in her poem.[4]

"REVISITATION"[5]

. . . No, I must go
Back to the places
Where you put your hand
To see them now without you
Gutted bare, swept hollow of your presence
I must stand alone and in their empty faces stare
To find another truth I do not know
To balance those unequal shifted planes of our existence
Yours and mine
To fix the whirling landscapes of the heart
In which I walk a stranger both to space and time . . .
Then I shall be able to refind myself
And also you.

But with the turn of the year, Anne's former life returned, its laws the same as they had been. On January 2, the madness took hold again—the crowds, the reporters, the frenzied energy of the human hunt. Everyone, from the ordinary spectator to the celebrated personality, craved the touch and feel of the Lindbergh kidnapping. It was as though the violation of an icon permitted them access to forbidden places within themselves. Energy rushed into the quiet town of Flemington, New Jersey, like air into a giant vacuum.

No one standing on Main Street on that bright winter morning, as the limousines and vans filled with celebrities and journalists moved like juggernauts through enemy territory, would have known that the nation was still in the grip of the Depression. The trial breathed new life into the town's faltering economy. The population doubled nearly overnight. The Union Hotel, across the road from the courthouse, hired sixteen new hands and filled all of its fifty rooms. Vendors filled the streets, selling trinkets and phony memorabilia: replicas of the three-piece ladder, bookends shaped like the courthouse, photographs of Lindbergh with false signatures, and snippets of baby hair sold by a young man with suspiciously fine curly blond locks.

In a perverse way, it was American capitalism at its best. Products flooded the market, and the market grew bigger every day. A hundred and fifty prospective jurors, a hundred reporters, fifty cameramen, twenty-five communications technicians, prosecution and defense lawyers, dozens of investigators, thirty court officials, and three hundred spectators, red-faced and cold, pushed up against the large courthouse windows, waiting for a glimpse of a celebrity.[6] The century-old courthouse, with its pillared façade, stood as a symbol of calm above the fray.

But inside, the unimposing nature of the courtroom, with few architectural details, blurred the edges of rank and function. It looked more like an Elizabethan playhouse than a court of law, and, in many ways, it had the intensity of theatre.

Hired by the *New York Times* because of her novelist's eye, Edna Ferber analyzed the voyeurism of the hovering crowds and the allegor-

ical quality of the unfolding drama. Disgusted by the behavior of the
publicity-seeking socialites who attended the trial for "trend rather
than tragedy," she wrote in her piece, "Vultures at the Trial," "we are
like the sans-culottes, like the knitting women watching the heads fall
at the foot of the guillotine."[7]

Indeed, there was the smell of execution in the air. The spectators
turned their gaze from Lindbergh to Hauptmann as they listened to the
opening words of the Attorney General for the State of New Jersey,
David T. Wilentz. Although he was an experienced prosecutor, he had
never before tried a criminal case, but he had appointed himself to the
task of representing the state when Hunterdon County could not afford
to support the case.

A Russian-born Orthodox Jew who had been brought to America at
the age of one, Wilentz had made his way up the legal and political hierarchy by his precise and scholarly mind. The thirty-eight-year-old father of three, small and wiry, with dark penetrating eyes and
slicked-back hair, dressed in stylish, double-breasted suits, a white felt
hat, and a Chesterfield coat.[8] But his air of restraint turned electric on
the floor of the courtroom as he paced among the desks and chairs, sitting, standing, waving his hands, and modulating the tone and power
of his voice to tell his story. Choosing his words with a storyteller's flair,
he addressed the jury of housewives, farmers, and laborers, taking them
through the ten-week ordeal, conjuring up images of violence, shock,
betrayal, and grief.[9] Hinging his case on murder committed in the act
of felony,[10] Wilentz told the jury that the state would prove that Bruno
Richard Hauptmann was a cold-blooded killer who, acting alone, had
kidnapped the Lindbergh baby for the sole purpose of extorting money.

Edward J. Reilly, the attorney for the defense, was so moved by
Wilentz's opening speech that he called it an "inflammatory summation" and asked that the case be dismissed as a mistrial. The judge denied the request. Reilly was Hauptmann's second lawyer,[11] hired by
Anna when the Hearst newspapers offered to pay a retainer of $25,000
in exchange for exclusive interview rights to the *New York Journal*.[12] At
the height of his career, Reilly had been known as one of the most suc-

cessful trial attorneys in New York City. Shrewd, skillful, and disarming, he had defended difficult cases—from bootleggers to female killers—two thousand in all, earning him the reputation of "the bull of Brooklyn." Now fifty-two years old, with a florid face from years of drinking, he was slow and plodding in comparison with the ubiquitous Mr. Wilentz. His courtroom demeanor had become erratic and his flamboyance had turned to eccentricity. Dressed in a black morning coat, striped pants, and spats, as though he were a groom at a brideless wedding, he shifted his eyes behind heavy-rimmed glasses and moved his hands in sweeping gestures. Using his low and resonant voice like a finely tuned instrument, he carefully formed his words. From the beginning, his self-conscious wit had tried the patience of the judge, who saw himself as a paternal figure, protecting the reputations and lives of all those within his courtroom.[13]

Thomas W. Trenchard was an experienced trial judge with a reputation for fairness. While some criticized his slow and deliberate manner and his liberal interpretation of his role, none questioned his integrity. After twenty-eight years on the bench, the seventy-one-year-old judge was known as a principled and compassionate man whose belief in the American court system and the inalienable rights of the accused had translated into a record rarely achieved. He had never ruled on a capital offense that was reversed on appeal.[14]

Anne and Charles were among the first to be called. As Anne rose to take her place on the witness stand on the morning of January 3, all sound and gesture ceased. The moment, one journalist wrote, hung in suspense so painful that one could not fail to register the gentle quality of her presence.[15] Unused to the rhythms of the court, Anne sat down too soon and was asked to rise to take the oath. She was dressed in a blue silk suit and a black satin beret, and sat tall and straight, her legs crossed and her eyes riveted on Wilentz's face. In a measured voice, formulating her responses with care, Anne followed Wilentz and told the story from the arrival of Betty Gow, on March 1, at the Hopewell estate, to the discovery of her baby's body ten weeks later. Without evidence of emotion, she examined each of her baby's sleeping garments, confirming their authenticity as those he had worn on the night of the kidnapping. Satisfied, Wilentz turned his witness over to the defense. As the court watched Reilly rise, no one could have anticipated the compassion of his words.

"The defense feels," he said softly, "that the grief of Mrs. Lindbergh needs no examination." Anne glanced gratefully at Reilly and then nearly leaped up from her chair.[16]

Charles was next. With a formality that almost smacked of the absurd, Wilentz opened with two simple questions.

"Are you the husband of the lady who was just in the stand?"

"I am," Charles said.

"What is your occupation?"

"My occupation is aviation."

Wilentz then led him into a moment-by-moment narrative, replete with charts and documents of the sequence of events from his arrival for dinner on the night of March 1, through the ransom exchange in the Bronx cemetery, to the identification of his child at the morgue in Trenton. For several hours, Charles answered Wilentz's questions in a precise and careful manner, noting exact times, dates, and places. To those unfamiliar with the case, Charles's narrative was a seamless story. But Reilly knew there were issues that Wilentz had deliberately left unaddressed.

Once Reilly took the floor, there were no holds barred. Moving back and forth in time, dealing with personalities and theories rather than facts, Reilly hacked away at Charles's composure, challenging both his memory and his judgment, forcing him to admit investigative possibilities that had gone unexplored: Charles's refusal to have lie-detector tests given to the Morrow and Lindbergh servants or to permit probes of their personal and professional backgrounds; his refusal to cooperate with the police except on his own terms, making unilateral decisions at key points in the investigation. Furthermore, the investigation was hindered by the dissension among the police agencies; the mishandling of the evidence at the scene of the crime; Condon's unusual role in the ransom exchange and possible complicity in the execution of the crime; and Charles's espousal of John Hughes Curtis's gang theory.

Pressed to articulate the reasons for his unconventional course of action, Charles stated that once the Condon-kidnapper liaison had been established, he decided "the events would probably be peculiar, not according to the ordinary logic of life."[17]

True to his reputation, without documents, facts, or substance, Reilly had exposed Charles as controlling and unreasonable. While all unexplored channels would remain in the realm of theory, it was clear that Anna Hauptmann had hired a masterly lawyer.

If Reilly had punctured Charles's persona, Anne had not noticed. Overwhelmed by the trauma of recounting the kidnapping of her child in a public forum, she left the courtroom, intending not to return. Charles, however, went every day, with a .38–caliber pistol strapped to his chest, in the company of his brother-in-law, Aubrey Morgan.[18] Sequestered at the Morrow home, Anne knew of the trial only what she viewed through her husband's mind.

For the moment, however, the trial had set her free. Finally, she believed, justice would be done. For the first time since Charlie's death, Anne stopped running, allowing her thoughts and her grief to come to the surface. Over and over she dreamed of Elisabeth, permitting herself to feel the loss. The Elisabeth of her dreams carried Anne through "strange temples" and long dark hallways. But one dream had an unexpected twist: Elisabeth was tired and upset, and Anne was beginning to feel like a burden. They went through a door into a large, enclosed piazza, and Anne sat down to read a magazine. Suddenly their roles were reversed; Anne was carrying Elisabeth, who sobbed and clung and demanded her comfort.[19]

Words were the key—Anne reflected when she awoke—not those written in the privacy of her diary, but in the open piazza, the public square. Only then could she stand on her own and carry the weight of Elisabeth's legacy.

Harold Nicolson, who was to write Dwight's biography, had become the unexpected midwife to Anne's work. He saw her as a gentle and sensitive young woman caught in a bizarre and punitive drama, and he labored daily to gain her trust. It was he, in fact, who had read her magazine article about her transatlantic flight and who made sure to let her know he thought it "excellent." Charles was too close to the experience and too invested in her work to be anything but critical; Nicolson, however, gave her hope that her slow "illogical mind" could understand aspects of life worth recording. The baby was dead, but she was alive, and she did not want her writing to be "crushed . . . smothered . . . hurt." If she couldn't write, "someone should kill this thing in me . . . [and] send me back to children."[20]

While Anne built barricades against the trial, the public knew no bounds, and those who strutted upon its stage moved with a heightened sense of drama. After the Lindberghs and their servants had been heard, those who professed to have seen Hauptmann took the stand, and Reilly gave the public the show it desired. The prosecution gathered circumstantial evidence, and the defense had nothing but theory. Witness after witness came to the stand, pointed at Richard Hauptmann, and became subject to Reilly's attempt to cast doubt on their credibility. His tactic was to belittle their character and to jar their memory, building suspicion in each juror's mind. Although he often lost the game, he played his hand well. He managed to make Hochmuth, the eighty-one-year-old neighbor of the Lindberghs who claimed to have seen the murderer on the day of the crime, look like a half-blind, incompetent meddler; he managed to undermine the reliability of Perrone, the taxi driver who had acted as the liaison between Cemetery John and Dr. Condon.

But Condon was a fierce opponent, one who could chase Reilly around the ring. The New York Times did not need a dramatist to describe the courtroom scene. Condon was the protagonist, the playwright, and the director. And there was justice in his tone of authority. Lindbergh had taken a ride, heard a voice, and paid a fee; it was Condon who had made a pact with the devil. But if he was the biggest star among the witnesses, he was also the prime target for the defense. While he and Wilentz smoothly walked through the ten-week sequence of events between the crime and the discovery of the baby's body, Condon and Reilly vied for the attention of the court. Recognizing Condon's narcissism, Reilly flattered his keen powers of observation and admired the quality of his physical prowess—and managed to press Condon against the ropes. But, to the delight of the spectators, not for long.[21]

As the contenders battled in public, Anne wrestled with her inner voices and sought comfort from her friends. Corliss Lamont, the gentle and philosophical son of the Morgan partner Thomas Lamont, had come to commiserate with her during the trial. To Anne's surprise, they discussed Elisabeth, love, and "a woman's place." She delighted in the generosity of Corliss's mind, grateful not only for his understanding but for his acceptance of who she was. What a relief, she wrote in her diary, that he didn't try to change her. "Why can't one keep that admirable distance when one is married, that respect for another person's solitude?"[22]

Her Englewood friend Thelma Crawford Lee tried to encourage her,[23] but it was Con's friend Margot Loines who drew Anne into the nourishing universe of ideas. An aspiring actress, Margot radiated a *joie de vivre* and moved with grace, precision, and femininity. Anne was quick to recognize the rare confluence of intellect, sensitivity, and strength. A Theosophist, Margot meshed Hindu sacred writings with Protestant ethics, challenging the duality of Christian virtue and sin. She taught Anne to seek, through meditation, a spiritual reality beyond her senses. She celebrated the human mind, validating its wickedness as well as its divinity. Anne later said that Theosophy satisfied her "hunger" to accept the "evil" within herself and in others.[24]

Charles worried that he was losing control of Anne. He believed Anne's dependence on her friends and her diary was a threat to their relationship. For the first time, Anne had secrets. When Anne wanted to meet Con in Boston for a show, Charles balked, insisting it was "disrespectful" to the trial. But there was an inconsistency to his thinking, Anne wrote. "C. so rarely cares about appearance." Still, Anne did as he said, even though her decision to stay home made her feel like a caged animal, imprisoned in a life she hadn't created and was powerless to change.

The trial had allowed the public eye to pierce the walls of her home, affecting even her movements among family. She had feared impropriety, but now there was a greater danger. She was afraid that her rebellious anger toward Charles would make every act, every thought, every dream, every emotion, seem to him an act of betrayal. She wrote:

> *I must not talk. I must not cry. I must not write—I must not think— I must not dream. I must control my mind—I must control my body— I must control my emotions . . . But last night, lying in bed . . . trying to be like a stone . . . I felt I could understand insanity and physical violence . . . anything.*[25]

Unable to sleep, Anne took long walks around the estate, seeing figures in the patterns of trees and snow, and reciting poetry. Her struggle with her thoughts seemed to work; she found the courage to write. She wished her writing could rise to the standards of Harold Nicolson's. She found the first five chapters of his biography of her father an astute and "charming" analysis. He had captured her father well, and, with him, her memories of Elisabeth. She confided to her mother about her book and revealed her grief about her father and Elisabeth. Finally, Anne wrote triumphantly in her diary, she was "purged" of herself.[26]

Meanwhile, at the trial, a wood technologist Arthur Koehler, of the U.S. Forestry Service, testified that the wood used for the ladder could be traced to a lumberyard in the northeast Bronx, where Hauptmann had worked. The ladder was linked to Hauptmann in four ways: the place where the wood was purchased; an incomplete sketch of a ladder and a dowel pin in one of his private notebooks; the distinctive tool marks made by Hauptmann's chisel and plane; and a section of the ladder that matched the floor planks in Hauptmann's attic. As he listened to the expert's testimony, Hauptmann, noted a journalist, looked as if the life had been sucked out of him. "His muscular frame sagged in his chair between his guards, and his pale face was whiter than ever."[27]

Hauptmann went back to his cell to scan photocopies of his bank and brokerage accounts. Even though four people, who claimed to have been eyewitnesses to the exchange of money and ransom notes, had identified him during the first week of testimony, Hauptmann believed he could prove his innocence by accounting for the money in his possession at the time of the arrest. He attributed his assets of $44,500 to stock investments and to his investments with his business partner, Isidor Fisch. He had already testified that Fisch, shortly before his departure for Germany and subsequent death, had left a package with Hauptmann for safekeeping. Hauptmann had put it on the shelf of his broom closet.[28] But it had since been proven that Fisch died homeless and penniless. Between 1932 and 1933, Fisch had made few deposits in his bank, none for more than $700. The Internal Revenue Service had evidence that Hauptmann had only $303.90 at the time of the crime, and that, though his total assets amounted to less than $5000 before April 2—the day of the ransom exchange—he had spent $15,000 in the subsequent two and a half years.[29]

Frustrated by Reilly's inconsistent and halfhearted efforts, Hauptmann took the stand in his own defense on January 24, three weeks into the trial.[30] Reilly tried to portray Hauptmann as a steady wage-earner and family man, living modestly, saving money, and enjoying the small pleasures of camping, playing cards, and making music with his friends. Dressed like a gentleman, in a gray suit, a light-blue shirt, and a dark blue tie, Hauptmann answered Reilly's questions in halting English. Together they established Hauptmann's alibis for the night of the kidnapping and the time of the ransom exchange, and reconstructed his relationship with Isidor Fisch. When Wilentz took over, he shot rapid-fire questions at the witness, attempting to expose the inconsistencies in his testimony.[31]

Hauptmann leaned forward, with a level stare, and responded in tempo to Wilentz's fire. Yet despite his effort at self-control, Hauptmann, unaware of his own inconsistencies, permitted Wilentz to establish a pattern of criminality, secrecy, hoarding money, and telling lies. Realizing that he was losing the game, but determined to maintain the battle of wills, Hauptmann taunted Wilentz with smiles, sometimes laughing aloud at the prosecutor's attempts to entrap him. On the second day, though, Wilentz began to break him down.

"This is funny to you, isn't it?" asked Wilentz. ". . . You think you're a big shot, don't you? . . . Yes. You are the man who has the willpower . . . Willpower is everything with you, isn't it?"

"No. Should I cry?" countered Hauptmann. ". . . I know I am innocent."

But when Wilentz accused him of lying in the face of God, Hauptmann pointed a finger at Wilentz and shouted, "Stop that! . . . Stop that!"[32]

No one could have fabricated a better story: the heroic Lindbergh couple, sweethearts of the world, victims of a brilliant and satanic mind bent on their destruction. That very day, millions read Hauptmann's testimony. The recording and the transmission of thousands of words a day was seen as a journalistic feat, meeting the demand of a voracious public. The *Times* called Hauptmann's self-defense nothing less than thrilling, a real-life masterpiece surpassing the best in fiction.[33]

Meanwhile, Judge Trenchard struggled to keep the crowds under control. More than a hundred "witnesses" were subpoenaed daily. Often, they turned out to be friends of the defense attorneys. No longer would the summonses be honored, the judge said. Using the prerogatives of New Jersey law, patterned on the British, Trenchard anguished over every nuance and detail, angering some and gleaming the admiration of others. Ford Maddox Ford, hired by the *New York Times* for his observations, noted that every one of the judge's statements "strikes you as the only thing that could be possibly said—by justice that is at once supremely impartial and benevolent . . . The whole assembly has an air of a family gathering."[34]

Anna Hauptmann gathered her strength to help her husband. She had moved with her baby to a friend's house in Flemington so that she could see him every day. As direct as her husband was evasive, as trusting as he was cautious, Anna declared his innocence with a shrill wail that seemed the very stuff of tragedy. But Anna's love for him took an ironic twist when she finally testified on his behalf. After establishing herself as a careful housewife, she could not explain why she hadn't seen on her closet shelf, for a year and a half, the box filled with thousands of dollars in gold notes. Try as she might to wash her husband clean, she succeeded only in tainting his testimony.[35]

Determined to get away from home, Anne disguised herself in bangs and dark brown glasses and went to dine with Margot Loines in the city. Margot was an oasis; along with her sister Con, Margot was among the few in whom Anne could confide. She shared with her the thoughts and impressions, even the contents of the cherished notebook in which she daily recorded snippets of prose and poetry to console and inspire herself.

Most often, she quoted the *Duino Elegies* of Rainer Maria Rilke, which captured her feelings of abandonment and spiritual alienation. One needn't go farther than the first lines of Rilke's *First Elegy* to see why Anne heard her voice in his words:

> *Who, if I cried out would hear me among the angels' hierarchies? and even if one of them pressed me suddenly against his heart: I would be consumed in that overwhelming existence.*[36]

If only she could learn to understand the voices of man, God, and nature, she might know what she needed to do, she told Margot.

On February 9, five weeks into the trial, Anne sneaked into the courtroom through the back door to avoid the camera and the crowds. It was her mother's turn to testify, and she had promised to be there. It was, she wrote, far worse than the day she testified. She had more time to think and feel and observe the ugly haggling over detail. "How incredible," she wrote, "that my baby had any connection with this!"[37] To Anne, the courthouse was little more than a child's toy stage set, the kind she had played with as a girl.

Three days later, the testimony completed, the lawyers vied for the jury's trust. Banging his fists and pointing his fingers, Reilly summarized the case for the defense much as he had laid it out at the beginning:

the unconfirmed character of the servants; the lost evidence at the scene of the crime; the mishandling of the ladder by police and press; the dog that never barked; the possible substitution of the attic plank; the money Hauptmann received from Fisch; and Hauptmann's alibis for the night of the kidnapping and the time of the ransom exchange. Reilly warned the jury, "Judge not lest you be judged."[38]

The next day, Wilentz summarized the case for the prosecution. Talking to the jury as if they were his living room guests, Wilentz cited the established evidence:[39] Lindbergh's gold certificates in the joists of Hauptmann's garage; the tracing of the ladder's wood to Hauptmann's attic and lumberyard; the fieldglasses; the maps; the sketches; the ransom note stationery; the IRS records that documented Hauptmann's finances before and after the crime; the implausibility of Fisch's role; the failure to incriminate the Lindbergh or Morrow servants. Exhausted, Wilentz made a personal and emotional plea for justice. Calling Hauptmann "un-American," and emphasizing his "animal quality," Wilentz demanded a conviction without mercy. "I know how difficult it is to believe that one person committed this crime," he said, "[but] that is not important, because if fifty people did it, if Hauptmann was one of them, that would be all there was to it . . . All the evidence leads to Hauptmann, only to Hauptmann."[40]

Judge Trenchard addressed the jurors with concluding remarks as trenchant as if the weight of civilized society hung on their decision. He pleaded with them to question all the evidence, to leave no facet unexamined, and to remember that the defendant was presumed innocent unless he was proved otherwise, beyond a reasonable doubt:

> *The evidence produced by the State is largely circumstantial. In order to justify the conviction of the defendant upon circumstantial evidence, it is necessary not only that all of the circumstances concur to show that he committed the crime charged, but that they are inconsistent with any other rational conclusion. They must exclude the moral certainty of every other hypothesis but the single one of guilt, and if they do not do this, the jury should find the defendant not guilty.*[41]

He reminded them that the charge was "murder committed in the course of a burglary," and although it was a charge of the first degree, the court could recommend a sentence of mercy: life imprisonment at hard labor.

Anne wrote in her diary, "Judge Trenchard's summation is cool, dignified, wise, and infinitely removed from petty human suffering and yet relevant, just, and true to life."[42]

As the jury deliberated, Anne, Charles, Con, and Betty, along with Harold Nicolson and Aubrey Morgan, sat down to dinner in the Morrow dining room. The wireless radio blasting from the pantry and the drawing room was so loud that jazz and jokes resounded through the house. Charles punctuated the dinner conversation with wild sneezes, the only ungoverned gesture in an otherwise remarkable show of manners and restraint. With dinner over and no verdict yet announced, they retired to the drawing room, noticeably upset. Betty, who conducted the evening as if she were a young teacher just out of Smith, insisted that they hold "a family council" about the "proper illustration" for Nicolson's book. Obediently, everyone complied, grateful for the diversion to get them through the evening.

It was past eleven when the jury, after ten hours of deliberation, reached a verdict. The crowds at the courthouse roared as the official radio announcement was made: Hauptmann was guilty—condemned to death, without mercy.

"A-tishoo! A-tishoo! from Lindbergh," Nicolson wrote home. "They were all sitting round—Con with embroidery, Anne looking very white and still."

"You have now heard," broke in the announcer, "the verdict in the most famous trial in all history. Bruno Hauptmann now stands guilty of one of the foulest . . ." A-tishoo! A-tishoo! A-tishoo. "Turn that off, Charles, turn that off." Then we went into the pantry and had ginger beer. And Charles sat there on the kitchen dresser looking very pink about the nose. "I don't know," he said to me "whether you have followed this case carefully. There is no doubt at all that Hauptmann did the

thing. My one dread all these years has been that they would get hold of someone as a victim about whom I wasn't sure. I am sure about this— quite sure. It is this way . . ." And then quite quietly, while we all sat round in the pantry, he went through the case point by point. It seemed to relieve all of them . . . Then we went to bed.[43]

Before she slept, Anne noted in her diary that it had been as bad as the first night at Hopewell.[44] The howl of the crowds echoed the howl of the wind that whipped around their house the night the baby was taken. Again, man and nature seemed to confirm the evil that killed her child.

Hauptmann, it was observed, was "a broken man." For the first time, he lost control, "sobbing wildly" alone in his cell.[45] Anne, too, felt broken—like "a broken pot."[46]

18

A Room of Her Own

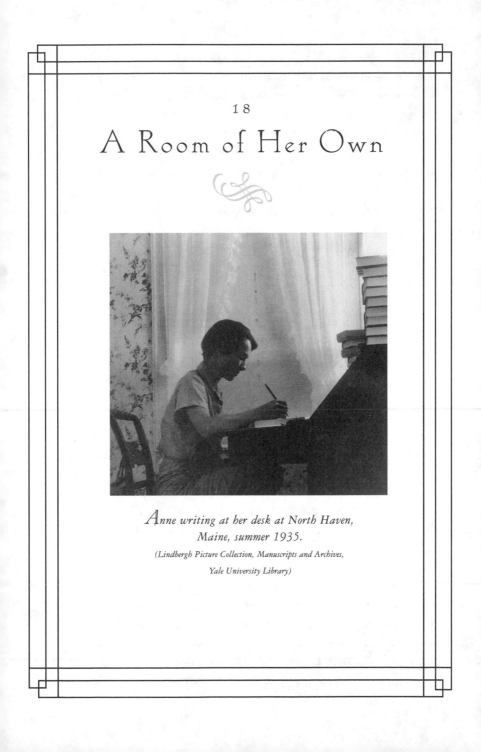

*Anne writing at her desk at North Haven,
Maine, summer 1935.*
(Lindbergh Picture Collection, Manuscripts and Archives,
Yale University Library)

*The extraordinary woman depends on the ordinary woman. It is only
when we know what were the conditions of the average woman's life—
the number of her children, whether she had money of her own, if she had
a room to herself, whether she had help in bringing up her family, if she
had servants, whether part of housework was her task—it is only when
we can measure the way of life and the experience of life made possible to
the ordinary woman that we can account for the success or failure of
the extraordinary woman as a writer.*

—VIRGINIA WOOLF,
Granite and Rainbow

SPRING 1935, NEXT DAY HILL,
ENGLEWOOD, NEW JERSEY

Anne sat at a desk in her mother's home, pouring her rage into
her diary. She felt like a victim of God and man, but what
could she do? Rail against an inscrutable God? Or her loving
husband, as much a victim as she? Or herself, for failing to protect her
child? It was impossible to unravel the threads of Charlie's death; each
path led nowhere.

She knew it was the ordinary things that mattered. They were the
"safety, the infinite safety and deliverance from terror." The hand on
one's shoulder, the leaning of one's head, the breath of her child, her
hand on his curls—these were "the great wells of security and faith"
that built the "precious structure of life."[1]

When Smith College offered Anne an honorary degree for her accomplishments in aviation, she was indignant. All she had done, she
wrote to Con, was be a good wife. She had done nothing that warranted
an award. Nevertheless, Charles was extraordinarily proud, she wrote.
Why, she wondered. Because she was a reflection of him?

Contemplating the poetry of Yeats, she wrote in her diary that "love has nothing to do with happiness, and marriage very little to do with love."[2]

In April, Anne submitted the final draft of her manuscript of *North to the Orient* to Harcourt Brace. Afraid that they might publish it only because she was Charles's wife, and just as afraid that they wouldn't publish it at all, she whipped herself into a panic. Charles panicked, too. On rereading the manuscript, he had said that if he read the first paragraph, he would not read the book. Throughout the week preceding the submission, Charles had edited the manuscript, going through every chapter with painstaking precision, changing the smallest words and phrases. Anne felt she would "burst" with anxiety, but it was better to burst than to die inside. Perhaps, she consoled herself, she should just have another child and worry about "fundamental" things.[3]

She had not expected a response for at least a week, but she was called by Mr. Harcourt the following evening, just as she was putting Jon to bed. "It is splendid," he said. "I would take it even if it were written by Jane Smith. It's a good story, it's moving, it's well-constructed, and parts of it border on poetry." He wanted to close the deal at his office the next day with her and Charles.[4]

Joyful beyond anticipation, Anne went out to the garden, just as she had as a little girl, to take stock of her life. This time she counted her moments of triumph, not her sins: the Jordan Prize for writing that she had won at Smith, her first kiss, Charles's asking her to marry him, the birth of her children, Harold Nicolson's confirmation of her ability to write. It wasn't happiness, she wrote; it was "something fiercer," and she wondered whether her joy and pride should make her ashamed. But she could not deny a sense of power. They couldn't be sins, she convinced herself at last. They connected her in a vital way to the flow of life. Finally, she had "a place and a reason for living." Finally, "I can hold my head up," she wrote.[5]

Within a week, though, reality set in. Writing a book was like having a baby, Anne concluded, and "publishers are like obstetricians." She would have to let go of the idea that she was "accomplishing God's mission."[6]

God's mission or not, the acceptance of the book made her "a real person"—capable, discerning, and articulate. She would never have the energy or the practicality of her mother or Charles, but she had found a way of life and a craft.

The public announcement of the Carrel-Lindbergh perfusion pump in June, however, confirmed her belief in Charles's superiority. When the papers proclaimed his feat as sensational, even more important than his historic flight,[7] Anne wrote, "[it] is not a fluke, not chance, not charm and youth and simplicity and boyishness, but the expression of a great mind."[8] She, like her mother, believed Charles was the ideal of manhood. Without Charles, she would be nothing. He was the fire through which she burned, the alchemy that changed her base metal into gold.[9]

And yet, the more she praised Charles, the more her own life pounded within, like "a giant," demanding to be free. By mid-August, the pounding stopped. *North to the Orient* received complete critical acclaim. *The Saturday Review* wrote, "Mrs. Lindbergh has a seeing eye and a singing heart"[10]; *Newsweek* wrote, "She can write as well as she can pilot."[11] Harcourt Brace had printed twenty-five thousand copies, but to everyone's surprise, including Mr. Harcourt's, by the end of the first week, Anne's book was into its third printing.[12] The Harcourt Brace salesmen had assumed it would sell on the Lindbergh name, whether or not it had any literary merits of its own, but once the book reached the stores, the dealers gave it their enthusiastic backing. The book was national as well as trade news. Many papers ran front-page stories. Later, it was chosen for a National Booksellers Award as the most distinguished book of general nonfiction for the year.

But the success fanned her fears. She anguished over what she would write next. Although Charles, as usual, gave her encouragement and perspective, she was beginning to see the price she paid for his borrowed strength. He made it clear that she had to play the game according to his rules. When he asked her to fly with him, she had to go.

As if to rediscover the roots of his childhood, Charles took Anne on

In September 1931, Anne and Charles arrived safely in Japan after a two-month-long flight through the northwest tundra of Canada to Alaska and down the Bering Strait. Much of the territory had never been seen from the air, and constant walls of fog forced them to fly blindly, with only Anne and her Morse-code radio to guide them. (Lindbergh Picture Collection, Manuscripts and Archives, Yale University Library)

Anne and Charles at a tea ceremony in Tokyo. Anne is moved by the spirituality of the ritual, which leads to self-knowledge through silence and meditation, a theme that will come to dominate her work. (Corbis/Underwood & Underwood)

Anne addresses the public on the state of the flooded regions in China, on behalf of the Federal Council of Churches, February 1932. (Culver Pictures)

In September of 1932, Anne and Charles and the Morrow family gather, as usual, at their estate on North Haven, Maine, for their end-of-summer reunion. Elisabeth, now thirty, is frail with heart disease; Constance, eighteen, is a student at Smith; and Dwight Jr., twenty-four, is a student at Amherst.
(Lindbergh Picture Collection, Manuscripts and Archives, Yale University Library)

After Jon's birth, Anne resumes flying with Charles as his copilot. She smiles in the cockpit of their newly equipped Lockheed Sirius, which will take them to Europe, Africa, and South America on a five-month survey tour of potential passenger air routes, summer 1933. (Lindbergh Picture Collection, Manuscripts and Archives, Yale University Library)

Anne Lindbergh in a kayak in Holstein, Greenland, during the Lindberghs' survey flight of 1933. (Lindbergh Picture Collection, Manuscripts and Archives, Yale University Library)

Anne and Charles land in Leningrad in September 1933 on a survey tour through Europe. Here she poses with a group of Russian sailors. (Popperfoto)

Anne and Charles arrive in Miami, Florida, on December 16, 1933, after their prolonged flight to South America and through the Caribbean. Anne is glad to be back after five months away from home. Her baby, Jon, waits for her in Englewood. (AP/Wide World Photos)

Charles Augustus Jr. celebrating his first birthday on June 22, 1931. (Popperfoto)

Charles A. Lindbergh, Jr., was abducted from his nursery in the new Lindbergh home in Hopewell, New Jersey, on March 1, 1932. The State Troopers and federal investigators comb the crime scene for clues. (UPI/Corbis-Bettmann)

Charles Lindbergh is among the first to testify at Bruno Richard Hauptmann's trial in Flemington, New Jersey, in January 1935. Charles came to the trial every day with a .38-caliber pistol strapped to his chest. (UPI/Corbis-Bettmann)

Hauptmann, the German-born carpenter accused of kidnapping the Lindbergh baby, being led to the courthouse in Flemington, New Jersey, for his trial, January 1935. (UPI/Corbis-Bettmann)

*R*eporters gather outside the courthouse to cover the trial of Bruno Richard Hauptmann. Hundreds of newsmen write thousands of words each day to feed the demands of a voracious public. The account of the trial in the newspapers was seen as "a real-life masterpiece," surpassing fiction. *(Corbis-Bettmann)*

*D*uring the final weeks of the trial, Colonel Norman H. Schwarzkopf, Superintendent of the New Jersey State Police, and Anne Lindbergh accompany Mrs. Morrow to testify at Hauptmann's trial. It was the second time Anne attended, preferring the seclusion of her parents' home. "Justice doesn't need my emotions," she said. *(AP/Wide World Photos)*

Anne and Margot Loines sailing off the coast of North Haven, summer 1935. Margot offers Anne new hope for spiritual reconciliation with death and evil through her belief in Theosophy. (Lindbergh Picture Collection, Manuscripts and Archives, Yale University Library)

Anne at her desk on North Haven, Maine, working on the manuscript of Listen! The Wind, *her travel account of the 1933 transatlantic survey tour, summer 1935. (Lindbergh Picture Collection, Manuscripts and Archives, Yale University Library)*

Anne and Jon, age four, with their guard dog Thor and their Highland terrier Skean in the garden of Long Barn, winter 1937. (Lindbergh Picture Collection, Manuscripts and Archives, Yale University Library)

*L*ong Barn, Kent, England, home of Vita Sackville-West and Harold Nicolson, which the Lindberghs rented in 1936-1937 to escape death threats to their son Jon and the intrusions of the American press. (Lindbergh Picture Collection, Manuscripts and Archives, Yale University Library)

*A*nne in a straw hat, writing on a terrace overlooking the gardens at Long Barn. The beauty and seclusion of the house and land restored Anne's faith in nature and life, permitting her once again to write. (Lindbergh Picture Collection, Manuscripts and Archives, Yale University Library)

*A*nne and Charles arrive in Germany, July 1936, flanked by Truman and Kay Smith. At the request of Smith, the U.S. military attaché, 1935-1936, Charles has been invited by the Reich to tour aviation factories and review developments in air warfare technology. (Ullstein Bilderdienst)

*I*n July of 1936, on their first trip to Germany, Air Minister Hermann Goering shows Charles his ceremonial saber while Anne, Kay, and Truman Smith look on. (Popperfoto)

*A*lexis Carrel, French surgeon, sociologist, and biologist who received the 1912 Nobel Prize for Medicine. Impressed with Charles's facility and skill, Carrel invited him to join his laboratory staff at the Rockefeller Institute as a technical consultant in 1932. *(UPI/Corbis-Bettmann)*

A cart delivering furniture to the Lindbergh house on Illiec, a small rocky island off the coast of Brittany, purchased by Charles in the spring of 1937 at the request of his mentor and collaborator, Dr. Alexis Carrel. In Carrel's laboratory on the neighboring island of Saint-Gildas, Charles and he designed apparatus that would preserve human organs in the hope of prolonging life and creating a superior human breed. *(Lindbergh Picture Collection, Manuscripts and Archives, Yale University Library)*

*A*ntoine de Saint-Exupéry, the French writer and aviator whom Anne met in New York in 1939 shortly after her return to America from Europe. An admirer of his essays and narratives, Anne felt an immediate spiritual kinship that inspired her later work. *(UPI/Corbis-Bettmann)*

*I*n May of 1941, Charles speaks at a rally for the America First Committee, a broad-spectrum political-pressure organization opposing aid to the Allies in World War II. *(UPI/Corbis-Bettmann)* a trip to visit his family in Michigan and Minnesota. In the last week of August, they flew to Detroit to see Charles's mother, whose mind, wrote Anne, was "tidy," "accurate," and "clear."[13] In Anne's view, at least as presented in her published diary, her mother-in-law had managed to rid herself of volatility and paranoia. Though Anne would always think of Evangeline as strange, she dutifully portrayed her as the essence of restraint and control.

She and Charles went on to Minnesota to visit Mrs. George Christie, Charles's half-sister Eva, who had married a newspaperman and lived in a small northern town, Red Lake Falls, with her son, George, and daughter, Lillian. Eva, the brainy and jealous daughter of Mary La Fond and Charles Sr., had blossomed into a pretty, dignified, and independent young woman, wrote Anne. After visiting Charles's Uncle Frank and Aunt Linda, Anne concluded that the Lindberghs were made of "stern stuff." On the way home, they returned to Detroit to see Charles's maternal relatives, the Lodges. They too were stern, recorded Anne, as well as "ascetic" and religious.[14]

Once home, Anne had had enough of the Lindberghs, including Charles. She was "oppressed" by his incessant demands. She wanted to be free of him, and she wanted to be alone. He belittled what she valued most—her desire to write letters to her family and friends. "I cannot write letters for I feel C.'s disapproval. I cannot write other things because he is there. I just sit."[15]

Anne convinced herself that she had to accept the extraordinary conditions of marriage to a man whose personality and fame obscured her gifts and dictated the course and direction of her life. How could she achieve the impossible, she asked herself? How could she satisfy Charles's demands, preserve the integrity of their relationship, and yet satisfy her needs as a woman and a writer? She was beginning to think that marriage was "an impossible ideal," that husband and wife should be "further apart."[16] Like Psyche holding a candle to her husband's face, Anne was beginning to understand that Charles, in spite of his public image, was painfully vulnerable. There were distortions in his personality that permeated their relationship, but she would never be free until she could define them.

In September 1935, Alexis Carrel published his book, *Man, the Unknown*.[17] In it, he proposed a relationship between mental acuity and moral perception and the influences of disease and environment on each person's physical and psychological health. He urged the reader to see himself in the context of both human history and his individual biological ancestry, and he set forth "scientific evidence" to support the genetic determination of one's mental and physical attributes. His bias became clear in his advocacy of constructing a "genetic elite" through the voluntary practice of eugenics—the sterilization of those who could not produce healthy and intelligent progeny. In this context, women were viewed as childbearing vehicles, measured according to their social use in creating a hereditary aristocracy. We must be "reasonable" and "economical," he wrote. Criminality and insanity could be prevented only by eugenics and by changes in education and social conditions. Prisons should be abolished. Criminals should be whipped, sterilized, or gassed. Conventional modes of thought and systems of ethics must be dismissed as sentimental in the face of necessity. "The development of human personality is the ultimate purpose of civilization," he wrote.

His book was reflective of the burgeoning eugenics movement in the United States,[18] legitimated by the 1927 Supreme Court decision *Buck vs. Bell*,[19] but it was still considered extreme and ridiculous by most educated people. The press deplored the pseudo-science that camouflaged the author's misogyny and racism. *Time* magazine called it a "wild rant" and "a colossal joke."[20] Proliferating reviews blasted Carrel for his racism, ignorance, and unscientific methods, but Anne and Charles remained publicly silent.

And then Anne, determined to write her book, and frustrated by Charles's demands and by the constant flow of her mother's "do-gooder friends," withdrew. Solitude, she wrote, made her less volatile and less vulnerable. She was most free when she was alone. Charles, as if fearing the separation Anne sought, frequently knocked at her closed door. He "whistled" for her when she was working on her book and invited her to fly with him. Though enraged by his intrusions, Anne complied and, for the first time, played with the idea of losing Charles. But just as the fantasy took hold, she raised him once again to the status of savior. Without his energy and competence, she would be "incredibly empty." "Without Charles, [she] would lose life and the whole purpose of life."[21] But it seemed as though she protested too much.

As she studied the plans for their transatlantic trip, Anne decided to write an allegorical narrative. While the allegory in *North to the Orient* seemed an afterthought, this time she patterned her book on a classical model. Each trip was an odyssey, a voyage "home," but this one had the taste of hell. Terribly discouraged by her lack of progress, she burrowed her way through "the pit," hoping to turn her rage into passion.

"The pit" was wider than she had imagined, and Harold Nicolson had fallen in. While Anne saw his biography of her father as a finely crafted "composition" that restored Dwight Morrow's legacy of "strength, tolerance, and wisdom," reviewers noted Nicolson's inability to put Morrow's life in historical perspective and to draw conclusions relative to the present.[22] In the end, it was clear that Nicolson did not understand Morrow, his accomplishments, or the American social phenomenon he had represented.

In the wake of Nicolson's failure, Anne realized the folly of her timidity. Instinctively, she knew she had to write, and she began to burst with ideas. She had so much to say that she could not write fast enough. She felt "rooted and unshakable," as she had never felt before. Even the wind had lost its potency. During a visit with the Guggenheims at Falaise, Anne looked at the sea and saw "eternity."

Determined to stop "running," Anne sought a quiet place outside her mother's home in which to write her book. In late November, just before the first anniversary of Elisabeth's death, Anne rented an apartment designated solely for her work. As she placed her books on the shelves and hung her paintings on the walls, Anne comforted herself with the "immortality" of Elisabeth's legacy: "Courage, memory, and love." Finally, Anne had given herself permission to write. Her talent, commitment, and affluence had produced that rare specimen of humanity that Virginia Woolf called the female writer.

But Anne's victory was as short-lived as it was momentous. In spite of the vigilance of the state and city police and the FBI, Jon, now three years old, was the object of constant threats. The final act of harassment came when reporters stalked Jon on his way to school. Sideswiping the Morrows' car, they pushed it off the road and pulled open the doors to take the boy's picture. Within hours, Charles and Anne decided to leave America.[23]

19

Crossing Over

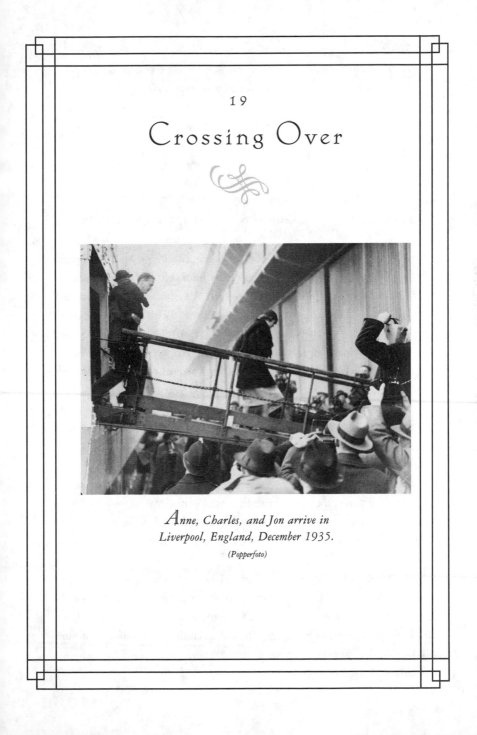

*Anne, Charles, and Jon arrive in
Liverpool, England, December 1935.*

(Popperfoto)

We, local and ephemeral as we are, are not one moment contented in the
world of time nor confined in it; we keep on crossing over and over to our
predecessor, to our descent and to those who came after us.

— RAINER MARIA RILKE,
Duino Elegies

DECEMBER 1935, ABOARD THE *AMERICAN IMPORTER*

In the early morning hours of December 22, 1935, the Lindberghs slipped quietly out to sea on a freighter bound for England. Standing bareheaded on the deck, Charles saluted the Statue of Liberty as they navigated the inland waters toward the open sea.[1] With a sense of betrayal as passionate as his Swedish grandfather's nearly eighty years earlier, Charles was crossing back to Europe in the hope of anonymity and peace.

At strict orders from Charles, the ship was empty, and no one came to say good-bye.[2] Betty Morrow and Con had waved to them from the big front door as their limousine disappeared around the curve down Next Day Hill. Arriving at the dock on Manhattan's West Side, they registered under assumed names and presented diplomatic passports. Even the crew didn't know who their only passengers were.

Christmas at sea would be lonely, but it would also be free from fear for the first time since the children were born. As Anne walked with Jon up the gangplank toward the forward deck and down through the darkened halls to their stateroom, she was tired and apprehensive but pleased with their decision.

She had felt rootless since leaving Hopewell. The lack of privacy at Englewood, the publicity surrounding the trial, and the efforts of the New Jersey governor to commute Hauptmann's death sentence had created an atmosphere of hostility.[3] "It was as though the Lindbergh family were living alone on a frontier, their home surrounded by savages," commented the *Times.*

On their second day at sea, amid the roar of wind and rain, Anne noted in her diary that their hasty exit had made quite a "splash." It was "rather shocking," she wrote, but it was as if, by their own hand, the American people had forced the exile of their native son.[4] While the Lindberghs blamed their departure on the intrusions and distortions of the press, the press was divided against itself, blaming its lowly tabloid brethren for pushing the Lindberghs to desperation. But not even the most self-righteous newspapers had resisted the Lindberghs' story. Front pages were filled with sensationalized versions of the facts, even as the editors preached holy abstinence. The *Christian Science Monitor* wrote that "newspapers more than kidnappers have exiled the Lindberghs," and *Time* magazine added that long ago "the Press at large concluded that Hero Lindbergh's real Herod was yellow journalism."[5] The cannibalization of the Lindberghs by the press reached the absurd when Viscount Rothermere printed an editorial, in the London *Daily Mirror,* entitled "Leave Them Alone" while simultaneously covering his front page with news of the Lindberghs' crossing.[6]

But the public searched for deeper reasons. On Christmas Day, there was an outcry in the United States against the "alien" and "criminal" elements responsible for the "outrage" of the Lindberghs' departure for England. Bruno Richard Hauptmann had become the xenophobes' symbol of the inferior, uneducated, and morally bankrupt "aliens" who had flooded the American cities at the turn of the century; to the eugenics movement, the Lindberghs were martyrs. Ironically, the public did not know that Charles was the grandson of a Swedish immigrant who had been a convicted felon and a fugitive from the law.

While the English public thrilled to the prospect of the Lindberghs' arrival, observers saw little to suggest that life in England would offer them much consolation. "It reminds one somewhat of the frog who dived into the pond to avoid getting wet in the rain," wrote a satirist for the Paris *Oeuvre.*[7] He couldn't see how the Lindbergh child could be any more secure in England than in the States. The frequency of child abduction was as high in England as in America, he wrote.

In fact, that was not true. During the preceding two years, there had been sixty-three kidnappings in America; in England there had been four, according to public record.[8] Furthermore, there was no complicated process of appeal in England. Criminals were punished swiftly and severely, by imprisonment or by hanging.[9]

As the storms at sea raged, and little Jon grew paler and more seasick each day, Anne cared for him with an intensity she had never achieved at home. Wholly responsible for Jon while Charles conferred and dined with the ship's captain, Anne's priorities were instantly rearranged. Suddenly, her anxiety became academic. Concentrating on the routine tasks of tending to Jon, she had no time to contemplate her writing. When a wave crashed through the window, threatening Jon with an "impersonal force" like the one that had overtaken Charlie, Anne wrote, "How could I have longed for anything else? Let me get safely there."[10]

In the stealth of the night, two weeks later, their ship lurched toward the docks of Liverpool on the Mersey River. The next morning, amid the pop of flashbulbs and the shouted queries of the British press, the Lindberghs stood on the deck in the rain while a platoon of bobbies hastily carved a lane through the waiting throng.[11] With Jon shielded in Charles's arms, the Lindberghs, smiling wanly, passed through the protective lines of the British police into their waiting limousine. They spent the afternoon in a local hotel, and then, under cover of darkness, drove to the childhood home of Aubrey Morgan, in the small country town of Llandaff, near Cardiff.[12]

Even though every newspaper in London ran the story of their arrival on its front page, once they were at the Morgan home, it was as if they had disappeared. Finally, they had earned the privacy they deserved.

Anne wrote to her mother-in-law that she felt safe in "this quiet garden."[13] At night she wasn't afraid to put Jon to bed and felt no compulsion to check his breathing.

But all too soon, Anne found she had traded safety for ennui. The status of the Morgan family could protect her from the public but not from the realities of middle-class motherhood. Without a home of her own, without domestic help and the leisure to write, Anne grew lonely, bored, and restless. She felt like a "flat-footed, red-nosed, and dowdy governess," unable to think, read, or even talk.[14] It was not a question of time, she wrote; it was a question of being disconnected from the world beyond the nursery.[15]

Again, she played games with herself, fighting despair by forcing her thoughts through the open branches of the oak trees into the effortless glide of the seagulls in the sky. Discouraged, she wondered whether her ability to write had been no more than an illusion she would now have to discard for the hard-edged realities of British domestic life. The lack of privacy, the consuming demands of Jon, and the conversation of the women she met in the suburbs of Cardiff made her sharply aware of the extraordinary quality of the life she was seeking. As consolation, friends of the Morgans gave her a book outlining the proprieties and responsibilities of English motherhood. Dutifully, Anne noted the advice in her diary: The gifts of women were lesser than those of men, in spite of their claims to equality. Rather than pretend she had something to contribute to society at large, a woman should stay at home with her "real masterpiece," her son. "I feel confident that her soup will be better than her poetry," the author concluded.[16]

To be a mother in England in 1936, that is, to bear and rear a male child, was to personify Christian values. Given the limited quality of her intellect, a woman's only "sane" solution was to dedicate her life to motherhood and housewifery.

What Anne sensed, but could not confirm, was that British attitudes toward women in the 1930s was a backlash against their full participation in public service, industry, and government during the First World War. Once the war was over, government, mirroring public opinion, provided incentives to lure women back to their homes, where they could fulfill their "natural" roles as wives and mothers. Dubbed "hussies" and "dole-scroungers" by men whose jobs were "stolen," the women who persisted in working in the open market were discouraged by national insurance and dole legislation, which sought to ease them out of the workplace. Working-class girls were educated in domestic skills, meant to be practiced not only in their homes, but as servants in the homes of the wealthy. The new women's magazines presented the shining ideal of the stay-at-home housewife, groomed to bear and educate a new generation of children, and thus make up for the ravages of war.

The feminist ideal did not extend much beyond the notion of suffrage. After 1928, when women were enfranchised, a complacency seemed to take hold, especially among younger women. To them, the battle for freedom had been won, and there was no longer a need for concerted action in the public arena. In 1936, as the Depression became more severe and the threat of war nearly palpable, the issue of women's rights seemed narrow. Women worked within the established social and political structure to deal with the exigencies of public need and foreign policy.[17] It was not surprising that Anne felt pangs of guilt and self-indulgence. A privileged and educated American woman, whose peers had confirmed her ambitions in spite of her own doubts, she found life in Wales reactionary and constrained. She was trapped in a life she had not chosen, and longed again for the independence she had had as a college girl. In her diary, she noted that she was still "Mother's little girl, Daddy's little daughter, C.'s little wife."[18] Her long struggle to define herself as a writer now seemed to have come to naught.

She hid her feelings from Charles; she no longer had the luxury of alienating him. Isolated and alone, needing his approval more than ever, Anne told Charles what he wanted to hear. She did not yearn for anything but a home, she said—a home, anywhere, with him and Jon.[19]

Back in the States, Con was learning that fighting against prevailing social expectation was a difficult task, even in the company of like-minded peers. Suddenly pretty and sure of herself, after graduating *summa cum laude* from Smith in 1935, Con had moved to Vermont with Margot Loines, intent on pursuing a career in the theater. Once back at home, she was thrust into the company of Aubrey Morgan, whose grief in the wake of Elisabeth's death had inspired her compassion.[20] Aubrey, nine years older and sophisticated in business and travel, had chaperoned Con and her mother the following summer on a tour of Europe. It was there, while Betty Morrow slept, that Aubrey and Con, talking into the morning hours, had fallen in love. Now they announced their plans to marry.

Anne was shocked. The pieces didn't fit. Wouldn't their marriage somehow diminish Elisabeth? She had appeared to Anne like a painted portrait, and now her fears were coming to pass—Elisabeth was lost forever behind a "glaze" of memory.[21]

Determined to begin again to set down their roots, Anne and Charles canvassed the English countryside in search of a home.[22] Cambridge didn't suit them, and Charles needed to be near enough to London to have something to do. For the first time, they realized they had cut all their ties. Time was suspended as they meandered through the small country towns with their Victorian structures, too large and too expensive to rent. London, they decided, was at least familiar, and that familiarity alone would root them in a country that grew more alien each day. They turned to Harold Nicolson for help.[23]

Nicolson gave them a tour of Parliament and, over lunch, discussed with them the possibilities of renting a home near London. When Anne said she wanted a house that would "welcome" her, Nicolson replied that he knew a house that would "jump all over her like a Spaniel." It was his beloved Long Barn, home to him and Vita for fifteen years after their return from government service in Constantinople in 1915.[24]

As Anne and Charles drove through the lush countryside of Kent toward the fourteenth-century village of Sevenoaks, their spirits rose with anticipation. Lost in the winding hills surrounding the village, they searched for the Nicolson home. "Crouching" over the brow of the next hill, shielded from the road by low feathery trees, the rambling house sat behind a gate at the end of a courtyard. As they opened the gate, Anne felt that it was like slipping into another realm. It was the sheltered and bucolic world she and Charles had imagined when they built their house in Hopewell four years earlier.[25] The house seemed to reach out to embrace them. Finally, they had found "security."[26]

Long Barn consisted of a fourteenth-century hall-house and a sixteenth-century L-shaped cottage and barn. Not quite two miles from

Vita's ancestral home, Knole, Long Barn had provided not only the consolation Vita craved for her lack of inheritance, but fertile ground for the art of gardening. It was here, in the intricately terraced gardens of Long Barn and in the long, poplar-lined vistas that spread like spikes into open fields, that Harold and Vita consummated their love of the earth, and it was here that Vita wrote her epic poem, "The Land." The gardens of Long Barn were the prelude to their floral masterpiece at Sissinghurst Castle, a medieval home only twenty-one miles away, on the outskirts of Kent.[27] Nicolson truly loved the place, and his offer to Anne and Charles was an act of generosity that Anne understood the moment she walked through the gates.

Her belief that the best gifts were those given lightly and gratuitously would later be turned into metaphor.

A L M S [28]

Like birds in winter
You fed me;
Knowing the ground was frozen
Knowing
You did not need my gratitude
Softly
Like snow falling on snow,
Softly, so not to frighten me,
Softly,
You threw your crumbs upon the ground
And walked away.

While Anne and Charles found refuge in the rolling hills of Kent, life in the United States was harder than ever. At a time when 38 percent of American families still had an income of less than a thousand dollars a year,[29] the Lindberghs gave no thought to conventional employment. As news of their life filtered back home, neither the public nor the press was eager to let them forget the price they had paid for their wealth and fame. It was reported that on the third anniversary of Charlie's abduction, Dwight Jr.'s room at Harvard had been scavenged by thieves.[30] They had stolen letters written by Betty Morrow to Dwight Jr. in the aftermath of the kidnapping and during the throes of the trial. The theft, though petty, underlined the continued violation of their privacy.

March 6 was moving day. Anne woke up singing a German song she sang only when she felt gay. She and Charles packed the back of their car while the nurse left for Sevenoaks by train. Followed by a reporter, they stopped on the way to buy two dozen narcissi and some anemones from a nice old man. When they arrived, Jon was eager to run and play, pleased with the gardens and the birds and the chance to throw stones into the pool. But the joy Anne felt on entering the house seemed suddenly to belong to someone else. As she surveyed the rooms and rearranged the furniture, Anne sensed Elisabeth's presence, as though she were coming to pay a visit. Even now, she didn't feel grown up. When she and Charles sat down to dinner that evening, it was as if they were "playing house."[31]

The next day, Anne sat on the stone steps above the rose gardens and thought of Hopewell and of the suspended days of waiting for little Charlie's return. The air had been warm and springlike, just like this, she thought. But her sadness seemed out of place amidst all this beauty. Anne felt profoundly alone, like a stranger in a strange land.[32]

That same day, March 7, Hitler stormed the Rhineland. While he hailed the act as a protest of the Franco-Soviet pact, it was a move calculated to test the Allied response. England, France, Belgium, Italy, and the League of Nations, though outraged, retreated in silence. Had they retaliated, Hitler later said, he would surely have fallen. In point of fact, Hitler had only four brigades.[33]

Ensconced in Kent, Anne and Charles argued about the morality of France's position. Anne took a pacifist view. Why, she wondered, was there war at all? Why couldn't there be trust among nations? Charles believed that war was an inevitable part of the cycle of life. They should have "crushed" Germany after the Great War, he said, shifting the blame to the Allies. The "middle course" of humiliation was what had created Hitler's frustration.[34]

Anne was puzzled by the seeming nonchalance of the English toward the imminent threat of war. While segments of the American population were outraged by the violation of the Treaty of Versailles, England and Germany played a game of denial, she wrote in her diary. Germany had violated the peace treaty, and England refused to respond. To Anne's surprise, the newspapers were clearly pro-German. If only they would stop acting like bullies in a schoolyard, attacking people just to prove they could.[35]

Denial seemed the order of the day, even back in New Jersey. Bruno Richard Hauptmann protested his innocence, buttressed by the howlings of his indignant wife and the sustained protest of Governor Hoffman. But the drama of the kidnapping was drawing to a close. In spite of Hauptmann's appeals and his thirty-day reprieve, the state court upheld its ruling, echoing the argument of the prosecutor, David Wilentz. Even if fifty people had conspired in the kidnapping, Hauptmann was one of them.

On April 4, 1936, Hauptmann walked in silence toward the execution chamber at the state prison. Fifty official witnesses and newspapermen watched behind a three-foot canvas barrier in the brightly lit execution chamber. Its tall white-washed walls, with the neat rows of wooden chairs, had the grotesque air of theater. Head held high, Hauptmann stepped quickly into the electric chair and his two spiritual advisers read to him from the Bible in German. The two-thousand-volt current was turned on at 8:44 P.M. Three and a half minutes later, he was pronounced dead by the attending physicians.[36]

Large crowds filled Times Square, waiting for the news to be flashed on the high electric sign. When it did appear, at 8:47, a strange whisper rose from the crowd, as if the sharpness of consonants might desecrate the moment. Slowly, the crowds drifted away.

On hearing the news of her husband's execution, Anna Hauptmann screamed, "Another man is guilty. There is another man."[37]

While Anna Hauptmann seemed betrayed by her inability to understand her husband, Anne, in England, was growing certain that she understood Charles. Love, she wrote in her diary, was "seeing in every little act of a person the essence" of who he is; she must teach herself to accept Charles exactly as he was. The essence of Charles was "fast," "concentrated," and "relentless." As he tore home from London on a narrow winding road through the darkness of a rainy night, his race seemed a metaphor.[38]

Anne's feelings of unworthiness dissipated amid the beauty and security of Long Barn. The house was a spiritual reservoir. She would hold it in her mind forever.[39] Just as people made permanent marks of peace on one another's lives, so could places. Their happiness brought Anne and Charles closer to each other and to Jon. They walked for miles each night through the open fields, savoring the beauty of early spring.[40] Charles had found that the people at the Pasteur Institute in London valued his previous work with Carrel, and had bought a row of books on big-game hunting in Africa. Anne prayed silently that he wasn't planning a trip to Africa.[41]

But the more Anne nestled in the security of Long Barn, the more she worried that it was an illusion. She feared everything in life, she told Charles, as though there were "great pits on either side" of her path, waiting to swallow all that she valued and loved. Charles, as usual, tried to assuage her fears.[42]

Social life in England was stiff and vacuous. Appearance and convention suffocated warmth and spontaneity. "Everyone calls everyone Darling," she wrote in her diary; everyone touched each other with their summer-white gloves. Everyone except the king; he was fascinating. He understood his role and played it well. Anne saw a piece of herself in the lonely king—a victim of tragedy. Like Shakespeare's kings, he struggled to fit his humanity into his crown. Anne sensed his frustration of trying to live an authentic life, trapped in the prison of convention.[43]

With Jon enrolled in the local school, Anne once again had time to write. She tried to keep alive the memory of her transatlantic trip, re-calling her experience and her desolation. The key to writing, she noted, was a moment of insight like a window to a distant landscape. The rest are just shells, structures to support your vision. You must be open to your subject, respectful and patient. But life, too, was an art, no less demanding and perhaps more important than writing. If only she could be like Charles or the Carrels. They lived artful lives of pre-cision and purpose.[44]

Developing a metaphor that would become a definition of contem-porary womanhood, Anne wrote that "everyday living" was like "walk-ing on a tightrope," demanding balance and strict control. Marriage was the most important thing in life, and her commitment to Jon was its essence. But as she worked daily on her narrative, Anne resolved to find standards and measures of her own.[45]

While Anne, in the walled English garden, contemplated the rela-tion between life and art, Kay Smith, in Germany, read the *International Herald Tribune* in her apartment in the center of Berlin. There, she found an item to tell her husband. Charles Lindbergh had been to Paris on an inspection tour for the French government. Impressed that the Lindberghs were no longer home-bound, she wondered aloud whether Charles would consent to inspect the German planes on behalf of the United States government.[46]

Kay's suggestion grew out of her husband's frustration. Truman Smith, the American military attaché in Berlin for the past year, saw factories and barracks springing up all around him, the unmistakable signs of a war machine. He had read *Mein Kampf* and took Hitler's plans seriously.[47] But he was an infantry man, an expert on guns and tanks and ground forces. He did not have the knowledge to analyze the military implications of aircraft. In spite of his well-cultivated contacts within the Reich, Smith had no information to send home to Washington. His new aviation assistant, Captain Theodore Koenig, also lacked the nec-essary experience and the technical knowledge.

Pursuing Kay's idea, Truman negotiated through Air Minister Hermann Goering and State Secretary for Air Erhard Milch with

Chancellor Hitler. Hitler was eager to strike a deal. The presence of Charles Lindbergh on the eve of the Olympic Games would thrust Berlin onto the center stage. Lindbergh, Hitler agreed, would be permitted access to factories, research facilities, and combat units, with full government protection, if he promised to attend the opening ceremonies of the Olympics.[48]

He wrote to Truman Smith that he and his wife were eager to see the German civil and military developments in aviation. Nonetheless, he had one major request. The government, he wrote, must promise to protect him from the sensational press coverage which had encumbered his foreign visits in the past. Hitler gave his word through his ministers to Smith that the government-controlled press would be severely restricted.[49]

On July 22, ten days before the Olympics, Anne and Charles took off from Penshurst, a secluded airport in Kent. In their small, gray low-winged monoplane, they rose high above the feathery grass and the sleepy fields of Kent. Anne saw the house, down below, looking small and unprotected, and the figure of Jon doing a war dance and waving a towel. As they flew over the Channel toward the coast of Belgium, Anne felt their plane was a sanctuary. No matter how life changed below, the sky would always remain the same. Cathedrals pulled the houses toward their center, making each town look like a wide-eyed daisy. By tracking the canals and railroad tracks, Anne and Charles could follow the maps through the fields and forests of Germany. They landed in Cologne, next to an octagonal stone tower; it appeared very German, noted Anne—"large and blocky."

In deference to Charles's demand for privacy, neither Hitler nor Goering was present when the Lindberghs landed. They were greeted by several officials, but few spectators. As the soldiers clicked their heels and saluted, Captain Koenig ceremoniously shook everyone's hand. Anne was struck by the formality of the assemblage and by the clipped speech and movements of the attending officers. Amid a flurry of *Heil Hitlers,* raised arms, and heel clicks, Anne was presented with a bouquet of roses.

To her relief, Hitler managed to control the crowds even at their official welcome in Berlin. The formalities increased, but Anne enjoyed the ceremonies. Charles, too, with rare generosity, consented to ride through the streets in an open car. Quickly, Anne was separated from him. "Ah, yes," she wrote, "the subservience of women in Germany." As the crowds cheered her husband, Anne rode in a closed car behind the entourage. Smiling, Anne wondered whether she would ever see him again.[50]

In fact, the antifeminist fervor in Germany far surpassed that in England. The Nazis glorified domestic life and saw the clamor for women's rights as a form of moral decadence. While the nationalization of industry in the Weimar Republic had accelerated industrialization, opening unspecialized jobs to women, the economic depression that paved the way for the Nazis had lessened the demand for unskilled labor. In Germany, as in England, women colluded with the government for the restriction of their freedom. The Housewives Union organized to restrain individual opportunity, thereby ensuring a supply of domestic servants. The union proposed and won an ordinance requiring a year's service for every German schoolgirl. But the constant propaganda had its dark side in laws that enforced compulsory sterilization to maintain racial purity. In the six years preceding the outbreak of World War II, 320,000 people, nearly half of 1 percent of the population at large, were sterilized.[51]

Sitting in the back car with attention focused on her husband, Anne resumed her role as observer. She was struck by the clean, treeless streets and the stark concrete buildings in a city that seemed to have sprung up overnight. Unlike London or New York, Berlin looked untouched by poverty and despair. There was an air of order and optimism, wrote Anne. The boulevards were filled with cars and bicycles and alive with pre-Olympic festivities. The avenues were draped with red Nazi flags and the white blue-ringed colors of the Olympics. Emblematic of the new "Aryan vision" was the Olympic stadium, garishly decorated with pseudo-Greek statues. While the German aesthetic felt alien to Anne—

clumsy and heavy and too ornate—it had a bold magnificence she could not deny.[52] It was a city eager to forget its past; it raised monuments to a future it could not yet articulate.

But no matter how visionary that future was, Adolf Hitler was certain that Charles Lindbergh personified it. His tall frame, his sandy-haired boyishness, his piercing blue eyes, made him the quintessential Aryan. The Nazis could not have constructed a more eloquent embodiment of their vision. Although Hitler had promised him privacy, Charles did not object when the press circulated portraits of him as an American hero, praising him for his indomitable will and his precision and skill as a pioneering aviator.[53]

Truman Smith marveled at Charles's knowledge and precision; Katharine Smith responded to his beauty and charms.[54] Smiling and hatless amid the stern German officers, Charles burst with vitality and confidence. His compelling presence underlined Anne's self-apologetic stance.[55] Kay sensed that Charles was the couple's "designated spokesperson."[56]

Hoping to shield them from unwanted publicity, the Smiths invited Anne and Charles to stay at their apartment in Berlin. Observing Anne daily, Kay saw only the façade of self-deprecation, not her intrinsic strength.[57] Anne's diary entries for her days in Berlin were replete with insight into people and events; she was intent on documenting a culture in the process of inventing itself.

In a sense, the Lindberghs' visit was another of Kay Smith's victories. She had a practical, intuitive intelligence, along with a desire to join the political fray. Under five feet, not more than a hundred pounds, Kay, like Anne, was a diminutive figure beside a strapping and athletic husband. Her pointed, birdlike features contrasted with Truman's solid, brawny frame, described by his daughter as befitting a "Grecian God."[58] But as smart and as competent as he was, Truman never knew "when to come in from the rain."[59] Kay, in short, kept Truman safe, governing his life while he commanded the lives of others.

Kay and Anne were mirror images of a common ideal: service to the

husband in a male-dominated culture, each woman as relentlessly vig-
ilant as the other, each ambitious and daring. Kay sought to master the
political scene while Anne honed her skills of observation. But Kay's
practicality was also her frailty. Her view of the world was cynical, un-
tuned to the nuances of Anne's complex personality, so different from
her own.

On the first day of their tour, Charles was scheduled to make a
speech to his hosts in the presence of the international press. But he
converted a perfunctory salutation into serious commentary. Speaking
at the Lufthansa headquarters at Templehof, the center of German commercial aviation, Charles reminded his fellow aviators of the heavy responsibility they bore:

> *We who are in aviation carry a heavy responsibility on our shoulders,
> for while we have been drawing the world closer together in peace, we
> have stripped the armor of every nation in war. It is no longer possible
> to shield the heart of a country with its army. Armies can no more stop
> an air attack than a suit of mail can stop a rifle bullet. Aviation has,
> I believe, created the most fundamental change ever made in war. It has
> abolished what we call the sense of warfare. It has turned defense into
> attack. We can no longer protect our families with an army. Our li-
> braries, our museums—every institution which we value most—is laid
> bare to bombardment. Aviation has brought a revolutionary change to a
> world already staggering from changes. . . . I find some cause for hope
> in the belief that power which must be bound to knowledge is less dan-
> gerous to civilization than that which is barbaric.* [60]

He finished his speech with a toast to aircraft: "May pursuit planes
get faster and faster" and may "bombers get slower and slower."

Charles was showing his ambivalence, and the Nazi officers were
confused. Was he warning or praising them? They smiled politely but
drank their wine "as if it had hairs." [61]

The government-controlled German press distorted Charles's
speech, toning down his admonitions, and the American reporters ap-

plauded him for his courage. Since he was viewed both as a spokesperson for the concerns of his countrymen and as an informed observer of the British military, his speech was regarded as an event of "cardinal importance"[62] and "a notable service"[63] to Europe and, perhaps, to the entire world.

Goering, delighted with Charles's Swedish roots, could not have been a more willing host. He was impressed with Charles's technical skill, his acute powers of observation, and his commitment to the development of aviation. As he paraded Lindbergh through the Heinkel and Junker factories, Goering permitted him to inspect an elite Luftwaffe group and to fly a JU–52, a standard bomber, and the Hindenberg, a four-motor experimental passenger plane. He took him to Adlershof, a major research facility, to show him engines and equipment no one had seen before, including the JU–87 Stuka, a dive bomber, and the Messerschmitt 109, which became Germany's prime combat plane.[64]

As they toured, Goering, a self-aggrandizing liar, fabricated statistics with the greatest of ease. He told Charles that Germany was producing between five hundred and eight hundred combat planes a month and would soon build twenty thousand a year. England, he noted, produced seventy a month; France, a mere fifty at best. Ironically, Goering's numbers corresponded with those of American intelligence, which was willing to accept "hot news," often unreliable and "wildly inaccurate," deliberately planted for its obfuscation.[65]

Toured by day and dined by night, Lindbergh would return to the Smiths' apartment to tell the attaché his impressions of the day. Often the lights would burn into early morning as the two men discussed and interpreted the information to send back to the War Department.[66]

But Lindbergh and Smith made a vital error in their assessment of German air power. They did not understand that the Luftwaffe was a tactical, not a strategic, force, designed to support the army but not to carry out long-range bombings. There were few four-motored aircraft and no heavy bombers. Deceived by Goering's hyperbole, they failed to see the inexperience and inefficiency of many of the Luftwaffe generals.

Their report to Washington was comprehensive and detailed, but fraught with exaggerated assessments of German air power.[67]

While Charles was being manipulated by the dissembling air minister, Anne was systematically courted. Officers flanked her daily at lunch at the Air Club, feeding her propaganda along with herring and Bavarian bread. Kay monitored Anne's every move, and recorded the drama faithfully in her diary.

Minister Milch approached Anne like a predator stalking his kill. Bowing stiffly, he began his rendezvous with the colonel's lady. Complementing her on her modest demeanor, he rendered a short history of German leadership, portraying Hitler as a man of peace. The Führer, said Milch, believed that enough lives had been lost on the battlefield. France would always be their enemy. But he wanted a bloodless victory. Their goal was not the conquest of people, merely the acquisition of land.[68] But on the streets, Anne noticed the young boys, in brown shirts and pants, goosestepping like soldiers.[69]

Influenced by his renewed worldwide approbation, Charles began to take his own opinions seriously. After six months in England with nothing to do, Charles was again the hero poised at the edge of history. The Germans, in a sense, had reinvented Charles in the image he had come to expect. And the Nazi leaders, masters of pageantry and drama, understood how to use his political power for their ends. Charles was eager to be of "use" for a cause and a culture that transcended his own. The spirit of the German people was "magnificent," he wrote to a friend, and, one may note, closely akin. They refused to admit that anything was "impossible or that any obstacle was too much to overcome." It was an attitude he feared the American people were losing.[70]

For the moment, he was hailed on both sides of the Atlantic. The Americans and the Germans believed him invaluable to the process of military preparations and international rapprochement. On a visit to the newly built Olympic stadium, Charles took a sprint around the track, to the delight of photographers and reporters. Now a world-class spokesman, he imagined himself a world-class athlete. Walking in the parklike surroundings of grass, trees, and flowers, Charles inspected every corner of the Olympic village and gave it his complete approval.[71]

Anne, however, was less exuberant. She sensed that Charles was playing the fool. She was tired of the ceremony and the raised arms, and sick of the press intruding despite the orders of Hitler's officers. She questioned the whole premise of Olympic competition and asked herself of what use was physical prowess. What about spiritual and intellectual pursuit? Would the Germans breed a race of brawny, insipid athletes?[72]

Persuaded by his friend Henry Ford, whom he had met after his flight in 1927, Charles accepted an invitation to see the ousted German crown prince, Eitel Friedrich van Hohenzollern. The Smiths were nervous, but Charles was determined. In fact, the visit turned out to be a trap. Although it was portrayed as a private social affair, the prince hoped the legitimacy associated with Lindbergh's presence would be construed as an insult to the Nazi regime. Reporters stalked the men from behind potted plants, and Kay Smith was appalled. At dinner she sat between a reporter and Charles to drown out the conversation between him and the prince. When the prince invited Charles out to the verandah for a "casual photo," and photographers came forward with their tripods, Kay became furious. She demanded that they stop, but the damage was done. The next day a photograph of Charles appeared in the morning news—an insult to his Nazi hosts.[73]

Kay later described Charles as a "naïve political thinker . . . It was the silliest thing for him to do because he was the guest of another government."[74]

Calling on her skills of observation, Anne tried to penetrate Goering's intentions. When the Lindberghs were invited to a state luncheon at Goering's home on the Wilhelmstrasse, in the heart of Berlin, Anne found a reception worthy of a ball. As in her parents' receptions for Charles in Mexico, guards lined the red-carpeted steps, and a flurry of footmen shuffled and bowed. Nazi officers paved the way to the formal reception. While the men conferred, the women formed a constellation around the yellow-haired wife of the German minister. Dressed in a long green-velvet gown, shimmering with diamonds, Frau Goering appeared to Anne no less than a queen. Moving closer, Anne realized that her diamond brooch was a swastika set in a sea of emeralds.[75]

In his coat of braided gold, Goering, too, had the air of royalty. At forty-three, he was less handsome than formidable, strutting like a peacock in a barnyard of chickens. But Anne sensed more than she saw. She later referred to him as an "inflated Alcibiades," comparing him to the Greek general who led his men into wars to suit his amoral ends.[76]

Anne was correct. Goering was a ruthless despot.[77] But on that summer afternoon, as he paraded into the hall to receive his guests, his charm was thick with honey. Unlike the English king who sought his humanity beneath his royal person, Goering enjoyed playing his role. He looked at people through veiled eyes, wrote Anne, turning to look at her only after she had already passed.

Second in command, with a breadth of influence unmatched in Hitler's regime, Goering sought to create the drama of a medieval royal court. Anne followed the other guests through hallways hung with huge tapestries into a luminous, glass-walled dining room.[78] While Truman and Charles dined at one end of the enormous table, Anne and Kay flanked the general at the other. Bored with Anne, Goering filled the silence with questions about Charles. Kay, annoyed by his impertinence, asked whether he was aware that Mrs. Lindbergh had been her husband's radio operator on his pioneering flights. Goering broke down in hysterical laughter. "That is the most ridiculous thing I have ever heard," he said. "How could such a shy and fragile woman be capable of such a thing?" Pleased with her own impudence, but appalled by his contempt, Kay did not translate his comment for Anne.[79]

While Charles was shuttled from factory to factory, Anne stayed with Kay. In the mornings, she would work on her transatlantic narrative, later to become *Listen! The Wind.* The women spent the afternoons lunching with officers' wives and visiting museums and shops. At night, the Lindberghs and Smiths would be transported by limousine from one formal reception to the next. But when the time came for them to leave, Charles wanted to stay for the entire week of the Olympics. Kay was "terrified" that he and Anne would extend their stay, because she had agreed to house the equestrian team after the Lindberghs' departure. She was certain her staff would balk at too large a number of guests, though one housemaid was heard to say, "This is the most important house in all Berlin."[80]

On August 1, the opening day of the 1936 Olympics, crowds streamed into Berlin and gathered in the new stadium. In unison, a hundred thousand spectators raised their arms to hail the Fuehrer. All the world was watching Hitler, and Charles Lindbergh had kept his promise. With Anne beside him, he was sitting only a few feet away from the leader of the German Reich.[81]

Charles, however, was disappointed. He had wanted to meet Adolf Hitler, but Kay and Truman had counseled against it. His momentary pleasure, they believed, would not be worth the publicity. They had worked hard to keep Charles away from politics and "in the air," and they held their ground. Charles acquiesced. Seated so close that they could nearly touch, neither Charles nor Hitler offered the other a word of greeting.[82]

When Anne and Charles left Germany the next day, it was with optimism and gratitude. Hitler had kept his promise to them; he had managed to keep the press at bay and their privacy inviolate. There was something to be admired in the power of one man who could control his citizens by the weight of his word. In America, they had been stalked by the public and the press; in Germany, they had been fiercely protected. They were certain that Hitler was good for the German people and that he carried the mark of "greatness."

It is "Puritanical," she wrote, to view dictatorship as necessarily "evil." Hitler was, she believed, a visionary who really wanted the best for his country. Regardless, Anne felt that the unity and spirit of the people were "thrilling." The democracies seemed unable to produce that effect. Nonetheless, Anne did worry that Hitler's fanaticism, potentially good, might become a weapon of "horrible destruction." She was uncomfortable with the Nazis' Jewish policy and their brutal denial of national integrity and human rights. These things were so repulsive to her that they could not possibly be "worth" the price.[83]

In short, German life was a surging wave, as amoral and undefined as anything in the "natural" world. The question was who would govern it and how.

Charles agreed. "Hitler is undoubtedly a great man who has done much for the German people," he wrote to his friend. But he pushed his observations one step further. Were the standards of American democracy worth saving? Were the principles by which it governed true? He wondered if it was self-delusion when "we attempt to run our government by counting the number of heads, without a thought to what lies between them." The Germans, he wrote, had other criteria by which to judge the rights of men that were not measurable by any political system yet conceived.[84]

20

Polish Bright His Hoofs

Anne at Long Barn, Kent, England, spring 1937.
(Lindbergh Picture Collection, Manuscripts and Archives,
Yale University Library)

UNICORN

Everything today has been
"Heavy" and "brown."
Bring me a unicorn
To ride about town! ...
And I will kneel each morning
To polish bright his hoofs
That they may gleam each moonlight
We ride over roofs!

— BY ANNE MORROW,
JANUARY 1927[1]

WINTER 1937, LONG BARN, SEVENOAKS, ENGLAND

The winter of 1937 was both a sleep and an awakening. The new pregnancy made Anne tired and slow, blunting the "sharp pointed flame" of her mind.[2] She could write for only two hours each morning, and even that time was less than productive. And yet her ideas had begun to coalesce—all her disparate glimpses of insight about women and family and creativity began to take form beneath her quietude. Anne knew that she could not follow Charles; he "raced ahead into new ideas, new countries, new schemes." She had to see life within her frame—narrow and near, deep and essential. She read books with a new energy and challenged herself to formulate conclusions.

Was it possible to reconcile her need to write with the responsibilities of motherhood? She wrote to her cousin Margaret Landenberger Scandrett, that she would not choose to work if it meant denying the needs of her family. "Deep down in my heart, I don't honestly want to be a 'woman writer' any more than I once wanted to be a 'woman aviator' . . . I am not prepared to sacrifice . . . those advantages and qualities that are truly feminine."[3]

Echoing the poetry of Lao-tzu, Anne wrote that a woman must stand at the hub of a wheel that moves toward a larger goal. Creative work was merely one spoke of the wheel, a ray of insight leading to and from a unifying core, essential to the balance of the wheel, without which her life would simply stop turning. Out of this way of life, she wrote, "some very great art might spring—not much but pure gold."[4]

The pattern of a woman's life, she implied, was determined not by talent but by values. Her walls were narrow but her wells were deep, serving as reservoirs of perception for her husband and children. Anne's theories, however, were about to be tested by a woman who had broken all the rules.

On January 15, Anne and Charles drove, for three and a half hours, north to Maidenhead to spend the night with Lady and Lord Astor at their home, Cliveden. High on a cliff overlooking the Thames, Cliveden was a huge and imperious Roman villa, built in 1850 and purchased by William Waldorf Astor[5] in 1893. The estate was a wedding gift given by Astor to his eldest son, Waldorf, on his marriage, in 1906, to Nancy Langhorne.

Small and delicate, with a finely-boned face and stately carriage, the quick-witted Nancy Langhorne had made her way easily into the turn-of-the-century British society. Born in Greenwoods, Virginia, to a large farming family that had lost its money during the Civil War, she was married at the age of eighteen and divorced at twenty-four. In 1903 she went, with her son, to England, where she met Waldorf Astor. At the time of their marriage, Astor was a Conservative member of the House of Commons, but in 1918, when he succeeded to the viscountsy, he became a member of the House of Lords. His father died in 1919, and Nancy won his seat in the House of Commons, becoming the first woman to sit in the lower house of Parliament. Before her swift and unprecedented political ascent, she had spent the early years of her marriage at her husband's side, serving an apprenticeship to public life.

This she did while raising four sons and a daughter. Her home, a grand salon, was frequented by the political and social elite. Nancy, savvy and brazen, with "volcanic" energy, had a natural flair for public speaking and an instinct for politics. Although she ran her campaign in 1919 on a platform of protective legislation for women and children, once she was seated, she earned a reputation as a right-wing spokesperson—a colonialist and an anti-communist with German sympathies. She thought of herself as a realist with a pragmatic view of foreign policy.[6]

By the time Anne and Charles met her, in 1936, her reputation was beginning to tarnish. Her propensity for talk had already earned her a reputation for political indiscretion. She blamed the rise of Hitler on the misjudgment of her countrymen and their allies. His strength was, she believed, an outcome of the folly of the Treaty of Versailles. If he had defects, so did English democracy, and whatever the unattractive aspects of his political philosophy, they were preferable to those of Soviet communism. But Hitler was beginning to look like a rogue, and Nancy's pragmatism was beginning to look like ideology. While "the Cliveden Set" had not yet become synonymous with German appeasement, the seeds of pro-German support were being sown. By January 1937, Nancy was demonized by the English public, along with those who moved in her circle.[7] And yet, Anne and Charles chose to dine with her.

On his return to England from Germany in August 1936, Charles hoped to convince Prime Minister Stanley Baldwin of the dimensions of German air superiority. Baldwin, however, brushed his theories aside, throwing Charles into a "cold rage." Privately, Charles derogated England's people and power as second-rate, and believed that its "best brains" had been killed in the Great War.[8] But many American State and War Department officials were eager to listen to him. Interested, too, were private citizens in France and England, among them the Astors and their friends.

Anne loved talking to Lord Astor at dinner, she told her mother. He was kind and responsive—not stuffy at all. Best of all was the tour, after dinner, when Lady Astor took her through the rooms of the house.

Unintimidated by its tradition or its splendor, Nancy Astor had stripped it of its Roman statues and busts and replaced its gloomy tapestries and furniture with chintz curtains and slipcovers, books, and flowers. In spite of its size, Anne found it warm and comfortable. Nancy showed Anne the dining room in which she had first met Anne's father and Elisabeth during their stay in London for the Naval Conference in 1930. With dramatic flair, she re-created the evening for Anne, and then guided her into the library. There, they sat in front of the fire, amid Dutch portraits of children, and talked of poetry, "Daddy," and Elisabeth.

When Anne returned to Long Barn from Cliveden, she pondered not only the patterns of womanhood but the moral justification of English aristocracy. Large estates were like social microcosms, reflecting a natural human hierarchy. The quality and ethics of life at the top trickled down through the ranks, bestowing pride and purpose on the servant class. Anne felt nothing but admiration for the Astors, and she was proud to say that Charles articulated his views on Germany with a precision worthy of the distinguished couple.[9]

Charles was planning a trip to India at the end of the month on behalf of Pan Am and British Imperial Airways, which wanted to link India's cities to a worldwide network of air-mail flights. Torn by her need to write and her desire to take care of Jon, Anne, now five months pregnant, reluctantly agreed to accompany Charles.[10] On the evening of January 21, Anne left Jon asleep in his bed, thinking how little he cared that they were going and how much it meant to her. As they flew across the Alps, in their new low-wing Miles Mohawk plane, they were wrapped in a shroud of fog. Lost and out of control, they dropped to earth, flying blindly, suspended between life and death. Caught, once again, in the nexus of "the timeless with time," Anne was no longer afraid. Later, the incident would become the core of her book *Steep Ascent* and a metaphor for her relations with Charles.[11]

They flew to Pisa and then to Rome, basking in color and sunlight after the gray days of an English winter. Anne delighted in the architecture of the ancient buildings and ruins, but her pleasure brought an unexpected loneliness. The richness of its history was lost on Charles, she wrote, who lacked the knowledge of those who had had a classical education. If only Elisabeth were here, she mused.[12]

They flew through Italy, across the Mediterranean, into Egypt and Palestine, and finally to Calcutta. While Charles was being treated with the deference of a religious icon,[13] Anne, in her letters home, analyzed the social texture of India. The size, the complexity, and the diversity of the people, along with the economic and social discrepancies, made it a land of injustices that would take generations to resolve. She was instinctively drawn to the Indian intelligentsia, yet she sensed their bitterness toward the English. But again, affirming the value of aristocracy, Anne wrote that the British had brought India peace, order, and a sense of national pride.[14]

For the moment, Charles had little patience with social analysis. He was worried about American military power in comparison with the developing German forces. Although America was still ahead, he wrote to his friend Harold Bixby, its lead was narrowing with "amazing rapidity." Russia's progress was unknown, but Italy was becoming another important competitor.[15]

Back at Long Barn, the spring passed quietly. The aubretia and daffodils bloomed in the soft April sunshine, and every morning the thrushes and the blackbirds sang. With her window open to the sounds of the spring, Anne sat at her desk with maps and photographs, trying to weave the facts and memories of their transatlantic flight into metaphor and narrative. She was happy to be pregnant, happy to be home with Jon, and grateful for her clarity of mind and the time to write.

As she had done in her early days in Princeton, Anne set up the nursery and counted her towels and blankets. She delighted in domesticity and spending time with Charles and Jon.[16] Seeing Jon in his "ragged red raincoat, thumping along with his boots," was consolation for anything.[17] She sat in the sun and walked slowly around the paths, cutting tulips, content to be waiting.[18]

On May 11, after two days of irregular pains, wondering whether she was going into labor, Anne asked Charles to drive her to the London Clinic. It was Coronation Eve,[19] and the crowds in the flag-draped streets were in holiday mood. Charles concentrated on getting through the mobs and traffic jams; Anne, overjoyed with excitement, looked at the candle-lit trees and remembered the beauty of her wedding night. Her labor continued through Coronation Day as she listened to the cheering crowds lining the streets. As her contractions came and went, she counted her breaths and read *The Years* by Virginia Woolf. By nightfall the pain was overwhelming, but she was determined to be conscious at the birth of her child. Between the whiffs of chloroform she caught Charles's eyes; his presence in the birthing room was enough to make the pain bearable. She was no longer tormented by fears of inadequacy and death, and the voice that had taunted her through the birth of Jon was silent. By morning, her third child, a son, was born. They named their "Coronation baby" Land, in memory of Charles's maternal grandparents.

Anne felt reborn—at peace and in control. With the pregnancy and birth behind her, she was suddenly "alive," eager to make up for lost time. Reviewing the year they had spent in England, she felt she had achieved nothing. Nonetheless, her time with Charles and Jon was "pure gold."[20]

While Anne dug her roots deep in Long Barn, Charles seemed to spin untethered. Several times a month he flew to Saint-Gildas, an island off the coast of Brittany, to work with Carrel in his summer laboratory.[21] After the visit to the Carrels' the previous August, Anne had little desire to return. The island had had a haunting beauty, bathed in a hazy green-gray light, but the Carrels had been less than hospitable to Anne. Solicitous and deferential toward Charles, they had insulted her with their categorical opinions. At once intimidated and repulsed by their arrogant notions of human types, she was troubled by their sanctimonious air. It was as though they were ordained vicars of God, looking down in judgment on lesser beings. They spoke of "auras," intangible currents of light and sensation that emanated from the bodies of human beings, defining and classifying personal value. Charles's aura, they said, was "deep, deep violet"; hers was "pale, pale blue."[22] Charles was incisive; she was superficial. Charles had greatness; she was condemned to mediocrity. But even as she understood the absurdity of their views, she wondered whether they had hit upon the truth. Were these the ideal measures of the Aryan spirit? Anne had always believed she was lesser than Charles. The Carrels' judgment was strangely liberating.

Charles's absence, however, and the consuming routine of caring for two children created a paradox. Anne was both happy and lonely, as if a piece of herself had died. In a letter to her friend Thelma Crawford Lee, Anne paraphrased a thought expressed by Rebecca West in her book *The Thinking Reed,* a rumination on the "price" women pay for their relations with men. A woman involved in a marriage, wrote West, especially a happy, absorbing marriage, seemed to lose her capacity for friendship. West wondered whether men had an unconscious desire to keep their women occupied so that they had no time for anything else. Anne wondered, along with West, whether only a part of her was expressed through marriage and other parts were wasted.

Anne confided in her friend that she had a feeling of emptiness that had no name; her commitment to her family seemed to fall short of happiness. She did not have the nourishment of people and responsibilities beyond her home, the sense of pride and purpose that she had before she was married.[23]

But if she was torn with conflict, no one around her knew. Two weeks later, on August 16, Margot and Dwight, on their honeymoon, arrived at Long Barn. Their love had germinated in the dark months of the Hauptmann trial, when Margot was a source of sustenance to the Morrow family. After Dwight's first year at Harvard Law School, assured by his doctors that he had been "cured" by psychotherapy,[24] they had married in May. They seemed a perfect union of opposites. Margot was strong, sturdy, and confident; Dwight was nervous, sensitive, and fragile. His neediness had given her a permanent place in the family she had come to love. But after three months, their marriage was beginning to falter, and Margot was desperate. It didn't take her long to realize that Dwight was still ill.[25]

While they were touring in Brittany, Dwight received notice that he had not made the school's law review. He went into a deep depression, hallucinating and talking to himself. Frightened, Margot took him to Long Barn, hoping that Anne would be able to console him. Anne understood him well; Dwight felt better almost immediately.

But the salve of Anne's presence would not last. Dwight returned to the States and resumed his studies at law school, but before the year was out, he was overwhelmed by paranoia and forced to leave Cambridge for home. Those close to him believed that the "fire and brimstone" of his early church education had filled him with the terror of damnation. As if in compensation, he had delusions of grandeur, imagining himself Jesus, saving the souls of the damned through his corporeal death. Sometimes, he would see himself as a "lighthouse," illuminating the way for those lost in the darkness.[26] There was a certain irony in his brother-in-law's achieving the public stature to which Dwight aspired.

In a sense, Dwight's terrors were not much different from Anne's. An alignment of genes, a biochemical shift, and the same voice that taunted Anne in the aftermath of Charlie's death might have found a way to consume her. She, too, feared sin and damnation and sought to be an incorporeal saint. In the summer of 1937, while Dwight Jr. succumbed to his fear and desperation, Anne sat in her second-floor office, overlooking the manicured gardens of Long Barn, seeking "salvation" through the written word. Each morning, between trips to school with Jon and feeding Land his milk and porridge, Anne wrote *Listen! The Wind*.

Listen! The Wind,[27] like *North to the Orient,* is a travel book suffused with myth. The book narrates ten days of the Lindberghs' five-month tour, from November 27 to December 6, 1933, to the Cape Verde island of Santiago off the coast of Africa and on to the English colony of Bathurst in Gambia. Anne struggled to write the book from her return home to Englewood in December 1933, through the Hauptmann trial in 1935, and their self-exile in England through the summer of 1937 at Long Barn.

While *North to the Orient* is a confrontation with death and a statement of loss, *Listen! The Wind* is an encounter with evil and an act of penance. Death is not "the answer" that will take Anne "home." She has to acknowledge the evil inside herself, renounce her moral righteousness, and come to terms with the "fallen" nature of man. Still hiding behind the façade of Charles's heroism, careful not to expose his vulnerability, Anne speaks for both of them. She unmasks the "sin" of their arrogance and carries the burden of insight and atonement.

Listen! The Wind is a sophisticated work with a strong narrative and an unyielding vision. It is written in layers to camouflage Anne's intent, but the linear narrative is precise in detail, time, and place. The second layer meshes two governing metaphors: Odysseus' descent to Hades on his journey home, and Dante's pilgrimage through the Inferno. The third layer is the relation between the two "Annes"—Anne the narrator, omniscient and omnipresent, and Anne the protagonist, living in the moment and vulnerable to the vicissitudes of time, place, and events. Using the literary technique of "doubling," Anne preserves her public image while subjecting herself to moral scrutiny and condemnation. Through the veil of the written word, Anne exorcises her demons and saves herself, pulling Charles, unaware, behind her.

While Anne the narrator, detached and confident, establishes the authority of herself and Charles, the certainty in her voice erodes her argument from within. She and Charles are equipped for everything, she tells the reader. They are independent and in control. They came like "giants on the wind," jumping from island to island, as though stepping on stones across the Atlantic.

As the Lindberghs descend from their "Olympian heights" to the wind-swept waters surrounding Cape Verde, Anne's narrative vision constricts and, with it, her sense of space and time. In the blazing heat of the African sun, Anne, like Dante, meets her counterpart in the world of the damned. Again, Anne the narrator "doubles" her characters as they approach a girl standing with a man on the pier. In spite of their race, age, and culture, they are mirror images of Charles and her.

But immediately Anne feels the presence of death. The man and the girl are thin, sick, reeking of decay. The man is a skeleton in an elegant suit; his child-wife is a phantomlike creature of burden. Like Anne, the girl is dressed in men's gear, too heavy for her delicate form. Her masquerade threatens to destroy her. Ruling the island with demonic force, sheathed in the grace of French hospitality, the man and the girl are instruments of evil, satanic creatures intent upon seducing Anne and Charles. While Anne resists, she knows she is no more righteous than they. She feels like a leper in the Bible, unclean—as though no amount of washing could remove her sins.

While Anne the narrator penetrates beneath the surface of the characters and events, Charles merely squirms in discomfort. Immediately, he distinguishes himself from the hosts, whose decadence he is forced to confront. Like Dante, Charles protests that he is just a pilgrim in a foreign land.

Charles is a shadowy, one-dimensional character, a thin figure of inflated stature, physically and morally absent. Unlike the "Charles" in *North to the Orient,* he is no longer the superior moral being, the contrast to Anne's inadequacy and weakness. In *Listen! The Wind,* they are partners in sin, roaming aimlessly in the land of the damned. Charles, the pilot, has the power to liberate them through flight; Anne, the narrator, has the vision to distill the meaning.

Time stops as life rushes like the wind above their heads. The wind, like a chorus, is a relentless presence that presages their actions and imbues them with meaning. The wind becomes the measure of their physical and spiritual vitality, the determining force of their salvation. It is the same wind that howled in Hopewell, obscuring the sounds that might have saved Charlie.

The wind dwindles to a distant roar, and Anne continues her struggle. As with the wave in her dream after Charlie was kidnapped, and the voice that taunted her during the birth of Jon, Anne is caught in a moment of terror. She can run, but she cannot be free. Their only hope is to get off the island—to radio Bathurst and get permission to land.

Released from the force that governs the island, the plane rises easily above the sea. But as they approach the coast of Africa, Anne the narrator lulls the reader into delusion. They are safe, she writes, in British territory—safe from the barrenness and decay of French colonialism. They are connected again to life and to time, to the running of the clock and to the rhythm of ordinary moral perception. People bustle and then stop to rest, policemen patrol the sunny streets of Bathurst in tropical attire, and the British flag waves in the soft wind.

But it is hot, Anne writes, incredibly hot; the seductive heat permeates their bodies and forces them to surrender. In spite of its veneer of civility, Bathurst, Anne implies, is just another ring of Hell. At least the French man and the girl on Cape Verde had succumbed to evil. The English people of Bathurst, numbed by convention and affluence, lack even the pretense of moral struggle.

Like Jacob, Anne does not know whether she wrestles with God or Man. The Almighty, she writes, can see everything. He has the vision and he has the power. Human perception is both partial and feeble. But the mention of God embarrasses her; she must pretend that Charles is still in control. She must help Charles harness and outwit the wind.

Systematically, they lighten their plane, stripping themselves of supplies and clothing and the aircraft of maps and charts. They discard the anchor and thirty miles' worth of fuel. Retaining only what they'll need for safety in the tropics, they prepare to leave with the morning wind.

That morning, an attempt at take-off fails, as do their efforts later in the day. In one of the most lyrical passages, Anne describes their surrender to the power of the elements:

> *The cliff below us fell abruptly to the sea. The sea poured out, a great wide circle to the smooth expanse, rolled out like heavy corded silk to the edge of the world . . . Here there was no struggle. Earth, sea, and sky— we had been in them this morning fight against them. Why, I wondered? . . . If only you could have your point of balance the sky! With such a pivot you could hold the world on your shoulders, another Atlas. In such an armor you could meet anything.*

A point of balance, the faith to surrender—these are the keys to salvation. They harness God's power and bridge the gap between man and the divine.

That night, as the wind rises with the moon, they take off into the "fathoms" of the night. Wrapped in layers of darkness, they plunge through the night with only the stars to guide them. Now stripped of all illusion, Anne the protagonist merges with Anne the narrator. The wind, as if in accord with Anne's self-knowledge, rises to lift them over the sea. They sail at daybreak, thanking God "as if we had been living in eternal night, as if this were the first sun that had ever rose out of the sea."

But Anne the narrator, powerful and visionary, must hide her journey through the rings of Hell, both from the reader and from her husband. As in the beginning, she affirms their heroism. Their visibility is unlimited, she declares, and her husband remains indomitable. Like Odysseus, they are sailing home. As though winking at the reader through her metaphor, Anne ends her story with a quote from Homer: "The men are sailing home from Troy and all the lamps are lit." But beyond the pretense, Anne's message is clear. Like Dante, she has made her pilgrimage through Hell. She has humbled herself in the face of God and is deemed worthy of salvation.

21

After the Fall

Anne on Illiec, 1938.
(Lindbergh Picture Collection, Manuscripts and Archives,
Yale University Library)

Winter Tree[1]

. . . The troubled mind
After the fall's deception reassured—
After the wind, after the winter storm—
By deep return to discipline of form.

—ANNE MORROW LINDBERGH

Summer 1937, Long Barn, Sevenoaks, England

While Anne sought salvation, Charles sought immortality. Three times in five weeks, in July and August, Charles flew to Brittany to work with Carrel.[2] Behind closed doors, they wrote their book, *The Culture of Organs.*[3] Carrel's vision had expanded beyond the mere sustenance of life. He prophesied a time when organs could be removed and healed at hospitals, when human life could be frozen and revived at will, when organs could be transplanted and reconfigured to create superior animal species, and when medical techniques could carry physicians into the realm of the living dead. Lindbergh's task was to develop the technological apparatus to support Carrel's theories of a new human breed. Labeled modern "Frankensteins" by the press, sea-locked on a wind-swept island, Carrel and Lindbergh tried to turn fiction into scientific reality.

Their flurry of activity elicited the unceasing interest of the press. The more secretive they were, the more the press intruded, until Carrel became enraged. In a letter to the Associated Press, he wrote, "You know that for scientific work, peace is a requisite. The attention of the public should not be attracted to this spot where we are working and on us."[4]

Europe was on the brink of war, and Lindbergh and Carrel knew that victory would be won on the battlefield, not in the laboratory. The spoils would belong to those who could master military technology. In a letter to Ambassador Robert Bingham, the English envoy to Germany, Charles wrote that one must "cost" devise such effective forms of counterattack as to make an offensive by the enemy prohibitive. One must deal with the enemy aggressively. "As civilization progresses, safety lies more in the ability to attack than in the ability to defend."[5]

In the middle of August, Charles planned his fourth visit to Saint-Gildas. This time Anne decided to go with him, but, discouraged by the thought of traveling with two children, she took the baby and left Jon behind. It was the first time she had left the serenity of Long Barn since the trip to India, before the baby was born. Sadly, she wrote, Charles had chosen to go during the week of Jon's birthday.[6]

In mid-September, when they were home, and Britain was condemning the Japanese attack on the Chinese cities of Nanking and Canton,[7] Kay and Truman Smith came to visit at Long Barn. In her diaries, Kay noted that the Lindbergh home was less than harmonious. She detected a sadism in Charles that extended even to his friendship with Truman. He once set Truman's newspaper on fire as they sat together reading in the car. Most obvious was his harsh treatment of Jon, who, at the age of four, was expected to behave like an adult. His meals and activities mimicked his parents'; if he did not follow their schedule, he was punished. In a bizarre reflection of Charles's life as the only child of an estranged marriage, alone with his mother in his father's absence, Charles compelled Jon to undertake the responsibilities of a man.[8] By intimidating him with adult standards, Charles expected to make Jon confident and self-sufficient. As a consequence, Jon developed the pose of maturity while hiding his fears in silence.

Kay also noted Charles's paranoia. The Lindberghs' German shepherd, Thor, policed the garden as the baby slept, alerting Anne and Charles to people who wandered in and out of his purview. When the dog barked, Charles would take his gun from the closet with eerie nonchalance.

In spite of their differences, Charles and Truman had work to do together. Since the Reich ministers had confidence in Charles, Truman wanted him to return to Berlin and inspect more engine and aircraft factories. Within a week the Lindberghs, with the Smiths, were in Germany; Jon and Land were at home. They arrived in Frankfurt on October 10 and in Munich on the eleventh. In an effort to shelter Anne and Charles from Nazi Party politics, the Smiths arranged for them to stay in the mountains of Bavaria, miles away from Berlin, at the home of Baron Cramer-Klett.[9] As Charles was shuttled to and from Munich by official car to attend meetings of the Lilienthal Aviation Society and to tour aircraft factories, Anne hiked through the mountains with the "ageless" baron, speaking of human frailty and the divinity of truth.[10] For Anne, this was a journey into the Middle Ages, a beautiful fairyland, insulated from the political turmoil of the German cities. Yet she found the atmosphere unsettling, as if something she could not discern lingered beneath the surface.

While Anne was charmed by the baron's manner, Kay investigated his political status. She found that he was in danger of being arrested by the Reich. A devout Catholic with a papal title, Cramer-Klett was passionately anti-Nazi. He had agreed to house and court the Lindberghs in exchange for his continued freedom.[11]

Minister Udet, eager to show Lindbergh his country's progress, took him to the testing bases of all the major aircraft—bombers, fighters, and training planes. He allowed him to fly the Storch, which Charles found comparable to American planes. For the second time, Lindbergh helped Smith write a formal report for the War Department, a general estimate of German air power as of November 1, 1937. Smith later admitted that they had dramatized their data, hoping to capture high-level attention. They reported that

> *Germany is once more a world power in the air. Her air force and her air industry have emerged from the kindergarten state . . . They would reach "full manhood" in years . . . it is one of the most important world events of our time. What it portends for Europe is something no one today can tell . . . The vision of Goering is fantastically large, but their humbleness of spirit has made them work harder.*[12]

As Charles was being shown through factories and fields and military air installations, Hitler was planning to take over Europe. In a reversal of policy, he now announced that *Lebensraum,* "living space" for his people, could be gained only by force. And he made clear his plans to annex Austria. When Italy and Japan joined Germany in a pact to annihilate communism, the military triangle—the Axis—evoked alarm in some quarters, but appeasement still reigned in Britain. That gave Hitler the confidence to proceed.[13]

Home once again, Anne busied herself. Delighting in the beauty and nearness of her children, she charged through her mornings writing at her desk, only to fall into breathless afternoons, racing Jon, wild with joy, through the mist and mud of the English autumn.

At night, she and Charles and Thor walked miles in the moonlight through open fields. In the soft light, with trees laced against the sky, they sat on the gate and looked through the tangled oaks toward the moon. When their reverie was disturbed by the roar of planes, it mattered little; they trudged toward the bright lights of Long Barn, tingling with excitement.[14]

As Britain and France announced a joint pact of neutrality, the Lindberghs traveled to the States for Christmas. The trip was hastily conceived, and it confused and mystified those around them. Charles had business in New York with Pan Am and experiments to complete at the Rockefeller Institute with Carrel.[15] But he left England, after two years there, with an air of urgency, as though it were time to accelerate his work.

It was terrible for Anne to leave Jon for Christmas, but Charles was intent on going, and she would not refuse.[16] She bought the Christmas tree early, and seating Jon on her knee, told the boy the story of the birth of Christ. Did the wise men go fast when they followed the star, he asked? They went by camel, not by car, Anne explained.

On December 1, Anne and Charles left Long Barn and the children, and boarded a ship bound for New York. Even though they were registered under the name "Gregory," they made no attempt to hide their identity.[17] In contrast to their crossing two years earlier, they appeared relaxed and comfortable. They lounged on the deck in the morning sun and sat at the captain's table at dinner.[18] And while they kept to themselves in the afternoon, it was clear, even to the press, that something new was in the air. Charles was re-entering the public arena, with a strong sense of personal influence. One magazine reported, "Lindbergh landed with probably more complete information of Europe's airways than any individual on this side of the Atlantic."[19]

Anne found life in New York crude. Having been moved by the bucolic life of Long Barn and the reserve of London, she felt out of place in the frenzied, acquisitive culture of New York society.[20] Its pace left her no room to breathe, and seemed to lack any trace of the spiritual.[21] Shopping on Fifth Avenue and living in the luxury of Next Day Hill, she had little cognizance of life on the street.[22] In fact, the economy was beginning to lose the early gains of the New Deal. In the first half of 1938, industrial production would drop precipitously, and by the end of the year two million people would lose their jobs.[23] But what Anne saw was magazines and shops full of luxurious clothes, furs, and jewels. It was all she could do not to be swept away by the mindless opulence.[24]

Meanwhile, the tension abroad was rising. Italy withdrew from the League of Nations, and on December 12 the Japanese bombed British and American gunboats on the Yangzte River. One day later, the Japanese staged the "rape" of Nanking, in which 200,000 civilians were slaughtered and 20,000 women were raped and murdered.[25]

The British foreign secretary, Anthony Eden, dissuaded an irate League of Nations from imposing sanctions. The British cabinet, however, overruled the aviation experts by approving a shift from the building of bombers to fighter aircraft. That dramatic change would later prove pivotal in Britain's defense.[26]

As preparations for war intensified, Carrel deepened his commitment to "civilization." In a bold attempt to sustain human organs in his laboratory, he used the pump designed by Charles to perfuse tissue with insulin, adrenaline, and other glandular extracts so that he could study the morphology and activities of the organs.[27] In a speech to an audience of Phi Beta Kappa members at Dartmouth, he called for the establishment of eugenics institutes throughout the world, for the express purpose of developing a higher breed of "civilized man."[28] Through December and January, Lindbergh worked at the Rockefeller Institute to further their experiments. Simultaneously, Carrel arranged to educate doctors in Italy and Germany in the techniques that he and Lindbergh were perfecting.[29]

By the turn of the year, Anne was eager to return to Long Barn. On January 17, she wrote in her diary that once again the pendulum of her life had swung too far. The visit to the States had been a frenetic attempt to see everyone and do everything. This hurried life was as numbing as the isolation of domesticity. As Anne would later write in *Gift from the Sea*, one must learn to navigate the sea between solitude and society.[30]

But Anne was about to get more than her share of isolation. At Carrel's suggestion, Charles had consented to buy an island near to St. Gildas called Illiec. From the moment Charles saw the tiny, four-acre slip of land, washed by tides and flooded by light, he wanted to own it. And the Carrels were eager to have him join them. In spite of its wild beauty, reminiscent of Maine, Illiec seemed to Anne little more than a pile of rocks with a house set in a grove of pine trees.

She must have remembered she hadn't married for happiness. Although she would have to leave Long Barn and the beauty and safety of its walled gardens and paths and the life they had carved in the small country village with Jon and Land, Anne knew she had to go. In spite of the fact that she disdained the Carrels and their racist views, Anne deluded herself that living on Illiec was what she should do.[31]

22

The Crossed Eagle

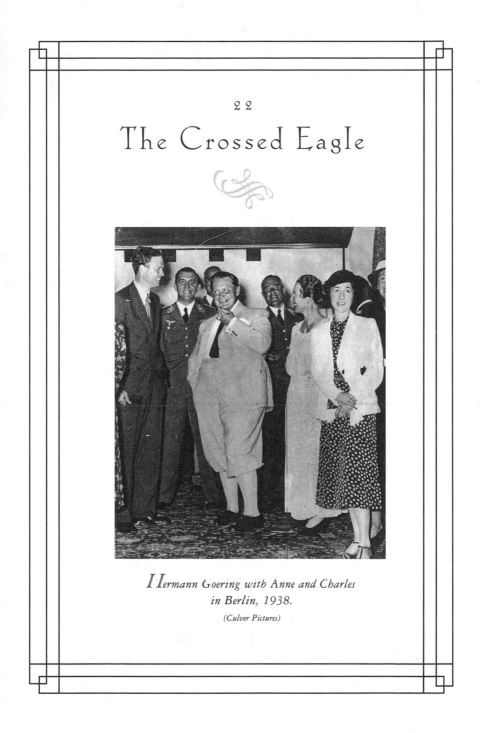

*Hermann Goering with Anne and Charles
in Berlin, 1938.*

(Culver Pictures)

EVEN — [1]

Him that I love
I wish to be free—
Even from me.

—ANNE MORROW LINDBERGH

APRIL 1938, ILLIEC, FRANCE

There is your island!" said Madame Carrel, pointing into the mist. Her eyes squinting against the cool April rain, Anne took the sighting on faith. No matter how hard she peered toward the open sea, Anne could not discern the shore.[2]

With their baby in a basket in the cockpit, Anne and Charles had landed in a field on the mainland. The Carrels, who had met them, drove to the coast of Brittany near Mont-Saint-Michel, and now, at high tide, they crossed by motorboat and moored on the cratered beach. When they climbed the pebbled spit of rocks toward a stone tower, a nineteenth-century manor house rose up to meet them. The wild beauty of the "galloping tides" and rocky coastline heightened the majesty of its imposing structure, and the gray light of the stormy sky bathed the rugged "gorse-covered" land with an air of medieval romance.[3]

Unfortunately, the house was dreadful inside, with no heat or plumbing or electricity. Built in the 1860s by the French composer Ambroise Thomas, it still had the look of an elegant mansion, but now it was in total disrepair.[4] Anne's mind was filled with possibilities as she walked the dark halls and surveyed the sparsely furnished rooms.[5]

Their decision to buy the island was spurred by both desire and desperation. When they returned from America in the dead of winter in 1938, the complacency of England was chilling. It was a land, they believed, at war with itself and steeped in self-delusion; they felt alienated from English society and politics.[6] But in part, the Rockefeller Institute had given them no choice. The board of directors had decided to discontinue its support of further collaboration by Charles and Carrel.[7] In early June 1937, in a sudden change of policy, the board had declared a mandatory retirement age of sixty-five, with a specific notice that those members reaching the age of sixty-four or over on July 1 of that year would be retired on July 1, 1939.[8] The date was just three days after Carrel's birthday, and he was the only member who would turn sixty-four in 1937. The decision seemed less than coincidental. Other members of the institute had been permitted to carry on with their work well into their late sixties and early seventies.

The institute could no longer tolerate Carrel's vision of a social order determined by eugenics. To have as a member of its staff a radical ideologue was unacceptable to an institution dedicated to objective inquiry. Furthermore, the presence of Charles, an unqualified layman, diminished the standards of their institution.[9]

Carrel, in retribution, sought to expose the institute as a "Jewish operation." He tried to intimidate the board by saying the institute was run by Jews who intended to replace him with one of their own.[10] But the board was implacable, and Carrel and Charles left. Carrel, certain that he would find sympathetic colleagues in Germany and Italy, wrote to a friend that he would train doctors in both Padua and in Berlin.[11]

When Anne and Charles prepared for their move, they found themselves embroiled in English politics. The Astors now counted them among their own and again invited them to dine. Charles, who had found his views confirmed during his second trip to Germany, was eager to take a political stand. Anne, however, was put off by the Astors' anti-Churchill, pro-German friends. She claimed she was too stupid to understand the wisdom of the intellectual elite,[12] but Charles "shock[ed] the life out of everyone" with his views on Germany.

Slowly, Anne came to believe that Charles was right. At a dinner at Cliveden on May 1, Anne summoned up the courage to tell Lord Astor, the perfect gentleman and host, that she and Charles agreed with his views. Accommodating Germany was the only hope of keeping peace.[13]

The next day, the Lindberghs and the Nicolsons conferred at Sissinghurst on the implications of the impending crisis between Germany and Czechoslovakia. Charles bombarded Nicolson with facts, noted Anne,[14] but Nicolson had impressions of his own:

> *Lindbergh is most pessimistic. He says we cannot possibly fight since we would surely be beaten. The German Air Force is ten times superior to that of Russia, France and Great Britain put together. Our defences are simply futile and the barrage-balloons a mere waste of money. He thinks we should give way and then make an alliance with Germany. To a certain extent his views can be discounted a) because he naturally believes aeroplanes will be the determinant factor in war; and b) because he believes in the Nazi theology, all tied up with his hatred of democracy as represented by the free press and the American public. But even when one makes these discounts, the fact remains that he is probably right in saying that we are outmastered in the air.[15]*

Nicolson may have exaggerated; he did not fabricate. Clearly, Charles saw the Third Reich as the embodiment of his values: science and technology harnessed for the preservation of a superior race, physically able and morally pure. While Charles valued democracy in the abstract, he had come to believe that its freedoms were not worth the price. Social and political equality, together with an ungoverned press, had produced a climate of moral degeneracy that had permitted the murder of his infant son. He did not disdain democracy so much as he did the common man—the uneducated and enfeebled masses, typified by Hauptmann, who lived like parasites on the body politic. America wallowed in decadence, the Russians sank into mediocrity, and England and France, at war with themselves, were weak, aimless, and morally defunct. To Charles, Germany under Hitler was a nation of true manhood—virility and purpose. The strong central leadership of a fascist state was the only hope for restoring a moral world order.

While Charles spoke his mind behind closed doors, Carrel publicly asserted his contempt. Democracy, he said, was an outright failure, incommensurate with the laws of nature. Human beings were not equal, and to build a system on such an ideology was to court failure. Eugenics and the government of the elite were the means for maintaining civilized life.[16]

At last, Charles had found a master, someone erudite and capable, whose courage to defy public opinion exceeded his own. If Charles had his master, so too did Anne. From the moment they moved to Illiec, on June 20, 1938, Alexis Carrel took over their lives. And for the first time, Charles willingly relinquished the reins. Everything from what the Lindbergh children ate and wore to how they slept and spent their days was submitted for the approval of Dr. Carrel.[17] A strong advocate of breast feeding and a staunch believer in the duty of women to care for their young,[18] Carrel deepened Anne's sense of inadequacy and guilt. She tried to obey his wishes and was constantly on the verge of collapse. Her head ached, her nerves were frayed, and she desperately longed for a place to rest. Although the wild beauty of the island and the sea had held the promise of new adventure, now even Jon seemed lost and lonely. Only Charles was pleased.[19]

As Charles trudged along the sand bars between home and laboratory, pondering the mysteries of life, Anne drowned in domestic chaos. The four members of her staff were under the eye of Dr. Carrel, and they rose in rebellion against his rules of childrearing.[20]

The same week the Lindberghs arrived in Illiec, President Roosevelt had sponsored a conference, in the French mountain resort of Evian, to discuss the immigration of the Jews. The United States promised to accept 27,370 from Germany and Austria; Britain refused to accept any. Australia declared, "As we have no real racial problem, we are not desirous of importing one."[21] New Zealand said the same; Canada, Colombia, Uruguay, and Venezuela agreed to accept only farmers. Nicaragua, Honduras, Costa Rica, and Panama jointly announced that they would not accept political insurgents or intellectuals. Argentina and France said they had reached saturation. Only Denmark and the

Netherlands responded to the plight of the Jews and agreed to open
their borders without qualification.

When she heard of the projected immigration of Jews, Kay Smith
articulated the sentiments of 70 to 85 percent of the American public:[22]
"At a time when we have some twelve million unemployed and the
number steadily mounting and a huge debt, this course is nothing short
of suicide." And, Kay continued, in a voice that expressed the extreme
of xenophobia:

> *I am beginning to think Hitler is right: a Jew is first of all a Jew and
> a national only when his interests are not involved. Certainly the Jews
> in America, where we have given them everything, now that the test has
> come, are proving themselves Jews and not Americans. Their constant
> agitation against those European nations which have discriminated
> against their race, the pressure they constantly put on Washington to
> protest, to get their relatives out of the countries and into America is done
> entirely without regard to our best interests.*[23]

What were the best interests of America? The question became a
national obsession. Intent on finding the answer in aviation, Charles resolved to study European military air power firsthand. At his request,
Roosevelt gave him permission to fly to Russia, Czechoslovakia, and
France.[24]

When Charles asked Anne to go with him, she was torn again by
her desire to stay with Jon and Land. But her fear of alienating Charles,
along with her delight in the beauty and freedom of flying, prevailed.[25]
As they flew over the English Channel, Anne reveled in the sight of the
"satin sea" and in the landscape rushing below.[26] While they were waiting in London for permission to fly to Russia, Berlin announced the
conscription of 750,000 men.[27] Anne feared for the British but felt contempt for their blindness. Why had they left themselves so vulnerable?[28]

On August 17, 1938, the Lindberghs flew to Moscow across
Germany and Poland on a route laid out by Russian officials; they were

able to avoid fortified zones. As the ground crews awaited their craft, squadrons of bright red pursuit planes circled in mock battle, entertaining the half million Russians who had flooded the city for the event. It was dusk before the Lindberghs' monoplane circled the field in Moscow, illuminated only by ordinary searchlights. Adjacent to the field, a captive balloon, high above the trees, supported a portrait of the commissar of war.[29]

The next day, Anne and Charles drove out to the countryside to meet "the people."[30] Anne had already accepted the views of the Carrels. To question them would have been tantamount to questioning Charles and taking a moral stand alone. The risk was too great. Instead, using her newly acquired standards, Anne judged the people they saw. She decided there were five Russian types: the stupid, the fanatical, the clever, the shallow, and the criminal. Using the Carrels' criteria, which had once dismayed her, she sorted the Russian population into these identifiable types, as though she could discern the quality of a human being by the length or shape of a nose or the refinement of a cheekbone.[31] While the government had built new official structures, wide boulevards, and underground trains, the life of the people on the street seemed impoverished. Their colorless lives and vacant faces seemed proof to Anne that they had sacrificed their spirit to the ideal of material progress.

Anne's impressions of life in Russia were not far from the truth. Living conditions had deteriorated so far that an air of apathy pervaded the country. Besides the terror of Stalin's purges, which had left the Russian people whispering inside their homes, the inefficiency of an economy and a labor force unable to keep pace with world industrialization had, by 1938, left the people wholly demoralized.

The malaise, however, had not affected those involved in aviation. Anne met three women fliers with "intelligent, healthy faces." She marveled that these professional women, whose attitudes and demeanor matched those of their male colleagues, were married and had children.[32] Unlike the British and the Germans, the Russians applauded the modern woman.[33] But a trip to the government-run nurseries for working women reversed her admiration. The freedom of the women to work had its price; the children were malnourished and neglected.[34] Although Anne felt more kinship with the Russians than with the Germans, she wondered how one could admire a system that accepted mediocrity.[35]

The professionalism and high morale of the aviation community, however, could not compensate, in Charles's judgment, for the mediocrity of the planes. Intent on impressing Charles, the Russian government put on an air show and guided him through their bases and factories. Charles remained unimpressed. What he saw, he said, was clearly inferior to German and English aircraft, though it was good enough for military combat.

After a visit to the countryside for a holiday, Anne could not wait to leave the "swarming" hordes.[36] Even the state dinners had ceased to be interesting. Tired of ceremony and social pretense, Anne wrote in despair, "I have lost my mask."[37]

As news of the Lindberghs' arrival in Russia filtered to the people, they were plunged into public demonstrations reminiscent of those during their early flying years. From Moscow, they flew to Kiev, to Odessa, and on to Rumania, where thousands awaited their arrival.[38] The crowds could not be controlled.[39] They were forced to stay at private homes rather than to risk being in public places. Police cars followed their every move.[40]

The landing in Prague several days later coincided with Hitler's declared threat to Czechoslovakia. But Anne was hopeful; the Czechs were well armed.[41]

As Charles inspected the aviation factories, and Anne visited libraries and museums, the Czech government suddenly conceded to all the German demands. Hitler accelerated his preparations for invasion. Then, when France called up its one million reservists,[42] Anne and Charles left Czechoslovakia. When they landed at Le Bourget across the Maginot Line, Anne was relieved.[43] The shops on the rue St. Honoré looked "wonderful."[44] And Charles looked wonderful to the government ministers of France. His survey trip had earned him credentials; they wanted his firsthand impressions of Russian and German air power.

On September 9, Anne and Charles spent the night in Paris, planning to meet American Ambassador William C. Bullitt and the French Air Minister Guy la Chambre in the morning. Ambassador Bullitt agreed with Charles that a direct German attack would cost the French three to four times as many casualties as the Germans. It would be "the death of a race," he had earlier written to Roosevelt in a message advocating appeasement.[45] A war would mean the end of civilization. Profoundly depressed, Guy la Chambre reported his conversation with Lindbergh to Premier Édouard Daladier and Foreign Minister Georges Bonnet. Bonnet concluded that "peace must be preserved at any cost," and, for the moment, Roosevelt agreed. The next day he confirmed his commitment to American neutrality; he told White House reporters that it would be "100 percent wrong" to assume that America would side with Britain and France.[46]

While Russia continued to urge France to take action, and while Britain maintained its silence, Czechoslovakia prepared to meet the Germans alone. On September 10, the Lindberghs departed from Paris in gloom, and arrived home too late to see Con and Aubrey, who had waited nearly a week for their return.[47]

Hurriedly, at low tide, Charles walked the rocky sand toward St. Gildas, eager to report his findings to Carrel. There, he met a house guest who would become his friend and confidant for life. James Newton was a successful businessman who had discovered his "genius" for making friends and had dedicated his life to the service of "uncommon men." In the wake of a religious epiphany that exposed his moral failings, he had joined the Moral Rearmament movement,[48] which preached a philosophy of purity, honesty, and unselfish love. A longtime admirer of Alexis Carrel's, Newton had jumped at the chance to meet him when their mutual friend Edward Moore suggested a trip to St. Gildas. The chance to meet Lindbergh doubled his interest.[49]

Anne liked Jim right away. He was warm and gracious, but probably more clear-headed than the typical American. But his notions of morality were a bit too simplistic for her taste. Newton believed that war could be prevented by a "re-armament" of the collective moral spirit. Although Jim was a man of humility, his philosophy seemed to her immature and arrogant.[50] Charles felt much the same, and Newton understood. Later, in his book, Newton explained that Charles was not an organization man and did not believe in a paternalistic God. Charles accepted life "on his own terms," he wrote.[51]

On September 14, while the Lindberghs supped in island darkness, Prime Minister Neville Chamberlain prepared to meet Hitler. One day before Hitler's deadline for capitulation, all of Western Europe was pitched for war. Bound to France, but sensing Daladier's ambivalence, Chamberlain feared he stood alone. He asked Hitler to state his minimum demands. Hitler claimed he wanted only what was his: those parts of Czechoslovakia inhabited by Germans. He promised Chamberlain not to invade until Chamberlain had conferred with his cabinet. Russia, bound by treaty to France, massed its troops in the Ukraine.[52]

On September 18, the Premier Daladier and Foreign Minister Bonnet met Hitler to establish the ground rules of annexation. Only those territories whose population was at last 50 percent German, they declared, would be conceded. The Czechs were not even offered a plebiscite. Abandoned and desperate, Prime Minister Eduard Beneš capitulated.

Heady with victory, Hitler three days later demanded the total and unconditional occupation of the Sudetenland. Chamberlain convinced his cabinet to concede. He warned Hitler, however, that if France fought, so would Britain. On September 27, France and Britain mobilized for war and 1.5 million Czech soldiers gathered at the German border.[53]

While the Czechs struggled with the devastating implications of an unprincipled peace, Charles was summoned to London to meet Joseph Kennedy, the American Ambassador to Britain.[54] As a result of their September 13 meeting, Charles drew up a four-page report to the ambassador on his views of German air superiority.

Kennedy and Lindbergh had met at Cliveden four months earlier and their isolationist, pro-German views made them fast friends. Kennedy fancied himself a maverick, an outsider with a businessman's sense, rather than an obedient career diplomat. He was known for breaking protocol and for taking initiatives. Frustrated with the slow workings of the State Department, he appointed himself a "super ambassador" who could resolve problems for all of Europe.[55] He believed the continent's only hope was a negotiated peace with Nazi Germany, and he used Lindbergh's report in an attempt to influence Roosevelt.[56] Charles had asked the Germans for permission to share their data with "his own people," and they had agreed. He made clear to Kennedy and Roosevelt, however, that he did not want his name associated with the information.[57]

"German air strength is greater than all other European countries combined," he wrote in his report. "They produce 500–800 planes per month and are capable of producing 20,000 per year." Their design, construction, and operation were "excellent."

> *It seems to be essential to avoid a general European war at any cost. I believe that a war now might easily result in the loss of European civilization. A general war would, I believe, result in something akin to communism running over Europe and, judging by Russia, anything seems preferable . . . I am convinced it is wiser to permit German's eastward expansion than to throw England and France unprepared into a war at this time.*[58]

In fact, Lindbergh's statistics were later proved wrong. The numbers he had were based on long-range plans, but Hitler's thirst for domination sabotaged them. Production would not hit its potential of 20,000 planes until the end of 1942.[59] Goering's estimates had been inflated not only to satisfy Hitler but to intimidate the Allies. Lindbergh was being used. The information leaked to him was meant to erode resistance. And, in fact, his derogation of Russian aircraft and his German production report to Roosevelt gave him new credibility and increased his access within the Reich.[60]

On receipt of Charles's letter of September 22, Ambassador Kennedy cabled the document to Secretary of State Cordell Hull in Washington. Two days later, Kennedy and Hull conferred by phone, with the understanding that Roosevelt had received the message. The president had already sent the memo to Chief of Staff Malin Craig and Chief of Naval Operations William D. Leahy.[61] On the same day, Kennedy had slipped a copy of the report to Chamberlain as he boarded a plane to meet Hitler at Bad Godesberg.[62] That evening, in London, Lindbergh spent two hours at dinner with Air Minister John Slessor and the next day had lunch with Air Marshal Sir Wilfrid Freeman. He also talked with others in the air ministry and in air intelligence.

As Londoners placed sandbags around doors and windows, Anne and Charles strapped on their gas masks. They spent the night of September 26 at Cliveden, listening to a broadcast of Hitler's speech. Anne felt as though she were watching a patient with a fatal illness. War seemed inevitable, but she was confused about the issues.

When her father was alive, the world had seemed smaller and less complicated. She was beginning to believe that his idealism was the "romantic" illusion of simpler times. He was certain of his loyalty to Britain, and committed to the Wilsonian vision of sovereign nations adhering to the laws of the international community.[63] Confused about the "right" or "wrong" of war, Anne nonetheless consented to return to Berlin later in the fall and to consider making it their permanent home.[64]

While Chamberlain prepared his declaration of war, Hitler conferred with Mussolini, at whose suggestion they agreed to meet the British and French in a last effort to avoid military confrontation. Within twenty-four hours, Chamberlain, Daladier, Hitler, and Mussolini were in Munich. Without the consent of Czechoslovakia or Russia, they signed an agreement in the early morning hours of September 30, conceding to all of Hitler's demands. Chamberlain arrived home waving the treaty, which promised enduring peace. He assured the crowds that had gathered to cheer him that he had brought them "peace with honor."

Anne was thrilled. In her diary she quoted the words Chamberlain had borrowed from Shakespeare's *Henry IV,* hoping with him that he had "out of this nettle, danger, we pluck this flower, safety." It was clear, she noted proudly, that Charles could be of influence.[65] Apparently, the French foreign minister thought the same.

On September 30, on their way home from London to Illiec, they stopped in Paris, where Charles once again talked to Ambassador William Bullitt and French economic minister, Jean Monnet. Recognizing Charles's sway with statesmen, as well as his public clout, they asked him to galvanize French public opinion in support of developing resources to resist the Germans. Their plan was to circumvent Roosevelt's pledge of neutrality by secretly manufacturing planes in the French air factories on the Canadian border, using manpower from Detroit and Buffalo.[66] Anne was torn between her father's views expressed by his old friend Jean Monnet and her husband's hard-nosed realities. But Charles remained implacable. Planes or no planes, he was convinced that a war with Germany would be a disaster, allowing communism to overrun Europe.[67] "Victory itself would be of little value, for it would leave no civilization able to appreciate or take advantage of it."[68] In short, if the Germans were to lose the war, the best blood of Europe would be dead. Certain that war would bring an end to Western civilization, and ridding himself of any moral responsibility, Charles refused to help. Jean Monnet abandoned his plans.[69]

The next morning, Hitler marched through the Sudetenland, occupying 10,000 square miles with a population of three and a half million, a fifth of whom were Czechs.[70]

Concerned about her children, Anne left Charles in Paris and returned to Illiec. The children were her source of strength.[71] And yet she was home not a week before she agreed to accompany Charles to Berlin. He was so pleased about her coming, he was "like a small boy."[72] Jon, however, turned away in tears, asking plaintively why she had to leave. Anne, filled with pain, had no answer.

Quite in harmony, Anne and Charles set out for Berlin and were invited to the Lilienthal Aviation conference. Charles attended on the tacit premise that he would be privy to new Luftwaffe developments. In the wake of their Munich victory and their successful invasion of Czechoslovakia, the Nazis saw Charles as a spokesman for their superior military might. The new pro-German American ambassador, Hugh Wilson, viewed Charles's presence as an opportunity to strengthen his connections within the Reich. And Truman Smith, like Charles, was eager to garner new military information.[73]

Later, Smith wrote that Charles had come to Berlin to help the Jews rescue their money from the hands of the Nazis.[74] But there is no evidence to support that claim. While Anne expressed revulsion at German anti-Semitism, both she and Charles viewed "the Jewish Problem" as a German internal matter, of little import in the prevailing political and military context. But their intimate connections with the Reich through Truman Smith, as well as their familiarity with street life in Berlin, leaves little doubt that they did understand Hitler's racial motives. Even if they had not read the hate-riddled pages of *Mein Kampf,* which is doubtful, the daily barrage of anti-Semitic propaganda, and the anti-Semitic laws that delineated the inferior legal and social status of the Jews, could not possibly have escaped their notice. By October 1938, there were nearly four hundred laws segregating, stigmatizing, and impoverishing Jews. In 1933, Jewish state employees had been dismissed. In an attempt to keep Jewish propaganda out of the press, Jewish editors were ousted and authors expelled. In 1934, Jewish students and professors were removed from college and universities, and in 1935 Jews were stripped of their German citizenship and civil rights. At the beginning of 1938, an intensified program of "Aryanization" had been launched, and Jewish businessmen were forced to sell out to Germans. Four out of five Jewish establishments were transferred to "Aryan" landlords. By the end of the summer, Jewish physicians and nurses had been forced to resign, and the middle names of all Jews were modified to bear the mark of their ancestors.

Every man would be known henceforth as "Israel" and every woman as "Sara."[75] All who had walked the streets of Berlin, all who had read any pages of *Mein Kampf,* and certainly all who sat within the walls of the American embassy understood the intentions of the Reich.

But Lindbergh's new moral order transcended the existence of any race or nation. In his view, no ideology or people were sacred; everything and everyone was expendable. The Jews, the Russians, the Asians, the British, and the French, even the principles of democracy, were subject to the same evolutionary laws. The strong would always dominate the weak, and the end would always justify the means. The Germans represented the archetypal model of virility, energy, efficiency, and excellence. The Jews, it seemed, were responsible for the economic and social chaos after the Great War. And their infiltration of German society was a problem that had to be resolved. If the Jews were sacrificed to preserve German moral and racial superiority, it was in the natural order of things.[76]

Anne may have been ambivalent about the destructive power of fascism, but, like Charles, she had become disillusioned with the freedoms inherent in democracy. If the ungoverned press—the ubiquitous voice of the common people—could create the moral degeneracy that inspired the murder of her child, perhaps democracy wasn't worth its price. Despite her deepest instincts, and the humanist teachings of her Presbyterian parents, Anne questioned its viability. Furthermore, there was something seductive about a society governed from the top. Under Hitler's rule, there seemed no room for the moral license that had killed Charlie. Germany was vigorous, purposeful, and productive at a time when the democracies seemed to shatter in the throes of economic depression and moral confusion. While in America the Lindberghs had lived in a state of "siege," there, in Germany, Hitler had promised them total protection from the public and the press. For the first time, they had the prospect of living a normal life with their children.

In the end, Anne cast her lot with Charles. She was willing to accept the validity of his views. Maybe history was Darwinian—the inevitable unfolding of natural laws. Maybe the strong would always dominate the weak; perhaps the fittest would always survive. Germany had the technology and the will to win a war. By force of nature, Hitler's domination was inevitable.

They were not alone in their indifference to the Jews. In American polls taken in 1938, Jews were last on the list of public concerns. An overwhelming majority of those questioned were repelled by the atrocities and perversions of the German Reich, but few wanted to do anything about them.[77] The words of Charles Lindbergh would echo around the world. By force of his celebrity and his ambition, he had placed himself at the crux of power, and it was his voice that was heard by those who governed. In 1938, he was still the untarnished hero of the technological age, as well as a world-renowned expert on aviation. Although his motives seemed enigmatic and mercurial, his voice carried the weight of "truth."

To Anne, Charles seemed "chosen" to walk among the superior few who could push forward the "natural" process. Who was she to hold it back? As his wife, wasn't she morally bound to his view? Like the virtuous woman defined by her ancestors, Anne was prepared to leave her country and her home, her children and her writing—in short, everything she held dear, to go "all the way" with her husband. Even if her loyalty to Charles violated her true instincts, she maintained her self-imposed silence. Only when the Nazis sought to honor him did she finally choose to speak.

Two and a half weeks after Munich, on October 18, Ambassador Hugh Wilson gave an official dinner at the American Embassy in Berlin to honor Charles and Field Marshal Goering. Among the Americans attending were Truman Smith, Albert Vanaman, Igor Sikorsky, Consul General Raymond Geist, and other officials of the American Embassy. Among the Germans were other high-level military advisers: Milch, Udet, Heinkel, Messerschmitt, and the chief of the Air Research division. The Italian and Belgian ambassadors to Germany also attended.[78] Because the event was a "stag dinner," Anne and Kay dined alone at the Smiths' apartment.

Within minutes of Charles's arrival, he was approached by Goering, who, with a few German words, handed him a small red-leather box. *"Im Nahmen des Fuehrer . . . ."*

As the voice of the translator echoed his words, Goering read from a parchment signed by Hitler, presenting Charles with the Service Cross of the Order of the German Eagle, a golden medallion with four small swastikas. *"Dienst Kreuz des Orden vom Deutschen Adler mit dem Stern."*

It was the second highest medal conferred on foreigners for service to the Reich. Hugh Wilson noted that Charles received it with unqualified pride. Smiles and applause accompanied Goering's declaration, and the evening proceeded with routine nonchalance.[79]

With Goering at one end of the dinner table, and Charles, the honored guest, at the other, conversation centered on the aftermath of Munich. Amid the clink and hum of Kate Wilson's finest crystal and china, and the shuffling deference of coat-tailed servants, Goering delivered his opinions on the adversaries of the Reich. Daladier, he said, was limited but honest. Chamberlain was a diligent statesman within his narrow abilities. And Anthony Eden was contemptible—a coward who had achieved a position incommensurate with his meager gifts. It was Sir John Simon, foreign minister and now chancellor of the exchequer, Goering reported brightly, who fully understood the mission of the Reich.[80] His views, coincidentally, reflected those of Charles.

As if by design, Goering and Charles "huddled alone" with their interpreters when dinner was over, and the others drew back, awaiting their return. Goering, pleased with his newly honored comrade, discussed his latest JU-88 bomber.[81]

When Charles returned to the Smith apartment with the small red box containing his medal, Anne immediately understood. He handed her the box in silence; it was as if the wave had finally crashed.

"The albatross," was all she said.[82]

23

Broken Glass

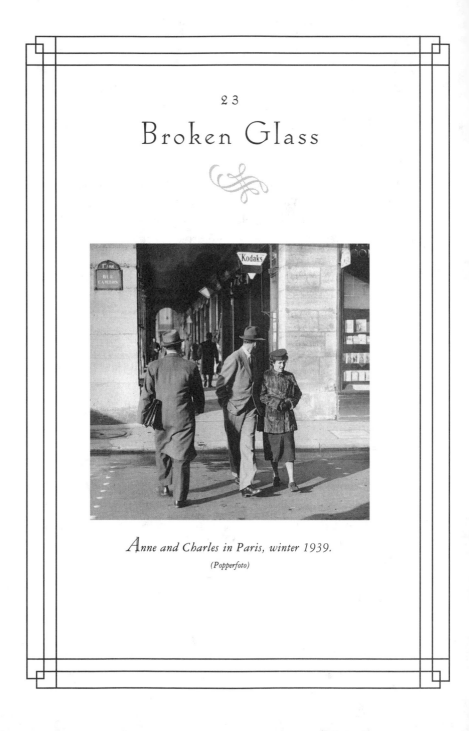

Anne and Charles in Paris, winter 1939.
(Popperfoto)

A Final Cry[1]

Praise life—Praise life
Before the fall of winter's knife,
They stand and call,
O man, praise life . . .

A final cry
From earth to sky,
Tree, fruit, and flower,
Before the hour
Of sacrifice:

Praise life, O man,
While yet you can.

—ANNE MORROW LINDBERGH

NOVEMBER 9, 1938, "KRISTALLNACHT," GERMANY

Three weeks later, flames shot through the November darkness as thousands of people scuttled amid the broken glass to escape the beatings of Hitler's henchmen. It was the Day of the Movement, an official holiday since Hitler had come to power, and his S.A. officers swaggered through the streets of cities throughout Germany, attacking synagogues and storefronts with equal abandon. While Hitler remained aloof and silent, issuing orders through Gestapo headquarters, Himmler announced that "anti-Jewish demonstrations" should not be hindered. As many Jews as possible were to be arrested by the Gestapo—especially wealthy Jews—for immediate incarceration at detention camps. Staged by Hitler as "spontaneous demonstrations" in reaction to the assassination of a German consul in Paris by a young irate

Jew two days earlier, Hitler assigned his civilian thugs, plucked from the general population, to kill the "abdominable Jews" for their crimes against the state. "The swine won't commit another murder . . ." Goering would say. "I would not like to be a Jew in Germany."[2]

By the early morning hours of November 10, 1938, as fire turned to smoke, tens of thousands of windows were broken, at least a hundred people had been killed, and thousands more had been subjected to wanton and sadistic violence. Seventy-five hundred businesses had been gutted, and two hundred sixty-seven synagogues burned. Almost all Jewish cemeteries had been desecrated, and at least a hundred and ninety-seven private homes destroyed. Later, it would be called Kristallnacht, the Night of Broken Glass.[3]

The official Nazi newspaper, the *Voelkischer Beobachter (The People's Observer)*, remained silent. It reported nothing on the number of Jews killed, injured, or arrested, or on the damage done to the Jewish homes and synagogues. It urged the German people to exercise discretion and discipline, to avert their eyes when they passed the ruins, and to remember the crimes committed by the Jews against the state.

The pogrom marked a turning; now even the general populace viewed the Jews as "fair game." Although most Germans were frightened by the violence in their midst, angry at the hundreds of thousands of Reichmarks the damage had cost the state, and fearful of the vengeance of the Jews, thousands watched through the night and the next day as the Jews were marched off to concentration camps.

A hundred thousand people attended a rally to hear the anti-Jewish propaganda of Julius Streicher, the publisher of *Der Stürmer* and one of the most rabid anti-Semites in Germany. A member of the Hitler Youth Movement said, "After Kristallnacht, no German old enough to walk could ever plead ignorance of the persecution of the Jews and no Jews could harbor any delusion that Hitler wanted Germany anything but *Judenrein,* clean of Jews."[4]

November 10 was a beautiful day on Illiec, mild and clear, with a cloudless sky and a gentle wind. As the news came over the radio, Anne wrote in her diary that she was "shocked." But Charles sat quietly at his desk, wondering whether this was simply a deterrent against further shooting incidents. Or was it a move to oust the Jews from Germany? A means to stir up international anti-Semitism? Or was it the indication of the German government's inherent hatred of the Jews?

"They have undoubtedly had a difficult Jewish problem," he wrote. "But why is it necessary to handle it so unreasonably?"[5]

Kay Smith recorded that Charles called them the morning after Kristallnacht to express his "outrage" and to inform them that he and Anne had canceled their plans to move to Berlin,[6] but on the same day, he wrote to Dr. Carrel expressing his regret at having to change his plans. He had hoped that living in Germany would enable him to understand the German viewpoint.

In fact, until the very morning of Hitler's Kristallnacht, Anne and Charles were continuing with plans to make Berlin their home. Since receiving the German Cross, Lindbergh's ties to Germany had tightened. He had spoken to Ambassador Hugh Wilson in confidence, asking his advice about taking a house in Berlin for the winter. Wilson counseled him to seek "a degree of immunity with the press" in the United States by speaking with William Randolph Hearst, Colonel Robert McCormick, and other newspaper publishers to work out a *modus vivendi*. Lindbergh vigorously objected to the position that the public had "a right to know" about his and Anne's private lives. He added that as far as attacks on him went, he "didn't give a damn." In any case, he was not ready to return to the United States with his family.[7] While Anne had felt strangely "starved" in the midst of plenty, Charles felt increasingly fulfilled. In exile, he had found a home. In the well-guarded Reich, he would no longer have to worry about the whim of a disapproving press or the fury of a volatile public. An official and permanent "bodyguard," assigned by the Reich, would protect Lindbergh and his home.

Viewing the streets of Berlin on the morning after Kristallnacht, Hitler, it was said, told his men that the success felt like a "dream," accomplished with a modicum of bloodshed and with the tacit blessings of the people. Through his skillful handling of a docile and able press, he had invented a monstrous propaganda machine and had turned his greatest enemy, the voice of a free people, back on itself. He had broken not only the public will, but the resolve of Western officialdom.

On November 12, as Charles left to confer with Finance Minister Monnet in Paris, all the papers, except those in Germany, attacked him. The German atrocity had stoked the fire. *Pravda* continued to call him a "stupid liar," a lackey and henchman of the Nazi Reich;[8] the British press began to wonder aloud whether Charles Lindbergh was a German spy.[9] The *Times* of London blackballed Anne's book *Listen! The Wind,* omitting it from its Christmas list,[10] and the American press reported demands that Charles return the Nazi medal.[11] Public pressure became so high in the United States that Transcontinental and Western Air were forced to drop Lindbergh's name from their advertising slogan.[12] While Charles remained "marvelously untouched,"[13] Anne had deep forebodings. She believed it would be an age full of hatred, lies and slander that would require her total commitment, even at the cost of her principle.[14]

To bolster her spirits, Betty Morrow shipped reviews of *Listen! The Wind* to Illiec. "Mrs. Lindbergh," declared the *New York Times,* "has written a nearly perfect little book . . . It is the personal record of one who writes at least as well as her husband is said to fly."[15] While *North to the Orient* had been touted as the book equal in expertise to her own flying, this time she was being treated as Charles's equal—a writer who could fly like a hero.

To Anne, it was as if they were writing about someone else. Charles, on the other hand, felt unreserved joy. Anne was immensely touched by his praise.[16]

In spite of the political snubs, *Listen! The Wind* did well in the American market. By November 1938, it was already in its fifth printing, in 1939, Anne would receive the American Booksellers Association Award for "favorite" nonfiction.[17] The praise came to her like a dove of peace from an American audience grown hostile. Now, the prospect of facing a public that admired her work, regardless of her husband's politics, along with the offer of an honorary degree from Amherst, encouraged her to consider a trip to the States in the spring.[18] For the moment, though, she and Charles had to decide where to live.

As Daladier's fear of invasion mounted,[19] and in spite of Hitler's obvious threat to France, the Lindberghs decided to move to Paris. Charles believed he would be welcomed there.[20]

Anne finished packing on December 3 and took one last walk with Charles around the island. Sitting on the huge rock overlooking the sea, she experienced a bright awareness. "Journey pride." She had felt it before; the very act of traveling, which defied the rhythms of the norm, seemed to carry the weight of sin. At eight P.M., as the cart waited at the door and the trunks were piled high, the shores of Illiec were reminding her that nothing important would ever change. Yet she did feel a vast uncertainty.

She awakened and dressed Land and handed him to Charles so that she could climb onto the high cart. From there, she said good-bye to the servants at the lighted door and to Thor, standing inside. Jon, dressed in his town coat and huge hat, sat beside her, and Land clung to her in his fuzzy Eskimo suit.

In one of the most lyrical passages of her diaries, Anne describes the sights and sounds of their "strange exit" from the island: her child singing to the rhythm of the cart, the soft cloudy "mackerel" sky, and the "three-quarter moon" gleaming on the rocky coast of the sea.[21]

While Anne was settling into their apartment on Avenue Maréchal-Maunouy, U.S. Secretary of the Interior Harold Ickes, speaking at a banquet of the Zionist Society in Cleveland, on December 19, blasted Charles:

Any American who accepts a declaration from a dictator automatically forswears his American birthright. How can any American accept a decoration at the hand of a brutal dictator who, with that same hand, is robbing and torturing thousands of fellow human beings?[22]

His comments were a reflection of the administration's anger toward its officials in Berlin. President Roosevelt could not reconcile the current wave of Nazi brutality with the reports coming from the embassy. Resolved to purge the State Department of all pro-German influence, he began to call his officers home. Truman Smith, summoned to Washington to be tested for diabetes, understood that his career was over. "Retirement at this crucial moment in history would be too cruel, too uselessly cruel," Kay Smith wrote in her diary.[23] Later, her daughter Kaetchen said that her father's involvement with Lindbergh in Berlin "all but destroyed his career."[24] An era in American diplomacy was over; the new ambassador, Hugh Wilson,[25] would also be recalled. Sympathetic to the Nazi regime, Wilson had been running the embassy as if it were an officers' club, a salon for the American and German military and intellectual elite.[26]

Walter Winchell, a New York journalist and radio broadcaster, quipped that the boys in Berlin must have been out playing baseball while the Nazis moved in.[27] In point of fact, it was golf and squash. Within the elegant American Embassy, the Wilsons and the Smiths and their entourage dined in splendor with their German guests. A meeting in the morning, a game at the club in the afternoon, a house filled with servants—the sinecure of serving in the Nazi Reich was not at all unpleasant, and the Truman Smiths, as well as the Wilsons, found it painful to leave. When Wilson was recalled to Washington, in the spring of 1939, he left his wife at the embassy in the hope of his swift return.[28]

"We do not love, we do not hate, we do not judge, we do not condemn," Wilson later said. "We observe, we reflect, we report."[29] Kay and Truman Smith echoed his claim when they were called home. "We did not look either right or left," Kay Smith said. "We were just there to do our job."[30]

As Roosevelt's cabinet denounced Charles as an American unworthy of his birthright, Anne moved in the rhythms of French society, though she was hungry for home.

For Anne, Elisabeth was a symbol of "home," and she again read Elisabeth's letters, in search of "another age and a more golden one."[31] When she later wrote the poem "The Little Mermaid," based on Hans Christian Andersen's story, she was composing a lament for the loss of childhood, family, and home—the exchange of innocence for moral doubt.[32]

Roosevelt now had little doubt that America would have to go to war. After the events of late 1938, he began to make his position clear, and called for a re-evaluation of the U.S. neutrality laws and a dramatic increase in the defense budget. On January 4, he said, "We have learned that when we deliberately try to legislate neutrality, our neutrality laws may operate unevenly and unfairly—may actually give aid to an aggressor and deny it to the victim."[33]

Anne felt like it was the end of the Roman Empire—not knowing what was coming, "waiting for the storm."[34]

Charles, however, was more certain than ever that eugenics was the answer to the degeneration of Western civilization.[35] On January 16, he returned to Berlin, ostensibly to procure engines for French aircraft. He talked to Air Minister Milch, who demanded to know what Lindbergh had said in London before the Munich conference. Apparently he was satisfied with Charles's answer and agreed to send engines to France.[36] His words, however, were as hollow as always. The Germans never intended to keep their promise. Once again, Charles had overestimated his power. He thought, to the Germans' satisfaction, that the force of his personality would deflect France and Germany from their collision course. Hitler was even then planning to invade Poland on his way to France.[37]

Charles returned to Paris, and Anne rejoiced. She was only alive when he was home.[38] She was proud that he had stood up for himself in the face of all the bad publicity.

At just this time, Goering accelerated the "evacuation" of the Jews, Mussolini renewed his support of Franco and the Spanish Nationalists, and France and Britain reaffirmed their alliance.[39]

While Charles believed the lessons they had learned while living in Europe would prove invaluable, Anne felt they "had exiled them forever." She would never see America the same way again.[40]

In the salons of Paris, they were greeted by an aristocracy steeped in delusion. To Anne, everyone looked like "the Queen in *Alice in Wonderland*" or, scarier yet, "Mary Queen of Scots." She found that her anger at public derision had given her new courage. After being so shy and reticent, she was able to talk to anyone.[41]

In February 1939, at a dinner at the American Embassy, Anne was approached by the Duke of Windsor. When he left England after abdicating so that he could marry Wallis Simpson, Edward roamed the salons of Europe. Like Charles, he was criticized by the press for his visits to Germany and his friendships within the Reich. Attracted by the rigor and vitality of the Reich, he, too, threw his support to the Nazis. It was later said that Hitler had promised to return Edward to his throne once Germany had conquered England.[42]

Anne spoke to the duke of their rootless life and of her fear of going home; he nodded in commiseration. They agreed that Germany was the best hope for the average worker and that the country was an important force, whether or not one agreed with its policies. As she had in London, Anne saw Edward as a kindred spirit, a sensitive man forced to conform to a public image. Soon the duchess and Charles joined the conversation. Drawn together by their isolation, the four exiles stood in the center of the room. They were "like a people in a foreign land who suddenly realize they speak the same language . . . A pair of unicorns meets a pair of unicorns," Anne wrote.[43]

As the press raged at Hitler, and Britain and France readied their troops, Anne's anger at Charles began to surface. She mourned her misspent youth and the time lost to Charles when she denied her own worth and directed her life and energy to his ends. And yet she tried to silence her doubts, to convince herself that her struggle for internal harmony was over. No longer would she dwell in "divided selves."[44]

But she was more confused than ever; like Anne the narrator in *Listen! The Wind,* she was trying to summon up moral courage. As if her life were imitating her art, Anne again adopted an attitude of helplessness.

At the end of January, Anne and Charles visited the Astors. On their way to Cliveden, passing through the drab suburbs of the working classes, Anne delighted once more in the beauty of the Astors' home.[45] Yet her new way of thinking cast a pall on both their wealth and their politics. Their self-conscious aristocratic behavior and their phalanx of servants seemed absurd. And this time there was a self-congratulatory manner that Anne had not seen before. Neville Chamberlain arrived, with a shy young "niece" who reminded Anne of her former self.[46] All at once, her detachment shattered, sending her crying into Lady Astor's arms. In spite of her distortions, Nancy seemed to Anne beautiful, courageous, and confident. She reminded her of Elisabeth, a feminine ideal to which Anne could only aspire. She realized how much she missed her sister and the depth of her loneliness.[47] With introductions from the Astors, they visited London salons where talk of books, poetry, social philosophy, and art distracted them from the news of impending war.[48]

But the more their reputations were tarnished, the more Charles clung to his ideal "images." In November, Charles had commissioned the French sculptor Charles Despiau to make a bust of Anne, and the New York designer and artist Jo Davidson to make a figure of himself.[49] But somewhere inside, Anne wondered whether it was a golden calf. By year's end, she was overwhelmed by a deep and heavy depression.

Anne blamed herself for a winter without purpose or accomplishment.[50] As had happened after Charlie's kidnapping, her unexpressed rage toward Charles made it impossible for her to write. Moreover, she could not conceive another child. With Carrel and Charles pushing her to perform her sacred role, Anne accepted her infertility as the final confirmation of her worthlessness.

On March 14, Chamberlain and Daladier renounced their commitment to protect the Czech border. Their agreement did not apply, they reasoned, since Czechoslovakia had not been attacked.[51] In Prague, George F. Kennan, stationed at the American Embassy, saw crowds of people weeping in the darkened streets at the "death knoll of their independence."[52]

Privately, Anne, too, condemned the Nazis. "All the Edens and Hulls are right. I can't bear it."[53]

When Roosevelt sought assurance from Mussolini that Germany

and Italy would not "attack or invade," Hitler and Mussolini called his appeal "absurd."[54] Anne remained in Paris while Charles took a ship to New York on business on April 14.[55] As the *Aquitania* sailed into port, the Carrels and Jim Newton rode the tugs to greet him. Embittered by events that had made them pariahs in their own land, Dr. Carrel and Lindbergh commiserated in Lindbergh's cabin aboard the ship while James Newton stood guard at the closed door.

As luck would have it, the arrival was the night of the photographers' annual ball. On hearing of Lindbergh's return, the conductor stopped the music, and the men, cameras in hand, rushed to meet the *Aquitania*. Stampeding on board, they hammered on Lindbergh's door. When he refused to open it, one photographer broke into the adjoining cabin, took photos, and fled.

Charles walked down the plank of the ship, swarmed by reporters shooting hundreds of flashbulbs into the air. "It takes the sweetness from the freedom of democracy," he thought as he scuttled across the broken glass.[56]

24

Which Way Is Home?

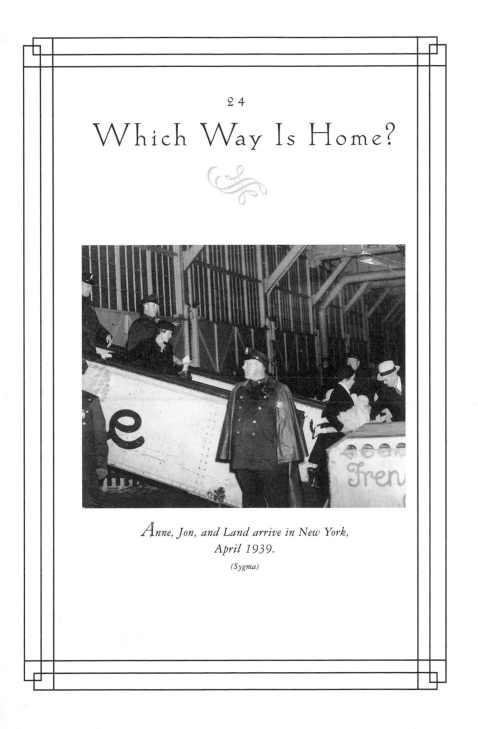

Anne, Jon, and Land arrive in New York,
April 1939.

(Sygma)

NO ANGELS[1]

You think there are no angels any more—
No angels come to tell us in the night
Of joy or sorrow, love or death—
No breath of wings, no touch of palm to say
Divinity is near.
Today
Our revelations come
By telephone, or postman at the door,
You say—
              Oh no, the hour when fate is near,
Not these, the voices that can make us hear,
Not these
Have power to pierce below the stricken mind
Deep down into perception's quivering core.
Blows fall unheeded on the bolted door;
Deafly we listen; blindly look; and still
Our fingers fumbling with the lock are numb
Until
The Angels come . . .

—ANNE MORROW LINDBERGH

APRIL 28, 1939, NEW YORK HARBOR

Two weeks later, Anne awoke to the brightening sky as the
Champlain paddled softly up the Hudson River toward the West
Side piers. The April air still held its chill, and rain tapped the
deserted deck outside her cabin. The quiet breathing of her young sons
was muffled by the sound of reporters gathering outside her door. She
wondered whether "coming home" was not just another plunge into the

nightmare she had left two years earlier. She hurried the children into their clothes, pulled their hats down over their eyes, and handed Land to his nurse. Dressed in black, as if in mourning, she grabbed Jon's hand and told the others to follow her. They all ran breathlessly down the gangplank and out to the waiting limousine. As police sirens carved a path through the moving traffic, Anne's car rumbled across the George Washington Bridge and turned northward to Englewood. Her mother and Margot were waiting at the door.[2]

Charles had made an important decision. Even before touching shore, he had cabled his friend General Henry (Hap) Arnold to say that he wished an army aviation post. Within two days of his return, after announcing to everyone that he would not stay long, Charles accepted the position President Roosevelt had reluctantly assigned him. Charles was to study the efficiency of aeronautical production in the United States,[3] and, though neither man trusted the other, they understood the need to bury their anger. Charles was convinced that nothing about his current work would evoke Roosevelt's opposition.[4]

Writing at her desk in their private suite at Next Day Hill, Anne assessed the quality of their lives since their return to America. She marveled at Charles's robust energy and his power to find fulfillment wherever he went. For the moment, Anne was content to relax in the luxury of her mother's home. The flowers were beautiful and the robins were huge, she wrote. Anne took much pleasure in the company of Margot, Con, and their babies, drinking it all in with the thirst of one who has been in an emotional desert.[5] The war in Europe seemed far away, and too unreal to feel its pain. But America with its speed and brightness offended her sensibilities. She felt herself an outcast in a corrupt land. Everything seemed "false . . . flashy and cheap," especially the movies and the press. She wanted her old America back—the one she had known in her innocence.[6]

There were many who would have welcomed a garish assault on their senses. To the German Jews, who feared for their lives, the bright face of America was an aspect of its democratic freedom. After Kristallnacht, nothing about America could deter the German Jews from banging on its doors. Throughout Germany, people searched for relatives abroad who would help them through the arduous and serpentine process of emigration. But the concerted efforts of Jewish and non-Jewish groups in the United States to persuade Roosevelt and the Congress to liberalize immigration laws proved fruitless. Even legislation to permit German-Jewish children to bypass the quota system failed, and pleas from the international committee established by the Evian Conference were viewed by attendant nations as "Jewish blackmail."

Only non-quota immigrants—university professors, research specialists, writers and artists—reached the United States in appreciable numbers. Nineteen thirty-nine was the biggest year: 56,347 German aliens were admitted. After that, the Nazi crematoria slowed the pace.[7] Even though many Americans believed the Jews in Germany were treated unjustly, they didn't, said one official, want boatloads of refugees arriving on their shores.[8]

After the Lindberghs and the Carrels were reunited on the same side of the Atlantic, Carrel, as usual, ran the show. He could not tolerate any disagreement; he would not accept any point of view but his own.[9]

Anne wanted to take a summer house in Washington, but the Carrels cautioned her against it. Charles's voice was conspicuously silent. But Anne was troubled by their rootlessness. She did not want to be an exile—another "Henry James American."[10] She wondered if she could ever feel at home again.[11] Even surrounded by the warmth of family, she felt alien, disconnected.

The American public, however, was proud to have the hero and his family back, and, for the moment at least, the press called a truce. *Commonweal* magazine pleaded with Lindbergh to assume good faith on the part of the press and to meet the American people graciously. And it asked the public to display discretion and forbearance.

Colonel Lindbergh is here again, summoned by the government to give his high abilities and exceptional experience to the aerial division of the national forces. May he be allowed to do so in peace.[12]

Charles "streaked" across the country in army pursuit planes, inspecting air corps centers and fighter-plane factories, and his colleagues were proud to have him in their ranks. Now that he was working for the United States government, doubts about his loyalty faded, as did any antipathy toward Anne and her books. Two weeks after their return, Anne's photograph appeared on the cover of *Life*. The editors explained:

> *The fine sensitive face on the cover belongs to the wife of America's*
> *greatest post-war hero. But Anne Morrow Lindbergh is now a celebrity*
> *in her own right. Her two beautifully written books,* North to the
> Orient *and* Listen! The Wind, *have won her wide acclaim.*[13]

But Anne resisted taking center stage. She wanted a simple life, alone with her children. She tried to justify her material comfort in the Morrow home by engaging in her mother's charitable activities, but she only felt harried, pushed, even more removed from herself and reality.[14] Even a quiet social evening with friends was impossible. With Con and Aubrey, Margot and Dwight, all staying in the house, there was constant jockeying for space and chauffeured cars. It was easier, she wrote, to be alone.[15] She and Charles, desperate for a place of their own, took the suggestion of Anne's friend Thelma Crawford Lee and looked at a house at Lloyd Neck, Long Island. Set on a high, cool peak, the white clapboard, light-filled house had a lawn that sloped down to the Sound. Almost immediately, Anne and Charles decided to rent it.[16]

Anne was relieved by the prospect of staying home. With Jon and Land, now seven and two, aware of her presence and uprooted for the third time, she did not want to travel with Charles. Since their return home, their relationship had loosened; without the bond of a common cause, the seams frayed. Charles again was the aviator hero, and he was going places Anne would not follow. She imagined Charles happy and carefree in his work, climbing "effortlessly into the sky,"[17] while she remained grounded in guilt and uncertainty.

To the world, Anne continued to appear contented. That spring, she was awarded two honorary doctorates, one from the University of Rochester and the other from Amherst, her father's alma mater. President Alan Valentine of Rochester congratulated her for her literary and aviation achievements, adding that her "greatest victory yet has been a victory of the spirit."[18] The irony cut her to the core.

On June 22, 1939, Anne's thirty-third birthday, she, Charles, and the children moved to the home in Lloyd Neck. The house looked new and fresh, and she was certain that the nearness of the sea would help her to find purpose in her work.[19] She had her desk placed in the garage, and with two maids, a nurse, and a cook to help her, she was able to turn completely to her writing. When she reread the letters she had written to Elisabeth during the early years of her marriage, she was surprised by the spontaneity of her emotions.[20] Through her words to her sister, Anne could see that she had betrayed herself for Charles. She prayed for the peace and clarity of mind to sustain their marriage and Charles's "spirit."

But Charles, it seemed, required little encouragement to maintain his belief in a new world order. He and Carrel made plans to establish the Institute for the Betterment of Man. Its purpose was articulated by Carrel:

> Politically naturalistic democracy is incapable of keeping the peace or of providing adequate food, shelter and clothing for its peoples. Physiologically, the race is degenerating. Morally, force and materialism predominate. We allow this collapse of civilization to proceed without using against it the powerful weapons which science possesses. Unintegrated and specialized resistance is offered. What we need is to assemble in one coordinated group all the weapons of knowledge and thought which are so abundantly available.[21]

The plan was to have a "nucleus" of men, with practical experience and "universalist minds," who would govern a group of fact-finding specialists studying contemporary issues crucial to the sustenance of a "civilized" society. The findings of the studies would become the basis for reforms in education, legislation, and all aspects of American life, from the breast-feeding of babies to labor law. American individualism would diminish and, in time, disappear, and the new state would promote the welfare of all. The governing nucleus would comprise Alexis Carrel and his closest friends, Charles A. Lindbergh, James Newton, and Edward Moore.[22]

The world according to Carrel would see that women accomplished their divinely ordained purpose of sustaining and educating a new generation. The women selected for the task would be governed by benevolent, visionary, and "civilized" men. Because the quality of civilization was determined by genetic pooling, Charles understood that "mating involves the most important choice in life." He had chosen well, not only in the individual he married, but in her "environment and ancestry." He had no doubt that Anne was capable of carrying the "species" forward.[23]

Their biggest obstacle in promulgating their theories, wrote Charles in his diary, would be the mindless intrusions of a free and ungoverned press. "Someday, they'll need friends and find them lacking," he wrote in his diary.[24] If only they could get rid of "British and Jewish propaganda."[25]

Charles's assessment of the American press echoed the Nazi view. The Jew, according to the German press, was the source of all evil in American society and was fast pushing America into conflict with foreign powers. The leading Nazi daily informed its readers that 97 percent of all American newspaper publishers were Jews, and that the abduction of the Lindbergh baby had been a Jewish plot, carried out for the purpose of obtaining the child's blood for a religious ritual.[26]

On a flight to Denver, a week after his meeting with Carrel, Charles climbed to an altitude of 20,000 feet to avoid an oncoming storm. Darting through the clouds, he "rode on top of them like a God," feeling as if he "owned the world." Piercing through the open sky, he mocked the arrogance of the mountains. Even the valleys belonged to him.[27]

Once again, he was prince of the sky. He had navigated the storm of public opinion, and now he would fill his role in governing the lives of his wayward countrymen.

Whenever Charles came home between trips, he scolded Anne for wasting her time writing letters when she should be writing books. Anne, believing he was right, planned a book of reminiscences. But the nearness to the sea had not kept its promise of renewal. Isolated and aimless, still unable to conceive a child or to write, Anne sank deeper into depression.

On August 4, just as she seemed to reach her nadir, Charles handed her a letter from the publisher of the French writer and aviator Antoine de Saint-Exupéry. The envelope also contained Saint-Exupéry's preface to the French edition of *Listen! The Wind.* He had read her book at the publisher's request while traveling to the States to promote his own book, *Wind, Sand and Stars.* Intending to write a one-page piece, Saint-Exupéry had instead written a nine-page essay. As Anne read his analysis, she felt he had plumbed the depth of her loneliness and self-doubt.

There is a little girl who runs more slowly than the others. Over there the others are playing. "Wait for me!" Already, she is late, they will get tired of waiting for her, they will leave her behind, she will be forgotten and left alone in the world. How can she be reassured? This kind of anguish is incurable.[28]

Saint-Exupéry's publisher relayed the author's desire to meet her on his arrival in New York. Quickly, she pulled *Wind, Sand and Stars* from the bookshelf and started to read. Riveted by its insights and poignancy, she wrote, "It is all I ever wanted to say and more of flying and time and human relationships."[29]

Like Anne, Saint-Exupéry reveled in the metaphysics of flight. It was both a laboratory and "a baptism," a means for stern self-examination and a spiritual journey toward salvation. The detachment and timelessness of flight produced for him, as it did for Anne, the paradox of clarity in oblivion. Flying removed the veneer from his daily life and laid bare his human frailty. The "lonely glaze" of his cockpit window, he wrote, confirmed the divinity of nature, the delusory arrogance of machine-age man, and the hope of redemption through human relationships.[30]

Anne, intimidated by his literary fame, asked Charles to call him at his hotel the next morning. But Charles, unable to speak French, had to hand the phone to Anne. Nervously, in her "hesitant" French, she invited him to dinner at Lloyd Neck that evening. Charles, she said, would meet him at his hotel at five o'clock.

Charles left early for a meeting in Cold Spring, New York, with Grace Lee Nute, a Minnesota historian who was writing a biography of his father. But his meeting with Miss Nute did not go as expected. In her research, she had uncovered evidence of his father's illegitimate birth and his grandfather's conviction for embezzlement. Charles, fearing the effects of the book's publication on his family, tried to persuade Miss Nute to drop the project.[31] Because his visit was longer than he had expected, he called Anne to meet Saint-Exupéry in his stead.

Anne raced to New York, frustrated by the Saturday traffic, and went to the Ritz-Carleton bar, where Saint-Exupéry awaited his host. At first look, she was disappointed. She found him to be a typical Slav—"bald," bent, and unattractive.[32] In fact, Anne was being kind. He had a chunky, undisciplined body, and a pasty face with bulging black eyes and large drooping ears[33]—the antithesis of the type Carrel would have deemed civilized.

She thought she recognized him, like a man she had seen in one of her "dreams." She explained her presence and, after a quick exchange of pleasantries, they crossed the street to her car, but no sooner had they gone around the block than the car stalled.[34]

By then, it hardly mattered. For Anne and Saint-Exupéry, time had stopped. While the Park Avenue traffic honked around them and a taxi driver tried to push their car, they were lost in conversation. Anne flitted from English to French, at once shouting out the window to the taxi driver, explaining the situation to Saint-Exupéry, and talking "furiously" about the unconscious rhythm of language and books.

After leaving the car at a repair shop, they went to Penn Station and took the train to Lloyd Neck. How unusual, they agreed, to have touched each other, from so far away, through the power of their written words. It was as if they spoke the same language, a language, Anne implied, that her husband didn't understand. They talked about writing and its limits within the walls of symbol and culture. They shared the sensation of being both a "spectator and an actor" in their work, of finding communion in physical separation and the difficulty of gaining philosophical distance on ordinary life. How wonderful to be understood, Anne later wrote.

"*Je sais, je sais,*" each murmured to the other, finishing sentences before the other could speak. The meeting was a consummation, and Anne, like a shy and inexperienced lover, wondered whether she could maintain "the pitch." He commented on the clarity and the classicism of her work; she on the metaphysical subtlety of his. She said how flying did not separate you from the elements, but, rather, bathed you in them—only to remember that he too had written those words. In his eyes, she saw her image, perfectly formed and immediately confirmed. The crowning moment was their discovery of their shared love of Rilke, who articulated everything they felt. Later Anne would quote the poet's words in her diary:

> *I feel as though I had been sleeping for years or had lain in the lowest hold of a ship that, loaded with heavy things, sailed through strange distances. Oh, to climb up on deck once more and feel the winds and the birds, and to see how the great, great nights come with their gleaming stars . . .*[35]

Anne felt liberated and completely understood by someone who was a perfect stranger. To her surprise, he treated her like his equal. She wrote in her diary, he ". . . fenc[ed] with my mind, steel against steel."[36]

Saint-Exupéry, too, was pleased. Anne was an attractive and cultivated woman who understood his maverick life. He had been born to an aristocratic family but had little facility for the military or politics. Much like Charles, his only gifts were a taste for adventure and a desire to fly. Trained as a civil pilot, he had charted the mail routes into South America and Africa, and his books had grown out of his long night flights and his experience when downed in the Sahara. In 1939, he had reached the pinnacle of his literary career, but his personal life had become a vacuum.[37]

His wife, Consuelo, was an aspiring and unconventional sculptor of bohemian tastes. A petite and delicate Latin beauty, as rash and capricious as a child, she had grown distant, unable and unwilling to understand his work. At one time he had delighted in her energy, but now he understood the price he had paid. If, as he had written, love was at the "essence" of life, he believed there was little hope for his "salvation." Anne had succeeded where Consuelo had failed. She had lived a creative life within the bounds of domesticity. The warmth and understanding he had sought from Consuelo flowed easily and effortlessly from Anne.

When Charles returned home, it was nearly ten o'clock, and Anne was relieved to be a mere spectator. Saint-Exupéry and Charles moved breathlessly from subject to subject, Anne wrote in her diary, finding a higher level than her own. They spoke of the machine and its role in society, and of the spiritual aspects of political nationalism. But Saint-Exupéry, unlike Charles, had little taste for political ideology. He believed the meaning of life was an ineffable mystery, and that men joined political "brotherhoods" to assuage their loneliness. If Charles believed in the superiority of "types" and chose to emphasize the differences among them, Saint-Exupéry believed that "each individual is an empire," and that there were as many truths as there were men who dreamed.[38] In his presence, it was as if, Anne later wrote, her name had been spoken in a room full of strangers.[39]

Saint-Exupéry stayed less than twenty-four hours, but their meeting had changed everything. He had done something no one else had done. He saw Anne apart from Charles. Through his eyes, she was not an appendage of her husband; she was a thinking, sensitive, and skilled artist. While others had seen *Listen! The Wind* as the account of a transatlantic flight, he had understood her journey through Hell. Saint-Exupéry was to Anne the truest of heroes, conscious of himself and alive to the meaning of every moment.

25

No Harvest Ripening

Anne Morrow Lindbergh, circa 1939.
(Brown Brothers)

No Harvest Ripening [1]

Come quickly, winter, for the heart belies
The truth of these warm days. These August skies
Are all too fair to suit the times—so kind
That almost they persuade the treacherous mind
It still is summer and the world the same.
These gaudy colors on the hills in flame
Are out of keeping with the nun's attire
We wear within—of ashes, not of fire.

Season of ripening fruit and seeds, depart;
There is no harvest ripening in the heart . . .

—ANNE MORROW LINDBERGH

Autumn 1939, Lloyd Neck, Long Island

Anne was afraid of Charles. She was afraid of following him and afraid of losing him. She was afraid of defying him and afraid of betraying him. Most of all, she was afraid of being left behind. Had she dared to express her doubts about German aggression, she would have been subjected to Charles's anger and ridicule. She knew he would never change his mind and that the rift might be impossible to repair. Saint-Exupéry was right. Anne did not have the courage to stand alone; that would have been an unbearable anguish.

Charles's beliefs, she wrote, were "beautiful and strong," yet they made her "tremble." In this "Armageddon," she wrote, there would be no middle ground. She would have to take sides, but she could not. Her thoughts resonated with her father's speeches and essays written during and after the First World War. Dedicated to the Covenant of a League of Nations, he had written, "Whether a single state wills it or not, it belongs to a society of states [which must] establish a civil society universally administering right in accordance with law." While national sovereignty was a moral imperative, he wrote, consonant with the growth of democratic principle, the actions of one state influenced the cooperative efforts of the community. The tension between the "ideal of liberty" and the "ideal of world order" must constantly be reconciled by law and reason.

A renegade state had no more right to aggression than a passive state had to neutrality. Reflecting the teachings of Leviticus, Morrow didn't believe in the luxury of "isolation"; of standing by to watch another state starve and die. To cut off "entanglements" was to cut off the "liveliness, comfort, and happiness of millions of people." Of course Morrow detested war and its devastation, but he believed it was often necessary to clear the path for human progress. The danger to America, he wrote, was measured not by military invasion but by its moral commitment to the international community. Growth required sacrifice and discipline. "Only then can we have the unity and courage to bring the world nearer to a dependable international guarantee of the territorial and political integrity of all nations, large and small."[2]

Now her mother was defending her father's words against the views of Charles. Torn by the conflict, Anne wondered naïvely why there was a need for war at all. She hated any show of force; it was against her nature. But how could she desert Charles? And how could she live without him?[3]

On August 22, Hitler told his generals that the "extermination" of Poland was about to begin. Although he had made a pact with the Soviet Union he vowed to crush Stalin. "Whether the world believes it doesn't mean a damn to me . . . Be hard . . . Be without mercy. The citizens of Western Europe must quiver in horror."[4]

One week later, sitting at her desk in Lloyd Neck, Anne wrote in her diary that negotiations between Poland and Germany had stopped. War, she was certain, was inevitable. The waiting stirred her darkest memories. In her mind, her failure to protect her baby and her complicity with Charles and his pro-German views, were synonymous. She wrote in her diary, "The child is dead in Europe."[5]

Anne's body pulsed to the sounds of war as she imagined guns booming in the distance. That night, unable to sleep, she sat by her window,
watching the moon rise against the trees and the dim gold lights of the
Connecticut shore. Suddenly, she found herself on her knees praying—
praying as she had not done since Charlie died. It was as if she had been
touched by God. She felt empty of anguish, clear and free. Like the birth
of her babies, it was both a death and a resurrection.[6]

But what and who had died? The next morning, as Anne sat on the
steps of her seaside house, peeling unripe chestnuts with Jon, the realization came. The realities of war were harsh, and her husband's stance
was implacable. No matter how repelled she was by his antiseptic pragmatism, it was her duty as his wife and the mother of his children to
submit to his views. Charles and the children were everything to her.
They were her microcosm, her war job, small and meaningless in the
scheme of things, but nonetheless an influence in a shattering world.[7]

Her thoughts turned to her friends in Europe and the terible fate
that lay ahead of them.[8] She imagined the horror of human suffering
and wanted to make it her own. And she saw something else—an
America "shocked out of its senses" and turning against Charles.[9]

Charles remained aloof, scanning the events with disciplined detachment. It was clear to him that Britain and France would not prevail against the Germans. Furthermore, he did not question the
justifications for Germany's transgressions. But he was concerned that
the American press might push the United States into a war.[10] Their influence made Charles wonder whether he could even think of living
permanently in New York.

As the Germans stormed Poland, Roosevelt declared a state of "limited national emergency," which authorized him to accelerate conscription and call reservists to active duty. On the night of September 15, in
a small broadcasting room in Washington, Charles spoke nationwide,
with Anne by his side, urging Americans to stay out of war.[11]

He set forth an isolationist doctrine, couched in the admonitions of
the Founding Fathers, that drew on the xenophobia of the public. What

good had the First World War done, he asked? It had cost over a hundred thousand men and millions of dollars, debts that we were still paying. Involvement in a European war was a fathomless pit that would put our country in debt for generations to come. And what did this war have to do with us? It was an internecine battle among "sister nations," not a threat to the "white race." The Versailles Treaty, which had reduced the size of Germany and demanded tens of billions of dollars in reparations, had proven that no one could legislate strength among nations. In 1936, when Hitler first came to power, the Allies might have persuaded Germany to disarm; now, they were paying for their errors. Anne found his speech visionary yet practical. It was Charles at his best.

We must not let our sympathies cloud our vision, he said. "We must be as impersonal as a surgeon with his knife," cutting off the infections of European affairs. Besides the costs in men and dollars, he said, we would turn our country into a war machine in which democracy might not survive. Let us tend to our own problems and regenerate our institutions, turning away the alien voices in our midst that call for war. Now, in a public forum, Charles attacked the Jewish influence in the press:

> *We must learn to look behind every article we read and every speech we hear. We must not only inquire about the writer and the speaker—about his personal interests and his nationality—but we must also ask who owns and who influences the newspapers, the motion pictures and the radio stations.* [12]

Ending with a plea for self-preservation and for a reliance on "logic" in our foreign policy, Charles, at Anne's urging, called for the salvation of Western civilization. "The gift of civilized life must still be carried on. It is more important than the sympathies, the friendship, the desires of any single generation."

Charles would later pay a price for his isolationist, anti-British, and anti-Jewish address, but for the moment he basked in the favorable comments of his friends and in the admiration of the fine physical "types" who rallied to his cause. Buoyed by his apparent "victory," he finished writing an article for the *Reader's Digest* and began to compose another radio address.

But the press was already murmuring in disgust. As Britain declared its resolve to conquer Germany, in the *Times* of London Beverly Baxter, a member of Parliament, a novelist, and a journalist, condemned Charles for turning against the nation that had given him security.[13] At the same time Dorothy Thompson, a columnist for the *New York Herald Tribune,* railed at Lindbergh's slander of the press; if the motives of the press were to be examined, she suggested, so should his. She portrayed Lindbergh as an anti-British instrument of fascist Germany.[14]

Betty Morrow, meanwhile, was polishing her own speaking skills. Smith College had asked her to serve as acting president, and on September 26 she accepted the post in Northampton. As she spoke with poise and simplicity to the large audience of teachers and students, Anne felt her mother looked young again. She thought her mother had finally found her mission—the higher education of women.[15]

On September 27, three weeks after the declaration of war, Poland surrendered to Hitler. More than 140,000 Polish troops laid down their guns. Two-thousand Polish soldiers and ten thousand civilians had died. Hitler signed a treaty with Stalin and declared his desire for peace, even as he told his military commanders he would "attack in the West as soon as possible."[16] He issued his "strength of Germanhood" decree, calling for the "elimination" of all alien populations, and began to deport Austrian and Czechoslovakian Jews to the concentration camps set up in Poland. He told his generals that France was next.[17]

Anne, as she struggled with her book on family reminiscences, worked daily on a short piece confirming Charles's vision of the European war. If this was not at the direct urging of Charles, it was certainly to his great pleasure. After reading her work-in-progress, he praised her lyrical expression of feeling. Anne's writing, he wrote in his journal, combines philosophy with delicacy unparalleled."[18]

A week later, on the eve of a congressional debate on the Neutrality Bill, Charles gave his second radio address.[19] This time he argued, with greater subtlety, to convince the public of its moral obligation to avoid war. Yes, he said, we must defend America if it is attacked, and, yes, we must defend the countries of the Western hemisphere whose physical integrity is vital to ours. But we must make no promises we are unable to keep, and we must not embroil ourselves in an international struggle that has no moral or physical imperative. This war is not about ideology; it is about power. It is not about democracy; it is about political borders. We are bound to Europe by race, not politics, he said, implying his belief in Aryan superiority. This war is a quarrel among equals, an incestuous battle among the white races of Europe, beyond the purview of American interest. The laws of evolution, not manmade justice, were the measure of war.

> *If the white race is ever seriously threatened, it may then be time for us to take our part in its protection, to fight side by side with the English, French and German, but not with one against the other for our mutual destruction.*

The first war taught us that political strength could not be legislated and that war was costly. If America were to enter the present war, it would become like "Shylock," demanding retribution for its wartime loans. He offered his listeners a moderate course: the "unrestricted sale of purely defensive armaments" and a refusal of credit to the belligerent nations.

While the subsequent outrage in England and France was predictable, the response in Congress was beyond anyone's expectations. The *New York Times* reported:

> *Senate debate on the Neutrality Bill today quickly turned into a free-for-all discussion of Colonel Lindbergh's radio speech last night, in the course of which three Administration leaders charged him with inconsistency and, in one case, with substantive approval of the "brutal conquest of democratic countries."*[20]

Senator Key Pittman, chairman of the Foreign Relations Committee, stopped just short of calling Charles a fascist; others, such as Senator Alben Barkley, pointed to the absurdity of distinguishing between "defensive" and "offensive" ammunition. Are planes right, but gunpowder and gasoline wrong? The consensus was that the famous aviator had gone beyond the bounds of his limited expertise.

Even Charles's friends began to denounce him. In an article in the *British Spectator,* Harold Nicolson tried to explain the source of Charles's opinions. He said Colonel Lindbergh, after his historic flight to France, had allowed his ideas to become not merely inflexible, but rigid; his self-confidence to become arrogance, and his convictions to harden into granite. "He began to loathe democracy," Nicolson said.[21]

Nicolson's article knocked Anne's breath away. She was shocked that he didn't deal with the issues. He had chosen instead to dissect his motives, as if Charles were a laboratory specimen. Under the pretense of analyzing his views, he made a cheap shot at someone he once considered his friend.[22]

An audience in London, echoing Nicolson, raucously sang a ditty: "Then there's Colonel Lindbergh/Who made a pretty speech/He's somewhere in America/We're glad he's out of reach."[23] Henry Breckenridge, even the Guggenheims, turned their backs on their once beloved friends. Aubrey Morgan, Con's husband, now assistant chief of the Bureau of British Information Services, refused to see them.

Carrel could not understand the public uproar. He asked Jim Newton to send him a copy of Charles's speech. He wrote, "We are wondering about the cause of this immense feeling of surprise and hatred growing against him."[24]

Charles wondered whether, given the public hostility, he could remain on the East Coast. Perhaps "a real and permanent" home could be found only in the West. Echoing his father's views, Charles said he wanted to find a place grounded on "sound agricultural principles," where human values were not distorted by urban life.[25]

But in truth, he was being pushed. Betty Morrow simply had had enough. For the first time she spoke out against Charles, denouncing his call for a munitions embargo.[26] She announced that she was joining William Allen White's Nonpartisan Committee for Peace Through

Revision of the Neutrality Law, passed by Congress and signed by Roosevelt in 1935. White, the editor of the *Emporia Gazette,* in Kansas, was known as a philosopher, a liberal Republican, and a patriot. The committee attracted broad bipartisan support, from Henry L. Stimson, Thomas Lamont, and Helen Hayes, to the labor leader David Dubinsky and the theologian Reinhold Niebuhr. They threw their support to Roosevelt in his effort to arm the British. Father Charles E. Coughlin, an anti-Semitic isolationist with German contacts, denounced the committee as a "dangerous fifth column."[27] She was bitter, but she was resigned. The only thing she could do was pray.[28]

Two weeks later, Charles's *Reader's Digest* article appeared. Laced with poetic and philosophical musings, which showed the artful touch of Anne, it presented the airplane as an instrument of a divine and natural struggle among racially disparate nations. Aviation, wrote Charles, was "a tool specially shaped for Western hands . . . one of those priceless possessions which permit the white race to live at all in a pressing sea of yellow, black, and brown." While the airplane, he said, could lead to worldwide conflagration, it was also an instrument for preserving racial purity. In his most vicious racial attack yet, he wrote:

> *Unless we act quickly to counteract it . . . the White Race is bound to lose, and the others bound to gain . . . It is time to turn from our quarrel and to build our White ramparts . . . We can have peace and security only so long as we band together to preserve that most priceless possession, our inheritance of European blood, only as long as we guard ourselves against attack by foreign armies and dilution by foreign races.*[29]

His article was both a plea for peace and a justification for racism and war. Lindbergh, said Heywood Broun of *The New Republic,* had developed a new political stance, "Pacifist Imperialism." "I honestly believe that our greatest danger lies in heeding the jingoes who come forward camouflaged as doves."[30] The Roosevelt administration was angry. Secretary of the Interior Ickes noted that even Roosevelt was beginning to take seriously Charles's reputation as a fascist.

Three days later, Congress repealed the Neutrality Law. "Cash and Carry" purchases were now permitted; U.S. manufacturers could sell arms to belligerents if the material was shipped under the flag of a foreign nation. The next day, Hitler set his date for the attack on France. Within three weeks, wearing the yellow star became compulsory for Jews in Poland.[31]

Anne worked relentlessly on her plea for peace, to be published in the Christmas issue of *Reader's Digest*. Defying her deepest instincts, she immersed herself in Charles's political world.[32] "I *make* myself someone else and I am calm and collected!"[33]

Assuming her usual apologetic stance, Anne began her article:

I am speaking as a woman, a weak woman, if you will—emotional, impulsive, illogical, conservative, dreaming, impractical, impulsive, pacific, inadventurous, any of the feminine vices you care to pin on me. I write knowing that all those vices cannot help but be used to undermine anything I say.[34]

Speaking for a "long-range attitude toward peace," using the metaphors of motherhood and domesticity, Anne reiterated Charles's theories one by one: (1) the military constraints of the Versailles Treaty created an embittered Germany; (2) violence and aggression are facts of human life; (3) war is justified and inevitable among nations of disparate power; (4) the need to prevent the destruction of Western civilization as we know it; (5) the need to effect an early peace.

Hitler isn't evil, she wrote, or at least no more evil than the rest of us. He is the "embittered spirit of a strong and humiliated people." Russia, not Germany, is the real threat. Its weak and spiritless "hordes," mindlessly tied to a false vision of equality that breeds decadence and mediocrity, will destroy not only Germany but all the people of Europe. Let the natural process of war among nations smother the weak. Why destroy everything we value in Western civilization for a democratic principle that has proven itself flawed?

If Hitlerism is a spirit and you cannot kill or incarcerate a spirit, how can you deal with it? It can only . . . be exorcised. To exorcise this spirit you must offer Germany and the world not war but peace.[35]

Truly, Anne had written like "someone else." For the sake of loyalty to Charles, she had elevated Hitler to an unconquerable "spirit," reduced democracy to an infirm ideal, and renounced America's responsibility to its allies. There was only one thing harder to bear than the truth, and that was the thought of separation from Charles.

26

Images

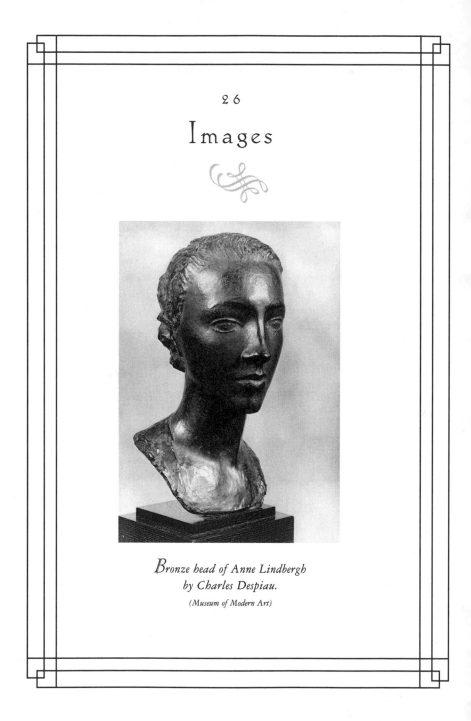

*Bronze head of Anne Lindbergh
by Charles Despiau.*
(Museum of Modern Art)

You have made an image of me.
Every image is a sin.

—ANNE MORROW LINDBERGH,
QUOTING STILLER IN CORRESPONDENCE[1]

JANUARY 1940, ENGLEWOOD, NEW JERSEY

Images of Anne—Charles couldn't get enough of them. As criticism of his pro-German stance intensified, he wanted to etch her onto the walls of his mind, as a sign of constancy in this pit-grave of politics. The task, however, was proving impossible. First Despiau and now Simon Elwes—painter of dukes, princesses, and kings—was summoned by Charles to perform the task. But no matter how many times the jovial painter put his brush to the cloth, the image turned out wrong. Elwes could not capture Anne's depth of character, Charles wrote in his diary. He would have to settle for mediocrity.

To Anne, however, the painter's brush was more than accurate. She felt sinful and useless, self-absorbed, and unworthy of Charles, Jon, and Land.[2]

On New Year's Day, Anne skied down the hills of Englewood, contemplating the chaos of war amid the simplicity of the winter landscape. As she "danced" with a hill,[3] all seemed tranquil and timeless, but she knew too well the illusion of the moment. Her thoughts turned toward possible American involvement in the war.[4]

Three days later, as if seeking approval from a higher source, Anne and Charles drove to Cambridge to visit Alfred and Evelyn Whitehead. When the tall, frail Mrs. Whitehead greeted them at the door, Anne felt an immediate kinship. Alfred, now eighty-two years old, was equally warm and engaging. His small bent frame played counterpoint to his fiery eyes. He spoke slowly and with precision, in beautiful prose, setting Anne at ease in spite of his penetrating mind and sardonic wit. He seemed to her a paradox of gentility and cynicism.[5]

Anne and Charles had read Whitehead's 1933 treatise *The Adventure of Ideas*. His mathematical mind had permitted him to distill the flux of history into thematic abstractions that confirmed Charles's view of an amoral universe. Recalling the fall of the Roman Empire and the age of decay that had augured its decline, Whitehead wrote,

> *My thesis is that a new reformation is in full progress. It is a reformation; but whether its issue be fortunate or unfortunate depends largely on the notions of comparatively few men . . . New directions require human misery . . . The vigor of the race has them pushed forward into the adventure of imagination so as to anticipate the physical adventures of exploration. The world dreams of things to come, and then, in due time, arouses itself to their realization.*[6]

To Anne, Charles Lindbergh and Alfred Whitehead were among the "vigorous race" who could dare to dream. The seriousness with which the esteemed philosopher treated Charles's ideas gave Anne new confidence.

The idea of change began to pervade her diaries. She had thought she craved the peace of Long Barn, only to find that something within her rebelled against the perfect and peaceful English world. In Illiec, she had found a natural rhythm as she moved according to its swelling tides, the thunder of the sea, and the howling of the wind, leaving behind all manmade falseness. She was beginning to see that harmony with life meant accepting the chaos and adapting to change.

The writings of Whitehead and Saint-Exupéry melded into one as Anne developed a metaphor that would dominate her work. We contain a "changeless element," she wrote, even as we submit to the rhythm of life. We must commune with that element or lose our power to create.

The opportunity to test her theory presented itself sooner than she had expected. Jim Newton, whom they had met through Alexis Carrel in Illiec three years earlier, had appointed himself their "guardian angel." Sensing their need to "get away," he had rented Anne and Charles a cottage on the island of Captiva, a remote island, only seven miles long, off the gulf coast of Florida.[7]

On January 21, Anne and Charles boarded a train for Tampa. Flirting with the public and the press, Charles ate in the dining car while burying his head in a mammoth book by H. G. Wells.[8] His *Outline of History* was an analysis of the patterns of human history from ancient Sparta to the Great War. While the trainmen and the other travelers gawked, Charles sat, head resting on his hand, contemplating the inevitable thrust of evolution.

They met Jim Newton at Haines City and drove to Fort Myers, where they crossed the bay to Captiva. From the moment Anne and Charles saw its shoreline, the barely inhabited island seemed a place beyond ordinary life. Separately, and yet in unison, Anne and Charles recorded their enchantment—the palms silhouetted against the sky, the shell roads, and the wide stretches of virgin beach.[9]

Newton had borrowed a thirty-foot cabin cruiser and hired a young game warden to help them navigate the Everglades. Guided by him, Jim lurched through the deep waters of the Shark River, chopping his way through the branches of the mangrove trees. As thousands of birds swarmed above them, reminiscent of the Minnesota woodlands one generation before, they made their way, spear-fishing by day, lighting campfires at night, and taking turns sleeping and keeping watch on their boat.

Determined to be "crew," Anne took her place beside the men. She was "steel," Jim later said, handling the big poles and spearing the lobsters.[10] "I have to do this," she insisted.

They returned home on February 5, pleased that Anne's article "Prayer for Peace" had been rated number one in a poll of readers. According to a concurrent Gallup Poll, only 23 percent of Americans wanted to join in the war against Germany.[11] Even the British Ministry of Information wanted to publish the article in pamphlet form.[12] Perhaps, Charles wrote, at last someone was listening.

One by one, the nations of Europe staked their territorial claims. In late February, 68,000 men died in the battles between Germany and Russia on the Finnish border, and Mussolini pledged his commitment to the fall of France. Britain announced that 400,000 children would be evacuated from the cities to the countryside.[13]

As Hitler's intent became clear, Charles's diaries assumed the tone of one who knew he must answer to history. He withdrew, seeking lessons from his past. On a trip to Washington, he retraced the steps through boulevards and corridors he had once walked with his congressman father. But all he saw was disorder and degeneration. He could not but wonder, he wrote, whether America was a country in "decline."[14] On a visit to the Smithsonian, he hid behind a statue of Martha Washington to view the crowd that paid homage to the *Spirit of St. Louis,* his now primitive airplane. He marveled now at his courage in flying the flimsy machine across the Atlantic. How wonderful it was in a museum, he wrote, never to be flown again, like an icon of the past.[15] Seeking courage from his accomplishments, he bought a big globe, on which he smeared in bold black ink the routes he had charted during their frontier flying days.[16] Acknowledging that Anne was at the core of his survival, Charles rewarded her for her love and loyalty. He remodeled the garage of the Lloyd Neck house. The structure, which stood on top of the hill, overlooking the sea, contained the room where Anne wrote. With a warm stove and an expansive view, Charles was sure she would be comfortable there.[17]

Anne, in turn, gave Charles a gift. She offered him *The Way of Life,* by Lao-tzu, a treatise on solitude and the balancing mechanism of a "changeless core."

Frequently nauseated, since her return from Florida, Anne took to her bed and gained a reprieve from the clamor of politics. Her doctor confirmed what she had hoped: she was pregnant again. The thought of having another child stirred memories of both her own childhood and the deaths of Elisabeth and Charlie.[18] Echoing her reading of Theosophy and the poetry of Rilke, Anne wrote, "There is no wall but time between the living and the dead."

While spring in Lloyd Neck dragged its heels, refusing to bloom beneath the rotting leaves, Germany invaded Norway and Denmark.[19] When the Norwegians and Danes were forced to surrender, Charles was pleased with the "amazing success" of the German army. It was not only a triumph of "air power," he wrote, it was also "a turning point in military history."[20] Anne, on the other hand, was shocked by the ruthlessness of the German troops.[21]

But with the arrival of spring, she felt closer than ever to Charles. She was certain, she wrote, that Whitehead was right. Events were ideas waiting to be born; like waves breaking against the shores of human experience, they swelled and receded according to a higher law. Human life was driven by notions of reality that were undefinable by existing language. Something good, though, would come; some hidden element for the good of mankind. Hitler's love for his people was no different from Roosevelt's. He, too, had instituted a kind of "New Deal." And he was just an accidental scourge, the means through which a new idea emerged. The Nazis were merely riding the wave.[22]

Unknown to Anne, Hitler had long since formulated the "final solution." Heinrich Himmler saw to the construction of Auschwitz and Bergen-Belsen in Poland, facilities for slave labor and the extermination of the Jewish population in occupied territory.[23]

As word—sparse and incomplete—of Jewish persecution filtered home, Charles noted in his diary that he was still pleased with his ancestry. But one's life, he wrote, was also determined by one's environment, and one must teach one's children to take care of themselves. Once again, mimicking his father's attempts to foster his manhood, Charles took Jon to a pasture near their home and left him alone to cope with a butting ram. Charles climbed over a fence and hid in an adjoining field to watch his son battle with nature. The ram got tired of butting, and Jon, wrote Charles, learned to protect himself.[24]

Unable to keep silent, Betty Morrow once again made known her opinions, so different from her children's. Appalled by the events in Norway and fearing the imminent invasion of France, she delivered a radio address that urged the public to extend active aid to the Allies. Known in the press as the mother-in-law of Charles Lindbergh, Betty sought to stand for herself. She told Anne she was doing it for "Daddy."

Her views reflected those of 51 percent of the public,[25] and she continued to urge the American government to send airplanes and money to the Allies and to stop the export of war materials that might find their way to the aggressors.[26] As her husband had done in *The Society of Free States,* published in 1919, Betty spoke of nationalism in the context of voluntary international cooperation, exercising her influence in her husband's name. As a widow, she became the man she married, a heroine in hero's shoes.

On May 10, 1940, Hitler launched a massive offensive; he broke through the French Maginot Line, and the British troops stationed in France withdrew to the beaches of Dunkirk.[27] The courage of the British, civilians and military men, in rescuing many of their soldiers was to be known as a miracle.

In a speech to the House of Commons on May 13, Churchill, referring to Dunkirk, turned defeat into inspiration. "We shall fight on the beaches, we shall fight on the landing grounds . . . until in God's good time the new world with all its power and might steps forth to the rescue and liberation of the old."[28]

And he asked Roosevelt to lend England fifty destroyers.

Three days later, Charles wrote in his diary that the press was "hysterical." They implied that America was just days away from attack.[29]

In response to Churchill's request, Roosevelt called for "sharply increased military spending" and the "modernization" of the United States Army and Navy.[30] Days later, Charles made another radio address, hoping to sway public opinion.[31] And on May 19, he urged the government to adopt a policy of "defense preparedness." Of course we need a greater army and navy, he said, but let us not be manipulated by propaganda. Let us not fear an invasion or commit ourselves to war. American editorials called him "ignorant" and "blind"[32]; the Italian press praised his speech as "cheering news."[33]

On May 24, as the Germans swept toward Paris, Anne lunched with her mother in New York at the Cosmopolitan Club. How the English and French "will *hate* us," Anne said to her. She realized that her loyalty to Charles would cost her her friendships; perhaps this was her contribution to the war.[34]

As Churchill called for a day of prayer in England, and crowds knelt in Ste. Genevieve in Paris, Anne prayed, too, not for victory, but for peace. "Thy will be done," she wrote.[35]

In fact, Charles, not God, was Anne's bulwark against despair.

Charles was one of the few men in the world who lived their lives on top of the facts. While her family and friends saw Charles as an "anti-Christ," Anne saw him as the image of the divine.[36]

Even as her mother's words were a monument to her father, Anne discarded his ideas.

The "old gods" were gone; the myth of democracy was dead; the optimism of her father had proved naïve. "Democracy," with its economic and social disorder and its political inefficiency, did not seem worthy of preservation. Desperately, as if damming a river, Anne began an article that would confirm her solidity with the Christian church and refute the charge that Charles was "anti-Christ." Later, Anne would call it "A Confession of Faith."

Charles spoke to America again on June 15 from the NBC studios in Washington.[37] He urged the United States to stay out of the war and recited his litany of warnings. England would inevitably fall to Germany, the strongest nation in human history. Any struggle to prevent this would be comparable to ancient wars; and to what purpose? To pit "one half of the white race against the other?"

Anne applauded his speech. It was beautifully delivered and all "of a piece." The criticism it provoked was proof of its validity; she was certain it would turn Americans against the war.[38]

Ten days later, Charles visited his old friend Henry Ford, hoping to convince him to support his cause. Charles had given Ford his first airplane ride after his flight in 1927. Now it was time for Ford to return the favor. He asked him to join his campaign against the war, to lend his fame and prestige to the cause. Ford needed little convincing. He had spent the past two decades making his views clear. The Jews, he believed, were international plotters pushing our country into war. Their materialism had brought about a decline in American morals, culture, values, products, and entertainment. In 1918, when Ford bought the small country newspaper the *Dearborn Independent,* he had considered it a ten-million-dollar investment to counter the distortions of the Jewish press. Within a year and a half, the paper had become a mass-circulation, anti-Semitic propaganda sheet, and by 1927, it had a world circulation of half a million. Ford

used it as the core of the four-volume *International Jew,* which he had deliberately chosen not to copyright so that it could be printed freely
throughout Europe and North America. It was said that Hitler had used
it as a model for *Mein Kampf.* It was also said that Hitler kept a picture of
Ford beside his desk and referred to him as "my inspiration."[39]

Lindbergh found the old man, now over seventy, "alert, agile, and
overflowing with new ideas." As they drove in a new Mercury on a tour
of factories dotting the River Rouge, they spoke of the future of
American industry, boys' camps, and the prospects of war. Charles had
a "great admiration" for Ford's unique genius and character. He felt that
even Ford's dreams were tinged with reality.[40]

What were Henry Ford's "dreams" between 1939 and 1945?:
Sustaining the leadership of Adolf Hitler to effect the military victory
of his Nazi Reich.

In April of 1940, just two months before Charles' visit to Dearborn,
a poem was published in an in-house magazine of the Ford Motor
Company's German subsidiary, when Henry Ford was still in complete
control of the German operation.

It read as follows:

> *The Fuhrer*
> *We have sworn to you once,*
> *But now we make our allegiance permanent.*
> *Like currents in a torrent lost,*
> *We all flow into you.*
>
> *Even when we cannot understand you,*
> *We will go with you.*
> *One day we may comprehend,*
> *How you can see our future.*
> *Hearts like bronze shields,*
> *We have placed around you,*
> *And it seems to us, that only*
> *You can reveal God's world to us.*

Later, in a U.S. Army Report, it would be revealed that German Ford served as an "arsenal of Nazism" with the consent of headquarters in Dearborn. Until Pearl Harbor, Dearborn made huge profits by producing war material for the Reich. German sales would increase by more than half between 1938 and 1943 and the value of the German subsidiary would double during the course of the war. Ford vehicles would be deemed crucial to the revolutionary military strategy of blitzkrieg, and approximately, one third of the 350,000 trucks used by the motorized German army as of 1942 would be manufactured by Ford. Furthermore, during this period, the U.S. Treasury Department would conclude that the Ford Motor Company cooperated with the Nazis through its subsidiary in France, encouraging executives to work with German officials overseeing the occupation.

In May of 1941, when Charles was still a full-time consultant to the Ford Motor Company, Nazi officials would praise the Ford operation for facilitating their military victory and cooperating in "the establishment of an exemplary social state."[41]

Unaware of his secret machinations but well versed in Henry Ford's anti-Semitic views, the press chastised Charles for meeting with him. When Anne sought comfort from her friends, they were surprised by her loyalty to Charles. Thelma Crawford turned away in disgust, and Sue and George Vaillant gave Anne little consolation. Only Mina Curtiss remained dispassionate. Later, she said that her attitude was a denial of her being Jewish. For the moment, however, she comforted Anne. And Anne was still defending Charles, reasoning that even if his views were wrong, they were not immoral.[42]

Roosevelt had taken steps to increase the military budget and had authorized the call-up of two million men. For the first time, Charles feared for his physical safety and faced the prospect of leaving Anne alone. In a moment of tenderness, he sought to free her from dependency on him. What would she do, he asked, if she had to make it on her own? She answered, simply, "I don't know."

Charles urged her to listen to him, and to remember that if she were ever left without him in times of need, she could earn her living as a writer, regardless of the government in power.[43]

"He frightens me," she wrote, as if he could see into the future. But ironically, he also gave her confidence.[44]

But if he aroused fear, he also incited her anger. In the hope of forcing her to face independence, he criticized her for not writing more. Only two books in nine years? Why didn't she compile an anthology so that her time since their return from France wouldn't be such a personal waste? She was torn by the children, the housekeeping, and her writing. It was impossible to keep her mind focused on daily matters and yet nourish the abstract thinking required for writing.

But, she confided in her diary, her inability to write was more than a matter of finding time. She didn't have the words. Her work before the war belonged to an era that no longer existed. Whitehead was right. The old world was dying and the new one had not yet begun.[45]

Charles, however, could not stop talking. On the sun-drenched afternoon of August 4, at a meeting in Chicago of Citizens to Keep-America-Out-of-War, Charles spoke to a crowd of forty thousand.[46] His speech was reminiscent of Anne's "Prayer for Peace." "The world," he said, "is not governed by principle or by Christian values; it is governed by power."[47]

Hitler apparently agreed. His economic minister touted the wisdom of Lindbergh's speech even as the Nazis were laughing at Charles's naïveté. American shores were not invulnerable. After Europe would come the conquest of the United States.[48]

As the Luftwaffe continued its assault on England, Anne finished her "Confession of Faith." Clothed in the religious and moral symbols of her childhood, her writing was a ritual form of self-absolution. The article would become her book *The Wave of the Future*.[49] In forty-one pages, more a pamphlet than a book, Anne crystallized the thoughts in her diaries and articles, portraying the destruction of Western civilization as a divine and natural inevitability. Her desperation gave the book a tone of extreme urgency. Once more she apologized for being a woman, as if to placate a wrathful God. But she had to speak out and be heard.

How are we to get at the "truth," she asks, and how are we to reevaluate the evil by the standard of Christian morality? Is it merely a question of good against evil? Is it a matter of launching a crusade? The demons who persecute, kill, and steal—do they not commit terrible sins? And what about the "democracies?" she asks, contemptuously placing the word in quotation marks. With fire and brimstone, Anne condemns them for their sins. "Democracies," she writes, are guilty of "sins of omission" and self-delusion. They can afford to be smug because they were among the "have" nations. Germany cannot, and the "democracies" refuse either to support them or to give them aid. If "territorial and economic concessions" had been made, there would be no Nazism and no war. She does not excuse Nazi evil; she merely explains it. Their evil springs from the barren earth of neglect.

Here all her theories coalesce in an attempt to paraphrase what she understands as Whitehead's theory of history. "The wave of the future is coming," and there will be no stopping it. It is a wave of human energy pushing toward a divine good, a conception of humanity, trying to come to birth, that obscures its purpose with horror and evil. Perhaps, she muses, it is retribution for our materialism and lack of spirituality. It is a war "we have begotten," and the evils we deplore are "the scum on the wave of the future."

Using an argument of Hitler's in *Mein Kampf,* she considers the evils of the French Revolution. Certainly we do not question its fundamental moral imperative. The old morality does not suffice; heroic enterprise is no longer respected. We have to let them go, and we have to let "democracy" die with them. It has failed economically and morally and has eroded the "hardiness of the race."

We cannot "save" civilization. The German "spirit" will crush our armies. Our own moral and spiritual disintegration is a greater threat to our existence than the possibility of invasion from abroad.

There is no fighting the wave of the future . . . We, unhappily, are living in the hiatus between two dreams. One is dying and the other is not yet born. America must confront its sins and have an infinite faith in the future.[50]

Her amoral logic fractures like light through a prism. The book stands as a philosophic consummation of all she and Charles believed. Finally their vision had a form.

Harcourt Brace rushed it to print. The book, published on October 3, 1940, the day after the birth of her daughter, Anne Jr., was a recapitulation of her husband's views. It sold fifty thousand copies within the first two months. The Italians and Germans called Anne "noble," and the American public regarded her as nothing less than satanic or, worse, Satan's "little wife." Male reviewers dismissed her as the mouthpiece for her husband's fascist views, and female journalists attacked her directly. The only exception was the gentle E. B. White, who criticized her logic but not her character.[51] But it was Dorothy Ducas who came closest to the truth. In *Who* magazine, she pegged Anne as an incompetent dreamer who lacked the courage of her idealistic parents. "The young woman," she writes, "[who] knows little of the rushing, pushing, world of reality," lives in a house divided against itself, caught between those she loves.[52]

Later, Anne would call it her "bridge book,"[53] her attempt to cross the divide between her father's Wilsonian principles and her husband's vision and practicality. Anne was convinced that her father would have agreed with its spirit if not its methods.[54] Once again, Anne was deluding herself. Dwight Morrow would have loathed both her methods and her ideas. Cold practicality would have held no weight for him in the face of Hitler's devastation of humanity. Man, believed Morrow, worked in partnership with God; there was no inevitability to "natural law." The future of a country rested on its moral fiber and ethics, not on momentary events. Morrow's loyalties to democratic principle and to the European democracies would have rendered his daughter's theories absurd. A humanist to the core, Morrow would have seen the notion of racial superiority as abhorrent. A man of diplomacy, dedicated to a covenant of nations, Morrow would have considered war the last resort, but he would have understood its moral imperative in certain crises.

To stop the walls of her marriage from crumbling, Anne sanctioned Hitler's charnel house. In the name of loyalty to her husband, Anne validated the vision of a madman.

27

Saint of the Midnight Wild

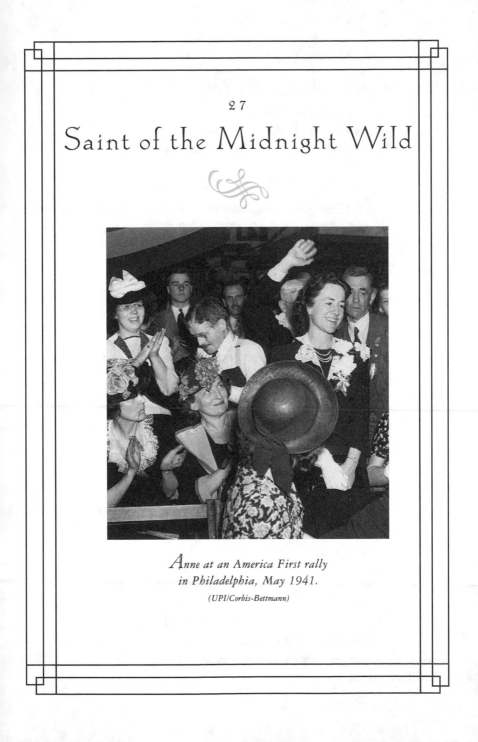

*A*nne at an America First rally
in Philadelphia, May 1941.
(UPI/Corbis-Bettmann)

SAINT FOR OUR TIME [1]

Christopher, come back to earth again.
There is no age in history when men
So cried for you, Saint of a midnight wild,
Who stood beside a stream and heard a child . . .

But who today will take the risk or blame
For someone else? Everyone is the same,
Dreading his neighbor's tongue or pen or deed
Imprisoned in fear we stand and do not heed.
The cry that you once heard across the stream
"There is no cry," we say, "it is a dream."

Christopher, the waters rise again,
As on the night, the waters rise; the rain
Bites like a whip across a prisoner's back;
The lightning strikes like fighters in attack
And thunder, like a time-bomb, detonates
The starless sky no searchlight penetrates.

The child is crying on a further shore:
Christopher, come back to earth once more.

—ANNE MORROW LINDBERGH

SPRING 1941, LLOYD NECK, LONG ISLAND

All Anne could do was pray. The grief of war, she wrote to a friend, was intensified by the wounds of thousands.[2] The world cried out for a saint who would carry the sins and pain of all men on his back.

But who were the new Saint Christophers, Anne asked? Winston Churchill? Adolf Hitler? Whoever they were, Anne was certain that Charles was meant to walk among them.

In the spring of 1941, Charles believed there was no turning back. Anne's book had lent nobility to his cause. When he reread his father's books, he saw history repeating itself; he was certain his father's beliefs were true. One need not be pro-British to be a "true" American, nor was it one's duty to stand by the president. It was the right of each citizen to challenge policy before or after it became law. Now, that right was again being violated by the machinations of warmongerers. Twenty years earlier, his father had believed that the Catholics formed an international conspiracy to bring America into a war with Europe. Charles believed it was now the Jews. The Jews, he wrote, were using the media to spread propaganda. And Roosevelt, a liar and a demagogue, was their puppet.[3] He had won election on a platform of peace, yet he was determined to lead the nation into war. Give England our destroyers? Protect them with American convoys? And now Lend-Lease? Whom was Roosevelt kidding? We were only a "step away" from sending our troops. Lindbergh would not be cowed into silence by Roosevelt's lies.

In fact, Charles's assessment of Roosevelt's view of the war was correct. By 1941, Roosevelt saw U.S. involvement as inevitable. It was a matter of convincing the public. But in early February 1941, 85 percent of the public polled by Gallup did not want America to go to war.[4] Knowing that time was running out, he had no choice but to move ahead.

Charles, too, sensed it was now or never. The time for aggressive attack had come. By the end of January, Charles joined the congressional debate. Representative Sol Bloom of New York, chairman of the House Committee on Foreign Affairs, asked him to offer the committee his case against Lend-Lease.[5] On January 23, 1941, Charles gave public testimony for the first time since the Hauptmann trial, in 1935, lending the proceedings an aura of theater.[6] Long before the doors of the committee room in the new House Office Building were opened, lines of spectators waited outside. Those lucky enough to be admitted broke the silence with a defiant show of applause for the Colonel.

With the air of a "veteran" and the voice of authority, he instructed the photographers to take their pictures at once and not to set off any flashbulbs while he was testifying. He read his prepared statement in a firm voice, handed it to the official stenographer, and settled back in his chair to await the questions. Reporters noted that when he spoke, all the witnesses who had gone before and all who were to follow "dropped to the status of aging and colorless extras." Cordell Hull and Henry Stimson and the others had been "eloquent but had sprung no surprises." Ambassador Kennedy appeared disingenuous and confused. "Serious" and "smooth-cheeked," with a touch of gray over his ears, Colonel Lindbergh responded with "infinite poise and infinite conviction," telling his audience, "I want neither side to win."[7]

The American press judged him "the perfect neutral," and the Germans called him one of the few true Americans.[8]

From Saint-Gildas, Carrel informed him that the French agreed. The military and air attachés of the Vichy government were with him "one hundred per cent." Thrilled with the news, Charles wrote in his diary: "I believe Dr. Carrel can be of great value to France at this time . . . to a reconstruction of France." Charles considered him "one of the great men of France in these times. If only he is able to make the right contacts."[9]

In the first week of March, feeling, once again, the need to "get away," Anne and Charles made their second trip with Jim Newton to Florida.[10] For Anne, it was a moment to regain perspective. She had begun to write her "feminist essay," an analysis of married women and creativity. The problems confronting the ambitious woman weighed heavily on Anne's mind. A married woman could not possibly write with the freedom and clarity of a man. Saint-Exupéry was the very essence of an artist, but he had the luxury of time and solitude, while she was pulled in different directions, always feeling rushed, guilty, and inadequate. She could not be the most important person in her children's lives and still manage to write and spend time with Charles. Life itself was her art. If only she could be everything to everyone.

While the Lindberghs chopped their way through the keys, the Lend-Lease legislation was passed by Congress and signed by Roosevelt.

This, said Roosevelt—as if to silence further dissent—"is the end of any attempt at appeasement in our land."[11] But Charles was prepared to counter Roosevelt's every move. He wrote "A Letter to Americans," which appeared in the March 1941 issue of *Collier's* magazine.[12]

Although he set forth the same arguments he had presented before, he now put them in the context of personal experience. At the suggestion of Anne, who had assumed the responsibility of editing his speeches,[13] he proclaimed himself the voice of reason and counseled France and England to cease the hopeless war. And he made one last request to the American people: before reaching a final decision, they should demand a full plan from those who preached the defense of democracy.

With simple elegance, Lord Halifax, the English ambassador to the United States, replied. The plan, he said, was a single word: "Victory."[14]

In fact, Charles's assessment of Allied military power was wrong. While America was not at the peak of its production—as it would be within six months—she and the Allies had enough power to keep the Germans at bay. At the time he wrote his article, Germany had approximately 3500 combat airplanes, the United States and Russia combined had 8000, and England had 3100. Within six months, the German force would decline to 2500, and the Allied forces, including the United States, would have 11,000 front-line combat planes.[15]

Contrary to Charles's assessment of Greenland as an unimportant military base, the U.S. acquired full defense rights for its operation.[16] Charles wrote in his diary that the moon rose "huge and blood red."[17]

Within the week, Charles joined the America First Committee, an event that made national news. Committee leaders convinced him that he was the only one with mass appeal that rivaled the President's. On April 17, Charles spoke to a crowd of 10,000 gathered under the committee's auspices in Chicago.[18]

America First had been conceived in the spring of 1940 after the fall of France. R. Douglas Stuart, Jr., a student at the Yale University Law School and the son of a vice president of the Quaker Oats Company, organized students and faculty on the Yale campus. They launched a petition that led to a nationwide anti-interventionist organization. Stuart's intent was to oppose the policies of the Roosevelt administration and preserve the Neutrality Act of 1939. On September 4, Stuart, as national director, assisted by General Robert E. Wood, chairman of Sears Roebuck, set forth the group's principles. The United States must build an impregnable military defense to protect itself against invasion. It must preserve democracy by keeping out of a European war and concentrating on its defense and the maintainance of its neutrality. To achieve these ends, the committee issued a resolution: "To bring together all Americans, regardless of possible differences on other matters, who see eye to eye on these principles. (This does not include Nazis, Fascists, Communists, or members of other groups that place the interest of any other nation above those of our own country)."[19]

While the organization attracted support across the political and social spectrum, its official stance reflected the interests of its main contributors—businessmen, manufacturers, agricultural-based enterprises—that is, industries dependent on consumer rather than military goods. Despite its conservative cast, however, America First contributed to several pacifist and socialist groups.

But the tide of public opinion was turning against the isolationists. President Roosevelt had managed to do the impossible. His personal approval rate was at 72 percent, and 59 percent of the public polled supported Lend-Lease. While 83 percent of the people did not want to go to war, the same number of people believed that we would. In fact, 68 percent believed it our moral duty.[20]

America was talking back, but Charles Lindbergh refused to listen. All he could hear was the roar of the crowds who flocked by the thousands to see him. They were the true mirror of America, he wrote. They were the pure and hearty Americans who were worth his voice and worth his life.

Harold Ickes, speaking this time at a benefit for the Jewish National Workers Alliance of America, dubbed Charles the "Number 1 Nazi Fellow Traveler," and described Anne's book, *Wave of the Future,* as "the bible of every American Nazi, Fascist, Bundist, and appeaser."[21]

At a rally on April 23 at the Manhattan Center, 35,000 people flooded the flag-draped hall. Amidst the flying colors, in his high-pitched, schoolmarm tone, Charles spoke for twenty-five minutes, to the intermittent applause of a thunderous crowd. Charles believed that "the crowd seemed one hundred percent with us,"[22] but a hundred policemen watched the hall anyway.[23] The press called it "the largest gathering of pro-Nazis and pro-Fascists since the Bund rallies in Madison Square Garden."[24] And while the German press called Charles "a real American of Swedish descent,"[25] Roosevelt called him a defeatist and an appeaser.[26]

Comparing him to Clement L. Vallandigham, the Civil War Copperhead who was banished by the North, Roosevelt questioned his integrity as an army officer.[27] Hurt and humiliated, Charles Lindbergh renounced his army commission.[28] "A point of honor" was at stake, he told his friend Truman Smith.[29]

To Anne, however, Charles remained "Sir Galahad." Yet she sensed that something was wrong. While the crowds hung on his every word, the caliber of the audience was not what it had been. Even the hall was shabby and garish. There was something "second-rate" to it all, she wrote. But she resolved to respond to the outspoken critics. Her article "Reaffirmation"[30] appeared in the June issue of *The Atlantic Monthly* and was billed as an explanation of *The Wave of the Future*. In truth, she confided to a friend, it was a form of self-exorcism. Even as she tried to dig herself out, though, she was sucked further into the quicksand.

Are we in America really good, she asks? No, she writes. "Scum is everywhere; it is not just personified in devils across the ocean; it is in our midst." Citing *Mein Kampf,* which refers to the infiltration of the Jews into German society, she writes, "Is it not possible that Nazism has come not only as a result of evils within Germany but also as a terrible antidote to other weaknesses in the Democracies themselves—as a fever is sometimes necessary to drive out a disease?"

The piece, she later told a friend, was a failure. Her message was too big for essays and articles; it was the stuff of novels and poetry. To herself, she admitted that it was a capitulation to Charles, tainted by her bitterness toward the press. It did not represent purity of thought. In short, there *were* principles worth dying for.[31]

On May 15, 1941, after Germany invaded the island of Crete in a spectacular air assault,[32] Henry Ford offered Charles and American First lavish funds to support the committee's cause: $250,000 for the first month.[33] On May 23, Charles was to give the keynote address at America First's meeting at Madison Square Garden,[34] an event he knew was sufficiently important to receive wide coverage. He was to share the stage with Norman Thomas, leader of the Socialist Party. Thomas, certainly neither pro-German nor a member of America First, was sympathetic to the isolationist cause and believed it crucial to educate as many as possible. He had addressed several America First rallies and accepted its funding and support for his radio broadcasts, tours, and books.

Anne and Charles drove to the Garden behind a fanfare of sirens. To Anne, the labyrinthine passages seemed a descent into Dante's Hell. Suddenly out of the passageways and into lights, accompanied by Norman Thomas, they were before the roaring crowds. Twenty thousand people, filling the hall to its dimly lit corners, marked Lindbergh's arrival with chants of "Lindbergh for President." Overwhelmed by the emotion, the noise and the lights, Anne imagined the sound of gunshots in her ears, but, with relief, glimpsed a policeman through the glare, seated at the feet of Charles, standing on the podium.

John T. Flynn, head of the New York chapter, called the meeting to order with the solemnity of a preacher. In a booming voice, he denounced the communists, fascists, and Bundists who were attempting to infiltrate the organization. Frozen, Anne watched the crowd grow wild with disapproval, booing and hissing at the well-known leaders of these radical groups. Did this outbreak presage a future revolution, she wondered?

Charles's presence seemed familiar yet strange. Once again, Anne became the child-wife who worshipped at her husband's feet.

Beginning his speech with his usual plea for "an independent American destiny," this time he dared to go a step further, portraying America as nothing less than a police state. Civil freedoms in America, he said, were little better than those in Germany. Without mentioning Roosevelt's name, he condemned the president as a self-serving dictator. "We in America were given just about as much chance to express our beliefs at the election last fall as the Germans would have been given if Hitler had run against Goering."

At Anne's request, Charles had included in the closing section a personal plea for commitment and a statement of his personal vision. But there was desperation in his words. His rhetoric had become so emotional that it lacked even the pretense of rational public policy.

Denounced from the pulpits of Presbyterian churches as an appeaser and a traitor,[35] damned by the White House to public oblivion, and labeled by the press as the voice of Hitler,[36] Charles was more desperate than ever to find the words that would set America free. Like a child who still believed in the magic of his will, he vowed to launch an attack on Roosevelt and the press, and, within the week, spoke again, this time to a crowd estimated at fifteen thousand.[37] Though Anne had begged him not to mention Roosevelt's name, Charles fiercely condemned him.

Anne resolved to make every sacrifice. No longer would she stay at home and indulge in fantasies of what might have been. She would squelch every doubt and follow him wherever he would go. She would throw herself headlong into Charles's life and give up the utopian vision.

But Charles, aware of Anne's sacrifices, tried again to set her free. The memory of his mother's youth spent in the shadow of his father's political views pained him. He told Anne to stay home and work, not only for the children but for herself. He wanted to protect her, even from himself.

On June 22, in the most ambitious attack in military history, Germany invaded the Soviet Union along its 1800–mile front from the Arctic to the Black Sea. More than three million troops, 600,000 vehicles, 750,000 horses, 3580 tanks, and 1830 planes were hurled against Russia's borders.[38] Charles calmly told the press that the invasion was "something that requires profound analysis."[39]

As the Einsatzgruppen pushed on through Russian villages, murdering thousands of Jews as they did so, Charles spoke at another
America First meeting in San Francisco.[40] He said, "I would a hundred
times rather see my country ally herself with England, or even with
Germany with all her faults, than with the cruelty, the Godlessness, and
the barbarism that exist in Soviet Russia."

The heat from the press made it clear to Anne and Charles that they
could no longer live in New York. In Lloyd Neck, they went into hiding, drawing shades and locking the doors. Margot Morrow encouraged
them to seek asylum in Martha's Vineyard near her family's summer
home. Desperate for escape, Anne searched for a home on the Vineyard
and found a small farmhouse, part saltbox, situated on the north shore
of the island, between Vineyard Haven and West Tisbury.[41] A cross
breeze came through the low-set doors and windows, and everywhere
were views of the sea.

In the wake of Anne's retreat to Martha's Vineyard, rumors of marital difficulties proliferated.[42] The press decided that Anne had broken
with Charles in favor of her parents' beliefs. But Anne, remaining
solidly by Charles's side, still believed he had integrity.

As Roosevelt and Churchill met in the mid-Atlantic to formulate
U.S.–British strategy, Anne slipped quietly into the rhythms of the sea.
She enjoyed the time alone with her children and her walks along the
beach. Except for the trees and the mild movements of the changing
tides, the island's climate and ambiance reminded Anne of Illiec.

Meanwhile, like a man with nothing to lose, Charles walked into
the eye of the storm, encountering hostility wherever he went. His
physical safety was constantly threatened; police officers watched his
every move. They accompanied him on motorcycles and fine-combed
every room in which he was to stay, checking the phones and x-raying
the furniture. They assigned a detective to every door of his meeting
halls and guarded the rooms beneath the speaker's stand. Nonetheless,
Charles insisted that the crowds adored him.[43]

Roger Butterfield commented in *Life* magazine,

Without {Lindbergh} the isolationist movement would be split into in-effective fragments. The magic of his legendary name, the appeal of his personality, the sincerity with which he comes before the microphone, have persuaded millions of Americans who were only half-persuaded before that there is no reason for the U.S. to fight or fear Hitler . . . The semi-hysterical response of the crowds is nothing less than "Fuehrer-worship."[44]

But Anne could tell that something had changed. Thwarted at every turn, Charles no longer masked his anger. The text of a speech he planned to give in Washington disturbed her. For the first time, he dared to give the enemy a name—"the British, the Jews, and the [Roosevelt] Administration."[45] She tried to dissuade him, but he would not bend. In an effort to protect him from Nazi epithets, Anne edited his speech, hoping that she would bring out his "true self."[46]

The public, of course, would believe what it heard and saw. Forced to appear outside Washington, for fear of retaliation by the government, Charles spoke on September 11 in Des Moines, surrounded by armed police and ferocious reporters. Even the crowd, numbered at only 7500, was unusually restless and unfriendly. When Charles rose to speak, a package thrown from the balcony onto the podium knocked down a vase on the table in front of him. He remained unperturbed.

Instead of agitating for war, the Jewish groups in this country should be opposing it in every possible way, for they will be among the first to feel its consequences. . . . I am not attacking either the Jewish or the British people. Both races I admire. But I am saying that the leader of both the British and the Jewish races for reasons which are as understandable from their perspective as they are inadvisable from ours, wish to involve us in the war. We cannot blame them for looking out for what they be-lieve to be their own interests, but we must also look out for ours. We can-not allow the natural passions and prejudices of other peoples to lead our country to destruction.[47]

Charles had made an irreversible leap from the abstraction of evolution theories to the "otherness," implying that the Jews were not Americans but had only self-serving allegiances. There was a hierarchy of human worth, even in America, and the civil rights of all citizens were not guaranteed. No longer were Jews merely cogs in the great wheel of history. They were dangerous to the survival of the body politic—an alien race deserving of public condemnation.

Defiantly, the crowd cheered Roosevelt's name eleven times during the course of his address, but Charles saw only their adulation. "Before long," he wrote in his diary, "we began to win over the crowd."

What he had won over was the admiration of Nazis, whose foot-high swastikas were displayed in storefronts as far away as Los Angeles. His speech in Des Moines was the final step in his public disgrace. Denunciation swept across the country, from Jews, Protestants, and Catholics. It came from Democrats and from Republicans, from government leaders and from grassroots Americans all charging him with anti-Semitism and Nazism. They called on America First, in the words of Reinhold Niebuhr, "to clear its ranks of those who would incite to racial and religious strife in this country."[48]

Several members of America First, however, supported Lindbergh, admiring his courage on "the Jewish Problem." On September 18, Lindbergh met with the committee, debating its public response for eight hours. The committee's statement, released on September 24, denied that Lindbergh and his fellow members were anti-Semitic. It blamed the interventionists for raising the issue of race, and it invited Jews to join the ranks.

Norman Thomas commented that "silence" would have been better. Privately, he castigated Lindbergh for singling out the Jews. In a letter to Flynn, however, Thomas went further, telling the organization that "many besides Jews have been at fault."

On October 3, at a rally in Fort Wayne, Lindbergh claimed that his motives and statements had been "falsely ascribed." He did not "speak out of hate for any individuals or any people." Nonetheless, John Flynn believed the damage had been done. At at time when Roosevelt accelerated efforts to repeal the Neutrality Act, Lindbergh, "acting alone," had discredited the anti-interventionist movement.

Even Anne could no longer abide his words. Charles's homecoming—indeed, the very idea of their marriage—was now a terrible burden. His bitterness had eclipsed his idealism, and Anne could no longer deny the meaning of his words. No matter what his intentions, his condemnation of the Jews was the anti-Semitism of Hitler's Reich. "I would prefer to see this country at war," she wrote.[49]

Perhaps the invasion of Kiev, portending the massacre of its 34,000 Jews, was at last too much. Perhaps, finally, she realized she could no longer defend his words to herself, to her family, or to her friends. She wrote to Mina Curtiss that some Puritan moral sense was taking hold of her.

28

Pilgrim

*Anne on a trip through the Florida Everglades
with Charles and their friend Jim Newton, 1941.*
(Lindbergh Picture Collection, Manuscripts and Archives,
Yale University Library)

PILGRIM [1]

This is a road
One walks alone;
Narrow the track
And overgrown.

Dark is the way
And hard to find,
When the last village
Drops behind.

Never a footfall
Light to show
Fellow traveler—
Yet I know

Someone before
Has trudged his load
In the same footsteps—
This is a road.

—ANNE MORROW LINDBERGH

DECEMBER 1941, MARTHA'S VINEYARD

Gathered in the darkness, the Japanese planes flew toward the island of Oahu. As light drenched the morning sky on December 7, 1941, waves of Japanese bombs pummeled Pearl Harbor. The U.S. Pacific Fleet, caught by surprise on a Sunday morning, was at anchor, off-guard and half-manned. Forewarned but unprepared, Admiral Husband E. Kimmel marshaled his sleeping men for counterattack, but within hours, 2334 American men were dead and 1347 lay wounded.[2]

At their home on Martha's Vineyard, Anne and Charles along with millions of Americans across the country, sat riveted by their radios as Roosevelt asked Congress to declare war on Japan. It was a date, said Roosevelt, "which will live in infamy."[3]

Charles knew better. "I am not surprised that the Japs attacked," he wrote in his diary. "We have been prodding them into war for weeks. They have simply beaten us to the gun."[4]

The next day hysteria took hold. Prewar ambivalence turned to fervor as thousands of men stormed naval recruitment centers.[5] In Germany, Adolf Hitler, fearing insurrection, went on a bloody rampage. He issued the Night and Fog Decree, enveloping enemies of the Reich in the folds of a winter night.

Anne hid beneath the bed covers, too weak to lift her head from the pillow. She was pregnant with her fifth child, but this malaise went beyond her pregnancy.[6]

She wrote to her friend Sue Vaillant that she would never publish anything under her name again and that Charles's reputation was ruined for good.

Charles would hear nothing of it. The war was on, and there was work to be done. Although he didn't trust Roosevelt, it was his duty to serve the president in his role as commander in chief.[7] Within days of Roosevelt's declaration, Charles offered his services to the War Department.[8] Secretary Stimson replied quickly: there was no way he would be permitted to serve, in any capacity. His loyalty, implied the letter, could not be trusted. Unless he retracted all his statements, his wartime activities would be shadowed by public doubt and fear. And for the most part, the press agreed. The best Charles could do, wrote the New York newspaper *PM,* was to retire.[9] *The Nation* magazine wrote that a commission to Charles Lindbergh would be "beyond the limits of safety."[10]

Outraged but adamant, Charles refused to give in to the War

Department's demands. A statement of retraction was out of the question. He still believed the war was wrong, but serving his country was a matter of honor. If he couldn't serve in the military, he would support the war through private industry. The problem was, the government was everywhere. No matter where he looked or to whom he spoke, it all came back to the decision by Roosevelt. While the War Department camouflaged its stance with amiable public statements, Charles was barred from company after company—first Curtiss-Wright, then United Airlines, then Pan Am. Discouraged, Charles called on his friend Henry Ford.[11]

Ford had instructed the men at his fledgling aircraft division at the plant in Dearborn to begin experimenting with high-altitude bombers. He was pleased with Charles's offer of help; the expertise would be more than welcome. This time, Roosevelt heartily agreed. Charles Lindbergh was suited to work with Henry Ford.

To the sound of the innocent laughter of her children at play, Anne began a gradual recovery. She sat in the island sunshine of early spring, trying to reconstruct her life. With her name synonymous with the "passive acceptance of totalitarianism," she feared not only public condemnation, but the loss of her family's and friends' good will. She still imagined she could have prevented the kidnapping and dammed the torrents of the war. If only she could achieve a state of grace, Anne thought she would be free of guilt and self-condemnation.[12]

In her despair, Anne turned again to the work of Saint-Exupéry for comfort. His new novel, *Flight to Arras,* a stream-of-consciousness narrative in the voice of a flier on a wartime mission, seemed to Anne "an act of forgiveness." He moved beyond the conventional notions of good and evil and beyond the confines of human "sin" to embrace the perversity of human nature. As if echoing Anne's deepest thoughts, he wrote, "I sat there longing for night, like a Christian abandoned by grace . . . alone and safely isolated in my beloved solitude. So that I might discover why I ought to die."[13]

Once more, his words seemed intended only for her. Anne no longer felt "exiled." Unlike the words of her husband, these were right and good and pure. Unlike the punitive voice of Calvinism during her childhood, they held the promise of forgiveness and grace.

In the spring of 1942, Anne was a pilgrim in search of God. She was willing to accept the dark uncertainties of life if only she could reclaim her faith.[14] But Anne's "darkness" mirrored the devastation of Europe. As she wrote, nearly a million German soldiers lay dead or wounded on the frigid white battlefields of western Russia. Hitler, confirming his right to rule, demanded that churchbells be taken down and collected. They would be melted to build airplane engines.[15]

Charles at last began to realize that German victory was far from certain, and he was worried. After all, to him "a Russian-dominated Europe would be far worse than German rule." He wondered how America could possibly win a war when the character of its people was in constant decline. If only we could do away with the "cheapness and immobility" of the motion picture industry, he wrote, America might stand a chance. While his patriotism condemned him to serve in a war he despised, he refused to profit from death and destruction. He would accept a salary of no more than $10,000 a year, he wrote—no matter what job he decided to take. It was the sum he would have received as a commissioned officer.[16]

Like Anne, he felt imprisoned by "fate." There is nothing worse than a caged animal, he wrote. The glaze in its eyes betrayed the death of its spirit. He, too, felt "hungry" and "deadened," but he hid his anguish to protect Anne.[17]

Anne believed that Charles was taking the war in stride. Nothing seemed to stop him. He was as tenacious and vibrant as ever.[18] Perhaps Charles's vitality came from his reconciliation with his past. It was as if, he later wrote, he sat on a hilltop and threw a beam of light on the road he had traveled. Not wishing for salvation, he hoped, at least, for self-understanding. He began to realize that the visions of his father and grandfather, which had pursued him during those long months before the war, were the source of his values, motives, and politics. He wanted to reclaim them and to make them his own. Using the story of his 1927 transatlantic flight, Charles wrote a narrative that overlaid bare fact

Summer 1943. Anne and her four children, Jon, Land, Scott, and Anne. While Charles worked as a technical consultant to the Ford Motor Company in Dearborn, Michigan, the Lindberghs rented a home in the affluent suburban enclave of Bloomfield Hills. For the first time, Anne becomes a part of a community of artists. (Lindbergh Picture Collection, Manuscripts and Archives, Yale University Library)

Charles arriving home from the South Pacific, September 1944. (UPI/Corbis-Bettmann)

Anne and her youngest daughter, Reeve, age three, summer 1948, North Haven, Maine. (Lindbergh Picture Collection, Manuscripts and Archives, Yale University Library)

Grandma Bee, Elizabeth Cutter Morrow, with her children and grandchildren on North Haven, summer 1948, at their annual reunion. (Lindbergh Picture Collection, Manuscripts and Archives, Yale University Library)

The once-spartan four-room cottage on Captiva Island off the west coast of Florida, which Anne rented in January of 1950. Strolling along the shell-laden beaches of the remote island, Anne conceived her book Gift from the Sea. *(Photographed by Susan Hertog in 1986)*

Dr. Dana Atchley, internist and pioneer in psychosomatic medicine at Columbia Presbyterian Hospital in New York City, on the beach at Treasure Island in the Bahamas, winter 1950. The Atchleys and the Lindberghs, neighbors in Englewood, traveled here together. Later, Anne and Dana would fall in love. (Lindbergh Picture Collection, Manuscripts and Archives, Yale University Library)

Anne's mother, Elizabeth Cutter Morrow, circa 1940. She had become an eminent champion of women's education, a philanthropist, and a political activist, calling for American intervention in World War II. (New York Times Pictures)

Charles is sworn in as a Brigadier General in the Air Force Reserves, regaining the commission he gave up after a dispute with President Roosevelt before World War II, April 1954. (U.S. Air Force Photo)

The Lindberghs' home in Maui, built in 1967 on five acres of land purchased from their friend Sam Pryor, whom Charles met in his early days of flying for Pan Am. While Charles loved the beauty of the land, water, and sky, Anne was often left alone, feeling isolated from her friends and family and hating the constant ocean's roar. (Lindbergh Picture Collection, Manuscripts and Archives, Yale University Library)

Anne and Charles, September 1969, in Darien, Connecticut, recently returned from a trip to Africa. (Richard W. Brown)

In 1971, Alden Whitman and Charles Lindbergh toured the Philippines. Whitman, a seasoned journalist and the editor of the obituary page of The New York Times, *was the first reporter in thirty years with whom Charles would speak. Whitman hoped to document Charles's environmental vision and projects. (Alden Whitman Papers, New York Public Library)*

Charles visiting his son Land on his cattle ranch in western Montana, April 1971. (Alden Whitman Papers, New York Public Library)

Charles in the kitchen of his boyhood home in Little Falls, Minnesota, on the shore of the Mississippi River, in 1971. His home is now a museum and a state park. (Alden Whitman Papers, New York Public Library)

*A*nne and her granddaughter Elizabeth Lindbergh Brown, Barnet, Vermont, Christmas, 1978. *(Richard Brown)*

*T*hree generations of Lindbergh women. Anne, her daughter Reeve, and her granddaughter Elizabeth at the dedication of the Lindbergh Terminal in Minneapolis, 1985. *(Photo by Robert E. Paulson, used by permission of the Anne and Charles Lindbergh Foundation)*

Anne, overcome with emotion, on the capitol grounds of St. Paul, Minnesota, in May 1985, at the dedication of a statue of Charles by sculptor Paul Granland. He is depicted as both a boy and an aviator. (AP/Wide World Photos)

Anne presenting an award to the Queen of Thailand for her efforts in environmental preservation at the Lindbergh Fund annual meeting, New York City, May 1995. (AP/Wide World Photos)

with metaphysical experience and stream-of-consciousness interpretation. It eventually took him seventeen years to write the book; in it, he defined his heroism as a response to the lives and views of his father and grandfather, and to his lonely, discordant, and vagabond childhood. He re-created his young self as a sensitive, frightened, and flawed child, whose desire to rise above personalities and ideologies drove him to seek the objective standards by which he could measure his life. While technology gave him a mechanism of control, flying gave him an almost "mystical" means of transcendence. The personal account of his public victory, *The Spirit of St. Louis,* is as technical and precise a book as it is a lyrical and poetic expression. It reveals his broad knowledge and his literary skill.[19] Although the story is dominated by masculine mythologies, thus minimizing the powerful influence of his mother—the prime sustaining force of his early years—it is an honest glimpse into the workings of his mind.[20]

Immediately, Anne understood the book. After reading the handwritten seventy pages of the first draft, she wrote, "I am humbled."[21] After all her anger and alienation, she could not resist the honest beauty of his words. Charles was "gold" and Anne was grateful—grateful for the luxury of loving her husband. This book was proof of Charles's integrity—a confirmation of the man she loved behind the maligned public image. And when Charles decided to take the job with Ford in Detroit, Anne could not bear the thought of living alone.

For the moment, pregnant and spiritually spent, Anne felt like a physical shell—a vehicle of nature, an object of someone else's desire. She felt empty and hollow, without moral or personal integrity. She feared that, left alone, she would crack. Charles's presence made her whole and "real." He was the keystone of her psychological survival. Twenty years later, Betty Friedan would call Anne's reaction a common one: "the problem without a name."[22]

In a double soliloquy, Anne and Charles grappled with the loneliness of physical separation. Their solitary contemplations suffused their letters with newfound passion and eternal commitment. Each saw in the other an idealized image.[23]

In the confines of a room at the Dearborn Inn in Detroit, Charles, too, tried to gain perspective on their marriage. In a letter to Anne he told her that his life without her would be barren and aimless—she was his window to a better world. He knew he was moving toward something beyond the mechanistic perversions of life, toward "something quite vague and indefinite, but something I know is there."[24]

But the more Anne pledged her undying love and idealized her marriage, the more the emptiness seemed to take hold. The farther she ran from the emotional truth, the more she plumbed the depths of her unhappiness. Again she felt like a prisoner in someone else's life. But if she was, she had no doubt that she was the one at fault. Charles, with his confidence, had set her free. It was not he, not marriage, that was the enemy. "But where is the real me?" she asked. "It is completely buried . . . Can one be a good mother and write? . . . It means disciplining myself—my two selves."[25] Creative freedom seemed another kind of prison; it cut her off from the mainstream of life. Her present work, she concluded, despite her dread of the months of pregnancy, was to have a child.[26]

At the end of June 1942, Anne did at last move with the children to Detroit. They rented a house in Bloomfield Hills, a suburb, Anne wrote, known for its beauty, its artistic interests, and the quality of its schools. Charles, rejoicing in Anne's arrival, was intent on encouraging her to write. Anne, though tired and worn and feeling out of "season" in her last months of pregnancy, cultivated a moment of optimism. She was hopeful, she told Charles, that he had found an enclave in Detroit—a place where they could begin again.[27]

But she felt displaced. Bloomfield Hills—in fact, the whole Midwest—she wrote, had the air of complacency attendant on the nouveauriches. From the garish rented house, to the manicured lawns and hedged gardens, to the insipid conversation at backyard barbecues, life was surrounded by unreality. Didn't anyone understand the war? Had no one heard of the mass executions? Did they know the Germans were advancing in Russia? How could anyone ever again trust the Germans?[28]

In fact, the Germans had accelerated the executions. Following the 1942 Wannsee Conference, where the systematic extermination of the Jews was set out in detail, camps were established in the occupied territories of the east. Bergen-Belzec, Sobibor, Treblinka, and Majdanek, all opened in that year, had a combined killing capacity of 60,000 a day. Between 1942 and 1944, the extermination capacity of Auschwitz would increase sevenfold.[29]

While Anne recoiled in terror at the news of Hitler's "final solution," Charles remained silent and unperturbed. But, then, the systematic destruction of the Jews could hardly have been a revelation. Between July 1936 and January 1938, in the course of Charles's six trips to Germany, he had witnessed firsthand the trajectory of Hitler's "eliminationist" goals. While Lindbergh could not have known the details of the plan to exterminate the Jews, their legal, economic, and social exclusion and the violence leading up to Kristallnacht made it clear that the Nazis were working hard to resolve the "Jewish problem."[30] The possibility of deporting the Jews to slave camps as retribution for their crimes against the state was discussed within the Reich and surmised in the press long before Lindbergh's decision not to return to Germany. Furthermore, his friendship with Henry Ford would have provided a direct link with the Nazi Reich. While Lindbergh would later state that he was not in contact with anyone in Germany after January of 1939, his friend and employer was a well-placed source of any information he might require.

In a bizarre refraction of feeling, Charles's compassion for the dying found expression in his treatment of his nine-year-old dog. Thor—tireless friend—was elevated to sainthood. Charles carried him around and planned his death, analyzing its logic and the meaning of its coming. He would poison him if it was necessary, he wrote. One should not interfere with death, but a dog should not suffer so much pain.[31] For Anne, the death of Thor had a different meaning. It was the end of an era—her childbearing years.[32] She sensed that the baby about to be born would be her last. As with Thor, there was nothing to separate her from death but the slow painful passage of time.

On August 12, with Charles away in New York, Anne was taken to the Henry Ford Hospital in active labor. Since the murder of Charlie, birth had become a communion with death, a journey into her unconscious. Yet for all the pain, it was a flight into the awareness from which her writing would grow.[33]

She counseled herself to "go *with* the pain"—to relax and release her body to its rhythm. Conjuring up a metaphor that would be crucial in her later work, Anne saw the contractions of birth as parallel to the movements of the sea. The ebb and flow of the tide would become the centerpiece of her book *Gift from the Sea.*

But then, once again, she was plunged into a bottomless pit and separated from Charles. Ironically, it was at this moment of darkness, in the throes of pain, that Anne understood that only when she could stand alone would she and Charles truly be married.

The voices that had haunted her at the birth of Jon again asked questions she could not answer. Strident and mocking, they asked: What is the secret of the universe? Did she deserve to live while others died? How could she bear a child with joy when so many children were tortured by the war? Her every answer was met with contempt. All was deception, the voices replied. As she railed against the nothingness, Anne gave birth to her fifth child.

The child was a boy—"strong, sound and 7½ pounds," noted Charles. They called him Scott, a name that had belonged to his maternal ancestors, the French-Canadian Lands.

Later, at home, Charles would record that Anne's experience was more than birth; it was a journey beyond "the science of psychology."[34] But for Anne, it proved a passage to nowhere. Once again buried beneath the weight of domestic chores, answering to the needs of her four children, anything beyond the moment seemed the stuff of dreams. To escape, she walked the fields of the Cranbrook School, which adjoined their home. By chance, she met, and found sanctuary in the home of the Swedish sculptor Carl Milles. And, despite her contempt for those who ignored the travails of war and history, Anne enjoyed the beauty and elegance of Milles's art and his commitment to the culture of prewar

France. In his home, at his studio, and with his friends, she found the friendship and encouragement she had been seeking.[35]

Struggling against the howl of the winter wind and the materialism of wartime Detroit, she found, through the study of sculpturing, the longed-for escape from domestic routine and from her obsession with the atrocities of war. Here, in an artistic community, she began a new book.[36] It would be a statement, she decided, of all she knew, a final testament, and an answer to Saint-Exupéry's article "To All Frenchmen Everywhere."[37]

With the publication of Saint-Exupéry's plea for French resistance, Anne saw again the cold-blooded practicality of Charles's views. In simple and elegant prose, Saint-Exupéry wrote a paean to war. Fighting a war, he wrote, was like building a cathedral. No amount of pain could justify one's reluctance. One fought one's enemies without doubt or judgment for the sake of one's god and one's country. Anne agreed.[38]

She and Charles argued about the atrocities of war, about human suffering, about the role of fate. Defending his understanding of the laws of nature, the inevitable rise and fall of civilizations, Charles affirmed the necessity of suffering and loss. Strong nations would always subdue the weak. It was better to have war, he said, than to nurture the seeds of civilized decay.

Desperate, Anne blurted out, "I want to be forgiven."

"For what? And by whom?" asked Charles.[39]

On Christmas Day 1942, Anne did not go to church. She prayed at home, reading the Bible to her children as they sat by the fire.[40]

29

Through a Glass Darkly

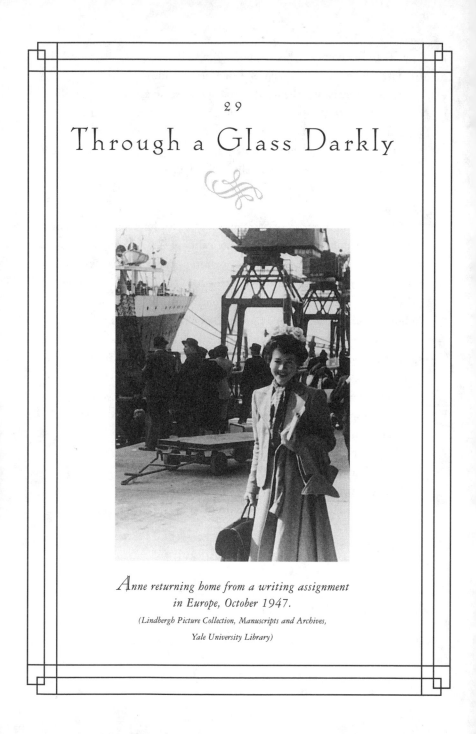

*Anne returning home from a writing assignment
in Europe, October 1947.*

(Lindbergh Picture Collection, Manuscripts and Archives,

Yale University Library)

A Dialogue of Self and Soul [1]

My soul. I summon to the winding ancient stair;
Set all your mind upon the steep ascent,
Upon the broken, crumbling embattlement,
Upon the breathless starlit air,
Upon the star that marks the hidden pole;
Fix every wandering thought upon
That quarter where all thought is done:
Who can distinguish darkness from the soul?

—W. B. YEATS

SPRING 1943, DETROIT, MICHIGAN

As the cold Michigan winter of 1943 thawed into spring, Anne awakened with new insight. Her exile in Europe, and now in Detroit, had convinced her that she must acknowledge the evil inside herself or renounce the possibility of an honest life.[2]

As if running out of time, she worked hurriedly on *Steep Ascent*. It was a fictional account of an incident that had occurred in February 1937, as she and Charles flew across the Italian Apennines and the Adriatic Sea toward India. Caught in a layer of shifting white clouds, they dared to climb into the sunlit world above. But, flying too high, they got lost in the mountains and were unable to find their way back on course. Without a sense of time or place, enveloped in clouds, they descended blindly through the fog, not knowing whether they would crash or survive. As they dived into the darkness, Anne prepared for the underworld, grateful for their children and the life they had. Then, as if from a dream, they awoke to the sea below and the steep green volcanic hills dotting the town.

Like *Listen! The Wind,* the book is a descent into hell. A journey that begins in the Garden of Eden ends in a birthlike whirl through the chaos of the "pit." Anne conceived it as the story of a "woman's ordeal," filtered through the metaphor of flight.

Eve, the protagonist, is an American married to an English flier, Gerald, the antithesis of the reader's conception of Charles. Indulgent, inefficient, stubborn, and injudicious, Gerald becomes Anne's laboratory specimen for her study of Charles. Clear and bold as never before, Anne the narrator watches his every move, analyzing the premises and dynamics of their marriage, testing her husband's strength against her ideal, and pitting her vision against his imperfect reality. No longer the child-bride of a God-like hero, the narrator is helpmate to a flawed and humbled man. This Eve has tasted the apple and can no longer deny the truth.

The view from the back cockpit is like none the reader has seen before. Eve, pregnant, impatient, and longing for home, sits in silence as Gerald gets lost in the fog. "Perhaps I can see something he can't," she thinks, "even in the back cockpit." But as they drop toward certain death on earth, all is suddenly and painfully clear. She has put her life in the hands of a man who is no wiser than she. And as death looms, Eve has a sudden conversion. She sees the truth in a blaze of light: virtue is more important than freedom. She must dedicate herself to her husband and children. Freedom is worthless without marriage and a family.

For a fleeting moment, Anne had set herself free. But the book, named for a nineteenth-century Presbyterian hymn,[3] remains a prototype of Victorian female virtue, even though it is Anne's first public expression of an ethical vision different from Charles's. Even as she repeats the Calvinist views of her ancestors, Anne's diary reveals her ambivalence.

The more clearly she saw Charles, the more frightened she became. She wrote in her diary:

> To write, I have decided, is to be possessed by the Demon lover the ballads talk of. . . . You are another person. . . . You don't love your children or your husband at all.[4]

Between the din of domesticity and the solitude of the written page, Anne observed and recorded the nuances of her feelings and relations. In the tradition of the woman novelist, not unlike Jane Austen, she used the written word to compensate for what she could neither do nor say.

She cleaned drawers, bathed the baby, wrote letters, nurtured Jon— and wrote and recopied every chapter. She struggled to find a core of strength, hoping to become one with God.[5]

But in spite of Anne's efforts to compartmentalize her feelings, Charles could measure the distance between them. When she told him of a dream of a perfect love, young and beautiful, he grew irritated by her self-absorption and turned away, frightened that he could no longer satisfy her. The thought of their being separate was unbearable, he told her.[6]

Her manuscript confirmed his view. It was not, he told her after reading it, a book she ought to publish now. It would not be well received by those who opposed their political views. Perhaps his reasons were more than political. Although Charles had begun to acknowledge his frailties, he could not bear public exposure. Seeing Eve's husband as a self-indulgent, pipe-smoking Englishman was seeing Charles as a fool—flawed, stubborn, and insensitive—no matter how "gallant" or courageous Anne had made Gerald.

She was disappointed, but she was also angry. She had thought that writing the book would have been enough. Now, she was not content to put it away.[7] In defiance of Charles, Anne sent the manuscript to Harcourt Brace. Alfred Harcourt did accept the book for publication but printed only 25,000 copies, half the number of *Listen! The Wind.*

Through the winter of 1943, Anne sought to reconcile the reality of her marriage, domestic life, and the Christian ideals she held true. Like her father, she went beyond the stern precepts of her ancestors' Calvinism; she was searching for the "changeless light," looking inside herself, trying to make peace with God.

But, as if her life were imitating her art, Anne silenced herself at the very moment she sensed her power. She surrendered the manuscript of

Steep Ascent to Charles, permitting him to edit her work. When he was finished, Anne hardly felt like celebrating. How far she had come from herself, she noted in her diary. Castigating herself for wasting time, she immersed herself further in studying sculpture.

In the summer of 1943, as the Allied forces prepared to invade Italy and to bomb German war plants, Anne sat in the studio of her friend Milles, learning to model clay. What a relief, she wrote, to escape from oneself and the war in a way one could never do in one's writing. She felt strangely anonymous, with no past and no future. But sculpture, Anne admitted, was hard work. Nonetheless, she felt productive and competent, excited by the Egyptian head that was taking form under her hands. Her work was reminiscent of Despiau, said one of her friends.

By Christmas, though, Bloomfield Hills was like a place of exile— so far from the realities of the war. The Allied movements had been swift and incisive, and as Roosevelt and Churchill set the date for freeing France from occupation, the Nazis accelerated operations in the crematoria. Millions of people had been killed, half of them civilians. To fill the ranks of Allied soldiers at the front, five hundred thousand American men had been drafted between July through September.[8]

By the start of 1944, Charles was getting restless. He had received permission from the Pentagon to test the Corsair bombers in the South Pacific, and was eager to go.[9]

On April 4, 1944, Charles left for Hawaii. Before leaving, as if to fortify himself, he went to the Smithsonian to look at his 1933 transpacific plane, the *Tingmissartoq*. He stood on the balcony above the craft and watched the men, women, and children filing past; then, as if to acknowledge his humility he walked below to touch the showcase glass. In the folds of his Brooks Brothers naval uniform, he had tucked the fifth draft of his flight narrative and a copy of the *New Testament*.[10]

Anne threw herself into physical work. She scrubbed the floors, washed the dishes, the children's socks, and the baby bibs. She felt vulnerable. Harcourt Brace had published her book, but the critics didn't seem to understand it. The Book of the Month Club did not select it, and the sales were lower than Harcourt had hoped. Only Mina Curtiss offered her comfort and perspective.[11]

Charles toured the Hawaiian, Gilbert, and Marshall Islands, recording his impressions with razor-sharp precision. With detail and thorough analysis, he described the jungle terrain and the untainted beauty of the natives and the wildlife. He recorded evidence of American atrocities against the Japanese: small mass graves, skulls, bones, and equipment, hung on barbed-wire entanglements, and the desecration of human bodies. He saw nothing in the war but the destruction of wildlife and native culture by the brutal American soldiers. There in the jungle he was never so certain that the universe moved according to evolutionary law, and that men, with all their moral pretensions, were no higher than animals.[12]

Ironically, Charles's noncommissioned status permitted him the luxury of moral distance. Committed to no one, except by choice, he stood in judgment of his officers and peers. Frustrated by the narrow limits of his mission, Charles flew, with the tacit approval of his superiors, on fifty combat and reconnaissance flights, adding up to 178 hours in the air. He locked horns with Japanese fighters and succeeded in downing at least one plane.[13] As he surveyed the vacant beaches of the islands and their jungles, he recorded his struggle to separate himself from the blood-sport and animalism of his commissioned comrades. Adopting once again Saint-Exupéry's stream of consciousness form, he wrote at the crux of "time" and "eternity." He described his temptation to kill a Japanese, unarmed and naked on a deserted beach. In war, he wrote, life and death balance on "a muscle's twitch." But at close range, with the power to kill at the press of a button, Charles saw the value of individual human life. The lives of our enemies are worth so much more than their deaths, he wrote.[14]

On June 6, 1944, D-day, the massive amphibious operation was launched by the Allies under the command of General Dwight Eisenhower. Within twenty-four hours, 176,000 troops landed on the northern coast of France between Cherbourg and Le Havre. By evening the United States V Corps established a beachhead. Six days later, all beachheads in Normandy were linked, constituting a fifty-mile-wide front. After four years, Charles de Gaulle made his triumphant return to France.[15]

Charles was virtually silent about the invasion, wondering only how many soldiers died; Anne knelt in prayer. The Allied victory was a testimony to democracy. She recognized the truth of her father's belief that there were certain ideals worth dying for.[16]

With no sign of Charles's return, Anne, for the first time, cultivated a "circle of friends." Resisting her desire to write, to think, or to wallow in her loneliness, she kept up her sculpture classes and attended exhibitions and neighborhood parties. Music, talk, art, writing—the conversations were fun, natural and free. Within an artistic circle, she believed she had found herself.[17]

In early July, Anne traveled by train to visit Margot in San Francisco. Through the windows of the Pullman car, she sought perspective in the rolling landscape, much as she had done seventeen years earlier on her way to Mexico to meet Charles for the first time. This westward journey, intended to be a vacation, became a quest for reconciliation with Charles, whom she hoped to greet in California. Free of domestic responsibility, Anne felt whole again. As she watched the fields of Iowa darken and the homesteads stand "courageous" among the flatlands like "oases in a desert," she was overcome with the richness of their lives. But even as she sensed that her marriage was crumbling, Anne sought to understand the value of their past. Anne quoted a poignant passage from John Jay Chapman in a letter to Charles:

> *How are the waters of the world sweet—if we should die, we have drunk them. If we should sin—or separate—if we should fail or secede—we have tasted of happiness—we must be written in the book of the blessed. We have had what life could give, we have eaten of the tree of knowledge, we have known—we have been the mystery of the universe.*[18]

Once in California, she grew tired of waiting. After a month-long visit with Margot, Anne returned to Detroit. Charles's homecoming had been delayed by an assignment to work with Douglas MacArthur in the Philippines, teaching pilots the efficient use of fuel. Acting on their decision to move back east, Anne spent August searching for a home in Westport, Connecticut.

On the morning of August 24, 1944, as Hitler committed Germany to "total war," the "liberated" tanks of a French armored division rolled into Paris. By 3:15 the following afternoon, the German commander had surrendered to a French brigadier general, and jubilant Parisians moved from house to house, clearing them of Germans.[19] Within a week, the new government turned the Palais des Sports into a detention camp for four thousand civilians accused of collaborating with the Germans. Among them was Alexis Carrel.[20]

After dismissing Carrel as director of the Vichy-supported Foundaton for the Study of Human Relations, also known as the Carrel Institute, the health minister publicly announced that "important new evidence" proved conclusively that Carrel had collaborated with the Germans. Though Carrel publicly denied the charges and asserted his loyalty to France, the American press did not hesitate to link this suspected collaborator to Charles Lindbergh.

While his former colleagues at the Rockefeller Institute acknowledged the possibility of Carrel's collaboration, they did not deny his genius.[21] His enemies, however, both here and abroad, insisted that he was a Nazi sympathizer who had finally got what he deserved. But Carrel was never tried in a court of law. Three months after his incarceration, the seventy-one-year-old doctor was dead.[22] His friends would say he died of a "broken heart"[23]—lonely, alienated, and far from the scientific brilliance of his youth. Charles and Anne, however, remained silent, commenting neither on his arrest nor his death. For the rest of their lives, though, they worked with his friends and biographers to dispute the charge of collaboration and clear his name.

By mid-September, Anne and the four children awaited the arrival of Charles in their new rented home in Westport. On September 19, dismissed from his duties in the Pacific, Charles flew to Texas and then to Pittsburgh, where he boarded the night train to New York.[24]

Photographers and reporters flocked to meet him at the station. Masked in a hat and glassless spectacles, Charles sprinted out the back of the train but was spotted and immediately surrounded by shouting, bulb-popping reporters.

"I'm sorry," he told them, "I have nothing to say."

Crouching and jumping, the photographers were like "monkeys," he wrote in his diary—not much different from the animals in the jungle. Nothing, during his six-month absence, had changed. America, he said, was still a lawless country.[25]

He was, though, overjoyed to see Anne and the children. The hills and woodlands of their new home held the promise of renewal. The house, located on Long Lots Road, was surrounded by lush foliage and trees. There was a big open field, intersected by a crystalline mountain brook. It was a much better place, Charles wrote, than he had dared to hope.[26]

For Anne, Charles's homecoming was a disappointment. After months of separation, during which she had cultivated both friendship and solitude, she discovered that his physical presence had lost its power. The insulation of Bloomfield Hills and now the humdrum suburban pace of Westport made her feel hungry, cheated of life.[27] And the suspected death of Saint-Exupéry, lost on a mission in North Africa, stirred again her dissatisfaction with Charles.

It was not that she was surprised by Saint-Exupéry's disappearance; she had expected it for a long time. He had, in a sense, achieved what he had set out to do: to sacrifice his life to a higher cause, to make his word flesh. Nonetheless, she felt a profound loss. Saint-Exupéry, she wrote, was the one person in the world who might have understood *Steep Ascent*. She had written it as a letter to a friend to explain who she was and where she was going. And now that he was gone, she was certain she was alone.[28] His work had become a touchstone for her—a facilitating principle, a validating voice. He had cracked the walls around her, and had spoken her language better than anyone she had known. And though she had seen him only once, she hoarded his memory to sustain her courage. Their war views, she mused, seemed to get in their way. She wondered whether he had forgiven her for *Wave of the Future.*

"Now," she wrote, "all the planes in the sky are going nowhere."

With the death of Saint-Exupéry, her last bastion of self-delusion was gone. She would measure herself by no one's standards but her own. As the Allies prepared to invade Germany, Anne wrote in her diary that she and Charles were "together" but "a little lost."[29]

In the spring of 1945, the capitulation of Germany, the liberation of the concentrations camps, the death of Roosevelt, the suicide of Hitler, and the assassination of Mussolini all changed the face of Europe. On May 8, the European war was officially over. Eager to witness the scene firsthand, Charles secured a commission from the War Department to study German developments in jet and rocket aircraft and to analyze their implications for postwar Europe.

His head pressed against the windows of his naval air transport as it prepared to land in France, Charles saw the bomb-dug craters, the roofless houses, and the ruins of monuments once testaments to tradition. "It reminded me of a Dali painting . . ." he wrote. "Creation without God."[30] And while he assumed the air of an objective observer, his written record seemed a justification of his wartime views. Men were predators, he wrote, no matter what their nationality. The only difference between the Allies and the Germans was the absurdity of the Allies' moral pretensions.[31] They treated the "Japs" and the Germans much as the Germans had treated the Jews. The Americans were merciless and cruel, delighting in the suffering of the homeless, starving citizens of conquered Germany. He condemned the "heinous delight" with which Americans "liberated" occupied territories, confiscating the best houses, and stripping others bare of food, with little concern for the plight of the townspeople. The Russians, Poles, and Frenchmen were even worse than the Americans. Who is clean? Who can condemn the Germans for their sins?

Ultimately, his message lay in his silence. Charles simply did not understand the moral distinction between the Allied soldiers who had fought for democracy, and the German troops on a bloody rampage for dominance and power. Six million Jews had been murdered by Hitler in the name of racial superiority, and Charles Lindbergh could not discern the difference between government-sanctioned genocide and the atrocities of war by some debased individuals. Hitler's systematic extermination of the Jews launched a worldwide conflagration that challenged the fundamentals of morality and law that, for thousands of years, had governed Western civilization.[32]

Nor was Charles content to survey the damage; he wanted to feel the pain of the vanquished. Hoping to see the war through Hitler's eyes, Charles traveled from Stuttgart to Berchtesgaden, Hitler's mountain retreat. Charles made his way through the rubble to a large gaping hole that was once Hitler's window. Standing at its frame, he composed an ode to the beauty of the countryside: "The high Alpine range—sharp gray crags, white fields of snow, saw-toothed peaks against the blue sky . . ."

> *It was in this setting, I realize, that the man Hitler, now the myth Hitler, contemplated and laid his plans—the man who in a few years brought the human world into the greatest convulsion it has ever known and from which it will be recuperating for generations. A few weeks ago he was here where I am standing, looking through that window, realizing the collapse of his dreams, still struggling desperately against overwhelming odds.[33]*

Charles contemplated the strength of prewar Germany and the potential "goodness" of Hitler's power. He was a man whose "dreams" had simply gone awry, resulting in evil and devastation. The best of Germany's youth, Charles explained, was dead. The population was not only homeless and hungry; it was vulnerable to what Hitler feared most: the Bolshevik armies of Soviet Russia. There was pathos in his words for the German people, but there was no hint of apology. To Charles, Hitler's demise was the very stuff of tragedy.

Only a trip to a concentration camp, and a tour through the rubble led by a "skeleton" boy, moved him to condemn the brutality of the

Germans. This kind of human destruction, he wrote in his diary, was not worth the fulfillment of political ends. But his questions remained. Was German brutality really very different from the American atrocities in the Philippines? "Only in the sky is there hope," he wrote, "only in that which man has never touched and which God forbid he ever will."

When Charles returned home to Connecticut in mid-September, he and Anne walked for hours among the trees, stopping at dusk in an open field. Again, they had been apart for six months, and yet, Anne wrote, the lines of their thoughts moved in parallel course. Was it the sight of the "skeleton" boy, the bombing of Hiroshima and Nagasaki, or was it Anne's newfound clarity? This, their public record doesn't reveal. But by year's end, Charles had made a spiritual turning, confirming his belief in a Christian God.

Charles had told Congress and the press of the need for Christian ideals in a technological society that had the power of mass destruction. In a statement that echoed his warning to the Germans on that July afternoon in Berlin a decade earlier, he pleaded for the restraint of a world organization to monitor military power with Christian ideals.

> *The philosoph{ies} of Christ may have been too intangible for the Nazi Government to understand . . . but in a deeper sense they affect every industry and every action. They cannot be left alone to Church and clergy. They must live in the philosophy of a nation, in the policies of a world organization, in the use of science and its great inventions.*[34]

For the moment, at least, the devastation wreaked by the Nazis humbled him. If Charles saw the error of his judgment, he glimpsed it, in part, through the eyes of Anne. And if one listened carefully to his words, one could hear Anne's voice pushing through his darkness.

30

Pure Gold

*Beach across the road from Anne's cottage
on Captiva Island, where she wrote* Gift from the Sea.

(*Photographed by the author*)

THE UNICORN IN CAPTIVITY[1]

Here sits the Unicorn
In captivity;
His bright invulnerability
Captive at last;
The chase long past,
Winded and spent,
By the king's spears rent
Collared and tied
To a pomegranate tree—
Here sits the Unicorn
In captivity,
Yet, free.

—ANNE MORROW LINDBERGH

SEPTEMBER 1945, WESTPORT, CONNECTICUT

Charles's homecoming was an intrusion. For the first time in fifteen years, Anne had planned her days to suit her own needs, balancing her work with the demands of the children. She had tasted not only the sweetness of solitude but the camaraderie of artists who were also friends. And just as she was feeling separate and whole, finding a language and a culture of her own, Charles was back and omnipresent.

As a special consultant to the air force, teaching pilots long-range fuel efficiency, Charles had a scattered and unpredictable schedule. Anne never knew when to expect him, but when he arrived, he took over the house, disciplining the children and demanding her attention. The placid quality of suburban Connecticut life, first in Westport and, a year later, in Darien, had deepened Anne's isolation and resentment.

She was thirty-nine years old; this was their tenth move in fifteen years; and she still didn't feel she was "home." The needs of four children under the age of thirteen and the household chores were consuming and incessant. Drives to music and dance lessons, PTA meetings and visits to the school, Saturday sports, doctors appointments, meals, laundry, buttons to be sewn and seams to be repaired—the everyday mechanics sapped Anne's strength and creativity. She may have glimpsed "the changeless light," but the gift of "grace" still alluded her.

Feeling captive to her husband's and children's lives, Anne buried herself in another pregnancy. Their sixth child, a daughter, Reeve, was born on October 2, 1945, on the fifth birthday of Anne Jr. The baby, named for her grandmother's great-uncle, urgently needed a blood transfusion from Charles; it was a gift for which Reeve would always be grateful.[2] But the fragility of the baby was evidence of Anne's physical exhaustion.

The following fall, at the age of forty, Anne conceived her seventh child, but this pregnancy was more difficult than the others. As usual, Anne felt weak and nauseated, but this time she had constant abdominal pain. At the suggestion of friends, she consulted a physician, Dana Atchley, a neighbor in Englewood who practiced in New York City at Columbia Presbyterian Hospital. He diagnosed the presence of gallstones, and recommended surgery to remove the obstruction. It was a routine operation, he explained, but it could jeopardize her pregnancy, and he suggested the possibility of an abortion.[3] The deliberate termination of a pregnancy, however, must have weighed heavily on Anne. The burden was relieved when, shortly before Christmas, she miscarried.

In February, following surgery for the removal of the gallstones, Anne spent many hours in Dr. Atchley's office, talking about her conflicts as an artist and a woman. Atchley was warm and engaging, with a smile that filled his face and his eyes. Fourteen years older than Anne, he had a paternal air, heightened by his thinning gray hair and rimless spectacles. He summoned up, perhaps, memories of her father.

In August 1947, after months of frustration with her work and bouts of depression, Anne was offered an assignment from *Reader's Digest* to write about the survival of "Christianity, Western Civilization, and Democracy" in postwar France, Germany, and England. Reluctant to leave home and the children, but encouraged by Charles, Anne gratefully accepted the time to write and travel, and to test the limits of her independence. When she arrived home two months later, Anne wrote daily in a trailer parked in the woodlands bordering Long Island Sound.

"Western values," she concluded, "were crumbling in the rubble" of a weary Europe devastated by war. Honing her material into five articles, some of which would later be published in *Life* and *Harper's* magazines, as well as *Reader's Digest,* Anne was pleased with her accomplishments. Hoping her work was the beginning of a new period of productivity, she wrote a poem called "Second Sowing," published in *The Atlantic Monthly.* Reminiscent of Psalm 24, which she believed hailed the second coming of Christ, it pulsed with the loss of her unborn child and her inability to nourish and sustain its life. She prays for the courage to break down "the bolded door" and harvest the "golden" crop "now hoarded in the barn, a sterile store."

But Anne's optimism was short-lived. Her miscarriage, linked inextricably with Charlie's death, triggered her anger and her self-contempt. She felt physically and mentally ill, fearing she would go "mad" and wanting to "die."[4] After so many years of guilt for not preventing Charlie's murder, for not taking a stand against the war, Anne's need for separation from Charles was finally breaking down her defenses. But the more she pulled away, the more frightened and helpless she became, the angrier Charles grew. When Anne sought the help of Dr. John Rosen,[5] the psychiatrist who had treated her brother Dwight, Charles punished her by moving out of the bedroom. For two months he refused to talk.

In Dr. Rosen, Anne found a sympathetic mind. He had saved her brother from being subjected to a frontal lobotomy and refused to diagnose him as hopelessly ill. At a time when schizophrenia was treated with bromides and "shock," Rosen applied the theories of Freud to the symptoms of psychosis. "Insanity" he considered the far end of a neurotic continuum, not a disease. Ascribing it to a developmental lag caused by "malevolent" mothering, he sought to counter that cause with "good" mothering—to become, in short, a foster parent. Driven, he would say, with a "Messianic" fervor, he would remove the patient from her "toxic" home and take control of her life. The most severely disturbed would move in to his quarters; others were given his part-time care.

Playing "father" to his child-patients, Rosen was as likely to swathe and bottle-feed them as he was to shame, curse, or tackle them to the floor; intimidation, he believed, was the key to cure. His theories, like Freud's, smacked of misogyny, but though his aim was to liberate a patient from the distortions of the mother's psyche, he had no taste for defying convention. Little boys were boys, and little girls were girls, and the nuclear family was a sacred institution. Because he also believed that the neurotic person could use his dreams as tools for understanding, he told Anne that she was not "sick" but was trapped in a developmental lag caused by her up-bringing. She should leave behind the "toxins" of family and home and, instead, pay heed to the "demons" that haunted her dreams. His desire to foster Anne's independence directly opposed Charles's desire to punish her. Once the salve to all her wounds, Charles now seemed poison.

Undaunted by Anne's illness, Charles continued to seek his place on the public stage. As much as he hated the "political game," he insisted on pressing his message. Ironically, his prewar pro-German position underwent a new interventionist twist. In April 1947, Charles declared the defeat of Germany a Pyrrhic victory.

We won the war, but lost the quality of Western Civilization. The world is weakened by famine, hatred, and despair. We have destroyed Nazi Germany . . . only to strengthen Communist Russia. The war might have been prevented, but now in its aftermath we owe Europe financial and military assistance. There is no cost too high to prevent the domination of an "aggressive power."[6]

Russia was strengthened, but Charles was wrong. The "quality of Western Civilization" was about to flourish. One year later, the American Marshall Plan and the British cosponsored Berlin airlift would save the German people from starvation and economic chaos.

In his 1947 book, *Of Flight and Life,* Charles wrote that the war had been a conflict between brothers damned by the same demon. Science and Technology, not the Germans, were to blame. A world disconnected from Nature and from God had bowed to a golden calf, wreaking death and destruction, and solving nothing with its pain. Surely the Bolsheviks would inherit the earth, now that the German spirit was crushed. Hope lay in the heart of Man if he turned himself inward toward the light of Christ. Charles was beginning to wonder whether that was possible.[7]

In 1948, Anne and Charles revisited Captiva Island with their children, staying in a house rented by Jim Newton. Anne recalled, from her first visit a decade earlier, the island's primeval beauty, which seemed to belong to another world.

In January 1950, when Anne was sturdy enough to resume her writing, she returned to Captiva alone. The house she rented, then, on the bend of the road that linked Sanibel Island to Captiva, belonged to 'Tween Waters Restaurant and Inn. It was a simple, four-room cottage across from a stretch of expansive beach.

The beach is gone now, hammered level by storms, its white-powdered width slashed by huge iron pipes that pump sand to stem the erosion of a battered shore. But in 1950, Anne could walk barefoot across the unpaved road and out to the wooden pier to watch the gulls "dip and dive" into the waves below.

In the mornings she would write in a bare, curtainless room, drenched in the light and the wind of the sea, and later, after lunch and household chores, she walked along the deserted beach, absorbing its "rhythms" and hoarding its "treasures."

"I collected shells," said Anne. "There was nothing else to do on an island like that, and everyone else seemed to be doing it. I recognized how wonderful the freedom was of not having to do things every day and being able to go into a room and just write what one felt . . . One sees through the writing. You sink into a more authentic place inside yourself." Living without writing is like "trying to paint a picture without any shadows and I think without any perspective . . . I wrote about the experience of a woman having a solitary experience—some time of her own."[8]

After returning to Darien in early spring, Anne met a woman who would become both a confidante and a midwife to her work. Ernestine Stodelle, a protégée of Doris Humphrey, ran an academy of dance in the basement of a local church. She was a vital, self-educated woman, the mother of three and the wife of the Russian theater director Theodor Komisayevsky. Married to a man she deemed a "genius," and dedicated to her home and children, Ernestine believed that the conflicts in her life were much like Anne's. But she felt like "pottery" to Anne's delicate "porcelain." Tall and lean, muscular yet graceful, with a sculptured face and riveting eyes, Ernestine was confident and unencumbered by guilt. She saw her commitment to theater and dance not as self-indulgence, but as a necessity to her living a whole and balanced life. "I knew how to live," said Ernestine:

> I was dealing with one reality on top of another. I was working all the time with the reality of one force pulling against another. I didn't have self-pity. I didn't feel like a suffering genius. I was caught up in life . . . But Anne was suffering—feeling thwarted. I tried to help her.[9]

She taught Anne to use dance as therapy, and she shared Anne's desire to read and to study. While Ernestine admired Anne's physical strength and mental precision, she believed her "rhythms were out of sync," and she taught her to balance "on a moment in time," at the nexus of breath, body, and spirit. It was a lesson Anne would carry back to her work, using the fluidity of dance to harmonize the dissonance of her feelings and thoughts.

Together, they read Greek, Christian, and Indian philosophy and mythology. They studied Freud and Jung and went to the theater and dance concerts. Comforting each other with their poetry and letters, they read the works of poets and novelists, hoping to find inspiration. As they studied the diaries of Katherine Mansfield, they taught one another the art of surrendering to universal truth and confronting the necessity of human suffering.

Like so many of the women from whom Anne had sought comfort—Mina Curtiss, Margot Loines Morrow—Ernestine was both strong and visionary, compassionate and provocative. Ernestine later said she gave Anne courage, "divining things in her that came to pass."

In the summer and fall of 1950, Anne worked on her manuscript in Darien and returned to Captiva in January. Margot and Anne's sister Con would come and go, grateful for their time together, away from their responsibilities of motherhood and home. Con and Aubrey Morgan now had three children and lived in Oregon. Margot, also the mother of three, was divorced from Anne's brother, Dwight, and was finding her way as a single parent. Together, the three women walked the shell-laden beaches, talking of religion, philosophy, and literature, and of their need to find balance in their domestic lives.

Anne completed the book in 1953. After setting it aside for several months, she took the manuscript, which she called "The Shells," to Kurt Wolff, publisher and editor at Pantheon Press. She had met him by chance at a meeting of the International Goethe Society in Aspen at Christmas 1948. Drawn to his incisive and cultured mind, Anne found him warm and responsive. He understood her needs as a writer as well as the demands of the literary marketplace. They had sustained their friendship through letters and visits, and now she sought his professional advice. Immediately, Kurt recognized the literary and commercial value of Anne's book. He published it in March 1955, under the title *Gift from the Sea*.[10]

The book, a prose poem, rose out of her diaries, her talks with her sisters, her family, and friends. It is the product of a quest for faith and harmony—for "grace," not in the theological sense, but a state of peace and blessedness. "I was not looking for God," she later said. "I was looking for myself."[11]

To accomplish her task, Anne makes a bargain with her reader. Come with me, she says, to a place where distinctions slip away; where there is no time, no culture, and no preconceived notion of sexual identity. Only then can we see who we are. The beach and its primeval rhythms will strip us of pretense, and the "twisted strands" of our lives will gain clarity, meaning, and perspective. But for all its literary and philosophic glaze, *Gift from the Sea* is a personal statement of "hunger and thirst," tempered by an implicit faith in Nature.

Faith was new to the feminist scene. The redefinition of American female roles had its roots in defiance. Anne's mother and other turn-of-the-century middle-class, urban, educated women had fought for suffrage. Women of the twenties and thirties had thrust open the doors of educational institutions, making their way into professions once bastions of male dominance. Law, medicine, even governmental service, became accessible to those willing to pay the price of loneliness, frustration, and prejudice. But in 1955 women had traded college for marriage. The average age of a woman at the time she married was twenty, and it was quickly dipping into the teens. The proportion of women attending college in comparison to men dropped from 47 percent in 1920 to 35 percent in 1958, and 60 percent dropped out of college to marry. By the end of the 1950s the birth rate in the United States was overtaking that of India.[12]

"Home" had become the focal point of the postwar social order. It symbolized a sinecure amidst the uncertainty of a cold war. It was a microcosm of an ideal world—peaceful, safe, and technologically advanced—in a sea of potential nuclear devastation. Later, Betty Friedan wrote,

> *The suburban housewife—she was the dream image of the young American women, and the envy, it was said, of women all over the world . . . She was healthy, beautiful, educated, concerned only about her husband, her children, her home. She had found true feminine fulfillment . . . She had everything that women ever dreamed of . . . but she wanted more.[13]*

By 1955, nearly six million women had entered the marketplace. Unlike twenty years earlier, 30 percent were married, and 40 percent came from the middle class. Furthermore, and perhaps most significant, 39 percent of women with school age children were employed. As a result of these changing patterns, a great debate broke out in American media: Could a woman be a wife and mother and still pursue a professional career? It was called "the woman problem," and scores of social theorists rose to explain it. Feminists believed women were unhappy because they were compelled to stay at home. Antifeminists blamed the discontent of housewives on their violation of tradition, dogma, and social role.[14] Amidst this conflagration of ideas, Anne retreated to Captiva to find her own solutions.

The universe Anne enters is Darwinian and amoral, governed by laws beyond human control. But for all its bare-boned obsession with death—the skeletal shells of wandering homeless creatures—she finds an affirming, life-sustaining force in the rhythmical turnings of nature and the sea.

It is a journey infused with classical literature and Christian doctrine, yet rooted in the teachings of Hindu and Buddhist philosophy. A circular metaphor, womblike and nourishing, is the unifying principle of *Gift from the Sea*. At its center is a maternal force, nameless and sacred, that enlightens and transforms all who enter. It is an oasis—both full and void— that connects the individual to her unconscious, and the unconscious to the collective whole. Camouflaging her Hindu and Buddhist sources beneath the words of Christian saints and modern poets and writers, Anne chooses to articulate only those concepts which mesh with the writings of Saint Augustine, Saint Catherine of Siena, and the works of William James, Charles Morgan, Rilke, John Donne, and Saint-Exupéry.

The book comprises eight essays, six of them represented by shells, which reflect not only Anne's process of revelation, but the biological and social life cycle of women.

Anne begins with the deserted shell of a snail-like creature called the Channeled Whelk. She, like the Whelk, has left her shell—her home in Darien—regressed in time and space to this soft, moist place. The simplicity of its form, the perfect spiral toward its apex, teaches Anne a "singleness of eye"—harmony in the midst of flux. The pattern of women's lives, Anne writes, breeds fragmentation, alienation, and the destruction of the "soul."

> *My mind reels with it. What a circus act we women perform every day of our lives. It puts the trapeze artist to shame. Look at us. We run a tightrope daily, balancing a pile of books of the head. Baby-carriage, parasol, kitchen chair, still under control. Steady now!*[15]

But fragmentation is not only a female problem; it is a human problem that goes beyond feminist ideology. Best illustrated by the wheel, whose spikes radiate from a "central mother-core," the problem is how to preserve the stability of the hub, no matter what shocks attack its periphery.

Anne has no answers, only clues, and they lie in the contours of her deserted shell. The act of "shedding"—the renunciation of clothes and objects—implies the loss of vanity, restraint, and pride. But this is only a "technique"; the road to "grace" lies inside.

The snail shell, glossy, round, and compact, has inner secrets to unfold. It is like the moon, powerful and solitary. It teaches women to confront their solitude and use it as a source of creativity. They must live in the present, like islands in time, respecting the boundaries of other shores. "No man is an island," she says, quoting Donne, but "I feel we are all islands in a common sea."

Anne rails at the insidious corruption of technology. Machines have made women's lives easier and freer, she acknowledges, but Virginia Woolf's ideal of "a room of one's own," formulated before women had a range of opportunity, shows us the limitations of economic independence. Many women who have time, money, and space have little knowledge of how to use it. Women have traded domesticity for the distortions of the marketplace. They have independence and affluence, but no tools for living the creative life.

We have lost not only the solitary hour in the sewing room, the kitchen, and the church, but that essential: the "right" to be alone. We no longer have the "uninterrupted moment" in which to nourish our individuality and wholeness. We perceive one another as collections of functions, as fragmented social beings. William James, she says, called it *"Zerrissenheit"*—the state of "torn to pieces-hood." It is a problem of the individual, but also a social disease endemic to a technological society that bows to the notion of progress.

A woman must not emulate the masculine pattern. To deny the value of traditional female life is to diminish humanity. A woman must cherish the powers of introspection—ways of listening and loving—provided by thousands of years of evolution. Anne implores the reader to dedicate time to creative work, something both separate and nourishing. Paradoxically, solitude is not selfish. To still one's center is to create the strength and integrity required to touch the lives of others. The well-being of family, society, even "our civilization," Anne writes, depends on women's self-knowledge. Betraying her sense of wartime guilt, Anne implies her weakness is not questioning her husband's views. Standing alone is a woman's moral duty.

But once a woman has learned the techniques of self-renewal, how does she sustain the relations on the circumference of her wheel? In her fourth, fifth, and sixth essays, Anne defines the three stages of marriage. The first, a romantic fusion of identities, resembles the Double-Sunrise shell. The second, the unwieldy years of childrearing, resembles the ugly Oyster shell. And the last, the independent stage, moves like the Argonauta, untethered and free.

The Double-Sunrise, she says, is pure and beautiful—simple, perfect, symmetrical and unified. But as each partner performs its biological and cultural roles, the purity and unity is obscured by the specialization that is integral to family life. While it is only a stage in an evolving relationship, it can be reclaimed by the enforcement of simplicity; by celebrating, even if only for short periods of time, the essence of its original form—time alone. Do not be fooled, Anne cautions the reader, by fantasies of duplicating the passion and romance of an earlier stage of marriage.

The second stage of marriage, the Oyster shell, ridged with responsibility, is a sign of middle age. As one approaches the end of one's childbearing years, death is both visceral and real. But middle age, Anne asserts, is wrongly interpreted as a time of degeneration. It is an opportunity for new self-definition and for the shedding of pride, vanity, and pretense. It is a "second-flowering," when one is free from the responsibilities of youth. There is time for the intellectual, cultural, and spiritual growth that was "pushed aside in the heat of the race."

The last stage of marriage, symbolized by the Argonauta shell, rides on "the chartless seas of imagination." It is a stage marked by full "becoming," that stage toward which every other moves. A play on words, Argonauta is not only an illusion to Jason the Greek adventurer in search of the Golden Fleece, it is also the name of a shell Anne found by chance on Treasure Island in the Bahamas—a mollusk with arms like an octopus, the female of which clings to a thin featherweight shell. With the shedding of biological and cultural specialization, this stage, Anne writes, offers both partners the freedom to find new patterns and connections. It is a marriage of two selves, two solitudes, unhinged and alone, yet united in a common purpose.

Here Anne's insight reaches its apex. It is the feminine "gold" for which she has been searching through twenty-five years of marriage to Charles. A true marriage, she writes, requires individual strength and separate borders. These are the principles on which marriage rests.

> Woman must come of age by herself. This is the essence of "coming of age"—to learn how to stand alone. She must learn not to depend on another, nor to feel she must prove her strength by competing with another. In the past, she has swung between these two opposite poles of dependence and competition, of Victorianism and Feminism. Both extremes throw her off balance; neither is the center, the true center of being a whole woman.[16]

As if she and Charles did not suffice as a model, Anne illustrates this stage by recounting "a perfect day" with her sister. Its perfection lay in a common rhythm, touching without intruding on each other's space.

Clothed in philosophical musing, it reads like a admonition to her husband.

> *The only real security is not in owning or possessing, not in demanding or expecting, not in hoping, even. Security in a relationship lies neither in looking back to what it was in nostalgia nor forward to what it might be in dread or anticipation, but living in the present relationship and accepting it as it is now, within their limits . . . islands, surrounded and interrupted by the sea, continually visited and abandoned by the tides.*[17]

Anne calls it "intermittancy"; it is an internal as well as a social imperative. One must respect the flow of personal experience and also the relation between oneself and society. Solitude and marriage are not sufficient for "grace." Grace implies dedication to others. Here Anne's Presbyterian teachings are manifest. Autonomy breeds selfishness, and women are the keepers of the family and social ethic. In the small circle of their home, women must lead themselves and their families through the path of "temptation," thereby regenerating the commitment to social values. Simplicity, solitude, and intermittency—these are the "gifts" one takes home from the sea.

Gift from the Sea marks Anne's coming of age. Finally, she stands alone. The book asserts her legitimacy as an artist and redefines marriage as a union of equals. For the first time, Anne speaks straight to the reader in a commanding voice. She strips contemporary womanhood of its Victorian limitations and challenges the distortions that devalue the traditional female voice. It is alchemy, fired by desperation, which changes the "forbidden" graven image—the written word—into a means of spiritual and ethical enlightenment. She has moved from the fundamentalist teachings of the Hebrew Bible to the New Testament revelations of John, finally giving herself permission to write.

"I've been a rebel," she says with pride and with anger, as though the very act of rebellion defined her personhood.[18] When asked, she can recite the list of acts that have earned her the role. But her only authentic rebellion, she implies, was to become herself—to shed the expectations of her parents and her husband, and to find the space and time to write.

The book was an immediate and unqualified success. Quickly, it climbed to the bestseller list, remaining at the top for eighty weeks. Within its first year, it sold more than 300,000 copies.[19] It was a rare phenomenon: a conflagration of individual insight and social consciousness which challenged the conventions of marriage and child-rearing. Like many feminists, Anne Lindbergh believed that biology was not destiny. It was, however, a moral responsibility. Women, she concluded, had the right to pursue their independent lives, but they must make certain that their choices reflected their values. She understood, too well, the price she and her family had paid for her own fame and ambition. The success of *Gift From the Sea* lay in Anne's moral vision: Women wanted distance from wife and motherhood without abandoning their children or destroying their marriages. They sought independence without discarding traditional values.

Gift from the Sea was "an awakening" in the classic feminist sense, no less poignant than that of Kate Chopin's heroine, Edna Pontellier, portrayed fifty years earlier. But unlike Chopin's book, *The Awakening,* which casts its heroine as a shameless adulterer, Anne's book represents female consciousness inextricably tied to Christian values. No less than Chopin's heroine did Anne understand the price she paid for marriage. She knew that her husband and her children possessed her; she knew she had bowed to social expectation. But while Anne felt constrained by her domesticity, she did confirm the value of a sacred ideal. She resolved not to abandon her family and her virtue for the solitary life of a writer and an artist. Chopin's heroine commits suicide, surrendering to the wild amorality of the sea; Anne nourishes her creativity and faith on its ebb and flow.

Some critics compared Anne's book to *Walden,* hailing her as a female counterpart to Henry David Thoreau, but Anne's philosophy challenges his individualism. Thoreau believed that the state derived its power and authority from the individual, who was free to break its laws at will. True to the Morrow ethic, the premise of Anne's philosophy is the sacredness of the whole—the inviolability of family, community, and state. Anne validates the supremacy of law over individual will on the assumption that it represents the common good. Both Anne Lindbergh and Henry David Thoreau confirm the lessons of nature in a mechanical age and the divinity of self-revelation through meditation. But Anne's solitude, unlike Thoreau's, had a singular purpose—to enrich and consecrate her relationships. Family, community, and the state—these were the institutions that exalted one's humanity. To live for oneself alone was the stuff of "sin."

While some saw Anne's book as "psychobabble," most found it a thoughtful analysis of contemporary life and the human condition, as pertinent to men as to women. And nearly everyone, no matter the point of view, saw *Gift from the Sea* as the work of a disciplined and accomplished poet.

31

Midsummer

*Anne Morrow Lindbergh on Treasure Island,
Bahamas, 1950.*

(Lindbergh Picture Collection, Manuscripts and Archives,

Yale University Library)

MIDSUMMER[1]

. . . suddenly I seem
Bogged down, stock still, knee deep
in tangled grass . . .

—ANNE MORROW LINDBERGH

MAY 1955, ENGLEWOOD, NEW JERSEY

Anne sat in the bare, darkened rooms of Next Day Hill amid the half-packed boxes of her mother's possessions. While her spare, curtainless room in Captiva had resounded with life and regeneration, her parents' home, stripped of its objects, seemed a woeful shell of death. Gone was the shine of tabletops and chandeliers, the deep softness of sofas and chairs, and the scent of fresh-cut flowers. Lost was the grandeur, and with it the ethic that had lifted the Morrows above the banality of pretense—puritan piety and public service.

Four months earlier, Anne's mother had died. During the week of Thanksgiving 1954, Betty, eighty-two, suffered a stroke, and as the paralysis progressed, she sank into a coma. Anne, constantly at her side, was relieved that she seemed free of pain. On January 24, 1955, her death was noted in the press: the passing of Mrs. Dwight Morrow, the wife of the ambassador and mother of Mrs. Charles Lindbergh, poet and wife of the famous airman.[2] Although Betty's poetry had received little attention, Anne's literary success heightened its value and its public acclaim. And so Betty was remembered not only as an educator and a public servant, but also as a writer and poet.[3] It was the eulogy Elizabeth Cutter might have wanted.

During the twenty-four years since her husband's death, Betty became the philanthropist she had set out to be. In Englewood, she served as a board member of the hospital, the library, and several schools, as well as director of the Community Chest. Above all, she was a champion of women's education. After her service as the first female acting president of Smith, in 1940, Betty remained a tireless fund-raiser and spokesperson for the college. In her will, she bequeathed nearly a million dollars to charities, including the institutions she had served in Englewood, as well as Union Theological Seminary and the churches she attended. But no institution, public or private, received more than Smith and Amherst. In profound gratitude for the opportunities given to her and Dwight, she bequeathed each college a hundred thousand dollars. The remainder of her $9.4 million estate was divided equally among her three children. Anne, Dwight, and Con each received life interests in trusts and $50,000 in cash.[4]

Shuttling between Darien and Englewood, Anne began the tortuous process of sorting through her mother's books, furniture and clothing. It was a tedious job which must have evoked memories of the loss of Charlie, Elisabeth, and her father. And yet, the house must have also resonated with the joy of Christmas, weddings, and good times. Within its walls her mother had never been happier, more productive or strong. But surrounded by the mere objects of her mother's life, Anne felt strangely disconnected from its meaning. Just as she had searched Charlie's closet to find "her boy," Anne soaked herself in the stark realities of settling the estate and preparing the house for occupation by The Elisabeth Morrow School. The cycle of life, nonetheless, seemed confirmed. After her work in Englewood was done, she planned to fly west to visit with her children. Her first grandchild, Christina, Jon's daughter, had been born that spring and Anne delighted in its promise of regeneration. Her only regret was that she could not enjoy it with her mother.[5]

For Anne and Charles, Christmas 1955 had fallen into shadow, darkened by the death of their mothers. Evangeline had died in September 1954, at the age of seventy-eight, after suffering for many years from Parkinson's disease. And now, with their parents gone and Next Day Hill in shambles, Anne had the task of reinventing Christmas. While the Morrows and the Lindberghs were fragmented without the glue of Grandma Betty, Anne, feeling like the matriarch of the Lindbergh clan, was determined to keep her own family together.

In December 1956, Anne and Charles traveled west to Colorado, with Anne Jr., sixteen; Scott, fourteen; and Reeve, eleven. They met Jon, now twenty-four; and Land, nineteen, in a rented cabin called Lazy T Ranch, a niche on Aspen Mountain.

Jon had married Barbara Robbins in March 1954, in secrecy, much as Anne and Charles had done twenty-five years earlier.[6] It was a private, unannounced family ceremony in Northfield, Illinois, at the home of Barbara's uncle William Miller, whose daughter was to become the wife of Anne's son Land. Now, two and a half years later, Jon and Barbara had two little girls, Christina and Wendy.

Shy and solitary, Jon had pursued Barbara with uncharacteristic tenacity, throwing pebbles at her dormitory window and following her around the Stanford University campus. Tall and graceful, with a chiseled face, Barbara had a compliant air that must have seemed familiar to Jon. The daughter of a domineering businessman and pilot, and a mother whose inability to assert her needs drove her to an early suicide, Barbara had a vulnerability akin to Jon's.[7] Now a recognized oceanographer and deep-sea explorer, Jon looked like a Morrow but carried himself with the restraint of his father. Sensitive yet demanding, Jon never said more than was necessary, and had a secret, closed-mouth smile.[8] Above all, he seemed to live in the same bubble of silence he had created as a boy in England.

For two weeks, Anne and Charles skied and sleighed through the snow-covered woodlands, playing with their children and grandchildren in the mountain sun. Gone were the lavish accouterments of Christmas at Next Day Hill—the poinsettias, the Mexican bands, the white-gloved servants, and the china and crystal. But three generations alone in the woods re-enacted the rituals that confirmed the values at the crux of the Morrows' life. For Anne, Christmas would always be "a prayer and a promise," an invocation of God, and a renewal of vision. But at the turn of the year, Anne returned to Darien to find herself the object of damnation.

In September 1956, Anne had published her first collection of poetry. Until then, she had published each poem individually, usually in *The Atlantic Monthly* or in *The Saturday Review,* never attracting critical attention or considering her work worthy of critical notice. But after the accolades for her lyrical prose in *Gift from the Sea,* Kurt and his wife, Helen Wolff, encouraged Anne to publish her poetry in book form. *The Unicorn and Other Poems* represented nearly thirty years of writing, from simple statements of feeling to diatribes against an indifferent God.

Pantheon, anticipating success, printed 25,000 copies of the book for September publication and another 40,000 for December. But despite the strong sales, *The Unicorn and Other Poems* was poorly received by the critics, and Anne was immediately embarrassed. Her poems were such "waifs," she wrote to a friend.[9]

The critics agreed that Anne had overstepped her bounds. She was an essayist—a woman's writer who had dared to enter a masculine realm. *Gift from the Sea* may have displayed a powerful female voice, but it also provoked a backlash of misogyny, even from women. The rules were clear: if she dared to speak about the lives of women, she would have to bear the weight of their preconceived frailties. Anne's achievement, wrote Bette Richart in *Commonweal,* was domestic, not poetic, "like flower arranging or china painting."[10] She was a Woman Poet, a "poetess," with the cultural fatuity of the "second sex."[11]

In January 1957, just as Anne thought the storm of criticism was over, John Ciardi launched a literary crusade. Fallen Catholic turned missionary poet, English professor turned literary critic, Ciardi was the newly appointed poetry editor of *The Saturday Review of Books.* From the moment he took that seat, he "systematically set out to uproot genteel poetry," the kind written, he explained, by celebrities with more face than substance, and "blue-haired old ladies" whose poetry reflected little more than the polite conventions of a bygone era. For Ciardi, Anne Lindbergh, wife of Charles and female spokesperson for the middle-aged middle class, seemed to "fill the bill perfectly."[12]

In the January 12 edition of *The Saturday Review,* Ciardi showed his contempt for Mrs. Lindbergh's collection. It was his "duty," he wrote, to expose her "offensively bad book—inept, jingling, slovenly, illiterate even, and puffed up with the foolish afflatus of a stereotyped high-seriousness, that species of esthetic and human failure that will accept any shriek as a true high-C." Her poems were mindless clichés, he wrote, with tortured rhymes and bad grammar.[13]

Unsatisfied with literary condemnation, Ciardi also attacked the "low-grade humanity" of her work, lacing his criticism with hell-fire damnation. "Mrs. Lindbergh's poetry," he wrote, "is certainly akin to Original Sin, and in the absence of the proper angel I must believe that it is the duty of anyone who cares for the garden to slam the gate in the face of the sinful and abusive . . . What will forgive Mrs. Lindbergh this sort of miserable stuff?"[14]

Ciardi's condemnation of Anne was probably a reflection of his spiritual turmoil. After spending a childhood begging for forgiveness from a devout Catholic mother who played on his fears of divine retribution, Ciardi had turned to the study of literature and poetry. The poet, he wrote, was a divine conduit for superior culture. A paternalistic leader who "lured" his readers through sound, imagery, symbol, and rhythm, the poet directed them to a higher law.

"Luring" intellects wasn't his only intent. Both at the University of Michigan, where he received his master's degree in 1939, and at Kansas City University, where he later taught, Ciardi had earned a reputation as a womanizer, intent on proving his sexual potency to female students and colleagues' wives. Conquest and control defined his relationships with women, and female poets were special targets.[15]

But clearly Mrs. Lindbergh was more to Ciardi than a pretentious lady with a penchant for rhyme. She was the wife of Charles Lindbergh, known for his political "sins." Ciardi had a political agenda of his own.

In 1947, he had been a spokesperson for the Progressive Citizens of America, a political action committee comprising many artists, academics, and political radicals who became disaffected with the Democratic Party after Franklin Roosevelt's death. At its prow was Henry Wallace, secretary of agriculture under Roosevelt and the 1948 presidential candidate for the Progressive Party. In 1940, Wallace had condemned Lindbergh as "the outstanding appeaser of the nation."[16] And in 1948, Ciardi campaigned for him throughout the summer, six nights a week, earning a reputation as Wallace's "right-hand, golden-tongued" pitchman.[17] But when Wallace lost the election to Harry Truman, Ciardi turned his attention to literary matters.

His criticism of Anne's poetry raised one of the largest outcries in the history of *The Saturday Review.* Hundreds of letters poured in, most of them in defense of Anne.[18] For Anne, the criticism was her self-damning voice reaching a deafening roar. Against all instinct and religious teaching, Anne had dared to become a writer, defying not only Old Testament prescript, but the bounds of traditional femininity. Although publicly silent, she was devastated—not certain she would ever write again.

Although Ciardi's moral condemnation was absurd, his assessment of Anne's poetry was, in a sense, right. Her poems were "imprisoned" in conventional verse and rhyme, bound, for the most part, in couplets and quatrains, giving the appearance of careless cliché. But buried inside the restraint of form were the anger and rebellion that had made *Gift from the Sea* possible. Encoded in her poems is the pain of her self-denial and her false quest for salvation through her marriage to Charles.

Published in volume form in the aftermath of her success, the poems gave the impression of spontaneous combustion, which belied the slow burn of their thirty years. Because they were arranged according to theme rather than chronology, the progressive sophistication of her work was not apparent. And Ciardi, eager to fit his theory to fact, neglected to read huge chunks of her book, concentrating in brutal detail on its weaknesses. While the great melodies of the Western canon— Shakespeare, Donne, Johnson, Rossetti, Dickinson, and Rilke—filtered through her lines, Anne's poems read more like conversations with her mother—attempts to analyze, challenge, and transcend the Victorian womanhood for which she stood. Her poems banter with her mother's, defying their precepts, embellishing their common truths, and imbuing Christian virtue, Greek myth, and biblical parable with raw psychological energy. Anne scrambles her mother's rigid quatrains and perfect sonnets, as if breaking her verse were an act of rebellion. Like Anne's travel books, bound by form, slouching toward art, her poems are meant to depict her emotions while protecting the integrity of her relationships.

The centerpiece of the collection is "The Unicorn,"[19] in which Anne's voice becomes lucid in its determination. Virtue is not externally imposed; it is not a rigid standard of measure. Virtue is a personal choice through which one barters freedom for responsibility. The poem reflects Anne's tension between duty and desire as much as it does her struggle to find a personal verse form. It finds completion when her emotion is spent. It is a confirmation of her message to women in *Gift from the Sea:* find the knowledge that will nourish and liberate your creativity within the bounds of marriage and convention.

But in her poem "The Stone,"[20] written during her breakdown and psychoanalysis, she exposes the pain of the struggle. In perfect couplets, Anne questions the value of everything—virtue, love, God, even the power of words—in explaining her pain. She tries to release herself from suffering, but a stone clogs "the stream" through which light, faith, and happiness flow. Here the Unicorn cannot transcend, and virtue is meaningless in a faithless world. Anne is not a saint after all. Life is uncertain, and the only "solvent" for the stone is love, yet she cannot find it, even in herself. The source of her suffering is faceless and inhuman; the only resolution is to embrace its darkness. It is from this paradox that her poetry rises. Though the rhyme itself may not be new, it serves to convey her personal rebellion. The Victorian symbol turns back on itself, presenting her with the possibility of survival.

It is not whim that names the collection *The Unicorn.* Anne wants to be seen as a virginal martyr who transcends her moral frailties through creativity and virtue. Resigned to her prison, she is reconciled to her role. The only power she has is her writing, and now, Ciardi had voiced her deep fears of blasphemy against a vindictive God.

Anne was shocked and humiliated by Ciardi's criticism.[21] Charles was rarely home, and without his presence or the rhythms of domesticity, the insights of *Gift from the Sea* seemed esoteric and untrue. Anne was hurt and lonely, not fertile with solitude. Not certain that she would ever write again, Anne sought consolation from Con, Margot, and her friends, including her long-time physician, Dana Atchley, now estranged from his difficult and quarrelsome wife, Mary. In Charles's absence he was a sympathetic listener to Anne's anger and fears, eager to encourage and support her.

During Charles's absence, Atchley was a frequent visitor to Anne's home in Darien, but in the fall of 1956, Anne rented an apartment in New York, at 146 East Nineteenth Street. It was a personal retreat and a place for her to be alone with Atchley. He often stayed for a martini and dinner, and for morning breakfasts with their friends. They even appeared together at dinner parties, restaurants, and the theater. Atchley loved Anne much as Saint-Exupéry had, for her warmth, sensitivity, and intelligence. She banished his troubles and rekindled his passion. Unlike Anne's relations with the French writer, her affair with Atchley was neither platonic nor fleeting.[22]

A year after Anne had preached that women were the bastions of Christian virtue and the saviors of Western civilization, she had a sexual liaison with a married man. Although Charles never knew, Anne's betrayal haunted her. Ciardi's condemnation had an ironic twist, freeing her to be the "sinner" she knew she was.

In the dead heat of summer, 1957, in her mother's garden in Maine, she composed a poem heavy with disillusion and death. Her earlier poems had depicted her as a victim and a martyr; in this, her last published poem, she admits her complicity in her demise. As if looking Ciardi squarely in the eye, Anne adopts a new form, controlling the rhythm and the rhyme. Still in the garden of Adam and Eve, she is both the serpent and the sinner. Mistress of the house that once embraced her family, surrounded by memories of her mother and father, of Charlie and Elisabeth, Anne discards the illusions of her youth.

She had been blinded by the summer of her youth, swollen with passion and bursting with bloom. Once she had raced with the tides of time; now she was mired in the tall tangled grass, suddenly prey to satanic temptations. Echoing her poem "No Harvest Ripening," Anne writes of the deception of summer which belies the coming of the frost.

But now Anne's pain is profound and visceral. While the poem resonates Christina Rossetti's "Springtime" and Emily Dickinson's "Hour of Lead," Anne challenges their faith in Nature. Winter is certain but spring, she says, may never come. The smiles of summer smolder with storms, and her perfectly formed couplets burn with anger and rebellion. Anne feels cheated and bitter at a life that should have yielded more than mediocrity and sin. She writes:

> *This is the summer of the body but*
> *The spirit's winter.*[23]

In one sweep of unstopped verse, Anne cries out for the fulfillment she believes she deserves. Her cry hangs unpunctuated, waiting for resolution—but there is none. Her fertility is waning, and the fruit is too long in the bearing. The "summer of the body" has sucked her spirit, and Anne passionately hungers for death.

It was the last poem Anne ever published.

32

Dearly Beloved

*A*nne and Charles at daughter
Reeve's wedding, 1968.

(© Richard W. Brown)

The earth is a nursery in which men and women play at being heroes
and heroines, saints and sinners; but they are dragged down from their
fool's paradise by their bodies: hunger and cold and thirst, age and decay
and disease, death above all . . . Here you call your appearance beauty,
your emotions love, your sentiments heroism, your aspirations virtue, just
as you did on earth; but here there are no hard facts to contradict you,
no ironic contrasts of your needs with your pretensions, no human
comedy, nothing but a perpetual romance, a universal melodrama.

— GEORGE BERNARD SHAW,
Man and Superman

FALL 1959, DARIEN, CONNECTICUT

Not quite autumn; there was a wilt to the trees, and the late-night air held the chill of fall. The hired car slipped through the streets of Darien, carrying Anne eastward toward the water's edge. The manicured foliage grew thin and straggly as the paved, well-marked road bent and narrowed toward a rustic bridge. As the car crossed over, the earth seemed to swing out from under it, jettisoning into an expansive sky. And then, encircled by water as if on an island, the car elbowed its way around Scott's Cove, turning in to an unmarked drive.

It was September 3, 1959, and, after three months in St. Denis, Switzerland, Anne relished the familiarity of home. The rambling stone-façade house, purchased in 1946, sat on four and a half acres of woodlands and meadows bordering the shore of Long Island Sound. To Anne, it had always looked "amorphous and ugly," a practical concession to housing five children in a suburban town noted for its schools. Once brightly lit and bustling with children demanding to be heard, tutored, and fed, it was now dark and empty. Anne had told her housekeeper to leave the door unlocked; she would arrive late.[1]

Anne opened the huge oak-paneled door and entered the small dimly lit vestibule. After the radiant alpine light, the heavily curtained rooms, hung with old tapestries and European paintings, seemed dense and dark. Red fabric draped the windows and walls, and thick textured cloths covered the sofas and chairs. A grand piano stood in one corner of the lamp-shaded room, walled by leather-bound volumes of encyclopedias. Only the sculptures—a wooden Saint Francis, a bronze head, and a Chinese horse—gave rhythm and flow to the unpatterned room.[2] But life itself had lost its pattern; time was paced by the cadence of Anne's thoughts. By now, she should have grown used to the silence. The children, except for Reeve, were rarely there, and Charles was almost never home.

In 1953, Charles had become a consultant to the technical committee of Pan American Airlines and traveled frequently to aircraft plants in California and England. He had first met Juan Trippe, Pan Am's chief executive, in 1927, when the fledgling company was bidding for airmail routes. They met again in the early 1930s, when Charles and Anne made their transcontinental and intercontinental survey flights. Trippe knew that his pilots would be eager to hear anything Lindbergh had to say. And his name, especially after the publication of *The Spirit of St. Louis,* which won the Pulitzer Prize the following year, enhanced his status.[3]

But by April 1954, Charles had to limit his time at Pan Am. In an effort to heal wartime divisions and to acknowledge his contributions to aviation, President Eisenhower nominated Charles for the rank of brigadier general and then asked him to join the Air Force Scientific Advisory Board, assigned to study ballistic missile defense. The committee traveled twenty thousand miles a year, screening four hundred locations, and visiting proposed rocket and missile sites in twenty-two states.[4] Charles rarely spent more than a few days in Darien.

For Anne, long-distance flight had become a burden; she no longer had the stamina. But in choosing to stay home, Anne had become the sole caretaker of their three teenage children: Anne Jr., Scott, and Reeve. Rambunctious and wild in their father's absence, eager to push the limits of his rules, they defied Anne and the household staff. They ran off without telling anyone and stayed out long after midnight, scrambling up drainpipes before their mother awakened.[5] Delighted to challenge Anne's emphasis on neatness, they would smuggle wild animals into their rooms.[6] Unwilling to be a stern taskmaster, overwhelmed by the burden of their total care, Anne withdrew to her writing room. It was as if she had retreated inside her body, feeling incapable of physical warmth. Although accessible to the children, willing to listen and give them comfort, she remained emotionally removed.

If Charles's absence created a vacuum, his presence was intoxicating. He never stopped talking or moving around, filling the air with frenzied sound and energy. During his short stays, he would turn the house into a military camp, instructing Anne, his lieutenant, in the proper workings of household and staff. Drilling his recalcitrant teenage troops with relentless questions and detailed checklists, he attempted to improve their moral standards with long-winded "pearls of wisdom," intended to prevent the "downfall of civilization."[7] Anne Jr., whom Charles thought too clever for her own good, named him "Alcibiades High Fly," after the Athenian politician and commander whose moral pretensions did not cloak his immoral self-indulgences.

It was as if their home could not contain him. His relentless energy and ceaseless movements were dissonant interruptions in the rhythm of their lives. The sound of his steps, the boom of his voice, his constant trips up and down the stairs, all day long and even at night, sent waves of tension throughout the house. If someone, anyone—a child or Anne herself—dared to transgress, all his energy focused on the accused with an intensity that was primitive and painful to bear, even to witness. And yet at times Charles could be warm and playful, dispensing bear hugs and long-armed embraces. He read to them, and encouraged them to write, and taught them to hike, swim, and sail.

Oddly, there was sadness when Charles left the house, as if "real life" had suddenly walked out the door. The house once again became hollow and dry. Everyone felt relieved and "free" but less alive and more vulnerable than before. Like his own father, Charles loved his children deeply but lacked the capacity for shared emotion that might have bred intimacy. He simply could not admit he had "feelings like other people."[8] Feelings held the promise of danger, while "reality" could be measured, analyzed, and mastered.

By 1958, Anne's ardor for Atchley had cooled to friendship, and in Charles's absence, Anne turned to her publishers and friends, Helen and Kurt Wolff, for consolation. Helen was a maternal and nourishing woman who was also a devoted linguist and translator with an instinctive sense of style and language. A meticulous craftswoman and editor, she was fluent in German, French, Italian, and English. Twenty years her senior, Kurt, a gentleman with a classic education, was excited by the evolving cultural landscape of books, art, and music. Together they were an extraordinary pair; they understood the synergy between writer and editor, and viewed publishing as a medium synonymous with art.

Kurt would write that "a publisher's relationship with his author must be like a love affair in which he asks nothing and has already forgiven every failing in advance."[9] But that unconditional acceptance was a gift bestowed to the exceptional few. Helen and Kurt saw Anne as a woman of great talent who needed their confidence to harness her will. They believed in Anne—in the beauty of her poetic prose, in her ability to perceive psychological truth, and in the sincerity of her desire to master herself and her relationships.

The half-Jewish son of a music professor, Wolff had left Germany in 1933, just as Hitler rose to power, with Helen, his second wife.[10] They made their way to England and then to France, where their son, Christian, was born. After being arrested by the Nazis in Italy in 1939, they were freed and immediately sailed for New York, in January 1940. In prewar Munich, under the imprint of Kurt Wolff Verlag and Pantheon International, Kurt had been an innovative publisher, as eager to foster the expressionistic movement as he was committed to preserving classical texts. Fascinated by the culture that emerged after the First World War, he gave voice to young talent. And undeterred by geographical and cultural boundaries, he translated and disseminated, throughout Europe, the writings of Heinrich

Mann, Franz Kafka, Anton Chekhov, Maxim Gorky, Émile Zola, and Sinclair Lewis.[11]

Nearly penniless on his arrival in New York, and unschooled in American business, he could not negotiate his way through established channels. But New York in 1941 was an extraordinary place, enriched by a vibrant European community that had arrived at the start of the war. Helen and Kurt acted as mediators, translating European titles for the United States market, and, within a year of their arrival, began a new publishing firm, named for the old Pantheon Press, in the cramped rooms of their Washington Square apartment.[12]

Gift from the Sea was Pantheon's first real commercial success. Having nursed her through the publication of her poetry and the John Ciardi ordeal, Kurt encouraged Anne to write a book about marriage, a fictional sequel to *Gift from the Sea.* But by September 1959, Anne had reached an impasse. After a feverish beginning, the book was barely moving. The characters, Anne believed, were sketchy, mere mouthpieces for her ideas. She was untutored in the imaginative demands of fiction, and found her language stiff and monotonous, her dialogue unnatural and stilted. Her intent was to examine Eros and Agapé—physical and spiritual love—but it was also the story of a disillusioned housewife.

Deborah, the protagonist, much like the narrator in Anne's poem "Midsummer," was suffocating beneath domestic responsibility, bogged down in time and self-delusion. Her creativity was sapped, her marriage was flawed, and she was trapped in an affluent and stifling suburb. This was the underside of *Gift from the Sea,* the knots tied in the back of Anne's philosophical tapestry. Anne conceived the book as a medley of voices speaking in testimony to a failed ideal.

When the children were young, Anne would retreat to her small, second floor writing room and sit at a table in a straight-backed chair. Strewn with shells and feathery quills, her desk held a tray of pens and pencils, a blotter, and a small blue writing pad. With the light of the window streaming over her left shoulder, Anne laid out her books and papers, much in the Morrow tradition, writing in long-hand, leaning back between her thoughts as she scanned her bookshelves and watched the birds skim the cove.

Later she would work in a small gray tool shed behind the house bordering Long Island Sound. Its walls, crossbeams, and shelves decorated with remnants of driftwood, cork, and seashells, it must have reminded her of her time at Captiva when she first understood the fullness of her solitude.

At first, the voices played easily in her head, clear and resonant and strikingly distinctive. Unaware of Anne's disappointment in Charles as well as her affair with Atchley, Kurt was confused by her lack of passion, by the dull gray palate she chose to use. Where were the strong, authentic feelings, he asked? Where were the extremes of egocentrism and possessiveness, the tenderness and rage that Eros and Agapé demanded? And where was the central theme of happiness by which dissonance could achieve melody? Surely it existed.

Intrigued by the musical structure of the piece, Kurt gave Anne a recording of the fugue from the Anna Magdalena Notebook by Bach. The intricate texture of chord and melody seemed to echo the emotions she was seeking. Although Anne was grateful for Kurt's genteel criticism, she was disturbed by what his comments revealed. She could not make happiness in marriage the central theme of her book. This was neither her belief nor her intent. To define the goal of marriage as happiness was to delude oneself. Of course, happiness was possible at fleeting, precious moments, she wrote, but harmony and selfless love seemed nothing more than a myth; the bride and groom and the wedding ceremony were symbolic expressions of eternal hope. Completely happy marriages, she wrote, were of certain types: (1) simple-minded; (2) very young; (3) very old; (4) European; and (5) second marriages in middle age.[13]

Anne no longer saw the world in the bright colors and stark boundaries of her youth. The landscape of middle-age love was gray, not black and white, but it had a beauty of its own—like the muted palate of a painting by Boudin. She no long indulged in idealized perceptions; like the Unicorn of her poem, Anne was resigned. And yet her vision had matured and softened in recent years. The message she wanted to carry forward was tinged with pain, but still held the promise of joy and love.[14]

Kurt wrote back, "I would not wish to change your palate. I would consider it a sin against the Holy Spirit. You have to follow your own law, and only then will you be able to reach not absolute perfection, which is a myth, but your own perfection. And now I wish you, with all my heart, a time of blessed creativity."[15]

But Anne's work was not blessed. After a year and a half, during which she produced nothing, Helen and Kurt began to worry. It was clear that Anne was anguishing over the book, and they feared she would abandon it. It would be a loss and a sin, Kurt admonished her. She had a rare gift for internal monologue, and she had touched a subject universal in meaning.[16]

After a summer in St. Denis, Anne struggled through the fall of 1958 and the winter of 1959, cutting, rewriting, and pacing the book. In Charles's absence, Anne "hungered" for the company of Helen and Kurt. In the summer she walked with them along the woodland paths outside their home in Zürich; in winter, along the "mechanized and hellish" streets of Manhattan. When she wasn't with them, she longed for their presence, and when family or work thwarted their meetings, Anne wrote them letters. Lovingly, they gave her advice and perspective through books, music, and literary quotations, constantly affirming the necessity of her struggle and the worth of its outcome. Helen summed up their views in a line from the French philosopher Jean Reverzy: "If I reconciled myself with life, I would be at odds with myself. That would never happen, for everything perishes except disorder."[17]

But reconciliation would not come. Life at home was a constant struggle. The children, difficult and rebellious, consumed her time and drained her will. Charles's mood swings had gotten worse; when he did come home, he continued to be dictatorial and angry. Again, Anne was smothered by domesticity and bereft of a husband who was also a partner.

Like a good friend, Helen understood that Anne needed a dose of her own medicine. Echoing the words that Anne had used in *Gift from the Sea* to inspire others, Helen counseled her to find her "center." Anne's creative energy, Helen noted, dissipated in the rush of daily domesticity. She must set herself free—discard her schedule and her endless caring for others. She must make her work the focal point of her life.[18]

By Christmas 1959, three years after Anne had begun the book, Kurt's encouragement turned to surrender. He wondered whether Anne could complete the book. He wished her patience, and the goodwill of the Gods, and he pledged his unfaltering friendship. Above all, Kurt wanted Anne to know that he believed in her and would always be there for her. Friendship, he mused, was like an eternal harvest—joyful, pure, and enduring.[19]

Clearly, Anne's characters were fragments of herself, and her book was more than a "story." Each voice became an instrument for analyzing her failing marriage and for assessing the options for reconciliation. Each character allowed her to examine every aspect of the marriage. With the precision of a fine watchmaker, she sought to put the pieces together again. How could she remain married to a man whose insensitivity and egoism evoked her contempt, whose presence was as vacant as his absence? Should she, like "Beatrice," get a divorce? Could she, like "Frances," become reconciled? Perhaps she would resign herself to loneliness.

Christmas, as usual, buoyed her spirits, but by the turn of the year, the Lindbergh name was again on the front page of the *Times.* An extensively researched biography, written by Kenneth Davis, pointed a finger at Charles's prewar Nazi entanglements. His friend Truman Smith tried to wash him clean by writing, in his published memoirs, that Lindbergh "was forced to accept the German medal. He was on a mission to ease the financial plight of Jews."[20] But Smith's comments were pathetically transparent, a frail attempt at protecting Lindbergh, as well as exonerating himself, a tinny challenge to accepted fact.

Anne passed the cold and rainy summer of 1960 in St. Denis and stayed on through the winter in Vaud. Switzerland had become Charles's central base for his Pan Am inspection tours, and neither she nor he had much interest in returning to Darien. They decided to build a cottage of their own in Vaud, and sell the large house on Scott's Cove, with the intention of building a smaller one on its eastern shore.

With Charles away and the children traveling or at school, Anne sat on her verandah, still intent on "attacking" her book. Her promises to the Wolffs, however, dissolved into nothing. Kurt, now ill with heart disease, feared that he and Helen had failed her. What had they done, he asked, and what could they do? The failure was inside herself, Anne answered.

But by Christmas 1960, something cracked; Anne's thoughts began to flow. Immersed as if in a dream, Anne abandoned housework for the book. She wrote, nonstop, all morning and most of the afternoon, emerging dazed from her writing room.[21] Deborah's friend "Beatrice," named perhaps for Dante's muse, who led the poet through Paradise, had finally taken form. Anne now returned to her portrait of the mother of the groom, "Frances," hoping she could bring the book to completion.

Alone in Darien through 1961, a year when Christmas seemed not to come, Anne struggled blindly to bring Frances to life.[22] Hungry and thirsty for the Wolffs' approval, Anne promised to repay them for their nourishment by handing them the final draft of the book.[23] In the summer of 1961, five years after her feverish beginning, Anne completed *Dearly Beloved*. For two weeks, Charles stayed home, correcting hundreds of small inaccuracies in language and expression, filtering out the errors. It was Charles who delivered the manuscript to Kurt.

Dearly Beloved[24] is the story of a family wedding in a suburban home much like Next Day Hill. The ceremony is reminiscent of Elisabeth's marriage ceremony to Aubrey Morgan thirty years earlier. The thoughts of Deborah McNeil, a middle-aged housewife, as she projects herself into the minds of her guests, are what construct the narratives. Through them, we see the diverse interpretations of the meaning and purpose of marriage.

It is also a moral allegory, a drama of ideas resonant with Biblical story and literary myth. Modeled on the Anna Magdalena fugue by

Bach, voices rise and fall and variant chords harmonize into a common melody encompassed by a prelude and coda. What begins as a playful minuet, suddenly darkens with the pounding clash of dissonant chords. Light and darkness struggle and chase, as the melody strives again to be heard. The melody is marriage, the variations are the internal monologues of the guests, and the embracing principle is Christian virtue.

Three generations of the Gardner family gather in a garden resplendent with flowers, blazing in reds that light the rooms and cast their glow on the faces. But it is the Garden after the Fall, after betrayal and deception, shame and divine punishment. It is Anne's vision of her moral exile after having broken her wedding vows.

Deborah, mother of the bride, allows the reader to know of her anger, inadequacy, and disillusion. Although she wants to sound a call for ethical and spiritual awakening, she fears that she is tainted with blasphemy, desecration, and temptation. As the bride and groom, symbols of "blessed union," walk toward the altar, and the words of the marriage ceremony are recited by the minister, Deborah's thoughts verge on madness.

Deborah, mad prophetess and suburban housewife, seeks the answer to her question. Is marriage a blessed union or a kind of suicide, a delusion that takes the place of emotional and sexual reality? Until this moment, the delusion of marriage is barely audible beneath the melody of the text. Now it takes control of the narrative. As the monologues of three generations converge in Deborah's mind, they become refractions of one another, living in the same dream.

Deborah casts herself out of the garden and into a private Hell. But this Hell of Deborah's, unlike the narrator's in *Listen! The Wind,* has no fatal disease, no demonic presence. The evil lives inside Deborah's mind, and Anne examines it in sordid detail. The book, written when Anne was fifty-five, is her first expression of her sexuality. Neither her published diaries nor her previous books reveal her sensuous nature.

Hell, Anne concludes, is the reality of one's mind—the unfulfilled hopes, the choices not made, the perfidies and betrayals, the lusts and temptations, the petty destruction caused by ordinary acts, the self-denial and self-delusion. But what kind of life has she created, Deborah asks? And who is this man she has married?

With little attempt to disguise Charles, Anne creates, in Deborah's husband, John, a hero who hides behind a mask of invulnerability. In her earlier books, Charles remains the shadow of a man; here, he is painted with merciless honesty. John, says Deborah, never cares about her problems or her daily decisions; he is content with platitudes. He speaks to Deborah in "a different language," a rational tongue alien to hers. A scientist who is governed by reason, he nails her with "the good strong nails of his logic."

Deborah rages as she mimics the sadism of her husband's diatribes, making herself into a Christ-like martyr.

> *Bang, bang, bang. Nailed to her faults forever, she couldn't move, couldn't walk away and leave them, like a goose nailed to the barn floor for a pâté de fois gras . . . Nailed through a webbed foot, forced to go on gorging forever.*

Shades of Saint-Exupéry give dimension to Anne's portrait of John, as Deborah remembers a Frenchman she might have loved, a man with whom conversation had been communion. But love, she reminds herself, is not the same as marriage.

As hellfire consumes, it also illuminates. Deborah represents triumph over the devil, and now she claims her victory. Through Beatrice, the virgin who leads the poet through Paradise, Anne makes the case for divorce. Through Frances, that is, Saint Francis, devoted to humility and poverty, she makes the case for marriage as self-sacrifice.

When the ceremony ends, Deborah has made a choice: the ideal of marriage is worth the sacrifice. Deborah's life, asserts Anne, is finally "real." She is the artist-mother she has always wanted to be: the composer of the wedding, the playwright of the scene, as creative as any writer or musician. In the garden of her private hell, she has eaten the apple, yet been blessed after her fall. All that remains is for her to love John, to confirm and to sanctify their imperfect union.

One can only imagine the conversation between Anne and Charles as they sat in their bed in Darien, with Anne's manuscript pages piled around them. As Charles scoured each page for "mistakes and inaccuracies," he must surely have sensed Anne's dissatisfaction, her emotional cry. Perhaps he wondered whether Anne, like Frances, had betrayed him. Or whether, like Deborah, she had sacrificed herself to preserve their tarnished marriage. Perhaps he even questioned his moral standards and wondered whether he could play according to Anne's rules.

33

Argonauta

*Eric, Peter, and Erin, three Lindbergh grandchildren,
on the beach near Argonauta, the Lindberghs' home
on Maui, Christmas 1972.*

(Lindbergh Picture Collection, Manuscripts and Archives,

Yale University Library)

The Garden of Eden is behind us, and there is no road back to innocence;
we can only go forward. The journey we started must be continued. With
our blazing candle of curiosity, we must, like Psyche, make the full
circle back to wholeness, if we are ever to find it.

—ANNE MORROW LINDBERGH, *Earthshine*

SPRING 1962, DARIEN, CONNECTICUT

Anne grew thin with insight. The equation was simple; less body, less pain. As she turned fifty-six, her vigor was cerebral. She wore her collars high and her buttons closed, lightly tied with a long, limp bow.

Dearly Beloved, published in the spring of 1962, received disappointing reviews. It was thrown into the stockpile of "women's books," viewed as a sequel to *Gift from the Sea,* lacking poignancy, substance, and drama. As Anne had feared, her "voices" fell flat, treated by critics as platitudes. Anne's now familiar housewife-saint was greeted with a critical yawn.

She wrote to Helen that the book was a failure. It was praised by those who did not understand it and rejected by those who thought they did. Now that the storm of publicity was over, Anne hoped to find the cool light of objectivity.[1]

Anne was right. Those who didn't toss the book out, still didn't seem to understand it. Virgilia Peterson of the *New York Times* saw it as a portrait of "three happy marriages" and called it nothing more than "flowers" arranged carefully in a jar.[2] The *Christian Science Monitor,* perhaps grasping the message of the story, brushed it off as something perverse.[3] But it was a commercial success; more than a hundred thousand copies in hardcover alone were sold and it immediately climbed to the top of the best-seller lists of the *Herald Tribune* and the *Times.* It stayed at the top of the *Times*'s list for nearly thirty weeks.

If the book did "fail," it was because Anne had not told her story. While demanding total honesty of herself, she had let the book play at the edge. As usual, the story was clothed in beautiful imagery, which camouflaged its intent. At first its publication released Anne's energy, spinning her back into domestic routine and spurring her to plan trips abroad with Charles. Then the poor reviews sent her back into retreat, and once again she sat alone in her room, wondering what she could possibly write next. In the winter of 1962–1963, she looked through her diaries, letters, and notes, hoping to find a kernel for another book. Writing, she wrote to Kurt, connected her to life in an essential way, fostering her growth and deepening her roots."[4]

Charles, now sixty years old, had grown solid and sturdy. No longer boyishly straight and "slim," he was finally filling the potential of his form. Still able to outdistance his sons, he walked with brisk, long-legged strides, and his whitening hair and pale cheeks heightened the penetrating blue of his eyes.

In 1961, after seven years as a consultant to the air force, and after being disillusioned by the encroachment of technology on the woodlands and farmlands he had known as a boy, he was back to flying for Juan Trippe at Pan Am. Now a director as well as a consultant, he crisscrossed Europe and America several times a year, meeting Anne in Darien or in their newly built chalet in Vevey. Dressed in a navy pinstripe suit, with his clothes and sock-wrapped razor stuffed into a small bag, he would pull the brim of his gray fedora over his eyes and board a commercial plane. After heading straight for the back, he would sprawl out with his papers and books, attracting little attention from tourists or staff. And yet all the attendants had been alerted to his presence. They whispered in the cockpit, "Lindbergh's aboard," but they had been forbidden to take notice or to engage in conversation. All were content to play his game, just glancing as they passed him, pretending that he was no one of any importance. Charles, now a detached observer, saddened by the antiseptic luxury of jet flight, would watch the stewardesses walk up and down the aisle serving full-course meals on household trays. It was, he found, hard to remember that they were 35,000 feet above the same Atlantic Ocean he had flown over thirty-five years earlier in a 300-horsepower plane.

He traveled for months at a time, often cutting a wide swathe through the gamelands of East Africa while also alloting time to Pan Am. His growing interest in wildlife conservation had convinced him that "civilization" was not "progress," and he sought to understand primitive human and animal life in the jungles of Tanzania and Kenya, places untouched by guns, planes, and "white men." He believed that, in spite of the advances of science and technology, Western culture had alienated man from his place in nature, denied him spiritual connection with life, and deprived him of the "miracles" of God's creation.[5]

There was an aspect of Charles's conservation philosophy that harked back to his childhood in Minnesota. On the front porch of his riverside home, he had listened to his father's spoken memories of dense virgin woodlands filled with deer and of clear skies blackened with wild geese. Later, he regretted having taken the path of scientific inquiry. The only true criterion by which to measure progress, he wrote in "Civilization and Progress," was the quality of human life. There was no reason to believe that the spear-thrusting Masai of Kenya lived less happily or well than his Pan Am colleagues in the boardrooms above the streets of New York.

Anne's time in Darien was punctuated by visits to and from the children—Jon and Land and their families out west, her brother Dwight, now a professor of history at Temple University, her son Scott, now enrolled at Amherst, and her daughters Reeve and Anne, students at Radcliffe. But the children seemed to register the strain of a marriage defined by their father's absences and their mother's loneliness and disappointment. Anne Jr., a blond Botticelli beauty with an incisive mind and acerbic wit, had grown severely depressed. When she talked of dropping out of school, and Anne encouraged her to see Dr. Rosen, Charles was furious. His anger was stoked by their son Scott, as argumentative and tenacious as he. Rebellious but sensitive, he would not comply with Charles's notions of "manhood" and discipline. Scott was opposed to the war in Vietnam, unhappy at Amherst, and hoped to find refuge at Oxford in England. He and his father fought incessantly about the responsibilities of "patriotism," and Charles demanded that Scott remain in this country and serve in the military. Anne would develop migraine headaches, feeling powerless to protect Scott from Charles.[6] When she did summon up the courage to defend Scott, asking Charles to see how deeply his criticism affected their son, she could not move him. Charles persisted in expressing his contempt for Scott's behavior.

The other children had developed their means of coping with Charles. Jon, earlier than the others, had learned to keep the peace by acting obedient and remaining silent; Land, now a cattle rancher in Montana, chose to keep the buffer of distance between them. Sunny-faced Reeve seemed unscathed until long into adulthood when she could face the emptiness of her father's absences and the fullness of his rage. Even as she treasured her mother's sensibilities, she questioned her timidity and emotional reticence.

Anne spent the spring of 1963 alone in their chalet in Vevey and often visited Helen and Kurt Wolff in Locarno. Weakened by heart disease and no longer able to bear the stress of independent publishing, Kurt had moved his and Helen's base to Locarno, expecting to make a full retirement. But William Jovanovich, at Harcourt Brace, lured them back with an offer so attractive that they could not refuse. He suggested they become his co-publishers, retaining both the name and the prestige of their imprint and protected by the financial resources of a large concern. Happy to resume his beloved work, Kurt once again traveled throughout Europe, reestablishing old contacts, meeting new authors, and bringing manuscripts to Helen to have translated and edited for the American and European markets. Totally engaged, Kurt seemed rejuvenated.[7]

On the afternoon of October 21, 1963, after their usual stop at the Bookfair in Frankfurt, Kurt and Helen took a detour through Marbach to visit the National Museum on their way to a meeting of Gruppe 47, a coterie of German-language poets, essayists, novelists, and dramatists who grappled with the social issues of Europe. Just seven kilometers from their destination, they stopped at a hotel in the small town of Ludwigsburg, and Kurt decided to take a walk. As he crossed a street, a tanker truck pulled into reverse. In his attempt to outrun it, Kurt was pinned by the force of its thrust. He died three hours later of massive internal injuries.[8] Those who knew him called his action thoughtless and impulsive, yet somehow consonant with his character. He died taking one more chance, believing his instincts would carry him through.

Helen received the news alone at the hotel. Three days later, surrounded by publishers and authors from all over the world, Helen buried Kurt in Marbach, home of the German Literary Archives, the largest collection of literature in Europe. His colleagues hailed him as "the most distinguished literary publisher of the twentieth century."[9]

To Anne, his sudden death must have seemed a familiar blow. Like the kidnapping of Charlie, the unexpected death of her father, and the disappearance of Saint-Exupéry, this death catapulted Anne from the lull of an ordinary day into the horror of loss. The man who had been a friend and a collaborator, who had loved her with "a purity" and a fullness of heart she had rarely known, was suddenly gone. As with Saint-Exupéry, when Anne wrote, she wrote for him. And once again, she had not had the chance to say good-bye.

The week before Christmas 1963, Anne Jr. married Julien Feydy, a young student she had met in Paris the year before. As usual, information was withheld from the press. It was a quiet service in the town hall of Dordogne, where the groom's father, a university professor, owned a large manor house and estate.[10] Within the week, Anne and Charles returned from France with Helen Wolff to spend Christmas in Darien.

On Christmas day, Charles declared that "everything will be the same."[11] Helen would edit, Anne would write, and he would ease their way. But as he watched the women grieve for Kurt, he must have wondered whether he could fill his place. Once again Anne's grief had taken her to a place where Charles could not follow, and he must have known how she had changed. To Anne, heroism was no longer a physical act; it was a journey toward enlightenment and awareness. Anne's magnificent "cathedral" of a husband, in spite of his noble intentions, was incapable of responding to her intellectual or emotional needs.

Nevertheless, in February 1964, Anne accompanied Charles to East

Africa. She had long been a passive listener to his stories about a place that stirred him as nothing had since his early days of flying. Her visit did indeed convince her of Africa's beauty—but she contracted viral pneumonia and had to remain in bed most of the spring.

By fall, Anne was hard at work again, reading and editing her letters and diaries. It was a project she had begun with Kurt, and now she was carrying it through, with the help of Helen. She wanted to shape a dramatic narrative, smooth enough for publication. Quite sure that she would never write another novel, she hoped that the story of her youth would be more compelling than any fiction she might imagine.

The bout with viral pneumonia in the spring of 1965 had left Anne physically exhausted, but it was an exhaustion she seemed eager to cultivate in order to free herself from Charles's schedule.[12] Nonetheless, Anne agreed again to accompany Charles to Africa during the Christmas holiday. Inspired, perhaps, by her memories of the trips with Charles in their "golden days," she invited the children to join them. The safari would be a family expedition. Land refused to travel with his father, but Jon and his wife, Barbara, Anne Jr. and Julien, Scott, and Reeve traveled with Anne and Charles, without guides or guns through the "big-game lands" of Serengeti, Lake Manyara, Kilimanjaro, Olduvai, Amboseli, and Ngorongoro. Charles assumed his usual military stance, commanding his family as if they were troops on a battlefield. In fact, nothing had changed since their honeymoon. Charles held the maps, decided their course, orchestrated the folding and unfolding of their gear, and delegated responsibilities according to what he saw as their collective needs. "This isn't a democracy," he was fond of saying; "this is a beneficent dictatorship."[13]

While Anne cooked their meals by campfire in the 120–degree heat, Charles went off scouting with the local game wardens. Feeling deserted by Charles, one day, in the Chumba Valley, Anne and the children staged an all-out mutiny, packing up the Range-Rovers so that they could head off for cooler and more temperate terrain. Charles returned and demanded that they unpack. Persuaded by Jon to obey, the children and Anne did as they were ordered.[14]

Though the family reunion was a failure, it was invaluable for Anne. On October 21, 1965, coincidentally the second anniversary of Kurt's death, Anne published "Immersion in Life" as the cover story of *Life* magazine. It was one of Anne's old-time travel pieces, reminiscent of *North to the Orient* and *Listen, The Wind:* a physical journey as a moral adventure, an exploration of the connections between man and nature and man and God. Writing in the first person, with the "innocence" of a child's eye, Anne piles image on image, wrapping the reader in sight, sound, and smell until he is enfolded in the landscape. It is a musical piece, as thunderous and dissonant as the *Dearly Beloved* fugue, but dominated by a sweeping, harmonizing melody. It is confident and commanding as never before, modulated and precisely controlled, strong in detail, yet lyrical in language. Like all her narratives, it is a disguised sermon, filled with the demands of her Calvinist ancestry. But it is also the exercise of literary imagination in the comprehension of God's will. It is the sanctification of literature as prayer.

On a trip to Paris in 1966, Charles took his usual place in the back of the plane, hiding behind his books and papers. But his long legs, thrust sideways between the seats, needed a stretch, and he walked down the aisle toward the back galley. Adrienne Arnett, a twenty-five-year-old stewardess who had seen him many times before, brushed by in the opposite direction. She was an attractive young woman, blond, buxom, and blue-eyed, distinctive in her jingling laugh and her direct, unabashed manner. Against company rules, Adrienne broke the silence.[15]

"You make me suspicious," she blurted out. To her surprise, Charles was not offended. He wheeled around, eager to banter, delving, in a teasing way, her apparent curiosity. Taking advantage of the opportunity, she told him that he was a man of "special destiny." It was no accident that he had flown the Atlantic, she said. His gifts were akin to those of all extraordinary men, no different from Thomas Jefferson's or Benjamin Franklin's. Intent on proving that she was more than she appeared to be, she told him that she was a metaphysician with a deep interest in the spiritual aspects of life. Before he left the plane, Charles asked for her address and handed her a copy of "Civilization and

Progress." There was a book he wanted to send her, he said: Lao-tzu's *The Way of Life.* It was a new translation of the book Anne had given him twenty years earlier.

For six years, Charles gave Adrienne many books—poetry, philosophy, even the works of Saint-Exupéry—and continued to see her in New York and Paris, London, Hawaii, California, whenever and wherever they happened to be. To Adrienne, he was "a gorgeous hunk of a man," with piercing blue eyes and a fascinating mind. She was eager to follow his thoughts, to learn what he had to teach.

Adrienne made life disarmingly simple. She cared about his comfort and understood his needs. And he could talk to her, he said, as he could never talk to Anne. Demanding of him no commitment, allowing him to come and go as he pleased, she was content to live in the moment. When they were together, they talked and laughed, sharing easy pleasures—a long walk, a good meal, and perhaps more passion than they cared to admit.

When Charles was with Adrienne, his anger dissipated; he was boyish. And though he was sometimes distant and preoccupied, he was a gentle and attentive friend and companion, much as he had been when he courted Anne. But most of all, Adrienne was not afraid of Charles. When his teasing became abusive or he got out of hand, she did not hesitate to throw him out. He would call the next morning, sheepish and apologetic and strangely grateful. If Charles was the hero with a "special" destiny, he was also a boy with lessons to learn who had found, perhaps for the first time, a female mentor strong enough and willing to teach him.

Anne knew nothing of Charles's visits with Adrienne.[16] Slipped into the seams of his scheduled flights, the relationship was invisible except to Charles and Adrienne. But Anne did notice the "emptiness" of the hours. Feeling old and tired and not needed by anyone,[17] she sought, as she had so many times before, to make sense of her marriage. Deeper than ever, she plunged into her diaries, hoping to find the "patterns" of their lives.

By the end of 1963, Anne and Charles had moved into a small house on the eastern side of their Darien property, built closer to sea level, "tucked among the marsh grasses with the shore birds of the Long Island

Sound."[18] Unlike the rambling Tudor in which their family had grown, the house, designed by Charles, was spartan and symmetrical, with stucco walls and teal-blue shutters. Gone were the dark, cavernous rooms, replaced by light-filled spaces and a simple, muted, streamlined décor. The only remnant of Anne's childhood was her father's desk from Next Day Hill, piled high with papers and books. They called the house Tellina, the name of a mollusk with a small, delicate body and spindly, powerful legs; it was as if it reflected the new shape of their lives.

By the end of the decade, Charles had become a strong advocate of wildlife preservation and a recipient of several national awards. As he had done in his early pit-stop flights, he canvassed the United States, meeting local leaders and speaking for his cause. Under the auspices of the World Wildlife Fund, he shifted his attention to the South Pacific, surveying the land and animal populations, lobbying foreign leaders to pass legislation on behalf of conservation.

In 1967, on one of his flights home from the Philippines, Charles stopped to visit a friend, Sam Pryor, at his ocean-front estate on the eastern shore of Maui, in Hawaii. Sam's uncle had been the president of the St. Louis bank that backed Charles in his 1927 flight, and he had known Sam since his early days at Pan Am. A man who could deftly handle the press, Sam had been "Trippe's man on the Hill," his liaison with government officials. He was a gregarious, hard-driving, salt-of-the-earth man in spite of his wealth, and he was given to hero-worship.[19] Charles understood Sam, and they enjoyed their shared commitment to the land and animals, as well as a spontaneous "little boy" sense of adventure. Sam was among the few who could match Charles's physical endurance and thirst for exploration. They had cultivated their relationship through the years, first at Pan Am, then as anti-Roosevelt men before the war, and also as neighbors in Fairfield County, Connecticut. In 1963, Sam and his wife, Tay, had purchased a hundred acres in Kipahulu, eleven miles outside the town of Hana. Their estate was a garden and a sanctuary, filled with flowers, shrubs, and trees, and home to Sam's menagerie of pet gibbons.

From the moment Charles's plane skimmed the surface of the island, he was taken by the line and color of its beauty. Its mountains sloped down to flat horizons, lush green terrain, and deep-dimpled craters of volcanic ash. Orange cliffs descended to black beaches washed by the deep blue sea. At early dawn, Charles would stand on Sam's beach to watch the sun rise. He would swim beyond the surf to the coral reefs, among the waving fronds and the brilliantly colored fish. But to his disappointment, the primitive ways of the native people had almost disappeared. European culture had eroded Hawaii's Polynesian past, and it had succumbed to the "modern."

Nonetheless, Charles believed it a perfect home base, developed and populated enough for Anne, yet accessible to him in his conservation work both east and west. In 1968, he had a house built on five acres of ocean-front land, transferred to his ownership through the generosity of Sam. The house was designed to buffet the ocean wind and rain, and its geometric lines married simplicity with technological precision. As if Charles wanted to touch the primitive within the refuge of impenetrable walls, he had the house constructed of three-foot-thick stone, its surfaces covered with granite tile. Built without Anne's consent, according to Charles's needs, the house, appropriately named Argonauta, never felt like home to Anne. It was cold and unforgiving, without the comfort of heat or electricity. Forced to cook and write by gaslight, eleven miles out of town, and thousands of miles away from family and friends, Anne was almost always alone. She used to stand on the cliffs above the shore and hold her ears against the deafening roar.

Preferring the sound of cowbells and the softness of mountain mist, Anne often retreated to her chalet in Switzerland. While Charles surveyed the rainforests of the Philippines, Anne sat in Vevey on her verandah, watching the cloud-hung mountains in the distance and working on her diaries and letters. Helen Wolff, in Locarno, read her manuscripts line by line. Since Kurt's death, Anne and Helen had become intimate friends; Anne trusted her literary instincts and her judgment. Her goal, Helen wrote to Anne, was to retain the honesty of her view while maintaining her professional objectivity. There was to be no record of marital disputes, children's problems, or family disharmony. In a sense, Helen, with the consent of Anne and Charles, created the "Anne" of her published diaries. Through Helen's eyes, Anne would become an asexual idealized woman, constantly struggling with herself for integrity. The flesh and blood Anne, with her rage and sensuality, would hover like a phantom beneath the text.

While Anne supported Charles in his land and wildlife conservation both in Maui and in Darien, she had no desire to follow him to the Philippines. Her jet lag, since the bout of viral pneumonia several years earlier, was growing more difficult, and "storms" of stomach pain would overwhelm her. Since Charles's first visit with President Ferdinand Marcos, in 1969, his goal had been to preserve the "core forests" from devastation and development by European loggers. Convinced that the islands would be reduced to a wasteland, he asked Marcos and his ministers to pass protective legislation. Emmanuel Elizalde, Marcos's minister of minority rights, a wealthy, Harvard-educated dilettante and playboy, was immediately intrigued by Charles's efforts. Hoping to use Charles's celebrity to advance his political ambitions, he granted Charles access to the interior jungles. After a survey flight of the islands in 1970, on which he was accompanied by *New York Times* reporter Alden Whitman,[20] Charles and a group of hand-picked journalists, photographers, and anthropologists, were air-lifted to the rainforests of Mindanao, at the southernmost tip of the Philippines. There he would live among a lost and isolated Paleolithic tribe discovered by Elizalde several months before.

As the helicopter hovered, Charles dropped to the jungle floor, greeted by an orchid-leaf-clad member of the Tasaday tribe.[21] After being guided six-hundred feet up to the stream-rippled mountain of this Stone Age, cave-dwelling society, Charles spent eleven days living and observing them. Convinced that they were pure specimens of "primitive man," he returned to Manila to consult with Marcos.[22]

Within days of Charles's return to Darien, Marcos had enacted legislation that transferred ownership of fifty thousand acres to the twenty-five-member Tasaday tribe. Refusing to heed the experts who thought

Elizalde's discovery a political hoax, Charles reveled in his victory. But after the November elections in the Philippines, and the decline of Elizalde's political fortune, it became clear to Charles that the passionate exponent was less than honest. For the next fifteen years, martial law thwarted the efforts of scholars to study the Tasaday tribe. In the 1980s, however, it became clear that they were modern-day forest dwellers who, having been bribed by Elizalde with guns, clothes, and golf carts, had masqueraded for the international press. Later seen in jeans and T-shirts, cavorting around Elizalde's Manila estate, they were understood to be pawns of his ambitions.[23] Once again, Charles was duped by smooth-talking politicians eager to harness his popularity to their ends. The Stone Age tribesmen were hired actors, and the Paleolithic tribe did not exist.

After his return from the Philippine expedition, Charles was ill. During the winter of 1971–1972 he lost twenty pounds and was plagued by colds, coughs, and fevers, as well as a case of shingles. Weak and fatigued, he curtailed his traveling and remained home. Anne, though she worried about his weakness and infections, enjoyed his uninterrupted presence. Throughout 1971 and 1972, they worked together in Maui and in Switzerland, editing, rewriting, and shaping Anne's diaries. As in the old days, Charles was both protective and strict. He would straighten up the kitchen and wash the dishes after sending her off to work. In the afternoon, when Anne was done, they corrected the details, the facts, and the presentation. They had published *Bring Me a Unicorn* and *Diaries and Letters 1922–1928* in 1971; in 1973 they completed the second volume, *Hour of Gold, Hour of Lead 1929–1932*.

By the summer of 1973, Charles knew that he was dying. He was diagnosed with lymphatic cancer, and told that the lesions had already spread to his lungs. Between the sessions of chemotherapy and radiation, he spent his time writing his memoirs, visiting his children and grandchildren, now numbering ten, and supporting efforts in behalf of land and wildlife preservation. In August 1973, he returned to his boyhood home, in Little Falls, to dedicate the family land as a state museum and park. In his speech he said, "If I had to choose between airplanes and birds, I would choose birds."

Charles had mellowed through the years. After his transatlantic flight, he was certain that aviation was the wave of the future; that technology would bring enlightened perspective. But after the devastation of Europe, Charles no longer believed in the beneficence of "progress." Technology was only as good as its masters; Science had to be governed by values. He turned back to nature in the hope of recapturing the lessons of his boyhood in the wilderness of Minnesota. His thoughts would echo his father's Jeffersonian principles, and confirm the relationship between agrarian society and moral virtue. Nonetheless, Charles Lindbergh would never rescind his wartime views.

By mid-July 1974, there was nothing more his doctors at Columbia Presbyterian Hospital could do. Defying their warning that he would not last the trip, Charles decided to return to Maui. Maui had come to feel like "home"—tinctured by memories of his boyhood on the Mississippi, and his childhood fantasies of solitary adventure in tropical jungles and warm island seas.[24]

Juan Trippe at Pan Am flatly refused to help him, but Sam Pryor was able to secure him a place on a United Airlines commercial flight. Carried into the cabin on a stretcher, Charles was cordoned off by curtains from tourists and staff. Anne, Land, and Jon sat by his side. His physician in Maui, Dr. Milton Howell, fearing that the Lindbergh home was too far from the medical clinic, borrowed a cottage on the sea three miles outside the town of Hana. For eight days, attended by two nurses around the clock, Charles lay in his seaside bed, taking charge of the preparations for his burial in the yard of an abandoned church he and Sam had restored several years earlier. He chose a eucalyptus coffin, sufficiently wide to accommodate his "broad shoulders," and instructed his native-born friend Tevy Kahalevah to see that the grave would be large enough to accommodate Anne, eventually. He sketched in detail the drainage pipe system and the rock configuration necessary to maintain the integrity of the grave's walls, and ordered for the gravestone a block of Vermont granite large enough not to tempt souvenir hunters. He chose lines from Psalm 139, his favorite, to be engraved exactly a quarter-inch into the surface of the stone, deep enough so that wind and rain could not wash the words away. They read: "If I take the wings of the morning, and dwell in the uttermost parts of the sea . . ."

But as if he could not bear his own vulnerability, Charles stopped short of the next verses:

Even there shall thy hand lead me, and thy right hand shall hold me.
If I say, Surely the darkness shall cover me, even the night shall be light
about me. Yea, the darkness hideth not from thee, but the night shineth
as the day: and the darkness and the light are both alike to thee.

Tired and weak, but alert and talkative, Charles juggled the apparatus to the end. He wanted to believe his inability to breathe was a matter of technical adjustment. Surrendering to a sedative and a painkiller, Charles slipped into a coma on Sunday evening, August 25. He died the following morning at seven-fifteen. Barefoot, clad in khakis, and wrapped in his favorite New England blanket, Charles was lifted into his eucalyptus coffin and set in the back of Tevy's pickup truck for the seven-mile journey along the winding seacliff road to the Congregational church in Kipahulu. The church was decorated with boughs of bougainvillea, stalks of ginger, and hibiscus and plumeria blossoms. One of his nurses, barefoot and silent, carried flowers in her apron to the coffin and scattered them, one by one, across its surface. His friend Henry Kaluhu led the singing of "Angel's Welcome" as Tevy lowered the casket into the grave alongside Sam Pryor's buried pet gibbons. Interred one hour earlier than stated on the public schedule, Charles, one last time, outwitted the press.

Anne was grateful to Charles's physician, Dr. Milton Howell. Because of him, Charles had been able to choose the rhythm and pace of his death. He wanted to confront it on his own terms, to maneuver its currents as he went, and to plan its details in the embrace of his family and the beauty of Maui he had come to love. Now it was time for Anne to grapple with her sadness and rebuild her life. One must have the courage to stay open and keep trying, she said, using nature and one's family as means of renewal. She felt fortunate she had children and a large family who cared for her.[25]

The children, too, had to reconcile themselves to their father's death. Reeve felt as if "half the world was gone." Even as her mother moved toward the center of her life, the "airless hollow" of her father's absence set the family adrift. While her mother loved and understood her, Reeve wrote, her father had seemed to hold and protect her. Without his lectures and frequent letters, like newsworthy bulletins yelled through a megaphone, the family felt fragmented and disconnected.[26]

Anne would rarely return to Maui alone. She felt the swift passage of time and was determined to define the pattern of her years. She chose to live instead in the comfort of her nest in Darien, surrounded by her birds. She visited her children and grandchildren in France, Vermont, Washington, and Montana, settled the affairs of Charles's estate, and dedicated herself to the editing of her diaries and letters and Charles's *Autobiography of Values.*[27] With the unflagging help of Helen Wolff, Anne published her third volume of diaries and letters, *The Flower and the Nettle,* in 1976 and the fourth volume, *War Within, War Without,* in 1980.

Her diaries and letters show us a nineteenth-century female mind grasping for consciousness amid the strictures of Victorian virtue. Magnificent testimony to her capacity to present scene, character, and dialogue, they are the "great American novel" Anne never wrote. In the end, the only protagonist worthy of her gifts was herself. While her diaries provide us with a window into the beginnings of twentieth-century feminist thought, they leave the image of her husband's heroism untouched. In the end, as in the beginning, Anne loved Charles passionately, and, though willing to forgive his frailties, she could not bear to portray him as he was. If meeting Charles was Anne's moment of rebirth, exposing him would be akin to suicide.

When Charles died, so did Anne's courage to write. Without his "rational" mind and his commanding presence, there was nothing for her to push against. She would record her experience in the quiet of her diary as if it were a daily offering to God, but she would never write another book.

Coda

Anne, 1979.
(Minnesota Historical Society)

BARE TREE[1]

Already I have shed the leaves of youth,
Stripped by the wind of time down to the truth
Of winter branches. Linear and alone
I stand, a lens for lives beyond my own,
A frame through which another's fire may glow,
A harp on which another's passion, blow . . .
Blow through me, Life, pared down at last to bone,
So fragile and so fearless have I grown!

—ANNE MORROW LINDBERGH

AUGUST 1989, SWITZERLAND

The train hugs the bank of Lake Geneva, wide and crystalline under the majesty of sky and mountains. Town after town punctuates the lake with stucco houses, clotheslines, and boats turned upside down in the morning sun. But the town of Vevey has been less than the enclave the Lindberghs anticipated. Once a village tucked into a valley, Vevey is a city in transition. Garishly colored high-rise department stores are neighbors to nineteenth-century cafés. Motorcycles and buses, cranes and bulldozers, disturb the tree-lined quiet of the village green. Only the mountains remain true to themselves.

The road cuts broadly up the hill, crisscrossing the lush vineyards and rolling farmlands. The cows graze in the pastures while the lake blurs through the mist. Like so many places where the Lindberghs have lived—Illiec, Maui, Martha's Vineyard, even Scott's Cove—the grandeur of the open sky dominates. Riding along the mountainside is like moving in a low-flying plane.

It has been two years since my first visit to Anne at her chalet. Her frail, bent body and angular face, with its wide-set brow, are fixed in my mind. I can describe the 1960s cut and color of the clothes she will be wearing, the cadence of her greeting, and the birdlike feel of her hand. I know that she will probably have coffee yogurt with her soup for lunch, tea with her afternoon croissant, and that any mention of the kidnapping will turn her face to stone.

The kidnapping occurred sixty years ago, yet Anne Morrow Lindbergh still has the manner of a violated woman. The murder of her infant son has become the recurring psychodrama that dominates her life. She still feels as though something will be taken from her; something innocent will be stolen and destroyed without her knowledge or consent. She is no longer wife or caretaker-mother; her fears have become insidious and symbolic. Her only legacy is her words, the feelings and thoughts that are testimony to her past. At eighty-two, she still plays the "victim," like the beautiful and chaste Unicorn of her poetry. Imprisoned by the sins of others, Anne finds strength in her martyrdom, hiding behind a mask of weakness and self-deprecation. When Charles was alive, this role sufficed, calling forth his paternal, protective instincts. But his death has cast her in a dual role: victim and guardian of their past. "Anne is the only citadel to their history," says one of her friends.[2] But, in truth, she doesn't guard it well. She is too humble and gentle to be a guard.

I walk the narrow stone steps to the house, welcomed only by the bark of Anne's Scottish terrier. Anne, aloof, greets me politely. Antennae up, she pauses for a moment. "You are early," she says, eyebrows raised above her blue-tinted glasses.

Her body seems swathed in darkness. Her shoulders bend inward as she draws her blue sweater around her. She raises her hand to her collar as she speaks, fingering its button as if it were a key in a lock.

She seems distressed, like an actress who has missed her cues. She apologizes for her hair and lack of lipstick and then goes into the next room to look at her clock.

"My clock stopped," she says, obviously embarrassed.

Anne has aged since our last visit. Her walk is tentative and slow. She is bent, dry as a fallen twig, now and then holding on to furniture as she walks.

"Old age," she says with an ironic smile, "isn't for sissies."

I have been told that she is impatient with herself, frustrated by her loss of memory and waning ability to care for herself. And yet she takes pride in her modest self-sufficiency, choosing to prepare our lunch of soup and salad. She putters around the kitchen, fumbling with the pot cover, forgetting the tea, not sure whether she should toast the bread.

"I'm not at all mechanical," she says apologetically. But mechanics, I realize, is not the problem. It is my presence—my unending questions, my unfathomed intent—that unnerves her. Our lunch is eaten among a medley of ideas, tossed between two women separated by a generation of attitudes and experience, yet bound by a kinship neither could explain.

As a biographer, I have dared to lift her mask, seeking her true self. I have come to know Anne not intimately but in ways she herself cannot or does not want to. I can see patterns, continuums, and curves of growth. I can correct her on dates and paint stories around her memories.

At times she delights in my knowledge, sinking into thought as we explore the origins of her ideas. But more often, my presence seems to threaten her. I am an intruder, a potential "thief" who may violate the integrity of her words. Recording her words on my high-tech machine, I am one more reminder that it is time to pass on. The idea of biography pains and burdens her. She is too enlightened to deny its necessity, but she is too tired to embrace its challenge. My presence reminds her of people long gone and things she might have done.

I must be like a voice from a distant past. Some people say Anne has lost touch with herself now. The passionate and prolific days of Anne Morrow Lindbergh—flyer, writer, and mother—have an air of unreality, like a story that she once read but can no longer remember, says a daughter. She has been known to recite words from her books and to forget that she is their author. She says she "can no longer think of myself as a woman." She is drawing closer, she says, to what Indian law calls "the great mysterious," to that pool of life to which children belong. The past no longer interests her, she says with a sweep of her hand. It is living in the present, enjoying each day "like a child," that gives her life meaning.

"There is a certain lack of responsibility in being old," she says. "I've made a lot of mistakes. I've done what I could. I have tried, and I think life is a journey toward insight, and that is all I can hope for."

But like the sudden conversions of the protagonists in her novels, Anne's words seem more wistful than true. Not even her work is a source of pride, says one friend. She is apologetic, as though her writing has no value. She acknowledges her work as if she wrote because she couldn't do anything else.

She still regrets that she did not write an actual work of fiction. It would have "let me be a little freer." Now she writes only in her diary, but she thinks of writing about widowhood. Publicly, she has compared it to adolescence, a stage in life when one finds one's true center alone. But widowhood is a quiet distillation. It is a relief, she says, a time of shedding excess baggage, possessions, ambitions, vanities, and duties. Stripped of the delusion of one's "specialness," one is more capable of understanding and of compassion. Privately, she acknowledges the loneliness and the pain; it takes so much to retain one's vigor and openness. The support of her children carries her along.

The dog starts barking. He is a gray, unkempt terrier, uninhibited, demanding, possessive, and insistent. "Okay, okay," she says with sweet annoyance, as one would talk to a young child. "You want to go out?" His presence gives her purpose and a sense of intimacy otherwise lost. She lets the dog out the door, and within minutes he is around the verandah, barking and clawing at the screen door.

"This dog is like a husband," she says with a laugh. "There are good things about living alone. Nothing to push against. You can take walks whenever you want, do what you want. And yet"—the twist of logic is one only the long-married can know—"at night, under the stars, I feel closest to Charles."

Suddenly, as if remembering something important, she gets up and goes to her bedroom. I hear her rummaging through papers. She appears with a postcard in her hand and slaps it down in front of me. It is a picture of the statues of men of the Reformation—Calvin and his followers—in the park in Geneva. They are stern, Bible-carrying figures. It is as though she has freed a long-buried feeling. For the moment, her sadness is gone. "Look at these people. They are so grim. This," she says in anger, "this is my heritage . . . There is nothing beautiful about the Presbyterian Church. There is so much emphasis on sin and self-control."

Obviously tired, she excuses herself and offers to drive me to the station at Vevey. As we leave, she pauses and points to the mantelpiece. "Do you see?" she says proudly. "I've arranged the flowers you brought me."

I admire her handiwork, remembering the words of her contemptuous critics. "It's the only art I have," she says, her eyes sad and haunted.

All her life Anne wanted to be a saint—a selfless, disembodied, servant of God. But her standard of sainthood taught her the wrong lessons. She felt tainted and corrupt, as though being human were not enough. Her biggest fear was that she was Bette Davis in disguise—a castrating selfish woman parading as a Quaker maid. But if she dueled like Davis in her dreams, her "sins" had the touch of passivity. Yes, Anne must be held accountable for the stances she didn't take and the words she didn't say, but she spent her whole life begging God for forgiveness and never made peace with herself.

But those of us who follow have a lens to her life beyond her own. Every day she dove down into the blackest gorges and every day she soared out again. Flying blind through the pain, the guilt, and the fear, she climbed like an eagle over the highest mountains. Her diaries, essays, novels, and poems were relentless acts of heroism in search of the "truth." They are her moral journey into enlightenment and her long-sought vehicle of grace and salvation.

Had she only written *Gift from the Sea,* it would have been enough.

Finally, she had found the courage to stand apart and to speak her mind according to her vision. At a time when women were constrained by social mores, Anne broke through to something real, giving millions of women a deeper understanding of their commitment as wives and mothers and the courage to live independent and creative lives.

In January 1991, Anne suffered a stroke. She is no longer able to live alone or to travel long distances from her Connecticut home, so her children built a replica of her Vevey chalet in the foothills of northern Vermont. There she lives part-time with her daughter Reeve. Anne Jr. died in 1993 at the age of fifty-three from melanoma, but she is visited by Jon, Land, and Scott, and by her grandchildren and great-grandchildren. She seems to move in and out of consciousness, sometimes lucid and sometimes removed. At first she was overtaken by anger—involuntary surges of rage. Ironically, her stroke had set her free from a life lived in homage to self-control.

Now she sits alone and quiet, content with her thoughts and her solitude, as if "pushing herself into the mind of an angel."[3] While she remembers little of the past, and the present moves in a diaphanous blur, sometimes, as if for no reason, she recites Rilke's poems. Perhaps Anne confirms what she has always known:

> . . . *The living are wrong to believe*
> *in the too-sharp distinctions which they themselves have created.*
> *Angels (they say) don't know whether it is the living*
> *they are moving among or the dead. The eternal torrent*
> *whirls all ages along in it, through both realms,*
> *forever, and their voices are drowned in its thunderous roar.*

— RAINER MARIA RILKE,
   Duino Elegies

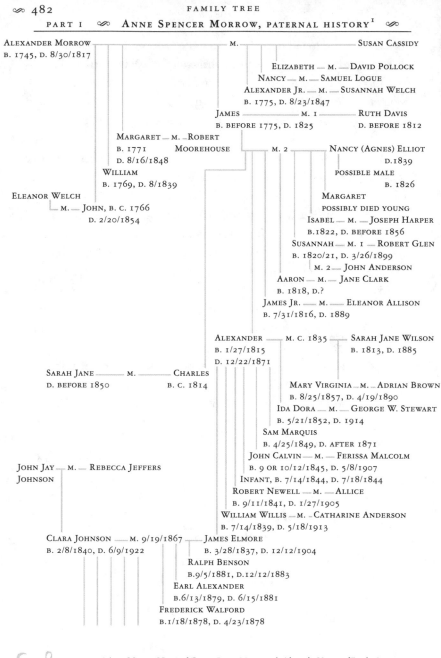

[1] Anne Morrow Nees and George Lester Morrow, ed. *Alexander Morrow of Brooke County,*
(W) Virginia and His Descendants, Including Morehead and Allied Lines, Baltimore:
Gateway Press, Inc. 1993.

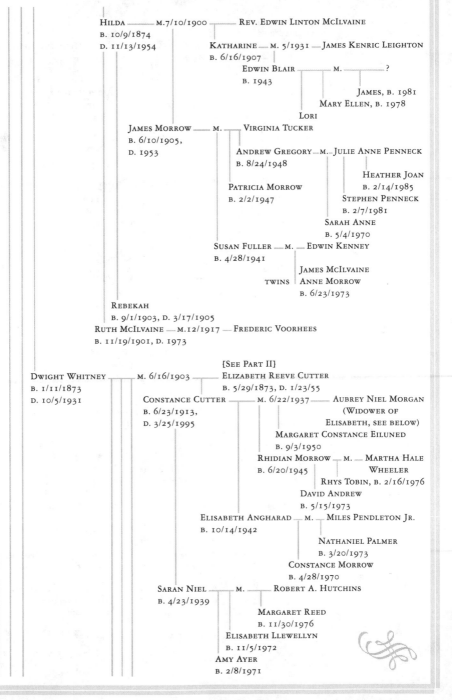

Hilda ———— M.7/10/1900 ———— Rev. Edwin Linton McIlvaine
B. 10/9/1874
D. 11/13/1954

Katharine — M. 5/1931 — James Kenric Leighton
B. 6/16/1907

Edwin Blair ———— M. ———— ?
B. 1943

James, b. 1981
Mary Ellen, b. 1978

Lori

James Morrow ———— M. ——— Virginia Tucker
B. 6/10/1905,
D. 1953

Andrew Gregory — M. Julie Anne Penneck
B. 8/24/1948

Heather Joan
B. 2/14/1985

Patricia Morrow
B. 2/2/1947

Stephen Penneck
B. 2/7/1981

Sarah Anne
B. 5/4/1970

Susan Fuller — M. — Edwin Kenney
B. 4/28/1941

James McIlvaine
twins │ Anne Morrow
B. 6/23/1973

Rebekah
B. 9/1/1903, D. 3/17/1905

Ruth McIlvaine — M.12/1917 — Frederic Voorhees
B. 11/19/1901, D. 1973

[See Part II]

Dwight Whitney ———— M. 6/16/1903 ———— Elizabeth Reeve Cutter
B. 1/11/1873   B. 5/29/1873, D. 1/23/55
D. 10/5/1931

Constance Cutter ——— M. 6/22/1937 — Aubrey Niel Morgan
B. 6/23/1913,   (Widower of
D. 3/25/1995   Elisabeth, see below)

Margaret Constance Eiluned
B. 9/3/1950

Rhidian Morrow — M. — Martha Hale
B. 6/20/1945   Wheeler

Rhys Tobin, b. 2/16/1976

David Andrew
B. 5/15/1973

Elisabeth Angharad — M. — Miles Pendleton Jr.
B. 10/14/1942

Nathaniel Palmer
B. 3/20/1973

Constance Morrow
B. 4/28/1970

Saran Niel ——— M. ——— Robert A. Hutchins
B. 4/23/1939

Margaret Reed
B. 11/30/1976

Elisabeth Llewellyn
B. 11/5/1972

Amy Ayer
B. 2/8/1971

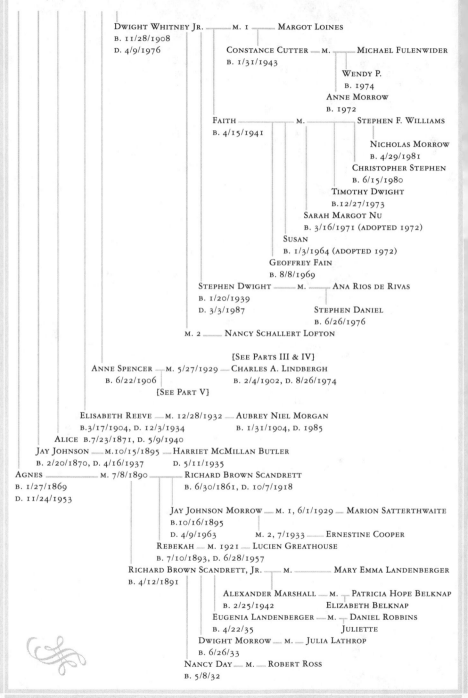

DWIGHT WHITNEY JR. ——— M. 1 ——— MARGOT LOINES
B. 11/28/1908
D. 4/9/1976

CONSTANCE CUTTER — M. ——— MICHAEL FULENWIDER
B. 1/31/1943

WENDY P.
B. 1974
ANNE MORROW
B. 1972

FAITH ——————— M. ——————— STEPHEN F. WILLIAMS
B. 4/15/1941

NICHOLAS MORROW
B. 4/29/1981
CHRISTOPHER STEPHEN
B. 6/15/1980
TIMOTHY DWIGHT
B.12/27/1973
SARAH MARGOT NU
B. 3/16/1971 (ADOPTED 1972)
SUSAN
B. 1/3/1964 (ADOPTED 1972)
GEOFFREY FAIN
B. 8/8/1969

STEPHEN DWIGHT ——— M. ——— ANA RIOS DE RIVAS
B. 1/20/1939
D. 3/3/1987
STEPHEN DANIEL
B. 6/26/1976

M. 2 ——— NANCY SCHALLERT LOFTON

[SEE PARTS III & IV]
ANNE SPENCER — M. 5/27/1929 — CHARLES A. LINDBERGH
B. 6/22/1906   B. 2/4/1902, D. 8/26/1974
[SEE PART V]

ELISABETH REEVE — M. 12/28/1932 — AUBREY NIEL MORGAN
B.3/17/1904, D. 12/3/1934 B. 1/31/1904, D. 1985
ALICE B.7/23/1871, D. 5/9/1940
JAY JOHNSON —— M.10/15/1895 — HARRIET MCMILLAN BUTLER
B. 2/20/1870, D. 4/16/1937 D. 5/11/1935
AGNES ——————— M. 7/8/1890 ——— RICHARD BROWN SCANDRETT
B. 1/27/1869   B. 6/30/1861, D. 10/7/1918
D. 11/24/1953

JAY JOHNSON MORROW — M. 1, 6/1/1929 — MARION SATTERTHWAITE
B.10/16/1895
D. 4/9/1963 M. 2, 7/1933 —— ERNESTINE COOPER
REBEKAH — M. 1921 — LUCIEN GREATHOUSE
B. 7/10/1893, D. 6/28/1957
RICHARD BROWN SCANDRETT, JR. ——— M. ——— MARY EMMA LANDENBERGER
B. 4/12/1891

ALEXANDER MARSHALL — M. — PATRICIA HOPE BELKNAP
B. 2/25/1942 ELIZABETH BELKNAP
EUGENIA LANDENBERGER — M. — DANIEL ROBBINS
B. 4/22/35   JULIETTE
DWIGHT MORROW — M. — JULIA LATHROP
B. 6/26/33
NANCY DAY — M. — ROBERT ROSS
B. 5/8/32

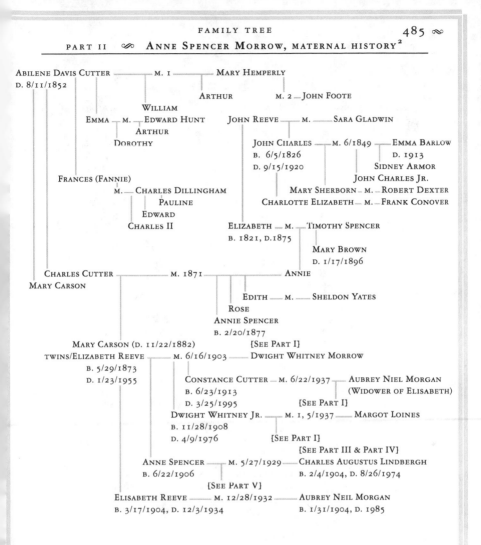

ABILENE DAVIS CUTTER ———— M. I ———— MARY HEMPERLY
D. 8/11/1852

ARTHUR   M. 2 — JOHN FOOTE

WILLIAM

EMMA — M. — EDWARD HUNT   JOHN REEVE ——— M. ——— SARA GLADWIN
ARTHUR

DOROTHY   JOHN CHARLES —— M. 6/1849 ——— EMMA BARLOW
B. 6/5/1826   D. 1913
D. 9/15/1920   SIDNEY ARMOR
JOHN CHARLES JR.

FRANCES (FANNIE)
M. — CHARLES DILLINGHAM   MARY SHERBORN — M. — ROBERT DEXTER
PAULINE   CHARLOTTE ELIZABETH — M. — FRANK CONOVER
EDWARD

CHARLES II   ELIZABETH — M. — TIMOTHY SPENCER
B. 1821, D.1875

MARY BROWN
D. 1/17/1896

CHARLES CUTTER ———— M. 1871 ———— ANNIE
MARY CARSON

EDITH — M. ——— SHELDON YATES
ROSE

ANNIE SPENCER
B. 2/20/1877
[SEE PART I]

MARY CARSON (D. 11/22/1882)
twins/ELIZABETH REEVE —— M. 6/16/1903 ——— DWIGHT WHITNEY MORROW
B. 5/29/1873
D. 1/23/1955   CONSTANCE CUTTER — M. 6/22/1937 ——— AUBREY NIEL MORGAN
B. 6/23/1913   (WIDOWER OF ELISABETH)
D. 3/25/1995   [SEE PART I]

DWIGHT WHITNEY JR. —— M. 1, 5/1937 ——— MARGOT LOINES
B. 11/28/1908
D. 4/9/1976   [SEE PART I]
[SEE PART III & PART IV]

ANNE SPENCER —— M. 5/27/1929 ——— CHARLES AUGUSTUS LINDBERGH
B. 6/22/1906   B. 2/4/1904, D. 8/26/1974
[SEE PART V]

ELISABETH REEVE ——— M. 12/28/1932 ——— AUBREY NEIL MORGAN
B. 3/17/1904, D. 12/3/1934   B. 1/31/1904, D. 1985

---

[2] Constance Morrow Morgan, *A Distant Moment: The Youth, Education & Courtship of Elizabeth Cutter Morrow*, Northampton, Massachusetts: Smith College, 1977; and Charlotte Reeve Conover, ed., *Dr. J. C. Reeve, M.D., LL.D., 1826–1920*, Dayton, Ohio: privately printer, October 1921, pp. 10-12, Sophia Smith Collection, Smith College Library.

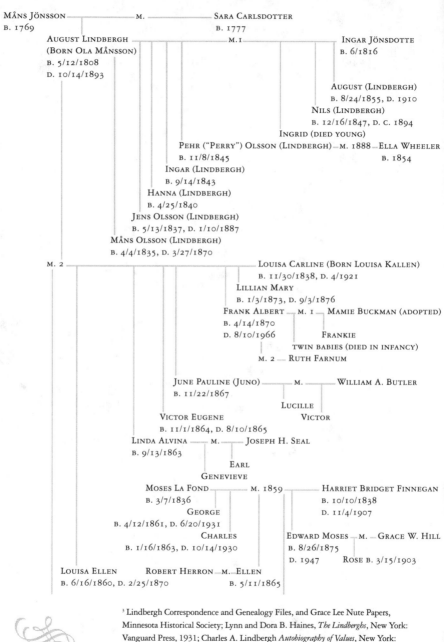

MÅNS JÖNSSON ——————— M. ——————— SARA CARLSDOTTER
B. 1769   B. 1777

AUGUST LINDBERGH ————————————— M. 1 ——————————— INGAR JÖNSDOTTE
(BORN OLA MÅNSSON)   B. 6/1816
B. 5/12/1808
D. 10/14/1893

                                    AUGUST (LINDBERGH)
                                    B. 8/24/1855, D. 1910
                                NILS (LINDBERGH)
                                B. 12/16/1847, D. C. 1894
                          INGRID (DIED YOUNG)
        PEHR ("PERRY") OLSSON (LINDBERGH) — M. 1888 — ELLA WHEELER
        B. 11/8/1845   B. 1854
      INGAR (LINDBERGH)
      B. 9/14/1843
    HANNA (LINDBERGH)
    B. 4/25/1840
  JENS OLSSON (LINDBERGH)
  B. 5/13/1837, D. 1/10/1887
MÅNS OLSSON (LINDBERGH)
B. 4/4/1835, D. 3/27/1870

M. 2 ——————————————————— LOUISA CARLINE (BORN LOUISA KALLEN)
                                  B. 11/30/1838, D. 4/1921
                            LILLIAN MARY
                            B. 1/3/1873, D. 9/3/1876
                      FRANK ALBERT — M. 1 — MAMIE BUCKMAN (ADOPTED)
                      B. 4/14/1870
                      D. 8/10/1966   FRANKIE
                                  TWIN BABIES (DIED IN INFANCY)
                            M. 2 — RUTH FARNUM

              JUNE PAULINE (JUNO) ———— M. ———— WILLIAM A. BUTLER
              B. 11/22/1867
                                          LUCILLE
          VICTOR EUGENE   VICTOR
          B. 11/1/1864, D. 8/10/1865
      LINDA ALVINA —— M. —— JOSEPH H. SEAL
      B. 9/13/1863
                  EARL
              GENEVIEVE
      MOSES LA FOND ————— M. 1859 ————— HARRIET BRIDGET FINNEGAN
      B. 3/7/1836   B. 10/10/1838
            GEORGE   D. 11/4/1907
      B. 4/12/1861, D. 6/20/1931
                  CHARLES   EDWARD MOSES — M. — GRACE W. HILL
            B. 1/16/1863, D. 10/14/1930   B. 8/26/1875
                                          D. 1947   ROSE B. 3/15/1903

  LOUISA ELLEN   ROBERT HERRON — M. — ELLEN
  B. 6/16/1860, D. 2/25/1870   B. 5/11/1865

[3] Lindbergh Correspondence and Genealogy Files, and Grace Lee Nute Papers,
Minnesota Historical Society; Lynn and Dora B. Haines, *The Lindberghs*, New York:
Vanguard Press, 1931; Charles A. Lindbergh *Autobiography of Values*, New York:
Harcourt Brace Jovanovich, 1976, pp. 404–5.

CHARLES AUGUST LINDBERGH ———————— M. 1, 4/4/1887 ———— MARY LA FOND
B. 1/20/1859, D. 5/24/1924   B. 5/1/1867, D. 4/16/1898

                                    EDITH (DIED AT AGE 10 OR 12)
                            LILLIAN — M. — LOREN ROBERTS
                            B. 1888
                            D. 1916   LOUISE, B. C. 1912
                            EVANGELINE ("EVA") ———— M. 1 ———— GEORGE WEST CHRISTIE
                            B. 9/12/1892   B. 1890, D. 7/1956
                            D. 1985   GEORGE WEST JR.
                                            LILLIAN L. — M. — EDMUND E. JOHNSON

                            M. 2 — GEORGE HOWARD SPAETH

                    [SEE PART IV]
M. 2, 3/27/1901 ———— EVANGELINE LODGE LAND
                    B. 1875, D. 9/7/1954

                                            [SEE PARTS I & II]
CHARLES AUGUSTUS LINDBERGH ———— M. 5/27/1929 ———— ANNE SPENCER MORROW
B. 2/4/1902, D. 8/26/1974   B. 6/22/1906
                                            REEVE MORROW
                                        SCOTT MORROW
                                    ANNE SPENCER
                                LAND MORROW   [SEE PART V]
                            JON MORROW
                        CHARLES AUGUSTUS JR.

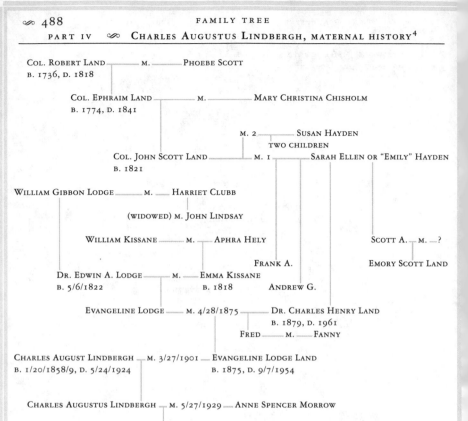

COL. ROBERT LAND ———— M. ———— PHOEBE SCOTT
B. 1736, D. 1818

        COL. EPHRAIM LAND ———— M. ———— MARY CHRISTINA CHISHOLM
        B. 1774, D. 1841

                M. 2 ———— SUSAN HAYDEN
                      TWO CHILDREN

           COL. JOHN SCOTT LAND ———— M. 1 ———— SARAH ELLEN OR "EMILY" HAYDEN
           B. 1821

WILLIAM GIBBON LODGE ———— M. ———— HARRIET CLUBB

        (WIDOWED) M. JOHN LINDSAY

           WILLIAM KISSANE ———— M. ———— APHRA HELY   SCOTT A. — M. —?

                           FRANK A.   EMORY SCOTT LAND

DR. EDWIN A. LODGE ———— M. ———— EMMA KISSANE
B. 5/6/1822   B. 1818   ANDREW G.

        EVANGELINE LODGE ——— M. 4/28/1875 ——— DR. CHARLES HENRY LAND
                             B. 1879, D. 1961
                    FRED ——— M. ——— FANNY

CHARLES AUGUST LINDBERGH — M. 3/27/1901 — EVANGELINE LODGE LAND
B. 1/20/1858/9, D. 5/24/1924   B. 1875, D. 9/7/1954

    CHARLES AUGUSTUS LINDBERGH — M. 5/27/1929 — ANNE SPENCER MORROW

              [SEE PART V]

[4] Charles A. Lindbergh, *Autobiography of Values*, New York: Harcourt Brace
Jovanovich, 1977, p. 405; Lindbergh Papers, Evangeline Lodge Land
"Notebook for Charles" Minnesota Historical Society.

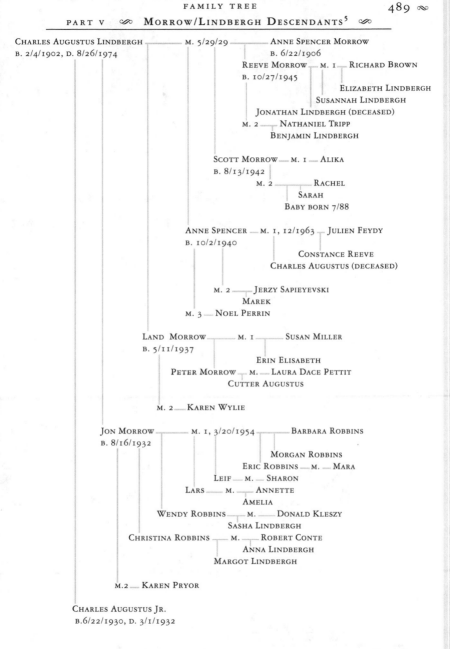

CHARLES AUGUSTUS LINDBERGH —— M. 5/29/29 —— ANNE SPENCER MORROW
B. 2/4/1902, D. 8/26/1974   B. 6/22/1906

REEVE MORROW —— M. 1 —— RICHARD BROWN
B. 10/27/1945

ELIZABETH LINDBERGH
SUSANNAH LINDBERGH
JONATHAN LINDBERGH (DECEASED)
M. 2 —— NATHANIEL TRIPP
BENJAMIN LINDBERGH

SCOTT MORROW —— M. 1 —— ALIKA
B. 8/13/1942
M. 2 —— RACHEL
SARAH
BABY BORN 7/88

ANNE SPENCER —— M. 1, 12/1963 —— JULIEN FEYDY
B. 10/2/1940

CONSTANCE REEVE
CHARLES AUGUSTUS (DECEASED)

M. 2 —— JERZY SAPIEYEVSKI
MAREK
M. 3 —— NOEL PERRIN

LAND MORROW —— M. 1 —— SUSAN MILLER
B. 5/11/1937

ERIN ELISABETH
PETER MORROW —— M. —— LAURA DACE PETTIT
CUTTER AUGUSTUS

M. 2 —— KAREN WYLIE

JON MORROW —— M. 1, 3/20/1954 —— BARBARA ROBBINS
B. 8/16/1932

MORGAN ROBBINS
ERIC ROBBINS —— M. —— MARA
LEIF —— M. —— SHARON
LARS —— M. —— ANNETTE
AMELIA
WENDY ROBBINS —— M. —— DONALD KLESZY
SASHA LINDBERGH
CHRISTINA ROBBINS —— M. —— ROBERT CONTE
ANNA LINDBERGH
MARGOT LINDBERGH

M.2 —— KAREN PRYOR

CHARLES AUGUSTUS JR.
B.6/22/1930, D. 3/1/1932

[5] The Lindbergh Foundation; Anne Morrow Nees and
George Lester Morrow, ed., op. cit.

Notes

ABBREVIATIONS:

AML: Anne Morrow Lindbergh
CAL: Charles A. Lindbergh
DWM: Dwight W. Morrow
ECM: Elizabeth C. Morrow
ERM: Elisabeth R. Morrow
CCM: Constance C. Morrow
ELLL: Evangeline Lodge Land Lindbergh
BMAU: AML, *Bring Me a Unicorn, Diaries and Letters, 1922–1928,* New York: Harcourt Brace Jovanovich, Inc., 1971.
HGHL: AML, *Hour of Gold, Hour of Lead, Diaries and Letters, 1929–1932,* New York: Harcourt Brace Jovanovich, Inc., 1973.
LROD: AML, *Locked Rooms and Open Doors, Diaries and Letters, 1933–1935,* New York: Harcourt Brace Jovanovich, 1974.
F&N: AML, *The Flower and the Nettle, Diaries and Letters, 1936–1939,* New York: Harcourt Brace Jovanovich, 1976.
WW&W: AML, *War Within and Without, Diaries and Letters, 1939–1944,* New York: Harcourt Brace Jovanovich, 1980.
NYT: New York Times
NJSPM: New Jersey State Police Museum and Learning Center Archives
All interviews not otherwise attributed were conducted by the author.

I. A NEW BEGINNING
∞

1 Details of Lindbergh's landing in Mexico are from excerpts of Elizabeth Cutter Morrow's diaries in the Dwight Morrow Papers, Amherst College Archives; *The Literary Digest*, 12/27/27 "Lindbergh's 'Embassy of Good-Will' to Mexico."

2 Description and biographical information of Morrow throughout this chapter are based on newsreels; interviews by Edwin G. Lowry, the biographer of Morrow initially commissioned by Betty Morrow; on Harold Nicolson, *Dwight Morrow*, New York: Harcourt Brace, 1935; on Ron Chernow, *The House of Morgan*, New York: Atlantic Monthly Press, 1990, pp. 287–301; and on the Dwight Morrow Papers in the Amherst College Archives.

3 Drawn from Ronald Steel, *Walter Lippmann and the American Century*, New York: Vintage Books, 1980; and Ron Chernow, op. cit.

4 The Campbellite Church, founded to bring unity and fundamentalist integrity to the Presbyterian Church, had become a sect that championed conservative adherence to New Testament values and straight-laced Christian virtue.

5 Dwight Morrow, "Two New Years," *Amherst Literary Monthly, 1892–93*, Amherst College Archives.

6 See correspondence of Dwight W. Morrow and Charles T. Burnett, 1895–1903, Charles T. Burnett Papers, Bowdoin College Archives.

7 Charles Lindbergh, *Autobiography of Values*, New York: Harcourt Brace Jovanovich, Inc., 1976.

8 The roof of the White House was being repaired. The temporary residence of the President was 15 Dupont Circle; from *The Saturday Evening Post*, "The Queen and Lindy," by Irwin H. Hoover, edited by Wesley Stout, 8/11/34, vol. 207, pp. 10–11.

9 Reflecting the movement away from identifying oneself in the context of patrimonial lineage, Ola Månsson's sons had changed their surname to Lindbergh, a contraction of the Swedish words for linden tree and mountain. Månsson adopted that name.

10 Details of the Månsson-Lindbergh ancestry and C.A.'s childhood and career are from the Lindbergh Family Papers, including a notebook by Evangeline Lodge Land Lindbergh that constitutes a memoir of family life until the time of CAL's flight, marked "For Charles A. Lindbergh Jr.," and the Lynn and Dora B. Haines papers and Dr. Grace Lee Nute's correspondence with Charles Lindbergh, all among the holdings of the Minnesota Historical Society. Additional information from Kenneth S. Davis, *The Hero: Charles A. Lindbergh and the American Dream*, Garden City, New York: Doubleday, 1959; Lynn and Dora B. Haines, *The Lindberghs*, New York: Vanguard Press, 1931; Ruth L. Larson, *The Lindberghs of Minnesota: A Political Biography*, New York: Harcourt Brace Jovanovich, 1971; and Brendan Gill, *Lindbergh Alone*, New York: Harcourt Brace Jovanovich, 1977.

¹¹ Haines and Nute papers, Minnesota Historical Society.

¹² Paul Tillich, *The History of Christian Thought,* New York: Simon and Schuster, 1967, pp.242–275.

¹³ Evangeline Lodge Land Lindbergh, Notebook "For Charles A. Lindbergh, Jr.," Minnesota Historical Society.

¹⁴ Information about Evangeline Lindbergh's mental state is from interviews recorded by Alden Whitman, *NYT,* and Charles Stone of the Lindbergh Museum in Little Falls, Minn. See Phyllis Chesler, *Women and Madness,* New York: Doubleday, 1972; Elaine Showalter, *The Female Malady: Women, Madness and English Culture, 1830–1980,* New York, Penguin, 1985; V. Skultans, *Madness and Morals: Ideas on Sanity in the Nineteenth Century,* London: Routledge Kegan Paul, 1975; and Theodore Lidz and Stephen Fleck, *Schizophrenia in the Family,* New York: International Universities Press, 1985.

¹⁵ In defense of her sanity, it must be noted that Evangeline earned a master's degree in education from Columbia University Teacher's College after her separation from C.A. and went on to teach high school chemistry for 35 years, in both Wisconsin and Detroit, until she retired shortly before her death, in 1954.

¹⁶ Lynn and Dora B. Haines, op. cit.

¹⁷ Evangeline Lodge Land Lindbergh, Notebook "For Charles A. Lindbergh, Jr."; Charles A. Lindbergh, *Boyhood on the Upper Mississippi,* St. Paul: Minnesota Historical Society, 1972; interview with AML.

¹⁸ At the turn of the century, divorce was becoming a frequent option for American women. Until then, it had been considered a byproduct of "moral turpitude and depravity." As more women gained employment, they became less dependent on their husbands, and marriage as a financial arrangement became less attractive. Moreover, between 1869 and 1887, thirty-three states and the District of Columbia gave women control over their property and earnings. This brought about higher expectations and a lower tolerance for unacceptable behavior and conditions. Through the judicial system, these attitudes changed the interpretation of "physical cruelty," the grounds for divorce. American marriages began failing at an unprecedented rate. Between 1867 and 1929, the population of the United States grew by 300 percent, the number of marriages increased by 400 percent, and the divorce rate rose by 2000 percent. The United States had the highest divorce rate in the world. From Elaine Tyler May, *Great Expectations: Marriage and Divorce in Post-Victorian America,* Chicago: University of Chicago Press, 1980, p. 2.

¹⁹ L. Laszlow Schwartz, D.D.S., "The Life of Charles Henry Land (1847–1922)" *Journal of the American College of Dentists,* March 1955, vol. 24, issue 1, pp. 33–51.

²⁰ CAL, *The Spirit of St. Louis,* New York: Charles Scribner's Sons, 1953.

²¹ Interview with AML.

²² CAL, *The Spirit of St. Louis.*

²³ Ibid.

[24] Details of CAL's aviation career are from *The Spirit of St. Louis;* Perry Luckett, *Charles Lindbergh: A Bio-Bibliography,* Westport, Connecticut: Greenwood Press, Inc., 1986; and Kenneth Davis, *The Hero,* New York: Doubleday, 1959.

[25] Irwin H. Hoover, "The Queen and Lindy," ed. by Wesley Stout, *The Saturday Evening Post,* 8/11/34, vol. 207, pp. 10–11.

[26] Dwight W. Morrow to Charles A. Lindbergh, 10/4/27, Dwight W. Morrow Papers (Series 1, box 31, Folder 47), Archives and Special Collections, Amherst College Library.

[27] Biographical information about Betty Morrow is based on Elizabeth Cutter Morrow Diaries, Dwight Morrow Papers, Amherst College Archives; Morrow Family Papers, Sophia Smith Collection, Smith College Library; Constance Morrow Morgan, *A Distant Moment: The Youth, Education and Courtship of Elizabeth Cutter Morrow,* Northampton, Massachusetts: Smith College, 1977; *BMAU*; and interview with Constance Morrow Morgan.

[28] Interview with neighbors of the Morrows in Englewood, Joan Johnson and her mother, Mrs. David Van Alstyne, and Janet Johnson and Sue Graham, two friends of Elisabeth's in Englewood who would become teachers at the Elisabeth Morrow School.

[29] Interview with Eleanor Rodale, a friend of Anne's at Smith College.

[30] Interview with Constance Morrow Morgan and correspondence between Dwight Morrow, Sr., and Dwight Morrow, Jr., Dwight Morrow Papers, Amherst College Archives.

[31] Interview with Reeve Lindbergh Tripp.

[32] This section is based in part on Kenneth Davis, *The Hero;* CAL, *The Spirit of St. Louis;* and Lindbergh Papers at the National Archives, Washington, D.C.; excerpts from Elizabeth Cutter Morrow Diaries, Dwight Morrow Papers, Amherst College Archives; and newsreels from the National Archives Motion Picture, Sound and Video library.

[33] CAL, *The Spirit of St. Louis.*

[34] CAL, *Autobiography of Values.*

[35] Ibid.

[36] Elizabeth Cutter Morrow Diaries, Dwight Morrow Papers, Amherst College Archives.

[37] Constance Morrow's letter to Anne Morrow, Dwight Morrow Papers, Amherst College Archives.

[38] Interview with AML and interview with Constance Morrow Morgan.

[39] *BMAU,* AML letter to ECM, 10/18/27, p. 74.

[40] *BMAU,* AML diary, 12/19/27, p. 79.

[41] Ibid., pp. 78–79; Interview with AML and interview with Constance Morrow Morgan.

[42] Dwight Morrow correspondence with Elisabeth Morrow, Dwight Morrow Papers, Amherst College Archives.

[43] *BMAU,* AML diary, 8/23/26, p. 38.

[44] Ibid., 12/21/27, p. 80.

[45] Ibid., p. 81.

[46] Ibid.

[47] *BMAU,* AML letter to ECM, 3/5/27, p. 62.

[48] *BMAU,* AML diary, 12/21/27, p. 81.

[49] Ibid.

[50] Ibid.

2. COMING HOME
∾

[1] *BMAU,* AML diary, "Christmas Eve Day," pp. 87–88.

[2] Ron Robin, *Enclaves of America: The Rhetoric of American Political Architecture Abroad, 1900–1965,* New Jersey: Princeton University Press, 1992, pp. 34–35, 67–69; and "New Embassy Building at Mexico City," *The American Foreign Service Journal,* October 1925, pp. 336–337.

[3] *Excelsior* (newspaper), Mexico City, 12/15/27 through 12/28/27.

[4] Many descriptive details in this chapter are derived from period newsreels and documentary films on file at the National Archives Motion Picture Sound and Video Library.

[5] *BMAU,* AML diary, 12/21/27, p. 84.

[6] The dialogue that follows is from *BMAU,* AML diary, 12/21/27, p. 82.

[7] Ibid., p. 83.

[8] Ibid., "Mexico City," p. 80.

[9] Ibid., "Sunday, Christmas Day," p. 91.

[10] Interview with AML.

[11] Elisabeth Reeve Morrow letters to Constance Chilton, 1925–1934.

[12] Ibid.; interview with Constance Chilton.

[13] *BMAU,* AML diary, 12/21/27, p. 86.

[14] Ibid.

[15] Ibid., "Sunday, Christmas Day," pp. 90–91.

[16] Details about Evangeline Lindbergh at the time of her visit to Mexico City are from the following sources: Alden Whitman's interview with Eva Lindbergh Christie Spaeth; ELLL Notebook "For Charles A. Lindbergh, Jr.," Interviews with AML; *Excelsior,* Mexico City, 12/15/27 through 12/28/27; Elaine Showalter, op. cit.

[17] *BMAU,* AML diary, 12/21/27, p. 87.

[18] Ibid., "Sunday, Christmas Day," p. 96.

[19] Details of Anne Morrow's first flight with Charles Lindbergh are from *BMAU,* pp. 95–99.

[20] Edgar Lee Masters, *Spoon River Anthology,* as quoted in Anne's diary *Bring Me a Unicorn.*

3. THE EARLY YEARS
∽

[1] AML, *The Unicorn and Other Poems,* New York: Vintage Books, 1972, p. 79.

[2] Morrow Family Papers, Sophia Smith Collection, Smith College Library; Alfred E. Stearns, *From an Amherst Boyhood,* Norwood, MA: Plimpton Press, 1946; Helen Lefkowitz Horowitz, *Alma Mater: Design and Experience in the Women's Colleges from their Nineteenth-Century Beginnings to the 1930's,* New York: A. A. Knopf, 1984; L. Clark Seelye, *The Early History of Smith College, 1871–1910,* Boston: Houghton Mifflin Co., 1923; Constance Morrow Morgan, op. cit. Harold Nicolson, *Dwight Morrow,* New York: Harcourt Brace, 1936.

[3] Constance Morrow Morgan, *A Distant Moment,* pp. 141–143.

[4] Ronald G. Mullins, *A Little About a Few Cutters, 1637–1980,* copyright 1980; William E. Foster, *Charles Ammi Cutter: A Memorial Sketch,* Public Library, Providence, Rhode Island, reprinted from the *Library Journal,* 1903.

[5] Constance Morrow Morgan, op. cit., p. 19.

[6] Barbara Miller Solomon, *In the Company of Educated Women,* New Haven: Yale University Press, 1985, pp. 62–65.

[7] Constance Morrow Morgan, op. cit., pp. 85, 139, 142.

[8] Ibid., p. 143.

[9] Harold Nicolson, op. cit.

[10] Constance Morrow Morgan, op. cit., p. 170.

[11] Ibid., p. 172.

[12] Ibid., pp. 177–179.

[13] *The City of Englewood, A Profile,* Englewood Chamber of Commerce, Englewood, New Jersey; Jewish Community Center, number 7; the Community Chest; and interviews with Mrs. David Van Alstyne and Janet Johnson, friends of the Morrows in Englewood.

[14] Harold Nicolson, op. cit., p. 81.

[15] Morrow Family Papers, Sophia Smith Collection, Smith College Library.

[16] Interview with AML.

[17] Information about the town of Quogue is from an interview with Quogue historian Pat Shuttleworth; Richard H. Post, *Notes on Quogue 1659–1959,* published

by the Quogue Tercentenary Committee, 1959; Scrapbook, "Old Long Island Towns, May 6, 1895," Suffolk County Historical Society; *One Hundred Years Ago in Quogue,* pamphlet, Quogue Public Library.

18 Morrow Family Papers, Sophia Smith Collection, Smith College Library.

19 *The Wheel,* Chapin School.

20 Morrow Family Papers, Sophia Smith Collection, Smith College Library.

21 Harold Nicolson, op. cit., p. 110.

22 Ron Chernow, op. cit.

23 Harold Nicolson, op. cit., pp. 128–131.

24 Karen J. Blair, *The Clubwoman as Feminist: True Womanhood Redefined, 1868–1914,* New York: Holmes and Meier, 1979.

25 Interview with Constance Morrow Morgan.

26 The following material is from essays, stories, and poems by AML published in *The Wheel,* Chapin School Archives.

27 Interview with AML.

28 Richard Harris and Lynn Seldon, *Hidden Bahamas,* Berkeley, CA: Ulysses Press, 1997, pp. 41–43.

29 Interview with AML.

30 *The Wheel,* Chapin School.

31 Harold Nicolson Diaries, Harold Nicolson Papers, Indiana University Archives.

32 Morrow Family Papers, Sophia Smith Collection, Smith College Library.

33 *The Wheel,* Chapin School.

34 Interview with Eleanor Rodale.

35 *The Wheel,* Chapin School.

36 Julie Nixon Eisenhower, *Special People,* New York: Simon and Schuster, 1977, p. 127.

37 Interview with Eleanor Rodale.

38 Barbara Miller Solomon, op. cit.

39 *BMAU,* AML letter to ERM, late September, 1922, pp. 5–7.

40 Catalogue of Smith College: Fiftieth Year, 1924–25, (Smith College: Northampton, MA), 1924–1928; Annual Report of the President of Smith College: Presented to the Board of Trustees, October 16, 1925; October 16, 1926; October 21, 1927; October 19, 1928, 1925, 1926, 1927, 1928.

41 Helen Lefkowitz Horowitz, op. cit., and L. Clark Seelye, op. cit.

42 *BMAU,* AML letter to DWM, 1/9/26, p. 25.

43 *BMAU,* AML letter to ECM, 3/5/27, p. 61.

44 Ibid., 11/4/26, p. 54.

45 Interview with Marilyn Bender; Mina Kirstein Curtiss obituaries, diaries, and papers, Sophia Smith Collection, Smith College Archives.

46 Anne Morrow, "Caprice," *Smith College Monthly,* October 1926.

4. A REBEL AT LAST
∽

1 *BMAU,* AML diary, February 1928, pp. 106–107.

2 Lydiard H. Horton, "On College Disappearances: The Analysis of a Case," *New England Journal of Medicine,* December 5, 1929, vol. 201, no. 23, pp. 1155–1163.

3 *BMAU,* AML diary, February 1928, p. 106.

4 Elisabeth Reeve Morrow letters to Constance Chilton, 1925–1934.

5 *BMAU,* AML diary, January 1928, p. 103.

6 *NYT,* 1/2/28, 27:5, "Extols Lindbergh as Good-Will Envoy."

7 Ibid., 2/14/28, 2:2, "Lindbergh Flew 9060 Miles."

8 CAL, *Autobiography of Values,* p. 90.

9 *NYT,* 1/25/28, 9:3, "Plan Lindbergh Holiday."

10 Ibid., 2/9/28, "Senate Authorizes Lindbergh Medal."

11 *BMAU,* AML diary, February 1928, p. 107.

12 Dwight Morrow Papers, Amherst College Archives.

13 Dwight Morrow Papers, Amherst College Archives.

14 *BMAU,* AML diary, Feb. 1928, pp. 108–109.

15 Ibid., pp. 109–110.

16 Ibid., 3/1/28, p. 114.

17 Ibid., 3/18/28, pp. 119–120.

18 Ibid., 3/1/28, p. 115.

19 Ibid., "April—still," p. 142.

20 Elizabeth Reeve Morrow letters to Constance Chilton, 1925–1934.

21 *NYT,* 3/2/28, "Col. Lindbergh Sees Mother Honored."

22 Ibid., 3/28/28, "Letters to the Times: Letting the Colonel Rest."

23 Ibid., 3/18/28, "Army Finds Col. Lindbergh in Perfect Health; Flier Says This Answers 'Breakdown' Reports."

24 Ibid., 3/25/28, "Lindbergh Weary of the Limelight but Won't Retire."

25 Ibid., 2/14/29, "Tell of Lindbergh Shyness."

26 CAL, *Autobiography of Values,* p. 122.

27 *BMAU,* AML diary, "Boston," pp. 155–156, 159.

28 Ibid., June 1928, pp. 163–164.

29 Interview with Reeve Lindbergh Tripp.

30 Dwight Morrow Papers, Amherst College Archives.

31 *BMAU,* AML diary, 3/18/28, p. 118.

32 Ibid., 3/26/28 through 4/5/28, pp. 124–134.

33 Ibid., 4/8/28, p. 137.

34 Elisabeth Morrow letters to Connie Chilton, 1925–1934; interview with Anne McGavrin.

35 Constance Morrow Morgan, op. cit., pp. 111–113.

36 Interview with Anne McGavrin.

37 *BMAU,* AML diary, "Cuernavaca," pp. 130–134.

38 Ibid., June 1928, p. 161.

39 Ibid., "3–11:30 in Laredo," p. 136.

40 Ibid., "After a reading at Smith College," p. 140.

41 Ibid., 5/3/28, pp. 145–147.

42 Information on Dwight Morrow's career in Mexico is based on Ronald Steel, op. cit., pp. 236–244, and Ron Chernow, op. cit., pp.287–301.

43 Dwight Morrow Papers, Amherst College Archives.

44 Ronald Steel, op. cit., p. 242.

45 *NYT,* 3/31/28, "Will Rogers Suggests Morrow as Candidate."

46 *BMAU,* June 1928, pp. 160–161.

47 Morrow Family Papers, Sophia Smith Collection, Smith College Library.

48 Ibid.

49 *BMAU,* AML diary, "Boston," pp. 157–158.

50 *NYT,* 2/18/28, 6:4, and 4/2/28, 26:3.

51 *BMAU,* AML diary, 7/13/28, p. 168.

52 CAL, *Autobiography of Values,* p. 123.

53 *BMAU,* AML diary, "Englewood, Wednesday Morning," p. 175.

54 Ibid.

55 *BMAU,* AML diary, "Evening," p. 179–180.

56 Ibid., p. 180.

57 *BMAU,* AML letter to CCM, 10/12/28, p. 181.

58 Ibid., p. 183.

59 Ibid., p. 182.

60 Ibid., p. 185.

61 Ibid., p. 186.

62 *BMAU,* AML diary, "Evening," p. 180.

63 Interview with Margot Wilkie.

64 *BMAU,* AML letter to CCM, 10/12/28, p. 181.

65 Ibid., p. 203.

66 Ibid., p. 188.

67 Ibid., pp. 189–195.

68 Ibid., 11/28, pp. 213–215.

69 Ibid., p. 214.

70 Ibid.

71 Interview with AML.

72 *BMAU,* AML letters to CCM, 10/27/28, p. 207, and 11/28, p. 214.

73 *BMAU,* AML letters to ERM, 10/26/28, p. 206, and 11/28, p. 219.

74 *BMAU,* AML letter to ERM, 11/28, p. 219.

75 *BMAU,* AML letter to CCM, 11/28, p. 214.

5 . PRESENTIMENT
∞

1   AML, *The Unicorn and Other Poems,* p. 77.

2   Elizabeth Cutter Morrow Diaries, Dwight Morrow Papers, Amherst College Archives.

3   Ibid.

4   Ibid.

5   Their house in Cuernavaca was named Casa Manana.

6   *NYT,* 1/1/29, "D. W. Morrows Hosts."

7   Elisabeth Reeve Morrow letters to Connie Chilton, 1925–1934.

8   Elizabeth Cutter Morrow Diaries, Dwight Morrow Papers, Amherst College Archives.

9   AML letter to James Newton, Feb. 1942, in James Newton, *Uncommon Friends,* New York: Harcourt, Brace, Jovanovich, 1987, pp. 256–257.

10 All around Anne convention prevailed. The "new woman" of the 1920s was not like her mother's generation, restless with rebellion and social defiance. In the wake of suffrage was a sudden realization that the reins of power had not changed. Women did not vote in large numbers nor did they form the political blocs anticipated by those who had fought for suffrage. While women enrolled in universities and joined the workplace in unprecedented numbers after the war, the demographics of marriage had changed. By the end of the 1920s, the marriage rate among educated women had doubled, and the task of balancing marriage and career became an identifiable social problem. (See Nancy Woloch, *Women and the American Experience,* New York: McGraw-Hill, 1996, pp. 241–279.) In 1925, when Anne was a freshman at Smith, the college opened the Institute for the Coordination of Women's Interests, resolving to ameliorate the "intolerable choice between career and home," but the institute folded. The experts concluded that women had no choice, given the prevailing social prejudice. (See Dolores Hayden, *The Grand Domestic Revolution: A History of Feminist Designs for American Homes, Neighborhoods, and Cities,* Cambridge, Mass.: MIT Press, pp. 266–277, and C. Todd Stephenson, "Integrating the Carol Kennicotts," in *Journal of Women's History,* 1992, vol. 4, no. 1 [Spring], pp. 89–113.) Even though Anne's contemporaries at Smith were preparing for a life of professional and financial independence, most would sacrifice their careers for the security of home and family within three years after graduation. (Alumnae Association of Smith College, *Alumnae Biographical Register,* 1935, Smith College Archives, pp. 338–357.)

11 *BMAU,* AML letter to CCM, 10/26/28, p. 199.

12 Elisabeth Reeve Morrow letters to Connie Chilton, 1925–1934.

13 Ibid.

14 *NYT,* 1/31/29, "Hoover's Cabinet Viewed as Formed."

15 Endicott Peabody letter to Dwight Morrow, Dwight Morrow Papers, Amherst College Archives.

16 *NYT,* 1/30/29, "Dwight W. Morrow at Stockbridge."

17 Ibid.

18 AML letter to Jim Newton, February 1942, in James Newton, op. cit., pp. 256–257.

19 *BMAU,* AML letter to Corliss Lamont, undated, pp. 227–228.

20 *NYT,* 2/13/29, "Col. Lindbergh Betrothed to Miss Anne S. Morrow; Lands in Cuba after Delay."

21 Ibid.

22 *NYT,* 2/14/29, "Tell of Lindbergh Shyness."

23 Ibid., "Comments on Engagement."

24 *NYT* 2/13/29, "Col. Lindbergh Betrothed to Miss Anne S. Morrow; Lands in Cuba After Delay."

25 Ibid., 2/17/29, "Miss Morrow Gained Honors in College."

26 Ibid.

27 Elisabeth Reeve Morrow letters to Connie Chilton, 1925–1934.

28 *NYT,* 2/25/29, "Flies from Eagle Pass," and 2/26/29, "Have Yet to Decide on Plans."

6. THE MERMAID'S BARGAIN

∾

1 AML, *The Unicorn and Other Poems,* p. 11.

2 *HGHL,* AML letter to CAL, 2/14/29, p. 17.

3 *HGHL,* introduction, p. 6.

4 *HGHL,* AML letter to CAL, 4/18/29, p. 36.

5 Interview with AML.

6 Interview with AML.

7 Elizabeth Cutter Morrow Diaries, Dwight Morrow Papers, Amherst College Archives.

8 Elisabeth Reeve Morrow letters to Constance Chilton, 1925–1934.

9 *HGHL,* AML letter to CCM, 3/8/29, pp. 18–20.

10 Ibid., p. 20.

11 *NYT,* 2/28/29, "Lindbergh Hurt, Fiancee Safe in Crash as He Lands Broken Plane in Mexico City; Shoulder Dislocated, Makes Light of It."

12 Ibid.

13 Both Charles Augustus Lindbergh and his father, Charles August Lindbergh, were named after Charles XIV, King of Sweden. Ola Månnson renamed himself August, meaning "of majestic dignity or grandeur," and Louise designated it as their baby's middle name.

14 *NYT,* 3/1/29, "Lindbergh Takes up Fiancée Three Times Despite His Injuries."

15 Ibid., letter to the editor from Will Rogers, 2/28/29.

16 Elizabeth Cutter Morrow Diaries, Dwight Morrow Papers, Amherst College Archives.

17 Elisabeth Reeve Morrow letters to Constance Chilton, 1925–1934.

18 Elizabeth Cutter Morrow Diaries, Dwight Morrow Papers, Amherst College Archives.

19 *HGHL,* AML letter to CCM, 3/14/29, p. 23.

20 *HGHL,* AML letter to CAL, 3/15/29–3/17/29, pp. 25–28.

21 "Consolation" from the musical comedy the *Golden Dawn,* lyrics by Otto Harbach and Oscar Hammerstein; music by Emmerich Kalman and Herbert Stothart,© 1927.

22 Elisabeth Reeve Morrow letters to Constance Chilton, 1925–1934.

23 *HGHL,* AML letter to CAL, 3/29/29, p. 33.

24 Ibid., 3/27/29, p. 32.

25 Elisabeth Reeve Morrow letters to Constance Chilton, 1925–1934.

26 Ibid.

27 *HGHL,* AML letter to ECM, early May 1929, pp. 39–40.

28 *HGHL,* AML letter to CAL, 4/18/29, p. 35.

29 Elisabeth Reeve Morrow letters to Constance Chilton, 1925–1934.

30 Ibid.

31 Elizabeth Cutter Morrow Diaries, Dwight Morrow Papers, Amherst College Archives.

32 Ibid.

33 Elisabeth Reeve Morrow letters to Constance Chilton, 1925–1934.

34 Elizabeth Cutter Morrow Diaries, Dwight Morrow Papers, Amherst College Archives.

35 Ibid.

36 Morrow Family Papers, Sophia Smith Collection, Smith College Library.

37 *HGHL,* AML letter to ECM, 5/27/29, p. 41.

38 Ibid.

39 Elizabeth Cutter Morrow Diaries, Dwight Morrow Papers, Amherst College Archives.

40 *HGHL,* AML letter to ECM, 5/27/29, p. 40.

7. HONEYMOON POLITICS
∽

1 *NYT,* 5/28/29, "Colonel Lindbergh Weds Anne Morrow in Her Home; May Fly on Honeymoon."

2 Ibid.

3 Ibid.

4 Elisabeth Reeve Morrow letters to Constance Chilton, 1925–1934.

[5] *Saturday Evening Post,* 8/3/29, "Lindbergh and the Press," by Julian S. Mason.

[6] *New Republic,* 6/22/29, "The High Cost of Fame."

[7] *HGHL,* AML letter to ECM, 5/31/29, p. 42.

[8] Ibid., pp. 43–44.

[9] Interview with Kaetchen Smith Coley, 5/25/85.

[10] Elisabeth Reeve Morrow letters to Constance Chilton, 1925–1934.

[11] Ibid.

[12] Bernard Spodek, ed., *Handbook of Research on the Education of Young Children,* New York: Macmillan, 1993, pp. 1–6, 91–97.

[13] *HGHL,* AML letter to ECM, 6/7/29, pp. 44–45.

[14] Ibid., 6/18/29, p. 46.

[15] Ibid., 6/28/29, pp. 50–51.

[16] Interview with AML, 8/30/88.

[17] *HGHL,* AML letter to ERM, 7/2/29, p. 52.

[18] Ibid., p. 53.

[19] *HGHL,* AML letter to CCM, 7/8/29, pp. 56–57.

[20] Ibid., 7/4/29, p. 55.

[21] Ibid., 7/9/29, p. 59.

[22] *HGHL,* AML letter to ECM, 7/13/29, p. 62.

[23] *HGHL,* AML letter to CCM, 8/6/29, pp. 67–68.

[24] *HGHL,* AML letter to ERM, 8/13/29, p. 69.

[25] Elizabeth Cutter Morrow Diaries, Dwight Morrow Papers, Amherst College Archives.

[26] *NYT,* 8/20/29, "Lindbergh Instructs Bride in Rudiments of Flying"; *NYT* 8/25/29, "Mrs. Lindbergh Flies 3 3-4 Hours."

[27] *NYT,* 8/24/29, "Mrs. Lindbergh Makes Her First Solo Flight; Colonel Smiles Broadly as Pupil Takes Off."

[28] Elizabeth Cutter Morrow diary, Dwight Morrow papers, Amherst College Archives.

[29] Interview with AML.

[30] *NYT,* 9/3/29, "Lindberghs Fly Back East."

[31] *HGHL,* AML letter to ECM, 8/26/29 ("Thursday"), p. 73.

8. THE ODYSSEY
∾

[1] Elisabeth Reeve Morrow letters to Constance Chilton, 1925–1934. In fact, Anne and Charles arrived in North Haven in a dual-controlled Kemo aero-marine monoplane. It was not surprising, considering their eagerness to return home, that the Lindberghs set a new speed record on their flight from St. Louis: 905 miles in five hours and twenty-one minutes.

[2] Roger G. Reed, *Summering on the Thoroughfare: The Architecture of North Haven,*

1885–1945, Portland, Maine: Maine Citizens for Historic Preservation, 1993; Norwood P. Beveridge, *The North Island, Early Times to Yesterday,* North Haven, Maine: North Haven Historical Society, 1976.

3 Elizabeth Cutter Morrow Diaries, Dwight Morrow Papers, Amherst College Archives.

4 Ibid., 9/12/29.

5 Elisabeth Reeve Morrow letters to Constance Chilton, 1925–1934.

6 *NYT,* 9/17/29, "Lindberghs Fly Tomorrow on 7,000-mile Trip; Stops Scheduled to Minute on 20-day Tour."

7 Elisabeth Stettinius Trippe.

8 *NYT,* 9/18/29, "Lindberghs to Take Four on Flight South."

9 Marilyn Bender and Selig Altschul, *The Chosen Instrument: Juan Trippe, the Rise and Fall of an American Entrepreneur,* New York: Simon and Schuster, 1982, pp. 135–146.

10 *NYT,* 9/23/29, "Lindbergh Log Sent by Radio Operator."

11 *HGHL,* AML letter to ECM, 9/20/29, p. 79.

12 Ibid., pp. 80–81.

13 *HGHL,* AML letter to ERM, 9/23/29, p. 88.

14 *HGHL,* AML letter to ERM, 9/23/29, p. 90.

15 *HGHL,* AML letter to CCM, 9/26/29, p. 93.

16 *Saturday Evening Post,* 2/1/30, "Exploring the Maya with Lindbergh," by William I. Van Dusen.

17 Dr. Austen Fox Riggs, trained in surgery, later joined his father-in-law, Dr. Charles McBurney, in studying the work of Dr. George Gehring who believed that "organic illness is interwoven with emotional upheaval." In 1913, Riggs began a formal practice of psychotherapy in Stockbridge, known as "not a sanitarium for the treatment of the psychoses (there were many of those), but a center for the treatment of the neuroses." The Austen Riggs Foundation was formally established in 1919. From Lawrence S. Kubie, M.D., *The Riggs Story,* New York: P. B. Hoeber, 1960.

18 Elizabeth Cutter Morrow Diaries, Dwight Morrow Papers, Amherst College Archives.

19 Elisabeth Reeve Morrow letters to Constance Chilton, 1925–1934.

20 Elizabeth Cutter Morrow Diaries, Dwight Morrow Papers, Amherst College Archives.

21 Anne used Reeve Hemperly, a contraction of old Cutter family names, as her *nom de plume.*

22 *NYT,* 11/21/29, "Morrow and Adams Join Naval Parley" and *NYT,* 11/29/29, "Larson Will Name Morrow to Senate."

23 *NYT,* 12/3/29, "House Delegation Favoring Morrow."

24 *NYT,* 12/17/29, "Start Morrow 1936 Boom."

25 Elizabeth Cutter Morrow Diaries, Dwight Morrow Papers, Amherst College Archives.

26 *HGHL,* AML letter to ECM, 11/6/29, p. 110.

27 *HGHL,* AML letter to CCM, 1/13–14/30, p. 121.

28 *HGHL,* AML letter to ECM, 1/30–31, p. 126.

29 Ibid., pp. 127–128.

30 *Literary Digest,* 4/12/30, "Motoring and Aviation: Husband and Wife Teams in the Flying Game," p. 39.

31 *HGHL,* AML letter to CCM, 4/10/30, p. 132.

32 *HGHL,* AML letter to ECM, 3/4/30, p. 129.

33 Ibid., p. 130.

34 *NYT,* 4/21/30, "Lindbergh Sets a Record from Coast of $14^3/4$ Hours with Wife as Navigator."

9. INTO THE CAULDRON
∞

1 AML, *The Unicorn and Other Poems,* p. 11.

2 *NYT,* 5/31/30, "Lindbergh Takes Morrow on Airplane Flight from Atlantic City to Newark in 45 Minutes."

3 *New Republic,* 11/5/30, "Dwight Morrow in New Jersey."

4 *HGHL,* AML letter to ELLL, 6/10/30, p. 137.

5 The sad fact is that the answers already existed but were inaccessible to the American medical community. Not until 1928 did Alexander Fleming notice the antibacterial qualities of mold. This observation led to the discovery of penicillin, which was used to treat many disorders, including rheumatic fever. The association between this fever and heart disease was already known, and in 1945, penicillin became a life-saving treatment. Unfortunately, the cure was not on hand for Elisabeth. See Blake Cabot, *The Motion of the Heart: The Story of Cardiovascular Research,* New York: Harper and Brothers, 1954, pp. 106–119.

6 Elisabeth Reeve Morrow letter to Charles Burnett, 9/17/30, Bowdoin College Archives.

7 *HGHL,* AML letter to ELLL, 6/10/30, p. 137.

8 New York *Daily News,* 6/23/30, " 'We' Now are Three," by Robert Conway.

9 *NYT,* 6/24/30, "Baby 'Adopted' by France."

10 Ibid., 6/25/30, "Messages and Gifts Flood the Lindberghs."

11 *HGHL,* AML letter to ELLL, 6/23 and 24/30, p. 138.

12 *NYT,* 6/26/30, "Birth Papers Filed for Lindbergh Baby."

13 *Outlook,* 12/3/30, "What's Wrong With Lindbergh?"

14 *HGHL,* AML letter to ERM, 7/30/30, p. 140.

15 John B. Watson, with the assistance of Rosalie Rayner Watson, *Psychological Care of the Infant and Child,* New York: W. W. Norton, 1928.

16 *HGHL,* AML letter to ERM, 7/30/30, p. 141.

17 Interview with Betty Gow.

18 Anne and Charles were unaware that officials in Mercer and Hunterdon counties competed over the location of the estate. After the Lindberghs bought their property, each county vied for the right to call the Lindberghs their own. Hunterdon County won, even though most of the land was in Mercer.

19 *HGHL,* AML letter to ELLL, 9/29/30, p. 144.

20 *HGHL,* AML letter to CCM, 11/10/30, p. 147.

21 *HGHL,* AML letter to ELLL, 8/20/30, p. 142.

22 Ibid., "Tuesday Morning, March," p. 155.

23 As a result, Charles and his half-sister Eva Christy donated the home and the land to the state of Minnesota, which designated it a park. The state's intent was to reconstruct the house as a museum and to use its ninety-three acres of woodlands for public recreation.

24 *HGHL,* AML letter to ELLL, 3/5/31, p. 153.

25 *HGHL,* AML letter to ECM, 4/19/31, p. 161.

26 Elisabeth Reeve Morrow letters to Constance Chilton, 1925–1934.

27 *NYT,* 5/14/31, "Denies Engagement of Elizabeth Morrow."

28 Partner in Morgan and Grenfell, London affiliate of J. P. Morgan and Company.

29 Elisabeth Reeve Morrow letter to Mary Chilton.

30 *HGHL,* AML letter to ELLL, 5/10/31, p. 162.

31 *NYT,* 5/30/31.

32 *NYT,* 6/20/31, "Into the Setting Sun with the Lindberghs."

33 AML, *North to the Orient,* New York: Harcourt, Brace and Company, 1935.

34 Eager to elevate the status of the Lindberghs, the press failed to note that the aviators Wiley Post and Harold Gatty flew a record-breaking flight over the Bering Strait in a direction opposite to that of June 1931.

35 AML, *North to the Orient.*

36 Interview with Janet Johnson; interview with Betty Gow.

37 *HGHL,* AML letter to ECM, 7/17/31, p. 163.

38 Interview with Betty Gow.

39 Elisabeth Reeve Morrow letters to Constance Chilton, 1925–1934.

10. BLACK OCTOBER
∽

1 Details pertaining to Morrow's death are drawn from the Dwight Morrow Papers, Amherst Archives.

2. Harold Nicolson, op. cit., p. 399.

3. *NYT,* 10/6/31, "His Last Address a Plea for Charity."

4 AML, *North to the Orient.*

5 *NYT,* 10/6/31, "Dwight W. Morrow Dies."

6 *NYT,* 10/7/31, "Funeral of Morrow to be Held Today."

7 *NYT,* 10/8/31, "Morrow Is Buried; Notables at Beir"; Plato, *Selected Dialogues,* Franklin Library, Franklin Center, PA., 1983, pp. 43–103.

8 Dwight Morrow letter to Reuben Clark, U.S. Ambassador to Mexico, 1/30/31, Dwight Morrow Papers, Amherst College Archives.

9 Letters of condolence to Elizabeth Cutter Morrow, Dwight Morrow Papers, Amherst College Archives.

10 Information about Betty Gow's summer in Maine and her relations with Red Johnson are from the following sources: Interview with Betty Gow; Betty Gow, Statements, 3/3/32 and 3/10/32, NJSPM; Finn Henrick Johnson, Statement, 3/8/32, NJSPM; and Johannes Junge, Statements, 3/9/32 and 4/14/32, NJSPM.

11 *HGHL,* AML letter to ELLL, 11/12/31, p. 204.

12 *HGHL,* AML letter to CCM, 11/16/31, p. 205.

13 Ibid., pp. 205–206; and interview with Joan Johnson.

14 William Raymond Manchester, *The Glory and the Dream: A Narrative History of America,* 1932–1972, Boston: Little, Brown, 1974.

15 *NYT,* 11/9/31, "Pershing Appeals with Col. Lindbergh for Idle in 'Crisis.' "

16 *HGHL,* AML letter to ELLL, 12/31, p. 207.

17 *HGHL,* AML letter to ECM, 1/32, p. 223.

18 *NYT.*

19 *HGHL,* AML letter to ELLL, 2/7/32, pp. 224–226.

20 *NYT,* 2/22/32, "Mrs. Lindbergh Aids China Flood Appeal."

II. WITHIN THE WAVE
∾

1 AML, *The Unicorn and Other Poems,* p. 78.

2 Details about the house, grounds, and surrounding area from a pamphlet published by Highfields/Albert Elias RGC, HighFields, East Amwell Township, New Jersey.

3 Elsie Mary Whateley, Statement, March 10, 1932, to Lt. John J. Sweeney and Det. Hugh J. Strong, Newark Police Department; Anne M. Lindbergh, Statement, March 11, 1932, to Lt. John J. Sweeney, Newark Police Department, NJSPM.

4 Anne M. Lindbergh, Statements, March 11, 1932, to Lt. John J. Sweeney, and on March 13, 1932, to Lt. John J. Sweeney and Det. Hugh Strong, NJSPM.

5 Ibid.

6 Jim Fisher, *The Lindbergh Case,* New Brunswick, New Jersey: Rutgers University Press, 1987, p. 47.

7 Septimus Banks, Statement, April 13, 1932, to Insp. Harry W. Walsh, Jersey City Police Department.

8 Jim Fisher, op. cit., p. 47.

9 In his article "Hunt for the Lindbergh Kidnappers," in the *Evening Journal,*

11/17/32, Insp. Harry Walsh, stated that it was Violet Sharpe who answered Whateley's call on the morning of Tuesday, Mar. 1, 1932. In Septimus Bank's statement to Inspector Walsh on 4/13/32, however, Banks claims that it was he who received the call and connected it to Betty Gow.

10 Betty Gow, Statement, March 3, 1932, to Lt. John J. Sweeney, Newark Police, Capt. Patrick J. Brady, Jersey City Police, and Trooper L. J. Bornman, New Jersey State Police, NJSPM.

11 Charles Henry Ellerson, Statement, April 12, 1932, to Insp. Harry W. Walsh, Jersey City Police Department, NJSPM.

12 Christen Christensen, Statement, April 15, 1932, to Insp. Harry W. Walsh, and Kristi Christensen, Statement, April 15, 1932, to Insp. Harry W. Walsh, NJSPM.

13 Betty Gow, Statement, March 10, 1932, to Lt. John J. Sweeney and Det. Hugh J. Strong, NJSPM.

14 Marguerite Junge, Statement, March 7, 1932, made to Sgt. Edward McGrath and Det. John F. Shaible, Newark Police Dept.; and Johann Junge, Statement, April 14, 1932, made to Insp. Walsh, NJSPM.

15 FBI Summary Report, New York #62–3057, Lindbergh Household and Employees, Charles A. Lindbergh, Jr., Aloysius Whateley, NJSPM.

16 Finn Hendrik Johnson, Statement, March 8, 1932, to Deputy Chief Frank E. Brex, Det. Hugh Strong, and Hobart A. Templeton of the Newark Police Department and to Sergeant Andrew Zaplosky of the New Jersey State Police Headquarters: "According to newspaper reports published shortly after the kidnapping, evidences were found by the New Jersey State Police of the apparent tapping of telephone wires at a point near Hopewell, presumably by agents of the kidnappers seeking to keep informed of the progress of the hunt for the kidnappers." The police found that the wires had been tapped after the kidnapping by someone trying to trace the call. FBI Summary Report, NJSPM, p. 127.

17 Charles Henry Ellerson, op. cit.

18 Betty Gow, Statement, March 10, 1932, to Lt. John J. Sweeney and Det. Hugh J. Strong, NJSPM.

19 *NYT,* 1/4/35, "Text of Trial Testimony by Col. and Mrs. Lindbergh."

20 Elsie Mary Whateley, Statement, March 10, 1932, to Lt. John J. Sweeney and Det. Hugh J. Strong, NJSPM.

21 FBI Summary Report, New York #62–3057, Lindbergh Household and Employees, Charles A. Lindbergh, Jr., Aloysius Whateley, FBI summary, NJSPM.

22 Betty Gow, Statements, March 3, 1932, and March 10, 1932, and Anne M. Lindbergh, Statements, March 11, 1932, and March 13, 1932.

23 The Tinkertoy is noted in the FBI report but not in the New Jersey State Police Archives. The FBI records that the toy remained intact after the kidnapping, implying, perhaps, that the baby had been handed out through the nursery window.

The FBI, however, was not first at the scene of the crime, nor did its men take photographs the first night. The inconsistencies between the reports makes this theory difficult to assess.

[24] Betty Gow, Statements, March 3, 1932, and March 10, 1932, and Anne M. Lindbergh, Statements, March 11, 1932, and March 13, 1932.

[25] Ibid.

[26] Anne M. Lindbergh, Statements, March 11, 1932, and March 13, 1932.

[27] Jim Fisher, op. cit., p. 130.

[28] Anne M. Lindbergh, Statements, op. cit., Col. Charles A. Lindbergh, Statement, March 11, 1932, to Lieut. John J. Sweeney, Oliver Whateley, Statement, March 3, 1932, to Capt. Patrick J. Brady, Jersey City Police, Trp. L. J. Bornman, NJ State Police, and Lieut. John J. Sweeney, NJSPM.

[29] Col. Charles A. Lindbergh, Statement, op. cit.

[30] Ibid., and Anne M. Lindbergh, Statements, op. cit.

[31] Betty Gow, Statement, March 10, 1932; Elsie Whateley, Statement, op. cit.; Oliver Whateley, Statement, op. cit.

[32] Betty Gow, Statements, op. cit.

[33] Ibid., March 10, 1932.

[34] Anne M. Lindbergh, Statement, March 13, 1932. Many accounts of the kidnapping adhere to Betty Gow's recollection of the dialogue in her statement made on 3/10/32, in which she quotes Charles as saying, "Anne, they have stolen our baby." In her own statement, however, Anne says twice that Charles was silent.

[35] *HGHL,* introduction to 1932 section, p. 211.

[36] Anne M. Lindbergh, Statement, March 13, 1932; Elsie Whateley, Statement, op. cit.

[37] *Literary Digest,* 3/12/32, "The Challenge of the Lindbergh Kidnapping."

12. THE WAR
∞

[1] There were two sets of footprints, one larger than the other. The New Jersey State Police theorized that the smaller ones were made by Anne that afternoon. The FBI noted that the smaller person was wearing moccasins, stockings, or cloth coverings over his or her shoes.

[2] Text of ransom notes from NJSPM; and J. Vreeland Haring, *The Hand of Hauptmann,* New Jersey: Hamer, 1937, p. 16.

[3] Fon W. Boardman, Jr., *The Thirties: America and the Great Depression,* New York, H. Z. Walck, 1967.

[4] *NYT,* 1/27/32, "279 Kidnapped in 29 States, Survey for 1931 Discloses"; 3/3/32, "A New Crime"; 3/6/32, "Kidnapping: A Rising Menace to the Nation"; Hugh A. Fisher and Matthew F. McGuire, "Kidnapping and the So-Called Lindbergh

Law," *New York University Law Quarterly Review,* vol. 12, pp. 646–662, June 1935; and Horace L. Bomar, Jr., "The Lindbergh Law," *Law and Contemporary Problems,* vol. 1, pp. 435–444, Oct. 1934.

5   It was public knowledge that Lindbergh had received $250,000 worth of stock when he had joined TAT.

6   Jim Fisher, op. cit.

7   Father of General Norman Schwarzkopf, commander-in-chief of the United States Desert Storm military operation.

8   Roger Cohen, and Claudio Gatti, *In the Eye of the Storm: The Life of General H. Norman Schwarzkopf,* New York, Farrar, Straus and Giroux, 1991; interview with General Norman Schwarzkopf, 2/21/97.

9   Jim Fisher, op. cit. p. 20.

10   *HGHL,* AML letter to ELLL, 3/5/32, p. 231.

11   Jim Fisher, op. cit.

12   *HGHL,* AML letter to ELLL, 3/2/32, p. 226.

13   Ibid., p. 227.

14   Jim Fisher, op. cit., p. 25.

15   *NYT,* 3/2/32, "Japanese Routing Chinese in Fierce Shanghai Battle; Death Toll Exceeds 2000."

16   Interview with Gen. H. Norman Schwarzkopf, 2/21/97.

17   Interview with Jim Fisher, 2/24/97.

18   *NYT,* 3/3/32, "100,000 in Manhunt."

19   *Commonweal,* 3/16/32, "The Lindbergh Case."

20   Jim Fisher, op. cit., p. 22.

21   Ibid., p. 23.

22   Jim Fisher, op. cit.

23   Ibid.

24   Jim Fisher, op. cit., pp. 24–25, 30.

25   Ibid., p. 24.

26   Wahgoosh was named after Charles's childhood dog, also a fox terrier. It had been beaten to death with a crowbar by an envious and deranged neighbor. See A. Scott Berg, *Lindbergh,* New York: Putnam, 1998, p. 53.

27   FBI Summary Report, New York #62-3057, NJSPM. There are differing reports regarding Wahgoosh's sleeping habits. Some say he slept in the servants' quarters; others say he slept regularly outside the baby's room.

28   Jim Fisher, op. cit. pp. 27–28.

29   See Note number 4.

30   Jim Fisher, op. cit., p. 28.

31   Ibid., p. 53.

32   *The Christian Century,* 3/16/32, "Behind the Empty Crib"; *Commonweal,* 3/16/32,

"The Lindbergh Case," and 4/13/32, "The Lindbergh Case"; *Literary Digest,* 3/26/32, "The Kidnapers' Threat to American Homes."

³³ See note number 4.

³⁴ *NYT,* 3/3/32, "Mother Meets Ordeal with Calm Fortitude."

³⁵ Ibid., "Diet Needed by Lindbergh Baby Listed by Mother for Captors."

³⁶ Jim Fisher, op. cit., p. 129.

³⁷ Betty Gow, Statement, 3/3/32, to Lieut. John J. Sweeney, Capt. Patrick J. Brady, and Trooper L. J. Bornman, NJSPM.

³⁸ Sidney B. Whipple, *The Lindbergh Crime,* New York: Blue Ribbon, 1935, p. 34.

³⁹ Report by Edward J. Reilly concerning Marguerite and Johannes Junge, 12/18/34, File #590, "re: Hauptmann," NJSPM.

⁴⁰ Ibid.

⁴¹ NYT, 3/13/32, "Brex Exonerates Johnson."

⁴² NYT, 3/11/32, "Lindbergh Search and Ransom Moves Fail on Ninth Day"; and Jim Fisher, op. cit., pp. 52–53.

⁴³ *NYT,* 3/5/32, "Still No Trace of Baby."

⁴⁴ Jim Fisher, op. cit., p. 32.

⁴⁵ *NYT,* 3/4/32, "World Waits Hopefully for News that the Lindbergh Baby Is Safe."

⁴⁶ Dudley Shoenfeld, *The Crime and the Criminal: A Psychiatric Study of the Lindbergh Case,* New York: Covici-Friede, 1936.

⁴⁷ *HGHL,* AML letter to ELLL, 3/5/32, p. 230.

⁴⁸ *NYT,* 3/6/32, "Lindberghs . . . Name Two Men to Represent Them."

⁴⁹ *NYT,* 3/3/32, "Capone Offers Reward."

⁵⁰ Jim Fisher, op. cit., p. 37.

⁵¹ Leonard Frank, *Uncle Frank: The Biography of Frank Costello,* New York: Drake, 1973, p. 250; Jim Fisher, op. cit., p. 37.

⁵² Dr. John F. Condon, *Jafsie Tells All!,* New York: Jonathan Lee Publishing Corp., 1936; National Archives Sound and Video collection 106.10; and Jim Fisher, op. cit., pp. 40–41.

⁵³ Dr. John F. Condon, op. cit., and Jim Fisher, op. cit., pp. 40–41.

⁵⁴ *Outlook,* 4/32, "Lindbergh and the Press," by Silas Bent.

⁵⁵ Jim Fisher, op. cit., pp. 45–46.

⁵⁶ Ibid., p. 46.

⁵⁷ Violet Sharpe, Statement, March 10, 1932, to Sgt. McGrath, Detectives Shaible and Strong; and Violet Sharpe, Statement, April 18, 1932, to Insp. Harry Walsh, NJSPM.

⁵⁸ John Lardner, "The Lindbergh Legends," in *The Aspirin Age, 1919–1941,* Isabel Leighton, ed., New York: Simon and Schuster, 1949, p. 205.

⁵⁹ Dudley Shoenfeld, op. cit.

⁶⁰ Jim Fisher, op. cit., pp. 50–51.

61 *NYT,* 3/13/32, "11 Days of Failure in Lindbergh Case."

62 Ibid., 1/10/35, "Testimony of Dr. Condon Identifying Hauptmann as Receiver of Ransom."

63 Ibid.

64 *HGHL,* AML letter to ERM, 3/18/32, p. 237.

65 Jim Fisher, op. cit., p. 64.

66 Details of ransom negotiations and payment are from *NYT,* 1/10/35, "Testimony of Dr. Condon Identifying Hauptmann as Receiver of Ransom," and Jim Fisher, op. cit.

67 AML, *The Unicorn and Other Poems,* p. 36.

68 Jim Fisher, op. cit. p. 77.

69 *NYT,* 1/8/35, "Miss Gow, on Stand, Details Her Movements after Tucking Baby in Its Crib."

70 The statement had a double meaning. John appeared to be talking about a biological relative, but implicit in his words was that the baby was with God.

71 Jim Fisher, op. cit., p. 88.

72 The story first appeared on 4/5/32 in the *Bronx Home News;* then, on 4/6/32, in the *Daily News,* and in *NYT,* 4/10/32, "Lindbergh Paid Ransom of $50,000, But Kidnappers Did Not Return Child."

73 Dr. John F. Condon, op. cit.

74 *NYT,* 4/7/32, "Curtis Says He Met Kidnappers' Agent."

75 *HGHL,* AML letter to ELLL, 4/8/32, p. 239.

76 Ibid., 4/10/32, p. 240.

77 The newspapers quotations in this paragraph are excerpted in *Literary Digest,* 4/23/32, "The Nation Outraged by the Lindbergh Fraud."

78 Dr. John F. Condon, op. cit.

79 *HGHL,* AML letter to ELLL, 4/13/32, p. 241.

80 *NYT,* 4/12/32, "Lindbergh Mediator Seeks New Contact; Ransom Bill Is Seen."

81 Ibid., 4/13/32, "Condon Deals Anew with Kidnappers and Reassures Them."

82 Ibid., 4/15/32, "Flier Asks Secrecy to Deal With Gang."

83 Ibid., 4/14/32, "Ransom Bill Found; Trail Lost in Bank."

84 *HGHL,* AML letter to ELLL, 4/18/32, p. 242.

85 *NYT,* 4/18/32, "Condon Reaffirms Contact With Gang."

86 *HGHL,* AML letter to Sue Beck, 4/25/32, p. 244.

87 Elisabeth Reeve Morrow letters to Constance Chilton, 1925–1934.

88 *HGHL,* AML letter to ELLL, 4/29/32, p. 244.

89 *HGHL,* AML diary, 5/11/32, p. 247.

90 Ibid., 5/12/32, p. 248.

13. ASCENT

∞

[1] AML, *The Unicorn and Other Poems,* p. 66.

[2] *HGHL,* AML letter to ELLL, 5/12/32, p. 249.

[3] *NYT,* 5/15/32, "The Worst and the Best."

[4] *HGHL,* AML diary, 5/16/32, p. 253.

[5] Ibid., 5/15/32, p. 252.

[6] AML, "Dogwood," in *The Unicorn and Other Poems,* p. 38.

[7] Ibid., p. 23.

[8] *NYT,* 5/16/32, "Five Men and Woman Believed Identified as Slayers of Baby."

[9] Ibid., "Would Call Army to Rout Lawless" by the Rev. Dr. Henry Howard.

[10] Ibid., "Five Men and Woman Believed Identified as Slayers of Baby."

[11] *HGHL,* AML diary, 5/16/32, p. 253.

[12] Ibid., pp. 252–253.

[13] *NYT,* 5/17/32, "Bronx Jury to Act on Ransom Today."

[14] *HGHL,* AML diary, 5/20/32, p. 256.

[15] Ibid.

[16] Ibid., 5/17/32, pp. 253–254.

[17] Ibid., p. 254.

[18] Ibid.

[19] *NYT,* 5/18/32, "Curtis Admits He Hoaxed Lindbergh in Kidnap Hunt."

[20] *NYT,* 5/20/32, "Lindbergh Reenacts Baby's Kidnapping"; and *HGHL,* AML diary, 5/19/32, p. 255.

[21] *HGHL,* AML diary, 5/18/32, p. 255.

[22] *NYT,* 5/14/32.

[23] *HGHL,* AML diary, 5/21/32, p. 257.

[24] Ibid., 5/22/32, p. 257.

[25] Amelia Earhart had fought for her life on the open sea in a plane twice as powerful and twice as fast as Lindbergh's *Spirit of St. Louis,* but she was unable to complete the flight.

[26] *NYT,* 5/31/32, "Lull in Lindbergh Hunt."

[27] *HGHL,* p. 262n.

[28] *HGHL,* AML diary, 5/25/32, pp. 260–261.

[29] Ibid., 5/28/32, p. 262.

[30] Ibid., 5/30/32, p. 263.

[31] Ibid., 6/1/32, p. 264.

[32] Violet Sharpe, Interrogation, 5/24/32, #30, NJSPM; and Jim Fisher, op. cit.

[33] Jim Fisher, op. cit., and NJSPM, Violet Sharpe letter to Miss (Fan) Simons of North Wales, 6/7/32: "I only weigh 7 stones." This letter also revealed the extent of her malaise. She concluded: "Life is getting so sad I really don't think there is much to live for any more."

[34] Jim Fisher, op. cit.

[35] Laura Hughes, Statement, 6/10/32, to Insp. Harry Walsh, NJSPM.

[36] *NYT,* 6/11/32, "Morrow Maid Ends Her Life; Suspected in Kidnapping."

[37] Interview with Betty Gow.

[38] *NYT,* 6/11/32, op. cit.

[39] *HGHL,* AML letter to ELLL, 6/13/32, pp. 274–275.

[40] But there was reason to believe that Anne figured greatly in Violet's fantasies. She longed to have violet eyes and airy adventures with a romantic prince. Violet copied into a notebook a poem that spoke of her wishes. NJSPM, Violet Sharpe File.

[41] *NYT,* 6/13/32, "Police Balk at Exonerating Girl"; and 6/16/32, "Miss Sharpe Is Buried; Inquiry Is Pressed."

[42] *HGHL,* AML diary, 6/11/32, pp. 272–273.

[43] The grandson of a Jewish immigrant who had earned his fortune in silver-mining, Guggenheim had been trained as a pilot during the war and had an interest in the commercial possibilities of aviation. He had met Dwight Morrow in 1925, when Morrow chaired Calvin Coolidge's Aviation Board.

[44] *HGHL,* AML diary, 6/11/32, p. 273.

[45] Harry Guggenheim, as quoted in AML diary, 6/11/32, p. 273.

[46] Ibid., p. 274.

[47] Ibid., 6/9/32, pp. 269–270.

[48] Ibid., 6/17/32, p. 279.

[49] Charles L. Morgan (1894–1958), also drama critic for the *London Times.*

[50] *HGHL,* AML diary, 6/21/32, p. 280.

[51] Charles Morgan, *The Fountain,* New York: A. A. Knopf, 1932, p. 333.

[52] Charles Morgan, as found in *HGHL,* AML diary, 6/21/32, p. 280.

[53] Anne would later find that the wheel metaphor was derived from a system of mystical Chinese thought set forth by Lao Tzu in the sixth century B.C. The circle is the symbol of life, and its center is the void through which one communicates with God.

[54] *HGHL,* AML diary, 6/22/32, p. 280.

[55] Hugh A. Fisher and Matthew F. McGuire, "Kidnapping and the So-Called Lindbergh Law," *New York University Law Quarterly Review,* vol. 12, June 1935, pp. 646–662; and Horace L. Bomar, Jr., "The Lindbergh Law," *Law and Contemporary Problems,* vol. 1, October 1934, pp. 435–444.

[56] *HGHL,* AML diary, 6/26/32, p. 282.

[57] Ibid., 6/27/32, p. 283.

[58] Ibid., 7/6/32, pp. 286–289.

[59] Ibid., 7/9/32, p. 289.

[60] Ibid., 7/17/32, pp. 292–293.

[61] Ibid., 7/24/32, p. 294.

[62] Ibid., 8/16/32, pp. 299–302.

[63] Interview with Betty Gow.

[64] *HGHL,* AML diary, 8/16/32, p. 302.

14. DEATH IS THE ANSWER

∾

[1] Rainer Maria Rilke, *Rilke: Poems,* Everyman's Library, Pocket Poets, New York: Knopf, 1996, p. 49.

[2] *HGHL,* AML diary, 9/4/32, p. 312.

[3] Ibid., 8/21/32, pp. 305–306.

[4] Ibid., 8/31/32, p. 310.

[5] Ibid., 9/2/32, p. 310.

[6] Interviews with Margot Loines Morrow Wilkie, 8/24/94 and 10/31/94; Reeve Lindbergh, *Under a Wing,* New York: Simon and Schuster, 1998.

[7] Interview with Margot Loines Morrow Wilkie, 8/24/94.

[8] Ibid.

[9] *HGHL,* AML diary, 9/17/32, p. 316.

[10] Ibid., 9/5/32, p. 312.

[11] Ibid., 10/15/32, p. 320.

[12] Ibid., 8/16/32, p. 303.

[13] *HGHL,* AML diary, 9/4/32, p. 312.

[14] Ibid., pp. 311–312.

[15] *NYT,* 8/17/32, "Second Son Is Born to the Lindberghs at the Morrow Home in Englewood."

[16] *HGHL,* AML diary, 9/8/32, p. 313.

[17] Ibid., 9/13/32, pp. 313–315.

[18] Ibid., 9/25/32, p. 318.

[19] *HGHL,* AML letter to ELLL, early October, p. 319.

[20] *NYT,* 11/4/32, "Held for Threat to Mrs. Morrow."

[21] Highfields, now Highfields/Albert Elias RGC, East Amwell Township, NJ. See *NYT,* 6/24/33, "Lindbergh Estate to Be Child Refuge"; 6/25/33, "Lindbergh Project Approved in Jersey"; and 6/26/33 "High Fields." After 1950, Highfields became a rehabilitation center for teenagers with criminal records.

[22] *HGHL,* AML letter to ELLL, 12/15/32, p. 321.

[23] Charles Lindbergh, introduction to Alexis Carrel's *The Voyage to Lourdes,* trans. from the French by Virgilia Peterson, New York: Harper and Brothers, 1950; and Charles Lindbergh, *Autobiography of Values,* pp. 16–17.

[24] Interview with Richard Bing.

[25] Interview with AML, 1/24/86.

[26] *HGHL,* AML diary, 12/28/32, pp. 322–325.

[27] Thirty years later, the wedding and her thoughts would be the subject of her book, *Dearly Beloved.*

28 *LROD,* AML diary, 1/16/33, p. 6.
29 Ibid., 1/6/32, p. 4.
30 AML, *North to the Orient.*

15. PURGATORY
∞

1 *LROD,* AML diary, 1/13/33, p. 6.
2 Ibid., 1/21/33, p. 8.
3 Victoria Glendinning, *Vita,* New York: Knopf, 1983, pp. 254–256.
4 Ibid.; Nigel Nicolson, ed., *Harold Nicolson, Diaries and Letters, 1930–1939,* New York: Atheneum, 1966, pp. 131–133; and *LROD,* pp. 8–12.
5 *LROD,* AML diary, 2/27/33, pp. 17–18.
6 Ibid., 3/17/33, p. 23.
7 Postmaster General Walter F. Brown decided to aid the transport industry by lobbying Congress to pass the McNary-Watres bill, encouraging the development of larger aircraft for mail, passenger, and freight. {*Legacy of Leadership,* published privately by Trans World Airlines Flight Operations, 1972, p. 45.}
8 *LROD,* AML diary, 4/26/33, p. 27.
9 Ibid., early May, pp. 32–33.
10 Ibid., 5/6/33, p. 35.
11 Anne Morrow Lindbergh, *Listen! The Wind,* New York: Harcourt Brace, 1938, forward by Charles A. Lindbergh, pp. v–ix.
12 *LROD,* AML letter to ELLL, p. 43.
13 *LROD,* AML diary, 7/8/33, p. 46.
14 Anne would later reflect on this moment in her book, *North to the Orient.* See also *LROD,* AML diary, 7/11/33, p. 48.
15 *LROD,* AML letter to ECM, 7/11/33, p. 48.
16 *LROD,* AML diary, 7/24/33, p. 63.
17 Ibid., 7/31/33, p. 69.
18 Ibid., 8/19/33, p. 92.
19 Ibid., 9/4/33, p. 107.
20 Ibid., 9/16/33, p. 112.
21 Ibid., 10/5/33, p. 124.
22 Ibid., 10/14/33, p. 127.
23 *LROD,* AML letter to ERM, undated, p. 136.
24 *LROD,* AML diary, 11/7/33, p. 141.
25 *LROD,* AML letter to ECM, 11/16/33, p. 150.
26 *LROD,* AML diary, 11/30/33, p. 163.
27 Humbert Wolf, as found in *LROD,* AML diary, 12/5/33, p. 169.
28 *LROD,* AML diary, 12/5/33, p. 170.

[29] Ibid., 12/9/33, p. 174–175.

[30] Ibid., 12/16/32, p. 181.

[31] Ibid., 12/19/33, p. 182.

[32] The plane had been named *Tingmissartoq,* meaning "big bird," by the Eskimos of Greenland.

[33] *LROD,* AML letter to ERMM, 12/31/33, p. 183.

[34] Elisabeth Morrow Morgan letter to Del, wife of the caretaker at the Elisabeth Morrow School, 1/30/34, Elisabeth Morrow School Papers.

[35] *LROD,* AML letter to ELLL, 1/24/34, p. 187.

[36] *NYT,* 2/1/34, "The Co-Pilot."

[37] Ibid., 3/1/34, "Elder Lindbergh Forecast the NRA."

[38] Norman E. Borden, *Air Mail Emergency, 1934: An Account of Seventy-Eight Tense Days in the Winter of 1934 When the Army Flew the United States Mail,* Freeport, Maine: Bond Wheelwright Co., 1968.

[39] Elisabeth Reeve Morrow to Elizabeth Cutter Morrow, Elisabeth Morrow School papers.

[40] *LROD,* AML letter to ERMM, 7/11/34, p. 193.

[41] NYT, 8/2/34, "Giant Seaplane Tops All Records; Lindbergh Hails Test of Clipper."

[42] *LROD,* p. 187n.

[43] *NYT,* 8/2/34, "Anne Lindbergh, in a Gay Humor, Writes Secrets of World Flight."

[44] Ibid., 9/14/34, "Lindberghs Down Again"; and 9/15/34, "Lindberghs Hold 'Court' for Throng."

[45] *LROD,* AML diary, 9/11/34, p. 200.

[46] *NYT,* 9/21/34, "Lindbergh Ransom Receiver Seized; $13,750 Found at His East Bronx Home; the Mystery Solved, Police Declare."

16. THE ARREST

∞

[1] Examination of Bruno Richard Hauptmann at the district attorney's office, Bronx, 10/3/34, between 3:30 and 5:15 P.M., reported by James H. Huddleson, M.D., to James M. Fawcett (Hauptmann's first defense attorney). Other alienists present were S. Philip Goodhart and Richard H. Hoffmann, representing Bronx County, and Doctors Connolly and Spradley, representing the state of New Jersey. Courtesy of Jim Fisher.

[2] Details and dialogue of Hauptmann's arrest are drawn from Jim Fisher, op. cit., and Ludovic Kennedy, *The Airman and the Carpenter,* New York: Viking Penguin Inc., 1985.

[3] Examination of Bruno Richard Hauptmann, reported by James H. Huddleson, M.D., to James M. Fawcett.

4 *NYT,* 9/21/34, "Lindbergh Ransom Receiver Seized; $13,750 Found at His East Bronx Home; the Mystery Solved, Police Declare."

5 Ludovic Kennedy, op. cit., p. 131, and Sydney B. Whipple, *The Trial of Bruno Richard Hauptmann,* New York: Doubleday, Doran, 1937, p. 32.

6 Sydney B. Whipple, op. cit., p. 30.

7 Examination of Bruno Richard Hauptmann, reported by James H. Huddleson, M.D., to James M. Fawcett, pp. 2, 8.

8 Sydney B. Whipple, op. cit., p. 29.

9 *NYT,* 9/22/34, "New Jersey Prepares Murder Charge Against Hauptmann in Kidnapping; Linked to Lindbergh Ransom Notes."

10 *NYT,* 9/21/34, p. 1, "Lindbergh Ransom Receiver Seized."

11 FBI Summary Report, New York #62–3057 re: Hauptmann's arrest, NJSPM.

12 Dudley D. Shoenfeld, op. cit.

13 *NYT,* 9/21/34, "Lindberghs' Tour Halted in West."

14 Ibid., 9/22/34, "Lindbergh Boy Returning"; and 9/24/34, "Lindberghs Spend Night in Arizona."

15 *LROD,* AML letter to ELLL, 9/28/34, pp. 202–203.

16 FBI Summary Report, New York #62–3057, Sept. 23, 1934, by Special Agent John L. Geraghty, pp. 4–6, courtesy of Jim Fisher. The bottle of ether was traced to the Raabe Pharmacy on White Plains Road in the Bronx.

17 *NYT,* 9/26/34, "New Clues Found in Hauptmann's Home"; *NYT* 9/27/34, "Hauptmann Is Indicted as Lindbergh Testifies; More Ransom Cash Found"; and Stanley R. Keith, metallurgical engineer and expert witness in the Hauptmann trial, "Bruno's Nails Built the Kidnap Ladder," 1935, King Features Syndicate, Inc.

18 *NYT,* 9/23/34, "Lindbergh Returning Home to Aid Hauptmann Inquiry"; J. Vreeland Haring, *The Hand of Hauptmann;* and Examination of Bruno Richard Hauptmann reported by James H. Huddleson, M.D., to James M. Fawcett, pp. 1–2.

19 *NYT,* 9/28/34, "Hauptmann Bail $100,000; Col. Lindbergh, Disguised, Sees Suspect Questioned"; and 10/9/34, "Col. Lindbergh Identifies Hauptmann by his Voice; Murder Indictment Voted."

20 Ibid., 9/21/34, "Lindbergh Ransom Receiver Seized; $13,750 Found at his East Bronx Home; the Mystery Solved, Police Declare."

21 Ibid., 10/6/34, "Hauptmann's Mind Is Called Normal by State Alienists."

22 Examination of Bruno Richard Hauptmann, reported by James H. Huddleson, M.D., to James M. Fawcett, pp. 1–2.

23 Later, Hauptmann would say that at the time of the kidnapping he was in the Bronx with his wife. He picked her up sometime between six-thirty and seven P.M. at the bakery where she worked, and they drove home; Jim Fisher, op. cit., p. 260.

24 *NYT,* 10/21/34, "Extradition Issue Is Often Debated."

17. TESTAMENT
∾

1 AML, *The Unicorn and Other Poems*, p. 26.
2 Interview with Margot Loines Morrow Wilkie, 10/31/94.
3 Letter from a Morrow family friend to Connie Chilton, 11/20/34.
4 *LROD*, AML diary, 12/3/34, pp. 223–224.
5 AML, *The Unicorn and Other Poems*, p. 83.
6 *NYT*, 1/3/35.
7 Ibid., 1/28/35, "Miss Ferber Views 'Vultures' at Trial."
8 *Literary Digest*, 1/12/35, 119:10, "They Stand Out from the Crowd"; Jim Fisher, op. cit., pp. 255–256.
9 *NYT*, 1/4/35, "Bookkeeper, 55, Carpenter, 60, Fill Jury, With Average Age Increased to $44^1/2$ Years."
10 Ibid., 1/13/35, "Prosecution's Task in Hauptmann Case," by Archibald R. Watson.
11 Anna Hauptmann had first hired James Fawcett, a friend of her cousin Harry Whitney. Fawcett was a Brooklyn-based defense attorney.
12 Anna Schoeffler Hauptmann, Statement, April 20, 1935, taken at the Hotel New Yorker by Ellis H. Parker, Jr., NJSPM.
13 Sidney B. Whipple, op. cit., p. 48.
14 Ibid.
15 *NYT*, 1/4/35, "Writer Marvels at Mother's Spirit."
16 Ibid., "Text of Trial Testimony by Col. and Mrs. Lindbergh."
17 Ibid.
18 "Lindy's Little Life-Saver" in *Guns and Ammo* magazine, Sept. 1982, pp. 80–81, 110.
19 *LROD*, AML diary, 1/12/35, pp. 237–238.
20 Ibid., 10/13/34, p. 210.
21 *NYT*, 1/10/35, "Condon Names Hauptmann as 'John' Who Got Ransom; Parries Defense's Attack."
22 *LROD*, AML diary, 1/10/35, p. 237.
23 Ibid., 1/15/35, p. 238.
24 Interview with AML, 6/7/88; and Interviews with Margot Loines Morrow Wilkie, 8/24/94 and 10/31/94.
25 *LROD*, AML diary, 1/20/35, p. 240.
26 Ibid., p. 241.
27 *NYT*, 1/24/35, "Expert Traces Tool Marks on Ladder to Hauptmann."
28 Ibid., 1/26/35, "Text of Hauptmann's Testimony Denying the Murder of the Lindbergh Baby."
29 U.S. Bureau of Investigation, 10/18/34, "Bruno Richard Hauptmann, Accounting Report"; Jim Fisher, op. cit.; and Sidney Whipple, op. cit. p. 32.

30 *NYT,* 1/25/35, "Hauptmann Takes Stand, Swears He Was at Home Night Ransom Was Paid."

31 Ibid., "Testimony of Hauptmann on Stand in Own Defense"; and 1/30/35, "Hauptmann Calm on Leaving Stand."

32 Ibid., 1/29/35, "Hauptmann's Testimony on the Second Day of His Cross-Examination by Wilentz."

33 Ibid., 1/25/35, "A Thrilling Trial."

34 Ibid., 1/26/35, "Tribute to Judge Paid by Novelist," Ford Maddox Ford.

35 *NYT,* 1/31/35, "Testimony of Mrs. Hauptmann Backing Triple Alibi Offered by Her Husband."

36 Rainer Maria Rilke, "Duino Elegies," *The Selected Poetry of Rainer Maria Rilke,* New York: Vintage International, 1984, p. 151.

37 *LROD,* AML diary, 2/9/35, p. 247.

38 *NYT,* 2/12/35, "Reilly Accuses Servants, Charges Police Frame-Up in His Final Plea to Jury."

39 Ibid., 2/13/35, "Young Prosecutor Emotional in Appeal; Talks to Jury as to Group of Friends," Craig Thompson.

40 Ibid., " 'No Mercy,' Wilentz Plea; Intruder Shouts at Court; Case Goes to Jury Today."

41 *NYT,* 2/14/35, "Justice Trenchard's Charge to Jury Stressing Burglary Element in Case."

42 *LROD,* AML diary, 2/13/35, p. 249.

43 Harold Nicolson, letter to Vita Sackville-West, 2/14/35.

44 *LROD,* AML diary, 2/13/35, p. 249.

45 *NYT,* 2/14/35, "Hauptmann in Cell Falls in Collapse."

46 *LROD,* AML diary, 2/18/35, p. 251.

18. A ROOM OF HER OWN
‰

1 *LROD,* AML diary, 5/16/35, p. 275.

2 Ibid., 3/19/35, p. 264.

3 Ibid., 4/30/35, pp. 268–270.

4 Ibid., pp. 270–271.

5 Ibid., p. 271.

6 Ibid., 5/8/35, p. 271.

7 *NYT,* 6/21/35, "Carrel, Lindbergh Develop Device to Keep Organs Alive Outside Body."

8 *LROD,* AML diary, 6/21/35, p. 278.

9 Ibid., 7/3/35, p. 279.

10 *Saturday Review,* 8/17/1935, "The Seeing Eye."

11 *Newsweek,* 8/17/1935, "Air-Jaunt: Mrs. Lindbergh Can Write as Well as She Can Pilot."

12 *Publishers Weekly,* 8/24/1935, "Anne Lindbergh's Book a Hit."

[13] *LROD,* AML diary, 8/28/35, p. 300.

[14] Ibid., 9/5/35, p. 305.

[15] Ibid., 9/15/35, p. 308.

[16] Ibid., 10/31/35, p. 324.

[17] Alexis Carrel, *Man, the Unknown,* New York: Harper and Brothers, 1935.

[18] By 1931, twenty-seven states had passed laws permitting sterilization. By 1932, more than 12,000 sterilizations had been performed in the United States, half of them in California. By 1935, the year Carrel's book was published, Denmark, Germany, Switzerland, Norway, and Sweden condoned enforced sterilization. To those who espoused it, sterilization of the socially unfit was simply a matter of reason and good economics. Source: J. H. Landman, Ph.D., J.D., J.S.D., *Human Sterilization: The History of the Sexual Sterilization Movement,* New York: Macmillan, 1932.

[19] *Time,* 9/16/1935, "Carrel's Man."

[20] *LROD,* AML diary, 9/17/35, pp. 312–313.

[21] *NYT,* 10/3/35, "Books of the Times."

[22] *LROD,* AML diary, 12/3/35, p. 328.

[23] *Newsweek,* 12/28/35, "Lindberghs Seek Threat-Free Exile as Hauptmann Seeks Life."

19. CROSSING OVER

ဏ

[1] *NYT,* 1/5/36, "Lindberghs at Landaff."

[2] Ibid., 12/23/35, "Lindbergh Family Sails for England to Seek Safe, Secluded Residence; Threats on Son's Life Force Decision."

[3] Ibid., 12/30/35, "Due in Liverpool Tomorrow."

[4] *LROD,* AML diary, 12/23/35, p. 333.

[5] *Time,* 1/6/36, "Hero and Herod," part I.

[6] Ibid., 1/13/36, "Hero and Herod," part II.

[7] *NYT,* 12/26/35, "Gangs Abroad Too, Lindbergh Is Told."

[8] British Sessional Paper 1936–1937, Command Paper #5520, vol. 26, p. 463.

[9] *NYT,* 1/3/36. "Letters to the Editor: Crime in England."

[10] *LROD,* AML diary, 12/29/35, p. 335.

[11] *Time,* 1/6/36, "Hero and Herod."

[12] *LROD,* AML diary, 12/31/35, p. 336; and *NYT,* 1/4/36, "Lindberghs Start Trip to Wales."

[13] *F&N,* AML letter to ELLL, 1/10/36, pp. 3–4.

[14] *F&N,* AML letter to CCM, 1/12/36, pp. 6–7.

[15] Ibid., p. 7.

[16] *F&N,* AML diary, 1/21/36, p. 10.

[17] Deirdre Beddoe, *Women Between the Wars: 1918–1939,* London: Pandora, 1989.

[18] *F&N,* AML diary, 1/28/36, p. 16.

[19] Ibid., pp. 11–12.

[20] Reeve Lindbergh, op. cit., pp. 143–144.

[21] The idea that art puts a glaze over reality recurs throughout Anne's work, permeating her books and poetry.

[22] *F&N,* AML diary, 2/3/36 through 2/15/36, pp. 17–22.

[23] Ibid., 2/19/36, p. 23.

[24] Ibid., 2/20/36, pp. 23–26.

[25] Ibid.

[26] Ibid., p. 25.

[27] Jane Brown, *Sissinghurst: Portrait of a Garden,* 1990; Anne Scott-James, *Sissinghurst: The Making of a Garden,* 1974; and Tony Venison, "The Garden Before Sissinghurst," *Country Life,* 169:924–6, 1981.

[28] AML, *The Unicorn and Other Poems,* p. 10.

[29] Fon W. Boardman, Jr., op. cit.

[30] *NYT,* 3/2/36.

[31] *F&N,* AML diary, 3/6/36, p. 29.

[32] Ibid., p. 30.

[33] Robert Goralski, *World War II Almanac: 1931–1945,* New York: Bonanza Books, 1981, p. 43.

[34] *F&N,* AML diary, 3/6/36, p. 31.

[35] *F&N,* AML letter to DWM, Jr., 3/25/36, pp. 40–41.

[36] *NYT,* 4/4/36, "Hauptmann Put to Death for Killing Lindbergh Baby; Remains Silent to the End."

[37] Ibid.

[38] *F&N,* AML diary, 4/21/36, pp. 42–44.

[39] Ibid., 5/16/36, pp. 53–55.

[40] Ibid., 4/23–26/36, pp. 44–46.

[41] *F&N,* AML letter to CCM, 3/23/36, pp. 36–40.

[42] *F&N,* AML diary, 4/30/36, pp. 46–47.

[43] Ibid., 5/12/36, pp. 48–53.

[44] Ibid., 6/24/36, pp. 71–72.

[45] Ibid., 7/4/36, pp. 72–73.

[46] Walter Ross interview with Kate and Truman Smith, 4/9/65; Interview with Katharine Smith, 5/14/85; Interview with Katharine (Kaetchum) Smith Coley, 5/25/85; Robert Hessen, ed., *Berlin Alert: The Memoirs and Reports of Truman Smith,* Stanford, CA: Hoover Institution Press, 1984.

[47] Interview with Katharine Smith, 5/14/85.

[48] Robert Hessen, ed., op. cit.

[49] Ibid.

[50] Preceding four paragraphs: *F&N,* AML diary, 7/22/36, pp. 80–84.

51 William L. Shirer, *The Rise and Fall of the Third Reich: A History of Germany,* New York: Simon and Schuster, 1959.

52 *F&N,* AML diary, 7/22/36, pp. 80–84.

53 *Time,* 8/3/36, "Airmen to Earthmen"; A perusal and examination of three representative newspapers of the Nazi Reich—*Voelkischer Beobachter, Berliner Tageblatt,* and *Deutsche Allgemeine Zeitung*—during this period reveals that Lindbergh was welcomed as an American hero, whose presence gave validation to the technological developments in aviation.

54 Walter Ross interview with Truman Smith, 4/9/65.

55 Interview with Katharine Smith, 6/18/85.

56 Ibid., 5/14/85.

57 Ibid., 6/18/85.

58 Interview with Katharine (Kaetchum) Smith Coley, 5/25/85.

59 Interviews with Katharine Smith, 5/14/85 and 6/18/85.

60 *NYT,* 7/24/36, "Lindbergh's Warning."

61 *Literary Digest,* 1/9/37, "English Garden: Lindbergh's Idyll."

62 Ibid.

63 *NYT,* 7/25/36, "Lindbergh Speech Praised by Steed," Wickham Steed.

64 Wayne S. Cole, *Charles A. Lindbergh and the Battle Against American Intervention in World War II,* New York: Harcourt Brace Jovanovich, 1974, p. 33.

65 John Slessor, *The Central Blue: Recollections and Reflections,* London: Praeger, 1957.

66 Interview with Katharine (Kaetchum) Smith Coley, 5/25/85.

67 Wayne Cole, op. cit., p. 36; Telford Taylor, *Munich: The Price of Peace,* New York: Doubleday, 1979, p. 762.

68 *F&N,* AML diary, 7/25/36, pp. 92–95.

69 Ibid., 7/26/36, pp. 95–97.

70 CAL, quoted in John Slessor, op. cit., pp. 218–219.

71 *NYT,* 7/25/36, "Lindbergh Hits at Bombing Planes in Toast."

72 *F&N,* AML diary, 7/24/36, pp. 88–92.

73 Walter Ross interview with Kate and Truman Smith, 4/9/65.

74 Ibid.

75 *F&N,* AML diary, 7/28/36, pp. 97–99.

76 Ibid.

77 David Irving, *Goering: A Biography,* New York: Avon Books, 1989.

78 *F&N,* AML diary, 7/28/36, pp. 97–99.

79 Interview with Katharine Smith, 6/18/85.

80 Ibid.

81 *NYT,* 8/3/36, "Lindbergh Ends Stay in Germany."

82 Walter Ross interview with Kate and Truman Smith, 4/9/65.

83 *F&N,* AML letter to ECM, 8/5/36, pp. 100–102.

84 CAL letter to Harry Davison, 1/23/37, as quoted in Wayne Cole, op. cit., p. 35.

20. POLISH BRIGHT HIS HOOFS

∽

1 Anne Morrow, *Smith College Monthly,* January 1927, p. 46.

2 *F&N,* AML diary, 4/20/37, p. 160.

3 *F&N,* AML letter to Mary Landenberger Scandrett, 1/13/37, p. 124.

4 Ibid., p. 126.

5 An heir to the Astor real estate fortune.

6 Christopher Sykes, *Nancy: The Life of Lady Astor,* London: Collins: 1972, pp. 79–99; Maurice Collins, *Nancy Astor: An Informal Biography,* London: Faber and Faber, 1960, pp. 22–34; Anthony Masters, *Nancy Astor: A Life,* London: Weidenfeld and Nicolson, 1981, pp. 20–23.

7 Christopher Sykes, op. cit., pp. 364–410; Claud Cockburn (recognized as the journalist who gave life to the term "Cliveden Set"), "Britain's Cliveden Set" in *Current History,* Feb. 1938, vol. 48, pp. 31–34.

8 Kenneth Davis, *The Hero,* New York: Doubleday, 1959, p. 375.

9 *F&N,* AML letter to ECM, 1/15/37, pp. 127–129.

10 Ibid., 1/22/37, pp. 129–131.

11 *F&N,* AML diary, 2/1/37, pp. 131–137.

12 Ibid., 2/6/37, pp. 141–142.

13 *NYT,* 3/5/37, "Lindbergh Embarrassed."

14 *F&N,* AML letter to ECM, 3/8/37, pp. 148–152.

15 CAL letter to Harold Bixby, 3/9/37, National Archives.

16 *F&N,* AML letter to ECM, 4/11/37, pp. 154–156.

17 Ibid., 4/17/37, pp. 156–157.

18 *F&N,* AML letter to "Grandma" Cutter, 5/3/37, pp. 159–160.

19 *NYT,* 5/25/37, "Third Son Is Born to the Lindberghs"; 5/26/37, "Lindberghs' Baby Born After a Race"; 5/30/37, "Lindbergh Birth Listed."

20 *F&N,* AML diary, 5/20/37, pp. 160–165.

21 *NYT,* 7/4/37, "Lindbergh Flies to Brittany"; 7/6/37, "Lindbergh Sees Carrel"; 7/7/37, "Lindbergh Returns to England"; 7/30/37, "Lindbergh Visits Dr. Carrel"; 8/9/37, "Lindbergh Visits France." Also, *F&N,* AML letter to Thelma Crawford Lee, 7/31/37, pp. 171–172.

22 Mme. Carrel, as quoted in *F&N,* AML diary, 8/30/36, p. 108.

23 *F&N,* AML letter to Thelma Crawford Lee.

24 After recovering from his breakdown in his senior year of high school, Dwight enrolled, in 1928, in Amherst College, where his manic episodes earned him a reputation as one of the "brashest" freshmen in school history. Later in his freshman year, Dwight was depressed again, and his parents placed him in a private hospital in Stockbridge, Massachusetts. There, the program worked, and Dwight returned to Amherst and performed so well that he earned the epithet given to his father: the student "most likely to succeed." In 1936, Dwight re-

ceived a master's degree in history from Harvard and in 1936, entered Harvard Law School.

[25] Interviews with Margot Loines Morrow Wilke, 8/24/94 and 10/31/94.

[26] Ibid.

[27] AML, *Listen! The Wind,* New York: Harcourt, Brace and Company, 1938.

21. AFTER THE FALL

∾

[1] AML, *The Unicorn and Other Poems,* p. 62.

[2] *NYT,* 8/9/37, "Lindbergh Visits France."

[3] Ibid., 7/14/38, "Carrel and Lindbergh Writing Book on Isle; Scientist Requests that Flier be Left Alone."

[4] Ibid., 9/18/37, "Dr. Carrel and Lindbergh Work on New Experiment"; 10/1/37, "Carrel, Back, Says We Talk too Much."

[5] CAL letter to Ambassador Bingham, 8/4/37, Library of Congress.

[6] *F&N,* AML letter to ELLL, 8/28/37, pp. 174–175.

[7] Robert Goralski, op. cit., p. 56.

[8] Katharine Alling Hollister Smith, *My Life: Berlin, August 1935–April 1939,* unpublished memoirs in the collection of the Hoover Institute.

[9] Ibid.

[10] *F&N,* AML diary, 10/12/37 and 10/13/37, pp. 183–187.

[11] Katharine Alling Hollister Smith, op. cit.; and Robert Hessen, ed., op. cit.

[12] Telford Taylor, op. cit., pp. 759–760.

[13] Robert Goralski, op. cit., p. 58.

[14] *F&N,* AML diary entry, 11/28/37, pp. 188–192.

[15] *NYT,* 12/6/37, "Lindberghs Arrive Home on Surprise Holiday Visit"; 12/11/37, "Bids Sought on Airliners to Carry 100 Passengers"; 12/11/37, "Lindberghs Visit Washington Again"; and *Time,* 12/20/37, "Transport: Technical Advisor."

[16] *F&N,* AML diary, 11/28/37, pp. 188–192.

[17] *NYT,* 12/6/37, "Lindberghs Arrive Home on Surprise Holiday Visit."

[18] Ibid.

[19] *Time,* 12/20/37, "Transport: Technical Advisor."

[20] *F&N,* AML diary, Dec. 1937, p. 192–193.

[21] Ibid.

[22] Ibid.

[23] Fon W. Boardman, Jr., op. cit.

[24] *F&N,* AML diary, Dec. 1937, pp. 192–193.

[25] Robert Goralski, op. cit., p. 60.

[26] Ibid.

[27] Arthur Train, Jr., "More Will Live," *Saturday Evening Post,* 7/23/38.

[28] Alexis Carrel, "The Making of Civilized Men: Oration at the 150th Anniversary of

Founding of the New Hampshire Alpha of Phi Beta Kappa," delivered at Dartmouth College, 10/11/37, Alexis Carrel Papers, Georgetown University Archives.

29 Carrel letter to Simon Flexner, 1/1/38, Rockefeller Archives.

30 AML, *Gift from the Sea,* New York: Pantheon Books, 1955.

31 Ibid., 2/25/38, p. 217.

22. THE CROSSED EAGLE
∞

1 AML, *The Unicorn and Other Poems,* p. 13.

2 *F&N,* AML diary, 4/7/38, p. 238.

3 AML, Forward to James Newton, op. cit., pp. *xi–xii.*

4 Ibid.

5 *F&N,* AML diary, 4/8/38, pp. 238–241.

6 *F&N,* AML diary, 4/1/38, p. 234.

7 *Ken* magazine, "The Future," 4/13/39, Rockefeller Archives.

8 Thomas Debevoise letter to Alexis Carrel, 5/12/38, Rockefeller Archives.

9 *Ken* magazine, op. cit.

10 Handwritten note by E. B. Smith, business manager of the Rockefeller Institute, in Rockefeller Archives file on Carrel's retirement; see also Thomas Debevoise's response to M. H. Dodge, 5/12/38, and subsequent correspondence (M. H. Dodge response to Debevoise, and Carrel to Sherman, 4/23/38, all in Rockefeller Archive files).

11 Alexis Carrel letter to Simon Flexner, 1/1/38, Alexis Carrel Papers, Georgetown University Archives.

12 *F&N,* AML diary entry, 5/1/38, p. 256.

13 Ibid.

14 *F&N,* 5/22/38, p. 271.

15 Nigel Nicolson, ed., op. cit., p. 343.

16 Alexis Carrel, op. cit.

17 *F&N,* AML diary entries 6/28/38, 6/29/38, 7/5/38, 7/12/38, 7/24/38, pp. 312–314, 320, 325, 330.

18 *Reader's Digest,* June 1939, "Breast-Feeding for Babies" and July 1939, "Married Love," both by Alexis Carrel.

19 *F&N,* AML diary entry, 7/12/38, p. 325.

20 Ibid., 6/28/39 and 6/29/39, pp. 312, 314.

21 Herbert A. Strauss, ed., *Jewish Immigrants of the Nazi Period in the USA,* vol. 6, New York: K. G. Saur, pp. 206–244; Leo Baeck Institute Yearbook XIII, 1968, New York: East and West Library, pp. 235–273; and Robert Goralski, pp. 68–69.

22 Robert E. Herzstein, *Roosevelt and Hitler,* New York: Paragon House, 1989, p. 237.

23 Katharine Alling Hollister Smith, op. cit.

[24] *F&N*, AML diary entry, 8/4/38, p. 336.

[25] Ibid., 8/5/38, p. 336.

[26] Ibid., 8/8/38, p. 340.

[27] Robert Goralski, op. cit., p. 69.

[28] *F&N*, AML diary entry, 8/13/38, p. 347.

[29] *NYT*, 8/18/38, "Russian Officials Greet Lindbergh."

[30] *F&N*, AML diary entry, 8/18/38, pp. 353–360.

[31] Ibid.

[32] *F&N*, AML diary entry, 8/18/38, p. 356.

[33] Ibid., 8/19/38, pp. 360–367.

[34] Ibid., 8/25/38, p. 383.

[35] Ibid., 8/19/38, p. 361.

[36] Ibid., 8/24/38, pp. 380, 382.

[37] Ibid., 8/25/38, p. 385.

[38] *NYT*, 9/1/38, "Lindberghs Visit Rumania."

[39] *F&N*, AML diary entry, 9/2/38, p. 400.

[40] *NYT*, 9/1/38, "Lindberghs Visit Rumania."

[41] *F&N*, AML diary entry, 9/3/38, p. 400.

[42] Robert Goralski, op. cit., p. 70.

[43] *F&N*, AML diary entry, 9/8/38, p. 401.

[44] Ibid., 9/9/38, p. 401.

[45] Orville H. Bullitt, ed., *For the President: Personal and Secret Correspondence Between Franklin D. Roosevelt and William C. Bullitt,* Boston: Houghton Mifflin Co., 1972, pp. 267–268.

[46] Robert Goralski, op. cit., p. 70.

[47] *F&N*, AML diary entry, 9/10/38, p. 403.

[48] Conceived by Frank Buchman, an evangelist minister and political opponent of C. A. Lindbergh, Sr., in the early nineteen-twenties, it was nondenominational organization based on established church dogma.

[49] James Newton, op. cit., pp. 121–122.

[50] *F&N*, AML diary entry, 9/13/38, p. 405.

[51] CAL, *Wartime Journals,* New York: Harcourt Brace Jovanovich, 1970, p. 298; James Newton, op. cit., p. 313.

[52] Robert Goralski, op. cit., p. 70.

[53] Ibid., p. 72.

[54] Michael Beschloss, *Kennedy and Roosevelt: The Uneasy Alliance,* New York: W. W. Norton and Co. 1980, p. 176; *F&N*, AML diary entry, 9/21/38, p. 409.

[55] Peter Collier and David Horowitz, *The Kennedys: An American Drama,* New York: Warner Books, 1985, p. 94; Telford Taylor, op. cit., pp. 765–766.

[56] Michael Beschloss, op. cit., pp. 176 and 235.

[57] Joseph P. Kennedy to Roosevelt (undated) and enclosed excerpt from Lindbergh

letter; President's Secretary's File, Navy 1938 folder, Franklin D. Roosevelt Papers, Franklin D. Roosevelt Library.

[58] Robert Hessen, op. cit., p. 154.

[59] Air Ministry of Great Britain, *Rise and Fall of the German Air Force 1933–1945*, London: Arms and Armour Press, 1983, pp. 19–20; John Ellis, *The World War II Databook*, Aurum Press, 1993, p. 231; I.C.B., Dear, *Oxford Companion to the Second World War*, Oxford: Oxford University Press, 1995, p. 22.

[60] *NYT*, 2/1/39, "In the Nation: The Invaluable Contribution of Colonel Lindbergh," by Arthur Krock.

[61] Joseph P. Kennedy to Roosevelt (undated) and enclosed excerpt from Lindbergh letter; Franklin D. Roosevelt to Chief of Staff and Chief of Naval Operations, February 10, 1938; President's Secretary's File, Navy 1938 folder, Franklin D. Roosevelt Papers, Franklin D. Roosevelt Library.

[62] Peter Collier and David Horowitz, op. cit., p. 106.

[63] *F&N*, AML diary, 9/26/38, p. 416; Her reference is to Dwight Morrow, *The Society of Free States*, New York: Harper and Brothers, 1919.

[64] Ibid., 9/24/38, p. 413.

[65] *F&N*, AML diary entry, 9/29/38, p. 419.

[66] Wayne Cole, op. cit., p. 57.

[67] Ibid., p. 58.

[68] Ibid., p. 57.

[69] Ibid.

[70] Robert Goralski, op. cit.

[71] *F&N*, AML diary entry, 10/2/38, p. 422.

[72] Ibid., 10/8/38, p. 425.

[73] Robert Hessen, op. cit., p. 127.

[74] *NYT*, 1/17/60, "Lindbergh's Move to Aid Jews Cited."

[75] William L. Shirer, op. cit., pp. 231–276. Also, exhibition at the Holocaust Museum in Washington D.C.

[76] CAL, *Wartime Journals*, 12/22/38, p. 131.

[77] Dr. George H. Gallup, *The Gallup Poll: Public Opinion 1935–1971*, New York: Random House, 1972.

[78] Wayne Cole, op. cit., p. 41.

[79] Hugh Wilson Papers, diary, p. 59, Herbert Hoover Presidential Library; Robert Hessen, op. cit.; Katharine Alling Hollister Smith, op. cit.

[80] Hugh Wilson Papers, Herbert Hoover Presidential Library.

[81] Robert Hessen, op. cit.

[82] Katharine Alling Hollister Smith, op. cit.; Robert Hessen, op. cit.

23. BROKEN GLASS

∞

[1] AML, *The Unicorn and Other Poems,* p. 21.

[2] Gerald Schwab, *The Day the Holocaust Began: The Odyssey of Herschel Grinspan,* New York: Praeger, 1990, pp. 19–32; William Shirer, op. cit., p. 434.

[3] Ibid.

[4] Daniel Jonah Goldhagen, *Hitler's Willing Executioners,* New York: Knopf, 1996, pp. 98–103.

[5] CAL, *Wartime Journals,* 11/13/38, pp. 115–116.

[6] Katharine Alling Hollister Smith, op. cit.

[7] Hugh Wilson diary entry 10/25/38, p. 61. Hugh Wilson Papers, Herbert Hoover Presidential Library.

[8] *NYT,* 10/16/38, "Adhesives from Abroad: Group of Soviet Airmen."

[9] Ibid., "Lindbergh's Activities Questioned in Britain; Newspaper Cites Praise of Reich Air Force."

[10] *F&N,* AML diary, 12/6/38, p. 467.

[11] *NYT,* 11/16/38, "Protest in Westchester"; and 11/28/38, "Expects Nazi Propaganda."

[12] *NYT,* 12/6/38, "Drops Lindbergh Slogan"

[13] *F&N,* AML diary, 12/10/38, p. 470.

[14] Ibid., 11/27/38, p. 462.

[15] *NYT,* 10/13/38, "Books of the Times: *Listen! the Wind.*"

[16] *F&N,* AML diary, 10/26/38, p. 438.

[17] *NYT,* 2/15/39, "Book About Plants Receives Award."

[18] *F&N,* AML diary, 1/30/39, p. 497.

[19] Robert Goralski, op. cit., p. 76.

[20] *NYT,* 12/13/38, "Lindberghs Occupy a Paris Apartment"; 12/14/38, "Lindbergh in Paris."

[21] *F&N,* AML diary, 12/3/38, p. 465.

[22] *NYT,* 12/19/38, "Ickes Hits Takers of Hitler Medals."

[23] Katherine Smith, op. cit.

[24] Interview with Katherine (Kaetchen) Smith Coley, 5/25/85.

[25] Hugh Wilson had been a junior staff member of the American Embassy in Berlin just before the outbreak of World War I. When that war broke out, he spent the duration in Austria and then Switzerland as chargé d'affaires. Back in Germany after the war, he served as chief negotiator for the peace and, later, as an effective negotiator of treaties for the League of Nations. But by the time he returned to Berlin in 1937, to replace the embittered William E. Dodd, he had come to believe that the vindictiveness of the Versailles Treaty and the ineffectuality of the League of Nations had made peace completely unenforceable.

26 Hugh Wilson Diaries, pp. 56–61, Hugh Wilson Papers, Herbert Hoover Presidential Library.

27 Hugh Wilson Papers, Herbert Hoover Presidential Library.

28 Katharine Alling Hollister Smith, op. cit.

29 *Current Biography,* May 1941, p. 926.

30 Interview with Kate Smith, 5/14/85 and 6/18/85.

31 *F&N,* AML diary, 1/14/39, pp. 487–488.

32 AML, *The Unicorn and Other Poems,* p. 11.

33 Robert Goralski, op. cit., p. 78.

34 *F&N,* AML diary, 1/14/39, p. 488.

35 Ibid., 1/7/39, p. 485.

36 CAL, *Wartime Journals,* p. 139.

37 William L. Shirer, op. cit.

38 *F&N,* AML diary, 1/18/39, p. 489.

39 Robert Goralski, op. cit.

40 *F&N,* AML diary, 1/30/39, p. 497.

41 Ibid., 2/7/39, pp. 501–512.

42 *NYT,* 8/1/57, 1:6, "Nazi Documents Show Plot to Win Duke of Windsor," Russell Baker.

43 *F&N,* AML diary, 2/7/39, pp. 501–512.

44 Ibid., 2/15/39, pp. 518–519.

45 Ibid., 2/24/39, pp. 524–525.

46 Ibid., 2/25/39, pp. 525–526.

47 Ibid., 2/27/39, pp. 534–535.

48 Ibid., 3/1/39, pp. 536–538.

49 Ibid., 3/13/39, pp. 550–551.

50 Ibid., 3/14/39, p. 552.

51 Robert Goralski, op. cit., p. 80.

52 George F. Kennan, op. cit., pp. 97–99.

53 *F&N,* AML diary, 3/16/39, pp. 554–555.

54 Robert Goralski, op. cit., p. 83.

55 CAL, *Wartime Journals,* pp. 182–183; James Newton, op. cit., pp. 175–176.

56 CAL, *Wartime Journals,* pp. 182–183.

24. WHICH WAY IS HOME?

∽

1 AML, *The Unicorn and Other Poems,* p. 23.

2 *WW&W,* AML diary, 4/28/39, p. 3.

3 CAL, *Wartime Journals,* p. 184.

4 Ibid., p. 187.

5 *WW&W,* AML diary, 4/28/39, pp. 3–4.

6   Ibid., 4/29/39, pp. 4–5.
7   Herbert A. Strauss, ed., op. cit., pp. 206–245; *Leo Baeck Institute Yearbook XIII, 1968,* pp. 235–273; and Robert Goralski, op. cit., 68–69.
8   Robert E. Herzstein, op. cit., pp. 236–237.
9   *WW&W,* AML diary, 5/2/39, pp. 5–6.
10 Ibid., 4/29/39, p. 4.
11 Ibid., 5/3/39, p. 6.
12 *Commonweal,* 5/5/39, "Colonel Lindbergh Returns."
13 *Life,* 5/15/39, photo caption.
14 *WW&W,* AML diary, 5/22/39, p. 8.
15 Ibid., 5/24/39, p. 9.
16 Ibid., 5/28/39 and 5/30/39, pp. 9–10.
17 Ibid., 6/11/39, p. 14.
18 *NYT,* 6/20/39, "Rochester Honor to Mrs. Lindbergh."
19 *WW&W,* AML diary, 6/23/39, p. 15.
20 Ibid., 7/20/39, p. 18.
21 "Memorandum as to a Proposed Center of Integrated Scientific Research," Alexis Carrel Papers, Georgetown University Archives.
22 CAL, *Wartime Journals,* p. 216.
23 CAL, *Autobiography of Values,* p. 16.
24 CAL, *Wartime Journals,* p. 216.
25 Ibid., p. 218.
26 Robert E. Herzstein, op. cit., pp. 36–37.
27 CAL, *Wartime Journals,* p. 222.
28 Antoine de Saint-Exupéry, *Wartime Writings,* New York: Harcourt Brace Jovanovich, 1982, p. 10.
29 *WW&W,* AML diary, 8/4/39, p. 21.
30 Antoine de Saint-Exupéry, *Wind, Sand and Stars,* New York: Harcourt, Brace and World, 1968.
31 CAL letter to Grace Lee Nute, 2/8/40, Minnesota Historical Society.
32 *WW&W,* AML diary, 8/5/39, pp. 21–22.
33 Stacy Shiff, *Saint-Exupéry: A Biography,* New York: Knopf, 1994, p. 9.
34 *WW&W,* AML diary, 8/5/39, pp. 22–28.
35 Rainer Maria Rilke, as quoted in *WW&W,* p. 25.
36 Ibid., p. 23.
37 Interview with Stacy Shiff.
38 Antoine de Saint-Exupéry, *Wind, Sand and Stars,* p. 191.
39 *WW&W,* AML diary, 8/6/39, p. 33.

25. NO HARVEST RIPENING

∞

1. AML, *The Unicorn and Other Poems*, p. 40.
2. Harold Nicolson, *Dwight Morrow*, pp. 186–192; and Dwight Morrow, *The Society of Free States*.
3. *WW&W,* AML diary, 8/17/39, p. 38.
4. Robert Goralski, op. cit., 8/22/39, p. 87.
5. *WW&W,* AML diary, 9/2/39 and 9/3/39, pp. 44 and 47.
6. Ibid., p. 46.
7. Ibid., 9/3/39, p. 49.
8. Ibid., pp. 48–49.
9. Ibid., p. 48.
10. CAL, *Wartime Journals,* 8/23/39, p. 245.
11. *NYT,* 9/16/39, "Lindbergh Urges We Shun the War."
12. Ibid.
13. *NYT,* 9/18/39, "Britton Chides Lindbergh."
14. *WW&W,* AML diary, 9/20/39, p. 59, and *New York Herald Tribune.*
15. *WW&W,* AML diary, 9/26/39, pp. 60–63.
16. Robert Goralski, op. cit., p. 96.
17. Ibid., pp. 96–97.
18. CAL, *Wartime Journals,* pp. 267–268.
19. *NYT,* 10/14/39, "Lindbergh Favors a Split Arms Ban."
20. Ibid., 10/15/39, "Lindbergh Speech Assailed in Senate."
21. Ibid., 10/22/39, "British Host Gives Lindbergh Excuse."
22. *WW&W,* AML diary, 10/28/39, p. 65.
23. *Time,* 10/30/39, "War and Peace."
24. Alexis Carrel, letter to Jim Newton, 10/24/39, Georgetown University Archives.
25. CAL, *Wartime Journals,* p. 278.
26. *NYT,* 10/22/39, "Mrs. Morrow Differs with Col. Lindbergh on Arms Ban, Joins Group Seeking Repeal."
27. Robert E. Herzstein, op. cit., pp. 308, 323.
28. *WW&W,* AML diary, 10/28/39, p. 64.
29. *Reader's Digest,* 11/1/39, "Aviation, Geography and Race," CAL.
30. *New Republic,* 11/1/39, "Shoot the Works: The Ambassador's Pajamas," Heywood Broun.
31. Robert Goralski, op. cit., p. 100.
32. *WW&W,* AML diary, 11/27/39, p. 68.
33. Ibid., 11/28/39, p. 69.
34. *Reader's Digest,* Jan. 1940, AML, "A Prayer for Peace," pp. 1–8.
35. Ibid.

26. IMAGES

∽

1   AML letter to the author, 7/31/86.

2   *WW&W,* AML diary, 1/1/40, p. 73.

3   AML, "Pas de deux—Winter," in *The Unicorn and Other Poems,* p. 65.

4   *WW&W,* AML diary, 1/1/40, pp. 73–74.

5   Ibid., pp. 74–76.

6   Alfred North Whitehead, *The Adventure of Ideas,* New York: Macmillan, 1933.

7   James Newton, op. cit., pp. 219–226; AML, *WW&W,* pp. 77–78; CAL, *Wartime Journals,* pp. 307–316.

8   CAL, *Wartime Journals,* 1/21/40, p. 307.

9   *WW&W,* AML diary, pp. 77–78.

10 Interview with James Newton, 6/27/91.

11 Dr. George H. Gallop, op. cit., p. 211; New York: interviewing date 2/2–7/40, survey #183-K, question #6.

12 CAL, *Wartime Journals,* 1/30/40, p. 312.

13 Robert Goralski, op. cit., 2/17/40–3/12/40, p. 107.

14 CAL, *Wartime Journals,* 3/27/40, pp. 327–328.

15 Ibid., 3/1/40, pp. 319–320.

16 Ibid., 3/16/40, p. 326.

17 Ibid., 3/15/40, p. 326.

18 *WW&W,* AML diary, 4/3/40, p. 78.

19 Robert Goralski, op. cit., 4/9/40, p. 108.

20 CAL, *Wartime Journals,* 4/11/40, pp. 331–332.

21 *WW&W,* AML diary, 4/16/40, p. 79.

22 Ibid., 4/23/40 and 4/29/40, pp. 79–81.

23 Robert Goralski, op. cit., 4/27/40, p. 111.

24 CAL, *Wartime Journals,* 4/28/40, p. 338.

25 George H. Gallup, interviewing date 5/16–21/40, survey #194-K, question #6.

26 *NYT,* 5/1/40, "Plan to Help Allies Is Widely Supported."

27 B. H. Liddell Hart, *History of the Second World War,* New York, Putnam, 1971, pp. 74–86.

28 Sir Winston Churchill, *Blood, Toil, Tears, and Sweat: The Speeches of Winston Churchill,* edited and with an introduction by David Cannadine, Boston: Houghton Mifflin, 1989.

29 CAL, *Wartime Journals,* 5/16/40, p. 348.

30 Robert Goralski, op. cit., 5/16/40, p. 114.

31 *NYT,* 5/20/40, "Lindbergh Decries Fears of Invasion"; and CAL, *Wartime Journals,* 5/19/40, pp. 349–350.

32 *NYT,* 5/20/40, "Col. Lindbergh's Broadcast."

33 Ibid., 5/21/40, "Italians Resigned to Active War Role."

34   *WW&W,* AML diary, 5/24/40, pp. 86–87.

35   Ibid., 5/26/40, p. 89.

36   Ibid., 5/31/40, p. 96.

37   CAL, *Wartime Journals,* 6/15/40, p. 358; *Vital Speeches of the Day,* "Our Drift Toward War," 6:549–551, July 1940; and *NYT,* 6/16/40, "Lindbergh Charges War Designs Here."

38   *WW&W,* AML diary, 6/15/40, p. 109.

39   Albert Lee, *Henry Ford and the Jews,* New York: Stein and Day, 1980, p. 46; Norman Cohn, *Warrant for Genocide: The Myth of the Jewish Conspiracy and the Protocol of the Elders of Zion,* New York: Harper and Row, 1966, pp. 159–185.

40   CAL, *Wartime Journals,* 6/27/40, p. 363.

41   Ken Silverstein, *Ford and the Fuhrer: New Documents Reveal the Close Ties Between Dearborn and the Nazis,* The Nation.com, issue 000124.

42   *WW&W,* AML diary, 6/28/40, p. 120.

43   Ibid., 7/19/40, p. 128.

44   Ibid.

45   Ibid., pp. 130–131.

46   *NYT,* 8/5/40, "Lindbergh Urges We 'Cooperate' With Germany if Reich Wins War."

47   *Vital Speeches of the Day,* 6:644–646, 8/15/40, "An Appeal for Peace."

48   William L. Shirer, *Berlin Diary,* New York: Knopf, 1941, pp. 467, 592–593.

49   AML, *The Wave of the Future,* New York: Harcourt, Brace and Company, 1940.

50   Ibid.

51   E. B. White, "One Man's Meat," *Harper's,* 2/1/42.

52   Dorothy Ducas, "Mother and Daughter," *Who,* 8/1/41.

53   Interview with AML.

54   *WW&W,* AML diary, 6/2/40, pp. 97–98.

27. SAINT OF THE MIDNIGHT WILD

∞

1   AML, *The Unicorn and Other Poems,* p. 45.

2   *WW&W,* AML letter to Mrs. Neilson, 1/22/41, p. 163.

3   CAL, *Wartime Journals,* 10/14/39, pp. 404–405; 5/1/41, p. 481.

4   Dr. George H. Gallup, *The Gallup Poll: Public Opinion 1935–1971,* p. 263.

5   CAL, *Wartime Journals,* 1/19/41, p. 441.

6   *NYT,* 1/24/41, "Lindbergh Sees Stalemate, So Urges Negotiated Peace; Doubts Air Invasion of U.S." by Harold Hinton; *Life,* 2/3/41, "Colonel Lindbergh Tells House Committee Neither Side Will Win War"; and CAL *Wartime Journals,* 1/23/41, pp. 442–443.

7   *Life,* 2/3/41, "Colonel Lindbergh Tells House Committee Neither Side Will Win War."

8 *NYT,* 1/25/41, "Lindbergh Praised by Reich Official."

9 CAL, *Wartime Journals,* 1/31/41, p. 444.

10 James Newton, op. cit., pp. 237–250; CAL, *Wartime Journals,* 3/6/41–3/27/41, pp. 455–471; *WW&W,* pp. 167–169.

11 Robert Goralski, op. cit., 3/11/41, p. 150.

12 CAL, "A Letter to Americans," *Collier's,* 3/29/41, pp. 14–15, 75–77.

13 *NYT,* 2/7/41, "Lindbergh Own Author, But Wife Sees Speeches."

14 Ibid., 3/27/41, "Victory Is Certain, Halifax Declares."

15 John Ellis, op. cit., p. 231.

16 Robert Goralski, op. cit., 4/9/41, p. 153.

17 CAL, *Wartime Journals,* 4/11/41, p. 474.

18 *NYT,* 4/18/41, "Lindbergh Calls War Lost by Allies"; CAL, *Wartime Journals,* 4/17/41, pp. 474–475.

19 Justus D. Doenecke, *In Danger Undaunted: The Anti-Interventionist Movement of 1940–1941 as Revealed in the Papers of the America First Committee,* Stanford, CA: Hoover Institution Press, 1990, p. 7.

20 Dr. George H. Gallup, op. cit., pp. 268–276, see also p. 278, question 15a.

21 *NYT,* 4/14/41, "Ickes Offers a List of Nazi 'Tools' Here."

22 CAL, *Wartime Journals,* 4/23/41, pp. 476–477.

23 *NYT,* 4/24/41, "British Seek Another A.E.F., Lindbergh tells 10,000 Here."

24 Ibid., 4/23/41, "Lindbergh to Lead Anti-Convoy Rally."

25 Ibid., 4/25/41, "Lindbergh Praised in Nazi Newspaper."

26 Robert Goralski, op. cit., 4/25/41, p. 156.

27 *NYT,* 4/26/41, "Nazis Near Athens, British Leave; Vast Equipment Reported Saved; U.S. Will Patrol Wider Sea Areas," by Frank L. Kluckhorn.

28 CAL, *Wartime Journals,* 4/27/41, p. 480; *NYT,* 4/29/41, "Lindbergh Quits Air Corps, Sees His Loyalty Questioned."

29 CAL, *Wartime Journals,* 4/26/41, p. 479.

30 *Atlantic Monthly,* June 1941, 167:681–686, "Reaffirmation" by AML.

31 *WW&W,* AML letter to Laura Stevens, 4/29/41, pp. 173–175.

32 Robert Goralski, op. cit., 5/20/41, pp. 159–160.

33 CAL, *Wartime Journals,* 5/15/41, pp. 489–490.

34 *Vital Speeches of the Day,* 6/1/41, vol. 7, no. 16., p. 1, "Election Promises Should be Kept"; *NYT,* 5/24/41, "Lindbergh Joins in Wheeler Plea to US. to Shun War"; CAL, *Wartime Journals,* 5/23/41, pp. 492–494; *WW&W,* AML diary, 5/23/41, pp. 186–192.

35 *NYT,* 6/2/41, "Calls This 'A Just War.' "

36 Ibid., 5/26/41, "Woollcott Takes Lindbergh to Task."

37 Ibid., 5/30/41, "Lindbergh Assails Roosevelt Speech," by Lawrence E. Davies; CAL, *Wartime Journals,* 5/29/41, pp. 497–498.

38 Robert Goralski, op. cit., 6/22/41, p. 164.

39 *NYT,* 6/23/41, "Lindbergh Sees Need for 'Profound Analysis.' "

[40] Ibid., 7/2/41, "Lindbergh Assails Tie with Russia."

[41] The area was once owned by a Dr. Shaler, a professor of geology at Harvard University. But with the coming of the First World War, the farm went broke and the Shalers were forced to parcel their land. Margot Loines Morrow's father had purchased one of those lots {Interview with Margot Loines Wilkie at Seven Gates Farm, 1994}.

[42] *WW&W*, AML letter to ECM, 8/8/41, p. 213.

[43] CAL, *Wartime Journals*, 8/9/41, pp. 524–525.

[44] *Life*, 8/11/41, "Lindbergh: A Stubborn Young Man of Strange Ideas Becomes a Leader of Wartime Opposition," by Roger Butterfield.

[45] *WW&W*, AML diary, 9/11/41, p. 220.

[46] Ibid., p. 221.

[47] *NYT*, 9/12/41, "Lindbergh Sees a 'Plot' for War"; and CAL, *Wartime Journals*, 9/11/41, pp. 536–537.

[48] Ibid.

[49] *WW&W*, AML diary, 9/14/41, p. 224.

28. PILGRIM
∞

[1] AML, *The Unicorn and Other Poems*, p. 44.

[2] Robert Goralski, op. cit., 12/7/41, pp. 186–189.

[3] Basil Rauch, ed., *Franklin D. Roosevelt: Selected Speeches, Messages, Press Conferences, and Letters*, New York: Rinehart, 1957.

[4] CAL, *Wartime Journals*, 12/8/41, p. 560.

[5] *NYT*, 12/9/41, "Rush of Recruits Crowds Stations."

[6] *WW&W*, AML diary, 2/18/42, p. 248.

[7] CAL, *Wartime Journals*, 12/12/41, pp. 566–567.

[8] *NYT*, 12/31/41, "Lindbergh Volunteers to Serve on Active Duty in Army Air Corps," and "Mr. Lindbergh Volunteers," editorial.

[9] As cited in *Newsweek*, 1/12/42, "Volunteers."

[10] *The Nation*, 1/10/42, "Charles Lindbergh's Offer to Serve."

[11] CAL, *Wartime Journals*, 3/16/42, p. 603.

[12] *WW&W*, AML letter to Margot Loines Morrow, 2/26/42, pp. 248–249.

[13] Antoine de Saint-Exupéry, *Flight to Arras*, New York: Reynal and Hitchcock, 1942.

[14] *WW&W*, AML diary, 3/15/43, p. 331.

[15] Robert Goralski, op. cit., March 1942, p. 207.

[16] CAL, *Wartime Journals*, 3/12/42, p. 602.

[17] Ibid., 3/26/42, pp. 609–610.

[18] *WW&W*, AML diary, 3/12/42, p. 251.

[19] Anne's function in the writing of this book is disputed. Some scholars say she had a role in editing and rewriting his book; others minimize her contributions.

20 CAL, *The Spirit of St. Louis,* op. cit.

21 *WW&W,* AML diary, 3/12/42, p. 252.

22 Betty Friedan, *The Feminine Mystique,* New York: Dell Publishing Co., 1963.

23 *WW&W,* AML letter to CAL, 4/8/42, pp. 257–258.

24 *WW&W,* CAL letter to AML, 4/10/42, pp. 259–260.

25 *WW&W,* AML diary, 11/6/41, pp. 236–237.

26 Ibid., 12/10–12/13/42, p. 242.

27 *WW&W,* AML letter to CAL, 5/26/42, pp. 266–267.

28 *WW&W,* AML diary, 7/18/42, pp. 272–276.

29 Elizabeth-Anne Wheal, Stephen Pope, and James Taylor, *A Dictionary of the Second World War,* London: Grafton, 1989, p. 105.

30 Daniel Goldhagen, op. cit., p. 98; and Ron Rosenbaum, *Explaining Hitler: the Search for the Origins of his Evil,* New York: Random House, 1998, pp. 42–43, 373–374.

31 CAL, *Wartime Journals,* 7/31/42, pp. 684–685.

32 *WW&W,* AML diary, 8/2/42–8/4/42, pp. 282–285.

33 Ibid., 8/12/42, pp. 287–294.

34 CAL, *Wartime Journals,* 8/13/42, p. 696.

35 *WW&W,* AML diary, "Coming Home," pp. 298–300.

36 AML, *Steep Ascent,* New York: Harcourt Brace, 1944.

37 Antoine de Saint-Exupéry, "To All Frenchmen Everywhere," *NYT Magazine,* 11/23/42.

38 *WW&W,* AML diary, 11/28/42, pp. 306–307.

39 Ibid., p. 309.

40 Ibid., 12/20/42, p. 312.

29. THROUGH A GLASS DARKLY
∾

1 *The Variorum Edition of the Poems of W. B. Yeats,* Peter Alt, ed., New York: Macmillan, 1987, p. 477.

2 *WW&W,* AML Diary, 1/26/43, pp. 320–322.

3 The title *Steep Ascent* came from a nineteenth-century Presbyterian hymn by Reginald Heber. Like Anne's poem "St. Christopher," it asks "Who will bear the burdens of Christ?" It speaks of the saints who sacrifice themselves in a war against tyranny and brute force. They are a noble army, not only of men and boys, but of matrons and maids, who will climb the Steep Ascent of Heaven. May all of us, wrote Heber, follow in their train and receive the gift of grace.

4 *WW&W,* AML diary, 2/18/43, pp. 325–326.

5 Ibid., 9/3/43, p. 386.

6 Ibid., 3/15/43, pp. 330–331.

7 Ibid., 4/17/43, p. 340.

8 Robert Goralski, op. cit., pp. 265–281.

9 CAL, *Wartime Journals*, 1/6/44, p. 756.

10 Ibid., 4/3/44, p. 775.

11 *WW&W,* 4/5/44, AML diary, p. 424.

12 CAL, *Wartime Journals*, 6/9/44, p. 847.

13 *St. Louis Post-Dispatch,* 3/11/50, "Lindbergh Flew 50 War Missions, Bombed and Strafed Japs in Pacific."

14 CAL, *Wartime Journals*, 5/24/44, p. 821.

15 Robert Goralski, op. cit., 6/6/44, p. 321.

16 *WW&W,* AML diary, 7/29/44, pp. 436–437.

17 Ibid., 6/20/44, pp. 426–427.

18 *John Jay Chapman and His Letters*, M. A. De Wolfe Howe, ed., as cited in *WW&W,* AML letter to CAL, 7/2/44, p. 429.

19 Robert Goralski, op. cit., 8/24/44 and 8/25/44, p. 340.

20 *Newsweek,* 9/11/44, "Collaboration Camp"; *NYT,* 8/31/44, "Dr. Carrel Arrested as Vichy Adherent"; *NYT,* 8/29/44, "French Health Chief Dismisses Dr. Carrel"; and *New York Herald Tribune,* 8/29/44, "Dr. Alexis Carrel Dismissed as Head of Institute in Paris."

21 Katherine Crutcher [Carrel's Assistant] letter to R. B. Wolf, 9/11/44, Rockefeller Archives.

22 *NYT,* 11/6/44, "Dr. Alexis Carrel Dies in Paris at 71"; *Time,* 11/13/44, "Died: Dr. Alexis Carrel"; *The Catholic World,* 12/1/44, "Noted Scientist Dies in Paris."

23 Letter from Brigadier General T. Bentley Mott to Mr. Frederic Coudert, Sr., 12/10/44, Rockefeller Archives.

24 *NYT,* 9/21/44, "Lindbergh Arrives Home."

25 CAL, *Wartime Journals*, 9/20/44, pp. 926–927.

26 Ibid.

27 AML, *The Gift from the Sea.*

28 *WW&W,* AML diary, 10/8/44, p. 447.

29 Ibid., 10/27/44, pp. 450–452.

30 CAL, *Wartime Journals*, 5/17/45, pp. 942–943.

31 Ibid., 5/18/45, pp. 946–951.

32 Lucy Dawidowicz, *The War Against the Jews, 1933–1945,* New York: Holt, Rinehart and Winston, 1975.

33 CAL, *Wartime Journals*, p. 949.

34 *NYT,* 12/18/45, "Lindbergh Urges Power-Backed Uno."

30. PURE GOLD
∞

1 AML, *The Unicorn and Other Poems*, p. 49. This chapter is based on interviews with Anne's family and friends. Everyone wanted to talk about *Gift from the Sea.*

However, James Newton, who had accompanied Anne and Charles on their early trips to Captiva, Margot Morrow Wilkie, who was among those who visited Anne during her stay, Ernestine Stodell Chamberlain, who read Anne's original manuscript, and their youngest child, Reeve Lindbergh Tripp, contributed most to my understanding.

² Interview with Reeve Lindbergh Tripp.

³ A. Scott Berg, op. cit., p. 481.

⁴ Interview with Margot Wilkie, 8/24/94.

⁵ Dr. John Rosen founded a branch of Freudian psychoanalysis, first known as direct analysis and later as direct psychoanalysis, in the late 1940s. Frustrated by the general reluctance to use psychoanalysis instead of pharmacology to treat pathology, Rosen studied psychiatry and published papers on his methods of resolving psychosis with direct analytic therapy. His approach gained momentum in the 1950s. By the 1960s, criticism of his methods exploded, and he was accused of "ignoring the plight of 60,000 retarded" in his position as chairman of the Philadelphia Health Department's Board of Mental Health and Mental Retardation. Former patients accused him of abuse, both physical and sexual, and one patient died in his care. Rosen, then 78, denied all charges, but two of his aides pleaded guilty to manslaughter. Dr. John Rosen File, Temple University Urban Archives.

⁶ *NYT,* 4/14/47, "Lindbergh Urges U.S. World Role."

⁷ CAL, *Of Flight and Life,* New York: Harcourt, Brace and Company, 1947.

⁸ Interview with AML.

⁹ Interview with Ernestine Stodell Chamberlain, 12/7/85.

¹⁰ Interview with Christian Wolff, 1/28/99; AML correspondence with Kurt Wolff, Kurt Wolff Papers, Beineke Rare Book and Manuscript Library, Yale University; *New Yorker,* "Profiles: Imprint," Herbert Mitgang, 8/2/82, p. 41 et seq.

¹¹ Interview with AML.

¹² Betty Friedan, op. cit., pp. 154–155; Barbara Miller Solomon, op. cit., p. 63.

¹³ Ibid., p. 13.

¹⁴ William H. Chafe, *The American Woman: Her Changing Social and Economic and Political Roles, 1920 to 1970,* New York: Oxford University Press, 1972, pp. 203–225.

¹⁵ AML, *Gift from the Sea,* p. 26.

¹⁶ Ibid., p. 96.

¹⁷ Ibid., p. 108–109.

¹⁸ Interview with AML.

¹⁹ *GFTS* would go on to sell 600,000 hardcover copies, and 3,000,000 copies in all English-language editions over the life of the title. Between 10,000 and 15,000 copies continue to be printed each year, and 26 publishers have printed *GFTS* in other languages.

31. MIDSUMMER
℘

[1] AML, "Midsummer," *Atlantic Monthly,* 12/57, p. 44.

[2] *NYT,* 1/24/55, "Mrs. Dwight W. Morrow is Dead; Educator Was Widow of Diplomat"; *NYT,* 1/27/55, "Rites for Mrs. Morrow"; *NYT,* 1/12/55, "Mrs. Dwight W. Morrow."

[3] Elizabeth Morrow also wrote short stories and children's books.

[4] *NYT,* 2/3/55, "Morrow Legacies Approach Million."

[5] AML letter to Eleanor Robson Belmont, 3/22/55, Columbia University Rare Book and Manuscript Library.

[6] *NYT,* 3/26/54, "Lindbergh's Son Weds Classmate"; *Newsweek,* 4/5/54 "Secret Wedding."

[7] Interview with Barbara Robbins, 10/1/93.

[8] Reeve Lindbergh, op. cit.

[9] AML letter to John Hall Wheelock, 12/5/56, Library of Congress.

[10] Bette Richart, "Since Sappho," *Commonweal,* 9/7/56, vol. 64:568–70.

[11] Ibid.

[12] John Ciardi, *Saturday Review of Literature,* 2/16/57, "The Reviewer's Duty to Damn."

[13] Ibid., 1/12/57, "A Close Look at the Unicorn."

[14] Ibid.

[15] Edward Cifelli, *John Ciardi: A Biography,* Fayetteville: University of Arkansas Press, 1997.

[16] Wayne Cole, op. cit., p. 147.

[17] *NYT magazine,* 2/8/48, "That Baffling Personality, Mr. Wallace," Cabell Phillips, p. 14 et seq.

[18] Norman Cousins, *Saturday Review of Literature,* 2/16/57, "John Ciardi and the Readers."

[19] "The Unicorn" was first published in *The Unicorn and Other Poems.*

[20] "The Stone" was first published in the *Atlantic Monthly,* 1/52, v. 189, p. 44. Perhaps the title "The Stone," has a double meaning, referring to her kidney stones and subsequent miscarriage, initiating a period of self-reflection and turmoil.

[21] Interview with Margot Loines Morrow Wilkie, 10/31/94.

[22] A. Scott Berg, *Lindbergh,* New York: Putnam, 1998, pp. 507–509.

[23] AML, "Midsummer."

32. DEARLY BELOVED
℘

[1] AML postcard to Martha Knecht, 8/31/59.

[2] Reeve Lindbergh, *Names of the Mountains,* New York: Simon & Schuster, 1992, pp. 76 and 144.

[3] Marilyn Bender and Selig Altschul, op. cit.

4 Letter to Walter Ross from USAF Major Gene Guerny, deputy chief, Magazine and Book Branch, Office of Information, 6/20/63.

5 Reeve Lindbergh, *Names of the Mountains,* op. cit.

6 Ibid.

7 Reeve Lindbergh, *Under A Wing.*

8 Reeve Lindbergh, *Names of the Mountains,* p. 179.

9 Michael Ermath, ed., *Kurt Wolff: A Portrait in Essays and Letters,* Chicago: University of Chicago Press, 1991, p. 7.

10 Ibid.

11 *New Yorker,* "Profiles: Imprint," Herbert Mitgang, 8/2/82, pp. 41 et seq.

12 Michael Ermath, ed., op. cit., and interview with Christian Wolff, 1/28/99.

13 Michael Ermath, ed., op. cit., p. 172.

14 Ibid.

15 Ibid., p. 175.

16 Kurt Wolff letter to AML, 2/21/58, Kurt Wolff Papers, Beineke Rare Book and Manuscript Library, Yale University.

17 Helen Wolff letter to AML, 11/24/60, Kurt Wolff Papers, Beineke Rare Book and Manuscript Library, Yale University.

18 Helen Wolff letter to AML, 3/13/59, Kurt Wolff Papers, Beineke Rare Book and Manuscript Library, Yale University.

19 Helen and Kurt Wolff letter to AML, 12/13/59, Kurt Wolff Papers, Beineke Rare Book and Manuscript Library, Yale University.

20 Robert Hessen, ed., op. cit.

21 AML letter to Kurt Wolff, 12/14/60, Kurt Wolff Papers, Beineke Rare Book and Manuscript Library, Yale University.

22 AML letter to Helen Wolff, 1/27/61, Kurt Wolff Papers, Beineke Rare Book and Manuscript Library, Yale University.

23 AML letter to Helen Wolff, 1/27/61 and AML letter to Kurt Wolff, 8/25/61, Kurt Wolff Papers, Beineke Rare Book and Manuscript Library, Yale University.

24 AML, *Dearly Beloved,* New York: Pantheon, 1962.

33. ARGONAUTA
∞

1 AML letter to Helen Wolff, 11/25/62, Kurt Wolff Papers, Beineke Rare Book and Manuscript Library, Yale University.

2 *NYT,* 6/10/62, Virgilia Peterson, "Memories of Married Life."

3 *Christian Science Monitor,* 6/21/62, p. 7.

4 AML letter to Helen Wolff, 11/25/62, Kurt Wolff Papers, Beineke Rare Book and Manuscript Library, Yale University.

5 Charles A. Lindbergh, "Is Civilization Progress?" *Reader's Digest,* July 1964.

6 Interview with Barbara Robbins, 10/1/93.

7 Kurt Wolff Papers, Beineke Rare Book and Manuscript Library, Yale University.

8 Interview with Christian Wolff, 1/28/99.

9 *NYT,* 10/23/63, "Kurt Wolff, Publisher, 76, Dies."

10 *NYT,* 12/27/63, "Daughter of the Lindberghs Wed to Student in France."

11 *New Yorker,* "Profiles: Imprint," Herbert Mitgang, 8/2/82.

12 Interview with Milton Howell, 7/6/88.

13 Reeve Lindbergh, *Under a Wing.*

14 Interview with Barbara Robbins, 10/1/93.

15 The account of Charles Lindbergh's meeting and friendship with Adrienne Arnett is based on the author's interview with Adrienne Arnett, 3/11/87.

16 It is said that Anne found Adrienne's letters among Charles's papers after his death.

17 A. Scott Berg, op. cit.

18 Reeve Lindbergh, *Names of the Mountains,* p. 76.

19 Marilyn Bender and Selig Altschul, op. cit.

20 Alden Whitman (1914–1990) was a retired reporter for the *New York Times* who pioneered the use of interviews of notable people to personalize their obituaries. In 1968, he became the first journalist in more than thirty years with whom Lindbergh talked at length. He traveled with Lindbergh in the Philippines and United States to gather information for a book he was planning to write about Lindbergh's later years and efforts to conserve land and wildlife.

21 *NYT,* 8/31/70, "Philippine Tribes Struggle to Survive," Alden Whitman.

22 John Nance, *The Gentle Tasaday: A Stone Age People in the Philippine Rainforest,* New York: Harcourt Brace Jovanovich, 1975, pp. 34–47.

23 Gerald D. Berreman, "Romanticising the Stone Age: The Incredible 'Tasaday' " *Cultural Survival Quarterly,* 1991, vol. 15, no. 1.

24 Reeve Lindbergh, *Names of the Mountains,* p. 31.

25 Interview with AML, 4/12/88; Interview with Milton and Roselle Howell, 7/6/88; lecture by T. W. Hunter in Little Falls, Minnesota, June 1981, Lindbergh Lecture series. Interview with Ernestine Stodelle Chamberlain, 12/7/85.

26 Reeve Lindbergh, *Under a Wing.*

27 Adrienne Arnett would later say that she was responsible for encouraging Charles to write the story of his life infused with his moral perceptions.

34 · CODA
∽

1 AML, "Bare Tree," in *The Unicorn and Other Poems,* p. 86.

2 Interview with Ernestine Stodell Chamberlain.

3 Reeve Lindbergh, *Under a Wing.*

Index

Illustration pages in boldface.

A

B

H

Index

M

Permissions

Many thanks to the sources who generously granted the author permission to print unpublished material. An excerpt from a letter by Dwight Morrow Charles A. Lindbergh, 4 October 1927, in Dwight W. Morrow Papers (Series 1, Box 31, Folder 47), is published by permission of Archives and Special Collections, Amherst College Library. Excerpt from Alexis Carrel's speech at Dartmouth on 10/11/37, "The Making of Civilized Men," excerpts from a draft entitled "Memorandum as to a Proposed Center of Integrated Scientific Research," and an excerpt from a letter by Alexis Carrel to Jim Newton, 10/24/39, are all printed by permission of the Georgetown University Library Special Collections Division. An excerpt from Alexis Carrel's letter to Simon Flexner, 1/1/38, an excerpt from Thomas Debevoise's letter to Alexis Carrel, 5/12/38, excerpt from E. B. Smith's undated note, excerpts from Katherine Crutcher's letter to R. B. Wolf, 9/11/44, and excerpts from a letter from Brigadier General T. Bentley Mott to Mr. Frederic Coudert, Sr., 12/10/44, all appear by permission of the Rockefeller Archive Center. Harold Nicolson's letter to Vita Sackville-West, 2/14/35, appears by permission of Nigel Nicolson and the Lilly Library, Indiana University.

Permission to quote 247 words from Anne Morrow Lindbergh's *Gift from the Sea,* Copyright © 1955, 1975, and 225 lines of poetry from *The Unicorn and Other Poems, 1935–1955,* Copyright © 1956, renewed 1984 by Anne Morrow Lindbergh, granted by Pantheon Books, A Division of Random House, Inc.

Photo Credits

Picture Research & Editing: Alexandra Truitt & Jerry Marshall
Cover: UPI/Corbis-Bettmann

INSERT PHOTOS

INSERT 1

Page 1 Amherst College Archives and Special Collections, Amherst College Library
Page 1 Lindbergh Picture Collection, Manuscripts and Archives, Yale University Library
Page 1 Photo by David B. Edmonston, Minnesota Historical Society
Page 2 Lindbergh Picture Collection, Manuscripts and Archives, Yale University Library
Page 2 Lindbergh Picture Collection, Manuscripts and Archives, Yale University Library
Page 2 Lindbergh Picture Collection, Manuscripts and Archives, Yale University Library
Page 3 Corbis/Underwood & Underwood
Page 3 UPI/Corbis-Bettmann
Page 3 Lindbergh Picture Collection, Manuscripts and Archives, Yale University Library
Page 4 Rinhart; George/Corbis-Bettmann
Page 4 Lindbergh Picture Collection, Manuscripts and Archives, Yale University Library
Page 5 UPI/Corbis-Bettmann
Page 5 Amherst College Archives and Special Collections, Amherst College Library
Page 5 Culver Pictures
Page 6 New York Times Co./Archive Photos
Page 6 AP/Wide World Photos
Page 7 Lindbergh Picture Collection, Manuscripts and Archives, Yale University Library
Page 7 UPI/Corbis-Bettmann
Page 7 Lindbergh Picture Collection, Manuscripts and Archives, Yale University Library
Page 8 Roger-Viollet/Liaison Agency
Page 8 Underwood & Underwood/Corbis-Bettmann
Page 8 AP/Wide World Photos

INSERT 2

Page 1 Lindbergh Picture Collection, Manuscripts and Archives, Yale University Library
Page 1 Corbis/Underwood & Underwood
Page 1 Culver Pictures
Page 2 Lindbergh Picture Collection, Manuscripts and Archives, Yale University Library
Page 2 Lindbergh Picture Collection, Manuscripts and Archives, Yale University Library
Page 2 Lindbergh Picture Collection, Manuscripts and Archives, Yale University Library
Page 3 Popperfoto
Page 3 AP/Wide World Photos
Page 4 Popperfoto
Page 4 UPI/Corbis-Bettmann
Page 4 UPI/Corbis-Bettmann
Page 4 UPI/Corbis-Bettmann
Page 5 Corbis-Bettmann

Page 5 AP/Wide World Photos
Page 6 Lindbergh Picture Collection, Manuscripts and Archives, Yale University Library
Page 6 Lindbergh Picture Collection, Manuscripts and Archives, Yale University Library
Page 6 Lindbergh Picture Collection, Manuscripts and Archives, Yale University Library
Page 7 Lindbergh Picture Collection, Manuscripts and Archives, Yale University Library
Page 7 Lindbergh Picture Collection, Manuscripts and Archives, Yale University Library
Page 7 Ullstein Bilderdienst
Page 7 Popperfoto
Page 8 UPI/Corbis-Bettmann
Page 8 Lindbergh Picture Collection, Manuscripts and Archives, Yale University Library
Page 8 UPI/Corbis-Bettmann
Page 8 UPI/Corbis-Bettmann

INSERT 3

Page 1 Lindbergh Picture Collection, Manuscripts and Archives, Yale University Library
Page 1 UPI/Corbis-Bettmann
Page 2 Lindbergh Picture Collection, Manuscripts and Archives, Yale University Library
Page 2 Lindbergh Picture Collection, Manuscripts and Archives, Yale University Library
Page 3 Photographed by the author
Page 3 Lindbergh Picture Collection, Manuscripts and Archives, Yale University Library
Page 4 New York Times Pictures
Page 4 U.S. Air Force Photo
Page 5 Lindbergh Picture Collection, Manuscripts and Archives, Yale University Library
Page 5 © Richard W. Brown
Page 6 Alden Whitman Papers, 1935–1986, Manuscripts and Archives Division, The New York Public Library, Astor, Lenox, and Tilden Foundations
Page 6 Alden Whitman Papers, 1935–1986. Manuscripts and Archives Division, The New York Public Library, Astor, Lenox, and Tilden Foundations
Page 6 Alden Whitman Papers, 1935–1986. Manuscripts and Archives Division, The New York Public Library, Astor, Lenox, and Tilden Foundations
Page 7 © Richard W. Brown
Page 7 Photo by Robert E. Paulson, Used with the permission of the Charles A. and Anne Morrow Lindbergh Foundation
Page 8 AP/Wide World Photos
Page 8 AP/Wide World Photos